INSIDE

LANGUAGE, LITERACY, AND CONTENT

PROGRAM AUTHORS

David W. Moore

Deborah J. Short

Alfred W. Tatum

Josefina Villamil Tinajero

Acknowledgments

Grateful acknowledgment is given to the authors, artists, photographers, museums, publishers, and agents for permission to reprint copyrighted material. Every effort has been made to secure the appropriate permission. If any omissions have been made or if corrections are required, please contact the Publisher.

Anthony Arrigo: "Preserving the Rural Environment" by Anthony Arrigo from www.starrynightlights.com. Used by permission of the author.

Acknowledgments continue on page 614.

Neither the Publisher nor the authors shall be liable for any damage that may be caused or sustained or result from conducting any of the activities in this publication without specifically following instructions, undertaking the activities without proper supervision, or failing to comply with the cautions contained herein.

Published by National Geographic School Publishing & Hampton-Brown
Sheron Long, Chief Executive Officer
Samuel Gesumaria, President

Editorial: Linda Alders, Amy Barbour, Lisa Berti, Chris Beem, Michael Beets, Renee Biermann, Ela Aktay Booty, Stefanie Boron, Janine Boylan, Susan Buntrock, Karen Cardella, Kristin Cozort, Darin Derstine, Amanda Gebhardt, Toni Gibbs, Trudy Gibson, Nadine Guarrera, Margot Hanis, Rachel Hansen, Fred Ignacio, Anne Kaske, Robin Kelly, Phillip Kennedy, Sarah Kincaid, Jennifer Kleiman, Jennifer Krasula, Joel Kupperstein, Phil Kurczewski, Mary Catherine Langford, Julie Larson, Kathleen Laya, Dawn Liseth, Daphne Liu, Nancy Lockwood, Jennifer Loomis, Kathleen Maguire, Cheryl Marecki, Andrew McCarter, Joyce McGreevy, Mimi Mortezai, Kimberly Mraovich, Amy Ostenso, Barbara Paulsen, Juan Quintana, Katrina Saville, Debbie Saxton, Thomas Schiele, Anastasia Scopelitis, Elizabeth Sengel, Heather Subba, Lin Sullivan, Seija Surr, Honor Teoudoussia, Jennifer Tetzloff, Joy Triche, Marietta Urban, Sharon Ursino, Beatrice Villar, Nora Whitworth, Virginia Yeater, Brown Publishing Network, Chapman Publishing Systems, MetaArts, Morrison BookWorks, Rainbow Creative Concepts, Words and Numbers

Art, Design, and Production: Marcia Bateman, Christy Caldwell, Andrea Cockrum, Kim Cockrum, Jen Coppens, Wendy Crockett, Denise Davidson, Alicia DiPiero, Carol Do, Darius Detwiler, Donna Jean Elam, Michael Farmer, Chanté Fields, Kathryn Glaser, Raymond Ortiz Godfrey, Raymond Hoffmeyer, Annie Hopkins, Karen Hunting, Jeri Gibson, Rick Holcomb, Cynthia C. Lee, Ernie Lee, Jean-Marie McLaren, Douglas McLeod, Mary McMurtry, Melina Meltzer, Rick Morrison, Russ Nemec, Marian O'Neal, Andrea A. Pastrano-Tamez, Leonard Pierce, Deborah Reed, Cathy Revers, Stephanie Rice, Scott Russell, Susan Scheuer, Janet Sandbach, Jeanne Stains, Sumer Tatum-Clem, Andrea Erin Thompson, Andrea Troxel, Donna Turner, Ana Vela, Alex von Dallwitz, AARTPACK, Brown Publishing Network, Chaos Factory & Associates, GGS Book Services, Rainbow Creative Concepts, Thompson Type, Vertis Inc., Visual Asylum

The National Geographic Society
John M. Fahey, Jr., President & Chief Executive Officer
Gilbert M. Grosvenor, Chairman of the Board

Manufacturing and Quality Management, The National Geographic Society
Christopher A. Liedel, Chief Financial Officer
George Bounelis, Vice President

National Geographic School Publishing
Hampton–Brown
www.NGSP.com

Printed in the United States of America
R.R. Donnelley, Willard, OH

ISBN: 978-0-7362-5342-0

ISBN (CA): 978-0-7362-5345-1

12 13 14 15 16 17   10 9 8

Contents at a Glance

We gratefully acknowledge the many contributions of the following dedicated educators in creating a program that is not only pedagogically sound, but also appealing to and motivating for middle school students.

Literature Consultant

Dr. René Saldaña, Jr., Ph.D.
Assistant Professor
Texas Tech University

Dr. Saldaña teaches English and education at the university level and is the author of *The Jumping Tree* (2001) and *Finding Our Way: Stories* (Random House/Wendy Lamb Books, 2003). More recently, several of his stories have appeared in anthologies such as *Face Relations*, *Guys Write for GUYS READ*, *Every Man for Himself*, and *Make Me Over*, and in magazines such as *Boy's Life* and *READ*.

Teacher Reviewers

Idalia Apodaca
English Language Development Teacher
Shaw Middle School
Spokane, WA

Pat E. Baggett-Hopkins
Area Reading Coach
Chicago Public Schools
Chicago, IL

Judy Chin
ESOL Teacher
Arvida Middle School
Miami, FL

Sonia Flores
Teacher Supporter
Los Angeles Unified School District
Los Angeles, CA

Brenda Garcia
ESL Teacher
Crockett Middle School
Irving, TX

Kristine Hoffman
Teacher on Special Assignment
Newport-Mesa Unified School District
Costa Mesa, CA

Dr. Margaret R. Keefe
ELL Contact and Secondary Advocate
Martin County School District
Stuart, FL

Julianne Kosareff
Curriculum Specialist
Paramount Unified School District
Paramount, CA

Lore Levene
Coordinator of Language Arts
Community Consolidated School District 59
Arlington Heights, IL

Natalie M. Mangini
Teacher/ELD Coordinator
Serrano Intermediate School
Lake Forest, CA

Laurie Manikowski
Teacher/Trainer
Lee Mathson Middle School
San Jose, CA

Patsy Mills
Supervisor, Bilingual-ESL
Houston Independent School District
Houston, TX

Juliane M. Prager-Nored
High Point Expert
Los Angeles Unified School District
Los Angeles, CA

Patricia Previdi
ESOL Teacher
Patapsco Middle School
Ellicott City, MD

Dr. Louisa Rogers
Middle School Team Leader
Broward County Public Schools
Fort Lauderdale, FL

Rebecca Varner
ESL Teacher
Copley-Fairlawn Middle School
Copley, OH

Hailey F. Wade
ESL Teacher/Instructional Specialist
Lake Highlands Junior High
Richardson, TX

Cassandra Yorke
ESOL Coordinator
Palm Beach School District
West Palm Beach, FL

Program Authors

David W. Moore, Ph.D.
Professor of Education
Arizona State University

Dr. David Moore taught high school social studies and reading in Arizona public schools before entering college teaching. He currently teaches secondary school teacher preparation courses in adolescent literacy. He co-chaired the International Reading Association's Commission on Adolescent Literacy and is actively involved with several professional associations. His twenty-five year publication record balances research reports, professional articles, book chapters, and books. Noteworthy publications include the International Reading Association position statement on adolescent literacy and the *Handbook of Reading Research* chapter on secondary school reading. Recent books include *Developing Readers and Writers in the Content Areas (5th ed.)*, *Teaching Adolescents Who Struggle with Reading (2nd ed.)*, and *Principled Practices for Adolescent Literacy*.

Deborah J. Short, Ph.D.
Senior Research Associate
Center for Applied Linguistics

Dr. Deborah Short is a co-developer of the research-validated SIOP Model for sheltered instruction. She has directed quasi-experimental and experimental studies on English language learners funded by the Carnegie Corporation of New York, the Rockefeller Foundation, and the U.S. Dept. of Education. She recently chaired an expert panel on adolescent ELL literacy and coauthored a policy report: *Double the Work: Challenges and Solutions to Acquiring Language and Academic Literacy for Adolescent English Language Learners*. She has also conducted extensive research on secondary level newcomer programs. Her research articles have appeared in the *TESOL Quarterly*, the *Journal of Educational Research*, *Educational Leadership*, *Education and Urban Society*, *TESOL Journal*, *Social Education*, and *Journal of Research in Education*.

Alfred W. Tatum, Ph.D.
Associate Professor and
Director of UIC Reading Clinic
University of Illinois at Chicago

Dr. Alfred Tatum began his career as an eighth-grade teacher, later becoming a reading specialist and discovering the power of texts to reshape the life outcomes of struggling readers. His current research focuses on the literacy development of African American adolescent males, and he provides teacher professional development to urban middle and high schools. He serves on the National Advisory Reading Committee of the National Assessment of Educational Progress (NAEP) and is active in a number of literacy organizations. In addition to his book *Teaching Reading to Black Adolescent Males: Closing the Achievement Gap*, he has published in journals such as *Reading Research Quarterly*, *The Reading Teacher*, *Journal of Adolescent & Adult Literacy*, *Educational Leadership*, *Journal of College Reading and Learning*, and *Principal Leadership*.

Josefina Villamil Tinajero, Ph.D.
Associate Dean, Professor,
College of Education
University of Texas at El Paso

Dr. Josefina Villamil Tinajero specializes in staff development and school-university partnership programs, and consulted with school districts in the U.S. to design ESL, bilingual, literacy, and biliteracy programs. She has served on state and national advisory committees for standards development, including English as a New Language Advisory Panel of the National Board of Professional Teaching Standards. She is currently Professor of Education and Associate Dean at the University of Texas at El Paso, and was President of the National Association for Bilingual Education, 1997–2000.

Finding Your Own Place

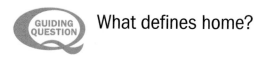 **GUIDING QUESTION** What defines home?

UNIT SKILLS

Pages 1W–31W

Unit 2

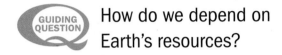

Water for Life

GUIDING QUESTION How do we depend on Earth's resources?

UNIT SKILLS

Pages 32W–93W

Natural Forces

How do people deal with the forces of nature?

UNIT SKILLS

Vocabulary Study

Literary Analysis

Listening & Speaking

Writing ✎
▶ **Narrative in a Friendly Letter**
▶ **Personal Narrative**

Pages 94W–137W

Unit **4**

CREEPY CLASSICS

 GUIDING QUESTION How can a powerful character inspire a range of reactions?

WRITING

INSIDE

LANGUAGE, LITERACY, AND CONTENT

Pages 138W–179W

Unit 5

The Drive to Discover

 GUIDING QUESTION How do discoveries change us and the world?

UNIT SKILLS

Pages 180W–245W

Unit 6

Struggle for Freedom

 GUIDING QUESTION How far will people go for the sake of freedom?

UNIT SKILLS

Pages 246W–281W

Unit 7

Star Power

 Why are both storytellers and scientists drawn to the stars?

UNIT SKILLS

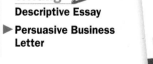

Pages 282W–321W

Unit 8

Art and Soul

 GUIDING QUESTION What do we learn about people from their artful expressions?

UNIT SKILLS

Pages 322W–355W

xx

Genres at a Glance

▼ Observatory in Mauna Kea, Hawaii

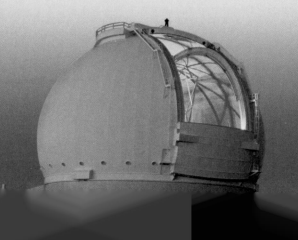

▲ Mariachi musicians in San Antonio, Texas.

Tia's Kitchen, 2003, Patssi Valdez. Acrylic on canvas, courtesy of Correia Gallery, Santa Monica.

△ **Critical Viewing** Would you feel comfortable in this kitchen? Explain.

Finding Your Own Place

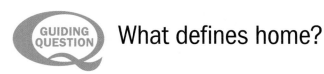

GUIDING QUESTION What defines home?

Read More!

Content Library

Communities Across America Today
by Sarah Glasscock

Leveled Library

Domitila
by Jewell Reinhart Coburn

Novio Boy
by Gary Soto

Pearl Harbor Is Burning!
by Kathleen V. Kudlinski

Internet
InsideNG.com

- Go to the Digital Library to explore different cultures around the world.
- Read stories of some new Americans.
- View family scrapbooks and make one of your own.

Focus on Genre

Organization of Ideas

▶ **Comparison and Contrast**

Writers want readers to understand their ideas. So they organize their ideas in clear, logical ways. If you pay attention to the organization, it will help you follow the writer's ideas.

How It Works

Before you read, preview the text to see what it is about. This will often give you a clue to the organization.

Comparison and Contrast Sometimes writers want to **compare** and **contrast** things, or show how things are alike and different. They organize the text in a way that makes the similarities and differences clear. Read the example and look for **signal words** that set up the comparison.

My New Neighborhood

I like my new neighborhood. I am beginning to feel at home. In my old neighborhood, we didn't have an outdoor basketball court. But my new school has one. I think I'll have to learn chess, though. Unlike the kids in my old neighborhood, the kids here really love it.

Another difference here is that the kids don't have to be home for dinner. My parents want me home by six o'clock. This is hard. Like most kids, I like to play sports at night.

One similar thing about my new and my old neighborhoods is that both have gingko trees. Grandfather told me that gingko trees grow in China, where he grew up. It is like having a piece of his homeland, he said. I feel the same way. For me, it is like having a piece of my old neighborhood.

▲ I play basketball in my new neighborhood.

Signal Words

Alike	Different
both	but
like	difference
same	however
similar	though
too	unlike

Academic Vocabulary

• **compare** (kum-**pair**) *verb*
   When you **compare** two things, you think about how they are alike and different.

Practice Together

Read the following passage aloud. As you read, listen for words that signal comparisons and contrasts.

City and Country

Javier feels at home in the city, but Ana likes to live in the country. When Javier leaves his apartment, he hears noisy cars, buses, and taxis. Unlike Javier, Ana hears birds chirping in the trees and the soft hum of insects. Sometimes Javier and Ana have

▲ A red-tailed hawk lands on a city building.

similar experiences. For example, they have both seen red-tailed hawks. Ana sees the hawks flying over her fields. Javier sees them land on buildings. However, Ana sees red-tailed hawks much more often than Javier does.

Try It!

Read the following passage aloud. How is the passage organized? How do you know?

Two Cities

Both New York City in New York and Mexico City in Mexico are home to millions of people. Both cities are important urban areas. Mexico City is the capital of Mexico, but New York City is not the capital of New York or of the United States. Both Mexico City and New York are made up of a collection of areas. Unlike Mexico City, the separate areas in New York City are called boroughs.

▲ Nearly nineteen million people live in and around Mexico City.

Focus on Vocabulary

Use Context Clues for Multiple-Meaning Words

Some words are spelled the same but have different meanings. A dictionary lists the different definitions. If you aren't sure which meaning of a word fits in a sentence, try looking at the **context** .

Suppose you are reading a passage about dogs, and you see:

> Some dogs have a loud **bark** that can really scare you.

Since you're reading about dogs, you know that the word *bark* means the noise a dog makes. But suppose you read this sentence:

> The woodpecker tapped on the thick **bark** of a tall tree.

Here the word *bark* must mean something else. You can use the **context** to figure out its meaning. The words *woodpecker tapped* and *tall tree* help you know that *bark* means the outer covering of a tree.

How the Strategy Works

When you read, you may come to a word that does not make sense to you. You may know one meaning of that word but not other meanings.
Look for **context** clues to help you figure it out. Follow these steps:

1. Think about what the sentence is about.
2. Look at the other words in the sentence.
3. Read the sentences nearby to find more clues, or hints.
4. Use the clues to think of a meaning that makes sense.

Use the strategy to figure out the meaning of each underlined word.

> My family left our homeland on a large boat. We all shared a tiny room. My brother and I had a bed in the left corner. Every day we ate one can of peas. I can still remember the awful taste!

☑ **REMEMBER** You can use **context** clues to figure out the meanings of multiple-meaning words.

Dictionary Entries

> **bark (bark)** *noun* **1** the sound a dog makes **2** the outer covering of a tree
> **can (kan)** *verb* **1** to be able to do something *noun* **2** a metal container in which food is sold
> **left (left)** *adjective* **1** located on the left side, the side of the body where the heart is located *verb* **2** the past and past participle of *leave*

Strategy in Action

" The paragraph is about moving to a new country. The word *homeland* gives me a clue that *left* means 'went away.'"

Academic Vocabulary

- **context** (**kon**-tekst) *noun*
  Context refers to the parts nearby that help explain the meaning.

Practice Together

Read this passage aloud. Look at each underlined word. Think about what the sentence is about. Use context clues to figure out the meaning of the underlined word.

The Arrival

People are getting off the boat onto the dock. Nadia holds her bag tightly. Inside are the jars of berry <u>jam</u> she made for the <u>trip</u>. She moves with the line. The air is hot. A <u>fly</u> lands on her nose. People are anxious to get off the boat. They <u>jam</u> tightly together. Nadia is pushed around. Two little boys <u>trip</u> and knock over her bag. The jars <u>fly</u> from her bag and break. The sticky jam goes everywhere.

Try It!

Read this passage aloud. What is the meaning of each underlined word? How do you know?

A New Land

Antonio looks out the window of the airplane. The plane will <u>land</u> soon. The <u>light</u> shines in Antonio's eyes. His sister and the <u>rest</u> of his family talk excitedly. Antonio picks up his small, <u>light</u> bag. He is ready to go. But he is so tired. He hopes to <u>rest</u> soon. The journey is long, and he will be happy to be in his new <u>land</u>.

▲ An airplane prepares to land.

fly (**flī**) *verb* **1** to move in the air *noun* **2** a small flying insect

jam (**jam**) *verb* **1** to push tightly together *noun* **2** a sweet food made with fruit and sugar

land (**land**) *verb* **1** to arrive *noun* **2** a country or place

light (**līt**) *adjective* **1** not heavy *noun* **2** brightness

rest (**rest**) *verb* **1** to sleep or relax *noun* **2** the part that remains

trip (**trip**) *verb* **1** to fall over something *noun* **2** a journey

Growing Together

by Carmen Agra Deedy
illustrated by David Diaz

Build Background

Meet the Author

Carmen Agra Deedy remembers how it felt to leave Cuba and call Georgia home.

Connect

Quickwrite Read each proverb. Tell whether you agree or disagree with it. Explain why.

Anywhere you live is your native land.
–Korean proverb

Go out from your village, but don't let your village go out from you.
–Afghan proverb

Digital Library

InsideNG.com
⊙ View the video.

▲ Havana, Cuba, is Carmen Agra Deedy's birthplace.

Language & Grammar

1 TRY OUT LANGUAGE
2 LEARN GRAMMAR
3 APPLY ON YOUR OWN

Express Ideas and Feelings

CD

Listen to the song and the poem.
Then sing along with the song, and read the poem.

SONG and POEM

Who I Am

I'll tell you who I am,
I'll tell you who I'm not.
What I feel is what I feel.
What I think are my own thoughts.

My New Home

This country is my new home.
There are things I must learn.
But I am not afraid.
I love my new home,
But Cuba is always in my heart.

Use Statements with *Am, Is,* and *Are*

A **statement** is one kind of sentence. It tells something.

A statement begins with a **capital letter** and ends with a **period**.

> EXAMPLE   **T**hey are from Brazil⊙

- Use **am** to tell about yourself.

  > EXAMPLE   I **am** American.

- Use **is** to tell about one other person, place, thing, or idea.

  > EXAMPLE   She **is** my sister.

Am, Is, Are

One	More Than One
I **am**	we **are**
you **are**	you **are**
he, she, it **is**	they **are**

- Use **are** to tell about yourself and another person or persons.

  > EXAMPLE   We **are** in a new place.

- Use **are** when you talk to one or more people.

  > EXAMPLE   You **are** my neighbor.

- Use **are** to tell about other persons, places, things, or ideas.

  > EXAMPLE   My friends **are** at the airport.

Practice Together

Say each sentence. Choose the correct form of the verb.

1. I (am/are) from Russia.
2. You (is/are) from Russia, too.
3. We (is/are) new students at this school.
4. The kids (am/are) nice.
5. The school (is/are) big, though.
6. Sometimes I (am/is) confused.

Try It!

Read each sentence. Write the correct form of the verb on a card. Then hold up the card as you say the sentence.

7. My parents (am/are) teachers.
8. They (is/are) happy with their new jobs here.
9. My brother (am/is) still in grammar school.
10. I (am/are) older than my brother.
11. You (am/are) the same age as me.
12. We (is/are) in middle school.

▲ **Russia is a beautiful country.**

Make a Self-Portrait

EXPRESS IDEAS AND FEELINGS

You are an artist! Draw a portrait of yourself. Write statements to describe your portrait.

Look at yourself in the mirror. Think about these questions. Then draw a picture of yourself that shows who you are.

- What kind of person are you?
- How do you feel about yourself?
- What things are important to you?

Exchange portraits with a partner. Look at your partner's portrait and read the statements. Express your ideas and feelings about them. Remember:

How to EXPRESS IDEAS AND FEELINGS

1. Tell what you see.

2. Tell how you feel.

3. Explain your thoughts about what you see and feel.

> You are happy in this portrait. I like this drawing. It shows what you are really like.

USE STATEMENTS WITH *AM, IS,* AND *ARE*

When you tell what you see and feel and explain your thoughts, you will use statements. When you make statements with **am**, **is**, and **are**, be sure to use the verb forms correctly.

EXAMPLES   You **are** a happy person.
I **am** able to see that in your eyes.
Your family **is** important to you.

Prepare to Read

Learn Key Vocabulary

Rate and Study the Words Rate how well you know each word. Then:

1. Pronounce the word. Say it aloud several times. Spell it.
2. Study the example.
3. Tell more about the word.
4. Practice it. Make the word your own.

Key Words

angry (an-grē) *adjective*
▶ page 15

When you are **angry**, you are mad at someone or something. An **angry** leopard hisses a warning.

change (chānj) *noun*
▶ page 14

A **change** is something new and different. A sudden **change** in weather can surprise people!

curious (kyoor-ē-us) *adjective* ▶ page 16

If you are **curious**, you want to know more about something. A **curious** person shows interest in things.

immigrant (i-mu-grunt) *noun* ▶ page 15

An **immigrant** is a person who comes to live in a new country. **Immigrants** say a pledge, or promise, when they become citizens.

learn (lurn) *verb*
▶ page 14

To **learn** means to know about a subject by studying or practicing it. You can **learn** many things by reading.

leave (lēv) *verb*
▶ page 15

When you **leave** a place, you go away from it. The bird **leaves** its nest to find food.
Past tense: **left**
Present participle: **leaving**

ordinary (or-du-nair-ē) *adjective* ▶ page 14

An **ordinary** thing is plain. The brown box looks **ordinary**.

strange (strānj) *adjective*
▶ page 15

Something that is **strange** is not familiar. The reflection in this mirror is **strange**.

Practice the Words Make a Study Card for each Key Word. Then compare your cards with a partner's.

> **angry**
>
> **What it means:** mad
>
> **Example:** how Mom felt after I ripped my new shirt
>
> **Not an example:** how I felt when I wore my new shirt

Study Card

Reading Strategy: Plan Your Reading

Before you read the personal narrative, look it over, or preview it. Try to decide what it is about and what might happen. This makes reading the text more meaningful.

HOW TO PREVIEW AND PREDICT

1. Read the title and look at the pictures.
2. Then begin to read the selection. Stop every few paragraphs to predict, or decide what will happen next. Record your ideas in a Prediction Chart.
3. Read on to find out if your predictions are confirmed, or if they actually happened. Make notes in your chart.

Strategy in Action

Here's how one student previewed and predicted.

Look Into the Text

title

Some days I still get homesick for Cuba, with its warm sea breezes and its mango trees. I live in Georgia now, far from the sea. There is winter here, when the days are short and cold. There is only one tree in my yard—a magnolia tree. It has no fruit, but it does bear flowers.

It is no ordinary tree. It has a story.

Prediction Chart

What the Text Says	My Prediction	What Happens
The title has the word *growing* in it.	Maybe this story is about plants.	
The author tells about a tree.	I predict that the text will tell about the tree.	

Practice Together

Follow the steps in the How-To box. Preview the selection. Then begin a Prediction Chart. As you read, check your predictions.

Focus on Genre

Personal Narrative

A personal narrative is nonfiction. It tells about a certain event in the life of a real person. The writer is also the **narrator**, or the person who tells the story.

Notice how the narrator **compares two important things** in her life.

> Some days I still get homesick for Cuba, with its warm sea breezes and its mango trees. I live in Georgia now, far from the sea. There is winter here, when the days are short and cold. There is only one tree in my yard—a magnolia tree.

Your Job as a Reader

Reading Strategy: Plan Your Reading

As you read, make and check your predictions.

YOU PREDICT

This story is about growing things.

THEN YOU READ

There is only one tree in my yard.

SO YOU DECIDE

The story is about that tree.
My prediction seems right.

Growing Together

by Carmen Agra Deedy

illustrated by David Diaz

Set a Purpose

A girl moves to a new country. Find out how she feels about her new home.

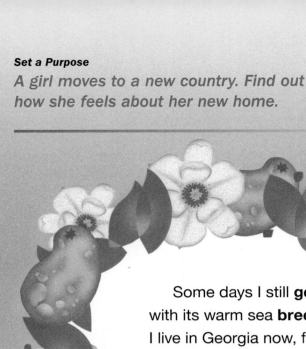

Some days I still **get homesick for** Cuba, with its warm sea **breezes** and its mango trees. I live in Georgia now, far from the sea. There is winter here, when the days are short and cold. There is only one tree in my **yard**—a magnolia tree. It has no fruit, but it does **bear** flowers.

It is no **ordinary** tree. It has a story.

When my family came to this small town in Georgia, it was a big **change** from our tropical island. In time, though, I started to like my new home. Soon I **learned** enough English to make a best friend. An American friend.

One day, we had a silly fight over a bike, and my friend called me **an ugly** name. I remember that Saturday as if it were today . . .

Key Vocabulary

ordinary *adj.*, plain; not special in any way

change *n.*, something new and different

learn *v.*, to know about a subject by studying it

In Other Words

get homesick for feel sad about moving away from

breezes winds

yard garden

bear make

an ugly a mean

My face is hot and red. I drop the bike in the driveway and run to find my father. I see him in the garden under the big magnolia. He is digging in the red **Georgia clay**. He stands up as I run to him. I cry **angry** tears.

A **moment** like this comes for every **immigrant** child.

It is hard to **leave** a home you know. It is even harder to make another place home. Everything is new. Everything is **strange**. Everything is different.

I tell Papi how I feel.

"I hate it here! I am not like them, and they are not like me!" I say to him.

Before You Move On

1. **Character's Point of View** On that Saturday, how did Carmen feel about her new home? Why?
2. **Personal Experience** Did you ever **leave** your home and move to a new place? How did it feel?

Key Vocabulary
angry *adj.*, mad
immigrant *n.*, someone who comes to live in a new country
leave *v.*, to go away
strange *adj.*, not familiar

In Other Words
Georgia clay sticky dirt found in Georgia
moment time

Predict

What will happen to make Carmen feel better?

Papi pulls out a **handkerchief** and **hands** it to me.

My father, the gardener, looks at me **intently** for a few moments. Then he asks, "Carmita, do you remember our mango tree in Cuba?"

"Yes," I **sniff**. I am **curious** now.

"Do you know what it means to graft a tree?"

I nod. "You take a branch from one tree and **attach** it to another tree. The branch and the tree grow together. Right?"

Key Vocabulary
curious *adj.*, wanting to know more about something

In Other Words
handkerchief cloth to dry my eyes
hands gives
intently right in the eyes
sniff say as I try not to cry anymore
attach join

"*Sí*, that is right," Papi says.

My father tells me that I am like a branch from that Cuban mango tree. He says Georgia is like the magnolia tree. I must wait. **Eventually**, the mango and magnolia will grow together.

I **lean** over and smell a sweet magnolia flower from the tree in our yard.

I smile. I will wait.

I am a tree that **gives forth** both mangoes and magnolias.

I am an American. ❖

About the Author

Carmen Agra Deedy

Carmen Agra Deedy (1960–) based this story on events from her childhood. She was born in Havana, Cuba, and came to the United States with her family in 1963. Deedy grew up in two cultures. She was always trying to find her own place. Her father's words were helpful.

"Sometimes I still feel like I don't fit in," Deedy says. "Then I remember Papi's story, and I know that I don't have to stop eating the fruit to smell the flowers."

In Other Words

Sí Yes (in Spanish)
Eventually After a while
lean bend
gives forth makes

Before You Move On

1. **Confirm Prediction** What does Papi tell Carmen that makes her feel better?
2. **Metaphor** In what way is Carmen like a tree that gives mangoes and magnolias?

When I Grow Up

by Janet S. Wong

I want to be an artist, Grandpa—
write and paint, dance and sing.

Be accountant.
Be lawyer.
5 Make good living,
buy good food.
Back in China,
in the old days,
everybody
10 so, so poor.
Eat one chicken,
work all year.

Grandpa, things are different
here.

In Other Words
accountant someone who keeps
track of the money a business
makes and spends
lawyer someone who knows about
laws
Make good living Earn a lot of
money

Before You Move On
1. **Author's Style** How many speakers
are in this poem? How does the
author show this?
2. **Compare and Contrast** How are
the speakers' ideas different?

Connect Reading and Writing

Vocabulary
angry

change

curious

immigrants

learn

leave

ordinary

strange

CRITICAL THINKING

1. SUM IT UP Draw the main events in the personal narrative. Show the **change** in Carmen's feelings. Then use the pictures to summarize the story.

2. Interpret What does the author mean when she says "A moment like this comes for every **immigrant** child"? Do you agree? Explain your answer.

3. Compare Compare the messages of "Growing Together" and "When I Grow Up." What does each one say about how people **learn** to fit in after **leaving** their home country?

4. Opinion Carmen Agra Deedy says, "I don't have to stop eating the fruit to smell the flowers." What does she mean by this? Do you agree? Explain.

READING FLUENCY

Intonation Read the passage on page 568 to a partner. Assess your fluency.

1. I read
  a. great   **b.** OK   **c.** not very well

2. What I did best in my reading was _____.

READING STRATEGY

Plan Your Reading
Review your Prediction Chart. Tell a partner how you made two of the predictions.

VOCABULARY REVIEW

Oral Review Read the paragraph aloud. Add the vocabulary words.

> My parents and I are _____ from a small country. There, we lived in a quiet, _____ town like any other. Our new home is _____ and different to me. Living here is a big _____. Everyone is busy all the time. I am _____ about why people hurry so much. I would like to _____ the reasons. My parents _____ early every morning for work and come home late, too. It makes me _____ that they are always busy. It is hard to compare my old life to my new life.

Written Review Write a journal entry from Carmen's point of view as an **immigrant**. Explain how she defines home. Use four vocabulary words.

WRITE ABOUT THE GUIDING QUESTION

Explore Finding Your Own Place
What do you think Papi means when he says the mango and the magnolia grow together? Reread the text to find support for your ideas.

Connect Across the Curriculum

Analyze Narrator's Point of View

Academic Vocabulary
- **analyze** (a-nu-līz) *verb*
  To **analyze** means to break down information into parts to understand it better.

The person who tells a story is the narrator. If the narrator is one of the characters, then the story has the **first-person point of view**. You can tell because the narrator uses words like *I* and *my*. In this passage from "Growing Together," the narrator tells her view of the events, not what other characters think or feel.

> I drop the bike in the driveway and run to find my father.
> I see him in the garden under the big magnolia.

A story may have the **third-person point of view** instead. The narrator in the following passage tells about Carmen. The narrator is not one of the characters in the story. When you read a story that has the third-person point of view, you may learn the thoughts and feelings of more than one character.

> Carmen drops the bike in the driveway and runs to find her father. He is thinking about the weather as he digs in the garden under the big magnolia.

Practice Together
Find Point of View Read and **analyze** this passage to figure out the narrator's point of view. Look for words like *I* and *my*.

> When my family came to this small town in Georgia, it was a big change from our tropical island. In time, though, I started to like my new home. Soon I learned enough English to make a best friend.

Change Point of View Retell the passage to change the narrator's point of view.

Try It!
With a partner, choose and **analyze** a passage in another personal narrative or fiction selection. How can you tell if the narrator is a character? Rewrite the passage to change the narrator's point of view.

Use Context Clues

Academic Vocabulary
- **explain** (ik-**splān**) *verb*
  When you **explain** an idea, you make it clear so people can understand it.

Some English words have the same spellings but different meanings. You can use **context clues** to figure out which meaning fits in a sentence.

Dictionary Entry

branch (**branch**) *noun* **1** a part of a tree that grows out from the trunk **2** a store or an office away from the main building

Read this sentence from the selection. You can use *tree* as a clue to figure out which meaning of *branch* makes sense in the sentence.

My father tells me that I am like a branch from that Cuban mango tree.

Use Context Clues With a partner, find these words in the selection. Take turns **explaining** which context clues help you figure out the meaning. Then find and copy the dictionary definition that fits.

1. cold, p. 14   **2.** yard, p. 14   **3.** drop, p. 15   **4.** cry, p. 15

Analyze Text Structure: Compare and Contrast

Academic Vocabulary
- **compare** (kum-**pair**) *verb*
  When you **compare** two things, you think about how they are alike and different.

Before authors write, they think about the best way to organize their ideas. One way is to make comparisons. A writer can **compare** and contrast two or more things to show how they are alike or different. In "Growing Together," the author **compares** her two homes, Cuba and Georgia.

Use a Chart Make a Comparison Chart like the one shown. Reread "Growing Together." Look for comparisons between Cuba and Georgia. Use your chart to keep track of how the author **compares** her two homes.

Comparison Chart

Cuba	Georgia
warm	cold

Talk About Text Structure Share your chart with a partner. Discuss how the comparisons helped you understand the events in the story. How did they help you understand Carmen's actions?

Literary Analysis

Analyze Poetry

> **Academic Vocabulary**
> • **arrange** (u-rānj) *verb*
>   To **arrange** means to put things in a certain order.

How Is Poetry Different? Poets often express an idea in few words. They also **arrange** the text in lines. These are two ways in which poetry is different from other forms of writing. In most fiction and nonfiction, the text is **arranged** in sentences and paragraphs.

The lines of a poem may be short or long. Some poems have a mix of short and long lines. A poet may **arrange** the lines to create a certain feeling, or **mood**. For example, short, simple lines may create a happy mood.

Practice Together

Look at the Poem Read the first two lines of the poem "When I Grow Up." Notice that the lines are about the same length. Look at the punctuation at the end of each line. Notice that the second line does not start with a capital letter or express a complete thought.

> I want to be an artist, Grandpa—
> write and paint, dance and sing.

Read and Discuss Reread the poem. Notice that the lines form three parts. The first two lines and the last two lines give one point of view. The other lines are from a different point of view. Tell who the speakers are.

Notice the space in the middle of the poem. Sometimes open space shows distance between people. Tell how it affects the meaning and the feeling, or mood, of the poem.

Try It!

Read the poem at the right. With a partner, answer these questions:

- What is the poem about?
- How are the lines **arranged**?
- How does the poem make you feel? What words or lines create that feeling?

Then share your answers with a group.

> The scuffle of feet,
> the trash on the floor,
> the jokes and the looks,
> the shouts and the roar.
> A new kid in school
> wishes he were home.
> He's caught in the crowd, but he's
>   Alone.

Express Ideas and Feelings

Act It Out Work in a group. Take turns acting out a feeling (such as being sad, angry, happy, or curious). Use your face and body language. Group members ask questions to guess your feeling. If they guess correctly, answer with a statement. After three guesses, say the correct answer.

> Are you jealous?

> Yes, I am jealous.

Write About Someone You Know

Study the Models When you write about someone you know, include enough details to make your statements clear and interesting.

JUST OK

My friend is Kimi. She is nice. I am usually at her house. Both our families are from another place. Kimi and I do things together.

> This writer leaves out a lot of details. The reader thinks: **"This is boring."**

BETTER

My best friend is Kimi. She is kind and nice. She makes me feel at home in my new neighborhood. I am usually at her house, or she is at my house. We are like sisters. Both our families are from Japan. Kimi and I cook Japanese food and sing Japanese songs together.

> Details make the statements interesting and clear.

Add Sentences Add two statements to the BETTER model above. Make the statements interesting and clear by adding details.

✐ **WRITE ON YOUR OWN** Write about someone you know who makes you feel at home. Include details. If you write statements with **am**, **is**, or **are**, be sure to use the verb forms correctly.

REMEMBER

There are different forms for the verb *be*.

One	More Than One
I **am**	we **are**
you **are**	you **are**
he, she, it **is**	they **are**

▲ Kimi and I like to be silly together.

KIDS LIKE ME
Voices of the Immigrant Experience

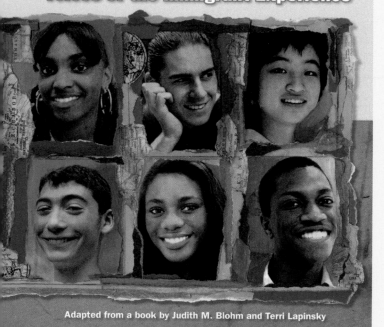

Adapted from a book by Judith M. Blohm and Terri Lapinsky

SELECTION 2 OVERVIEW

▸ **Build Background**

▸ **Language & Grammar**
Ask and Answer Questions
Use Questions and Statements

▸ **Prepare to Read**
Learn Key Vocabulary
Learn a Reading Strategy
Plan Your Reading

▸ **Read and Write**
Focus on Genre
Interview
Apply the Reading Strategy
Plan Your Reading
Critical Thinking
Reading Fluency
Read with Expression
Vocabulary Review
Write About the Guiding Question

▸ **Connect Across the Curriculum**
Literary Analysis
Analyze Text Structure: Compare and Contrast
Vocabulary Study
Use Context Clues
Listening/Speaking
Use Cultural Expressions
Research/Speaking
Research Population Change
Language and Grammar
Ask and Answer Questions
Writing and Grammar
Write a Message

Build Background

Listen to Teens

People from all over the world move to the United States. Teens have a lot to share about their experience as immigrants.

Digital Library

InsideNG.com
▸ View the video.

▲ It can be hard to make friends when you move to another country.

Connect

Anticipation Guide Think about a time when you had to adapt to a new place. Read each statement. Tell whether you agree or disagree.

Anticipation Guide

	Agree	Disagree
1. A good way to adapt is to change the way you look.	_____	_____
2. You should keep your traditions no matter where you live.	_____	_____
3. Making friends is the first thing you should do in a new place.	_____	_____

Language & Grammar

Ask and Answer Questions

Look at the photos. Listen to the questions and answers.
Then ask your own questions about the photos.

PICTURE PROMPT

What is this place?

It is Pike Place Market.

Where is the market?

The market is in Seattle.

When is the market open?

The market is open every day.

Who is the man?

The man is a fish seller.

Use Questions and Statements

You ask a **question** to find out something. Some questions start with *Am*, *Is*, or *Are*. The answer to these questions is a **statement** with *Yes* or *No*.

EXAMPLES   **Are** you from Miami?   **Yes**, I'm from Miami.

Is he from Miami?   **No**, he is from Chicago.

Some questions start with *Who*, *What*, *When*, or *Where*. Ask these questions to get information.

EXAMPLES   **Who** is that boy? He is my cousin.

What is that in his hand? That is his lunch.

When is lunch time? It is at 12:00.

Where is a good place to eat? That spot under the tree is a good place to eat.

Question Word	Asks About
Who?	person
What?	thing
When?	time
Where?	place

Practice Together

Ask these questions. Answer questions 1–3 with a *Yes* or *No* statement. Answer questions 4–6 with a statement that gives information.

1. Is this recipe from your home country?
2. Am I a good cook?
3. Are the potatoes ready?
4. Where is the sauce?
5. Who is here for dinner?
6. When is Asha coming?

Try It!

Ask these questions. Write a *Yes* or *No* statement to answer questions 7–9. Write a statement that gives information to answer questions 10–12. Hold up each answer as you say it.

7. Is this Room 12?
8. Am I in the right place?
9. Are you in my class?
10. What is your name?
11. Who is the teacher?
12. When is class over?

▲ **Where are the students? They are in class.**

Ask About Photos

ASK AND ANSWER QUESTIONS

Find a photo you like. Choose a photo of your family or friends or a photo from a magazine. Trade photos with a partner.

Look at your partner's photo. Decide what questions to ask. Make a chart to record your ideas. Use the four question words as headings.

Question Chart

Who?	What?	When?	Where?
Who is the woman in red?	What is in her hand?		

Now ask your partner the questions about the photo. Listen to the answers. Then change roles. Remember:

HOW TO ASK AND ANSWER QUESTIONS

1. To find out something, ask a question. You can start a question with *Am, Is, Are, Who, What, When,* or *Where.*

2. To answer a question, give a *Yes* or *No* statement or give information.

> Who is the girl?

> The girl is my friend Ayaka.

USE QUESTIONS AND STATEMENTS

When you answer a question about your photo, think about what the question word asks. Then form your statement.

EXAMPLES
Is this your mother?
No, that is my aunt.

Who is the man?
He is my uncle.

▲ **Where are they? They are in Morocco.**

Prepare to Read

Learn Key Vocabulary

Rate and Study the Words Rate how well you know each word. Then:

1. Pronounce the word. Say it aloud several times. Spell it.
2. Study the example.
3. Tell more about the word.
4. Practice it. Make the word your own.

Rating Scale

1 = I have never seen this word before.

2 = I am not sure of the word's meaning.

3 = I know this word and can teach the word's meaning to someone else.

Key Words

adjust (u-just) *verb*
▶ page 36

To **adjust** means to change in order to become comfortable with something. I hope I can **adjust** to my new school.

appreciate
(u-**prē**-shē-āt) *verb* ▶ page 36

To **appreciate** means to care about something or someone. The boy shows he **appreciates** his mom by giving her flowers.
Synonyms: **enjoy, like**

culture (kul-chur) *noun*
▶ page 32

The ideas and way of life for a group of people make up their **culture**. Baseball and jazz are both part of American **culture**.

different (di-fu-runt)
adjective ▶ page 32

Something that is **different** is not the same. The red flower is **different** from the others.
Antonym: **alike**

opportunity
(ah-pur-**tü**-nu-tē) *noun* ▶ page 33

An **opportunity** is a good chance to do something. The sign tells about a job **opportunity** at the restaurant.

relative (re-lu-tiv) *noun*
▶ page 34

A family member is a **relative**. The mother and daughter are **relatives**.
Synonym: **family**

understand (un-dur-stand)
verb ▶ page 36

To **understand** something is to know it well. This teacher **understands** the math problem and explains it to his students.
Past tense: **understood**

value (val-yū) *noun*
▶ page 35

A **value** is something that people care about. Respect is an important **value** in Japan.
Synonym: **ideal**

Practice the Words Work with a partner. Make a Word Web of Examples for each Key Word.

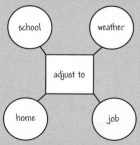

Word Web of Examples

Reading Strategy: Plan Your Reading

Before you read the interview, look it over. Notice the features, like the title and subtitle, to get an idea of what the selection is about. Look at the headings, pictures, maps, and charts. Then set a purpose, or reason, for reading.

**Reading Strategy
Plan Your Reading**

HOW TO PREVIEW AND SET A PURPOSE

1. Look at the title. Then look at other features. Think about what the interview is about.
2. What do you want to learn from the interview? Write questions that you would like to answer.
3. Read to answer your questions.

Strategy in Action

Here's how one student previewed the text and set a purpose.

Look Into the Text

title >

KIDS LIKE ME

subtitle > ## Voices of the Immigrant Experience

Meet six teens who are from different parts of the world. Now they live in cities and towns across the United States. They have families and friends in the U.S. Yet they remember and still observe some of the customs of their culture from "home." This is true whether their native country is South Korea, Peru, French Guyana, Iraq, Somalia, or Ethiopia.

How are these kids like me?

What customs do they still observe and why?

Practice Together

Read the passage again. Follow the steps in the How-To box. Set your purpose by writing a question about what you want to learn from the interview.

Focus on Genre

Interview

An interview gives information and opinions. In an interview, one person asks **questions** and one or more people **answer**.

When two **speakers** answer questions, you can compare and contrast their answers. That is, you can see how the answers are different or alike.

Q: **Why did you come to the United States?** ◁ question

Eunji: My dad is in business school. We followed my dad. ◁ answer

Hewan: Education is a top priority in my family. ◁ answer

Your Job as a Reader

Reading Strategy: Plan Your Reading

Before you read the interview, preview it and set a purpose. Write questions about what you want to learn.

Why did these kids come to the United States?

KIDS LIKE ME
Voices of the Immigrant Experience

Adapted from a book by Judith M. Blohm and Terri Lapinsky

Online Coach

Meet six teens who are from **different** parts of the world. Now they live in cities and towns across the United States. They have families and friends in the U.S. Yet they remember and still **observe** some of the **customs of** their **culture** from "home." This is true whether **their native country is** South Korea, Peru, French Guyana, Iraq, Somalia, or Ethiopia.

Where the Teens Come From

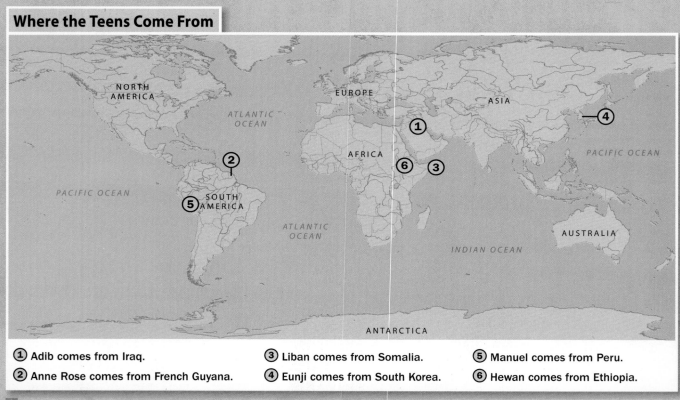

① Adib comes from Iraq.
② Anne Rose comes from French Guyana.
③ Liban comes from Somalia.
④ Eunji comes from South Korea.
⑤ Manuel comes from Peru.
⑥ Hewan comes from Ethiopia.

▲ Interpret the Map Find where Hewan's home country is. Whose home country is near hers?

Key Vocabulary	In Other Words
different *adj.*, not the same **culture** *n.*, the ideas and way of life for a group of people	**observe** follow **customs of** ways of doing things from **their native country is** they were born in

Q: Why did you come to the United States?

Eunji: My dad is in business school. We **followed** my dad.

Hewan: Education is **a top priority** in my family. My mother, older brother, and I are here for my education. Getting into medical school is my goal. My family **supports** this.

Liban: We are in the U.S. to have a better life. We are now away from the wars. We can get a good education for me and my sister. We are also free to be ourselves.

Adib: We are here because of war in our home country.

Anne Rose: My parents are from Haiti. They moved to French Guyana where I was born. Now we are in the U.S. We moved because my parents want a better and safer life for our family.

Manuel: I want a better education. I also want more **opportunities** to **succeed** in life. Unfortunately, my parents are still in Peru. They are working and taking care of my eight-year-old brother. I live with my aunt.

Key Vocabulary
opportunity *n.*, a chance to do something

In Other Words
followed came with
a top priority one of the most important things
supports wants to help me with
succeed do well

Before You Move On

1. **Categorize** List four reasons that these teens' families came to the United States.
2. **Viewing** Look at the map. Which teens are from countries in South America? Which ones are from African countries?

Q: What is different about living in the United States?

Eunji: School rules in Korea are a lot **stricter** than here. In Korea, we cannot have pierced ears or noses. We cannot have long hair or even colored hair clips.

Hewan: American families do not seem **that close-knit**. However, Ethiopian families are. Unlike American families, we share our food from one big plate. The entire family sits around the table. Then we all eat out of one dish.

Liban: In Somalia, there is no bus transportation. Everyone walks. People have cars, but everyone is close by. The store is next door. Your uncle is next door.

Adib: My mom says she noticed that in the U.S. you do not have as many **relatives** living with you as we do in Iraq and Lebanon.

Another thing that is different is school. There are more classes in school in Iraq and Lebanon.

Also, children and teens have to be **more polite** than American kids are to adults. When you talk to your teacher or when you are called on in class, students must first stand. Then you can ask or **respond to** a question.

Key Vocabulary
relative *n.*, a family member

In Other Words
stricter more difficult
that close-knit very close to each other
more polite nicer, more respectful
respond to answer

Anne Rose: There are many **similarities** between French Guyana and America.

Manuel: In Peru, family is the main value. Families always get together on weekends or at any holiday. The people in communities in Peru are closer to each other than in the neighborhoods in the U.S. The people in Peru don't have a lot of extra money to spend. So people are more helpful to each other. They try to find a way to help each other. They do things like selling food at **cheap** prices.

Immigrants to the United States in 2006

More than 1.2 million people came to the United States in 2006. Most are from Asia or Latin America. This chart shows the top ten home countries.

Home Country	Number
Mexico	173,753
People's Republic of China	87,345
Philippines	74,607
India	61,369
Cuba	45,614
Colombia	43,151
Dominican Republic	38,069
El Salvador	31,783
Vietnam	30,695
Jamaica	24,976

Source: U.S. Department of Homeland Security, Computer Linked Application Information Management System, Legal Immigrant Data, 2006.

▲ **Interpret the Chart** Which country did most immigrants come from in 2006?

Key Vocabulary
value *n.*, something that people care about; a worthy idea

In Other Words
similarities things that are alike
cheap low

Before You Move On

1. **Compare and Contrast** According to these teens, how are families in other countries closer than they are in the United States?
2. **Vocabulary** What are some examples of **values** in a **culture**?

Q: What advice do you have for people who move to the United States?

Eunji: Ask many questions. That way, you learn about the person you are talking to. You can also learn about American culture.

Hewan: Quickly make friends in order to learn the language and culture. With their help, it is easier to settle into a new country. Friends can also make it easier to **adjust** to the different customs and ideas.

Liban: Be yourself. That is the main thing. Do not **put yourself down**. Do not let anybody put you down. Work hard. Talk to people. Ask for help if you need it. Say what you want to say (other than bad words).

Adib: Play sports to meet new people. **Make an effort** to be social and talk with people in your classes. This is hard at first.

Anne Rose: Get involved in everything you can. The more things you **get into**, the more opportunities you have to learn, **understand**, and **appreciate** life.

Manuel: I have one **piece of advice**. Don't be lazy! ❖

Key Vocabulary
adjust *v.*, to become comfortable with
understand *v.*, to know
appreciate *v.*, to care about; to see the worth of something

In Other Words
put yourself down think badly of yourself
Make an effort Try hard
Get involved Be active; Take part
get into do
piece of advice helpful idea

Before You Move On

1. **Compare and Contrast** How is the advice of these teens alike? How are their ideas different?
2. **Judgment** Which advice do you think is most helpful? Explain why.

Connect Reading and Writing

Vocabulary
adjust
appreciate
cultures
different
opportunity
relatives
understands
values

CRITICAL THINKING

1. SUM IT UP Make a chart with the interview questions on pages 33–36. Use a few words to list answers from the **different** teens. Refer to the chart to summarize "Kids Like Me."

Summary Chart

Teen	Why did you come to the United States?	What is different about living in the United States?
Eunji	for my dad's schooling	
Hewan		

2. Evaluate What do you think is the most important idea to **understand** in "Kids Like Me"?

3. Analyze Look at the Anticipation Guide on page 24. Do you want to **adjust** any of your answers? Discuss with a partner.

4. Compare Name **values** that the six different teens share.

READING FLUENCY

Expression Read the passage on page 569 to a partner. Assess your fluency.

1. I read
  a. great   **b.** OK   **c.** not very well

2. What I did best in my reading was _____.

READING STRATEGY

Plan Your Reading
Did you learn what you thought you would learn from the interview? Share with a partner.

VOCABULARY REVIEW

Oral Review Read the paragraph aloud. Add the vocabulary words.

> Many immigrants come to the United States for the _____ to have a better life. Sometimes they bring their parents and other _____ to live with them. It can be difficult for immigrants to _____ to living in a country that is new and _____. It can be easier if someone speaks and _____ the language. People soon learn that most Americans enjoy, or _____, differences among people. The country has many ways of life, or _____. However, people share many of the same _____, such as freedom.

Written Review Why do so many people come to the United States from **different** countries? Write your opinion. Use four vocabulary words.

 **WRITE ABOUT THE** GUIDING QUESTION

Explore Finding Your Own Place
Do you think it is easier for teens or for adults to **adjust** to living in a new country? Use examples from the text to state your opinion.

Connect Across the Curriculum

Analyze Text Structure: Compare and Contrast

Academic Vocabulary
- **compare** (kum-**pair**) *verb*
  When you **compare** two things, you think about how they are alike and different.

Sometimes writers organize nonfiction text by **comparing** and contrasting ideas. They often use **signal words** to communicate the structure. Some signal words point to a comparison or a contrast. The chart at the right shows examples of signal words.

Signal Words

Comparison	Contrast
also	but
and	however
just like	unlike
too	yet

Practice Together

Look for Signal Words Read this passage from "Kids Like Me." Notice the **signal words**.

> **Hewan:** American families do not seem that close-knit. However, Ethiopian families are. Unlike American families, we share our food from one big plate. The entire family sits around the table. Then we all eat out of one dish.

▲ Ethiopian food is served in one big dish.

Use a Diagram You can use a Venn Diagram to show how things **compare** and contrast. The text in the middle shows how two things are alike. The other text shows how they are different.

Copy the diagram and complete it for the passage.

Venn Diagram

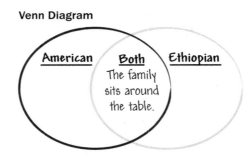

American | Both | Ethiopian
The family sits around the table.

Try It!

Make a Venn Diagram Work with a partner. Make a Venn Diagram for another passage from "Kids Like Me." Show how two things are alike and different.

Use Context Clues

> **Academic Vocabulary**
> • **context** (**kon**-tekst) *noun*
>   Context refers to the parts nearby that help explain the meaning.

Use a Dictionary Many English words have more than one meaning. The meanings are numbered in a dictionary. You can figure out the correct meaning of a word from the **context** .

Dictionary Entry

> **value** (**val**-yū) *noun* **1** a fair price for something **2** an idea that people care about

Read this passage from "Kids Like Me."
You can figure out the meaning of *value* by using *family* as a clue. Here, *value* means "an idea that people care about."

> **Manuel:** In Peru, family is the main value.

Define Words Find each of these words on page 33. Write the **context** clues you use to figure it out. Then look up the word in a dictionary and copy the best meaning.

1. top   **2.** goal   **3.** support   **4.** free   **5.** country

Use Cultural Expressions

SOCIAL
SCIENCE

> **Academic Vocabulary**
> • **explain** (ik-**splān**) *verb*
>   When you **explain** an idea, you make it clear so people can understand it.

Suppose you ask a friend about her math teacher. She answers, "His bark is worse than his bite!" You may not know this expression. Your friend may need to **explain** it. She means that the teacher is nicer than he seems.

1 **Interpret an Expression** Suppose you and a friend go somewhere new. You don't know any other people there. Your friend says, "I feel like a fish out of water!" In a group, discuss what this expression means.

2 **List Expressions** Think of other common expressions. What do they say about the culture?

3 **Share with the Class** Present an expression to the class. **Explain** what it means. Speak slowly and clearly. Check that your listeners follow what you say.

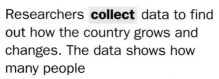

Research/Speaking

MATH

Research Population Change

> **Academic Vocabulary**
> • **collect** (ku-**lekt**) *verb*
>   To **collect** means to get from two or more different places.

Researchers **collect** data to find out how the country grows and changes. The data shows how many people

• live in each city and state
• go to school
• work in offices, restaurants, hospitals, and other places.

Government leaders can use the data to plan for the future. They use it to figure out how many schools or roads to build, for example.

▲ Researchers **collect** data about how many people live in cities like New York.

❶ **Conduct Research** Find out how your community has changed. Use the Internet to **collect** data.

> **Internet** InsideNG.com
> ⊘ Find out the population of your town now and in past years.

❷ **Make a Graph** Use the data to make a graph like this one.

Bar Graph

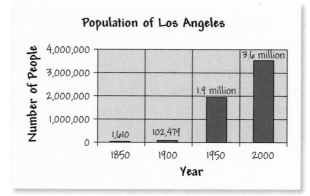

❸ **Report Your Findings** Display your graph for the class. Tell what it shows. Has your town grown quickly? How do you know? Speak clearly, and make eye contact with your classmates. Explain where your information comes from.

Ask and Answer Questions

Play Twenty Questions Imagine you are an animal, place, or thing. Your classmates will ask you questions with *Is* or *Are* to guess what you are. Answer only with *Yes* or *No* statements. If they can't guess in twenty questions, tell them the answer.

> Is your home in the forest?

> No, my home is in the jungle.

Write a Message

Study the Models When you write a message to someone you don't know well, you can make your writing more interesting by including both statements and questions. Readers are more likely to enjoy and understand what you write if it has variety.

JUST OK

Dear Ankur,

My name is Jay Resnik. What are your hobbies? Where is your favorite place to go on the weekends? Who are your best friends?

Jay

The writer mostly asks questions. The reader thinks: **"I wish Jay would tell me something about himself."**

BETTER

Dear Ankur,

My name is Jay Resnik. I am a student in Los Angeles, California. My teacher gave me your name to be my pen pal. What are your hobbies? I swim and play the guitar. Where is your favorite place to go on the weekends? I usually go to the movies with my friends. Who are your best friends?

Jay

Now the writer uses questions and statements. This is more interesting for the reader.

Add Sentences Pretend that you are Jay. Add one statement and one question to the BETTER model above.

WRITE ON YOUR OWN Imagine that you have a new pen pal. Write an e-mail message to your pen pal. Include statements and questions.

REMEMBER
- To tell something, make a **statement**.
- To find out something, ask a **question**.

Familiar Places
by Elizabeth Boylan

Build Background

See How Places Change

Communities change over the years. Take a tour of a city with a longtime resident. Explore the community's history.

Connect

TV Commercial Imagine you and some friends are in charge of encouraging visitors to come to your city. Think about special events, customs, and places in your community. Then plan and present a short TV ad for your town.

Digital Library

InsideNG.com
View the video.

▲ Every town has its own history.

Language & Grammar

Give Commands

Listen to the rap. Then listen again and chime in.

RAP

COME TO THE MARKET!

Come to the marketplace!
See the choices. Look!
Come to the marketplace!
Taste the samples. Yum!
See it! Try it!
Taste it! Buy it—
If it doesn't cost too much.

Use Statements and Commands

A **statement** tells something. It begins with a capital letter and ends with a period.

> EXAMPLE **W**e are hungry⊙

A **command** tells someone to do something. A command begins with a capital letter. It often ends with a period.

> EXAMPLE **T**ry the Italian restaurant⊙

A strong command ends with an exclamation point.

> EXAMPLE Be careful⨀

To make a polite command, use the word *please*.

> EXAMPLE **Please** get in the taxi.

Practice Together

Say each sentence. Tell whether it is a statement or a command. Then tell why.

1. This neighborhood is interesting.
2. Look at the signs.
3. They are in English and Vietnamese.
4. I see a newspaper stand.
5. Please buy me a paper.
6. The restaurant across the street is good.
7. There are a lot of cars.
8. Stay away from the curb!

▲ **This neighborhood in Westminster, California, is called Little Saigon.**

Try It!

Read each sentence. Write *statement* or *command* on a card. Hold up the card as you say the sentence. Then tell why the sentence is a statement or a command.

9. I like this festival.
10. The bright lights are pretty.
11. Listen to the music.
12. It has a great beat.
13. Smell that chili!
14. Get two plates for us, please.

Act Out a Market Scene

GIVE COMMANDS

Imagine you are at a market. Work with a partner to act out a scene.

One of you plays the customer, or the person who is buying. The other plays the vendor, or the person who is selling. Include commands in your conversation.

First, decide who will be the customer and who will be the vendor. Then decide what kind of market you are going to. Is it a fruit or vegetable market? A fish market? A food stand? A clothing market?

Draw or list things you can find at the market. Add the prices.

Now role-play the scene. Use as many commands as you can. Remember:

HOW TO GIVE COMMANDS

1. When you want to tell someone to do something, use a command.

2. Use *please* to make a polite command.

Please give me an apple.

USE STATEMENTS AND COMMANDS

When you want to tell something, make a **statement**. When you want somebody to do something, give a **command**.

EXAMPLES

Customer: I want a pumpkin.
Please give me an orange one.

Vendor: Look at the white ones!
They are very nice. They are $4.00 each.

▲ The farmer sells her produce at an outdoor market.

Prepare to Read

Learn Key Vocabulary

Rate and Study the Words Rate how well you know each word. Then:

1. Pronounce the word. Say it aloud several times. Spell it.
2. Study the example.
3. Tell more about the word.
4. Practice it. Make the word your own.

Key Words

agree (u-**grē**) *verb*
▶ page 50

When you **agree** with someone, you have the same ideas. A handshake shows that people **agree** to something.
Antonym: **disagree**

community
(ku-**myū**-nu-tē) *noun* ▶ page 50

A **community** is a place where people live, work, and carry out their daily lives. This **community** has an outdoor market.
Synonyms: **neighborhood, town**

familiar (fu-**mil**-yur)
adjective ▶ page 51

Something that is **familiar** is already known. The man was happy to see a **familiar** face at the party.
Antonym: **unfamiliar**

festival (**fes**-tu-vul) *noun*
▶ page 54

A **festival** is a special event or party. Dancers perform at the **festival**.
Synonyms: **celebration, fiesta**

native (**nā**-tiv) *adjective*
▶ page 53

Something that belongs to you because of where you were born is **native** to you. People wave flags from their **native** countries.

neighborhood
(**nā**-bur-hood) *noun* ▶ page 52

A **neighborhood** is a place where people live and work together. This **neighborhood** is in Boston.
Synonym: **community**

population
(pah-pyu-**lā**-shun) *noun* ▶ page 50

Population means the number of people who live somewhere. Many people live in New York City. It has a large **population**.

tradition (tru-**di**-shun) *noun*
▶ page 50

A **tradition** is an activity or belief that people share for many years. It is a **tradition** for this family to celebrate Kwanzaa every December.
Synonym: **custom**

Practice the Words Work with a partner. Write a question using one or two Key Words. Answer your partner's question. Use at least one Key Word in your answer. Take turns until you have used all the Key Words twice.

Questions	Answers
Do you have any traditions in your community?	Yes, we have a festival every spring.

Reading Strategy: Plan Your Reading

You can get more from reading nonfiction if you preview it
and set a purpose before you read.

Reading Strategy
Plan Your Reading

HOW TO PREVIEW AND SET A PURPOSE

1. First, look at the title and headings. Then, look at photos, captions, and other text features. Think about what kind of information they give.
2. Decide what you want to learn as you read. Write questions that you would like to answer.
3. Read the selection to answer your questions.

Strategy in Action

Here's how one student previewed the text and set a purpose in
"Familiar Places."

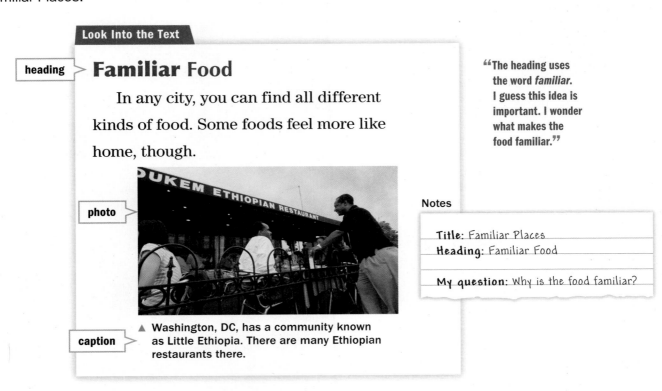

Look Into the Text

heading > ## Familiar Food

In any city, you can find all different kinds of food. Some foods feel more like home, though.

"The heading uses the word *familiar*. I guess this idea is important. I wonder what makes the food familiar."

photo >

Notes

Title: Familiar Places
Heading: Familiar Food

My question: Why is the food familiar?

caption >

▲ Washington, DC, has a community known as Little Ethiopia. There are many Ethiopian restaurants there.

Practice Together

Preview the rest of the selection. Follow the steps in the How-To box. List the
headings. Write questions to set a purpose. Read on to find the answers.

Focus on Genre

Expository Nonfiction

Expository nonfiction gives information and facts. Usually, the text is divided into sections. A **heading** tells the topic, or what the section is about. The text that follows includes a **main idea** that tells more about the topic.

Familiar Food ◁ heading

In any city, you can find all different kinds of food. Some foods feel more like home, though.

Your Job as a Reader

Reading Strategy: Plan Your Reading

As you preview the text, list the headings and write your questions. Read to find the answers.

Heading: Familiar Food

My question: What are some examples of familiar food?

▼ Chinatown in New York City is home to many people who moved to the United States from China.

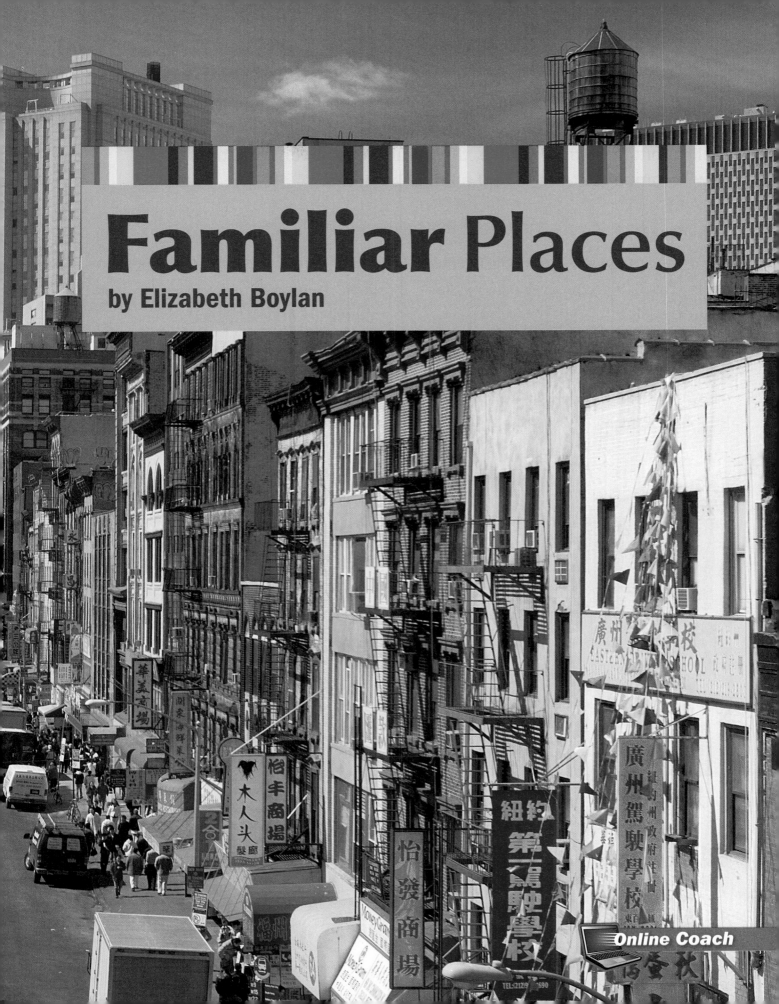

Familiar Places

by Elizabeth Boylan

Online Coach

People are the heart of any **community**. When the **population** changes, so does the community. People bring their clothes, their furniture, and, of course, their **traditions**. Over time, the new community starts to feel a little like home.

Familiar Food

In any city, you can find all different kinds of food. Some foods feel more like home, though.

Ethiopian people who move to Little Ethiopia **agree**. The community has many restaurants that serve **delicious** Ethiopian foods.

Walk into a restaurant. Order some food. **Tear** some of the *injera* to scoop up the hot **stews**. Taste the seasoned vegetables and spicy sauces.

The right food makes a new place feel like home.

◄ Washington, DC, has a community known as Little Ethiopia. There are many Ethiopian restaurants there. The first Ethiopian restaurants in Washington, DC, opened in the 1970s.

Key Vocabulary
community *n.*, where people live
population *n.*, the number of people in a place
tradition *n.*, an activity or belief that people share
agree *v.*, to have the same idea

In Other Words
delicious very good
Tear Pull off
injera Ethiopian flat bread ►
stews thick soups

Familiar Clothes

In a community, shops sell many different kinds of clothes. Some clothes look more **familiar**, though.

Indian people who go to Little India agree. There are many clothing and jewelry shops there.

Walk into a shop and feel the soft **fabrics**. Look at the colorful *saris*. Try on a *kameez*.

Familiar clothes can make a new place feel like home.

▲ Many people from India moved to Chicago, Illinois, in the 1960s. They opened shops that sell Indian clothes, food, and jewelry. The community is called Little India.

Key Vocabulary
familiar *adj.*, already known

In Other Words
fabrics cloth
saris long, flowing dresses
kameez long shirt

Before You Move On

1. **Explain** How do the people of Little Ethiopia make their **community** feel like home?
2. **Main Idea and Details** What is each section mainly about? What details tell about the main idea?

Familiar Sounds

There are sounds all around a **neighborhood**. Some sounds are more familiar, though.

Haitian people who move to Little Haiti agree. The sounds you hear in Little Haiti are like the sounds you hear in Haiti. Walk into a shop and hear people speak Haitian Creole and French. Listen to the *compas* **music**. **Sway** to the strong beat.

Familiar sounds can make a new place feel like home.

▲ Thousands of Haitians moved to Miami, Florida, in the 1980s. They formed a neighborhood called Little Haiti. Dancers move to the music at a street market.

Key Vocabulary

neighborhood *n.*, a place where people live and work together

In Other Words

compas **music** Haitian music
Sway Move your body back and forth

Familiar Language

When a language is new to you, the words can look so different. Sometimes it is nice to see your **native** language.

Korean people who move to Koreatown agree. In Koreatown, you can find words in English and Korean. Read the *hangul* **signs**. Buy a book in Korean. Find a Korean newspaper.

Familiar words can make a new place feel like home.

▲ Many Koreans moved to Los Angeles, California, in the 1960s. Now many businesses have signs in Korean and English.

Key Vocabulary
native *adj.*, belonging to the place someone was born

In Other Words
hangul **signs** signs that use Korean writing

Before You Move On

1. **Interpret** What are some of the sounds you might hear if you go to Little Haiti?
2. **Main Idea and Details** According to the text, what **familiar** things can Korean immigrants find in Koreatown?

Familiar Celebrations

Everyone likes to **celebrate**! There are always many reasons to have fun. Some celebrations are more familiar, though.

Every September, the people of Little Italy hold a **festival**. Look at the **decorations** and watch the parade. Then eat *cannoli* while you dance and sing Italian songs.

Familiar celebrations can make a new place feel like home.

Familiar foods, sounds, and celebrations can make you feel at home in a new neighborhood. As new people move in, the neighborhood will continue to change and become their home, too. ❖

▲ New York City, New York, has a neighborhood called Little Italy. Many Italians moved there in the late 1800s. Not many Italians move there now, though. People in Little Italy still celebrate Italian traditions.

Key Vocabulary
festival *n.*, a special event or party

In Other Words
celebrate have a party
decorations special lights and other things that people put up for the party
cannoli an Italian dessert

Before You Move On

1. **Evidence and Conclusion** Which words explain why **communities** often change over time?
2. **Inference** How can **festivals** help make a new place feel like home?

Connect Reading and Writing

Vocabulary

agrees

community

familiar

festival

native

neighborhoods

population

traditions

CRITICAL THINKING

1. SUM IT UP Make a Summary Chart. List the five **neighborhoods** in the selection. Record details about each. Use your chart to give a summary to a partner.

Summary Chart

Little Ethiopia	Little India	Little Haiti	Koreatown	Little Italy
many restaurants				

2. Paraphrase Look back at the first paragraph of the selection. Use your own words to tell how **communities** change.

3. Make Judgments What do you think makes a new place feel comfortable? Do you **agree** with the author, or do you have different ideas? Explain.

4. Analyze Why do you think **familiar** things are important to immigrants? Explain.

READING FLUENCY

Phrasing Read the passage on page 570 to a partner. Assess your fluency.

1. I read

　　a. great　　**b.** OK　　**c.** not very well

2. What I did best in my reading was _____.

READING STRATEGY

Plan Your Reading
Look back at the questions you wrote before you read. Did you find the answers? What else did you learn?

VOCABULARY REVIEW

Oral Review Read the paragraph aloud. Add the vocabulary words.

> In the 1880s, a _____ in Vancouver, Canada, was known as Chinatown. Today many Chinese people also live in other _____. Nearly one third of the city's _____ speaks a main Chinese language. Many people are _____ Chinese speakers even though they were born in Canada. Everyone _____ that art, music, and celebrations keep _____ alive. The Dragon Boat Festival is well-known, or _____, to nearly everyone in Vancouver. This _____ takes place on the water.

Written Review What **festivals** or special **traditions** does your **community** have? Write a TV ad for one of them. Use four vocabulary words.

 **WRITE ABOUT THE** **GUIDING QUESTION**

Explore Finding Your Own Place
Look back at the photos in the selection. How might these **neighborhoods** change in the future? Write your opinion, and support it with reasons.

Connect Across the Curriculum

Analyze Text Structure: Main Idea

> **Academic Vocabulary**
> ● **topic** (**tah**-pik) *noun*
>   A **topic** is the subject of a piece of writing or
>   of a discussion.

Writers of nonfiction usually organize their text into sections.
Each section has a **main idea**—what the writer is mostly
telling about the **topic**. The section heading often gives a
clue to the **topic** of the section.

Practice Together

Read for the Main Idea Read this section from "Familiar
Places." Use the heading to figure out the **topic**. Then look
for a sentence that gives the **main idea** about the **topic**.

Familiar Clothes ← heading

In a community, shops sell many
different kinds of clothes. Some clothes
look more familiar, though.

Indian people who go to Little India
agree. There are many clothing and jewelry
shops there.

Walk into a shop and feel the soft
fabrics. Look at the colorful saris. Try
on a *kameez*.

Familiar clothes can make a new place
feel like home.

▲ Many people from
India moved to
Chicago, Illinois, in
the 1960s.

Try It!

Look for the Main Idea Read the text on page 53.
Tell what the **topic** is. Then find the main idea of
the section.

Share with a Partner Compare your thoughts with a
partner's. Tell how the main idea relates to the **topic**.

Use Context Clues

> **Academic Vocabulary**
> • **context** (**kon**-tekst) *noun*
> Context refers to the parts nearby that help explain the meaning.

When you find a word that has multiple meanings, use **context** to try to figure out the correct meaning. Then check a dictionary.

Read a Dictionary Entry In a dictionary, **entry words** are listed in alphabetical order. The entry tells what the word means and gives other information.

pronunciation

stew (stū) *noun*

part of speech

meaning 1 **1** meat, fish, or vegetables cooked for a long time on the stove

meaning 2 **2** a state of worry: *He is really in a stew.*

example sentence

Find the Meaning Read this sentence from "Familiar Places." Use nearby words to figure out the meaning of *stew*.

Tear some of the *injera* to scoop up the hot stews.

Which dictionary meaning matches your meaning?

Look Up Words Work with a partner. Find each word in the selection. Use **context** to figure out the meaning. Then check the word in a dictionary, and copy the correct definition.

1. heart, p. 50   **2.** serve, p. 50   **3.** beat, p. 52   **4.** watch, p. 54

SOCIAL SCIENCE

Give Directions

> • **explain** (ik-**splān**) *verb*
> When you **explain** an idea, you make it clear so people can understand it.

Suppose your neighborhood is having a festival. You invite a friend who lives in a different part of town. How will you **explain** how to get to the festival?

1 **Draw a Map** Make a drawing that shows the main roads. Write the name of each road your friend will use. Label where the festival is. Include a compass rose to show north, south, east, and west.

2 **Think of Landmarks** A landmark is a point along a route that helps you figure out where you are. Parks, monuments, and special buildings like a post office are good landmarks. Think about what your friend will see.

3 **Write Directions** Tell a partner how to get to the festival. Your partner writes the directions as a list: *Turn right at the third street past the library. Go north one mile.*

Tell About Traditions

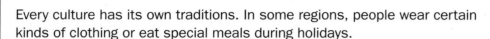

SOCIAL SCIENCE

> **Academic Vocabulary**
> • **collect** (ku-**lekt**) *verb*
>   To **collect** means to get from two or more different places.

Every culture has its own traditions. In some regions, people wear certain kinds of clothing or eat special meals during holidays.

1 **Choose a Topic** Choose a culture to research. It can be your own or another culture that you want to know more about.

2 **Research Traditions** Find out about the traditions of that culture. Use books, magazines, and the Internet. Look for details and stories to share.

Internet InsideNG.com
↻ Explore different traditions.

3 **Use a Chart** Make a Traditions Chart to record the information you **collect** .

Traditions Chart

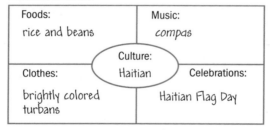

Foods: rice and beans	Music: compas
	Culture: Haitian
Clothes: brightly colored turbans	Celebrations: Haitian Flag Day

4 **Plan Your Presentation** Decide which details and stories to share. Also decide which ones not to share.

Think about the best order to present your ideas. You may:

• Tell a little about several traditions and a lot about one tradition.

• Use a calendar and tell about traditions that happen at different times of the year.

• Tell about many traditions that relate to a topic such as food harvest.

Consider bringing photos or other items such as traditional clothing or recordings of traditional music.

5 **Present the Traditions** Talk loudly enough so that everyone in the room can hear you. Relax and speak at a normal pace—not too fast and not too slow.

▲ Indian teens wear traditional clothing.

After your presentation, answer questions from your audience.

Give Commands

Pair Talk Imagine your partner is a visitor to your neighborhood. Describe some interesting places to visit. Tell your partner how to get to the places and what to do. Use commands. Switch roles.

> Try the Thai Garden. Go to 8th Street and turn right. Get there early!

Write About a Special Event

Study the Models When you write about a special event, use a variety of sentence types. Include **statements**, **questions**, **exclamations**, and **commands** to communicate your ideas and engage your readers.

JUST OK

The International Parade in our neighborhood is a lot of fun. I like to go and see the costumes. Some of my friends are always in the parade. Ahmet wears traditional Turkish clothing. Nestor and Cande are in the Caribbean band. Shivaani dresses as an Indian dancer.

This writer only uses statements. The reader thinks: "**The topic is interesting, but the writer presents it in a boring way.**"

BETTER

Have you ever been to a Cinco de Mayo celebration? It's really fun. Dancers wear colorful Mexican costumes. They swirl to the beat of lively folk music. There are games and good things to eat. There's even a jalapeño-eating contest! So mark next May 5 on your calendar. Come and join the fun!

This writer uses a variety of sentences. The text is more interesting.

Revise It Look back at the JUST OK passage. Work with a partner to improve it. Use a variety of sentences.

✎ **WRITE ON YOUR OWN** Imagine you are at a special event or celebration in your community. Write a description of it. Be sure to include different kinds of sentences.

REMEMBER

- A statement ends with a period (**.**).
- A question ends with a question mark (**?**).
- An exclamation ends with an exclamation point(**!**).
- A command ends with a period (**.**) or an exclamation point (**!**).

Compare Across Texts

Compare People

"Growing Together," "Kids Like Me," and "Familiar Places" tell about **immigrants** to the United States. Choose two people or groups of **immigrants** in the texts, and **compare** how they feel about their new homes.

How It Works

Collect and Organize Ideas Make a Venn Diagram to **compare** the feelings of two people you read about—Carmen and Liban. In the outside areas of the diagram, write different feelings that they have. In the center area, write feelings they share.

Practice Together

Study and Compare Ideas Use the information you collected in the Venn Diagram to write two sentences that **compare** Carmen's and Liban's feelings. In the first sentence, tell how their feelings are different. In the second sentence, tell how their feelings are the same.

> Carmen has nice memories of sea breezes and mango trees in Cuba, but Liban remembers wars in Somalia. Both people think that you should be strong and stand up for yourself.

Venn Diagram

Carmen — misses the warm sea breezes and mango trees in Cuba

Both — think you shouldn't let anyone call you an ugly name or put you down

Liban — is happy to be away from the wars in Somalia

Try It!

Make a Venn Diagram to **compare** two other people or groups of **immigrants** in the selections. Write two sentences about the information. You may want to use a frame like this one to help you express your comparison.

_____ feels _____, but _____ feels _____. Both people feel _____.

Academic Vocabulary
- **immigrant** (i-mu-grunt) *noun*
  An **immigrant** is someone who comes to live in a new country.
- **compare** (kum-**pair**) *verb*
  When you **compare** two things, you think about how they are alike and different.

Finding Your Own Place

 What defines home?

Reflect on Your Reading

Think back on your reading of the unit selections. Discuss what you did to understand what you read.

Focus on Genre **Organization of Ideas**
In this unit, you learned that sometimes writers organize text to compare and contrast things. Choose a selection from the unit, and draw a diagram, chart, or picture to show how the writer compares and contrasts two things. Use your drawing to explain the organization of the text to a partner.

Reading Strategy **Plan Your Reading**
As you read the selections, you previewed the text, made predictions, and set purposes for reading. Explain how you will use this strategy in the future.

Explore the

Throughout this unit, you have been thinking about what defines home. Choose one of these ways to explore the Guiding Question:

- **Discuss** With a group, discuss what immigrants do to make a new place feel like home. Give details from the selections that support your ideas.
- **Ask Questions** Ask someone who has moved to the United States how his or her home country and the U.S. are alike and different. Share with the class.
- **Draw** Create a map of your neighborhood. Label places or areas that are important to you. Share your map with a classmate, and explain how your neighborhood is a home for you and your neighbors.

Book Talk

Which Unit Library book did you choose? Explain to a partner what it taught you about the meaning of home.

UNIT LIBRARY

Content Library

Leveled Library

The Last Salmon Run (detail), 1990, Alfredo Arreguín.
Oil on canvas, private collection.

▲ **Critical Viewing** Notice the details in the painting. What do you think is the artist's message about natural resources?

Water for Life

 **GUIDING QUESTION** How do we depend on Earth's resources?

Read More!

Content Library

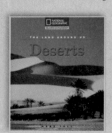

Deserts
by Mary Tull

Leveled Library

20,000 Leagues Under the Sea
by Jules Verne, adapted by Judith Conaway

Knights of the Round Table
by Gwen Gross

The Dragon Prince
by Laurence Yep

Internet
InsideNG.com

- ⊘ Go to the Digital Library to learn more about water resources.
- ⊘ Find out how people use water in the United States.
- ⊘ Watch a video about water.

Focus on Genre

Fiction and Nonfiction

There are two major kinds of text: **fiction** and **nonfiction**. Fiction is written to entertain the reader. It is a made-up story with events that form a plot. Nonfiction is usually written to inform or explain. It includes facts that can be proved.

How It Works

Before you read, preview the text to determine if it is fiction or nonfiction. This will tell you whether the text tells a story or gives facts.

Fiction The events in fiction are the **plot**. The **characters** are the people or animals that create the action. The writer also may include **dialogue** .

An Exciting Day

It is a lazy day at the lake. Even the fish are too lazy to swim. Josephina sighs. "Nothing exciting ever happens," she says.

Just then, a huge wind roars. Josephina has to tie her shoelaces to a tree to stay put. The wind blows until the entire lake, fish and all, is gone.

Then a thick, black cloud moves overhead. Like a sponge being squeezed out, the cloud dumps rain and fills the lake again.

"Well," Josephina exclaims. "That was exciting," she says.

Dialogue is what the characters in a story say.

Nonfiction Nonfiction writing gives facts about a **topic** . Writers organize the information to make it clear and easy to understand. For example, a writer may state the **main idea** about the **topic** . Then the writer gives details that tell more about the main idea.

Forms of Water

Water has different forms. As a liquid, water has no shape. Pour it into any container and water fits right in. If you freeze water, it becomes a solid. If you heat water, it will turn to steam and disappear as a gas. When it cools, it goes back to its liquid form.

Main idea

Details

Academic Vocabulary

- **topic** (**tah**-pik) *noun*
  A **topic** is the subject of a piece of writing or of a discussion.

Practice Together

Read these passages aloud. As you read, listen for clues that tell you if the passage is fiction or nonfiction.

Water Cycle

Water moves in a cycle that never ends. Above Earth, water is in the form of clouds. Clouds are made of tiny water drops or ice crystals. At some point, they fall to Earth as rain or snow. The water soaks into the ground or returns to rivers and oceans. Heat from the sun evaporates water from the surface of Earth, and water returns to the sky as clouds.

Calling the Wind

Sage had an idea for bringing rain to the dry fields. She climbed the highest hill and called to Wind. "Wind, you are weak!"

That angered Wind. "You dare to call me weak!"

Sage shrugged and said, "You are not strong enough to blow a cloud this way." Wind began to howl. It blew until the sky filled with clouds and rain fell.

Try It!

Read these passages aloud. What kind of text is each passage? How do you know?

A Mystery

Chang discovers all kinds of interesting things at the beach.

Today no one else is there. Even the birds are gone. Chang sees something purple rolling in the waves on the shore. He goes closer. It is a bottle, and it has something in it!

Chang reaches down to pick it up. Then he hears a voice. "Help me! I'm trapped in this bottle."

Chang knows a lot of folk tales. He knows that a voice in a bottle could be big trouble. So he turns around and walks away.

Bodies of Water

Earth has very large bodies of water on its surface. The largest is the Pacific Ocean. It is about 15 times bigger than the United States.

The largest body of fresh water is Lake Superior. The lake is almost 2,800 miles around. You could fit Rhode Island in the middle of it.

The Missouri River is one of the longest rivers in the world. It stretches 2,341 miles in length. People use these bodies of water for food, transportation, and recreation.

Focus on Vocabulary

Relate Words

Synonyms are words that have nearly the same meaning. For example, one word might create a stronger feeling than its synonym does. Knowing the exact meanings of synonyms can help you better understand what you read.

EXAMPLE   The Great Lakes are all **big**, but Lake Superior is **enormous**.

How the Strategy Works

The more words you know about an idea, the better you'll understand what people say and the better you will be able to express yourself.

1. Whenever you read, take time to learn new words.
2. Put words into groups, or **categories**. This web shows two **categories** of words related to water.

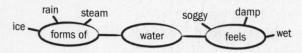

3. Then use a Synonym Scale to rank words in the same **category** in order of their strength.

Synonym Scale

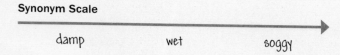

Use the strategy to sort out shades of meaning for the underlined words.

Rain in Washington

Washington State is known for its <u>damp</u> climate. Every year, it rains an average of 38 inches. In 1996, however, the state was <u>drenched</u>. That year, Seattle had almost 51 inches of rain. The ground was <u>soaked</u>. A few years later, in 2000, Seattle had only about 29 inches of rain. It was still a <u>moist</u> year, but it was tolerable.

Strategy in Action

" *Damp* and *drenched* both describe a shade of *wet*, but *drenched* is much stronger. 1996 was a very wet year in Washington!"

☑ REMEMBER Knowing the exact meaning of synonyms will help you understand what you read.

Academic Vocabulary
- **category** (**ka**-tu-gor-ē) *noun*
  A **category** is a group of items that are related in some way.

Practice Together

Read this passage aloud. Work with your class to make a Synonym Scale for the underlined words. Then discuss how using the scale helps you understand how the animals move.

River Fish

Last summer, my family went camping near a river. We had a great time watching all the different fish <u>swim</u> around. Big fish <u>moved</u> slowly from one dark spot to another. Tiny fish <u>zoomed</u> around the rocks. We even saw a river eel <u>glide</u> through the water! We all laughed as my dog <u>paddled</u> around, chasing them all.

▲ **Fish swim in the river.**

Try It!

Read this passage aloud. Notice the underlined synonyms. What are the fastest and slowest ways that river water moves, according to this writer? How do you know?

Moving Water

Have you ever thought about how river water moves at different speeds all the time? In deep, wide areas, the water <u>flows</u> gently. It <u>splashes</u> through rocky, shallower areas. Then it <u>speeds</u> down a hill and <u>rushes</u> over a waterfall. When it comes to a flat area, it <u>crawls</u>. It even <u>stands still</u> in pools at the edge of the river.

▲ **River water moves quickly over the rocks.**

THE SECRET WATER

by Daphne Liu

Illustrated by Jean and Mou-sien Tseng

SELECTION 1 OVERVIEW

▶ **Build Background**

▶ **Language & Grammar**
Express Needs and Wants
Use Nouns

▶ **Prepare to Read**
Learn Key Vocabulary
Learn a Reading Strategy
Monitor Your Reading

▶ **Read and Write**
Focus on Genre
Legend
Apply the Reading Strategy
Monitor Your Reading
Critical Thinking
Reading Fluency
Read with Expression
Vocabulary Review
Write About the Guiding Question

▶ **Connect Across the Curriculum**
Literary Analysis
Analyze Plot
Vocabulary Study
Create Word Categories
Research/Writing
Write About China
Listening/Speaking
Compare Tales Across Cultures
Language and Grammar
Express Needs and Wants
Writing and Grammar
Write About a Situation

Build Background

Visit a Village

"The Secret Water" takes place in a village in China. Often, people in villages have to walk to a stream or a river to get water.

Connect

Quickwrite Imagine that you live in a mountain village in China long ago. Every day you walk to a river a mile away and return with two buckets of water that weigh 20 pounds each. Describe what it is like to carry the water each day. Share your writing with a partner.

Digital Library

InsideNG.com
▶ View the video.

▲ Villagers collect water from a river.

Language & Grammar

Express Needs and Wants

Listen to the song. Then sing along with it.

SONG

We Need Water!

I carry two buckets.
You carry one.
We need water.
We work in the sun.

I carry one bucket.
You carry two.
We cannot rest.
We have work to do!

Use Nouns

A **noun** names a person, place, thing, or idea.

- A singular noun names one person, place, thing, or idea.

  EXAMPLE   The **farmer** carries a **bucket**.

- A plural noun names more than one person, place, thing, or idea.

  EXAMPLE   All the **farmers** carry **buckets**.

Spelling Rules

1. To make most nouns plural, just add **-s**.

  EXAMPLE   **vegetable + -s = vegetables**
  They grow many **vegetables**.

2. If the noun ends in s, z, sh, ch, or x, add **-es**.

  EXAMPLE   **lunch + -es = lunches**
  He prepares all the **lunches**.

3. If the noun ends in y after the consonant, change the y to i and add **-es**.

  EXAMPLE   **family + -es = families**
  Twenty **families** live in the village.

Practice Together

Change the noun in the box to the plural form. Say it. Then say the sentence and add the plural form of the noun.

1. | house | There are many _____ in the village.
2. | box | They look like small _____.
3. | field | Almost everyone works in the _____.
4. | baby | The grandparents take care of the _____.

Try It!

Change the noun in the box to the plural form. Write the plural form on a card. Then say the sentence and add the plural form.

5. | stream | Two _____ flow by the village.
6. | bush | Some _____ grow near the water.
7. | basket | Kids bring their _____ every morning.
8. | berry | They pick the ripe _____.

▲ The villagers work outside.

Make and Play a Memory Game

EXPRESS NEEDS AND WANTS

What's the difference between *need* and *want*? Form a group and explore this topic. Think about different situations when you need or want something. Make a chart. Write the situations and your responses.

Response Chart

Situation	I need . . .	I want . . .
I am thirsty.	water	lemonade
I am hungry.	a sandwich	
I am cold.		
I am hot.		
My homework is hard.		
I'm in a new country.		

Now play a memory game on the topic. Write each response on two cards. Turn the cards face down and mix them up. Spread them on a table.

Take turns with a partner or in a group. Turn over one card. Read the response. Explain how it might be something you need or want. Then turn over another card. If the response is the same, keep the pair and go again. If it is different, place the cards face down and let another person take a turn. Remember:

HOW TO EXPRESS NEEDS AND WANTS

1. Use words like *must* and *need* to tell about important things. If you need something and do not get it, you could have problems.

2. Use *want* to talk about things you like or do not like. If you do not get what you want, you may be unhappy. But it does not cause a problem.

I need to do my homework.

I want to see a movie.

USE NOUNS

You will often use **nouns** to express needs and wants. When you do, use singular nouns to talk about one thing you need or want. Use plural nouns to talk about more than one thing.

Singular Noun: **pen**

Plural Noun: **pens**

Prepare to Read

Learn Key Vocabulary

Rate and Study the Words Rate how well you know each word. Then:

1. Pronounce the word. Say it aloud several times. Spell it.
2. Study the example.
3. Tell more about the word.
4. Practice it. Make the word your own.

Key Words

available (u-vā-lu-bul)
adjective ▸ page 76

When something is **available**, it is here and ready for use. Fresh fruit is **available** in the summer.
Antonym: **unavailable**

perfect (**pur**-fikt) *adjective*
▸ page 76

Something that is **perfect** is just right. This girl makes a **perfect** dive into the water.
Antonyms: **wrong, bad**

plan (plan) *noun*
▸ page 80

A **plan** is an idea about how to do something. Drawings show the **plans** for building a new house.
Synonym: **blueprint**

problem (prah-blum) *noun*
▸ page 80

A **problem** is something that is wrong. A **problem** needs to be solved or fixed. This driver has a **problem**. His truck is stuck in the mud.
Antonym: **solution**

secret (sē-krut) *adjective, noun* ▸ page 78

1 *adjective* Something that is **secret** is hidden from others. **2** *noun* A **secret** is something you hide from others. Can you keep a **secret**?
Synonym: **private** (*adjective*)

statue (sta-chü) *noun*
▸ page 80

A **statue** is a model of a person or thing. This **statue** shows Abraham Lincoln.

village (vi-lij) *noun*
▸ page 76

A **village** is a very small town. Not many people live in this farming **village**.

worry (wur-ē) *verb*
▸ page 78

To **worry** about something means to feel unhappy and afraid about what may happen. People often **worry** when they are late.
Antonym: **relax**

Practice the Words Make a Vocabulary Example Chart for each Key Word. Then compare your charts with a partner's.

Word	Definition	Example from My Life
perfect	just right	100% on my math test

Vocabulary Example Chart

Reading Strategy: Monitor Your Reading

When you read, make sure you understand the text. If there is something you do not understand, reread or read on to make it clear, or to clarify ideas.

HOW TO CLARIFY IDEAS

1. When you do not understand the meaning of the text, reread the paragraph.
2. If you still do not understand, then read on. The meaning may become clear in the text you read later.

Strategy in Action

Here's how one student clarified ideas.

Look Into the Text

Shu Fa lives with Uncle and Auntie in a village by the mountain. The land is dry and dusty. There is no water available for the villagers.

Every day, people must walk over the steep mountain to get the precious water. They fill their buckets with the water and carry it home.

One day, Shu Fa goes up the mountain. Near the path, she discovers a turnip. It is perfect for lunch. She pulls it out of the ground.

> I do not understand why there is no water available.

> I reread to find out. I learn that the land is dry. They probably had no rain for a long time.

> Then I read on. The people fill their buckets with water. I guess they do not have faucets in their homes.

Practice Together

Reread the passage above. Follow the steps in the How-To box to clarify any text you don't understand. Share your ideas with a partner. Tell how rereading or reading on helped you clarify ideas.

Focus on Genre

Legend

A legend is a very old story, usually about a hero, or person who acts with courage. Legends are mostly fiction, but some details may be true.

The **characters** are the people in the legend. The **setting** is where and when it happens.

> Shu Fa lives with Uncle and Auntie in a village by the mountain. . . . One day, Shu Fa goes up the mountain. Near the path, she discovers a turnip. It is perfect for lunch. She pulls it out of the ground.

Your Job as a Reader

Reading Strategy: Monitor Your Reading

Make sure you reread to clarify ideas. Read on if you still don't understand.

YOU WONDER

What is a turnip?

READ ON

It is perfect for lunch.

YOU DECIDE

It must be something to eat.

THE SECRET WATER

by Daphne Liu

Illustrated by Jean and Mou-sien Tseng

Online Coach

Set a Purpose
Shu Fa's village needs water.
Find out how she helps.

Shu Fa lives with Uncle and Auntie in a village by the mountain. The land is dry and dusty. There is no water **available** for the villagers.

Every day, people must walk over the steep mountain to get the **precious** water. They fill their buckets with the water and carry it home.

One day, Shu Fa goes up the mountain. Near the path, she discovers a **turnip**. It is **perfect** for lunch. She pulls it out of the ground.

Snap! Water pours from the hole left by the turnip. Shu Fa is **amazed**! Now the villagers will not have to walk so far for water.

Key Vocabulary
village *n.*, a small town
available *adj.*, here and ready for use
perfect *adj.*, just the right thing

In Other Words
precious valuable and important
turnip vegetable ▶
amazed very surprised

Cultural Background
This story takes place in China, where most people still live in the country. Many people in China, and in the world, have too little water. They dig wells or carry water using buckets.

Suddenly, a strong wind blows in from the mountain. It pushes the turnip back into the hole. A loud voice **roars**, "You cannot take my water!"

Shu Fa asks, "Who are you?"

"I am the Voice of the Mountain. This is MY water. You cannot take it."

"But my village needs water! Can you share it with us?" Shu Fa asks.

"No, I do not share!" the Voice says. Then it **warns her**: "If you tell anyone about the water, you will be punished!"

In Other Words
roars says with force
warns her tells her in a strong way

Before You Move On

1. **Character** What kind of person is Shu Fa? How can you tell?
2. **Cause and Effect** What happens when Shu Fa pulls the turnip?
3. **Confirm Prediction** Did Shu Fa do what you predicted? Explain.

Shu Fa runs home. She wants to tell everyone about the **secret** water. But she is afraid.

Many days pass. Shu Fa sees how hard the villagers work to get water. She **worries** so much that her long, black hair turns white.

One day, Uncle walks over the mountain to get water. But he **trips** and hurts his head. *"Aiya!"* he cries.

Shu Fa cries, too. She knows now that she must help. She must bring the water to her village.

Shu Fa runs up the mountain and **smashes** the turnip. Water pours out of the hole. It becomes a river that goes into the village. The villagers dance with joy!

Then the Voice of the Mountain shouts, "Shu Fa, you told my **secret**! Now you must live in my river forever."

Shu Fa cries. She **begs** the Voice to let her say goodbye to her family. The Voice **grumbles**, "Go, but you must return here tonight."

Key Vocabulary	In Other Words
secret *adj.*, hidden; *n.*, something that is hidden	**trips** falls down
worry *v.*, to feel unhappy and afraid about what might happen	***Aiya!*** Oh no! (in Chinese)
	smashes breaks
	begs asks
	grumbles says unhappily

Before You Move On

1. **Inference** Why does Shu Fa's hair turn white?
2. **Confirm Prediction** Was your prediction correct? What happened that you did not expect?

How will Shu Fa solve her problem?

Shu Fa runs back to the village. "What can I do?" she asks herself. "I do not want to live in the river!" She decides to tell Uncle about the problem.

Uncle thinks for a few minutes. Then he says, "I have a **plan**."

Uncle works all day to **carve** a **statue** out of stone. The statue looks just like Shu Fa. He thinks the statue will trick the Voice of the Mountain.

"I just need one thing," Uncle tells Shu Fa. He cuts Shu Fa's long, white hair and attaches it to the statue. Then he places the statue in the river. Water flows over the statue. It carries the white hair over the mountain like a waterfall.

The Voice of the Mountain sees the statue. It says, "Hello, Shu Fa!"

The trick worked!

Today, the waterfall still flows to the village. The land is green, and the people are happy.

Once again, Shu Fa has long, black hair. ❖

Key Vocabulary

problem *n.*, something that is wrong

plan *n.*, an idea about how to do something

statue *n.*, a model of a person or thing

In Other Words

carve make, cut

Before You Move On

1. **Character's Motive** Why does Shu Fa tell Uncle the **problem**?
2. **Paraphrase** How does Uncle's **plan** save Shu Fa?
3. **Viewing** What clue in the picture tells you if the trick worked?

Connect Reading and Writing

Vocabulary
available
perfect
plan
problem
secret
statue
village
worries

CRITICAL THINKING

1. **SUM IT UP** Make a Character Description Chart for Shu Fa. List things that she does, including how she solves the **problem**. What do her actions say about her? Discuss your ideas with a partner.

Character Description Chart

What Shu Fa Does	What It Shows About Her
carries water	

2. **Infer** Most legends are set in the past. How can you tell that what happens in Shu Fa's **village** takes place long ago? Find details in the story.

3. **Interpret** Explain the title. What is **secret** about water in this story?

4. **Analyze** What is the Voice of the Mountain like? Describe this character, based on the dialogue.

READING FLUENCY

Expression Read the passage on page 571 to a partner. Assess your fluency.

1. I read
   a. great   **b.** OK   **c.** not very well

2. What I did best in my reading was _____.

READING STRATEGY

Monitor Your Reading
Tell a partner one place where you clarified the meaning of the text. How did rereading or reading on help you?

VOCABULARY REVIEW

Oral Review Read the paragraph aloud. Add the vocabulary words.

I live in a _____ where we eat a lot of fish. Fish are always _____ from the lake. No one ever _____ about hunger! To honor the fish, artists carved a large _____. They wanted to keep it a _____, so they didn't tell anyone. Then the artists had a _____ to solve: Where should they put the statue? They thought about it and decided on a _____. They found a _____ setting! The statue will sit in the lake!

Written Review Write a sentence to go with each illustration in "The Secret Water." Tell about the characters and the **village**. Use five vocabulary words.

 **WRITE ABOUT THE** **GUIDING QUESTION**

Explore Earth's Resources
Reread the selection. When is it OK to take an **available** resource from somebody to help others? Support your idea with examples from the text.

Connect Across the Curriculum

Analyze Plot

Academic Vocabulary
- **series** (**sear**-ēz) *noun*
  A **series** is a group of related things that are put in a certain order.

What Is Plot? A plot is the **series** of events that make up a story. A plot usually has a problem and a solution. Most stories tell the problem at the beginning. They tell the solution, or how the problem is fixed, at the end. This passage shows the **problem** in "The Secret Water."

Shu Fa lives with Uncle and Auntie in a village by the mountain. The land is dry and dusty. There is no water available for the villagers.

Every day, people must walk over the steep mountain to get the precious water. They fill their buckets with the water and carry it home.

Practice Together

Read and Discuss You can use a Problem-and-Solution Chart to keep track of what happens in a story. Look at the chart.

Problem-and-Solution Chart

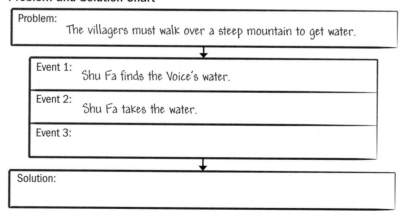

Problem:
The villagers must walk over a steep mountain to get water.

Event 1: Shu Fa finds the Voice's water.

Event 2: Shu Fa takes the water.

Event 3:

Solution:

Begin a Chart Copy the chart above, but add several more "Event" boxes. Fill in the boxes as shown.

Try It!

Finish the Problem-and-Solution Chart as you reread the story. Use as many "Event" boxes as you need. Be sure to add the solution. Then share your chart with a partner.

Create Word Categories

> **Academic Vocabulary**
> - **category** (ka-tu-gor-ē) *noun*
>   A **category** is a group of items that are related in some way.

Words that relate to the same topic form a **category** . *Turnip* and *carrot* form a **category** because they are both related to the topic *vegetables*. Words within a **category** may be more specific than the topic of that **category** . *Turnip* and *carrot* are more specific than *vegetable*.

Name a Category Work with a partner. Think of a **category** , which can be a word or a phrase, for these words:

village	farm	house	city

Work in a group to list more words that belong to the same **category** . Explain how each word fits in the **category** .

Name Related Words With a partner, play a word game. One person names a topic, such as weather. The partner names three words that belong in that **category** . Change roles.

Write About China

HISTORY

> **Academic Vocabulary**
> - **topic** (tah-pik) *noun*
>   A **topic** is the subject of a piece of writing or of a discussion.

❶ **Use Research Questions** Research the **topic** of life in China. Focus on these questions:

- When did China get technology such as television, cell phones, and computers? How did people communicate before then?
- How does geography affect communication between people in China and the rest of the world?

▲ A man who lives in the mountains in China uses his computer.

❷ **Conduct Research** Write your research questions on note cards. Use the cards to guide you as you look for information in textbooks, encyclopedias, and nonfiction library books about China.

❸ **Write a Journal Entry** Imagine that you are living in China long ago. Describe the setting. Tell how the land makes communication difficult.

Compare Tales Across Cultures

SOCIAL SCIENCE

Academic Vocabulary

• **compare** (kum-**pair**) *verb*
When you **compare** two things, you think about how they are alike and different.

Shu Fa helps save her village. You can find stories of strong women like her in many cultures.

1 **Read Another Story** Read the story of She-Who-Is-Alone, from the Comanche people. Think about what the character is like and what she does.

2 **Compare Characters** Work with a group to make a Venn Diagram. **Compare** Shu Fa and She-Who-Is-Alone. In the outside areas of the diagram, write ways in which the women are different. In the middle, write ways in which they are alike.

Venn Diagram

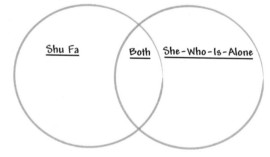

Shu Fa   Both   She-Who-Is-Alone

3 **Develop Theories** Pay attention to the similarities between the characters. Why do you think two different cultures would have stories about characters that are so similar? Also think about any other stories you know with a similar character. Discuss your ideas with a group.

Bright blue flowers called bluebonnets relate to the legend of She-Who-Is-Alone. ▶

Express Needs and Wants

Act It Out Work with a group, and imagine you are the characters in "The Secret Water." Use your own words to act out the story events and to tell what the characters need and want. Use precise, or exact, nouns.

> I want to get a bucket of water from the river.

Write About a Situation

Study the Models When you write about a situation, like the need for water, choose **nouns** that let readers picture exactly what you are saying. Be sure to spell plural nouns correctly.

NOT OK

> The sun beats down on the **plants** in the **fieldes**. The farmers worry because there is no rain. **Ladys** watch the **flowers** in their gardens turn brown. **Pets** just lie in the shade. It is even too hot for **childrens** to play.

The writer spells some plural **nouns** incorrectly. The reader is confused: "These words look wrong."

OK

> The water pipe on our street is broken. It is hard for all the **families**. At my house, dirty **glasses** and **plates** sit by the kitchen sink. The stack must be two **feet** high! Dirty **socks** fill the laundry basket. We can't even take **baths**.

The writer spells plural **nouns** correctly. The nouns also add details. The reader thinks: "I can really picture the writer's house."

Revise It Look back at the NOT OK passage. Work with a partner to revise it. Change *plants*, *flowers*, and *pets* to precise nouns. Fix the incorrect plural forms.

WRITE ON YOUR OWN Imagine a time when you did not have enough water. Use nouns that will help your reader picture what you are saying. Pay attention to the spelling of plural forms.

Spelling Rules

1. To make most nouns plural, just add **-s**.

 street + **-s** = streets

2. If the noun ends in *s, z, sh, ch,* or *x*, add **-es**.

 dish + **-es** = dishes

3. If the noun ends in *y* after the consonant, change the *y* to *i* and add **-es**.

 story + **-es** = stories

4. Some nouns, such as *woman* (*women*), have special plural forms.

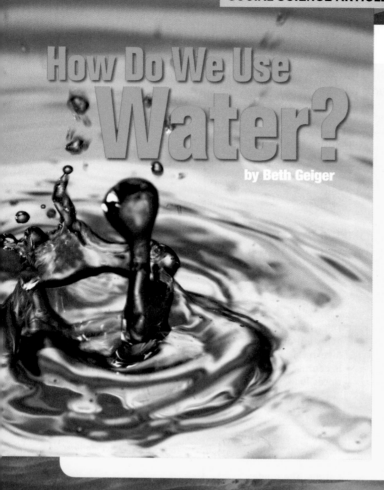

How Do We Use Water?

by Beth Geiger

Build Background

Discuss How We Use Water

People use water every day. Look at each photo and talk about how many ways water was used in the scene.

Digital Library

InsideNG.com
◉ View the images.

◀ Water covers much of Earth's surface.

Connect

Class Survey Find out how your class used water today. Use a chart like this to record information. What do the results tell you about the importance of available water?

Survey Chart

Daily Uses of Water	Times in One Day	Total Uses
to drink	〤〤 〤〤 〤〤	15
to prepare food		
to wash hands or face		
to brush teeth		

Give Information

CD

Listen to the rap and the facts. Then repeat the lines of the rap after the rapper, and chime in with the facts.

RAP and FACTS

Some Watery Facts

Earth is a watery planet.
Twenty-five percent is land.
The rest is oceans, ice, rivers, and lakes.
So learn to swim if you can.

Ocean water tastes salty.
Fresh water has salts in it, too,
But not enough to make you sick.
So that's a good thing for you.

Earth is a watery planet.
But there is no water to waste.
Only 3 percent of our water is fresh.
So don't use too much,
Unless you love the taste . . .

of salt.

Fact 1:
If the salt in the oceans could be spread out on land, it would cover all the continents. The salt would rise 500 feet!

Fact 2:
Seventy-five percent of Earth's fresh water is frozen. It makes the polar ice caps and all the world's glaciers.

Fact 3:
If you leave the water on when you brush your teeth, you use two gallons of water.

Fact 4:
A person can live without water for about one week.

OK, it's been a week!

Use Complete Sentences

A complete sentence has a **subject** and a **predicate**.

All people drink water.
subject   predicate

To find the subject in a sentence, ask yourself: Whom or what is the sentence about? The sentence above is about people.

The **complete subject** includes all the words that tell about the subject. The most important word in the complete subject is usually a **noun**.

EXAMPLE **All people** drink water.
subject

The **complete predicate** often tells what the subject does. The **verb** shows the action.

EXAMPLE All people **drink water**.
predicate

Practice Together

Say each group of words. Add a subject with a noun, or add a predicate that tells what the subject does. Then say the complete sentence.

1. washes the dishes.
2. My sister
3. saves the dirty water in the sink.
4. My father
5. carries buckets of water to the garden.
6. Beautiful flowers

Try It!

Read each group of words. Think about how to make a complete sentence. On a sheet of paper, write a subject with a noun, or write a predicate that tells what the subject does. Then say the complete sentence.

7. All animals
8. drink water.
9. live in water.
10. A bird
11. Bugs
12. wash pets in water.

▲ The elephants drink water.

Make a Chant

GIVE INFORMATION

What information about water can you give? Work with a group to write a chant with water facts.

Record facts about water. Use the water facts on page 87. Add other water facts. Make sure the information is correct.

> You can waste two gallons of water when you leave the water on while you brush your teeth.

Now choose some of the facts for your chant. Put fact sentences together. Use rhyming words, like *sea* and *me* or *fish* and *wish*.

Practice your chant. Then perform it for the other groups.

Remember:

HOW TO GIVE INFORMATION

1. When you give information, give facts about the topic.
2. Be sure the facts are correct.

> You brush your teeth. You leave the water on.

> Two gallons of water now are gone.

USE COMPLETE SENTENCES

When you give information, speak in complete sentences. This will help you present the facts clearly. Remember, a complete sentence has a **subject** and a **predicate** .

EXAMPLE   **Earth** **has a lot of water.**

Prepare to Read

Learn Key Vocabulary

Rate and Study the Words Rate how well you know each word. Then:

1. Pronounce the word. Say it aloud several times. Spell it.
2. Study the example.
3. Tell more about the word.
4. Practice it. Make the word your own.

Key Words

alive (u-līv) *adjective*
▶ page 96

Something that is living is **alive**. This girl looks happy to be **alive**.
Antonym: **dead**

amount (u-mount) *noun*
▶ page 94

An **amount** is the total number or quantity. What **amount** of wood is in this pile?
Synonym: **quantity**

crop (krop) *noun*
▶ page 96

Crops are plants that farmers grow. Corn, beans, and peaches are different **crops**.
Synonym: **produce**

depend (di-pend) *verb*
▶ page 98

When you **depend** on something, you need it. Babies **depend** on their parents for everything.
Synonym: **require**

globe (glōb) *noun*
▶ page 94

A **globe** is a model of Earth. The **globe** shows the shape of the land. The blue represents oceans.
Synonym: **world**

material (mu-tear-ē-ul) *noun* ▶ page 97

Materials are things you need to make a product or to do a project. Paint and brushes are **materials** you need for painting.
Synonym: **supplies**

rainfall (rān-fawl) *noun*
▶ page 96

Rainfall is the total rain, snow, or sleet that falls in a period of time. There has been a lot of **rainfall** this year.
Synonym: **rain**

resource (rē-sors) *noun*
▶ page 94

A **resource** is something that people need and use. Air, soil, and water are natural **resources**.

Practice the Words Work with a partner. Write four sentences. Use at least two Key Words in each sentence.

> The amount of rainfall this year will affect the crops.

Reading Strategy: Monitor Your Reading

As you read, you may see words that you don't know. Sometimes you can skip a word, keep reading, and still understand the text. Other times, you need to figure out the word in order to understand what you are reading.

Reading Strategy
Monitor Your Reading

HOW TO CLARIFY VOCABULARY

1. When you come to a word or phrase you don't know, reread the words and sentences nearby.
2. Look for context clues. Think about how the word is used and what the paragraph is about. Use the clues to figure out what the word means.
3. Replace the word you don't know with the meaning you figured out. Does that meaning make sense in the sentence?

Strategy in Action

Here's how one student clarified vocabulary.

Look Into the Text

All the World's Water

An incredible amount of water covers Earth. Look at a globe. The blue area represents the water. There are about 200 billion liters (53 billion gallons) of water for each person on Earth!

There is not always enough water to drink, however.

Most of Earth's water is salty ocean water. Salt water is fine for sea creatures. But it is not fine for humans and most other animals.

> What does *incredible amount* mean here? When I reread the sentence, I still don't understand.

> Billions of liters is a lot! Maybe *incredible amount* means "a lot." "A lot of water" makes sense.

Practice Together

Follow the steps in the How-To box to clarify the meaning of the word *fine* in the passage above. Discuss how you used the strategy.

Prepare to Read **91**

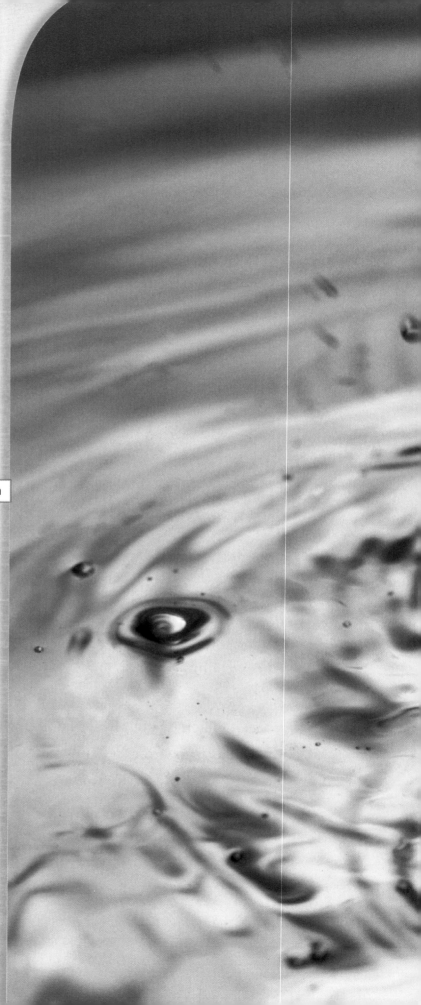

Focus on Genre

Social Science Article

A social science article explains facts and ideas. **Photos** and **captions** support the text or add details.

> Only 3 percent of Earth's water is fresh water. Fresh water is an important resource that we need every day.
>
>  ◁ **photo**
>
> ◁ Water in rivers, lakes, and streams is fresh water. ◁ **caption**

Your Job as a Reader

Reading Strategy: Monitor Your Reading

As you read, remember to clarify any words or phrases you find confusing. Use context clues to help you figure out the meaning.

> **YOU READ**
>
> Most of Earth's water is salty ocean water. . . . Only 3 percent of Earth's water is fresh water.
>
> **YOU THINK**
>
> What does *fresh* mean here? It must mean "not salty." Only 3 percent is not salty.

How Do We Use Water?

by Beth Geiger

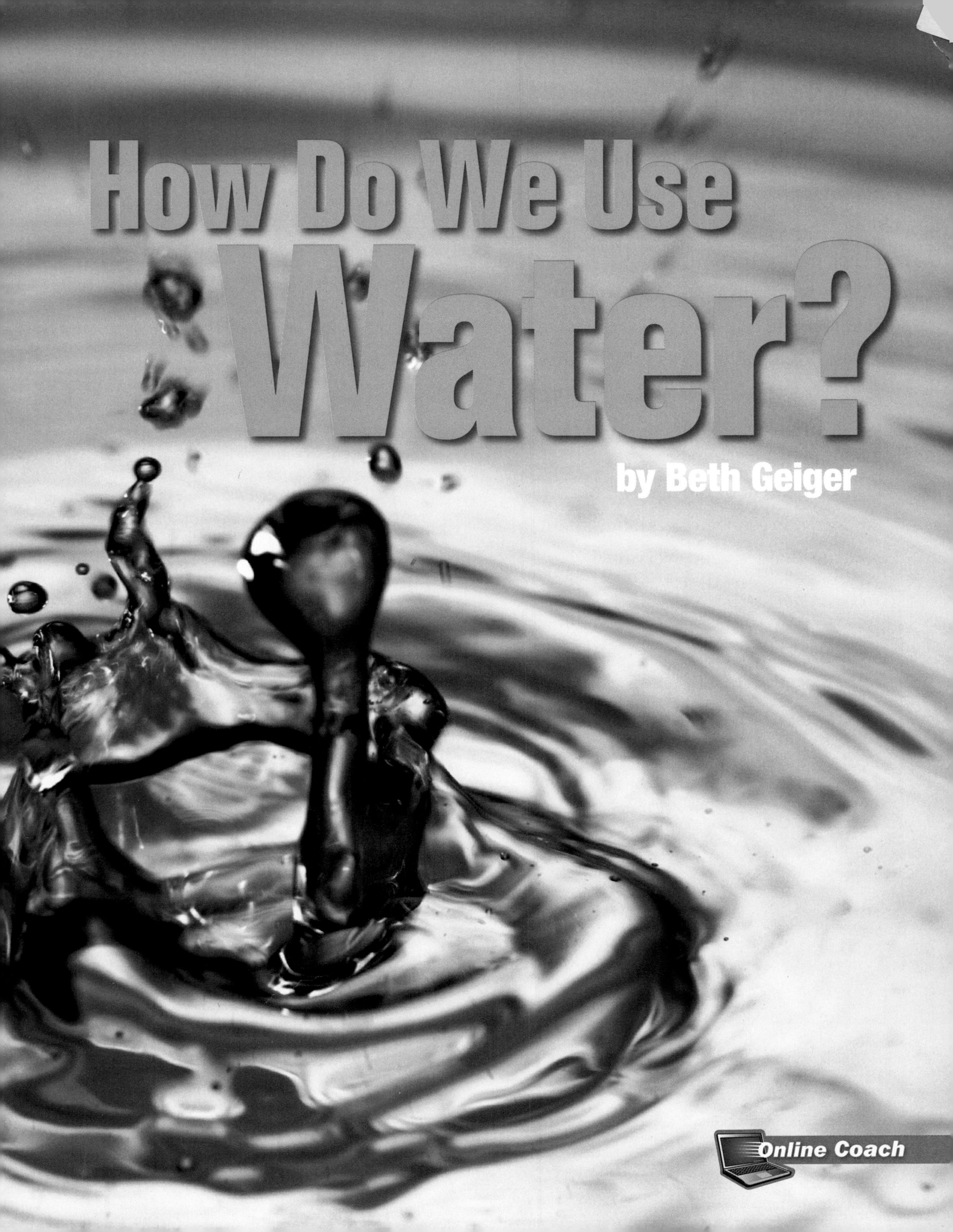

Online Coach

All the World's Water

An incredible **amount** of water covers Earth. Look at a **globe**. The blue area **represents** the water. There are about 200 billion liters (53 billion gallons) of water for each person on Earth!

There is not always enough water to drink, however.

Most of Earth's water is salty ocean water. Salt water is fine for **sea creatures**. But it is not fine for humans and most other animals.

Only 3 percent of Earth's water is fresh water. Fresh water is an important **resource** that we need every day.

Water in the ocean is salt water.

Water in rivers, lakes, and streams is fresh water.

Key Vocabulary

amount *n.*, the total number, the quantity
globe *n.*, a model of Earth
resource *n.*, something found in nature and used by people

In Other Words

represents shows
sea creatures animals that live in the sea

Water for Everyday Living

We need to drink fresh water to live. All day, we lose water from our bodies. We lose it when **we sweat** and when we **get rid of waste**. We drink water to **replace** the water we lose.

We use fresh water in other ways, too. Think about the water you use to wash dishes and to cook. You use water to brush your teeth. You also use water when you take a shower or bath.

People drink fresh water.

▲ Oceans cover most of Earth's surface.

In Other Words

we sweat our bodies work hard and give off water
get rid of waste use the toilet
replace put back

Before You Move On

1. **Explain** Why is there not always enough water for people to drink?
2. **Recall** What are some ways people use water every day?

Water for Farming

Farmers use fresh water to grow **crops**. Much of the fresh water in the United States is used for farming.

Many farms are in **areas without** much **rainfall**. Farmers irrigate to keep their crops **alive**. This means that they bring in water for their crops.

Farmers use fresh water to irrigate their crops.

Some crops, like cotton, need a lot of water.

Key Vocabulary	In Other Words
crop *n.*, plants that farmers grow	**areas without** places that do not have
rainfall *n.*, the total rain that comes down	
alive *adj.*, living, not dead	

Water for Building

People also use water as a resource to build things. They use water to mix **concrete** for floors and walls. They use water to make the paint that adds color to buildings.

People use water to make metal and glass, too. They need these **materials** to make most buildings.

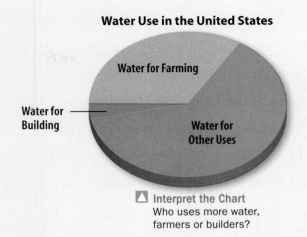

Water Use in the United States

Water for Farming

Water for Building

Water for Other Uses

▲ Interpret the Chart
Who uses more water, farmers or builders?

People use water when they mix concrete.

Key Vocabulary

material *n.*, something that is needed to make a product

In Other Words

concrete a blend of sand, small rocks, and cement

Before You Move On

1. **Inference** What do you think happens if farmers cannot get water for their **crops**?
2. **Main Idea and Details** How do people use water for building?

It All Adds Up!

People **depend** on fresh water every day. They use it for drinking, for growing food, and for building.

People in the United States use a lot of fresh water. Each person uses about 378 liters (100 gallons) of water each day. That amount would fill two and a half bathtubs. That is a lot of water! ❖

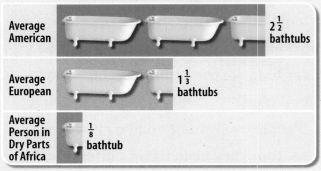

Water Used by One Person Each Day

Average American	$2\frac{1}{2}$ bathtubs
Average European	$1\frac{1}{3}$ bathtubs
Average Person in Dry Parts of Africa	$\frac{1}{8}$ bathtub

🔺 **Interpret the Graph** Who uses the most water each day? Who uses the least?

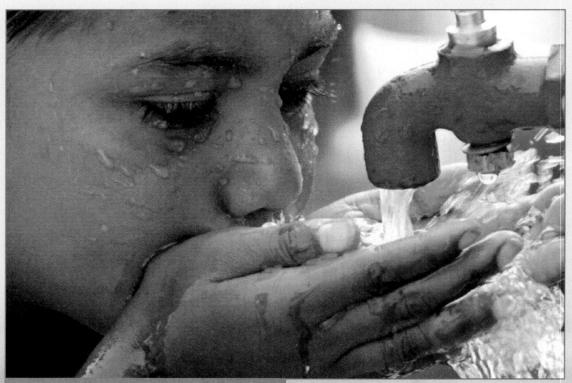

Everybody needs water, especially when it's hot! This boy drinks water on a hot summer day.

Key Vocabulary
depend *v.*, to need, to require

Before You Move On

1. **Evidence and Conclusion** What details show that Americans use a lot of water?
2. **Fact and Opinion** Facts can be proved. Opinions are people's ideas about something. Name one fact and one opinion on this page.

Connect Reading and Writing

Vocabulary
alive
amount
crops
depend
globe
materials
rainfall
resource

CRITICAL THINKING

1. SUM IT UP Create an Idea Web. Look for details in the text, captions, and graphics. Use your web to discuss ways we **depend** on water.

Idea Web

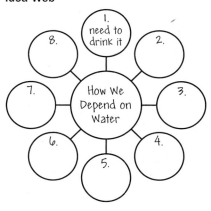

1. need to drink it

How We Depend on Water

2. Conclusion Some farmers do not rely on **rainfall** . What other sources of water could they use to grow **crops** ?

3. Evaluate We need water to stay **alive** . List the many uses of water in order of their importance. Explain the order.

4. Infer Look at the chart on page 98. Why do you think people in the United States use a greater **amount** of water than people in other parts of the world?

READING FLUENCY

Phrasing Read the passage on page 572 to a partner. Assess your fluency.

1. I read
  a. great   **b.** OK   **c.** not very well

2. What I did best in my reading was _____.

READING STRATEGY

Monitor Your Reading
Tell a partner how you determined the meanings of two words. Point out the context clues you used.

VOCABULARY REVIEW

Oral Review Read the paragraph aloud. Add the vocabulary words.

A _____ , or model of Earth, shows surface water. Some water, like _____ , comes from clouds. Water is underground, too. We can reach this natural _____ with pipes made of sturdy _____ . Some farmers live where there isn't enough rain to water their plants, or _____ . They _____ on a large _____ of ground water. They irrigate to keep the plants _____ .

Written Review Pick a photo in the article. Explain how people **depend** on water in that scene. Use four vocabulary words.

WRITE ABOUT THE GUIDING QUESTION

Explore Earth's Resources
Reread the selection. How would your life change if you had a smaller **amount** of water to use? Support your ideas with examples from the text.

Connect Across the Curriculum

Analyze Text Structure: Main Idea and Details

> **Academic Vocabulary**
> - **support** (su-**port**) *verb*
>   When you **support** an idea, you give reasons or examples for it.

No matter what topic writers choose, they want you to get the **main idea**, or what they are mostly saying about the topic.

How do you know if you are getting the main idea when you read the text? Sometimes writers tell you directly. They may include a main-idea statement in the text. Other sentences add details to **support** the main idea.

Practice Together

Read for the Main Idea Read this passage from "How Do We Use Water?" Notice that the first sentence states the **main idea**.

> People also use water as a resource to build things. They use water to mix concrete for floors and walls. They use water to make the paint that adds color to buildings.
> People use water to make metal and glass, too. They need these materials to make most buildings.

Chart the Main Idea Make a Main-Idea Chart to show how the main idea in the passage is connected to the details. Write the main idea in the top box. In the boxes below, write details that **support** the main idea. Copy this chart, and complete the last two boxes.

Main-Idea Chart

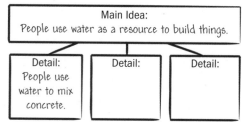

Main Idea: People use water as a resource to build things.

Detail: People use water to mix concrete.

Detail:

Detail:

▲ People use water when they mix concrete.

Try It!

Make a New Chart Make a Main-Idea Chart for the section on page 95. Compare your chart with a classmate's.

Use Synonyms

Academic Vocabulary
- **specific** (spi-**si**-fik) *adjective*
  Something that is **specific** is exact.

Synonyms are words that have almost the same meaning. You can use synonyms to make your writing more interesting.

EXAMPLES   I <u>drink</u> the water.

I <u>gulp</u> the water.

Drink and *gulp* have almost the same meaning, but *gulp* is more **specific** . **Specific** words help readers to picture the meaning.

Revise Sentences You can use a thesaurus to find synonyms. Use alphabetical order to locate the word. Find a synonym for each underlined word. Then rewrite the paragraph below and use the synonyms.

Thesaurus Entry

drink *v.* swallow, gulp, pull, drain

    The worker has to make concrete quickly. First, she <u>pours</u> the mix in a wheelbarrow. Then she <u>goes</u> to the hose. She <u>turns</u> the handle of the faucet. Water <u>comes</u> out. She <u>pulls</u> the hose to the wheelbarrow. The dry mix <u>goes</u> everywhere! She <u>laughs</u>.

Share your sentences with a partner. Compare synonyms.

Conduct a Survey

MATH

Academic Vocabulary
- **record** (ri-**kord**) *verb*
  To **record** means to put something in writing.

1 **Survey Classmates** Ask five people: "How many glasses of water do you drink each day?" **Record** the answers.

2 **Find the Average** An average is the middle point for a set of numbers. To calculate the average for your survey results:
   a. Add the five numbers.
   b. Divide the sum by the number of people you surveyed, which is five.

3 **Share Your Results** How many glasses of water, on average, do people drink, based on your survey? Discuss why the findings may be different. Listen to your classmates' ideas. Then respond.

Research/Writing

Research Water Use

HEALTH & SCIENCE

> **Academic Vocabulary**
> • **topic** (**tah**-pik) *noun*
>   A **topic** is the subject of a piece of writing or of a discussion.

Suppose a leaky faucet drips once per second. According to the U.S. Environmental Protection Agency, the leak adds up to 3,000 gallons of water per year!

Fixing a leak is one way to save water. There are many other ways. Research the **topic** of water use. Then write one way people can save water.

▲ A leaky faucet wastes a huge amount of water.

❶ **Focus Your Research** People use water at home for cooking, cleaning, and gardening. How can they use less water? Search for answers using library books or the Internet. Narrow your **topic** by choosing one way to save water.

> **Internet** InsideNG.com
> ➋ Find out what you can do to save water.

❷ **Take Notes** As you research, write the important information you find. Include facts, or things that can be proved. Find short statements from experts on the **topic**. Note where you find the information so you can go back to it if you need to.

❸ **Write a Paragraph** Begin with a sentence that tells how people can use less water. Add sentences with the facts and statements you found. If you use the exact words of the statement, put quotation marks around the words. Be sure to tell who said the statement. For example: "It is everyone's responsibility to save water," Professor Lin believes.

❹ **Present Your Ideas** Read your paragraph to a group. Then listen to other people's ideas about water use.

Give Information

Share Information Tell a classmate three ways people in your community use water. Use action verbs. Then listen as your classmate names three ways. Use complete sentences to report the information to the class.

> Big trucks clean the streets with water.

Write About Water

Study the Models When you share what you know about a topic like water, it is important to express your thoughts completely. If you leave out the subject or the predicate in a sentence, the reader will get confused.

NOT OK

The biggest ocean on Earth. The Pacific Ocean covers more space than all the land on Earth. Has the deepest areas on Earth. Has powerful storms, too. You would not guess this because the word _pacific_ means "peaceful."

The writer leaves out important parts of sentences. The reader is confused: "The thoughts are not complete."

OK

The biggest ocean on Earth **is the Pacific**. The Pacific Ocean covers more space than all the land on Earth. **It** has the deepest areas on Earth. **The Pacific** has powerful storms, too. You would not guess this because the word _pacific_ means "peaceful."

The writer adds a missing **predicate** and two missing **subjects**. Now the writer's sentences are complete.

Revise It Read the passage below. Work with a partner to revise it. Add one subject and one predicate.

Water covers nearly three-fourths of the surface of Earth. A tiny amount of this water is fresh water. All the rest of the water. Earth's salt water is divided into five oceans. Are the Atlantic, Pacific, Indian, Arctic, and Southern Oceans.

WRITE ON YOUR OWN Choose an ocean, river, lake, or stream you know about. Write a paragraph about it. Make sure every sentence expresses a complete thought.

REMEMBER

A complete sentence has a subject and a predicate.

The lake is huge.

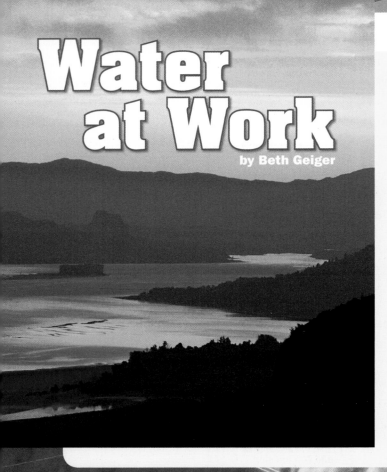

Water at Work

by Beth Geiger

SELECTION 3 OVERVIEW

▶ **Build Background**

▶ **Language & Grammar**
Elaborate
Make Subjects and Verbs Agree

▶ **Prepare to Read**
Learn Key Vocabulary
Learn a Reading Strategy
Monitor Your Reading

▶ **Read and Write**
Focus on Genre
Social Science Article
Apply the Reading Strategy
Monitor Your Reading
Critical Thinking
Reading Fluency
Read with Intonation
Vocabulary Review
Write About the Guiding Question

▶ **Connect Across the Curriculum**
Literary Analysis
Analyze Text Structure:
Main Idea and Details
Vocabulary Study
Use Synonyms and Antonyms
Research/Speaking
Research Floods
Discuss Hydroelectric Power
Language and Grammar
Elaborate
Writing and Grammar
Write About a Day at a River

Build Background

See How We Use Water

People can use a body of water such as a lake or river in numerous ways. They use it to move things, to make things, and just to play in.

Digital Library

InsideNG.com
⊘ View the video.

◀ Some people love to sail on the water.

Connect

KWL Chart Think about what you know about how people depend on rivers. Write your ideas in column 1 of a KWL Chart. In column 2, write what you want to know. Use column 3 to list what you learned after you read the article.

KWL Chart

WHAT I KNOW	WHAT I WANT TO KNOW	WHAT I LEARNED
Some rivers have dams.	What do the dams do?	

Language & Grammar

Elaborate

When you elaborate on a topic, you tell more details and give examples about it. Look at the photo and listen as one person tells about it. Then listen to the other people elaborate.

PICTURE PROMPT

Make Subjects and Verbs Agree

A **verb** must always agree with its **subject**. Study the forms of the verbs *be*, *have*, and *do*. Use the form of the verb that matches the subject.

Subject	Forms of *Be*	Forms of *Have*	Forms of *Do*
I	am	have	do
he, she, it	is	has	does
we, you, they	are	have	do

The **subject** of a sentence usually comes before the **verb**.

EXAMPLE   **We are** at the river.
              The river has a dam.

Practice Together

Say each sentence. Choose the correct form of the verb.

1. We (am/are) at the lake.
2. The lake (have/has) pine trees around it.
3. It (am/is) really pretty.
4. We (do/does) many things.
5. My friends (have/has) fishing poles.
6. I (have/has) a ball.
7. Our picnic lunch (is/are) great, too.

Try It!

Say each sentence. Write the correct form of the verb on a card. Then hold up the card as you say the sentence.

8. My cousins (have/has) exciting jobs.
9. They (am/are) tour guides on white-water rafting trips.
10. They (do/does) this every summer.
11. The river (have/has) wild waves and many turns.
12. I (am/is) amazed at what they do!

▲ The people have fun on the river.

Describe a Photo

ELABORATE

When you elaborate on something, you tell more about it. Work with a partner to elaborate about a photo of a river.

Find an interesting photo of a river. Look in magazines, books, and on the Internet. Think about the main idea you want to share about the photo. Then use an Idea Web to collect ideas about it.

Idea Web

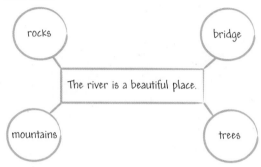

Show your photo to a group. One partner tells about the photo. The other elaborates, or tells more about it. Keep going until you have no more to say about the photo. Remember:

HOW TO ELABORATE

1. Think about the main idea of your discussion.
2. Add details.
3. Tell more. Add examples.

> The river is a beautiful place.

> The water is still and clear. Trees grow around the water.

MAKE SUBJECTS AND VERBS AGREE

When you elaborate, be sure to use the correct forms of *be*, *have*, and *do*. Also be sure to say the **subject** before the **verb**.

EXAMPLES   **The river** **has** a bridge.
The trees **are** tall.
We **do** sports in all seasons at the river.

▲ The river has a bridge.

Prepare to Read

Learn Key Vocabulary

Rate and Study the Words Rate how well you know each word. Then:

1. Pronounce the word. Say it aloud several times. Spell it.
2. Study the example.
3. Tell more about the word.
4. Practice it. Make the word your own.

Key Words

arrive (u-rīv) *verb*
▶ page 115

To **arrive** means to reach a place. A plane **arrives** at an airport.
Synonym: **enter**
Antonym: **leave**

electricity
(i-lek-**tri**-su-tē) *noun* ▶ page 114

Electricity is a form of energy. Lamps and computers use **electricity** to work.

flow (flō) *verb*
▶ page 115

To **flow** means to move freely. A river **flows** without stopping.
Synonyms: **go, move**
Antonym: **stop**

generate (je-nu-rāt) *verb*
▶ page 114

To **generate** means to make something. Windmills **generate** energy that people can use.
Synonyms: **make, produce**

goods (goodz) *noun*
▶ page 116

Goods are things that people buy and sell. Stores sell **goods**. For this meaning, **goods** is always plural.

power (pow-ur) *noun*
▶ page 114

Power is energy that makes things work. A dam collects water to use as a source of **power**.
Synonym: **force**

safely (sāf-lē) *adverb*
▶ page 113

To do something **safely** is to do it without danger. The girl is working **safely** because her eyes are protected from the chemicals.
Antonym: **dangerously**

treat (trēt) *verb*
▶ page 113

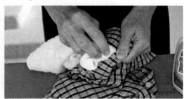

When you **treat** something, you change it. You can **treat** a dirty shirt with soap to get stains off.

Practice the Words Work with a partner. Make an Expanded Meaning Map for each Key Word.

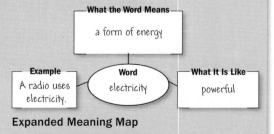

What the Word Means
a form of energy

Example
A radio uses electricity.

Word
electricity

What It Is Like
powerful

Expanded Meaning Map

Reading Strategy: Monitor Your Reading

When you read, you may come to a word that you don't understand.
Use this set of strategies to figure out the meaning.

Reading Strategy
Monitor Your Reading

HOW TO CLARIFY VOCABULARY

1. Ask: "Have I seen the word before? What do I already know about it?"
2. If you still do not understand the word, find context clues around the word. The clues may help you understand the meaning.
3. If the word is still not clear, break the word into parts. Do any of the word parts help you figure out the word's meaning?
4. If you are still confused, ask someone for help, or look up the word in a dictionary.

Strategy in Action

Here's how one student clarified vocabulary.

Look Into the Text

Making Boxes and Bags

Down the river, the water arrives at the Longview paper plant. Alan Whitford watches as recycled paper falls into huge tanks. The recycled paper is mixed with water from the river. Machines turn this mixture into paper boxes and bags. Then most of the water from the plant flows back into the Columbia River.

> I know a *plant* is something that grows. I don't think it means that here. I'll try Step 2.

> This paragraph is about making paper. A *plant* must be the place where paper is made. Step 2 helped me with this word.

Practice Together

Reread the passage "Making Boxes and Bags" above. Follow the steps in the How-To box to clarify the meaning of *mixture*. What helped you figure out the meaning?

Social Science Article

Social science articles give main ideas and details about topics such as geography, history, and transportation.

Articles often have maps that show features discussed in the text.

Map

Your Job as a Reader

Reading Strategy: Monitor Your Reading

Social science articles may include many important words to know. As you read, use the strategies you learned to clarify vocabulary.

YOU READ

> Kevin stops at an irrigation pipe. He turns a big wheel on the pipe. Water spouts from sprinklers . . .

YOU THINK

> What is an *irrigation pipe*? If water comes from sprinklers when he turns a wheel on the pipe, an irrigation pipe must supply water.

Water at Work

by Beth Geiger

The Columbia River runs through the states of Oregon and Washington. Millions of people depend on its water. How do they use it?

Columbia River

Growing Cherries

At **5 a.m.** it is still dark outside. But Kevin Aiken has been awake for an hour. Kevin is a farmer. He grows cherries near Wenatchee, Washington. In the **orchard**, Kevin stops at **an irrigation pipe**. He turns a big wheel on the pipe. Water **spouts from sprinklers** under the cherry trees.

This area does not have enough rainfall to grow fruit trees. Instead, Kevin uses water from the Columbia River to water the trees. Pumps move the river water to the cherry trees.

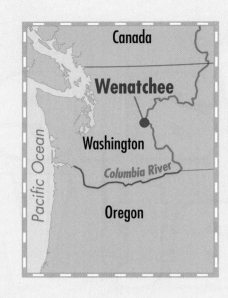

▼ Water from the Columbia River is used to grow cherry trees.

In Other Words

5 a.m. 5 o'clock in the morning
orchard field of fruit trees
an irrigation pipe a pipe that carries water to his trees
spouts from sprinklers sprays from tiny holes in the pipe

Cleaning the Water

Farther down the Columbia River is the city of Pasco, Washington. Roberto López plays basketball at his school there. Roberto stops for a drink of water. The water in the water fountain comes from the Columbia River.

Before the water reaches Roberto's school, though, it has to be cleaned. People cannot **safely** drink water **directly from** rivers. The water is **treated** at a **water treatment plant** first.

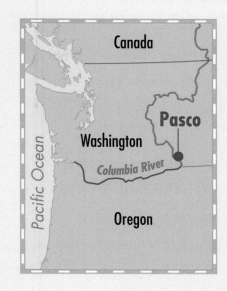

▲ Water is cleaned in a water treatment plant.

Key Vocabulary
safely *adv.*, without danger; without being hurt

treat *v.*, to change something

In Other Words
directly from right out of

water treatment plant special place for cleaning water

Before You Move On
1. **Main Idea and Details** Why does Kevin Aiken use river water to grow cherry trees?
2. **Inference** What do you think happens when people drink water that is not **treated**? Explain your answer.

Making Power

Farther down the river is the Dalles Dam. A dam is a **barrier** built across a river. It holds back the water. The water can then be used as a resource for different things.

The Dalles Dam makes **electricity**. Water rushes through the dam. It turns machines that **generate** electricity. The Dalles Dam generates enough electric **power** for two cities.

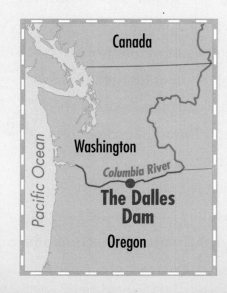

Canada

Pacific Ocean

Washington

Columbia River

The Dalles Dam

Oregon

▼ The Dalles Dam makes electricity.

Key Vocabulary

electricity *n.*, a form of energy

generate *v.*, to make

power *n.*, energy that makes things work

In Other Words

barrier big wall

Making Boxes and Bags

Down the river, the water **arrives** at the Longview **paper plant**. Alan Whitford watches as **recycled** paper falls into huge tanks. The recycled paper is mixed with water from the river. Machines **turn this mixture** into paper boxes and bags. Then most of the water from the plant **flows** back into the Columbia River.

▲ This paper plant makes big rolls of paper. Then they use the paper to make boxes and bags.

Key Vocabulary
  arrive *v.*, to reach a place
  flow *v.*, to move freely

In Other Words
  paper plant place that makes paper
  recycled used
  turn this mixture change the mix of paper and water

Before You Move On

1. **Explain** How do dams use water to **generate electricity**?
2. **Steps in a Process** How are boxes and bags made from recycled paper? Tell the steps in order.

Carrying Goods

Boats carry people and things along the Columbia River. One type of boat is called a barge. It is a long, flat boat. Barges carry wheat, **fuel**, and other **goods**. They take their goods to cities like Astoria, Oregon.

The Columbia River empties into the Pacific Ocean near Astoria. From its beginning to its end, the river helps many people in many ways. ❖

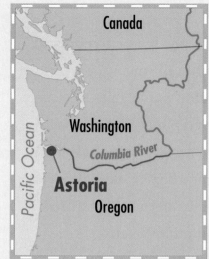

▲ This barge moves goods.

Key Vocabulary
goods n., things that people buy and sell

In Other Words
fuel coal or tanks of gas

Before You Move On

1. **Details** Describe where Astoria is along the Columbia River.
2. **Viewing** Look at the picture. Why do people use barges to move **goods**?

Connect Reading and Writing

Vocabulary
arrives
electricity
flow
generate
goods
power
safely
treated

CRITICAL THINKING

1. **SUM IT UP** Complete column 3 of the KWL Chart you started on page 104. Use your chart to summarize the article.

KWL Chart

WHAT I KNOW	WHAT I WANT TO KNOW	WHAT I LEARNED
Some rivers have dams.	What do the dams do?	The dams generate electricity.

2. **Infer** Dams make **electricity**, but they also create barriers. How can dams affect, or change, the lives of river wildlife?

3. **Predict** Millions of people use the Columbia River. What could happen if there is not enough water and the river stops **flowing**?

4. **Synthesize** Businesses depend on the Columbia River. They also depend on each other for **goods** and services. Give two examples of how.

READING FLUENCY

Intonation Read the passage on page 573 to a partner. Assess your fluency.

1. I read
   a. great   **b.** OK   **c.** not very well

2. What I did best in my reading was _____.

READING STRATEGY

Monitor Your Reading
Find a phrase that you did not know. Tell a partner the meaning. Change roles. Compare the strategies you used to clarify the meanings.

VOCABULARY REVIEW

Oral Review Read the paragraph aloud. Add the vocabulary words.

> Rivers that _____ through a dam have force and _____. The force is used to _____, or create, _____. With power, towns light up and factories produce _____. With the help of pumps, water _____ at your home. Dirty water from sinks, tubs, and washing machines travels back out through pipes to plants where it is _____. After this process, water can be returned _____ to the environment.

Written Review Imagine that you **arrive** in one of the places in the selection. Write a paragraph about what you see and hear. Use four vocabulary words.

 **WRITE ABOUT THE** GUIDING QUESTION

Explore Earth's Resources
Why do cities and towns often develop near rivers? Explain why people settle where a river **flows**. Include facts from the articles "How Do We Use Water?" and "Water at Work" as you write your paragraph.

Connect Across the Curriculum

Analyze Text Structure: Main Idea and Details

> **Academic Vocabulary**
> - **support** (su-**port**) *verb*
>   When you **support** an idea, you give reasons or examples for it.

The text in an article usually is organized into sections. All of the sections provide details for the whole article. Together, they **support** the main idea of the article.

Practice Together

Read for the Main Idea The topic of the article "Water at Work" is the Columbia River. What is the writer mostly telling you about the river? She states the **main idea** directly.

> The Columbia River runs through the states of Oregon and Washington. Millions of people depend on its water. How do they use it?

Make a Main-Idea Chart Copy this chart. Use it to show how the sections **support** the main idea of the article. Write the main idea in the top box. Find details in the first two sections that support the main idea. Write them in the boxes under the main idea.

Main-Idea Chart

Main Idea of Article: Millions of people depend on water from the Columbia River.

Detail from Section 1: People in Wenatchee, Washington, use the river water to grow fruit trees.

Detail from Section 2:

Try It!

Complete the Chart Add more boxes, and complete your chart for the other sections. Compare your chart with a classmate's. Did you find the same details?

Use Synonyms and Antonyms

Academic Vocabulary
* **relate** (ri-lāt) *verb*
  When you **relate** two things, you think about how they are connected.

Synonyms are words that have about the same meaning. Antonyms are words that have opposite meanings. You can use a scale to show how words **relate** to each other.

Compare the three words on the scale at the right. They are all synonyms for *run*. *Jog* is the slowest kind of run. *Sprint* is the fastest kind of run. Look at the order.

Scale

sprint

run

jog

The words at the opposite ends of the scale below are antonyms.

Scale

cold   cool   lukewarm   warm   hot

Make a Scale Work with a partner. Make a scale for the antonyms *huge* and *tiny*. Think of other words that **relate**. Write them in order on the scale.

Research Floods

HISTORY

Academic Vocabulary
* **resource** (rē-sors) *noun*
  A **resource** is something that people need and use.

The Columbia River is an important **resource**. With too much rain, rivers can flood and cause damage.

1 Use an Almanac Almanacs have facts on topics such as floods. Work with a partner. Use an almanac to find out about recent or famous floods.

▲ A flooded river covers a road in Bihar, India.

2 Find Out More Use library books or the Internet to learn more about a particular flood. Where and when did it happen? What damage did it cause? How did it affect people? Take notes.

Internet InsideNG.com
   Find out about a historic flood.

3 Share Your Findings Tell what you learned about the flood.

Research/Speaking

Discuss Hydroelectric Power

HEALTH & SCIENCE

Academic Vocabulary

• **resource** (rē-sors) *noun*
A **resource** is something that people need and use.

We use different natural **resources** to produce electricity. Some **resources**, like coal and oil, may be gone forever if we use them up. Others, like water, sunlight, and wind, can be used again and again.

Hydroelectric plants use the power of moving water to make electricity. They make less than 10 percent of the electricity in the United States. Why don't they make more? Work with a partner to find out.

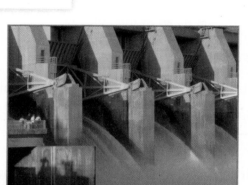

▲ **The power of water in motion can be used to make electricity.**

① **Gather Facts** Use different sources for your research. Ask an expert. For example, talk to someone who works for a power company. Or talk to someone who works for an environmental group. Use library books and the Internet. Take notes.

Internet InsideNG.com
⊘ Learn how hydroelectric power plants work.
⊘ Read about the costs to the environment.

② **Organize the Facts** Make a Comparison Chart. List reasons for using rivers to produce more electricity. Then list the problems.

Comparison Chart

Reasons For	Reasons Against
Water can be used again and again.	It costs a lot of money to build dams.

③ **Make a Decision** Put the facts together and decide your position. Should we produce more hydroelectric power? Or should we use other **resources** instead?

④ **State Your Position** Tell your opinion. Explain your reasons. Listen to other people's ideas. Do you still have the same opinion?

Elaborate

Pair Talk Say one fact about how people use rivers. Your partner then gives more information about that fact. Then you tell something more. Keep going until you cannot elaborate anymore. Use precise action verbs as you elaborate. Then switch roles to tell a new fact.

> *Farmers use river water.*

> *They irrigate the farm with the water.*

Writing and Grammar

Write About a Day at a River

Study the Models When you write about things that happen, you use action verbs. Precise and interesting action verbs help bring your writing to life. They help readers get a clear picture of actions and events. Each verb must agree with the subject of the sentence.

NOT OK

> Mr. Roja has a barge business on the Mississippi River. His barge **carry** passengers on trips down the river. The big barge **moves** down the Mississippi like a long, low box. It **passes** under bridges. It **travel** past towns. Passengers **walk** around the decks.

Some of the writer's action verbs are not precise. Other action verbs don't agree with their subjects.

OK

> Mr. Roja has a barge business on the Mississippi River. His barge **carries** passengers on trips down the river. The big barge **floats** down the Mississippi like a long, low box. It **drifts** under bridges. It **travels** past towns. Passengers **stroll** around the decks.

The writer uses precise action verbs. All the verbs agree with their subjects.

Add Sentences Think of two sentences to add to the OK model above. Tell what one passenger does. Use precise action verbs. Be sure the verbs agree with their subjects.

WRITE ON YOUR OWN Imagine people spending the day at a river. Tell what happens. Be sure to use precise, interesting action verbs. Make sure each verb agrees with the subject of the sentence.

REMEMBER

- Add **-s** to the end of an action verb that tells what one other person or thing does.
  The barge float**s**.
- Do not add **-s** to an action verb when the subject names more than one.
  The barges float.

Compare Across Texts

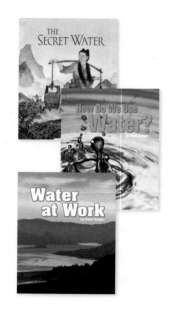

Compare Ideas

"The Secret Water," "How Do We Use Water?" and "Water at Work" tell about the importance of water as a **resource**. **Compare** the ideas in these texts.

How It Works

Collect and Organize Ideas Use a chart to organize what you know.

Comparison Chart

	The Secret Water	How Do We Use Water?	Water at Work
Fiction	✓		
Nonfiction		✓	✓
Why Water Is Important:			

Practice Together

Analyze Ideas This comparison paragraph tells how two types of text express ideas about water.

> "The Secret Water" is fiction, and "How Do We Use Water?" and "Water at Work" are nonfiction. "The Secret Water" uses imaginary characters and dialogue to express ideas about water. The other two texts give facts about water.

Try It!

Complete the chart to tell what each text says about the importance of water as a natural **resource**. Write a paragraph that **compares** the ideas across the texts. You may want to use this frame to help you write your paragraph.

"The Secret Water," "How Do We Use Water?" and "Water at Work" tell why people need water. In "The Secret Water," water is important because _____. "How Do We Use Water?" gives facts about _____. "Water at Work" explains how people in Oregon and Washington _____.

Academic Vocabulary
- **resource** (rē-sors) *noun*
  A **resource** is something that people need and use.
- **compare** (kum-**pair**) *verb*
  When you **compare** two things, you think about how they are alike and different.

Water for Life

 GUIDING QUESTION How do we depend on Earth's resources?

Reflect on Your Reading

Think back on your reading of the unit selections. Discuss what you did to understand what you read.

Focus on Genre   **Fiction and Nonfiction**

In this unit, you learned about the differences between fiction and nonfiction. Make a T Chart to compare "The Secret Water" with one of the other selections. List characteristics of each type of text. Use your chart to explain the texts to a partner.

Reading Strategy   **Monitor Your Reading**

As you read the selections, you learned to clarify ideas and vocabulary. Explain to a partner how you will use the strategy in the future.

Explore the

Throughout this unit, you have been thinking about Earth's resources. Choose one of these ways to explore the Guiding Question:

- **Discuss** With a group, discuss the Guiding Question. Remember, there can be many answers. Give details from the selections that support your idea.
- **Report** With the class, brainstorm a list of Earth's resources. Write each resource on a slip of paper, and put the papers in a container. Then form groups. Each group draws a paper. The group researches and reports to the class about how people depend on that resource.
- **Write and Draw** Make a brochure that tells how to save Earth's resources.

Book Talk

Which Unit Library book did you choose? Explain to a partner what it taught you about Earth's resources.

UNIT LIBRARY

Content Library

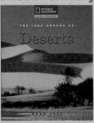

Leveled Library

A rescue worker and a trained rescue dog search for people after an earthquake in Peru.

Natural Forces

 **GUIDING QUESTION** How do people deal with the forces of nature?

Read More!

Content Library

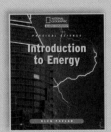

Introduction to Energy
by Glen Phelan

Leveled Library

Hercules
by Paul Storrie and Steve Kurth

Tornado
by Betsy Byars

Bearstone
by Will Hobbs

Internet
InsideNG.com

⊘ Go to the Digital Library to learn about the forces of nature.

⊘ See images of different natural forces.

⊘ Learn facts about different types of disasters.

Focus on Genre

Narrative Writing

▶ **Fiction**
▶ **Nonfiction**

Narrative writing can be fiction or nonfiction, but it always sounds like a story. In **narrative fiction**, the writer imagines the details of the story. In **narrative nonfiction**, the writer tells about real people and events.

How It Works

In **narrative** fiction, the **setting**, **characters**, and events are often believable, even if they are not real.

A Dark Storm

At eight o'clock in the morning, it was already hot and dry. Uncle Roy walked into the kitchen. He had gone to work in the field just a few minutes before, so Aunt Doris was surprised to see him.

"What's wrong?" she asked.

"There's a storm coming," he replied. "But it's not like any storm I have ever seen."

The sky got darker and darker. They could hear the wind. It wasn't rain that was blowing, though. It was dust.

The **characters** are the people in the story.

In **narrative** nonfiction, the **setting**, **people**, and events are real. Oleta Belezzuoli lived in Oklahoma in the 1930s. She tells about a dust storm.

The First Dust Storm

We were living in Oklahoma. I remember the first sandstorm. We were walking home probably three or four miles and this huge, huge black cloud came. We thought it was going to be a thunderstorm or a rainstorm, but it was only dust. And it just blotted out the sun. It was just like night. People had to use their car lights. The town lights went on. Afterwards, sand piled up two feet high in front of the door. It went through windows and every place.

Oleta is the narrator. She tells her own story, so she uses the words *I* and *we* a lot.

Academic Vocabulary

• **narrative** (**nair**-u-tiv) *adjective*
  Narrative writing tells a story.

Practice Together

Read the following text aloud. It is fiction. As you read, find the character and the setting. Look for the events that move the story along.

An Oklahoma Farm

It was 1933. Karen was living on a tiny farm in Oklahoma. The first few years on the farm were wonderful, but this year was hard.

There had been no rain all year, and the winds blew the dusty ground. The dust came in through the cracks of the house.

Karen wiped her finger along the table in the living room. It left a clear line in the layer of dust. She sighed and looked out at the dry fields around the house.

Karen unfolded the bedsheet she was holding. She climbed onto a chair and carefully pinned the sheet over the big front window.

"Maybe this will keep out some of the dust," she said aloud.

Try It!

Read the following text aloud. Ida Rockwell lived in Kansas in the 1930s. Who are the people she talks about? What is the setting? What events happen?

Leaving Home

It seems like the entire state of Kansas is covered in dust. There is no rain. Not one stick of corn will grow, and without corn, we can't make money.

We had to leave. Albert sold the tractor. We said good-bye to our friends. Everything we own is in our little car, and we are on our way West. We hear there is no dust out there.

Around noon, we ran out of gas. We were just outside of Augusta. Albert walked into town, bought the gas, came back, and we went on.

Then, before we had gone a mile, a tire went flat. The man from the garage helped us again. This time when Albert asked for the bill, the man just said, "Best of luck on your journey, folks."

That turned our day around. The car acted great, and we were in great spirits. We found a wonderful campground where we'll sleep well tonight. And I'll dream of rain.

Focus on Vocabulary

Use Word Parts

Some English words are made up of meaningful parts, including **base words** and **suffixes**. A base word makes sense alone, with no other parts attached to it. A suffix is a word part that comes at the end of a word. It changes the meaning of a word or how the word is used.

Sometimes you can put two or more smaller words together to form a **compound word**.

EXAMPLES

The suffix *-ly* means "in a certain way."

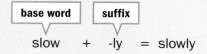

slow   +   -ly   =   slowly

Slowly means "in a way that is slow."

Everything is a compound word.

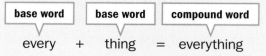

every   +   thing   =   everything

Everything means "all things that exist."

How the Strategy Works

When you read, you may come to a word that you don't know. Look for word part clues to help you **define** the word.

1. Look at words nearby for clues to the word's meaning.
2. Break down the word into meaningful parts.
3. Think about the meaning of each part.
4. Put the meanings together to **define** the whole word.
5. See if the meaning makes sense.

Follow the strategy to **define** each underlined word.

> It rained all night, from <u>sunset</u> until <u>sunrise</u>. What a <u>downpour</u> it was! The streets <u>quickly</u> became flooded. When the <u>rainstorm</u> <u>finally</u> ended, we went <u>outside</u>. What a mess! There was water and mud <u>everywhere</u>.

Strategy in Action

" I see meaningful parts in *sunset*. The *sun* is an object in the sky. *Set* means 'to go down.' A *sunset* is when the sun seems to go down. That meaning makes sense."

☑ **REMEMBER** Sometimes you can use word part clues to figure out the meaning of a whole word.

Academic Vocabulary
- **define** (di-**fin**) *verb*
  When you **define** something, you tell what it means.

Practice Together

Read this passage aloud. Figure out the meaning of each underlined word. Look for the word parts. Put their meanings together and **define** the underlined word.

Suffix	Meaning	Example
-ful	full of	hopeful
-ive	having qualities of	creative
-ly	in a certain way	quietly
-ment	action or process	payment

The Flood of 1993

When there is too much <u>rainfall</u>, rivers can <u>overflow</u>. Towns can get flooded. People who live near rivers may grow <u>fearful</u> when it rains for a long time.

A terrible flood happened in 1993. The Mississippi and Missouri Rivers both spilled over. About 50 people died.

Thousands more had to leave their homes. <u>Wildlife</u> suffered, too.

After days of rain, dirty water <u>quickly</u> covered roads and homes. Many <u>hardwood</u> trees fell down. Birds, turtles, and fish suffered, too. It was a difficult time for <u>everyone</u> in the Midwest.

Try It!

Read this passage aloud. What is the meaning of each underlined word? How do you know?

Storm Safety

If you prepare <u>properly</u>, you can survive a bad storm. Make a plan with your family. Have a radio, a <u>flashlight</u>, water, and a snack ready in a <u>backpack</u>. Go to your family's safe place. Stay there until an <u>announcement</u> tells you that you can <u>safely</u> leave. When you leave your safe place, be <u>careful</u> of <u>active</u> power lines and trees that are down.

▲ Power lines that come down during a storm can be dangerous.

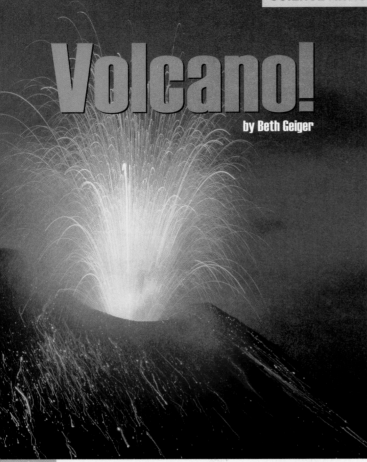

Volcano!

by Beth Geiger

Build Background

View Volcanoes

Volcanoes are powerful forces that begin deep inside the Earth. They create mountains and islands. They can also destroy life.

Digital Library

InsideNG.com
⊘ View the video.

▲ A huge crater was left after the volcano Mount St. Helens erupted.

Connect

Classify Senses Imagine that you are near a volcano by the ocean. Lava is flowing into the water. What do you see, hear, and feel? How does the air smell? Write your ideas in a chart.

Classification Chart

I see . . . thick red rivers of lava	I hear . . . crackling lava
I feel . . .	I smell . . .

Language & Grammar

Engage in Conversation CD

Look at the picture as you listen to the conversation.
Then practice the conversation with a partner.

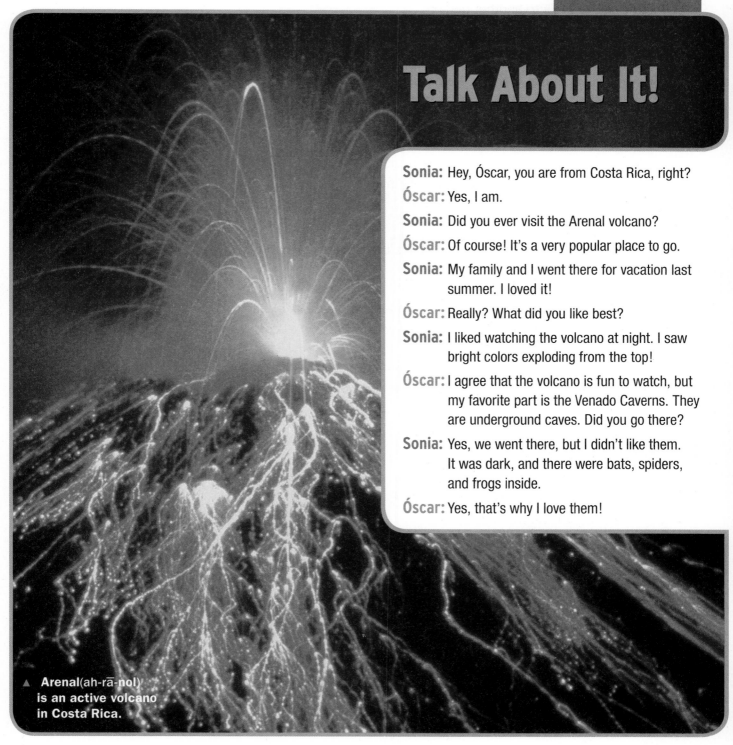

CONVERSATION

Talk About It!

Sonia: Hey, Óscar, you are from Costa Rica, right?

Óscar: Yes, I am.

Sonia: Did you ever visit the Arenal volcano?

Óscar: Of course! It's a very popular place to go.

Sonia: My family and I went there for vacation last summer. I loved it!

Óscar: Really? What did you like best?

Sonia: I liked watching the volcano at night. I saw bright colors exploding from the top!

Óscar: I agree that the volcano is fun to watch, but my favorite part is the Venado Caverns. They are underground caves. Did you go there?

Sonia: Yes, we went there, but I didn't like them. It was dark, and there were bats, spiders, and frogs inside.

Óscar: Yes, that's why I love them!

▲ **Arenal**(ah-rā-nol)
**is an active volcano
in Costa Rica.**

Use Subject Pronouns

Use a **subject pronoun** as the subject of a sentence.

- Use **I** when you talk about yourself.

  EXAMPLE   **I** visited a volcano.

- Use **you** when you talk to another person.

  EXAMPLE   **You** visited a volcano, too.

- Use **he** when you talk about one man or one boy.

  EXAMPLE   Juan has a camera. **He** takes photos of volcanoes.

- Use **she** when you talk about one woman or one girl.

  EXAMPLE   My aunt is a scientist. **She** studies volcanoes.

- Use **it** when you talk about one thing, one place, or one idea.

  EXAMPLE   Kilauea is a volcano. **It** is very interesting.

Subject Pronouns
Singular
I
you
he, she, it

Practice Together

Say each sentence or pair of sentences. Choose the correct pronoun from the chart above.

1. _____ am studying volcanoes in school.
2. My science teacher is Mr. Lin. _____ makes the subject exciting.
3. My sister helped me make a model of a volcano. _____ is a good artist.
4. Here is the model. _____ took a long time to make!
5. Mr. Lin asked me, "Do _____ want to display your model at the science fair?"

Try It!

Read each pair of sentences. Write the correct pronoun on a card. Then hold up the card as you say the sentences with the pronoun.

6. My mother visited Pompeii. _____ liked it very much.
7. Pompeii is an ancient city. _____ was destroyed by a volcano.
8. Luis is writing a report about Pompeii. _____ knows a lot about it.
9. Luis gave me his report. I read it. _____ learned a lot from it.
10. "This is great," I told Luis. "_____ are a good writer."

▲ Pompeii is in Italy. It is near the active volcano Mt. Vesuvius.

Reading Strategy: Make Connections

The text you read becomes more meaningful if you link it to your own life, to things you have read or seen, or to the world around you.

Reading Strategy
Make Connections

HOW TO MAKE CONNECTIONS

Use sticky notes to track connections. Tell how the connections help you understand the text better.

1. **Text to Self** If a fact or an idea reminds you of something from your own life, write T-S next to it. Explain the connection.
2. **Text to Text** If a fact or an idea reminds you of something you read or saw, write T-T next to it. Explain the connection.
3. **Text to World** If a fact or an idea relates to a problem or an issue in the world, write T-W next to it. Explain the connection.

Strategy in Action

Here's how one student made connections.

Look Into the Text

A Dangerous Job

Joanne Green walks by a glowing river. This river has no water, however. Instead, it is made of hot liquid rock, or lava.

The lava river is extremely hot, and so are the rocks surrounding it. "If you aren't careful," she says, "you'll melt your boots on the hot rock. Or worse!"

> "The text says the river is made of hot liquid rock."

In a movie, I saw some factory workers who poured hot melted metal. It looked dangerous! (T-T)

Practice Together

Reread the passage above, and make a connection of your own. Follow the steps in the How-To box. Put your sticky note next to the text.

Science Article

Science articles give information about the natural world. They often have **diagrams** that explain information in the text. The **title** and **labels** in the diagram help you know what it is about.

Diagram

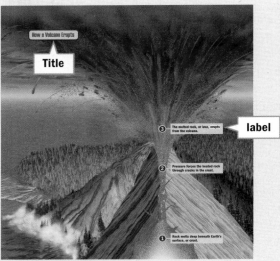

Your Job as a Reader

Reading Strategy: Make Connections

As you read, make connections to your own life, to things you have read, and to the world around you.

> Green is studying Kilauea, a volcano in Hawaii. Green studies other volcanoes, too. Earth has thousands of them.

I read a news story about a volcano that erupted. The lava burned everything.

(T-T)

This volcano in Stromboli, Italy, erupts and shoots out melted rock, or lava. ▶

Volcano!

by Beth Geiger

Online Coach

◀ Some people study volcanoes. They wear special clothing to protect themselves from hot rocks.

A Dangerous Job

Joanne Green walks by a glowing river. This river has no water, however. Instead, it is made of hot liquid rock, or lava.

The lava river is extremely hot, and so are the rocks surrounding it. "If you aren't careful," she says, "you'll melt your boots on the hot rock. Or worse!"

Green is used to these dangers. They are part of her job. She is a volcanologist, a scientist who studies **volcanoes**.

Green is studying Kilauea, a volcano in Hawaii. Green studies other volcanoes, too. Earth has thousands of them.

Volcanoes on Earth

Most people think that volcanoes are simply large mountains that pour out lava. But a volcano actually starts deep beneath Earth's **surface**, or crust.

The **layer** of rock below the Earth's crust is called the mantle. But the **pressure** and high temperature near the center of the Earth change the rock to liquid. The pressure can **force** the liquid rock upward. It moves up through cracks in the Earth's crust. This can form a volcano.

Key Vocabulary
volcano *n.*, an opening in Earth from which lava pours
surface *n.*, the outside part
layer *n.*, a section that is on top of or under another
force *v.*, to push strongly

In Other Words
pressure push from inside Earth

Language Background
The ancient Romans believed in many gods. The word *volcano* comes from the name of their god Vulcan. Vulcan was the god of fire.

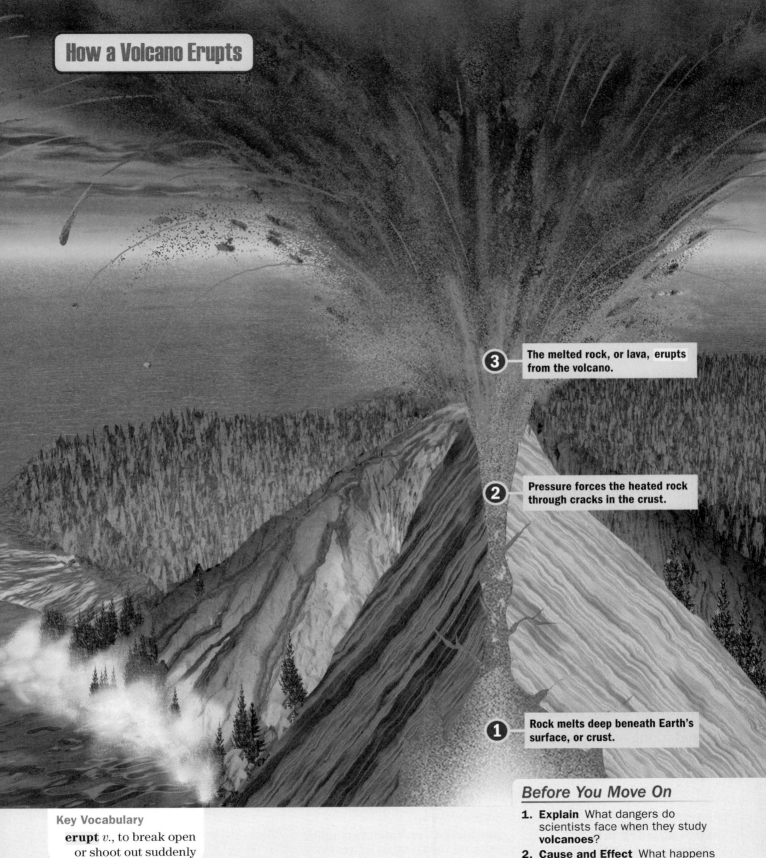

How a Volcano Erupts

3 The melted rock, or lava, erupts from the volcano.

2 Pressure forces the heated rock through cracks in the crust.

1 Rock melts deep beneath Earth's surface, or crust.

Key Vocabulary
erupt *v.*, to break open or shoot out suddenly

Before You Move On

1. **Explain** What dangers do scientists face when they study **volcanoes**?
2. **Cause and Effect** What happens to make a **volcano erupt**?

It's About the Lava

About 1,500 of Earth's volcanoes are **active**. An active volcano is one that can erupt lava.

Some volcanoes make runny lava. The lava flows fast, like **pancake batter**. It piles up in thin layers. Over time, it forms low, wide mountains.

Other volcanoes erupt thick lava. It flows slowly, like toothpaste. It piles up in thick layers. Over time, it forms tall, steep mountains.

▲ Cooling lava forms rock. That is how the Hawaiian Islands developed.

The Ring of Fire

Volcanoes are found all over Earth. Some form on land. Others rise up from the bottom of the ocean.

Most volcanoes are near the Pacific Ocean. They form a circle of volcanoes known as the Ring of Fire.

These volcanoes are found in areas where big pieces of Earth's surface, or plates, meet. Many volcanoes are formed along such **plate boundaries**.

THE RING OF FIRE

EURASIAN PLATE

JUAN DE FUCA PLATE

GORDA PLATE

NORTH AMERICAN PLATE

EURASIAN PLATE

PHILIPPINE PLATE

Ring of Fire

PACIFIC PLATE

CARIBBEAN PLATE

COCOS PLATE

AFRICAN PLATE

ARABIAN PLATE

SOMALI PLATE

INDIAN PLATE

NAZCA PLATE

SOUTH AMERICAN PLATE

AUSTRALIAN PLATE

PACIFIC OCEAN

SCOTIA PLATE

ANTARCTIC PLATE

△ **Interpret the Map** Name the largest plate within the Ring of Fire.

Key Vocabulary
active *adj.*, likely to show action

In Other Words
pancake batter a watery mixture
plate boundaries areas where Earth's plates meet

Living with Volcanoes

Many people live near volcanoes. Some live close to the **base** of the mountains. Others farm nearby land. **Ash** from volcanoes is good for **soil**, so crops grow well.

▼ This farmer works near Mount Agung, a volcano in Bali.

In Other Words
base bottom, lowest level
Ash The dust that comes from burnt rocks
soil the dirt

Before You Move On
1. **Summarize** What is the Ring of Fire?
2. **Evidence and Conclusion** Which details explain why people farm the land near **volcanoes**?

A Dangerous Surprise

Living near a volcano can be **dangerous**, though. Volcanoes can erupt without **warning**.

That is just what happened in 1980 in Washington. On May 18, a volcano named Mount St. Helens erupted. Hot ash and steam blasted out of the volcano.

Few people were ready for it. Even scientists did not know it would happen that day. The volcano had not erupted since 1857.

The burning ash poured down the mountain, killing all the trees and **wildlife** in its path. The blast produced millions of tons of dust that covered 230 square miles.

MT. ST. HELENS ERUPTS

May 18, 1980 • 8:27:00 a.m.
Mount St. Helens looked calm and peaceful. It wasn't. Scientists knew something would happen. But no one knew exactly when.

May 18, 1980 • 8:32:37 a.m.
The mountain exploded at 8:32 a.m. Ash soared 60,000 feet into the air.

May 18, 1980 • 8:32:51 a.m.
The blast produced 400 million tons of dust. It blanketed 230 square miles.

Key Vocabulary
dangerous *adj.*, not safe
warning *n.*, a sign that something bad may happen

In Other Words
wildlife animals

Math Background
In the United States, people often measure large areas of land in *square miles*. A square mile is one mile long and one mile wide.

Life Returns

More than 20 years have passed since that day. Trees have now grown back. Animals live in the forests. Life has returned to Mount St. Helens. The people there will not forget what happened, though.

▲ Visitors compare an old photo of Mount St. Helens to the volcano today.

▲ Trees now grow on Mount St. Helens.

Before You Move On

1. **Sequence** Tell what happened to Mount St. Helens between 8:27 a.m. and 8:33 a.m.
2. **Compare and Contrast** How did Mount St. Helens look before it **erupted**? How does it look today?

A Force on Earth

Volcanoes are all over the world. Some are active and some are not. Some, like Mount St. Helens, could erupt without much warning. Volcanoes are one of the **forces** on Earth that we live with but cannot control. ❖

People in this village in the Philippines used umbrellas to protect themselves from ash. Nearby, Mount Pinatubo was erupting. Ash from the volcano darkened the sky.

Key Vocabulary

force *n.*, a great power in nature

Before You Move On

1. **Make Decisions** If you lived near an **active volcano**, what would you do?
2. **Viewing** Look at the picture. How can you tell that a **volcano** is **erupting**?

Connect Reading and Writing

Vocabulary
active
dangerous
erupt
forces
layers
surface
volcano
warnings

CRITICAL THINKING

1. SUM IT UP Create a Fact Web. Write at least six facts about **volcanoes**. Then use your web to sum up the selection.

Fact Web

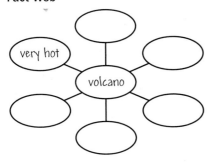

very hot

volcano

2. Make Judgments Why do people live near **active** **volcanoes**? Do you think they should? Explain your reasoning.

3. Classify Describe two different kinds of lava. Tell about the type of **layers** and mountains that each kind of lava forms.

4. Infer Many **volcanoes** form along the edges of big plates, or pieces of Earth's **surface**. Why do you think this is so? Use facts in the text to support your answer.

READING FLUENCY

Phrasing Read the passage on page 574 to a partner. Assess your fluency.

1. I read

   a. great   **b.** OK   **c.** not very well

2. What I did best in my reading was _____.

READING STRATEGY

Make Connections
What connections did you make to your own life, to other texts, and to the world? Tell a partner about one of each.

VOCABULARY REVIEW

Oral Review Read the paragraph aloud. Add the vocabulary words.

> A _____ is not just a mountain with hot lava. An _____ volcano is one that can _____, or explode. Pressure in the center of Earth _____ hot liquid rock through cracks in the crust. The hot rock, or lava, can be extremely _____! Scientists try to give _____ so people can escape. When lava from an explosion eventually cools, it adds new _____ to the _____ of Earth.

Written Review Pretend that you are a radio announcer. Write a **warning** about a **volcano** in your area that may **erupt**. Use five vocabulary words.

WRITE ABOUT THE GUIDING QUESTION

Explore Natural Forces

Imagine that you are going to work with Joanne Green, the volcanologist in the selection. How do you prepare for this **dangerous** job? Reread the selection and look for details that support your answer.

Connect Across the Curriculum

Literary Analysis

Analyze Text Structure: Cause and Effect

> **Academic Vocabulary**
> • **create** (krē-āt) *verb*
>   To **create** means to make something new.

How Is Text Organized? Some nonfiction writers use **cause and effect** to organize their ideas. A cause is an event that leads to another event, called the effect. Authors use cause and effect to explain why something happens and how one thing leads to another.

Practice Together

Note Causes and Effects Read this passage from "Volcano!" Think about how the forces of Earth **create** volcanoes. Focus on the causes and effects.

> The layer of rock below the Earth's crust is called the mantle. But the pressure and high temperature near the center of the Earth change the rock to liquid. The pressure can force the liquid rock upward. It moves up through cracks in the Earth's crust. This can form a volcano.

Make a Chart A Cause-and-Effect Chain shows how one event leads to another. The first box tells the first cause. The next box shows the effect of that cause. The third box shows what follows next. Work with your class to complete a Cause-and-Effect Chain for the passage above.

Cause-and-Effect Chain

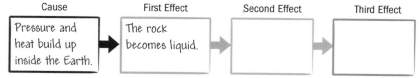

Cause	First Effect	Second Effect	Third Effect
Pressure and heat build up inside the Earth.	The rock becomes liquid.		

Try It!

Make a New Chain Work with a partner and follow these steps:

- Reread the text about the eruption of Mount St. Helens on pages 142–143.
- **Create** a Cause-and-Effect Chain to tell about the events.
- Add as many boxes as you need.

Use Word Parts

> **Academic Vocabulary**
> • **define** (di-fīn) *verb*
> When you **define** something, you tell what
> it means.

A compound word is made up of two or more smaller words. Sometimes you can **define** a compound word if you know the meanings of the smaller words, or you can use context clues to figure out the meaning. For example:

wild + life = wildlife   *Wildlife* is another word for plants and
                          animals that live in their natural habitat.

Define Compound Words Work with a partner. Write the meaning of each underlined word. Explain how you **defined** it.

1. The earthquake shook the house.
2. Books were scattered everywhere.
3. We went to stay with my grandparents.
4. Every morning we ate pancakes for breakfast.
5. We brushed our teeth with mint toothpaste.

MEDIA & TECHNOLOGY

Report on a Volcano

> **Academic Vocabulary**
> • **report** (ri-**port**) *verb*
> When you **report** on an event, you describe
> what happened.

Work with a partner to give a slide show that **reports** on a famous volcano.

❶ **Evaluate Information** Choose a volcano to research. Collect facts about the volcano, using reliable print and online sources.

> **Internet** InsideNG.com
> ↗ Gather information about a volcano.

❷ **Prepare Your Slide Show** Organize your ideas and write a script that **reports** the facts. Download photos and diagrams. Use only the visuals that you have the right to use. Put them together to make a slide show.

❸ **Give Your Slide Show** Speak clearly and loudly as you read your script. Answer your classmates' questions afterwards.

▲ **Mount Batur is a volcano in Bali, Indonesia.**

Research/Speaking

Research Plate Tectonics

Academic Vocabulary
- **force** (fors) *noun*
  A **force** is a great power in nature.

You learned about the Ring of Fire in the article "Volcano!" Find out more about the plates and the **forces** below Earth's surface that cause the plates to move and change. Then share what you learn.

▲ The wavy pattern of rock and soil here shows that the Earth has moved over time.

❶ Frame Questions Decide what questions you want to answer. For example:

- Where are the plates located?
- What causes the plates to move?
- How do the plates move?
- What happens when the plates move?

❷ Conduct Research Find books about geology, the study of the Earth. Use the table of contents to find out if the book has the information you want.

A table of contents is at the beginning of a book. Most tables of contents list chapter titles, main headings, and page numbers. If any of the contents in the book are about plates, use the listed number to find that section of the book. Read and take notes to answer your questions.

❸ Plan a Presentation Put your notes together. Organize your ideas around one main point. Write an introduction and a conclusion. Define technical terms. Draw pictures or make a model to explain your ideas.

Table of Contents

Contents

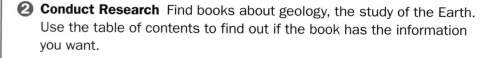

chapter titles   page number

❹ Present Your Findings Use your notes and your pictures or model to explain what you learned. Choose words carefully, and speak clearly.

Engage in Conversation

Group Talk With a group, look at the photos of Mount St. Helens on pages 142–143. Share your thoughts and ideas about the photos. Use subject pronouns.

> Animals probably ran away if they could.

> You're right. They were probably terrified.

Write About an Interesting Place

Study the Models When you write about an interesting place, it's important not to repeat words too many times. Your writing will be choppy and hard to read if you keep using the same words. Using subject pronouns in place of the subject can help make sentences smooth.

NOT OK

Paricutín is a small volcano in Mexico. **Paricutín** started in a cornfield in 1943. **Paricutín** eventually destroyed the nearby town of San Juan. My **uncle** visited San Juan. My **uncle** took pictures of the town. My **uncle** told me that no one was killed by the lava and ash. The **town** is almost completely covered in lava rock, though. The **town** is a strange place.

> The writer repeats **nouns** in the subjects. The reader thinks: "**This is not very easy to read.**"

OK

Paricutín is a small volcano in Mexico. **It** started in a cornfield in 1943. **It** eventually destroyed the nearby town of San Juan. My uncle visited San Juan. **He** took pictures of the town. **He** told me that no one was killed by the lava and ash. The town is almost completely covered in lava rock, though. **It** is a strange place.

> The writer replaces some nouns with **subject pronouns**.

WRITE ON YOUR OWN Write about an interesting place that you or someone you know visited. When you can, use subject pronouns to make your sentences smooth.

REMEMBER

There are singular and plural subject pronouns.

Singular	Plural
I	we
you	you
he, she, it	they

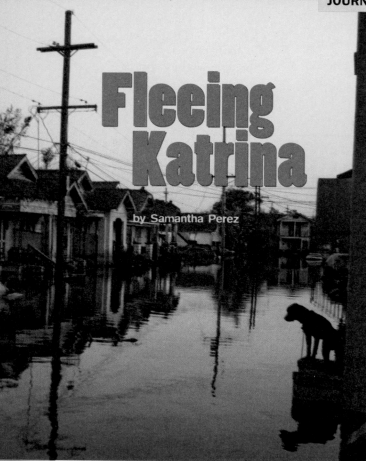

Fleeing Katrina
by Samantha Perez

SELECTION 2 OVERVIEW

▶ **Build Background**

▶ **Language & Grammar**
Ask and Answer Questions
Use Correct Pronouns

▶ **Prepare to Read**
Learn Key Vocabulary
Learn a Reading Strategy
Make Connections

▶ **Read and Write**
Focus on Genre
Journal
Apply the Reading Strategy
Make Connections
Critical Thinking
Reading Fluency
Read with Expression
Vocabulary Review
Write About the Guiding Question

▶ **Connect Across the Curriculum**
Literary Analysis
Analyze Facts and Opinions
Vocabulary Study
Use Word Parts
Research/Speaking
Retell a Personal Narrative
Media/Speaking
Compare Media Accounts
Language and Grammar
Ask and Answer Questions
Grammar and Writing
Write About a Natural Disaster

Build Background

Explore Hurricanes

A hurricane is a storm that gathers power as winds blow over the warm ocean. Find out why hurricanes can be so destructive.

Digital Library
InsideNG.com
◉ View the video.

◀ **A hurricane hits the coast of Florida.**

Connect

Collaboration In a group, share what you know about Hurricane Katrina. Record facts and details.

HURRICANE KATRINA
- When:
- Where:
- Damage:
- Health and Safety:

Language & Grammar

Ask and Answer Questions CD

Listen to the conversation. Then act out the dialogue with a partner.

DIALOGUE

After the Hurricane

Kate: Does your family still have a house in New Orleans?

Marcus: Yes, we do, but it is completely destroyed.

Kate: Do you miss New Orleans?

Marcus: Yes, I miss it a lot.

Kate: Does your whole family live in Houston now?

Marcus: Yes, they all live here now.

Kate: Does your mother like living in Houston?

Marcus: No, she doesn't. She really misses our home.

Kate: Do you think you will go back to Louisiana soon?

Marcus: No, I don't think so.

Kate: Does your family plan to go back someday?

Marcus: Yes, we do!

Use Correct Pronouns

Remember, the subject of a sentence can be a pronoun.

- Use **I** when you talk about yourself.
- Use **you** to talk to one or more persons.
- Use **we** to talk about another person or persons and yourself.
- Use **he**, **she**, or **it** to talk about one person, place, or thing.
- Use **they** to talk about more than one person, place, or thing.

A **subject pronoun** can refer to a **noun** in another sentence.

- If the noun is a man or a boy, use **he**.
  If it is a woman or a girl, use **she**.

  EXAMPLES   **Dan** is from Louisiana. **He** lost his house in a hurricane.

  Laila left her town. **She** came back after the hurricane.

- If the noun is a place or a thing, use **it**.
  If the noun is plural, use **they**.

  EXAMPLES   The **house** was flooded. **It** is a mess.

  My **relatives** lost their home. **They** are living with us.

Practice Together

Say each pair of sentences. Replace the
underlined subject with the correct subject pronoun.

1. The hurricane in 2005 was a big storm.
   <u>The hurricane</u> hit Cuba forcefully.
2. Winds pounded the island. <u>Winds</u> were
   very powerful.
3. Grandfather was in Cuba. <u>Grandfather</u>
   watched the storm.
4. Grandmother was in the United States.
   <u>Grandmother</u> felt worried.

▲ A hurricane is dangerous. It brings strong winds.

Try It!

Read each pair of sentences. Replace the underlined subject
with the correct subject pronoun. Write it on a card. Hold up
the card as you say the sentences with the pronoun.

5. Dave turns on the radio. <u>Dave</u> hears a weather report.
6. The storm is approaching. <u>The storm</u> is dangerous.
7. Waves hit the coast. <u>Waves</u> are huge.
8. Mom calls everyone. <u>Mom</u> gets the dog, too.

Discuss Natural Forces

ASK AND ANSWER QUESTIONS

Many people experience the destructive forces of nature. Strong winds can knock down a tree, or heavy rains can flood a house. What powerful forces of nature do you know about? Write your ideas in a web.

Idea Web

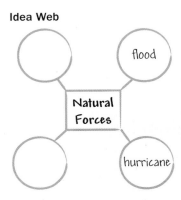

Work with a group to learn more about one of the forces in the Idea Web. Write questions to ask another group about the forces of nature they are studying. Take turns asking and answering questions with another group.

HOW TO ASK AND ANSWER QUESTIONS

1. You can use the words *Do* or *Does* to start a question.

2. You can answer a *Do* or *Does* question with *Yes* or *No*.

3. You can also give a short or long answer to a *Do* or *Does* question.

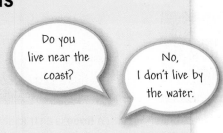

USE CORRECT PRONOUNS

When you ask and answer a question, use the correct pronoun. The **subject pronoun** in an answer often refers to a **noun** in the question.

Question: Does **California** have a lot of tornadoes?
Answer: No, **it** doesn't.

Question: Do your **parents** buy extra food before a blizzard?
Answer: Yes, **they** do.

Prepare to Read

Learn Key Vocabulary

Rate and Study the Words Rate how well you know each word. Then:

1. Pronounce the word. Say it aloud several times. Spell it.
2. Study the example.
3. Tell more about the word.
4. Practice it. Make the word your own.

Key Words

evacuate (i-va-kyū-āt) *verb*
▶ page 158

To **evacuate** means to leave or to get out. The woman **evacuated** the building when the fire alarm rang.

fortunate (for-chu-nut) *adjective* ▶ page 164

Someone who is **fortunate** is lucky. The family is **fortunate** that their house did not burn in the fire.
Base Word: **fortune**

future (fyū-chur) *noun*
▶ page 166

The **future** is what will happen in the time to come. I am going to a concert at some time in the near **future**.

hurricane (hur-u-kān) *noun*
▶ page 158

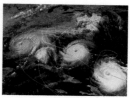

A **hurricane** is an ocean storm with strong winds. From space, a **hurricane** looks like a spiral of white clouds.

levee (le-vē) *noun*
▶ page 163

A **levee** is a structure that keeps a river from flooding. If rainfall is heavy for a long time, a river could rise and the water could spill over the **levee**.

necessity (ni-se-su-tē) *noun*
▶ page 160

A **necessity** is an item that someone needs. Food and water are the most basic **necessities** of life.

severe (su-vear) *adjective*
▶ page 158

Something that is **severe** is very serious or dangerous. Dad could not read because he had a **severe** headache.

untouched (un-tucht) *adjective* ▶ page 166

Something that is **untouched** is not changed or hurt in any way. Few areas of the world have been **untouched** by humans.
Base Word: **touch**

Practice the Words Work with a partner. Write a question using a Key Word. Answer your partner's question using a different Key Word. Keep going until you have used all the words twice.

Questions	Answers
What would you take if you evacuated your home in an earthquake?	I would take water, food, and other necessities.

Reading Strategy: Make Connections

As you read, make connections to your life, to other texts, and to the world. Think about how the links add to your understanding of what you read.

Reading Strategy
Make Connections

HOW TO MAKE CONNECTIONS

1. **Identify** As you read, stop occasionally and think about what you can link to the text.
2. **Evaluate** Does the connection help you understand the events? If so, write it down. Tell what you connect to and why you make the connection.
3. **Label** Tell what kind of connection it is: T-S (text to self), T-T (text to text), or T-W (text to world). Tell how it helps you better understand the text you are reading.

Strategy in Action

Here's how one student made connections while reading this journal.

Look Into the Text

Monday, August 29, 2005

Last Days in St. Bernard Parish

I lived in a place called St. Bernard Parish, Louisiana, a town just southeast of New Orleans. I say that I lived there, because I don't anymore. I don't live anywhere.

Friday night we heard that a hurricane in the Gulf of Mexico might be coming our way. Not a big deal, I thought.

> I saw some hurricanes on TV. They destroyed a lot of homes. Maybe this hurricane destroyed the writer's home.
> (T-W)

Practice Together

Now make a connection of your own as you read the journal entry above. Follow the steps in the How-To box.

Focus on Genre

Journal

A journal can be narrative nonfiction. People usually write journals to record their personal experiences, feelings, and thoughts. A journal often has **dates** that tell when events happen.

Tuesday, August 30, 2005 ◁ date

Fleeing Katrina

I grabbed the last of my things and turned off my light. Mom and I were in the car a minute later.

Your Job as a Reader

Reading Strategy: Make Connections

As you read, make connections to increase your understanding. Think about how the text connects to your own life, to things you have read, and to the world around you.

I grabbed the last of my things and turned off the light. Mom and I were in the car a minute later.

I know how they feel. A few years ago, our house was on fire, and we had to get out quickly.

(T-S)

New Orleans, Louisiana, on September 10, 2005, two weeks after Hurricane Katrina hit. ▶

Fleeing Katrina

by Samantha Perez

Monday, August 29, 2005

Last Days in St. Bernard Parish

I lived in a place called St. Bernard Parish, Louisiana, a town just southeast of New Orleans. I say that I lived there, because I don't anymore. I don't live anywhere.

Friday night we heard that a hurricane in the Gulf of Mexico might be coming our way. Not a big deal, I thought.

Dad called from his work and suggested **evacuating**. Since **Hurricane Ivan** last year, he'd been fairly **paranoid** about hurricanes.

By Saturday morning, the hurricane's **projected** path showed New Orleans getting a direct hit. Dad doubled the efforts of his evacuation campaign.

By Saturday night, the decision had been made: we had to leave. Hurricane Katrina was now a **severe Category 4**, and it was coming straight for the city. We needed to get out of the parish.

Hurricane Katrina's Path, August 23–30, 2005

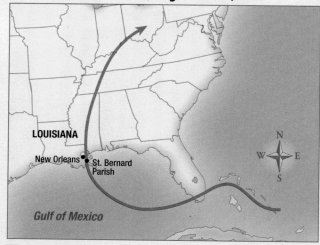

▲ Interpret the Map How many states did Hurricane Katrina pass through?

Key Vocabulary
hurricane *n.*, an ocean storm with strong winds
evacuate *v.*, to leave, to get out
severe *adj.*, very serious

In Other Words
Hurricane Ivan a hurricane that hit Louisiana
paranoid worried, nervous
projected expected, likely
Category 4 hurricane with winds of 131 to 155 miles per hour

▲ This business in St. Bernard Parish, Louisiana, was destroyed by Hurricane Katrina.

Science Background

Hurricanes have winds of 119 kilometers (74 miles) or more per hour over a long period of time. When they occur in the Atlantic Ocean, they can affect the eastern United States. The winds turn around a central point, called the eye. The eye is the calmest part of a hurricane.

hurricane

eye

◄ Hurricane Rita passed over the Gulf of Mexico in 2005.

I filled a big plastic container with my clothes. I took my books off my shelves and stacked them high in my room so, just in case we did get water, they would be safe. I stacked everything **atop** my desk, bookshelf, and dresser, so it would all be safe.

. . . just in case we did get water, the books would be safe.

I looked at my pretty dress a lot that night. I was going to wear it to my senior **prom** this year. It was strapless, this beautiful shade of pastel pink. It was just hanging in my near-empty closet. I wanted to bring it so badly, but Mama said no. No room for dresses, only **necessities**.

Key Vocabulary
necessity *n.*, an item that someone needs

In Other Words
atop on top of
prom dance

Tuesday, August 30, 2005, part 1

Fleeing Katrina

I grabbed the last of my things and turned off my light. Mom and I were in the car a minute later.

It took almost nine hours to get to the hotel in Bossier City. It didn't take any longer than it normally would, and we were lucky because there was very little traffic.

We spent the whole evening watching the news. Katrina's course had changed only slightly. **The track led it to make landfall** just east of New Orleans.

I looked at the projected path. The eye was going to pass over my parish. The storm was a Category 5 now, the highest possible.

▽ Samantha's family left quickly. Later, the roads were full of people leaving their homes before the hurricane arrived.

Science Background

There are five categories of hurricanes. For Category 5, the winds are greater than 155 miles per hour. Hurricane Katrina was a Category 5 over the Gulf of Mexico, before it reached land.

In Other Words

The track led it to make landfall It would cross from the ocean onto land

Before You Move On

1. **Summarize** Tell how Samantha's family gets ready to **evacuate**.
2. **Problem and Solution** What problem does Samantha face as she packs **necessities** to take with her? Tell how she solves it.

▲ This home was damaged by the mud and water that covered New Orleans after Hurricane Katrina.

Predict

What will happen to Samantha's family and her home?

Tuesday, August 30, 2005, part 2

First News from Home

We lost our home. The **levees** broke and water spilled into the streets.

Our home is gone. St. Bernard is completely under the water, and we have nothing now.

Saturday, September 3, 2005

Just Darkness and the Cry of a Million Crickets

I want to go home. I miss so many things about my home. We don't even know how long it'll be before they'll let us back into the parish, to save what we can and realize all that we lost.

Friday, September 16, 2005

Guilt and Doubt

Now my family is in Ponchatoula, Louisiana.

We're living on a **lot** that used to belong to our friend's grandmother. The three of us are living in the **camper**, and it's tight.

Here, I have some friends from my old school, and even though I was never really close with any of them, it's comforting looking around and seeing something familiar.

Key Vocabulary

levee *n.*, a structure that keeps a river from flooding

In Other Words

Crickets Small insects
lot piece of land
camper trailer

Before You Move On

1. **Confirm Prediction** Was your prediction correct? What happened that you did not expect?
2. **Evidence and Conclusion** Does Samantha's family go back to their home? How do you know?

Saturday, September 17, 2005

Going Home

I went home. But it wasn't home. Home isn't really there anymore.

Mud was **caked** everywhere on the ground. Things were brown and gray, not green as they used to be. It was like I stepped into some other **reality**. This wasn't the St. Bernard I remembered.

We **turned into** my neighborhood, and it was strange. Usually, I see green grass, green bushes, green shrubs, and trees. Now, the salt water had killed all of those things. It was brown now, an old, dry brown.

Dad stopped the truck in the middle of the street, and we spilled out.

When Mom walked onto the porch and looked through the front room door, I knew she wasn't expecting what she saw. And the smell was horrible. Mold and rotten food and mud scents mixing together.

. . . the smell was horrible.

I walked to the hall. There was mold growing everywhere on the walls. It was as if we had put up some **demented** circle-pattern wallpaper for fun.

My bedroom door was open, so I walked right in. Nothing was in its right place. My bed had flipped over. My bookshelf had fallen over. Papers were on my floor.

I climbed over my bed to get to the closet where my dresses had been hanging.

I was gasping for breath as I lifted a plastic bag and looked at my pink dress. It was fine, and I started yelling for my mom to come and see. My dress was fine!

As we drove away, I thought about walking around my house and seeing things that I had once treasured.

I realized that it didn't really matter anymore, any of it. I lost papers and stories and clothes, but I'm **fortunate** that I didn't lose the people that matter to me.

Key Vocabulary
fortunate *adj.*, lucky

In Other Words
caked stuck
reality place, world
turned into arrived in
demented crazy, wild

▲ After the flood, mold and mildew covered the walls, ceiling, and furniture of this home in New Orleans.

Sunday, May 14, 2006
A Pink Dress at the Prom

Last night, my new school had its senior prom. My best friends from my old school and I decided to go together as a group. So this prom was a **reunion**, which in some ways was so much better than any dance normal kids can have.

And I had the chance to wear my pretty, pastel pink dress. The one that survived the hurricane. We had it cleaned a few weeks before, and it came out great. The smell of mold was gone, and it looked **immaculate** and **untouched**.

Tuesday, August 29, 2006
One Year Since Katrina

It's been a year now, one year since Hurricane Katrina destroyed people's lives, dreams, and homes.

I am wiser than before. I have learned to adapt to whatever comes my way. And I've learned that if I work hard enough, I can make things better for the **future**. ❖

About the Author

Samantha Perez

Samantha Perez (1988–) was born in New Orleans, Louisiana. She is a proud resident of St. Bernard Parish, just southeast of New Orleans, where she has returned to rebuild in the wake of Hurricane Katrina. Her journalism for ReadTheTattoo.com brought attention to her hometown and won several awards, including the Scholastic Press Forum's Professor Mel Williams Award for Writing Excellence and a resolution praising her from the Louisiana State Senate in 2006. She is currently a student at Southeastern Louisiana University.

Key Vocabulary
untouched *adj.*, not hurt in any way
future *n.*, what will happen in the time to come

In Other Words
reunion time to be together again
immaculate clean, perfect

Before You Move On
1. **Recall and Interpret** What happens to Samantha's prom dress?
2. **Confirm Prediction** Was your prediction correct? How does the event change Samantha?

Connect Reading and Writing

Vocabulary
evacuated
fortunate
future
hurricanes
levees
necessity
severe
untouched

CRITICAL THINKING

1. SUM IT UP Make a Sequence Chain to show what happens to Samantha and her family before, during, and after the **hurricane**. Use your Sequence Chain to sum up the selection.

Sequence Chain

On Friday, Dad says they should leave.

2. Paraphrase In your own words, describe what Samantha sees in her home after the storm. How **severe** is the damage?

3. Analyze A special object is left **untouched** by the storm. What does it represent?

4. Draw Conclusions Samantha feels **fortunate** and thinks about the **future**. What do her thoughts tell you about her personality?

READING FLUENCY

Expression Read the passage on page 575 to a partner. Assess your fluency.

1. I read
   a. great   **b.** OK   **c.** not very well

2. What I did best in my reading was _____.

READING STRATEGY

Make Connections
What connections did you make during reading? Share one with a partner.

VOCABULARY REVIEW

Oral Review Read the paragraph aloud. Add the vocabulary words.

> All _____ develop in the ocean. Cities on the coast are damaged by some of these storms but _____ by others. In 2005, New Orleans was hit by Hurricane Katrina. Many people left, or _____, but others were not so _____. New Orleans is in a low area of land, with water all around. The city has wall-like structures, or _____, to keep water out. These structures are a real _____! In 2005, flood water broke through and did _____ damage. Engineers will make the levees stronger in the _____.

Written Review Suppose you had to **evacuate**. Write a paragraph about one thing you would take that was not a **necessity**. Use four vocabulary words.

WRITE ABOUT THE GUIDING QUESTION

Explore Natural Forces
Why was the impact of Hurricane Katrina more **severe** than other natural events in recent U.S. history? Write your opinion. Use examples from the text to support your ideas.

Connect Across the Curriculum

Analyze Facts and Opinions

> **Academic Vocabulary**
> • **discuss** (di-**skus**) *verb*
>   When you **discuss** something, you talk about it.

In her journal, Samantha includes both facts and opinions.

- An **opinion** is a personal judgment. Words like *I believe* or *I think* sometimes signal an opinion.

> Friday night we heard that a hurricane in the Gulf of Mexico might be coming our way. Not a big deal, I thought.

- A **fact** is something that can be proved. For example, you can check the weather report to prove this fact:

> By Saturday morning, the hurricane's projected path showed New Orleans getting a direct hit.

Practice Together

With a group, read this passage about another teen's experience during Hurricane Katrina. **Discuss** it. Notice the **facts** and **opinions**.

> On the news, the reporter said the wind is blowing at over 120 miles per hour in my hometown. We packed and went to a shelter right away. I feel safer here than I did at home. This shelter has room for more than 7,000 people, but it is almost full. This is a scary time for all of us.

Try It!

Read another passage about the teen and **discuss** it. How could you prove the facts? Which words are opinions? How do you know?

> It has been a month since the hurricane. Our family has a trailer to live in. There are only two beds, so space is a little tight. But we are glad to be together in our own place. There are five other trailers on our block. One of my friends lives in one of them. Everything is so different in my neighborhood, so I'm very glad that there is someone I know nearby.

Use Word Parts

Suffix	Meaning
-hood	quality of
-less	without
-ly	in a certain way
-ness	state of

Academic Vocabulary
- **locate** (lō-kāt) *verb*
  To **locate** something is to find it.

A suffix changes the meaning of a word and how the word is used in a sentence. For example:

base word	suffix

fear + -less = fearless

The suffix *-less* means "without," so when you add it to the noun *fear*, you create the adjective *fearless*. Someone who is fearless is without fear.

Define Words Work with a partner. **Locate** the suffix in each word and cover it. Tell the meaning of the base word. Uncover the suffix. Use the meaning of the suffix and the meaning of the base word to tell what the word means. Use the whole word in a sentence to tell about "Fleeing Katrina."

1. fairly   **3.** badly   **5.** completely   **7.** hopeless

2. strapless   **4.** slightly   **6.** darkness   **8.** neighborhood

---

Retell a Personal Narrative

HISTORY

Academic Vocabulary
- **narrative** (nair-u-tiv) *noun*
  A **narrative** is writing that tells a story.

❶ **Research Hurricane Katrina** Use magazines, books, newspapers, and the Internet to find a personal **narrative** about Hurricane Katrina. Note the interesting details that tell about the person's experience and feelings.

    Internet InsideNG.com
    ↻ Find a personal narrative about Hurricane Katrina.

❷ **Retell the Personal Narrative to the Class** Begin by giving background so that listeners will understand what was happening at the time. Tell what the person saw and how he or she felt. Explain why the event was memorable.

▲ Hurricane Katrina ruined this fisherman's boat, home, and business.

Connect Across the Curriculum, continued

MEDIA & TECHNOLOGY

Compare Media Accounts

Academic Vocabulary
- **explanation** (ek-splu-**nā**-shun) *noun*
  An **explanation** is a statement that makes an idea clear.

Nonfiction gives facts through words and text features, including charts, diagrams, and maps. It can be print or other media like video. The **explanations** in nonfiction help readers and viewers learn about interesting things that have happened or are happening.

Writers of nonfiction tell what they think is important. What they choose to tell or omit affects the opinions of readers and viewers.

1 **Conduct Research** Look through newspapers and magazines and on the Internet. Find an interesting article about Hurricane Katrina. Read it carefully.

> **Internet** InsideNG.com
> 🧭 Find an article about Hurricane Katrina.

2 **Analyze Text Features** Identify the text features, including photos, captions, maps, diagrams, and charts. Analyze the words and images that the writer uses. Think about

- what the writer chooses to tell about
- how the writing affects you
- whether the nonfiction piece is accurate
- what kind of information the features add.

▲ News articles often include photos that touch readers' emotions. How does this photo of hurricane damage affect you?

3 **Recall the Video** Think about the video you saw on Hurricane Katrina before you read this selection. Think about the images it shows and the main ideas it tells. Why do you think the writer chose those images? What opinion do you think the writer wants you to have about the event?

4 **Compare Accounts** Work with a small group. Compare the ideas in the print piece and in the video. Decide how each one causes you to think about the event. Which nonfiction piece gives a more effective **explanation** of what happened? Why?

Ask and Answer Questions

Interview a Classmate Wind, rain, lightning, and thunder are forces of nature. List others. Ask a classmate questions about different forces of nature. For example: "Do you like snow? Does lightning scare you?" Switch roles. Use correct subject pronouns.

> Do you like thunder?

> Yes, thunder is exciting. It can be dangerous, though.

Write About a Natural Disaster

Study the Models You may want to write about your experience with a storm or another natural force. Be sure to write sentences that are clear, so readers can follow what you write. One way to write clear sentences is to use the correct pronoun.

NOT OK

> Last **winter** was difficult. **He** was long and cold, and there were several snowstorms. My **sister** slipped on the ice during one storm. **They** broke her ankle. My **brother** fell off his bike on an icy road. **It** was OK, but the bike was damaged. My **parents** also had trouble. **She** had to cancel their vacation because the airport was closed.

The writer thinks: "**I'm confused. The nouns and pronouns don't seem to go together.**"

OK

> **Danny Boy** is my dog. **He** survived Hurricane Katrina. My **family** had to leave in a hurry. **We** could not take Danny Boy. A **lady** rescued him after the storm. **She** found him all alone in front of our house. The **house** was empty. **It** was filled with water. I am so happy Danny Boy is back with us!

The reader can understand the text because the **pronouns** agree with their **nouns**.

Revise It Look back at the NOT OK passage. Work with a partner to revise it. Fix the pronouns so they agree with the nouns.

✎ **WRITE ON YOUR OWN** Write about your own experience in a storm or a natural disaster, or write about a natural disaster you have read about. Use the correct pronouns.

REMEMBER

- Use **he** to refer to a male.
- Use **she** to refer to a female.
- Use **it** to refer to a place or thing.
- Use **they** to refer to more than one person, place, or thing.

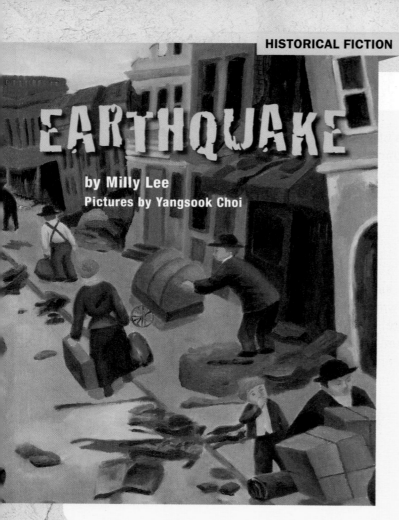

EARTHQUAKE

by Milly Lee
Pictures by Yangsook Choi

SELECTION 3 OVERVIEW

▶ **Build Background**

▶ **Language & Grammar**
Give Advice
Use Helping Verbs

▶ **Prepare to Read**
Learn Key Vocabulary
Learn a Reading Strategy
Make Connections

▶ **Read and Write**
Focus on Genre
Historical Fiction
Apply the Reading Strategy
Make Connections
Critical Thinking
Reading Fluency
Read with Intonation
Vocabulary Review
Write About the Guiding Question

▶ **Connect Across the Curriculum**
Literary Analysis
Analyze Setting and Character
Vocabulary Study
Use Word Parts
Research/Writing
Write a How-To Article
Research/Speaking
Research Earthquakes
Language and Grammar
Give Advice
Writing and Grammar
Write Advice

Build Background

Connect

Anticipation Guide What do you know about the dangers of earthquakes? Tell whether you agree or disagree with each statement.

Anticipation Guide

	Agree	Disagree
1. People should not live where earthquakes occur.	_____	_____
2. No building is really earthquake safe.	_____	_____
3. Earthquakes are scary but fun.	_____	_____

Discuss the Great Quake

How did the 1906 earthquake affect people in San Francisco? How do earthquakes affect people today?

Digital Library
InsideNG.com
⊘ View the images.

▲ Buildings collapsed after the earthquake in 1906.

Language & Grammar

Give Advice

CD

Listen to the rap. Listen again and chime in.

RAP

Earthquake

When an earthquake strikes,
When an earthquake strikes,
Things can tumble.
A wall could crumble.
Glass might crash
And fall on you.

So take my advice:
Stay calm, stay nice.
Get under your desk
And do your best
To protect yourself
When an earthquake strikes,
When an earthquake strikes.

Use Helping Verbs

- A **helping verb** is a verb that works together with another verb. The **main verb** shows the action or state of being. The helping verb supports the main verb's meaning.

    EXAMPLE   Earthquakes are scary. They **can shake** buildings.

- The verbs *can*, *could*, *may*, *might*, and *should* are helping verbs. Use *can* to tell what someone or something is able to do. Use *could*, *may*, or *might* to tell what is possible. Use *should* to tell what is good for someone to do.

    EXAMPLES   I **can** read information about earthquakes on the Internet.
    An earthquake **might** happen. It **could** create panic.
    You **should** stay calm.

Practice Together

Say each sentence. Add *can*, *could*, *may*, *might*, or *should*. More than one answer is possible.

1. An earthquake _____ strike our area soon.
2. Many people _____ be in danger.
3. They _____ get help from the government.
4. Other countries _____ help.
5. They _____ send food, supplies, and money.

Try It!

Read each sentence. Write *can*, *could*, *may*, *might*, or *should* on a card. Then hold up the card as you say the sentence with the helping verb. More than one answer is possible.

6. We _____ need an earthquake kit.
7. We _____ make one this afternoon.
8. I _____ find a flashlight for the kit.
9. Ben _____ have some batteries.
10. He _____ give them to us.
11. You _____ fill those containers with water.
12. We _____ have candles and matches in the house.

▲ **You might need these items during an earthquake.**

Share Safety Tips

GIVE ADVICE

How can people stay safe during an earthquake or another dangerous situation? What advice could you give them?

With a group, brainstorm dangerous situations that people might face. In a chart like this one, write what might happen in the situation. Then write what people should do to stay safe.

Idea Chart

Danger	What might happen?	What should you do?
earthquake	• Objects in the house might fall. • Windows might break.	• Hide under sturdy furniture. • Stay away from windows.
biking in traffic	• A car might hit you. • You might hit something.	• Wear a helmet. • Be careful when you ride.

Then work with a partner. Take turns giving advice for different situations on the chart. Remember:

HOW TO GIVE ADVICE

1. To give advice, tell what might happen.
2. Then give commands to tell people what to do.

> Heavy rains can flood your house. You should get sandbags. Put them at the bottom of your doors.

USE HELPING VERBS

When you brainstorm what might happen, use the **helping verbs** *can*, *could*, *may*, or *might*. When you give advice, use the helping verb *should*.

EXAMPLES   In an earthquake, windows **might** break.

The glass **could** hurt you.

You **should** stay away from windows during an earthquake.

Prepare to Read

Learn Key Vocabulary

Rate and Study the Words Rate how well you know each word. Then:

1. Pronounce the word. Say it aloud several times. Spell it.
2. Study the example.
3. Tell more about the word.
4. Practice it. Make the word your own.

Key Words

carefully (kair-foo-lē)
adverb ▶ page 182

To act **carefully** means to act with care. You should carry an egg **carefully** so it does not break.
Base Word: **care**

collapse (ku-**laps**) *verb*
▶ page 180

To **collapse** means to fall down. The old building **collapsed**.
Synonym: **crumble**

confused (kun-**fyūzd**)
adjective ▶ page 183

To be **confused** means to be unsure or not clear. They are **confused** by the instructions of this recipe.
Base Word: **confuse**

earthquake (**urth**-kwāk)
noun ▶ page 180

An **earthquake** is a sudden shaking of the Earth. Strong **earthquakes** cause damage to roads and buildings.
Word Parts: **earth, quake**

equipment (i-**kwip**-munt)
noun ▶ page 180

Tools or machines for a certain use are **equipment**. Hospitals have **equipment** for treating people who are sick or hurt.

frightened (**frī**-tund)
adjective ▶ page 183

To be **frightened** is to be afraid or scared. When I'm **frightened** at the movies, I cover my face with my hands.
Base Word: **fright**

prepare (pri-**pair**) *verb*
▶ page 182

To **prepare** means to get ready. Dad is **preparing** vegetables for dinner tonight.

shelter (**shel**-tur) *noun*
▶ page 188

A **shelter** is a place where people can safely stay. An umbrella provides **shelter** from the rain.

Practice the Words Work with a partner to complete an Expanded Meaning Map for each Key Word.

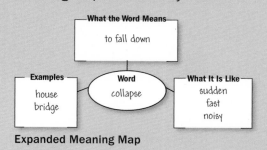

What the Word Means
to fall down

Examples
house
bridge

Word
collapse

What It Is Like
sudden
fast
noisy

Expanded Meaning Map

Reading Strategy: Make Connections

As you read, make connections between what you already know about a topic and what you read about it. Think about how the links add to your understanding.

How to MAKE CONNECTIONS

1. **Identify the Topic** As you read, figure out the topic—what the selection is mostly about.
2. **Look for Links** As you read, pay attention to what you already know about the topic.
3. **Build Understanding** Review the links you made. Use what you know to add to the text.

Strategy in Action

Here's how one student made connections.

Look Into the Text

❝ This is about an earthquake. I know that strong earthquakes can cause buildings to fall down.❞

This morning the earth shook and threw us from our beds. We were not hurt, just stunned.

Drawers spilled, dishes crashed, pots and pans clanged as they fell. Ancestral portraits flew off the walls.

PoPo packed up all we could carry—bedding, clothing, food, utensils; Kwan Yin and ancestors, too.

❝ People can take only necessities when they leave quickly. That's why PoPo packs these things.❞

Practice Together

Make connections of your own as you reread the passage above. Follow the steps in the How-To box.

Focus on Genre

Historical Fiction

Historical fiction is a type of narrative writing. The **characters**, or people in the story, are based on people who really lived. The **setting**—where and when the story takes place—and the events are based on facts of history. The story also includes details and **dialogue** that the writer creates.

> In the early dawn, confused and frightened, we gathered at Portsmouth Square. All of Chinatown must have been there.
>
> "You must go to Golden Gate Park!" shouted the policeman. — dialogue

Your Job as a Reader

Reading Strategy: Make Connections

As you read, make connections between what you already know about earthquakes and what the text says.

> The earth shook again. We stopped, and watched in fear as buildings crumbled around us.

I remember how scared I was in a small earthquake. If buildings are falling, everyone must be terrified.

EARTHQUAKE

by Milly Lee
Pictures by Yangsook Choi

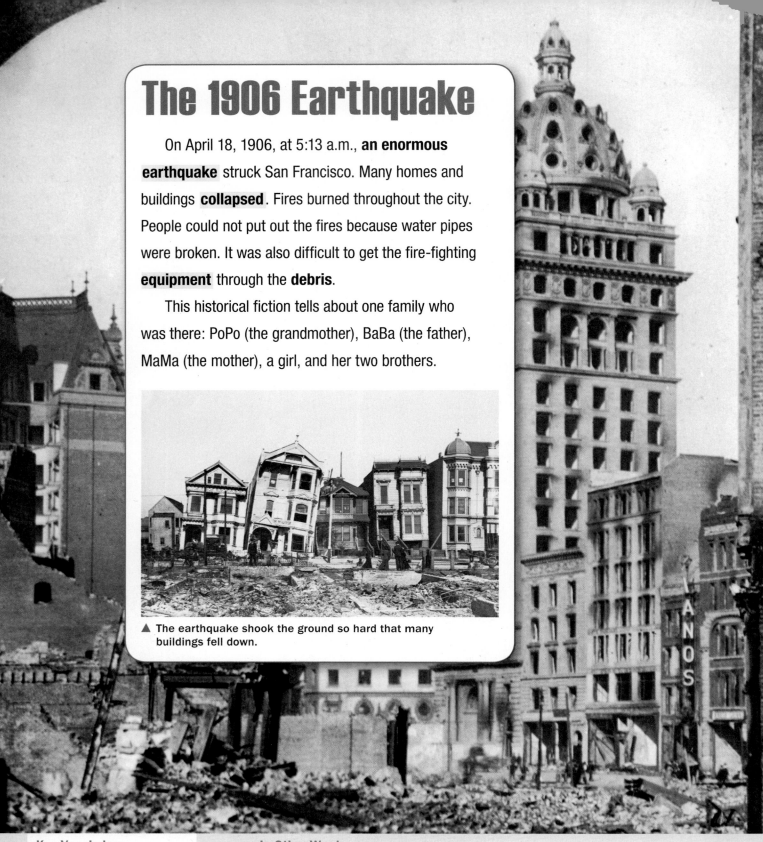

The 1906 Earthquake

On April 18, 1906, at 5:13 a.m., **an enormous earthquake** struck San Francisco. Many homes and buildings **collapsed**. Fires burned throughout the city. People could not put out the fires because water pipes were broken. It was also difficult to get the fire-fighting **equipment** through the **debris**.

This historical fiction tells about one family who was there: PoPo (the grandmother), BaBa (the father), MaMa (the mother), a girl, and her two brothers.

▲ The earthquake shook the ground so hard that many buildings fell down.

Key Vocabulary
earthquake *n.*, a sudden shaking of the Earth
collapse *v.*, to fall down
equipment *n.*, tools, machines

In Other Words
an enormous a very big
debris bricks, wood, and other parts of broken buildings

**The earthquake hits. Find out
what the family does.**

This morning the earth shook and threw us from our beds. We were not hurt, just **stunned**.

Drawers spilled, dishes crashed, pots and pans clanged as they fell. **Ancestral portraits** flew off the walls.

PoPo packed up all we could carry—bedding, clothing, food, **utensils**; Kwan Yin and ancestors, too.

In Other Words
stunned surprised
Ancestral portraits Pictures
 of family members
utensils tools for cooking
 and eating

Cultural Background
Kwan Yin is a popular Chinese
goddess of kindness and forgiveness.
Many Chinese families keep a statue
of Kwan Yin in their homes to
honor her.

MaMa told us to hurry, wear extra layers of clothes, and **prepare** to leave for safety.

BaBa hurried out to **seek** help and returned with a cart and two **kinsmen**.

Carefully and slowly we made our way down the stairs to load the cart with **our belongings.**

In the early dawn, **confused** and **frightened**, we gathered at Portsmouth Square. All of Chinatown must have been there.

"You must go to Golden Gate Park!" shouted the policeman.

"The city is on fire. Go quickly now!" Dark smoke hurt our eyes. **Gritty** dust filled the air, our mouths and noses, too.

Key Vocabulary
confused *adj.*, not clear, unsure
frightened *adj.*, scared

In Other Words
Gritty Rough, Sandy

The earth shook again. We stopped, and watched in fear as buildings **crumbled** around us.

Elder Brother, Younger Brother, and I cleared a path for the cart carrying MaMa and PoPo and our belongings.

In Other Words
crumbled fell into pieces

We were hot and thirsty until we **shed** the extra clothing and drank some cold tea.

In the early-morning rush to leave, we had not eaten anything.

PoPo gave us crackers and dried fruit.

Up the steep hills, across the city, we pushed and pulled the heavy cart.

In Other Words
shed took off

Before You Move On

1. **Paraphrase** Tell what the family did after the **earthquake**.
2. **Setting** What time of day is it now in the story? What clues give this information?
3. **Inference** How do you think the family feels carrying their belongings through the city?

All around us, frightened people struggled with **loads too dear** to leave behind.

Terrified dogs, cats, and horses joined the people hurrying to safety.

Until, at last, we were away from the spreading fires. Away from falling buildings.

In Other Words
loads too dear things that were too important
Terrified Scared

In Golden Gate Park there was food, water, and tents for **shelter**.

PoPo, BaBa, MaMa, Elder Brother, Younger Brother, and I rested and ate.

We were safe for now while the city still burned and the earth still shook. ❖

About the Author

Milly Lee grew up in San Francisco's Chinatown. Her parents, grandparents, uncles, aunts, cousins, and siblings all lived together in the same house. Lee speaks English and Cantonese, a language of China.

In her books, Lee tells about the part that Chinese Americans play in history. "I want my readers to know that 'we were there, too,'" she explains. "Earthquake" is the story of Lee's mother, who was 8 years old in 1906.

Key Vocabulary
shelter *n.*, a place where people can safely stay

Before You Move On

1. **Confirm Prediction** What happens to the family at the end? What happened that you did not expect?
2. **Make a Connection** Tell in your own words why the park is a safe place.

Connect Reading and Writing

Vocabulary
carefully
collapsed
confused
earthquake
equipment
frightened
prepare
shelter

CRITICAL THINKING

1. **SUM IT UP** Make a card for each vocabulary word. Use at least five of the words to describe the **earthquake** and the family's journey to Golden Gate Park.

> collapse
>
> confused
>
> prepare

2. **Evaluate** Review your Anticipation Guide on page 172. With a group, discuss how people deal with the dangers of **earthquakes**.

3. **Infer** When the family **prepares** to leave, PoPo packs pictures of ancestors. Later, BaBa asks family members to help. What do these clues tell you about the family?

4. **Compare** Imagine yourself in the pictures on pages 181–187. Would you be more **frightened** by the fires or by the falling buildings? Explain.

READING FLUENCY

Intonation Read the passage on page 576 to a partner. Assess your fluency.

1. I read
   a. great   **b.** OK   **c.** not very well

2. What I did best in my reading was _____.

READING STRATEGY

> **Make Connections**
> Tell a partner about one connection you made while reading. How did it help you understand what you read?

VOCABULARY REVIEW

Oral Review Read the paragraph aloud. Add the vocabulary words.

> In 1906, San Francisco had an awful _____. Buildings _____, fires burned, and water pipes broke. No one had been able to _____ for this unexpected disaster. People were scared, or _____. They did not know where to go, so they were _____. They walked quickly but _____ through the streets. The U.S. Army came to help. They brought supplies and special _____. They provided food, water, blankets, and tents for _____.

Written Review Imagine you are the mayor of San Francisco in 1906. Write a request to the army for more **equipment**. Use five vocabulary words.

WRITE ABOUT THE **GUIDING QUESTION**

Explore Natural Forces
How can people **prepare** for, deal with, and recover from **earthquakes**? Give examples from the text.

Analyze Setting and Character

> **Academic Vocabulary**
> ● **element** (e-lu-munt) *noun*
>   An **element** is a basic part of a whole.

Setting and **character** are important **elements** of fiction. Characters have **traits**, or special features, like kindness or courage. They also have **motives**, or reasons for their thoughts and actions. The setting and the characters' traits and motives affect the events in a story.

Practice Together

Read this story. Think about how the setting and the characters' traits and motives affect what happens.

> In 1850 the trip from Missouri to Oregon took months. The Jensons packed their tiny wagon with food and other necessities. They also brought a few things to remind them of home.
>
> After a few days on the trail, Mr. Jenson saw that the wagon was overloaded. He hesitated but then asked his wife for help. Mrs. Jenson took out a heavy box of fine dishes. She lifted the lid gently and touched a delicate dish painted with pink flowers. Then she wiped away her tears and placed the box on the muddy trail.

Make a Chart Make a Character Chart like the one below. Complete it for Mrs. Jenson. Then imagine how the events would be different if the Jensons were traveling from Missouri to Oregon today. Discuss how the events are linked to the setting.

Character Chart

Character	Traits	Motives	Actions
Mr. Jenson	practical	wants to get to Oregon	has to unload wagon, asks his wife for help
Mrs. Jenson			

Try It!

Work with a partner. Make a Character Chart for the characters in the story "Earthquake." How do the setting and the characters' traits and motives affect what happens?

Use Word Parts

Suffix	Meaning	Changes . . .
-ment	act or process	a verb (*pay*) to a noun (*payment*)
-ness	state of	an adjective (*kind*) to a noun (*kindness*)
-y	having the quality of	a noun (*dirt*) into an adjective (*dirty*)

Academic Vocabulary
- **discuss** (di-**skus**) *verb*
  When you **discuss** something, you talk about it.

A suffix changes the meaning of a base word and how the word is used in a sentence. For example, the word *grit* is a noun that means "a tiny piece of sand or stone." If you want to describe something that feels like sand, you could add the suffix *-y* and make the adjective *gritty*. Sometimes you need to change the spelling of the base word when you add a suffix.

base word   **suffix**

grit   +   -y   =   gritty

Define Words Work with a partner. Cover the suffix in each word below. Tell the meanings of the base word and the suffix, using the chart above. **Discuss** how the suffix changes the base word. Use the word in a sentence to tell about the selection "Earthquake."

1. equipment   **2.** kindness   **3.** forgiveness   **4.** foggy   **5.** thirsty

Write a How-To Article

SOCIAL SCIENCE

Academic Vocabulary
- **explanation** (ek-splu-**nā**-shun) *noun*
  An **explanation** is a statement that makes an idea clear.

❶ **Research Earthquake Safety** How can families prepare for an earthquake? Use magazines, books, or the Internet to find out.

    Internet InsideNG.com
    🔄 Find out about earthquake preparedness.

❷ **Write a Safety Article** Give an **explanation** of how to prepare for an earthquake. Write a list of steps that people can follow to stay safe at home if an earthquake happens. Put the steps in order.

❸ **Read the Article** Read your article to the class. Ask your listeners to name one thing they learned from your **explanation** .

▲ For safety, a water heater should be attached to the wall properly.

Connect Across the Curriculum, continued

Research Earthquakes

HEALTH & SCIENCE

> **Academic Vocabulary**
> • **define** (di-**fin**) *verb*
> When you **define** something, you tell what it means.

Nonfiction books, such as textbooks and reference books, often include tools to help readers.

- A **glossary** is a list of special terms used in the book and their meanings. It lists the terms in alphabetical order. It is usually near the end of the book.

- An **index** is a list of topics with page numbers. The topics are in alphabetical order. The numbers tell you the pages where you can find information about the topic. The index is usually at the end of the book.

Glossary

aftershock earthquakes that occur after the main earthquake

bedrock hard, solid rock under the soil

creep slow, continuous movement of plates on Earth's surface

epicenter point on Earth's surface above the cause of the earthquake

fault a break in Earth's crust where earthquakes happen

Index

aftershock 82, 83–85, 88

bedrock 14, 16–19, 22

creep 43, 47–50

epicenter 56, 58, 60–63

fault 24, 33, 35–37

focus 66–70

hypercenter 71, 73, 75, 77–80

Use the glossary and the index in a book to find out about earthquakes.

❶ Use Tools Find a nonfiction book about earthquakes. Then:
- Use the glossary to find and **define** terms about earthquakes.
- Choose one term. Use the index to look up more information.

❷ Share Your Research **Define** the term for a group. Then tell what else you learned about it. Discuss how using a glossary and an index helped you with your research.

▲ An earthquake can cause serious damage.

Give Advice

Role-Play Work in pairs. Choose roles from "Earthquake." Each partner gives advice about what to do after the earthquake. Use helping verbs like *can*, *could*, *may*, *might*, and *should*.

> People at Golden Gate Park can help you. You should go there quickly. Only take what you need.

Write Advice

Study the Models When you give people advice, give them ideas of what they should do. Include enough details to explain why they should do it, too.

NOT OK

> An earthquake **can** be dangerous. You **should** be prepared. You **should** secure your belongings.

> The writer uses some **helping verbs** to give advice, but there are not many details.

OK

> An earthquake **can** be dangerous. Vases **could** tumble off shelves and hit you. Bookshelves and other furniture **may** fall over on you.
>
> You **should** be prepared. You **should** secure your belongings. You **can** use special wax to attach vases to the shelves. You **should** fasten bookshelves and furniture to the walls.

> Now the reader has more information. The writer uses more **helping verbs** to add details.

Add Sentences Think of two sentences to add to the OK model above. Use *can*, *could*, *may*, *might*, or *should*.

✏️ **WRITE ON YOUR OWN** Imagine that a friend has moved to an area that has earthquakes. Write a letter with advice about what your friend should do and why.

REMEMBER

- Use **can** to tell what someone or something is able to do.
- Use **could**, **may**, or **might** to tell what is possible.
- Use **should** to tell what is good for someone to do.

◀ The people should stay away from the hole in the road.

Compare Across Texts

Compare How Information Is Presented

"Volcano!" "Fleeing Katrina," and "Earthquake" tell about violent **forces** of nature. Each selection tells about this topic in a different way.

How It Works

Collect and Organize Notes To compare across texts, organize notes in a chart. Consider how the kind of writing affects how information is presented.

Comparison Chart

Selection	Kind of Writing	How the Writer Gives Information
"Volcano!"	science article	facts, photos, diagram, map, narrative writing
"Fleeing Katrina"	journal	
"Earthquake"	historical fiction	

Practice Together

Study and Analyze Look at the notes in the second column of the Comparison Chart. Write an explanatory paragraph like this one to compare the different kinds of writing.

> The selections tell about different natural disasters. The science article "Volcano!" includes narrative writing that tells a story. "Fleeing Katrina" is a journal that tells a real-life story. "Earthquake" is a fictional story that is based on a real event in history.

Try It!

Copy and complete the chart above. Then write a paragraph to compare different ways in which writers give information. You may want to use this frame to help you express your comparison.

> Each writer tells about a force of nature in a different way. "Volcano!" uses _____ to tell about volcanoes. "Fleeing Katrina," tells about Hurricane Katrina through _____. In "Earthquake," the writer tells about a historic earthquake through _____.

Academic Vocabulary
● **force** (**fors**) *noun*
  A **force** is a great power in nature.

Natural Forces

GUIDING QUESTION How do people deal with the forces of nature?

Reflect on Your Reading

Think back on your reading of the unit selections. Discuss what you did to understand what you read.

Focus on Genre **Narrative Writing**

In this unit, you learned about narrative writing. Choose a narrative selection. Make a web. Write the name of the selection in the center. Around it, write clues that tell you why the selection is narrative. Use your web to explain the genre to a partner.

Reading Strategy **Make Connections**

In this unit, you learned to make connections to the reading. Explain to a partner how you will use this strategy in the future.

Explore the

Throughout this unit, you have been thinking about natural forces. Choose one of these ways to explore the Guiding Question:

- **Discuss** With a group, discuss the Guiding Question. Talk about ways in which people deal with natural disasters.
- **Dramatize** With a group, dramatize a talk show that includes a host, a volcano expert, a hurricane expert, and an earthquake expert.
- **Draw and Tell** If a force of nature were a person, what would it look like to you? Would an earthquake look like a giant that stomps on the ground, for example? Draw a character that represents a force of nature. Share it with classmates and tell about it.

Book Talk

Which Unit Library book did you choose? Explain to a partner what it taught you about natural forces.

UNIT LIBRARY

Content Library

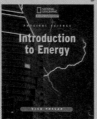

Leveled Library

Untitled, 1982, Jerry Uelsmann.

▲ **Critical Viewing** What makes this image creepy?

CREEPY CLASSICS

GUIDING QUESTION

How can a powerful character inspire a range of reactions?

Read More!

Content Library

Peering into Darkness
by Rebecca L. Johnson

Leveled Library

Frankenstein
by Mary Shelley, adapted by Larry Weinberg

The Metamorphosis
by Franz Kafka, adapted by Peter Kuper

Othello
by Julius Lester

Internet
InsideNG.com

- Go to the Digital Library to see classic monsters.
- Read about a classic monster.
- Learn about monster films.

Focus on Genre

Elements of Fiction

► **Plot**
► **Characters**
► **Setting**

Writers create fictional stories to entertain their readers. They use the **elements** of fiction—**plot**, **characters**, and **setting**—to build their stories.

Plot: How It Works

The plot is what happens in a story.

- Plots are built around a **conflict**, or problem that the main character faces.
- The **events** are what the characters do.
- The **turning point** is the most important event of the story.
- The **resolution** is the event that solves the problem.

Read "The Night Walker" to see examples of the **elements** of fiction and the stages of the plot.

The Night Walker

The swamp smelled rotten in the night air. Isabella wrinkled her nose. She poked a stick at the piles of green slime in the water. Suddenly, a patch of slime rose up. It was the Blob!

This terrible creature swallowed everything in its path. Isabella screamed and ran. The slimy Blob slipped out of the swamp and slithered onto the path. As Isabella reached for the handle of her car door, the Blob grasped her foot.

Isabella managed to get the door open. She grabbed the spray bottle of cleaner she always kept in her car. She blasted the creature with cleaner. At each squirt, the Blob grew smaller and weaker. In a few minutes, it was just a lifeless puddle. Isabella stood up and smiled. Then she wiped the puddle away with an old towel.

▲ The Blob lives in the swamp.

Setting
Character

Conflict

Turning point

Resolution

Academic Vocabulary
- **element** (e-lu-munt) *noun*
  An **element** is a basic part of a whole.

Plot: Practice Together

Read "The Night Walker" again, and tell where the events go on this Plot Diagram.

Plot Diagram

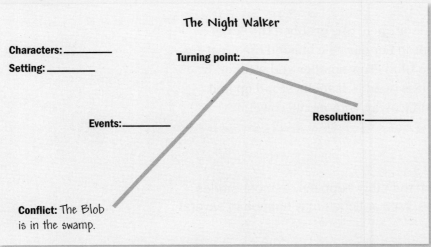

The Night Walker

Characters: _____

Setting: _____

Turning point: _____

Events: _____

Resolution: _____

Conflict: The Blob is in the swamp.

Character: How It Works

Characters are the people or animals that take part in the plot. A writer tells about each character through

- a description of what the character looks like
- the character's actions and words
- how other characters think about or act toward the character.

See these techniques in action as the writer characterizes the Blob.

> This terrible creature swallowed everything in its path. Isabella screamed and ran. The slimy Blob slipped out of the swamp and slithered onto the path. As Isabella reached for the handle of her car door, the Blob grasped her foot.

Tells about the character directly

Tells how others react to the character

Shows the character's actions

You can use a Character Description Chart to keep track of what the characters are like.

Character Description Chart

Character	What the Character Is Like	How I Know
the Blob	terrible	swallows everything in its path tries to grab Isabella

Character: Practice Together

Now read the rest of the story aloud with your class. As you read, listen for the ways the writer characterizes Isabella. After you read, make a Character Description Chart for Isabella.

> Isabella managed to get the door open. She grabbed the spray bottle of cleaner she always kept in her car. She blasted the creature with cleaner. At each squirt, the Blob grew smaller and weaker. In a few minutes, it was just a lifeless puddle. Isabella stood up and smiled. Then she wiped the puddle away with an old towel.

Setting: How It Works

Setting is the time and place in which the story happens. In most stories, the setting is one place and one time. Longer fiction may happen in several places and times.

See how the writer uses the **elements** of setting in "The Night Walker."

> The swamp smelled rotten in the night air. Isabella wrinkled her nose. She poked a stick at the piles of green slime in the water. Suddenly, a patch of slime rose up. It was the Blob!

The time and place

A normal thing to find in that place

Setting: Practice Together

Now read a different version of this story aloud with your class. As you read, listen for details about the setting. After you read, complete the activities below the passage.

> The city smelled clean after the evening rain. Isabella made her way through the crowd of people. As she crossed the street, she accidentally stepped in a puddle. Suddenly, something rose from the water. It was the Blob!

Work with a partner to answer these questions.

1. Describe the time and place in the second version.
2. Compare the different settings in these two versions of the story.
3. Predict how the plot of the second version would be different from the first plot.

Try It!

Read the following passage aloud, and answer the questions about the **elements** of fiction.

1. What is the setting?
2. Who are the characters and what are they like?
3. What is the conflict?
4. What is the turning point?
5. What is the resolution?

King Kong Lives

Alfonzo stretched sleepily as the morning sun warmed him. He loved camping in the woods. He had never been to this spot before, so he took time to look around him.

When he first saw the creature, he thought it was

▲ King Kong

a mountain in the distance. But then he saw it move. He saw its huge, hairy arms rip up trees like toothpicks. He saw it coming straight for him. Alfonzo knew what this creature was. It was King Kong, the beast that he had seen on the news. Everyone was trying to catch this gigantic, terrible creature.

King Kong crashed through the trees toward Alfonzo. Soon Alfonzo could hear it breathing. He stood frozen in fear.

Suddenly, the tree tops started shaking behind him. Five helicopters came speeding through the sky straight toward King Kong.

King Kong looked up and swung his massive arms at the helicopters. Alfonzo heard several loud pops and then a crash.

The people in the helicopters had hit King Kong with sleeping darts. Now the creature lay sleeping, inches from Alfonzo's feet. The helicopters landed and crews poured out. Within minutes, the crews came down, tied up the creature, and lifted it away.

Alfonzo shook his head in disbelief. Then he packed up his things and started the hike home.

Focus on Vocabulary

Use Word Parts

Some English words are made up of parts. These parts include **base words** and **prefixes**. You can use the parts as clues to a word's meaning.

A prefix is a word part that is added to the beginning of a word. It changes the meaning of the base word. The chart shows some common prefixes.

Common Prefixes

Prefix	Meaning	Example
dis-	opposite	disagree
im-	not	impolite
pre-	before	preview
re-	again; back	review

How the Strategy Works

When you read, you may come to a word you don't know. Sometimes you can use word parts to figure out the meaning of an unknown word.

1. Look at the surrounding words for clues to the new word's meaning.
2. Break the word into parts. **Identify** word parts you know.

   EXAMPLE   rearrange → re- + arrange

3. Think about the meaning of each word part. If you don't know the base word, look it up in a dictionary.

   | again | put in order | put in order again |

   re- + arrange = rearrange

4. Put the meanings of the word parts together to understand the whole word. Check that the meaning makes sense in the passage.

Use the strategy to figure out the meaning of each underlined word.

For hundreds of years, people have told stories about the Loch Ness Monster, which some think lives in a lake in Scotland. In modern times, people <u>renamed</u> the monster "Nessie."

Every time people <u>retell</u> the story about Nessie, they describe the monster differently. Some say that Nessie is a giant sea snake. Others say that the monster looks like a dinosaur with fins. One story seems to <u>replace</u> another!

☑ **REMEMBER** Sometimes you can use the meanings of a prefix and a base word to figure out what the whole word means.

Academic Vocabulary
- **identify** (ī-**den**-tu-fī) *verb*
  To **identify** means to find out or to show what something is.

Practice Together

Read this passage aloud. Look at each underlined word. Find the prefix and the base word. Put their meanings together to figure out the meaning of the underlined word.

True Monsters

When explorers first came to the deserts of the Southwest, they found a true monster: the Gila monster. This lizard seemed <u>unreal</u> to them. The creature was truly <u>unbelievable</u>.

Gila monsters come out at night to feed on small animals, birds, and eggs. A Gila monster moves slowly, but if its prey takes one <u>misstep</u>, it will get caught. A Gila monster can quickly <u>overpower</u> its prey with a poisonous bite. However, human deaths from Gila monsters are extremely <u>uncommon</u>.

Try It!

Read this passage on your own. What is the meaning of each underlined word? How do you know?

A Real Monster

You may think that all monsters are fictional. That is <u>untrue</u>. At least one monster, the giant squid, is based in reality.

After trying and <u>retrying</u> to find a live giant squid, researchers in Japan finally succeeded. They caught a 24-foot squid.

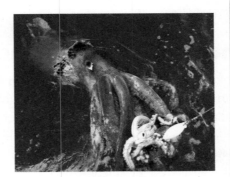

▲ Scientists caught this young squid in the Pacific Ocean.

Although it was attached to a fish hook, the giant squid was not <u>inactive</u>. In fact, it was quite strong. It fought hard to <u>untangle</u> itself from the hook.

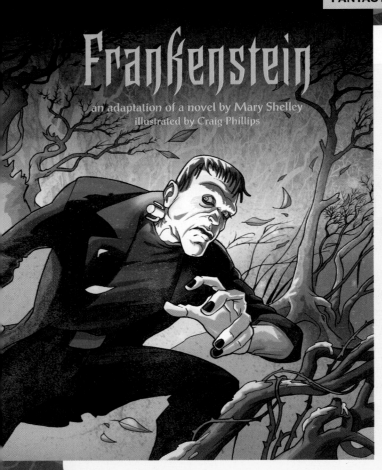

Frankenstein

an adaptation of a novel by Mary Shelley
illustrated by Craig Phillips

SELECTION 1 OVERVIEW

▶ **Build Background**

▶ **Language & Grammar**
Describe People and Places
Use Adjectives

▶ **Prepare to Read**
Learn Key Vocabulary
Learn a Reading Strategy
Visualize

▶ **Read and Write**
Focus on Genre
Fantasy
Apply the Reading Strategy
Visualize
Critical Thinking
Reading Fluency
Read with Expression
Vocabulary Review
Write About the Guiding Question

▶ **Connect Across the Curriculum**
Literary Analysis
Analyze Character Development
Analyze Theme
Vocabulary Study
Use Word Parts
Research/Writing
Research a Time Period
Language and Grammar
Describe People and Places
Writing and Grammar
Write About a Creepy Situation

Build Background

See Familiar Characters

Horror characters like Frankenstein's monster and Godzilla are featured in many stories. What makes them so popular?

Digital Library

InsideNG.com
↗ View the video.

◀ In this model, Godzilla terrorizes a city.

Connect

Reaction Chart Make a chart to show how different story characters make you feel. List the characters from stories, books, and movies. Draw a face to record your reaction. Share your chart and explain it.

Reaction Chart

Character	My Feelings
Godzilla	☹
Frankenstein's monster	😮

Language & Grammar

Describe People and Places

CD

Look at the picture and listen to the description.
Then describe something in the picture.

PICTURE PROMPT

Dear Edwin,

    A dark, creepy mansion sits on the hill at the end of the street. A strange old man lives there. He always makes me feel afraid. He wears a long, gray coat and black gloves. He only comes out at night to walk his big dog. His dog has sharp teeth and cruel, yellow eyes.

        Be careful,

        Alana

Use Adjectives

You can describe people, places, or things with **adjectives**. Use **adjectives** to describe:

- how something looks

    EXAMPLE   The **large** monster growls.

- how something sounds

    EXAMPLE   I hear his **loud** footsteps.

- how something feels, tastes, or smells

    EXAMPLE   I see his **rough** skin and smell his **rotten** breath.

Often the **adjective** comes before the **noun** you are describing.

    EXAMPLE   The **scary werewolf** has **silver fur**.

If two **adjectives** both describe the noun, separate them with a comma (**,**).

    EXAMPLE   The **small**, **thin boy** sees a **large**, **gray** dog.

Practice Together

Say each sentence with an appropriate adjective from the box.

green	huge	tiny	hot	long	sharp

1. A _____ monster climbs a building in Tokyo.
2. Godzilla looks down at the _____ people.
3. He has _____, fiery breath.
4. He has _____, scaly skin.
5. Look at Godzilla's _____ teeth!
6. Look at his _____, powerful tail.

Try It!

Read each sentence. Write an appropriate adjective from the box on a card. Hold up the card as you say the sentence.

dark	slimy	thin	quiet	sour	yellow

7. The creature lives in a _____ cave.
8. It has small, _____ eyes.
9. It has long, _____ fingers.
10. At night it walks around the _____ village.
11. It likes to eat _____ weeds.
12. It drinks water from a _____ pool.

▲ Godzilla looks scary.

Create a Character

DESCRIBE PEOPLE AND PLACES

What kind of creepy character can you imagine?

Visualize a creepy character and where it lives. Picture details in your mind. Then draw a picture of it. Give your character a name.

Study your picture. How would you describe the character and place? Jot down your ideas. Share your drawing and description with a partner.

HOW TO DESCRIBE PEOPLE AND PLACES

1. Tell what a person or place is like.
2. Give details.
3. Use descriptive words.

> What is Old Molly like?

> Old Molly is a crazy woman with long, bony fingers.

USE ADJECTIVES

When you describe people and places, you use **adjectives**. Adjectives help your listeners picture what you are saying.

Describe a person: Old Molly has **long**, **black** hair.

Describe a place: She lives in a **wooden** shack.

▲ This woman has bony fingers and large, round eyes.

Prepare to Read

Learn Key Vocabulary

Rate and Study the Words Rate how well you know each word. Then:

1. Pronounce the word. Say it aloud several times. Spell it.
2. Study the example.
3. Tell more about the word.
4. Practice it. Make the word your own.

Key Words

create (krē-āt) *verb*
▶ page 214

To **create** means to make something new. The artist **creates** a work of art in his studio.
Synonyms: **make, produce**

creature (krē-chur) *noun*
▶ page 212

A **creature** is a real or imaginary living thing. A dragon is an imaginary **creature**.
Base Word: **create**

destroy (di-stroi) *verb*
▶ page 216

To **destroy** something means to take it apart or to ruin it. Workers **destroy** this building.
Antonym: **create**

evil (ē-vul) *adjective*
▶ page 214

Something that is **evil** is very bad or harmful. Some people believe rattlesnakes are **evil** because their bite is dangerous.
Antonym: **good**

experiment (ik-**spair**-u-munt) *noun* ▶ page 214

An **experiment** is an activity that someone does to test an idea. The students are doing an **experiment** in their science class.

hideous (hi-dē-us) *adjective*
▶ page 216

Something that is **hideous** is very ugly. A mask can make someone look **hideous**.
Antonym: **beautiful**

lonely (lōn-lē) *adjective*
▶ page 212

To be **lonely** means to be alone, without friends. Do you feel **lonely** when your friends are away?
Base Word: **lone**

scientist (sī-un-tist) *noun*
▶ page 214

A person who studies science is a **scientist**. The **scientist** uses a microscope to study small objects up close.
Base Word: **science**

Practice the Words With a partner, take turns telling a story using the Key Words.

> **EXAMPLE:** **PARTNER 1:** Nina wanted to **create** a machine that could walk and talk.
>
> **PARTNER 2:** By mistake, she made a giant **creature**.

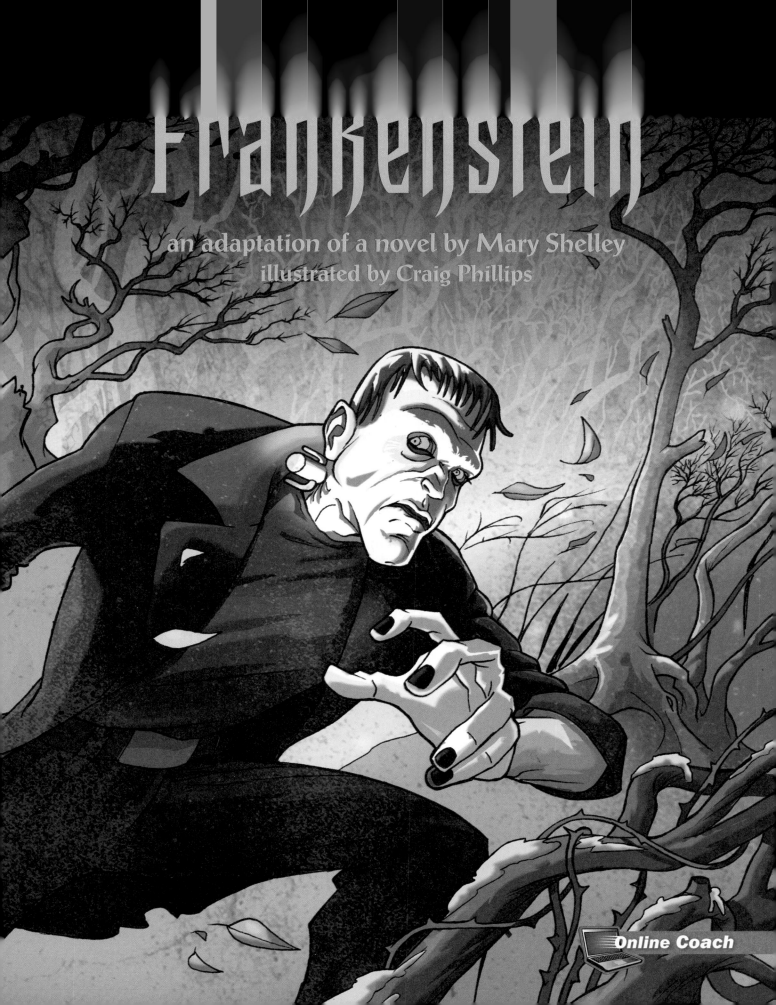

Set a Purpose
A man writes a letter to his sister.
Find out what he says.

August 19, 17_

My dear sister,

This long **voyage** has been so terribly **lonely**. The chilling frost and snow here in the Arctic completely surround our ship.

Three weeks ago, a remarkable thing happened. We saw a huge, ugly **creature** driving a sled pulled by dogs and racing north. The next morning, we saw a different dogsled drifting toward us on a sheet of ice. The poor dogs were dead, and the **weary** driver was barely alive. He wouldn't **accept** our help until we told him we were **heading** north.

The stranger will tell me his story tomorrow. I will **record it** and send it to you.

Key Vocabulary
lonely *adj.*, alone, without friends
creature *n.*, a living thing

In Other Words
voyage trip
weary tired
accept take; agree to
heading going
record it write it down

Geography Background

The Arctic is the area around the North Pole. It includes northern Canada and Greenland. Traditionally, people used dogsleds to travel across the ice and snow there.

Arctic Circle

Before You Move On

1. **Author's Style** Why do you think the author begins this story with a letter?

2. **Recall and Interpret** What does the letter say? Why did the man write this?

3. **Setting** Where and when does the first part of the story take place?

Predict
Do the creature and the man
know each other?

The Stranger's Story

My name is Victor Frankenstein. I **created** an **evil** monster. The terrible things that the creature has done are all because of me. No one else must ever know how to do what I have done— I will **take that secret with me to my grave**.

After many years of study, I had discovered how to bring something to life. I was eager to use what I had learned, so I devoted two years to making a new creature out of bones and body parts from graveyards and **slaughterhouses**.

At last, my **experiment** was ready. An enormous, lifeless creature lay on the table in my lab. I thought my creation would show the world what a great **scientist** I was. I did not know how wrong I was!

That cold November night, I brought my creature to life. I remember the moment his black lips moved. His skin, stretched and sewn together, **quivered**. He took a **rasping** breath and opened his watery, yellow eyes. Then that **repulsive** creature sat up and looked at me.

Key Vocabulary

create *v.*, to make something new
evil *adj.*, very bad
experiment *n.*, an activity that someone does to test an idea
scientist *n.*, a person who studies science

In Other Words

take that secret with me to my grave never tell that secret
slaughterhouses places where animals are killed for meat
quivered shook, moved
rasping scratchy, rough
repulsive ugly

Before You Move On

1. **Confirm Prediction** Was your prediction correct? How do you know? What happened that you did not expect?
2. **Visualize** Describe the **creature**.

Instead of feeling proud, I **was disgusted**. I could not even stand to look at him. So I ran away, asking myself, *What have I done?*

I hid in my room and nervously **paced** the floor, trying to determine what to do. But, because I had been hard at work for so long, I had not **slumbered** for many days, and I soon fell onto my bed and slept.

An odd, gurgling noise woke me up. The terrible creature was standing over me, grinning and making baby noises. He came closer and reached out one of his enormous hands to touch me. I leapt up and ran until I **crumpled** onto the street. A good friend found me and took me to his home. I lay there, sick for several months.

Much later, I learned what had happened to my creature while I was unwell.

What have I done?

He had wandered the streets. He was a newborn—a **hideous**, giant newborn. He knew nothing, he could not talk, and he did not even understand his own feelings.

People who saw him were terrified. Some people ran away screaming. Others threw stones and bricks at him. One man shot him in the arm.

The frightened, lonely creature hid in **a vacant** shed next to a cottage. He taught himself to speak and read by listening to the family in the cottage. Then he learned that I was his creator.

He found me and begged me for a **companion**. I felt sorry for him, so I agreed to create a wife for him. But when it came time to bring the female creature to life, I couldn't do it. I **destroyed** her instead. He was very angry and promised to make my life as unhappy as his life was. I was now his enemy.

Key Vocabulary
hideous *adj.*, very ugly
destroy *v.*, to take apart, to ruin

In Other Words
was disgusted felt sick; was shocked
paced walked back and forth across
slumbered slept
crumpled fell down
a vacant an empty
companion friend

The creature **terrorized** me for many years. First he found and killed my dear brother. Then he killed my best friend. Finally he killed my sweet bride on our wedding night. I **vowed** to stop this horrible beast.

I searched the world for him, and he has led me to this frozen land. But I have become weak from chasing him, and I know I am dying.

Now I realize I was wrong to create the monster and then **abandon him**. Now I know his **misery** is my fault, not his.

In Other Words
terrorized scared
vowed promised
abandon him go away from him
misery unhappiness

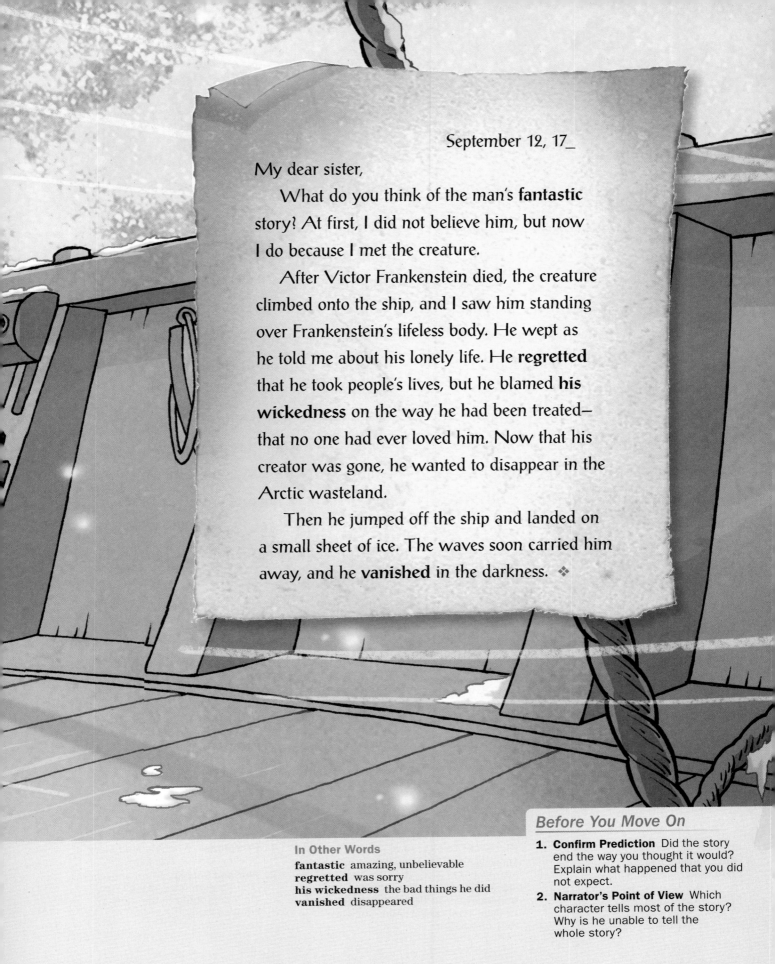

September 12, 17_

My dear sister,

What do you think of the man's **fantastic** story? At first, I did not believe him, but now I do because I met the creature.

After Victor Frankenstein died, the creature climbed onto the ship, and I saw him standing over Frankenstein's lifeless body. He wept as he told me about his lonely life. He **regretted** that he took people's lives, but he blamed **his wickedness** on the way he had been treated— that no one had ever loved him. Now that his creator was gone, he wanted to disappear in the Arctic wasteland.

Then he jumped off the ship and landed on a small sheet of ice. The waves soon carried him away, and he **vanished** in the darkness. ❖

In Other Words
fantastic amazing, unbelievable
regretted was sorry
his wickedness the bad things he did
vanished disappeared

Before You Move On

1. **Confirm Prediction** Did the story end the way you thought it would? Explain what happened that you did not expect.
2. **Narrator's Point of View** Which character tells most of the story? Why is he unable to tell the whole story?

How Frankenstein Began

by Mary Shelley

Mary Wollstonecraft Shelley 1797–1851

People often ask: *How did I think up such a hideous story when I was still a young woman?* Here is how it came about.

In the summer of 1816 my husband and I went to Switzerland. There we became friends with our neighbor, the famous poet Lord Byron.

It was a very wet summer. The rain often kept us in the house for days, so we read ghost stories to pass the time.

One day, Lord Byron suggested, "We will each write our own ghost story." I tried hard to think of a story that would make the reader afraid, but I had no ideas.

One day, I listened to a **conversation** between Lord Byron and my husband. They wondered if a dead person could live again. They wanted to know if body parts could be made, put together, and brought to life.

It was very late before we went to bed. I put my head on my pillow, but I did not sleep. Instead, my mind was filled with **vivid images** of pieced-together monsters.

I opened my eyes in terror!! I could not get the dream out of my head. I knew I must try to think of something else. So I thought of my unwritten ghost story. If I could only think of a story that would frighten my reader as much as I had been frightened by my dream!

That's when the idea hit me: I only have to describe the monster in my dream. What terrified me will terrify others.

The next day I announced that I had thought of a story. I began that day and wrote out the details of my dream.

In Other Words
conversation talk
vivid images colorful pictures

Historical Background
Mary Wollstonecraft Shelley wrote *Frankenstein* when she was nineteen. She was married to Percy Shelley, a well-known poet. Her parents, Mary Wollstonecraft and William Godwin, were also writers.

Before You Move On

1. **Paraphrase** What inspired Mary Shelley to write *Frankenstein*?
2. **Plot and Setting** When and where did this event take place? How did it contribute to the story of *Frankenstein*?

Connect Reading and Writing

Vocabulary
created
creature
destroys
evil
experiment
hideous
lonely
scientist

CRITICAL THINKING

1. **SUM IT UP** Make a card for each vocabulary word. Use at least five of the words to explain Dr. Frankenstein's **experiment** and what happened.

create

hideous

destroy

2. **Compare** Do you think the **hideous** monster in Mary Shelley's dream and story is as frightening today as it was in her time? Why or why not?

3. **Predict** What do you think the **lonely** creature does for the rest of his life? Explain.

4. **Make Judgments** Do you think Dr. Frankenstein is responsible for the **evil** things the **creature** does? Explain.

READING FLUENCY

Expression Read the passage on page 577 to a partner. Assess your fluency.

1. I read
   a. great   **b.** OK   **c.** not very well

2. What I did best in my reading was _____.

READING STRATEGY

Visualize
What pictures did you see in your mind as you read? What feelings did the pictures create in you? Tell a partner.

VOCABULARY REVIEW

Oral Review Read the paragraph aloud. Add the vocabulary words.

> I am a _____ who used to study animals. Last year, I set up an _____ to test ideas about growth. It was wrong! I used a rabbit named Ruff, who used to be a cute, furry little _____ . I _____ a _____ , ugly monster from him. Ruff Rabbit grew into a 200-pound furball. He is not an _____ monster, but he is dangerous. He hops on cars and _____ them. My friends no longer visit me, so I get _____ . I'm busy, though, raising acres of carrots, clover, and alfalfa.

Written Review Pretend you knew Dr. Frankenstein before his **experiment** . Write him a letter telling him why he should not **create** the **creature** . Use five vocabulary words.

WRITE ABOUT THE GUIDING QUESTION

Analyze a Classic Character
Reread the selection. If you saw the **creature** , what feelings would you have? Support your explanation with examples from the text.

Connect Across the Curriculum

Analyze Character Development

> **Academic Vocabulary**
> • **element** (e-lu-munt) *noun*
>   An **element** is a basic part of a whole.

What Is Character Development? Usually, main **characters** do not stay the same throughout a book or a movie. As a story progresses, characters change how they think, feel, and act.

Many **elements** in a story can cause a character to change and develop:
- setting, or where and when the story takes place
- events, or what happens to a character
- motivations, or what a character needs and wants

Practice Together

Analyze Character Read this passage from "Frankenstein." Think about how the creature's feelings toward Dr. Frankenstein have changed.

▲ The creature is angry with Dr. Frankenstein.

> He found me and begged me for a companion. I felt sorry for him, so I agreed to create a wife for him. But when it came time to bring the female creature to life, I couldn't do it. I destroyed her instead. He was very angry and promised to make my life as unhappy as his life was. I was now his enemy.

Think about what the creature wants and what happens in the story. Explain how the story **elements** cause the creature to change.

Try It!

Now think about Dr. Frankenstein. Find examples in "Frankenstein" that show how the setting, events, character traits, and motivations of the character cause him to change.

Present Your Analysis Share your examples with your classmates. First, pose a key question like this: Why does Dr. Frankenstein want to create the creature? Then explain how and why Dr. Frankenstein changes.

Use Word Parts

Prefix	Meaning	Example	Word Meaning
in-	not	inactive	not active
de-	do the opposite	defrost	to take the frost off something
bi-	two	bicolored	two-colored

Academic Vocabulary
- **locate** (lō-kāt) *verb*
  To **locate** something is to find it.

Many English words are made of word parts, including prefixes and base words. If you know the meaning of the word parts, you can sometimes figure out what the whole word means.

Combine Word Parts Figure out the meaning of each word. Look at the chart above. **Locate** the meaning of the prefix. If you don't know the base word, look it up in a dictionary. Put the meanings of the word parts together. Compare your definitions with a partner's. Use a dictionary to confirm.

1. incorrect   **3.** bicycle   **5.** insane

2. decode   **4.** biweekly   **6.** debug

Research a Time Period

HISTORY

- **relate** (ri-lāt) *verb*
  When you **relate** two things, you think about how they are connected.

Where and when an author lives can influence what the author writes.

❶ **Conduct Research** Find out how Mary Shelley's story **relates** to the time period when she wrote it. Choose appropriate resources that tell or show what was happening in England. Focus on the period between 1714 and 1830.

> **Internet** InsideNG.com
> ◔ Explore England between 1714 and 1830.

❷ **Narrow Your Topic** Choose one event or idea to focus on. Look for facts and important details that **relate** to "Frankenstein."

❸ **Write a Short Report** Tell about the event or idea. Clearly explain how it may have influenced Shelley. Include facts that support your ideas.

❹ **Read Your Report** Share your report in a group. Discuss how "Frankenstein" might be different if Shelley were living today.

Analyze Theme

Academic Vocabulary
- **theme** (thēm) *noun*
  A **theme** is the main message of a story.

The **theme** is the main message of a story. Usually, a **theme** says something important about life or the world. An example of a **theme** is "Nature is more powerful than people."

Authors usually don't tell you the **theme**. You have to figure it out from clues in the story.

When you read a story, pay attention to what the characters do, think, feel, and say. Look at the pictures, too. Use these clues to identify the **theme**.

Practice Together

Look for Clues Reread "Frankenstein." Make a Character Chart to track clues about what Dr. Frankenstein does, thinks, feels, and says. Then make a similar chart for the creature.

Character Chart

Actions	Thoughts/Feelings	Words
Dr. Frankenstein creates an evil monster.	He believes the creature will show the world what a great scientist he is.	I did not know how wrong I was!

Put the Clues Together Discuss the clues on your charts. What ideas about life or the world do you get from these clues? State what you think the author is trying to tell you.

Most stories have more than one **theme**, so you and your classmates may not agree on the author's message. Also, readers interpret **themes** in different ways. Each reader has a personal idea about the **theme**.

Try It!

State a Theme Reread a story you read earlier in this book, such as "The Secret Water" or "Earthquake." As you read, record clues about the characters. Then write a sentence that states the **theme**.

Share Your Ideas With a partner, discuss your interpretation of the **theme**. Do you and your partner have the same idea about the **theme**? Did you interpret it in a similar way?

Describe People and Places

Class Story Tell a story about someone lost in a scary place. Have one person start. Take turns adding a sentence. Use adjectives. Continue around the room until the story ends.

> It is a stormy night.

> A tall girl runs through a dark village.

Write About a Creepy Situation

Study the Models When you write a story or a description, include interesting, descriptive **adjectives** . Adjectives help your readers picture what you are writing about.

JUST OK

> My brother and I follow a path through the woods. It is a **cold** night. Suddenly, I hear a sound behind me. My brother whispers, "What was that noise?" We turn around and see a pair of eyes in the bushes. It is a wolf!

> This story is a little dull. The writer uses only one descriptive **adjective** .

BETTER

> My brother and I follow a **narrow** , **winding** path through the **dark** woods. It is a **cold** night. Suddenly, I hear a **growling** sound behind me. My brother whispers, "What was that noise?" We turn around and see a pair of **silver** eyes in the bushes. It is a **large** , **gray** wolf! We are **terrified** !

> The writer uses **adjectives** to describe how things look, sound, and feel. The reader thinks: **"I can really picture the scene."**

Revise It Work with a partner to revise the following passage. Add adjectives. Include one predicate adjective.

> A woman lives in this mansion. Every evening she walks in her garden. She wears a cape and carries a candle. A bird sits on her shoulder. At midnight the woman goes inside her house. She puts the candle in that window up there.

▲ A candle sits in the dark, creepy house.

✎ **WRITE ON YOUR OWN** Imagine a creepy situation and describe it. Use descriptive adjectives in your writing.

REMEMBER
- Adjectives usually come before nouns.
- **Predicate adjectives** come after forms of *be*.
  The wolf is **scary**.
- **Demonstrative adjectives** signal where things are.
  These creatures live here.

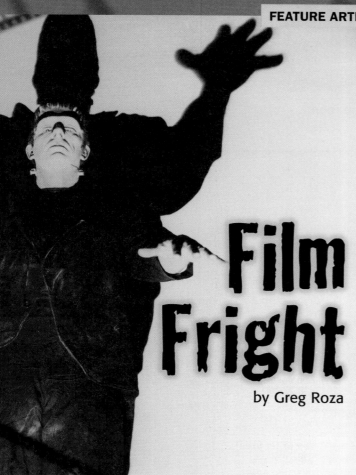

Film Fright

by Greg Roza

Build Background

Meet Movie Monsters

Mary Shelley created Frankenstein's monster nearly 200 years ago, and it was terrifying. How does it compare with modern versions?

Digital Library

InsideNG.com
● View the video.

◀ This 1940 horror movie features a monster that people now call "Frankenstein."

Connect

Describe a Monster Think of a movie you've seen that includes a monster. Write your thoughts and ideas about what makes the monster scary. Share with a group.

The monster's name:

What makes it scary:

How it was created (for example, with makeup or special effects):

Language & Grammar

Make Comparisons

CD

Listen to the song. Listen again and chime in.

SONG

The Wolf Man is not very handsome,
In fact, he's not handsome at all.
In fact, he looks really quite scary,
In Hollywood's *Monster Ball*.

Frankenstein isn't too friendly,
In fact, he's not friendly at all.
In fact, he is scarier than Wolf Man
In Hollywood's *Monster Ball*.

But Frankenstein's Bride is quite pretty.
In fact, she's the prettiest of all.
In fact, there is no one who's prettier
In Hollywood's *Monster Ball*.

Use Adjectives to Make Comparisons

- Add **-er** to many **adjectives** to compare two things.

    EXAMPLE   Frankenstein is **taller** than Wolf Man.

- Add **-est** to many **adjectives** to compare three or more things.

    EXAMPLE   Godzilla is the **tallest** monster of all.

To describe one thing	tall
To compare two things	taller
To compare three or more things	tallest

- Sometimes you need to make a spelling change before you add **-er** or **-est**. If the adjective ends in a consonant plus **y**, you usually change the **y** to **i** before you add **-er** or **-est**.

    gloomy + -er = gloomier   **crazy + -est = craziest**

Practice Together

Say each sentence. Choose the correct adjective.

1. This monster movie is (longer/longest) than that one.
2. It is the (creepy/creepiest) movie I have ever seen.
3. It is about the (uglier/ugliest) monster in the world.
4. The creature is (hairier/hairiest) than Wolf Man.
5. Its teeth are (sharper/sharpest) than a knife.
6. Its skin is (scaly/scalier) than a crocodile's skin.

Try It!

Read each sentence. Write the correct adjective on a card. Then hold up the card as you say the sentence.

7. The Monster Museum is the (odder/oddest) place I have ever visited.
8. One creature was (slimy/slimier) than an eel.
9. It had the (skinnier/skinniest) legs I have ever seen.
10. The (scarier/scariest) monster in the museum had long claws.
11. The (silly/silliest) monster of all looked like a blob of jelly.
12. It felt (softer/softest) than a pillow.

▲ This monster was scarier than others in the museum.

Make a Movie Poster

MAKE COMPARISONS

Look at the movie poster below and the one on page 227. Also look at the poster on page 235 in "Film Fright." Then create your own poster for a movie monster.

Choose or invent a movie monster. Draw the character on a large piece of paper. Make up a movie title. Write it in large letters. Make your poster exciting!

Now form a group and compare monsters and movie titles. You may want to use words like *dirty*, *funny*, *green*, *sharp*, *mean*, *slimy*, *smart*, and *spooky*.

> ## HOW TO MAKE COMPARISONS
> **1.** Tell how two or more things are alike.
> **2.** Tell how two or more things are different.

My monster is short.

My monster is short, too, but he's stronger than your monster.

USE ADJECTIVES TO MAKE COMPARISONS

When you use an **adjective** to make a comparison, you usually have to change the word. Add **-er** to many **adjectives** to compare two things. Add **-est** to many **adjectives** to compare three or more things.

EXAMPLES   The bride of Frankenstein has **crazy** hair.

It is **crazier** than the creature's hair.

In fact, her hair is the **craziest** hair in the movie.

▲ This movie poster is for two movies: *Son of Frankenstein* and *The Bride of Frankenstein*.

Prepare to Read

Learn Key Vocabulary

Rate and Study the Words Rate how well you know each word. Then:

1. Pronounce the word. Say it aloud several times. Spell it.
2. Study the example.
3. Tell more about the word.
4. Practice it. Make the word your own.

Key Words

actor (ak-tur) *noun*
▶ page 236

An **actor** is a person who acts in a movie or play. The **actors** are working on a new movie.
Base Word: **act**

character (kair-ik-tur) *noun*
▶ page 234

A **character** is someone in a story. They acted out the role of the **characters** in the play.

classic (kla-sik) *adjective*
▶ page 238

Something that is **classic** is old but good. **Classic** cars are expensive if they are in good shape.

fascinated (fa-su-nā-tud)
adjective ▶ page 234

To be **fascinated** means to be very interested in something. The student is **fascinated** by the model.
Base Word: **fascinate**

original (u-rij-u-nul)
adjective ▶ page 235

Something that is **original** is the first of its kind. Mary Shelley's novel is the **original** story of Frankenstein.
Base Word: **origin**

process (prah-ses) *noun*
▶ page 236

A **process** is a set of actions taken to get a certain result. Workers are part of a **process** for making goods.
Synonyms: **system, procedure**

successful (suk-ses-ful)
adjective ▶ page 234

To be **successful** means to have a good result or to be well liked. The team was **successful** at the science fair.
Base Word: **success**

terror (tair-ur) *noun*
▶ page 235

To feel **terror** means to have much fear. The man runs away from the bear in **terror**.

Practice the Words Make a Study Card for each Key Word. Then compare your cards with a partner's.

> **process**
>
> **What it means:** a set of actions taken to get a certain result
>
> **Example:** a recipe
>
> **Not an example:** watching TV

Study Card

Reading Strategy: Visualize

When you visualize, you form mental images—pictures in your mind.
As you read an article, visualize the people, places, and events in the text.
This helps you understand and remember what you read.

Reading Strategy
Visualize

HOW TO FORM MENTAL IMAGES

1. **Find Details** Look for words that describe people, places, or events. Look for descriptive words that explain ideas.
2. **Focus on the Words** Use the words to create pictures in your mind.

Strategy in Action

Here's how one student formed mental images while reading.

Look Into the Text

The first motion pictures were made in the 1890s. They were usually very short and simple. Some were only thirty seconds long! People were fascinated with moving images.

In 1910, Thomas Edison made the movie *Frankenstein*. It was only sixteen minutes. It terrified moviegoers, though. In the 1920s, a horror movie revolution began. People made numerous silent horror films.

> In my mind, I picture a short movie without fancy costumes or scenes.

> In my mind, I see a movie theater full of people who look amazed.

Practice Together

Try visualizing as you reread this passage about horror films. Look for descriptive details. Use the words to create pictures in your mind. Then write a sentence to tell what you visualize.

Focus on Genre

Feature Article

A feature article features, or focuses on, one topic. Writers use interesting facts and **descriptive details** to tell about a real-life topic in an entertaining way.

> Jack Pierce was a makeup artist. He created the monsters in *Frankenstein Meets the Wolf Man*. Pierce used glue and animal hair to make the Wolf Man.

Your Job as a Reader

Reading Strategy: Visualize

As you read, look for descriptive words in the text. Concentrate on these words. Use them to create pictures in your mind.

> I picture a man using glue to stick hair onto an actor's face.

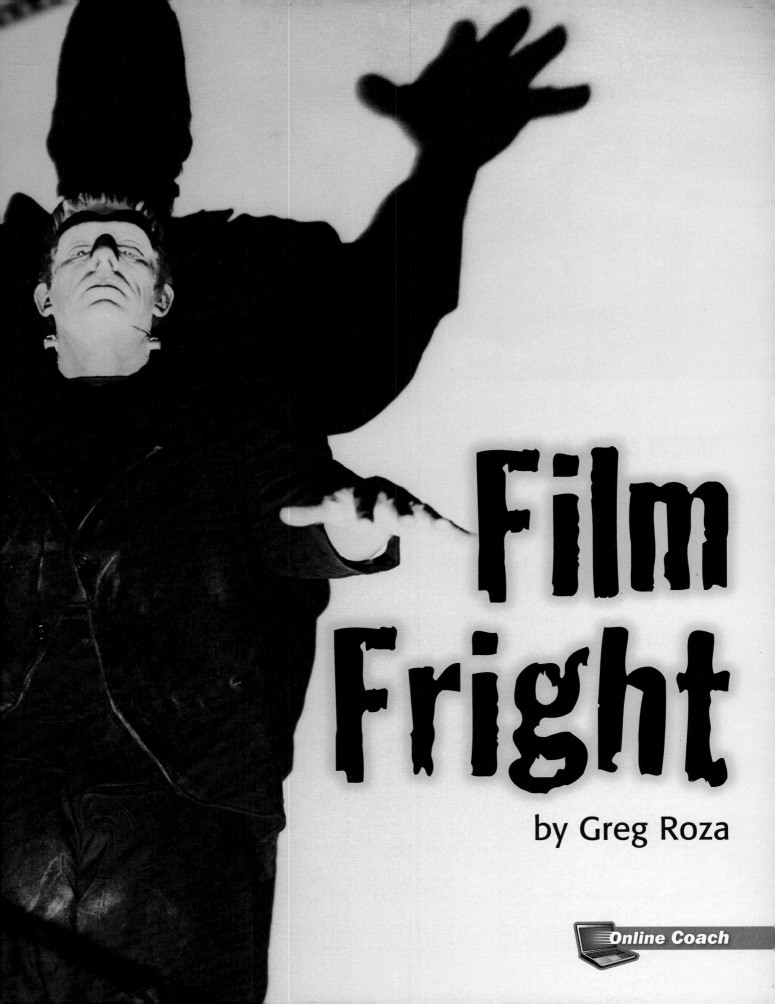

Film Fright

by Greg Roza

▶ Boris Karloff played Frankenstein's monster in the 1931 *Frankenstein* movie.

HISTORY OF HORROR FILMS

The first motion pictures were made in the 1890s. They were usually very short and simple. Some were only thirty seconds long! People were **fascinated** with moving images.

In 1910, Thomas Edison made the movie *Frankenstein*. It was only sixteen minutes. It **terrified moviegoers**, though. In the 1920s, a horror movie revolution began. People made **numerous** silent horror films.

Movie studios made many **popular** monster movies from 1920 to 1950. In 1931, Universal Studios released *Dracula* and *Frankenstein*. These films were two of the most **successful** horror movies of the time. The studios also made movies about other **characters**. These characters included the Wolf Man, the Invisible Man, and the Creature from the Black Lagoon.

Key Vocabulary
fascinated *adj.*, interested in something
successful *adj.*, having a good result; well-liked by many people
character *n.*, someone in a story

In Other Words
terrified moviegoers frightened the people who saw it
numerous many
popular well-liked

STUDIO MONSTERS

The studios made several movies about the Frankenstein monster during this time. The **original** one tells about **mad** Dr. Frankenstein. He creates a monster from body parts. Then he brings it to life. The next movie was *The Bride of Frankenstein*. The monster forces Dr. Frankenstein to build him a monster wife. In *The Son of Frankenstein*, Frankenstein's son wakes up the monster. The **terror** begins all over again. *The Ghost of Frankenstein* includes a monster more terrible than ever.

In the 1940s, studios began **teaming up movie monsters**. *Frankenstein Meets the Wolf Man* is an example. It joins the story of Frankenstein's monster with the story of the Wolf Man.

In *The Wolf Man*, Lawrence Talbot tries to save a woman from **a werewolf**. Talbot kills the werewolf. But he is bitten by it. At the next full moon, Talbot turns into the Wolf Man.

▲ This movie poster shows the classic monster team of the 1940s.

In Other Words
mad crazy
teaming up movie monsters putting different monsters in the same movie
a werewolf someone who is part human and part wolf

Before You Move On

1. **Paraphrase** Use your own words to tell the early history of horror movies.
2. **Main Idea and Details** What details show that horror movies were popular?

THE MEN WHO MADE THE MONSTERS

Jack Pierce was a makeup artist. He created the monsters in *Frankenstein Meets the Wolf Man*. Pierce used glue and animal hair to make the Wolf Man. The makeup was very uncomfortable. The **actors** had to sit still for many hours. It could be a **grueling** experience. The results were **spectacular**, though.

John P. Fulton was a cameraman. He worked on *Frankenstein Meets the Wolf Man*. Fulton used stop-motion photography. This **process** takes a very long time.

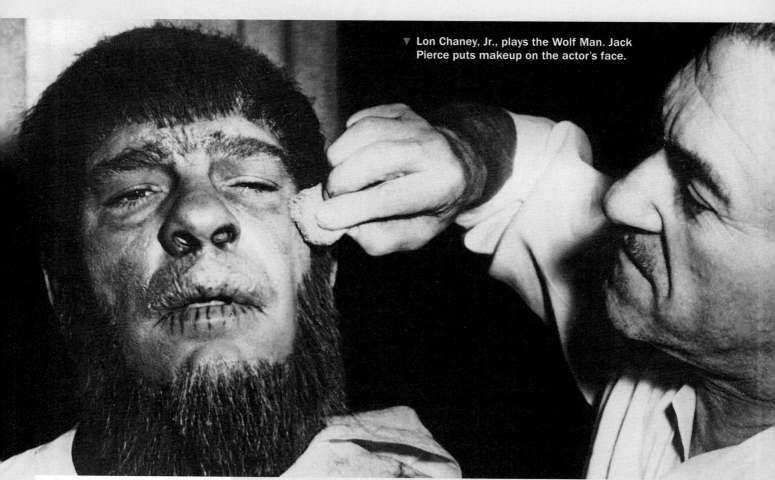

▼ Lon Chaney, Jr., plays the Wolf Man. Jack Pierce puts makeup on the actor's face.

Key Vocabulary

actor *n.*, a person who acts in a movie or play

process *n.*, a set of actions taken to get a certain result

In Other Words

grueling difficult
spectacular wonderful, incredible

Fulton used this **technique** to show Talbot **transforming** into a werewolf. First he filmed the actor without makeup. Then he stopped the camera. Jack Pierce **applied** the first layer of makeup. Then Fulton filmed for a few more seconds. Fulton and Pierce repeated this process many times.

Fulton put all the pieces together. On screen, Talbot turned into the Wolf Man. The transformation on film took ten seconds. The actual process took about six hours!

▲ These photos show how the actor transforms into the Wolf Man.

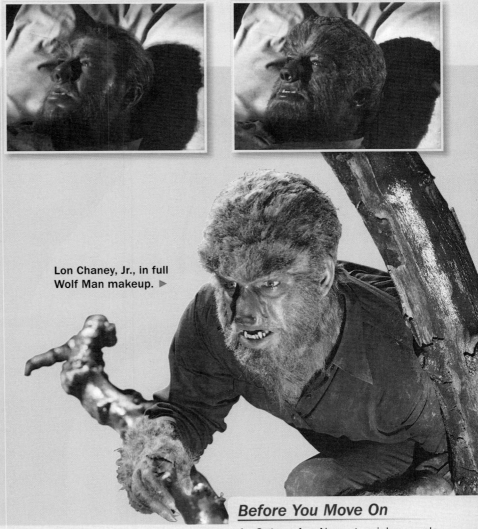

Lon Chaney, Jr., in full Wolf Man makeup. ▶

In Other Words
technique special way of doing things
transforming changing
applied put on

Before You Move On

1. **Categorize** Name two jobs people do to make monsters.
2. **Steps in a Process** Tell how John Fulton and Jack Pierce changed an actor into a werewolf.

Film Fright **237**

THE LEGACY

By the 1950s, U.S. movie studios stopped making these types of monster movies. New horror movies began to take their place. The **classic** monsters were not forgotten, though.

In 1974, Mel Brooks and Gene Wilder made *Young Frankenstein*. They filmed it where the original Frankenstein series was filmed. Their movie is a comedy. It makes fun of the old Frankenstein films. It also **honors** them.

▼ The movie *Young Frankenstein* is a comedy. The actor Gene Wilder plays Dr. Frankenstein. The director, Mel Brooks, is shown at the right.

Key Vocabulary
classic *adj.*, old but good

In Other Words
honors shows respect for

FRANKENSTEIN RETURNS

In 1994, Kenneth Branagh made *Mary Shelley's Frankenstein*. His movie follows the same basic plot as Shelley's novel. In this movie, Frankenstein's monster is not a flat-headed, growling monster. It is **an intelligent and sensitive** creature.

Frankenstein's monster in *Mary Shelley's Frankenstein* is like the character in the classic novel. ▶

STAMP OF APPROVAL

The movie monsters of the 1930s and '40s have had a lasting effect on popular culture. In 1997, the U.S. Postal Service made the Classic Movie Monsters postage stamps. These stamps also honored the work of makeup artist Jack Pierce.

The work of **these horror movie pioneers** helped make the monsters popular. Because of them, Frankenstein's monster and the Wolf Man continue to be popular today. ❖

▲ This stamp of Frankenstein's monster is one in a series that honors classic movie monsters.

Before You Move On

1. **Evidence and Conclusion** What information tells you that **classic** monsters were not forgotten?
2. **Compare** How is the movie *Mary Shelley's Frankenstein* like the **original** story?

FRANKENSTEIN MAKES A SANDWICH
by Adam Rex

When Frankenstein
prepared to dine
on ham-and-cheese on wheat,

he found, instead,
5 he had no bread
(or mustard, cheese, or meat).

What could he do?
He thought it through
until his brain was sore,

10 And thought he ought
to see what he could
borrow from next door.

In Other Words
prepared to dine on got ready
    to eat
brain was sore head hurt

Cultural Background
Frankenstein is not the name of
the monster in the original story
by Mary Shelley. The scientist
who created the monster was Dr.
Frankenstein. As this classic story
changed over time, people began
calling the monster Frankenstein.

His neighbors gawked
as Frankie walked
15 the paths up to their porches.

Each time he tried,
the folks inside
would chase him off with torches.

"A MONSTER! EEK!"
20 the people shrieked.
"Oh, make him go away!"

The angry hordes
unsheathed their swords,
pulled pitchforks out of hay.

25 They threw tomatoes,
pigs, potatoes,
loaves of moldy bread.

And then a thought
struck Frankenstein
30 as pickles struck his head.

In Other Words
gawked stared
shrieked screamed in fear
hordes unsheathed groups
of people took out
moldy spoiled, rotten

It's true, at first

he thought the worst:

His neighbors were so rude!

But then he found

35 that on the ground

they'd made a mound of *food*.

He piled it high

and waved good-bye

and shouted, **"Thanks a bunch!"**

40 Then stacked it on

a plate and ate

a big, disgusting lunch. ❖

In Other Words
rude mean, unkind
mound pile

Before You Move On

1. **Rhyme** Which words in this poem rhyme, or sound alike?

2. **Tone** The tone of a poem is what the writer thinks of the topic. What is the tone of this poem? Which words tell you?

Connect Reading and Writing

Vocabulary

actor

characters

classic

fascinated

original

process

successful

terror

CRITICAL THINKING

1. SUM IT UP Create a time line of the major events in the history of **classic** horror films. Use the time line to summarize the selection.

Time Line

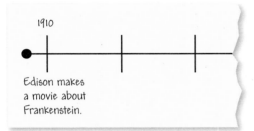

1910

Edison makes a movie about Frankenstein.

2. Compare How is Frankenstein in the poem like the Frankenstein **characters** in the movies? How is he different?

3. Speculate Many people go to horror films. Why do you think they are **fascinated** by evil **characters** and **terror**?

4. Generalize Think about **classic** monsters in the movies. What traits make these **characters** memorable?

READING FLUENCY

Phrasing Read the passage on page 578 to a partner. Assess your fluency.

1. I read
   a. great   **b.** OK   **c.** not very well

2. What I did best in my reading was _____.

READING STRATEGY

> **Visualize**
> Which descriptive details did you use to visualize? Show examples to a partner. Describe your mental images.

VOCABULARY REVIEW

Oral Review Read the paragraph aloud. Add the vocabulary words.

> Boris Karloff, an _____ in many movies, has played many _____. His role as the monster Frankenstein was his most popular, or _____. Karloff went through the long _____ of putting on monster makeup every day of filming. It created a new look for the creature, unlike the one in the _____ story. Audiences were _____. They were in _____ as they watched the frightening monster. Today, the 1931 movie *Frankenstein* is a _____ movie that people watch on DVD with amusement.

Written Review Would you rather be an **actor** or a makeup artist for a horror movie? Write a job description for the job you chose. Use five vocabulary words.

 **WRITE ABOUT THE** **GUIDING QUESTION**

Analyze a Classic Character
Reread the selection. Why is the **character** of Frankenstein's monster still part of our culture? Support your opinion with evidence from the text.

Connect Across the Curriculum

Analyze Rhythm in Poetry

> **Academic Vocabulary**
> • **locate** (lō-kāt) *verb*
>   To **locate** something is to find it.

Prose is the kind of writing you see in a story or a novel. Poetry is different from prose. Poets use a small number of words to express their feelings and ideas. They often arrange the words in lines. Look at the line breaks in this passage from "Frankenstein Makes a Sandwich":

> When Frankenstein
> prepared to dine
> on ham-and-cheese on wheat,

Poetry also has a musical sound. This comes from **rhythm**, or a pattern of beats. One form of rhythm is **meter**, which is a pattern of stressed and unstressed sounds. To get an idea of what meter is like, make a loud clap and then a soft clap. Continue the pattern of beats.

Sound is important in poetry. It helps communicate the **mood**, or feeling, of a poem. It also helps express a poem's meaning.

Practice Together

With the class, read aloud "Frankenstein Makes a Sandwich." Listen as you clap out the rhythm. **Locate** each strong beat, or stressed sound. Notice that the rhythm, or beat, is quick and lively. This adds to the silly, playful mood of the poem. Discuss how the rhythm adds to the meaning, too.

Try It!

Analyze a Poem With a partner, find a short poem in a book or magazine. Read the poem aloud together. Clap out the rhythm and **locate** each strong beat. Then discuss the poem:

- What does the poem mean?
- What is the mood, or feeling, of the poem?
- How does the rhythm add to the mood? How does it add to the meaning?

▲ When you read the poem aloud, emphasize the rhythm.

Read a Poem With your partner, read the poem aloud for the class. Emphasize the rhythm. Then tell about the poem.

Use Latin and Greek Roots

Root	Origin	Meaning
dict	Latin	tell
gram	Greek	write
scrib	Latin	write
sect	Latin	cut
tele	Greek	far

Academic Vocabulary
- **relate** (ri-lāt) *verb*
  When you **relate** two things, you think about how they are connected.

Some English words are made up of word parts, including Greek or Latin roots. A root is a central word part that has meaning. Unlike a base word, however, it cannot stand on its own.

If you know the meanings of the word parts, you can figure out the meaning of the word. For example:

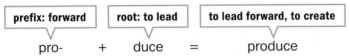

| prefix: forward | root: to lead | to lead forward, to create |

pro-   +   duce   =   produce

Use Roots Work with a partner. Define each word. Use the chart above and a dictionary to find the meanings of the word parts and of the words. Discuss how the meaning of each root **relates** to the meaning of the whole word.

1. predict   **2.** bisect   **3.** program   **4.** prescribe   **5.** telegram

Analyze Structure of Poetry

Academic Vocabulary
- **structure** (struk-chur) *noun*
  Structure is the way something is organized or put together.

Some poems have short lines grouped in verses. Some poems have a single column of long lines. The font, or the style of the letters, can vary, too. The **structure** of a poem can add to a poem's mood and meaning.

Discuss Structure Look at the short lines and the big, colorful letters in some of the verses from "Frankenstein Makes a Sandwich." As a group, discuss how the length of the lines and the style of the letters add to the feeling of the poem and to its meaning.

Dramatize the Poem With a group, act out "Frankenstein Makes a Sandwich." Speak clearly and with expression. Use body language and movements to add meaning. Notice how the poem's **structure** helps you know how to communicate its mood and meaning.

Connect Across the Curriculum, continued

MEDIA & TECHNOLOGY

Research a Special Effects Technique

> **Academic Vocabulary**
> • **specific** (spi-si-fik) *adjective*
>   Something that is **specific** is exact.

John P. Fulton used stop-motion photography to show how the character turns into the Wolf Man. Filmmakers use special effects such as this to trick viewers. This is one of many special effects techniques.

1 Explore the Topic Look through books and articles to explore the topic of special effects. Check out resources on the Internet, too.

> **Internet** InsideNG.com
> ◯ See how special effects are used in some films.
> ◯ Get a historic view of special effects in filmmaking.

Look for techniques such as

- optical effects, including double exposures, skip frames, and blue screens
- animation and scale modeling
- computer graphics.

Preview the text. Scan the descriptions. Make a list of techniques that interest you.

2 Narrow Your Topic Choose one technique to focus on. Focus on a **specific** part of it. Collect interesting facts and details to include in a report.

3 Write a Report Tell what you learned. Include pictures or graphics.

4 Share Your Information Present your report to the class. Remember to

- speak so everyone can hear
- display the graphics to help listeners focus
- answer people's questions about your report.

▲ A special effects artist helps make a movie about dinosaurs.

Make Comparisons

Interview a Classmate Ask a classmate to describe characters that he or she thinks are scary. Switch roles. Compare your descriptions and ideas. Use adjectives that compare.

> A troll is a scary character.

> A goblin is scarier than a troll.

Write to Compare Monsters

Study the Models When you write, use **adjectives** to make comparisons. Effective comparisons help your readers understand your thoughts and add details to your writing.

NOT OK

I think monster movies are the **goodest** movies of all. A monster movie is **scary** than a film without a monster. For example, on Saturday I watched the movie Swamp Thing, and then I watched a funny movie. Swamp Thing was **most exciting** than the other movie because of the creepy makeup and costumes.

The writer uses **adjectives** to compare but uses the wrong forms.

OK

I think monster movies are the **best** movies of all. A monster movie is **scarier** than a film without a monster. For example, on Saturday I watched the movie Swamp Thing, and then I watched a funny movie. Swamp Thing was **more exciting** than the other movie because of the creepy makeup and costumes.

The writer uses **adjectives** correctly to make comparisons. The reader thinks: **"Now I understand the writer's thoughts."**

Revise It Work with a partner to revise this passage. Fix the comparisons.

I like the movie Mary Shelley's Frankenstein. I think it is the greater Frankenstein film ever made. It is best than the 1931 movie Frankenstein. The monster in Mary Shelley's Frankenstein is more smarter than the monster in the other film. I think the worse movie of all about the monster is The Ghost of Frankenstein.

✎ **WRITE ON YOUR OWN** Choose two monsters or monster movies and compare them. Be sure to write comparisons with adjectives correctly.

REMEMBER

- Add **-er** or **-est** to most adjectives.
- If a word ends in a consonant plus **y**, change the **y** to **i** before you add **-er** or **-est**.
- Use **more** or **most** before long adjectives.
- Use special forms for **good**, **bad**, and **many**.

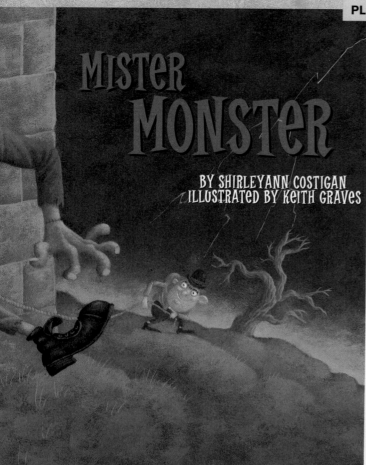

MISTER MONSTER

BY SHIRLEYANN COSTIGAN
ILLUSTRATED BY KEITH GRAVES

SELECTION 3 OVERVIEW

▶ **Build Background**

▶ **Language & Grammar**
Describe an Event or Experience
Use Adverbs

▶ **Prepare to Read**
Learn Key Vocabulary
Learn a Reading Strategy
Visualize

▶ **Read and Write**
Focus on Genre
Play
Apply the Reading Strategy
Visualize
Critical Thinking
Reading Fluency
Read with Intonation
Vocabulary Review
Write About the Guiding Question

▶ **Connect Across the Curriculum**
Literary Analysis
Compare Literature
Vocabulary Study
Use Word Parts
Research/Speaking
Explore TV Commercials
Listening/Speaking
Perform a Play
Language and Grammar
Describe an Event or Experience
Writing and Grammar
Write About a Performance

Build Background

Discuss Plays

In some ways, plays and movies are alike. In other ways, they are different. Look at the photos and talk about how plays are special.

Digital Library

InsideNG.com
⊘ View the images.

▲ Actors perform a play in special costumes.

Connect

Quickwrite Which do you think is more fun to watch, a play or a movie? Why do you think so? Take about three minutes to write your ideas. Save your writing. You may wish to use this frame.

Watching a _____ is better than watching a _____ because _____ .

Language & Grammar

Describe an Event or Experience

CD

Look at the photo. Listen to how the people describe the show. Then pretend you are there and describe something.

PICTURE PROMPT

▲ The play *Wicked* is based on the characters of the Wicked Witch and the Good Witch from the book *The Wizard of Oz* by L. Frank Baum.

> This show is exciting! The costumes are wonderful.

> The music is wonderful, too. Both actresses sing beautifully.

Use Adverbs

- Use an **adverb** to describe a **verb**. Adverbs often end in **-ly**.

    EXAMPLES   The actress **sings** loudly .   (how)
    The dancers **jump** high .   (where)
    The song **starts** immediately .   (when)

- Use an **adverb** to make an adjective or another adverb stronger.

    EXAMPLES   The singer is really pretty.
                                    adjective

    The dancer moves very slowly.
                                    adverb

- **Adverbs** add details and bring life to your writing.

    EXAMPLES   The performers bow gracefully . The people in the audience
    stand up and cheer. Everyone claps wildly .

Practice Together

Say each sentence with an appropriate adverb from the box. Explain
whether the adverb tells how, where, or when about a verb, or whether it
makes an adjective or adverb stronger.

| colorfully | really | exactly | there |

1. The theater opens _____ at 7:00.
2. We are going _____.
3. The actors are _____ good.
4. They dress _____.

Try It!

Read each sentence. Write an appropriate adverb
from the box on a card. Hold up the card as you say
the sentence. Does the adverb tell how, where, or
when about the verb? Does it make an adjective or
adverb stronger?

| frequently | out | skillfully | very |

5. We go to shows _____.
6. The performers say their lines _____.
7. Tonight's show will start _____ soon.
8. The performers are coming _____!

▲ These actors are very talented. Their characters are
really believable.

Relive an Experience

DESCRIBE AN EVENT OR EXPERIENCE

Think of something special that you did. Maybe you went to a party, a big game, or a concert. What was the experience like? List details to help you remember it.

Response Chart

What was the event?	Who was there?	What did I see and hear?	How did I feel?
a classic car parade	my family and friends; crowds of people	cool cars; the hum of motors; horns honking	excited; interested in all the cars

Review the details on your chart. Close your eyes and try to relive the experience. Then think about how you would describe it to someone.

HOW TO DESCRIBE AN EVENT OR EXPERIENCE

1. Tell what happened.

2. Give details.

3. Use descriptive words.

> I saw a classic car parade. The chrome on the cars sparkled brightly.

Get together with a partner and describe the event.

USE ADVERBS

You can make your description more interesting by including **adverbs**.

Tell *how*: The horns honked **loudly**.

Tell *when*: The parade started **precisely** at noon.

Tell *where*: Other old cars parked **nearby**.

▲ The cars move slowly down the street.

Prepare to Read

Learn Key Vocabulary

Rate and Study the Words Rate how well you know each word. Then:

1. Pronounce the word. Say it aloud several times. Spell it.
2. Study the example.
3. Tell more about the word.
4. Practice it. Make the word your own.

Key Words

amazed (u-māzd) *adjective*
▶ page 256

To be **amazed** means to be very surprised. They are **amazed** that the experiment worked so well.

apply (u-plī) *verb*
▶ page 256

To **apply** means to ask for or to request something. People often fill out forms when they **apply** for a job.

audience (aw-dē-unts) *noun*
▶ page 266

An **audience** is a group of people who watch or listen to something. The **audience** claps during the show.
Synonyms: **viewers, crowd**

commercial (ku-mur-shul)
noun ▶ page 262

A **commercial** is an ad on TV or the radio. Most TV **commercials** show products that viewers can buy.
Synonym: **advertisement (ad)**

disappear (dis-u-pear) *verb*
▶ page 263

To **disappear** means to no longer be seen. When the bell rang, the students left quickly. They **disappeared**.
Base Word: **appear**

mascot (mas-kot) *noun*
▶ page 256

A **mascot** is a character that represents an organization. This basketball team's **mascot** cheers for the team.

offstage (awf-stāj) *adverb*
▶ page 256

To be **offstage** means to be at the side of the stage. The dancer waits **offstage** and gets ready to perform.
Base Word: **stage**
Related Word: **onstage**

response (ri-sponts) *noun*
▶ page 266

A **response** is what people think or say about something. She raises her hand to give a **response** to the question.
Synonyms: **answer, reply**

Practice the Words Make a Vocabulary Example Chart for the Key Words. Compare your chart with a partner's.

Word	Definition	Example from My Life
amazed	very surprised	I am always amazed when I see a full moon.

Vocabulary Example Chart

Reading Strategy: Visualize

When you read a play, try to visualize the characters and action. Use the actors' dialogue and stage directions—the instructions about how to act and what the stage looks like—to form mental images of the story.

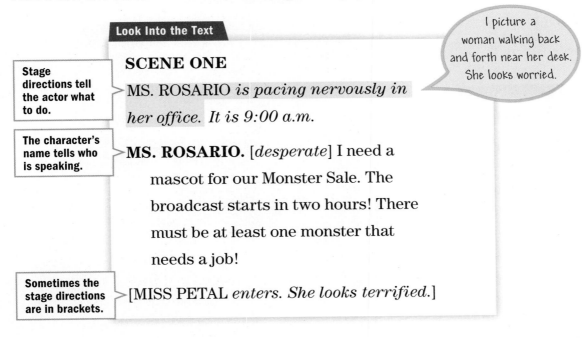

Reading Strategy
Visualize

HOW TO FORM MENTAL IMAGES

1. Look for words in the dialogue and stage directions that describe the characters, their actions, and events.
2. Focus on words that describe. Use them to form mental images.
3. Draw pictures to show what is happening. You may want to draw quick sketches the second time you read the play to help make the scenes clear in your mind.

Strategy in Action

Here's how one student formed mental images of a play.

Look Into the Text

I picture a woman walking back and forth near her desk. She looks worried.

Stage directions tell the actor what to do.

SCENE ONE

MS. ROSARIO *is pacing nervously in her office. It is 9:00 a.m.*

The character's name tells who is speaking.

MS. ROSARIO. [*desperate*] I need a mascot for our Monster Sale. The broadcast starts in two hours! There must be at least one monster that needs a job!

Sometimes the stage directions are in brackets.

[MISS PETAL *enters. She looks terrified.*]

Practice Together

Reread the passage above and form mental images of the characters and action. Follow the steps in the How-To box.

Focus on Genre

Play

A play is a story that is written for actors to perform. Plays have **dialogue**, or the words the characters speak. Plays also have **stage directions** that tell the actors how to look and act.

MISS PETAL. Ms. Rosario, someone is waiting to see you for the mascot job.

MS. ROSARIO. Great! Show him in.

[MISS PETAL *leaves, still looking terrified.*]

dialogue

stage directions

Your Job as a Reader

Reading Strategy: Visualize

When you read a play, picture the scenes to bring them to life. Look for words in the dialogue and stage directions that describe the characters and events.

> I picture Ms. Rosario looking excited, because she says, "Great!" Because of the word *terrified*, I picture Miss Petal looking afraid.

MISTER MONSTER

BY SHIRLEYANN COSTIGAN
ILLUSTRATED BY KEITH GRAVES

CHARACTERS

MS. ROSARIO, the manager of Dollar Rite Department Store

MISS PETAL, her assistant

YGOR, a lab assistant

VICTOR FRANKENSTEIN, a scientist

THE MONSTER, Dr. Frankenstein's creation

Online Coach

Set a Purpose
A store needs a mascot.
Find out who wants the job.

SCENE ONE

MS. ROSARIO *is **pacing nervously** in her office. It is 9:00 a.m.*

MS. ROSARIO. [*desperate*] I need a mascot for our Monster Sale. The **broadcast** starts in two hours! There must be at least one monster that needs a job!

[MISS PETAL *enters. She looks terrified.*]

MISS PETAL. Ms. Rosario, someone is waiting to see you for the mascot job.

MS. ROSARIO. Great! Show him in.

[MISS PETAL *leaves, still looking terrified.*]

[YGOR *enters, holding a thick rope that is pulled tight. At the other end of the rope is* THE MONSTER, *hidden **offstage**.* MS. ROSARIO *stares up at* THE MONSTER. *She looks **amazed**, then overjoyed.*]

MS. ROSARIO. Perfect.

YGOR. My name is Ygor Manic. [*points to* THE MONSTER, *still offstage*] This is my friend Frankensteinz. He wants to **apply** for the job you **advertised**.

MS. ROSARIO. [*still staring at* THE MONSTER] Frankensteinz?

YGOR. Yes, Frankensteinz is his first name. It's spelled with a *z*.

Key Vocabulary

mascot *n.*, a character that represents an organization
offstage *adv.*, away from the area where people can see
amazed *adj.*, very surprised
apply *v.*, to ask for, to request

In Other Words

pacing nervously walking back and forth in a worried way
desperate hopeless
broadcast TV show
advertised said you had open; are looking to fill

Cultural Background

Ygor does not appear in the original Frankenstein story. He was created for the movie *Son of Frankenstein*, which was released in 1939. Since then, Ygor has become a regular part of the Frankenstein story.

MS. ROSARIO. What is his last name?

YGOR. Monster.

[*Offstage*, THE MONSTER *makes a loud* **grunt**. *A cat* **howls**. THE MONSTER *tugs the rope impatiently, pulling* YGOR *toward him.* MS. ROSARIO *pulls the rope back.*]

YGOR. No, Frankie! Leave the cat alone! [*turning to* MS. ROSARIO] I think he's hungry. He hasn't eaten since he was born.

[MS. ROSARIO *makes a cell phone call.*]

MS. ROSARIO. [*on her cell phone*] Miss Petal, call Cluck-Cluck Chicken. Order a bucket of chicken and a broccoli salad. And **hop to it**, if you love your cat!

[*The rope loosens suddenly.* YGOR *and* MS. ROSARIO *fall to the floor.* MS. ROSARIO *gets up immediately and brushes herself off.*]

MS. ROSARIO. [*calmly*] Let's take Mr. Monster to the lunchroom. We can sit down. And I can tell you about the job.

YGOR. And how much it pays.

MS. ROSARIO. Yes, I can tell you that, too.

In Other Words
grunt short, low sound
howls gives a long, loud cry
hop to it make it quick

Before You Move On

1. **Explain** Why does Ygor bring Frankensteinz Monster to Ms. Rosario's office?
2. **Character's Motive** Why does Ms. Rosario tell Miss Petal to order lunch?

SCENE TWO

Later that morning. MS. ROSARIO gives orders to MISS PETAL, who takes notes.

MS. ROSARIO. We must hurry. The broadcast begins at 12:30. Call the **makeup department**. Tell them that Mr. Monster looks too scary. They should cover some of **his stitches**. Call **wardrobe**. Say we won't need them.

MISS PETAL. [*breathlessly*] Yes, Ms. Rosario.

[*Noises offstage: tin plates clatter.*]

THE MONSTER. [*from offstage*] More food!

YGOR. [*from offstage*] Eat your broccoli.

[*From offstage, MISS PETAL's cat howls.*]

In Other Words
makeup department people who make actors look good on camera
his stitches the sewing marks on him
wardrobe the people in charge of Mr. Monster's clothes

YGOR. [*from offstage*] No, Frankie!
Not the cat!

[MS. ROSARIO *and* MISS PETAL *look nervously at each other.*]

MS. ROSARIO. And order more chicken.

MISS PETAL. Cooked?

MS. ROSARIO. [*sounding overwhelmed*]
Whatever.

Before You Move On

1. **Confirm Prediction** Does the monster get the job? How do you know?

2. **Character's Point of View** Why does Ms. Rosario sound overwhelmed at the end of the scene?

SCENE THREE

That afternoon, MS. ROSARIO *watches a* **commercial** *on TV from her desk. She looks impressed.*

VOICE OF SALESMAN ON TV. [*very jolly*]

So, come to Dollar Rite Department Store right away! Discover our **monster bargains**. Shake hands with our monster mascot . . .

VOICE OF FRANKENSTEINZ ON TV. More food!

VOICE OF SALESMAN ON TV. [*laughing*]

Shake hands if you dare!

[MS. ROSARIO *turns off the TV.* MISS PETAL *enters the office with* DR. FRANKENSTEIN.]

MISS PETAL. Ms. Rosario, this gentleman wants to speak with you.

[*She points to the man as she leaves.*]

DR. FRANKENSTEIN. [*speaking angrily to* MS. ROSARIO] My name is Dr. Victor Frankenstein. You stole my creation!

MS. ROSARIO. [*surprised*] Your what?

Key Vocabulary
commercial *n.*, an ad on TV or radio

In Other Words
monster bargains very low sale prices

DR. FRANKENSTEIN. My creation! I put him together from a hundred dead bodies! I created him. I did not **give you permission to** use him in your commercial.

[YGOR *enters the office, pulling on the rope.* THE MONSTER *is offstage, at the other end of the rope.*]

DR. FRANKENSTEIN. [*pointing at* YGOR] You! You stole my creature to make money!

YGOR. We need the money. Do you know how much it will cost to **keep** this monster?

[*As* YGOR *argues with the doctor, he drops the rope mistakenly. The rope* **disappears** .]

YGOR. The cost of food alone will **break our backs**!

DR. FRANKENSTEIN. That's my problem! I created him. I gave him life!

Key Vocabulary
disappear *v.*, to no longer be seen

In Other Words
give you permission to say that you could
keep take care of
break our backs be very expensive

YGOR. Oh, yes, you gave him life. But did you give him love? Did you give him a name? Did you give him breakfast?

[MS. ROSARIO ***notices*** *that the rope is gone.*]

MS. ROSARIO. Uh, gentlemen? Gentlemen?

[DR. FRANKENSTEIN *and* YGOR *continue to argue, pointing at each other.*]

DR. FRANKENSTEIN. You, you . . . listen . . . !

YGOR. No, you listen!

MS. ROSARIO. [*shouting*] Gentlemen!

YGOR AND DR. FRANKENSTEIN. [*turning toward* MS. ROSARIO] What?

MS. ROSARIO. He's gone.

DR. FRANKENSTEIN. [*looking around*] Oh no!

[YGOR *and* DR. FRANKENSTEIN *both turn toward* MS. ROSARIO.]

DR. FRANKENSTEIN. Call the police!

YGOR. Call the highway patrol!

DR. FRANKENSTEIN. Call the hospital!

YGOR. Call the **Recycling Center**!

[*The phone rings.* MS. ROSARIO *answers it. She listens quietly and then hangs up.*]

MS. ROSARIO. He's in the lunchroom.

[YGOR *and* DR. FRANKENSTEIN *rush out of the office.* MISS PETAL *enters.*]

In Other Words
notices sees, realizes
Recycling Center place that
 collects trash to be used again

MISS PETAL. Here's the **audience's response** to the commercial. [*reading from her notepad*] **Seventy percent** loved the new mascot. Fifteen percent thought he was just OK. Nine percent thought he was disgusting. Six percent couldn't stop screaming. And . . . oh yeah, Mr. Monster **got two movie offers**.

[*Noises offstage: a loud crash, then the cat howls. MS. ROSARIO smiles and* **sinks** *into her chair.*]

MS. ROSARIO. [*softly*] A star is born. ❖

Before You Move On

1. **Conflict** Why does Dr. Frankenstein argue with Ms. Rosario and Ygor?

2. **Confirm Prediction** Was your prediction correct? What happened that you did not expect?

Connect Reading and Writing

Vocabulary

amazed

applied

audience

commercial

disappears

mascot

offstage

response

CRITICAL THINKING

1. SUM IT UP Draw important scenes from the play. Use the drawings to retell the story.

2. Compare In the play, what is the **response** of Dr. Frankenstein to his creation? How is this different from the way Dr. Frankenstein acts in Mary Shelley's story?

3. Explain How does the action **offstage** add to the humor of the play? Give examples.

4. Classify Look back at the reaction of the **audience** to Frankensteinz on page 266. Which group would you be in if you saw the **commercial**?

READING FLUENCY

Intonation Read the passage on page 579 to a partner. Assess your fluency.

1. I read
   a. great   **b.** OK   **c.** not very well

2. What I did best in my reading was _____.

READING STRATEGY

Visualize
Show a partner the parts of the play you visualized. Tell how **applying** the strategy helped you understand the play.

VOCABULARY REVIEW

Oral Review Read the paragraph aloud. Add the vocabulary words.

> After Act 1 of Frankie's first play, the _____ claps loudly. Frankie's _____ is to look surprised and _____. He smiles as he walks _____ for the break. He remembers when he _____ to drama school to take acting lessons. "I'm so glad I got in," he thinks as he _____ into a dressing room. Then Frankie thinks about the acting job he got in the ad, or _____, based on his acting lessons. The ad was for Chow Down dog food. He wasn't the star, though. The company _____, a dog named Wolf, got all the attention!

Written Review Imagine that your favorite monster and Frankensteinz are **mascots** in a **commercial**. Write a paragraph describing the ad. Use five vocabulary words.

WRITE ABOUT THE GUIDING QUESTION

Analyze a Classic Character

What emotions does this version of Frankenstein inspire in people? Read the selection again, and support your analysis with examples from the text.

Connect Across the Curriculum

Compare Literature

> **Academic Vocabulary**
> • **style** (stī-ul) *noun*
>   A **style** is a certain way of expressing an idea.

Language changes over time. Think about an old movie you have watched or a book you have read that took place long ago. The characters probably did not speak the way people speak today.

Language changes for many reasons. New words and expressions enter the language. Social attitudes and habits change. As a result, the **style** of speech changes. The **style** of language changes in literature, too.

Practice Together

Compare the Text "Frankenstein" tells a story from the 1800s. It is a historical text. "Mister Monster" is a modern story, even though some of the characters come from the historical text.

Compare the language in these two stories to see how the **style** is different. Look for passages that tell something similar. For example, look at the passages where Dr. Frankenstein tells about creating the monster.

Make a Chart Record what the character or narrator says.

Comparison Chart

"Frankenstein"	"Mister Monster"
I devoted two years of my life to making a new creature out of bones and body parts from graveyards and slaughterhouses.	I put him together from a hundred bodies!
Now I know his misery is my fault, not his.	That's my problem!

Analyze Language Patterns Notice that the historical text uses long sentences and some difficult words. The character uses words and expressions that people do not say very often anymore. The **style** is formal. The play uses everyday language, with short sentences and simple words.

▲ Frankensteinz scares the cat.

Try It!

Analyze Language Patterns With a partner, find and compare other examples in the selections.

Share Your Findings Read aloud a passage from each selection. Compare the vocabulary, or words, and the sound and **style** of the language. How does each piece of writing reflect its time period?

Use Word Parts

> **Academic Vocabulary**
> • **identify** (ī-**den**-tu-fī) *verb*
> To **identify** means to find out or to show what something is.

Prefix	Meaning	Example	Word Meaning
im-	not	impatiently	not patiently
mis-	wrongly	mistakenly	done wrongly
over-	a lot or too much	overjoyed	having a lot of joy

A prefix is a word part that is added at the beginning of a word. It changes the meaning of the base word.

Define Words Read each word and **identify** the prefix. Use the chart above to help you define the word.

1. overpower **3.** impossible **5.** imperfect **7.** misbehave

2. misread **4.** misjudge **6.** overcharge **8.** overreact

Compare your definitions with a partner's. Then look up the words in a dictionary and discuss the definitions.

Explore TV Commercials

MEDIA & TECHNOLOGY

> **Academic Vocabulary**
> • **classic** (**kla**-sik) *adjective*
> Something that is **classic** is old but good.

Television programs have changed over the years. Commercials have changed, too. Modern commercials are in color and often use computer graphics. Conduct research to find out about some **classic** TV ads. Then compare **classic** ads with commercials you might see on TV now.

❶ **Select a Research Question** *TV commercials* is a big topic, so think of one part of it that you would like to learn about. Write a research question to guide you. For example: "When were the first TV commercials made?"

❷ **Research Online** Look for information as well as photos or videos of commercials that relate to your question. Collect information and visuals that you can use in your presentation.

Internet InsideNG.com
◯ View some classic TV ads.

❸ **Present Your Findings** In a group, share what you learned. Read aloud your research question. Use the information and images to answer the question for your classmates.

❹ **Analyze Commercials** Think about the **classic** ads you saw. Discuss with your group how graphics, color, sound, and other technologies have changed the way people communicate their messages in TV ads.

Perform a Play

DRAMA

> **Academic Vocabulary**
> • **structure** (struk-**chur**) *noun*
>   **Structure** is the way something is organized or put together.

Bring "Mister Monster" to life by performing it in class.

1 Assign Roles Begin with the cast of characters on page 255 of "Mister Monster." Decide who will play which role. Don't forget other parts, such as the cat and the voice of the salesman on TV.

2 Assign Other Tasks Many people, besides actors, work hard to put on a play. You will need a director and a stage manager. Other important jobs include

• copying and distributing the script
• helping the actors learn their parts
• creating the sets
• making costumes and props
• designing and performing sound effects.

3 Study the Script Notice the **structure** of the play. How many scenes, or sections, is it divided into? Then review these dramatic elements:

• dialogue: the words the actors speak, or their lines
• stage directions: instructions that describe how the actors look and act, and what the stage looks like

▲ This prop could be used in Scene Two of "Mister Monster."

4 Rehearse With the help of the director, decide where the actors should stand and move on the stage during each scene. Actors should use the correct tone of voice, gestures, and expressions to communicate the meaning. Speak clearly and loudly. Other students can practice their jobs, such as changing the sets, putting out the props, and making sound effects.

5 Perform the Play Invite family members or another class to the performance.

Describe an Event or Experience

Tell About a Picture Find a picture of an event, such as a football game or a concert. Describe the event to a partner. Switch roles. Use adverbs in your descriptions.

> The coach yells angrily at the players.

Write About a Performance

Study the Models When you tell about a performance you have seen, you can use **adverbs** to let your readers know how, where, and when things happen. Adverbs add details to your writing and make it more interesting.

JUST OK

> We go to a concert. The band starts to play. The singer sings the first song. After the song, the audience claps **wildly**.

This is just OK because the writer uses only one **adverb**.

BETTER

> We go to a concert **downtown**. The band starts to play **loudly** and **clearly**. The singer sings the first song **perfectly**. **Immediately** after the song, the audience claps **wildly**.

The extra **adverbs** add details. They tell where, when, and how things happen.

Revise It Work with a partner to improve the following passage. Add more adverbs that tell how, where, and when.

> The curtain rises. Two actors stand in the middle of the stage. They begin to speak. They play their parts. The audience laughs. The play is great. It is called "Mister Monster"!

▲ **Ms. Rosario and Ygor pull the rope firmly.**

✎ WRITE ON YOUR OWN Write about a play or another type of performance that you have seen. Be sure to include adverbs.

REMEMBER

• Use an adverb to describe a verb. Adverbs often end in **-ly**.

• Use an adverb to make an adjective or adverb stronger.

Compare Across Texts

Compare Themes in Different Media

Monsters are featured in cartoons, TV shows, movies, and books. Compare the **themes** of **classic** monster tales.

How It Works

Collect and Organize Ideas To compare **themes** of different monster stories, organize your ideas in a chart. Add one **classic** monster story you have seen on TV or film. Tell what it's about. Then tell one **theme**, or message it says about life.

Comparison Chart

	What It's About	One Theme
"Frankenstein"	A scientist creates a monster that promises to make him unhappy.	You can never make up for the harm you do to others.
The Wolf Man movie	A man becomes a werewolf after he tries to save someone.	You cannot be rewarded for doing a good deed.

Practice Together

Study and Describe Write a paragraph to compare the **themes** of two **classic** monster stories, including one from a movie or TV show. Include appropriate details from your chart.

> The story "Frankenstein" and the movie The Wolf Man have different themes. Dr. Frankenstein treats his creation badly, and the monster threatens him. The story shows that you cannot make up for the harm you do to others. In contrast, the main character in The Wolf Man becomes a werewolf after he tries to help someone. The story proves that you cannot be rewarded for doing a good deed.

Try It!

Write a paragraph to compare two other **classic** monster stories. You may want to use this frame to express your ideas.

The story of _____ is about _____. The message is _____. In contrast, the story of _____ is _____. The message it tells about life is _____.

Academic Vocabulary
- **theme** (thēm) *noun*
  A **theme** is the main message of a story.
- **classic** (kla-sik) *adjective*
  Something that is **classic** is old but good.

CREEPY CLASSICS

 GUIDING QUESTION How can a powerful character inspire a range of reactions?

UNIT LIBRARY

Content Library

Peering into **Darkness**

Leveled Library

FRANKENSTEIN · THE METAMORPHOSIS · OTHELLO
JULIUS LESTER

Reflect on Your Reading

Think back on your reading of the unit selections. Discuss what you did to understand what you read.

Focus on Genre **Elements of Fiction**

In this unit, you learned about plot, characters, and setting. Choose one of the fiction selections and make a Plot Diagram. Use your diagram to describe the plot, characters, and setting to a partner.

Reading Strategy **Visualize**

As you read, you learned to visualize. Explain to a partner how you will use this strategy in the future.

Explore the GUIDING QUESTION

Throughout this unit, you have been thinking about the characters of classic monster stories. Choose one of these ways to explore the Guiding Question:

- **Discuss** With a group, discuss the Guiding Question. Talk about how you reacted to the characters in the different selections. Which character inspired the most powerful reaction in you? Give details from the text to explain.
- **Create a Character** Imagine you are a movie producer. What character can you create that would inspire strong reactions in people? Draw or make a model of your character and present it to a group. How do your classmates react to it?
- **Role-Play** With a partner, role-play Ms. Rosario, Miss Petal, or Ygor meeting one of the movie monsters from "Film Fright" for the first time.

Book Talk

Which Unit Library book did you choose? Explain to a partner what it taught you about classic monsters.

▼ A scientist explores Lechuguilla Cave in New Mexico.

The Drive to Discover

 **GUIDING QUESTION** How do discoveries change us and the world?

Read More!

Content Library

Earth, Sun, Moon
by Glen Phelan

Leveled Library

Dr. Jekyll and Mr. Hyde
by Robert Louis Stevenson, adapted by Kate McMullan

Can You Feel the Thunder?
by Lynn E. McElfresh

Breaking Through
by Francisco Jiménez

**Internet
InsideNG.com**

- Go to the Digital Library to explore places of discovery.
- Find out how scientists make discoveries about the world.
- View maps of discovery and exploration from the Library of Congress.

Focus on Genre

Organization of Ideas

▶ **In Sequence**
▶ **By Main Ideas and Details**

In fiction and nonfiction, writers **organize** their ideas in different ways. Understanding the organization will help you follow the writer's ideas and remember details.

How It Works

Before you read, preview the text to figure out the topic and see what type of writing it is. This will often give you a clue to the organization.

In Sequential Order A writer may want you to understand the order in which events happen. If so, the writer may organize ideas in time **sequence**. Study this example and watch for **time words**.

Cavern Exploration

Last summer, my family and I went to the Grand Canyon Caverns in Arizona. I didn't know what we would find. First, we took an elevator ride down 210 feet underground. Then we walked into the huge cave. During our tour, a scientist told us that the bones and prints from animals that lived long ago have been found there.

Time words help to show the order of events. Some time words are:

after	next
finally	soon
first	then

Ordered by Main Idea and Details Sometimes writers want to explain something. A writer might state a **main idea** and then provide several <u>details</u> to explain more.

The Grand Canyon Caverns

Scientists have made many discoveries inside the Grand Canyon Caverns. They found prints and bones of the giant ground sloth and now know more about this extinct animal. Scientists have also discovered a dead but well-preserved bobcat and a new type of cave cricket. What will they discover next?

Main Idea

Details

Academic Vocabulary

● **organize** (**or**-gu-nīz) *verb*
   To **organize** is to put things in a certain order.
● **sequence** (**sē**-kwens) *noun*
   The **sequence** of events is the order in which the events happen.

Practice Together

Read the following passages aloud. As you read, listen for clues that show how each is organized.

A Rainy Discovery

Walter Peck discovered a secret cave one rainy night in 1927. He was going to visit some friends when he slipped and almost fell into a large hole. The next day, he returned to the spot with his friends. They tied a rope around one man's waist and then lowered him into the hole. The man went down 150 feet. Finally, he reached the floor of the hole. The rocks in the cave sparkled like gold. Soon many people knew about Walter Peck's discovery—now called the Grand Canyon Caverns.

A Visit to the Grand Canyon Caverns

Many visitors see fascinating sights as they tour the Grand Canyon Caverns each year. They take an elevator 210 feet down to view the caverns. They enter the main room, which is bigger than a football field. As they explore the caverns, they see Snowball Palace and The Giant's Keyhole. Visitors also learn how the caves were formed during the past 35 million years!

Try It!

Read the following passages aloud. How is each passage organized? How do you know?

Summer Vacation

Last summer, I went on a wonderful trip to Arizona with my family. On the first day, we went into the Grand Canyon Caverns. It was dark and my little brother got scared. The next day, we went for a hike above ground. The desert sun was very bright and hot—even the lizards stayed in the shade! On the final day, we took a horseback trip. We rode to a waterfall. The horses were very friendly, and the waterfall was cool and beautiful.

Exploring a Cave

Exploring a cave is a lot of fun, but you must be well-prepared. Caves are dark, so you need a good, strong light. A helmet with a light is best, because it protects your head and leaves your hands free. You should wear waterproof shoes because caves can be wet—some even have streams and waterfalls. Make sure you have warm clothes and plenty of snacks. A backpack is good for carrying these supplies. Most important, never go into a cave alone!

Focus on Vocabulary

Use Word Parts

Words that share the same base word look **similar**. But a **prefix** or a **suffix** added to a **base word** makes a word with a different meaning.

EXAMPLES

The prefix *re-* means "again."

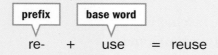

re- + use = reuse

Reuse means "to use again."

The suffix *-ful* means "full of."

use + -ful = useful

Useful means "full of use."

How the Strategy Works

When you read, you may come to a word you don't know. Look for word parts to help you understand the meaning.

EXAMPLE   We **reuse** paper bags.

1. Look closely at the word to see if you know any of the parts.
2. Cover any prefixes or suffixes.   re**use**
3. Think about the meaning of the base word.
4. Uncover any prefixes or suffixes and determine their meanings.
5. Put the meanings of the word parts together to understand the whole word. Be sure the meaning makes sense in the passage.

Use the strategy to figure out the meaning of each underlined word.

> What is it like to climb Mt. Everest, the world's tallest mountain? Samantha Larson, an 18-year-old from California, knows. Samantha, her father, and several <u>helpful</u> guides made the climb in 2007. During the climb, they often had to test and <u>retest</u> their equipment to make sure it was safe. After a month of climbing, they reached the top of the mountain. What a <u>joyful</u> occasion!

Strategy in Action

" I see the suffix *-ful* in this word. I'll cover it. There is the base word *help*. I know *-ful* means 'full of.' So *help* + *-ful* means 'full of help.' "

☑ **REMEMBER** You can use the meanings of word parts to figure out the meaning of an unknown word.

Academic Vocabulary
- **similar** (si-mu-lur) *adjective*
  Things that are **similar** are almost the same.

Practice Together

Read this passage aloud. Look at each underlined word. Find the word parts. Put their meanings together to figure out the meaning of the underlined word.

So Much to Discover on EARTH

People have often gone to new places because they want to <u>discover</u> something new. A discovery can be many things. It can be a place that someone sees for the first time. It can be art that was lost for thousands of years. It can even be a new idea.

What lies at the bottom of the ocean? What treasures are hidden deep in the earth? <u>Scientists</u> who ask <u>thoughtful</u> questions like these sometimes find important answers. They write about their findings so people in the world can learn more.

Try It!

Read this passage aloud. What is the meaning of each underlined word? How do you know?

Dive into Monterey Bay

Most ocean floors on earth are too deep for a human <u>diver</u> to reach. But in Monterey Bay, a robot travels to the very bottom of the sea to learn about life down deep. This little <u>traveler</u> takes pictures of <u>unusual</u> sea creatures, including one that sends out a glow-in-the-dark

▲ The robot is launched from a research ship.

cloud to scare away its enemies! The robot has also placed a tool on the ocean floor to learn about earthquakes. Scientists are <u>hopeful</u> that they will gather a lot of valuable information from this robot.

Return to Titanic

by Susan E. Goodman

SELECTION 1 OVERVIEW

▶ **Build Background**

▶ **Language & Grammar**
Ask for and
Give Information
Use Present and Past
Tense Verbs

▶ **Prepare to Read**
Learn Key Vocabulary
Learn a Reading
Strategy
Ask Questions

▶ **Read and Write**
Focus on Genre
History Article
Apply the
Reading Strategy
Ask Questions
Critical Thinking
Reading Fluency
Read with Intonation
Vocabulary Review
Write About the
Guiding Question

▶ **Connect Across the Curriculum**

Literary Analysis
Analyze Text Structure:
Sequence

Vocabulary Study
Use Word Parts

Media/Speaking
View the Wreck
of *Titanic*

Listening/Speaking
Conduct a Career
Interview

Language & Grammar
Ask for and
Give Information

Writing & Grammar
Write About the Past

Build Background

See Discoveries in Action

What does it feel like to make a discovery? Robert Ballard knows. In 1985, he discovered the wreck of *Titanic.* This big, beautiful ship sank on its first trip in 1912.

Connect

Team Brainstorm You are an explorer on Robert Ballard's team in 1985. You know that *Titanic* sank 12,000 feet to the bottom of the ocean. You want to find *Titanic*, but if you search for it you will be in danger. What does your team of explorers decide to do? Why?

Digital Library

InsideNG.com
⊘ View the video.

▲ A 1912 postcard shows *Titanic*'s great size.

Language & Grammar

1 TRY OUT LANGUAGE
2 LEARN GRAMMAR
3 APPLY ON YOUR OWN

Ask for and Give Information

CD

Listen to the chant and the interview.
Chime in on the chant, and role-play the interview.

CHANT and INTERVIEW

Get the Facts

Get the facts. Get them now.
Ask *Who? What? When? Where? Why?* and *How?*

▲ An iceberg in the North Atlantic Ocean

What was *Titanic*?

> *Titanic* was a huge ship. It was built in 1912.
> On its first trip, it sank.

How did *Titanic* sink?

> *Titanic* sank because it hit an iceberg.
> It broke into two pieces.

Who discovered the lost ship?

> Robert Ballard discovered the lost ship.

Where was *Titanic* found?

> *Titanic* was found at the bottom of the Atlantic.

When did Ballard find the ship?

> Ballard found the ship in 1985. He looked for it
> for many years.

Why was *Titanic* famous?

> *Titanic* was famous because it was the biggest ship ever built.

▼ *Titanic*, 1912

Use Present and Past Tense Verbs

The tense, or time, of a **verb** shows when an action happens.

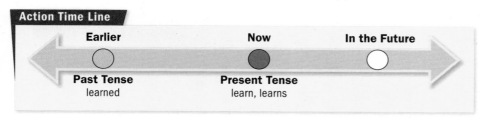

Action Time Line

Earlier	Now	In the Future
Past Tense	**Present Tense**	
learned	learn, learns	

- Use the **present tense** to tell about an action that happens now or often.

    EXAMPLES   Scientists **learn** about the ocean every day. *(happens often)*

    Today, they **look** for an old ship at the bottom of the ocean. *(happens now)*

    Use **-s** at the end of a verb that tells what one other person or thing does.

    EXAMPLE   My friend **learns** about the ship, too.

- Use the **past tense** to tell about an action that has already happened.

    EXAMPLES   Yesterday, we **looked** at a video about the ship.

    Last week, we **learned** about the divers on the team.

    Add **-ed** to most verbs when you talk about a past action.

    learn + -ed = learned   look + -ed = looked

Practice Together

Change the verb in the box to the past tense. Say it. Then say the sentence and add the past tense verb.

1. | call | One diver _____ out, "Let's go!"
2. | jump | Then all the divers _____ into the water.
3. | start | They _____ their search for the old ship.
4. | stay | They _____ together for safety.

Try It!

Change the verb in the box to the past tense. Write the past tense verb on a card. Then say the sentence and add the past tense verb.

5. | discover | The divers _____ the ship near the shore.
6. | hunt | They _____ for a way in.
7. | open | One diver _____ an old, rusted window.
8. | reach | She _____ inside the window.

▲ Divers discover an old ship.

Explore the Ocean

ASK FOR AND GIVE INFORMATION

There is a lot to learn about the ocean. What do you want to find out about it? Do you want to know more about lost ships, animals in the ocean, or how people use the ocean?

Work with a team to complete a question chart. Write six questions, one for each question word.

Question Chart

Question Word	The Answer Will Be	Question
Who?	a person	Who keeps the treasures from a lost ship?
What?	a thing	
When?	a time	
Where?	a place	
Why?	a reason	
How?	an explanation	

Then trade questions with another team. Find out the answers to their questions. Share your questions and answers with the whole group.

HOW TO ASK FOR AND GIVE INFORMATION

1. When you want information, you ask questions. Start your questions with *Who, What, When, Where, Why,* or *How.*
2. When you give information, you tell your main point and give some details.

> How did the divers discover the ship?

> They talked to people on the island. An old man pointed to a place on their map.

USE PRESENT AND PAST TENSE VERBS

When you give information, you may tell about something that happens often. If so, use a verb in the **present tense** . Or you may tell about something that already happened. If so, use a verb in the **past tense** .

In the Present: Who **looks** for old ships?

Scientists and treasure hunters **look** for old ships.

In the Past: Who **looked** for this old ship?

A scientist **looked** for this ship. He **wanted** to learn more about the ancient culture.

Prepare to Read

Learn Key Vocabulary

Rate and Study the Words Rate how well you know each word. Then:

1. Pronounce the word. Say it aloud several times. Spell it.
2. Study the example.
3. Tell more about the word.
4. Practice it. Make the word your own.

Key Words

alarm (u-larm) *noun*
▶ page 290

An **alarm** warns people of danger. A smoke detector is one kind of **alarm**.

discover (dis-ku-vur) *verb*
▶ page 292

To **discover** means to find something that is lost or hidden. The boy **discovers** a starfish at the beach.

explorer (ik-**splor**-ur) *noun*
▶ page 292

An **explorer** travels somewhere to study something. **Explorers** find out what is special about a new place.
Base Word: **explore**

famous (**fā**-mus) *adjective*
▶ page 288

Something that is **famous** is very well known. Many people have seen the **famous** Statue of Liberty.
Base Word: **fame**

ocean (**ō**-shun) *noun*
▶ page 290

An **ocean** is a large area or body of salt water. **Oceans** cover most of the Earth.

passenger (pa-sen-jur) *noun* ▶ page 288

When you ride in a car, boat, or other vehicle, you are a **passenger**. The bus driver took ten **passengers** to the school.

search (surch) *verb, noun*
▶ page 292

1 *verb* When you **search** for something, you look for it. You might **search** for something you lost.
2 *noun* A **search** is the act of looking for something.

wreck (rek) *noun*
▶ page 293

A **wreck** is what is left after a crash. A **shipwreck** is a broken ship that crashed.

Practice the Words Make a Study Card for each Key Word. Then compare your cards with a partner's.

wreck

What it means: what is left after a crash

Example: car after an accident

Not an example: new car

Study Card

Reading Strategy: Ask Questions

Do you ever wonder about something when you read? Do you ever get confused? Then ask yourself a question, and look for the answer in the text.

HOW TO SELF-QUESTION

1. As you read, ask yourself questions about the text.

2. Ask questions based on the 5Ws and H: *Who?*, *What?*, *When?*, *Where?*, *Why?*, and *How?* Write your questions on sticky notes.

3. To find the answers, you can usually reread or read on. If the answer is not in the text, look in another resource or ask someone else.

Strategy in Action

Here's how one student asked questions.

Look Into the Text

How big was Titanic?

It was as long as four city blocks.

" To answer, I just **read on**. The answer is right there. "

The Wonder Ship

On April 10, 1912, hundreds of people packed a dock in Southampton, England. They came to see *Titanic*, a ship that was about to leave on its first trip. And what a ship it was!

Titanic was the largest ship in the world—as long as four city blocks. Many people called it the "wonder ship." It was like a floating palace, with a swimming pool, carved wood, and fancy gold lights. It also had many rich and famous passengers who wanted to be the first to ride on this great ship.

Why was Titanic such a great ship?

It had a pool and fancy things.

" To answer, I had to **reread** the text. "

Practice Together

Reread the passage about *Titanic* and ask yourself two questions. Follow the steps in the How-To box. Put your sticky notes by the text above.

History Article

A history article tells about real events that happened in the past. The **headings** in the article tell what each part is about.

Many history articles present information in **sequence**. Look for **time words** that show the order of events.

> # The Wonder Ship ⟨ heading
>
> On April 10, 1912, hundreds of people packed a dock in Southampton, England. They came to see *Titanic*, a ship that was about to leave on its first trip.

Your Job as a Reader

Reading Strategy: Ask Questions

As you read, ask questions. Pay attention to the headings so you know what each part is about. You can even turn a heading into questions by using the 5W and H words.

> HEADING
>
> ## The Wonder Ship
>
> QUESTIONS
>
> **What** was the wonder ship?
> **Why** was the ship a wonder?

Return to
Titanic

by Susan E. Goodman

Titanic was meant to be the biggest and best ship of its day, but it sank on its first trip. Yet it is still the best-known boat on Earth.

The broken ship still sits at the bottom of the ocean. ▶

Online Coach

The Wonder Ship

On April 10, 1912, hundreds of people **packed a dock** in Southampton, England. They came to see *Titanic*, a ship that was about to leave on its first trip. And what a ship it was!

Titanic was the largest ship in the world—as long as four city blocks. Many people called it the "wonder ship." It was like a floating **palace**, with a swimming pool, carved wood, and fancy gold lights. It also had many rich and **famous passengers** who wanted to be the first to ride on this great ship.

▲ One of *Titanic's* grand stairways

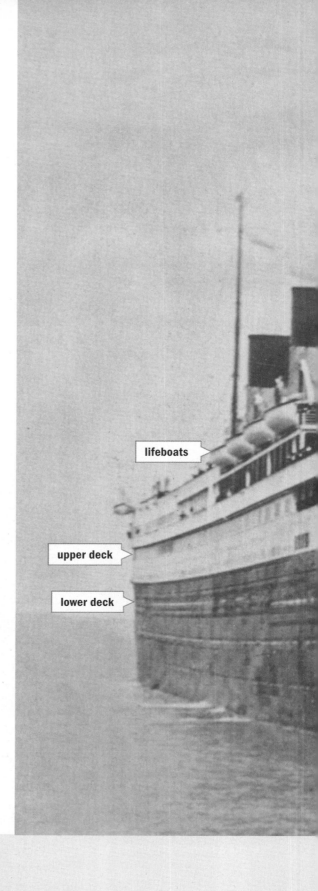

lifeboats

upper deck

lower deck

Key Vocabulary
famous *adj.*, very well known
passenger *n.*, someone who rides in or on a vehicle, such as a boat, bus, or car

In Other Words
packed a dock filled the place where a ship stops
palace house that is very large and fancy

▽ *Titanic* left England for New York in 1912. Poor passengers had to stay in the lower decks. Only the rich could use the top four decks.

passengers

Before You Move On

1. **Details** What made *Titanic* a floating palace?
2. **Text Features** What information do you learn from the caption on this page?

Danger Ahead!

Titanic **set off for** New York. At first, the ride was like a party. By April 14, the ship was in the middle of the Atlantic **Ocean**. That night, the weather was clear, and stars twinkled against the dark sky. On the ship, people danced late into the night. No one knew that danger was near.

Shortly before midnight, a sailor **on lookout** saw something in the darkness. He knew it could be only one thing. It was an iceberg, a floating mountain of ice. The sailor raised the **alarm**: "Iceberg ahead!" Next, the **crew** tried to turn *Titanic* away from the iceberg, but it was too late. Finally, the ship scraped along the ice.

Hulton archive, Getty Images; Illustration by Ken Marschall © 1992, from *Titanic: An Illustrated History*. A Hyperion/Madison Press book.

passengers in a lifeboat

▲ After the ship broke apart, it sank 12,000 feet to the bottom of the ocean.

Key Vocabulary
ocean *n.*, a large body of salt water
alarm *n.*, a signal to warn people of danger

In Other Words
set off for began sailing to
on lookout watching for problems
crew workers

Water Rushes In

The problem did not seem too bad at first. Then water started pouring into the ship, and nothing could stop it. The ship was going to sink!

The crew tried to get help. They shot off fireworks to **attract** the attention of nearby ships. Crew members on those ships thought the fireworks were for fun, so they did not stop to help.

Passengers began climbing into the lifeboats on *Titanic*. Women and children mostly went first, but there was not enough room for everyone. When the last lifeboat was lowered into the water, there were still 1,500 people on the sinking ship.

A Ship Torn Apart

Soon passengers heard a terrible sound. It was the sound of the ship **ripping apart**. The ship sank just 20 minutes later, with most of the passengers and crew still on board.

▲ A newsboy in London sells papers telling about the **disaster**. The disaster **shocked** people around the world.

In Other Words
attract get
ripping apart breaking into pieces
disaster horrible event
shocked surprised and saddened

Before You Move On

1. **Cause and Effect** Why did the ship sink?
2. **Explain** What happened to the **passengers** when the ship went down?
3. **Inference** Do you think most of the people who lived through the disaster were men or women? How do you know?

A Boy's Dream

Titanic sank to the ocean floor and stayed there for 71 years. Then Robert Ballard set out to find it. As a kid, Ballard had loved reading about *Titanic*. "My dream," he says, "was to find this great ship."

Ballard became an ocean **explorer** and **studied the ocean floor**. Although he made many discoveries, he never forgot his dream: he still wanted to find *Titanic*. People said it was impossible. They said that the shipwreck was too deep, but Ballard did not agree.

Hunting for Titanic

In 1985, Ballard **teamed up** with a French scientist and began his **search** for *Titanic*. The two men sailed to where *Titanic* had sunk. They used **high-tech** tools to **search** the ocean floor. For weeks, they found nothing. Then they sent down Argo, an underwater machine that took pictures and sent them back to the crew.

Argo searched the ocean for a few days without finding anything. Then a big metal object came into view. It was a ship's engine. The team began to cheer. They knew that they had **discovered** *Titanic*!

▼ Robert Ballard and a crew member look at images of *Titanic* from their ship's control room.

Key Vocabulary

explorer *n.*, a person who goes to a new place to find out about it

search *n.*, the act of looking for something; *v.*, to look for something

discover *v.*, to find something that is lost or hidden

In Other Words

studied the ocean floor used tools to learn about the bottom of the ocean

teamed up worked

high-tech modern

A Closer Look

Ballard saw the bow, or front, of *Titanic* stuck in mud. He saw cups, beds, shoes, suitcases, and other objects from the ship. It was like visiting a museum. Ballard wanted to see more, but he had run out of time and had to return home.

In 1986, Ballard came back to the ship. This time, he traveled down to the **wreck**, riding in a submersible, which is an underwater craft. He brought a deep-sea robot that was able to look inside the ship.

▲ *Titanic* sank in 1912. Yet some of its windows are still unbroken.

Saving the Past

As Ballard explored *Titanic*, he took pictures of the shipwreck. He did not take anything away, though. He left things just as they were. Each object helps to tell the sad story of *Titanic*. ❖

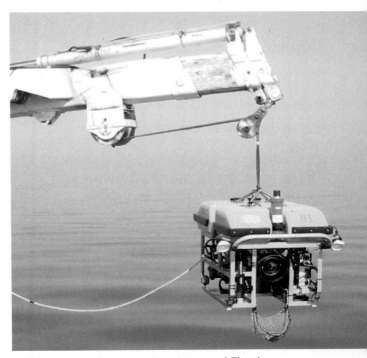

▲ This robot took underwater pictures of *Titanic*.

Key Vocabulary

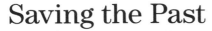

wreck *n.*, what is left of a ship or other vehicle after a crash

Language Background

The name *Titanic* comes from the word *titan*, meaning "a giant." With a partner, list other words to describe the gigantic ship.

Before You Move On

1. **Summarize** How did Ballard **discover** *Titanic*?
2. **Opinion** Do you think it was important to find the ship? Why or why not?
3. **Vocabulary** What other words are related to the word **explorer**?

Talking with Robert Ballard

▲ Robert Ballard

Robert Ballard has explored many parts of the ocean. In this interview, he talks about his work.

How did you get interested in ocean exploration?

I always loved the book *Twenty Thousand Leagues Under the Sea* by Jules Verne. It was all I could think about. I wanted to see what was deep in the ocean!

How did you become an explorer?

My parents wanted me to have a good education. I went to college and studied the ocean. Later, I joined the navy.

There have been many shipwrecks. What is special about *Titanic*?

Titanic's story interests people. The ship was full of people when it sank. Many were scared. Many were brave. Many were also very famous. People want to hear their stories. They want to know how we study the shipwreck.

Why is it a bad idea to take items from the wreck?

The objects are part of history. Seeing them in place tells a lot. For example, we can learn how the ship sank. That information is lost if you take things away from the wreck.

What was it like to find *Titanic*? How did you feel?

Finding *Titanic* was **a dream of mine**. So discovering it made me happy.

◄ Ballard found many objects on the wreck, including a passenger's watch.

In Other Words
a dream of mine one of my goals in my life

Before You Move On

1. **Text Features** In this interview, which text shows the questions? Which shows the answers?
2. **Judgment** Was Ballard right to leave all the items with the wreck? Why or why not?

Connect Reading and Writing

CRITICAL THINKING

1. SUM IT UP Make a card for each vocabulary word. Use at least five of the words to explain how Ballard explored the **ocean** to find *Titanic*.

famous

passenger

ocean

2. Analyze Describe *Titanic* to a friend. Use details from the text to give a clear picture. Tell why *Titanic* is **famous**.

3. Conclusion Which picture best shows why so many people wanted to **search** for *Titanic*? Support your conclusion.

4. Interpret Robert Ballard says, "Information is lost if you take things away from the **wreck**." Do you agree? Why or why not?

READING FLUENCY

Intonation Read the passage on page 580 to a partner. Assess your fluency.

1. I read
   a. great   **b.** OK   **c.** not very well

2. What I did best in my reading was _____ .

READING STRATEGY

Ask Questions
How did you find the answer to a question you asked during reading? Tell a partner.

Vocabulary
alarm
discover
explorer
famous
ocean
passengers
search
wreck

VOCABULARY REVIEW

Oral Review Read the paragraph aloud. Add the vocabulary words.

> Most ships are safe, but some ships face terrible danger. Sometimes there is no warning or _____ and a ship crashes into rocks. The ship may sink into the _____. The _____ may lose their lives. People may _____ for the _____ of a lost ship for many years before they _____ it. An _____ who studies a well-known, or _____, shipwreck can learn new information.

Written Review Imagine you are an **explorer**, diving to see the **wreck** of *Titanic*. Write a journal entry about it. Use five vocabulary words.

 **WRITE ABOUT THE** **GUIDING QUESTION**

Explore the Drive to Discover
Why do you think Robert Ballard put his life in danger to **discover** *Titanic*? Read the selection again. Support your opinion with examples from the text.

Connect Across the Curriculum

Analyze Text Structure: Sequence

> **Academic Vocabulary**
> • **sequence** (sē-kwens) *noun*
>   The **sequence** of events is the order in which the events happen.

How Is Writing Organized? Some writing is organized by time. Time words show when things happen and help readers put events in **sequence**.

Practice Together

Note Sequence As you read the passage, use the **time words** to identify the **sequence** of events.

> On April 10, 1912 . . . *Titanic* set off for New York. At first, the ride was like a party. By April 14, the ship was in the middle of the Atlantic Ocean. That night, the weather was clear. . . . Shortly before midnight, a sailor on lookout saw something in the darkness.

Make a Time Line The time line shows events from "Return to *Titanic*." What happened April 10, 1912? The answer is listed under the date.

Time Line

Sometimes several important events occur on the same date. Reread the part of the text that describes the events of April 14. Use the time words to identify the **sequence**. List these events on the time line.

Try It!

Finish the time line by rereading the rest of the text and using the time words. Be sure to add the discovery of *Titanic*.

Internet InsideNG.com
➔ Find out what has happened with *Titanic* recently. Add to the time line.

Give an Oral Presentation Use your time line to tell what happened to *Titanic*, in **sequence**. Use time words to tell

• a date or time, such as *April 14, 1912* or *at midnight*
• the order of events, such as *first, next,* and *then.*

Use Word Parts

Word Part	Meaning
dis-	the opposite of
un-	not; the opposite of
-able	can be done
-er, -or	one who
-ful	full of

Academic Vocabulary
- **similar** (si-mu-lur) *adjective*
  Things that are **similar** are almost the same.

Words that share the same base word can look **similar**. But a prefix or a suffix changes the meaning of the base word. For example:

- *pack* means "to put things in a container."
- *packer* means "someone who packs," because the suffix *-er* means "one who."
- *unpack* means "to take things out of a container." Explain how the meanings of the word parts add up to this definition.

Figure Out Word Meanings Work with a partner. Cover the prefix or suffix in each word. Find the base word. Uncover the prefix. What does it mean? Then put the meanings together and write the meaning of the word.

1. sailor
2. disappear
3. explorer
4. unclear
5. lovable
6. comfortable
7. visitor
8. hopeful

View the Wreck of *Titanic*

MEDIA & TECHNOLOGY

Academic Vocabulary
- **fact** (fakt) *noun*
  A **fact** is a piece of information that is true.

Use visual media to learn more about *Titanic*:

❶ **Locate Videos for Research** *Titanic* sank almost one hundred years ago. Find videos of the wreck online, and collect more **facts** about *Titanic*.

> **Internet** InsideNG.com
> ⊘ Take a virtual tour of *Titanic*.

❷ **View the Videos** Pay attention to details and **facts**. What kinds of plants and animals do you see? What parts of the ship do the videos show? Jot down words you want to look up, like *starboard* or *plankton*.

❸ **Discuss Your Findings** Share the **facts** you learned with a partner. Ask each other questions. Then discuss whether you would like to explore a shipwreck like *Titanic*.

▲ Ocean plants and animals now cover parts of *Titanic*.

Conduct a Career Interview

CAREER STUDY

Academic Vocabulary
- **interview** (**in**-tur-vyū) *noun*
  In an **interview**, one person finds out about another person by asking questions.

If you want to make discoveries about people, you can conduct an **interview**.

1 **Decide Whom to Interview** Tell the person what you want to learn. For example: "I want to find out about important discoveries that geologists make." Research your topic before the **interview**.

2 **Prepare the Questions** Basic questions will help you gather specific information about your topic. Open-ended questions will encourage more complex answers.

Basic Questions	Open-ended Questions
What is your job?	Why did you become a geologist?
How did you train for the job?	Why are rocks interesting?

Both types of questions are necessary to make your **interview** interesting and complete. Brainstorm with a small group to write some additional basic questions and open-ended questions.

3 **Practice the Interview** Role-play your **interview** with a partner. Ask questions. Your partner can provide imaginary answers to give you practice in asking questions and listening actively. Then switch roles.

4 **Conduct the Interview**
Follow these steps:
- Introduce yourself. Make eye contact.
- Ask your questions. Take notes or record the **interview**.
- Ask the person to explain any information that you don't understand.
- Thank the person for the **interview**.

▲ **Make eye contact with the person you interview.**

5 **Tell What You Discovered** Tell your class what you discovered during your **interview**. Speak clearly and slowly. Use tone and facial expressions to show that you are interested in the subject.

Ask for and Give Information

Role-Play With a group, act out a news conference with explorers of *Titanic*. Some of you ask questions as news reporters. The explorers answer. Use past tense verbs. Trade roles.

> Where did you search?

> We searched the part of the Atlantic Ocean near New York.

Write About the Past

Study the Models When you write about an event that already happened, you use verbs in the **past tense** . Once you choose a verb tense for your writing, stick with it.

NOT OK

> I **walk** through the door of the museum and **looked** at a boat that was 1000 years old! I **wanted** to know if it was real. So I **tap** on the side of the boat and **touched** the surface.

This writer confuses the reader by switching between **past tense** and **present tense** .

OK

> I **walked** through the door of the museum and **looked** at a boat that was 1000 years old! I **wanted** to know if it was real. So I **tapped** on the side of the boat and **touched** the surface.

This writer sticks to the **past tense** .

WRITE ON YOUR OWN Write about something you discovered when you were younger. Pay attention to the tense of your verbs. Check your verbs for correct spelling, too.

REMEMBER
- Use the past tense to tell about something that already happened.
- Many past tense verbs end in -**ed**.

    learn**ed**   walk**ed**

Spelling Rules

1. Often, you just have to add -**ed**.

look + -ed = looked   The guard **looked** right at me.

2. If a verb ends in silent **e**, drop the **e** before you add -**ed**.

like + -ed = liked   He **liked** his job.

3. If the verb has one syllable and ends in one vowel and one consonant, double the consonant.

plan + n + -ed = planned   He **planned** to walk to the museum.

4. If the verb ends in a consonant + **y**, change the **y** to **i**. Then add -**ed**.

study + -ed = studied   He **studied** ways to protect old ships.

The Forgotten Treasure

an adaptation of a Nigerian folk tale

Extended Family, 2006, Jimoh Buraimoh. Beads on board, Via Mundi Gallery, Atlanta, Georgia.

◩ Critical Viewing: Design How is this family portrait like others you have seen? How is it different?

SELECTION 2 OVERVIEW

▶ **Build Background**

▶ **Language & Grammar**
Engage in Discussion
Use Verb Tense:
Be and *Have*

▶ **Prepare to Read**
Learn Key Vocabulary
Learn a Reading Strategy
Ask Questions

▶ **Read and Write**
Focus on Genre
Folk Tale
Apply the Reading Strategy
Ask Questions
Critical Thinking
Reading Fluency
Read with Expression
Vocabulary Review
Write About the Guiding Question

▶ **Connect Across the Curriculum**
Literary Analysis
Analyze Text Structure: Sequence
Analyze Theme
Vocabulary Study
Use Word Parts
Research/Speaking
Discover Tools of the Past
Language and Grammar
Engage in Discussion
Writing and Grammar
Write About the Past

Build Background

Connect

Anticipation Guide Think about an object that is really important to you. What would you do if you lost it? Tell whether you agree or disagree with these statements.

Anticipation Guide

	Agree	Disagree
1. I would never forget about it. I would keep on looking and remembering, even after many years.	_____	_____
2. I don't worry about what is lost. I would find something new.	_____	_____

Meet a Griot

"The Forgotten Treasure" takes place in Nigeria. Nigeria has a long history of oral storytelling by griots. These storytellers, poets, and wandering musicians travel across the country, singing traditional songs and telling tales like this one.

Digital Library

InsideNG.com
◉ View the video.

Nigeria

Nigeria is in West Africa. ▲

Language & Grammar

Engage in Discussion

CD

Listen to the chant and chime in. Then listen to a discussion. In a discussion, you discover other people's ideas—agreeing with some and disagreeing with others. You share your own ideas, too.

CHANT and DISCUSSION

Talk It Over

Hear what others have to say.
You'll understand much more that way!
Focus on the topic—
That's what it's all about!
When it's your turn to speak,
Get the main points out.

Use Verb Tense: *Be* and *Have*

The tense of a verb tells when an action happens. The verbs *be* and *have* use special forms to tell about the **present** and the **past**.

Forms of *Be*	
Present Tense	**Past Tense**
I **am**	I **was**
you **are**	you **were**
he, she, or it **is**	he, she, or it **was**
we **are**	we **were**
they **are**	they **were**

Forms of *Have*	
Present Tense	**Past Tense**
I **have**	I **had**
you **have**	you **had**
he, she, or it **has**	he, she, or it **had**
we **have**	we **had**
they **have**	they **had**

Use the correct form of the verb.

EXAMPLES **Forms of *be***

Present: He **is** interested in folk tales.

Past: He **was** interested in folk tales.

Present: We **are** in eighth grade.

Past: We **were** in seventh grade.

EXAMPLES **Forms of *have***

Present: Our class **has** many students.

Past: Last year, our class **had** only a few students.

Present: The students **have** lots of stories to tell.

Past: Last year, we even **had** a folk tale festival.

▲ The friends have a lot of stories to share.

Practice Together

Say each sentence. Then say it again and change the verb to the past tense.

1. I <u>am</u> interested in folk tales.

2. Ana and I <u>are</u> storytellers.

3. We <u>have</u> a favorite story.

4. It <u>is</u> a tale from Mexico.

Try It!

Say each sentence. Write the past tense of the underlined verb on a card. Then say the sentence and add the past tense verb.

5. We <u>have</u> a folk tale performance.

6. Ana <u>has</u> the best voice!

7. I <u>am</u> good at different sounds.

8. The show <u>is</u> a success.

Discuss Stories

ENGAGE IN DISCUSSION

Are stories really that important? Discuss your ideas with a group.

HOW TO ENGAGE IN DISCUSSION

1. Give your ideas. Include examples to support them.
2. Ask and answer questions.
3. Show you are listening to other people's ideas. Respect their opinions.

> Stories are fun to hear, but I'm not sure they are that important.

> That's interesting. Why do you think that?

Remember that everyone can have different ideas. When you discuss ideas, you are just sharing what you think. Other people may agree or disagree.

USE VERB TENSE: *BE* AND *HAVE*

When you discuss ideas, be sure to use the correct form of *be* and *have*.

In the Present: I **am** a big fan of stories! Stories **are** important. I **have** a great book of fables. Each fable **has** a moral, or lesson. One moral **is** "There **is** always another side of the story."

In the Past: When I **was** little, I **had** a book of stories. They **were** all scary. The book **had** scary pictures in it, too. I **had** bad dreams from those stories! I **was** happy to give the book to my older cousin.

Prepare to Read

Learn Key Vocabulary

Rate and Study the Words Rate how well you know each word. Then:

1. Pronounce the word. Say it aloud several times. Spell it.
2. Study the example.
3. Tell more about the word.
4. Practice it. Make the word your own.

Key Words

beautiful (byū-ti-ful)
adjective ▸ page 310

Something that is **beautiful** is very pretty. The flowers are **beautiful**.
Base Word: **beauty**

forest (for-ust) *noun*
▸ page 309

A **forest** is a place that has lots of trees.
Synonym: **woods**

forget (fur-get) *verb*
▸ page 308

When you **forget** something, you stop thinking about it. The boy leaves without his shoes. He **forgets** them.
Past tense: **forgot**
Past participle: **forgotten**

locate (lō-kāt) *verb*
▸ page 312

To **locate** something is to find it. The woman tries to **locate** something she lost.

loss (laws) *noun*
▸ page 309

When you no longer have something important, you feel the **loss**. A terrible **loss** is the death of a loved one.

remember (ri-mem-bur)
verb ▸ page 308

When you **remember** something, you think of it again later. The man goes to the monument and **remembers** his friend who died.

skeleton (ske-lu-tun) *noun*
▸ page 312

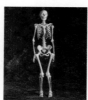

A **skeleton** is the set of bones in an animal or a person. The model shows a human **skeleton**.

treasure (tre-zhur) *noun*
▸ page 308

A **treasure** is something very special and important. These decorated eggs are **treasures**.

Practice the Words Work with a partner. Write a question using two Key Words. Answer your partner's question. Use at least one Key Word in your answer. Keep going until you have used all of the Key Words twice.

Questions	Answers
Do you remember how to locate your house?	Yes. I will never forget my address.

Reading Strategy: Ask Questions

When you read, ask yourself questions about the text. Then look for the answers. Sometimes the answer to a question is right there in the text. Other times you have to link the details to find the answer.

Reading Strategy
Ask Questions

HOW TO FIND ANSWERS TO YOUR QUESTIONS

1. As you read, ask yourself questions. Write them down. Begin with *Who, What, Where, When, Why,* and *How.*

2. Read the text to find any answers that are right there. See the example on the blue note below.

3. If the answer is not there, think about the details. Try to put them together to come up with the answer. See the example on the yellow note below.

Strategy in Action

Here's how one student found answers.

Look Into the Text

Who is this story about?
It's about a hunter, his wife, and their sons.

Once there was a hunter who lived with his wife and their four sons. Each son had eyes like shiny black stones. The hunter looked at his sons and smiled. "Some men have gold, but my sons are better than gold. They are my treasures."

Every morning, the hunter said to his family, "You are all my treasures. If you care about me, remember me always."

"I can point to the text and show that the answer is right there."

Why does the father tell his sons what to do?

"I link details. He cares about his sons and wants them to care, also."

Practice Together

Now ask a question of your own. Then look for details that will help you answer it. Is the answer right there in the text? Or do you have to put details together to get it?

Folk Tale

A folk tale is a story that has been told and retold for many years. The words and actions of the **characters** , or people in the story, show what is important.

> Once there was a hunter who lived with his wife and their four sons. Each son had eyes like shiny black stones. The hunter looked at his sons and smiled. "Some men have gold, but my sons are better than gold."

The events of a folk tale usually happen **in sequence**. Look for time words to help you know when things happen.

Your Job as a Reader

Reading Strategy: Ask Questions

As you read, ask questions about the folk tale. For example, you may want to ask questions about the characters.

> QUESTION
>
> Why are sons better than gold?

The Forgotten Treasure

an adaptation of a Nigerian folk tale

Extended Family, 2006, Jimoh Buraimoh. Beads on board, Via Mundi Gallery, Atlanta, Georgia.

▲ Critical Viewing: Design   How is this family portrait like others you have seen? How is it different?

A man leaves his family to go hunting. Find out what happens.

Once there was a hunter who lived with his wife and their four sons. Each son had eyes like shiny black stones. The hunter looked at his sons and smiled. "Some men have gold, but my sons are better than gold. They are my **treasures**."

The hunter's wife was going to have a fifth baby. Sometimes she could feel it kick. "It will be another boy," she would say. "Another **fine** boy, just like his brothers."

Every morning, the hunter said to his family, "You are all my treasures. If you care about me, **remember** me always."

Every morning, his sons would say, "Father, we do not need to remember you. Every day you go out, but every day you come back. You are always here, so how could we ever **forget** you?"

African Hunter, 2002, Emmanuel Yeboa. Oils and batik on calico, courtesy of Novica, Los Angeles.

△ **Critical Viewing: Character** Which character in the folk tale could this be? Explain.

Key Vocabulary
treasure *n.*, something that has great value or importance
remember *v.*, to keep in mind; to think of again
forget *v.*, to stop thinking about someone or something

In Other Words
fine good

One day, the hunter went out into the **forest** with **his spear, his bow, and his arrows**. At the end of the day, he did not come home. His wife and his four sons stayed up all night waiting for him, but still he didn't come home. A week passed but still he did not come home. His wife and his sons cried for their **loss**.

Weeks went by, but the hunter did not come home. His wife and his four sons dried their tears.

A month went by and the hunter still did not come home. His wife and his four sons forgot about him. They forgot all about the hunter with his spear, his bow, and his arrows.

Many months went by. The new baby boy was born, and he was just like his brothers. The baby grew. First, he **crawled**. Then he walked. But he did not play.

Through the Window, 1992, Tilly Willis. Oil on canvas, private collection.

▲ **Critical Viewing: Character** Which sentence in the folk tale do you think goes best with this painting? Explain why you think so.

In Other Words
his spear, his bow, and his arrows the tools that he used for hunting
crawled moved on his hands and knees

Before You Move On

1. **Vocabulary** The father says that his sons are his "**treasures**." What does he mean?
2. **Sequence** What happens when the hunter does not come home? What happens a month later?

Every day, the mother gave the little boy a shiny stone or a **beautiful** feather, but the boy would not even look at it. Every day, the brothers took turns trying to find him something nice. One day it was a colorful leaf. Another day it was a smooth red shell. Still another day it was a sparkling spider web. But the boy would not look at the gifts.

"I want our treasure," said the little boy.

His family laughed. "We have no treasure!" they said in **response**. "We are just an ordinary family."

The little boy looked at his mother and told her again, "I want our treasure!"

"Little one," said the mother, with a smile. "Today you want a treasure. Tomorrow you will forget and want something good to eat. That is how it is with little ones."

The little boy, whose eyes were like shiny black stones, looked at his four brothers. "I want our treasure," he said. "Don't you want our treasure, too?"

They covered their faces with their hands. "Oh! Our treasure! We forgot him! We forgot all about him! He went into the forest and never came home."

The mother said, "My sons, you must find your father."

The next morning, the four brothers set off together into the forest. First, they found a spear on the ground. Then they found the bow and arrows. Next, they found the hunter's white bones, which were almost covered by fallen leaves.

Key Vocabulary
beautiful *adj.*, very pretty

In Other Words
response answer
They covered their faces with their hands. They felt ashamed, or bad about themselves.

African Sunset, 2005, Angela Ferreira. Oil on canvas, collection of the artist.

▲ **Critical Viewing: Setting** Describe the setting of this painting.

Before You Move On

1. **Confirm Prediction** Was your prediction correct? What happened that you did not expect?
2. **Inference** Why doesn't the little boy want the gifts from his mother and brothers?
3. **Cause and Effect** What causes the brothers to **remember** their father?

And so the sons **located** their father, but how could they help him? The first brother said, "It's a good thing I know how to bring the bones together!" As he sang over his father's bones, the bones jumped up and made a **skeleton**.

The second brother said, "It's a good thing I know how to put skin on the bones!" As he sang over his father's skeleton, skin covered the bones.

The third brother said, "It's a good thing I know how to put life into the body!" As he sang over his father's body, the hunter's heart began to beat.

Egungun costume and mask, Nigerian Yoruba culture.

△ Critical Viewing: Design What details make this object like a painting? How is the object different from a painting?

Key Vocabulary

locate *v.*, to find exactly where something or someone is

skeleton *n.*, all the bones of an animal or person

The fourth brother said, "It's a good thing I know how to make the body move!" As he sang to his father's heart, the hunter sat up and looked around.

"Where have I been?" the father asked. His sons answered, "You were lost, but we have found you."

The father smiled at his sons. "You are my treasures," he said. Then he picked up his spear, his bow, and his arrows and went home with his sons.

At first, the wife was happy to see her husband. Then she looked away from him **in shame**. "You were gone for so long that we forgot you," she said.

"You are my treasures."

The hunter smiled at his wife. "You are my treasure," he said. He sat down by the fire, picked up a knife and a lump of wood, and began to **carve**. His sons watched him. He carved all night. He carved for a week. He carved for a month. He carved for a year.

The hunter made the most beautiful carving that his wife and sons had ever seen. The carving showed every animal in the forest. It showed every tree and every flower.

The father looked at his family. "This carving is for the one who saved my life," he said.

In Other Words
in shame because she felt bad
carve cut shapes onto the wood

Father and Son, 1989, Paul Nzalamba. Batik, collection of the artist.

▲ **Critical Viewing: Character** What are the characters in this painting like?

His wife said, "Then it is mine. I sent your sons to find you."

The first brother said, "No, it is mine. I put your bones back together."

The second brother said, "No, it is mine. I put skin back on your bones."

The third brother said, "No, it is mine. I made your heart beat again."

The fourth brother said, "No, it is mine. I made you move again."

The hunter looked at them all. He smiled and shook his head. "No," he said. "This is for the little one. He is the one who remembered me. As long as a person is remembered and treasured by someone, he is not really lost." The hunter lifted the fifth son onto his knee. Then he put the beautiful carving into his son's hands. ❖

Stories and Storytellers

Charlotte Blake Alston

No one knows who made up "The Forgotten Treasure," but people have been telling stories like it for thousands of years. In West Africa, a storyteller is called a *griot* (**grē-ō**). Stories are not written down, so griots must be able to remember them all. Griots are also the keepers of history.

Today, many American storytellers tell stories aloud. **Charlotte Blake Alston** gathers folk tales from West Africa. She visits schools to share the stories. Alston uses the "power of the voice" when she performs.

Before You Move On

1. **Confirm Prediction** Was your prediction about the hunter coming home correct?
2. **Opinion** Does this story have a happy ending? Explain.

There Is No Word for Goodbye

by Mary Tall Mountain

Sokoya, I said, looking through
the net of wrinkles into
wise black pools
of her eyes.
5   What do you say in Athabaskan
when you leave each other?
What is the word
for goodbye?
A shade of feeling rippled
10   the wind-tanned skin.
Ah, nothing, she said,
watching the river flash.
She looked at me close.
We just say, Tlaa. That means,
15   See you.
We never leave each other.
When does your mouth
say goodbye to your heart?

She touched me light
20   as a bluebell.
You forget when you leave us,
You're so small then.
We don't use that word.
We always think you're coming back,
25   but if you don't,
we'll see you some place else.
You understand.
There is no word for goodbye.

In Other Words
Sokoya Aunt (in Athabaskan)
Athabaskan your Native American
    language
rippled moved
bluebell flower

Before You Move On

1. **Inference** Is Sokoya young or old? Find details that go with your answer.
2. **Opinion** Do you think the speaker **forgets** about people when they leave? Explain.

Connect Reading and Writing

Vocabulary

beautiful

forest

forget

located

loss

remember

skeletons

treasures

CRITICAL THINKING

1. SUM IT UP Ask a partner to role-play a character from "The Forgotten Treasure." Conduct an interview with the character. Ask questions about the important parts of the story.

> What did your father tell you every morning?

> He said we were his treasures.

2. Explain Look again at the Anticipation Guide on page 300. Do you want to change your responses? With a group, discuss if you prefer to **remember** or **forget** about something you lose. Tell why.

3. Compare Tell about the **loss** and the discovery in "The Forgotten Treasure" and "There Is No Word for Goodbye."

4. Analyze Why does the father put so much care into the **beautiful** carving?

READING FLUENCY

Expression Read the passage on page 581 to a partner. Assess your fluency.

1. I read

   a. great   **b.** OK   **c.** not very well

2. What I did best in my reading was _____.

READING STRATEGY

Ask Questions
With a partner, compare the questions you asked as you read the selection. Tell what steps you took to **locate** the answers.

VOCABULARY REVIEW

Oral Review Read the paragraph aloud. Add the vocabulary words.

> I dreamed I found _____ jewels, gold, and other _____ in the woods. I put them in a paper bag, which I lost. I was upset about my _____. I tried to _____ where I had last seen the bag. I looked near every tree in the _____. The branches looked like bones, or _____. At last, I _____ the bag. I will never _____ about that dream!

Written Review Write a paragraph that tells about a **treasure** of your own. Use at least five vocabulary words in your paragraph. Then draw a picture of your treasure.

 **WRITE ABOUT THE** GUIDING QUESTION

Explore Personal Discoveries
Choose a character from "The Forgotten Treasure." Tell how the discovery of the father changed the character. Have you ever made a discovery like that? Give examples from the text and your life.

Connect Across the Curriculum

Analyze Text Structure: Sequence

> **Academic Vocabulary**
> • **sequence** (sē-kwens) *noun*
>   The **sequence** of events is the order in which the events happen.

Time words give you clues to the **sequence** of events. Read this passage from "The Forgotten Treasure." Notice the **time words**.

> One day, the hunter went out into the forest with his spear, his bow, and his arrows. At the end of the day, he did not come home. His wife and his four sons stayed up all night waiting for him, but still he didn't come home. A week passed but still he did not come home. His wife and his sons cried for their loss.

Practice Together

Begin a Sequence Chain You can use a **Sequence** Chain to keep track of the events in a story. The chain shows the order of events. It is different from a time line because it does not show exact dates. Compare the events in this **Sequence** Chain to the text above. Then work with your class to add two more events.

Sequence Chain

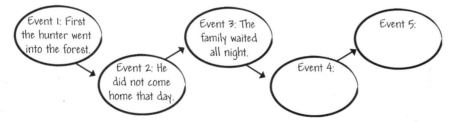

Event 1: First the hunter went into the forest.
Event 2: He did not come home that day.
Event 3: The family waited all night.
Event 4:
Event 5:

Try It!

Make a Sequence Chain Make a **Sequence** Chain for the rest of the story.

• Draw ovals. Connect them with arrows.
• Write an event in each oval. Use time words such as *first*, *then*, and *next* to show the right order for the events.
• Number the events in **sequence**.

Use Word Parts

Suffix	Meaning
-er, -or	one who
-ful	full of
-ous	full of, having
-y	like, having that quality

Academic Vocabulary
- **record** (ri-**kord**) *verb*
  To **record** means to put something in writing.

When you add a suffix to a base word, you change the meaning.

base word   suffix

color + -ful = colorful

The suffix *-ful* means "full of," so *colorful* means "full of color."

Spelling Rules

1. If the suffix begins with a consonant, make no change to the base word unless it ends in *-y*.

   hope + -ful = hopeful   beaut~~y~~i + -ful = beautiful

2. If the suffix begins with a vowel, you may need to make a change.

   fam~~e~~ + -ous = famous   shin~~e~~ + -y = shiny   hunt + -er = hunter

Build Words Add a suffix to each base word. Use the chart above. **Record** the new word and use it in a sentence.

1. courage
2. dirt
3. plenty
4. work
5. carve
6. danger
7. visit
8. faith

Discover Tools of the Past

HISTORY

Academic Vocabulary
- **organize** (**or**-gu-nīz) *verb*
  To **organize** is to put things in a certain order.

In "The Forgotten Treasure," the father uses a spear, a bow, and arrows. What other tools did early humans use?

❶ **Conduct Research** Work with a partner to do research. Take notes.

   Internet InsideNG.com
   Find out how early humans developed tools and used fire.

❷ **Prepare a Presentation** Review your notes. Write each main idea on a card. Write examples for each main idea on separate cards. **Organize** your cards. Draw or gather pictures to illustrate the information. Then practice using your cards and pictures to present the information.

❸ **Present the Information** Use your cards to give your presentation. Speak in a clear voice. Display your pictures. Use meaningful gestures. For example, show how people used certain tools.

Analyze Theme

> **Academic Vocabulary**
> • **theme** (thēm) *noun*
>   A **theme** is the main message of a story.

The **theme** of a story is its main message. One way to discover the **theme** is to look for clues in the title, the setting, the thoughts and actions of the characters, and the plot.

When you read, pay attention to the problems that the characters face and how they solve those problems. Put the clues together to determine the **theme**.

Practice Together

Begin a Theme Chart Use a **Theme** Chart to collect the clues you discover. Copy the chart below. Then think about the title of the selection. What message do the words tell you? Talk with a partner and find one more clue from the characters, setting, or plot.

Theme Chart

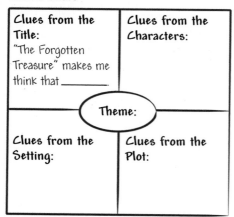

Clues from the Title:
"The Forgotten Treasure" makes me think that _____.

Clues from the Characters:

Theme:

Clues from the Setting:

Clues from the Plot:

Try It!

Complete the Theme Chart Add more clues from the setting, the characters, and the plot that lead to the main message, or **theme**, of the story. Then write a sentence that tells the **theme** of the story.

Remember that a story may have different **themes**. Share yours with a partner. How do your **themes** compare?

Engage in Discussion

Group Talk Imagine that the family in "The Forgotten Treasure" did not listen to the youngest son. What do you think might have happened? Use present and past tense verbs in your discussion.

> I agree with you. I felt bad for the youngest son, too. What did you think about the family?

Write About the Past

Study the Models At almost any age, people make personal discoveries. When writers tell about a discovery, they let the reader know when things happen.

NOT OK

> Last year, I **am** very shy. I was afraid to speak in front of the class or to join groups. Then a new student came to our class. She **has** no friends. I **decide** to say hello. I discovered that I was not so shy after all! Soon, Dana and I were good friends.

The writer uses some **present tense** verbs to tell about the past. The reader is confused: "I can't tell if the narrator is still shy."

OK

> When I **was** a little kid, I **was** different from a lot of my friends. They **screamed** when they **saw** big, ugly bugs, but I just **wanted** to learn more about them. I **collected** insects and **studied** them. One day I **learned** about entomology, or the study of insects. I **was** so excited! Today, I **work** at a university. I **am** an entomologist.

The reader can tell from **past tense verbs** when things happened.

This part is about today, so the writer uses the **present tense**.

Revise It Look back at the NOT OK passage. Work with a partner to revise it. Fix verb tenses so they don't confuse readers.

WRITE ON YOUR OWN Write about a personal discovery of your own. Use correct verb tenses.

REMEMBER

	Regular Verbs		Forms of *Be*			Forms of *Have*	
Present Tense	discover	learn	am	is	are	have	has
Past Tense	discover**ed**	learn**ed**	was	was	were	had	had

Mysteries
of the Ancient Past
by Reyna Eisenstark

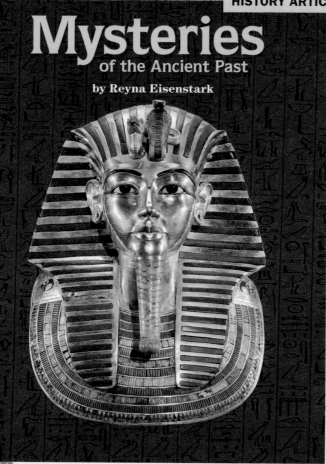

Build Background

Discuss the Ancient Past

Scientists discover many things when they dig up the past. Look at the photos, and identify signs of ancient people.

Digital Library   InsideNG.com
⊙ View the images.

▲ These pyramids are in Egypt.

Connect

KWL Chart Tell what you know about pyramids. Write your ideas in column 1 of a KWL Chart. In column 2, write what you want to learn about pyramids. Use column 3 to list what you learned after reading.

KWL Chart

WHAT I KNOW	WHAT I WANT TO KNOW	WHAT I LEARNED
Pyramids are very old buildings.	Why were they built?	

Language & Grammar

Define and Explain

CD

Study the photo and listen to the explanation.
Then explain something else in the picture.

PICTURE PROMPT

archaeologist

skeleton

hand tool

An archaeologist studies human life in the past. Archaeologists often use hand tools. They dig up old buildings, pots, and bones. They work slowly and carefully so they do not break anything.

Use Past Tense Verbs

The tense of a verb tells when an action happens.
- Add **-ed** to most verbs to show that an action already happened.
- Use special **past tense** forms for irregular verbs.

Present	Past	Example in the Past
do, does	did	I **did** my research on pyramids.
go, goes	went	I **went** to the library.
feel	felt	At first I **felt** tired.
know	knew	I **knew** nothing about pyramids.
see	saw	Then I **saw** pictures of them.
tell	told	"This is interesting," I **told** myself.

Practice Together

Say each sentence. Choose the past tense form of the verb.

1. Last year, my parents (did/do) something amazing.
2. They (go/went) to Egypt.
3. Mom and Dad (felt/feel) so excited.
4. They (see/saw) some pyramids.
5. They (told/tell) us all about them.
6. We never (know/knew) that pyramids could be so interesting.
7. Mom and Dad (told/tell) us that they want to go back to Egypt some day.

Try It!

Say each sentence. Write the past tense form of the verb on a card. Then hold up the card as you say the sentence with the past tense verb.

8. The professor (went/goes) to Egypt every year.
9. He (does/did) research on life in the past.
10. He (saw/sees) bones and old buildings.
11. He (went/goes) to many interesting places.
12. He (felt/feels) excited about his job.
13. He (knows/knew) a lot about life long ago.
14. He (tells/told) us all about it.
15. We (saw/see) his photos, too.

▲ Scientists went to this site to study bones.

Describe a Favorite Topic

DEFINE AND EXPLAIN

What do you enjoy? Tell a partner about a game, sport, or other topic that you know well. Define the difficult words.

First, use a Word Web to gather the important words that go with the topic. Here is a Word Web about Egypt.

Word Web

Decide which words you may need to define for your partner. Write the meanings. Use a dictionary if you need help.

Then talk with a partner. When you give your explanation, define at least one word.

HOW TO DEFINE AND EXPLAIN

1. **Define:** Tell what the word means.
2. **Explain:** Give details and examples to make the definition clear.

> A mummy is a body that has been treated so it doesn't fall apart. A mummy is wrapped in cloth. In ancient Egypt, the dead were made into mummies.

USE VERB TENSES

Be sure to use the correct verb tense when you speak. When you define something, you can use the **present tense verbs** is or are.

EXAMPLES   The Nile **is** an important river in Egypt.
The pyramids **are** special buildings in Egypt.

When you give an explanation, you may tell about something that already happened. If so, use **past tense verbs**.

EXAMPLES   Last year, I **went** to a museum. I **saw** a mummy up close. It **was** covered in cloth. The guide **told** us that the mummy **was** 2000 years old.

Learn Key Vocabulary

Rate and Study the Words Rate how well you know each word. Then:

1. Pronounce the word. Say it aloud several times. Spell it.
2. Study the example.
3. Tell more about the word.
4. Practice it. Make the word your own.

Rating Scale

1 = I have never seen this word before.

2 = I am not sure of the word's meaning.

3 = I know this word and can teach the word's meaning to someone else.

Key Words

ancient (ānt-shunt) *adjective*
▶ page 330

If something is **ancient**, it is very old. People built this **ancient** temple long ago.
Antonym: **new**

archaeologist
(ar-kē-ah-lu-jist) *noun* ▶ page 332

An **archaeologist** studies the way people lived in the past. Bones, buildings, and tools help **archaeologists** learn about the past.
Base Word: **archaeology**

artifact (ar-ti-fakt) *noun*
▶ page 333

An **artifact** is an object, or the remains of one, that represents a culture. An old statue is an **artifact**.

bury (bair-ē) *verb*
▶ page 337

To **bury** means to place in the ground. The dog **buries** a bone.
Synonym: **cover**

civilization
(si-vu-lu-zā-shun) *noun* ▶ page 330

A **civilization** is the culture of a specific place, time, or group of people. Greece has a very old **civilization**.

clue (klü) *noun*
▶ page 330

A **clue** is a piece of information that leads to a solution. The man looks for **clues** to the crime.
Synonyms: **hint, sign**

pyramid (pear-u-mid) *noun*
▶ page 330

A **pyramid** is a building with a square base and four sides that are triangles. This **pyramid** is in Egypt.

tomb (tüm) *noun*
▶ page 334

A **tomb** is a grave, or a special place for the body of a dead person. This is the inside of a **tomb** in Italy.

Practice the Words Work with a partner to complete an Expanded Meaning Map for each Key Word.

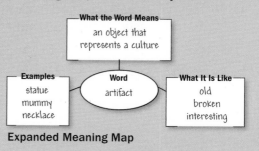

Expanded Meaning Map

Reading Strategy: Ask Questions

Sometimes the answers to questions are right there in the text.
Other times you need to put together information to get the answer.

HOW TO FIND ANSWERS TO YOUR QUESTIONS

1. Write your question on a sticky note.

2. See if the words that answer the question are right there in one of the sentences. If so, write the answer.

3. If not, gather information from different sentences or paragraphs. Put together all of the information you find. Write your answer.

Strategy in Action

Here's how one student found answers.

Look Into the Text

What is an archaeologist?
Someone who studies old objects.

"The answer is right there."

Archaeologists study objects from the past to learn about the people who made or used those objects and left them behind when they died. Archaeologists gather clues in many places. They look in old buildings. They also look for objects buried under the ground. Archaeologists often have to dig to find what they are looking for.

How do archaeologists get their clues?

"I need to gather ideas and put them together."

Practice Together

Reread the passage above. Follow the steps in the How-To box to answer the question on the yellow note.

History Article

A history article is **nonfiction**. It tells about something that really happened in the past. The headings show what each section is about. The text also explains hard words, or **technical terms**.

> **Objects from Long Ago** ⟨ heading
>
> The objects that archaeologists study are called **artifacts**. Artifacts are clues that tell archaeologists how people lived in ancient times.

The paragraphs in a history article often tell about one **main idea**. They include **details** to support the main idea.

Your Job as a Reader

Reading Strategy: Ask Questions

As you read, ask questions to gather information. Pay attention to the technical terms.

TECHNICAL TERM

artifact

QUESTION

What is an artifact?

Mysteries
of the Ancient Past

by Reyna Eisenstark

Online Coach

Discovering the Past in
ANCIENT EGYPT

Egypt

Ancient Egypt was home to a great **civilization**. The people who lived there left **clues** about how they lived. One clue is the **pyramids**, buildings that have stood in the desert for thousands of years.

Who built the pyramids, and why did they build them? What lies inside these mysterious buildings? These are some of the questions that scientists and **historians** try to answer.

Key Vocabulary
ancient *adj.*, very old
civilization *n.*, the culture of a specific place, time, or group
clue *n.*, a piece of information that leads to a solution
pyramid *n.*, a building with a square base and four triangular sides

In Other Words
historians people who study history

▼ King Tut was a teenager when he died. This is a detail, or part, of the **coffin** in which his body was placed.

In Other Words
coffin container

Before You Move On

1. **Explain** Who was Howard Carter?
2. **Inference** Read the caption and study the photo on this page. How do you think **ancient** Egyptians felt about King Tut? Explain.

ANCIENT EGYPT

Mediterranean
Sea

Nile River

EGYPT

Red
Sea

■ **Archaeological Sites**

▲ Interpret the Map Where are most of the archaeological sites located?

In Other Words

Archaeological Sites Places
where archaeologists think ancient
people stayed for a period of time
and left artifacts

Lost Treasures

Ancient Egyptians **buried** their dead kings in special tombs. Some tombs were in pyramids. Others were in the Valley of the Kings. Many archaeologists wanted to find these tombs so they could study the valuable artifacts inside. Often, though, when they opened the tombs there was nothing left inside, because people had stolen the treasures long before.

▲ Archaeologists dig for artifacts.

Looking for King Tut

Howard Carter had a plan. He read stories of Egypt's history. He learned about a leader named Tutankhamun, or King Tut. No one knew where King Tut was buried, though.

Carter wanted to look for King Tut's tomb. He decided to look in the Valley of the Kings. Carter got a map of the valley and marked the tombs that had already been found. Carter thought King Tut's tomb might be nearby. He began to dig in 1917.

▲ Carter and his team dig in search of King Tut's tomb.

Key Vocabulary
bury *v.*, to place in the ground

Before You Move On

1. **Details** What was special about the Valley of the Kings?
2. **Cause and Effect** How did Carter decide where to look for King Tut's tomb?

A statue of young King Tut ▶

Stairs to a Door

Carter searched for many years. At first he found nothing. But he kept looking. He was determined to find King Tut's tomb. On November 4, 1922, his luck changed. Carter's team discovered a step that was cut into some rock.

The team kept digging. Soon they found fifteen more steps. The steps led to an ancient doorway. The door seemed to be **sealed**. It had the name Tutankhamun written on it.

▲ Carter and his team entered the tomb through this door.

The Room Beyond

The team took nearly three weeks to clear the staircase. Carter slowly made a hole in the door. He was **stunned** by what he found. Through the door was a series of rooms. One room held King Tut's mummy. Other rooms were filled with artifacts that had been buried with King Tut thousands of years before.

▲ The Egyptians believed that this statue would protect King Tut.

In Other Words
sealed closed tight
stunned amazed

The Glint of Gold!

The ancient tomb held more than 3,500 artifacts. It held jewels, statues, paintings, and lots of gold. King Tut's coffin was solid gold. The dead king had a gold mask and throne, too.

Howard Carter carefully studied all of these artifacts, which showed the great riches of Egyptian kings. They also gave clues about life in ancient Egypt. It took Carter **a decade** to finish work on King Tut's tomb.

▲ Howard Carter uses a brush to clean an artifact.

A Famous King

King Tut died more than 3,000 years ago and **reigned** for only a decade or so. He had little **claim to fame**. He is well-known today, though, simply because of Howard Carter's amazing discovery.

King Tut's tomb has taught us a lot about life in ancient Egypt. For example, it proves that ancient Egyptians believed in life after death. It also shows that people honored their king. And it shows the great riches of the ancient Egyptian civilization. ❖

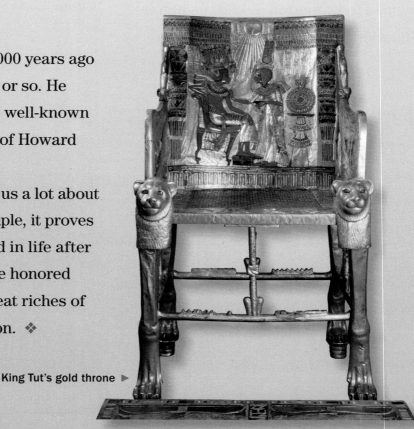

King Tut's gold throne ▶

Before You Move On

1. **Explain** Why is King Tut famous today?
2. **Summarize** What does King Tut's tomb teach us about life in **ancient** Egypt?

Connect Reading and Writing

Vocabulary

ancient

archaeologists

artifact

buried

civilization

clues

pyramid

tomb

CRITICAL THINKING

1. **SUM IT UP** Point to pictures in the selection as you give a summary of the main ideas. Use these ideas to make a Five-Ws Chart about **archaeologists**.

Five-Ws Chart

Who?	archaeologists
What?	
Where?	
When?	
Why?	

2. **Explain** Return to the KWL Chart you made on page 322. Write what you learned about **pyramids** in column 3. Discuss your chart with a group.

3. **Interpret** How do **artifacts** give us **clues** about people of the past?

4. **Infer** Why do you think it took Carter so long to work on King Tut's **tomb**?

READING FLUENCY

Phrasing Read the passage on page 582 to a partner. Assess your fluency.

1. I read
   a. great   **b.** OK   **c.** not very well

2. What I did best in my reading was _____ .

READING STRATEGY

Ask Questions
Ask your partner a question about the text. Have your partner find the answer and tell if he or she found the answer "right there" or had to gather ideas and put them together.

VOCABULARY REVIEW

Oral Review Read the paragraph aloud. Add the vocabulary words.

A museum had a very old statue from the grave, or _____, of a dead king. The handmade object, or _____, was beautiful. It had been created during the time of a great _____. One day the _____ statue was stolen from the museum. Some _____ and other scientists decided to search for it. They solved the mystery by looking for _____ to follow. They found the statue, where it was _____ underground, near the base of a _____.

Written Review Imagine you are an **archaeologist**. Write a paragraph to tell about your work. Use at least four vocabulary words in your paragraph.

 **WRITE ABOUT THE** **GUIDING QUESTION**

Explore Discoveries of the Past
How do the discoveries of Howard Carter's team of **archaeologists** change us and the world? Read the selection again and look for details that support your answer.

Connect Across the Curriculum

Analyze Text Structure: Main Idea and Details

> **Academic Vocabulary**
> • **organize** (or-gu-nīz) *verb*
>   To **organize** is to put things in a certain order.

Nonfiction writers begin with a **topic**. The topic is what the text discusses. Writers usually **organize** the text so the ideas are clear to readers. They state the **main idea**—what they want to say about the topic—and then give **details** about the main idea.

Looking for King Tut ⟨ heading

Howard Carter had a plan. . . . Carter wanted to look for King Tut's tomb. He decided to look in the Valley of the Kings. Carter got a map of the valley and marked the tombs that had already been found. Carter thought King Tut's tomb might be nearby. He began to dig in 1917.

Practice Together

Use a Chart When you look closely at how the writer **organizes** the text, it helps you understand the ideas. You can use a chart to keep track of the main idea and details of each section.

To make a chart, first determine the main idea. Find it by looking at the headings and what the writer is saying about the topic. Then add details about that idea. Compare this chart to the text above.

Main-Idea Chart

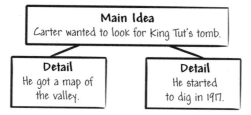

> **Main Idea**
> Carter wanted to look for King Tut's tomb.
>
> **Detail**
> He got a map of the valley.
>
> **Detail**
> He started to dig in 1917.

Try It!

Make a Chart Choose another section of the article. Make a Main-Idea Chart for it.

- Figure out the topic. Use the section heading to help you.
- Find the main idea—what the section is saying about that topic.
- Write the details about the main idea.

Use Word Parts

Prefix	Meaning
dis-	opposite
mid-	middle
mis-	wrongly
pre-	before
super-	above

> **Academic Vocabulary**
> • **record** (ri-**kord**) *verb*
>   To **record** means to put something in writing.

A prefix can be added to the beginning of a base word. It changes the word's meaning.

prefix   base word

mis- + judge = misjudge

The prefix *mis-* means "wrongly," so *misjudge* means "to judge wrongly."

Build Words Start with a base word and then add a prefix from the list to make a new word. **Record** each new word you make. Keep the spelling of the prefix and the base word the same. Say what the new word means, and use it in a sentence.

1. star   **3.** way   **5.** agree   **7.** cook

2. night   **4.** trust   **6.** spell   **8.** market

Research Pyramids

HISTORY

> **Academic Vocabulary**
> • **fact** (**fakt**) *noun*
>   A **fact** is a piece of information that is true.

1 **Conduct Research** Learn some **facts** about pyramids. Find out how they were built and what is inside of them. Take notes about an aspect of the pyramids that interests you.

> **Internet** **InsideNG.com**
> ➋ Take a virtual tour inside a pyramid.
> ➋ Read about some important pyramids.
> ➋ Study diagrams of pyramids.

2 **Prepare a Presentation** Use your notes to help you prepare an oral report. Decide which facts you will tell about and how you will organize them. Then:

- Think of an interesting introduction, or way to begin your talk. What will grab your classmates' attention right away?
- Create a good conclusion, or ending. Briefly sum up what you said.

3 **Present Your Findings** Practice giving your talk. Then tell your classmates what you learned.

Listening/Speaking

Explore Egyptian Art

HISTORY

> **Academic Vocabulary**
> • **discover** (dis-**ku**-vur) *verb*
>   To **discover** means to find out something you didn't know before.

You can **discover** a lot about a civilization when you look at its art. Ancient art can give you clues about the crops that people grew or the metals they got from the earth. You can also **discover** their beliefs, customs, and values. Learn about ancient Egyptian art. Share your **discoveries** with the class.

1 **Search for Art** With a partner, search for photos of and information about ancient Egyptian art. Look for any type of art, including sculpture, jewelry, pottery, painting, and architecture.

> **Internet** InsideNG.com
> 🔘 Take a virtual tour of an ancient Egyptian art display.

2 **Study the Art** Choose a piece of art to tell about. Think about what the art shows and what materials and colors the artist used. Take notes about important details, such as where the art comes from, when it was made, and what it was made from. Note interesting facts, such as what the art represents and how it was used.

3 **Plan a Talk** What idea do you want to tell your listeners? Turn this idea into a key question. That's how you can begin your talk. For example: "What was life like in ancient Egypt?" Your question should relate to the details you collected.

Review your notes. Find the facts that answer your question. Write each fact on an index card. Include enough facts to inform your listeners and to keep them interested. Then use the index cards to practice your presentation.

4 **Share Your Findings** Display the picture of the art so everyone can see it. Begin with your key question. Use your cards to guide your presentation. Speak clearly so everyone can understand. At the end, ask if anyone has questions.

▲ This Egyptian statue is made of pressed glass.

Define and Explain

Be an Expert Work with a partner. List the technical terms in the selection. Take turns choosing a term to define. Tell what it means and give an example. Use past tense verbs when it makes sense.

> Artifacts are objects made by people. A toy or a bowl can be an artifact.

Write About the Past and Present

Study the Models When you write about a discovery, it's important to let your readers know when it happened and how it affects people today.

NOT OK

> Some archaeologists **go** to Egypt. They **bring** special tools for digging up artifacts. Some workers **find** a large tomb. Today, scientists **study** the artifacts and **learn** about ancient Egypt.

This is not OK because the writer uses present tense to tell about the past.

OK

> Some archaeologists **went** to Egypt. They **brought** special tools for digging up artifacts. Some workers **found** a large tomb. Today, scientists **study** the artifacts and **learn** about ancient Egypt.

The writer uses past tense to tell what happened and present tense to tell how the discovery connects to today.

Add Sentences Think of two sentences to add to the OK model above. Be sure to use the correct tense.

✏ **WRITE ON YOUR OWN** Choose a moment in history that you know about. Write about it, and tell how it connects to something that is happening today. Pay attention to the verb tenses.

REMEMBER

Add **-ed** to most verbs to show past tense. Some verbs use special forms to show action in the past.

	Regular Verbs		Irregular Verbs					
Present Tense	discover	study	bring	find	go	know	see	take
Past Tense	discover**ed**	stud**ied**	brought	found	went	knew	saw	took

Compare Across Texts

Compare Important Ideas

"Return to *Titanic*," "The Forgotten Treasure," and "Mysteries of the Ancient Past" tell about people who **discover** things. Compare the ideas in the texts.

How It Works

Collect and Organize Ideas To compare ideas across several texts, **organize** them in a chart. List two or three questions to get the big ideas.

Comparison Chart

Big Idea Question	Return to Titanic	The Forgotten Treasure	Mysteries of the Ancient Past
1. Do discoveries make a difference?	The discovery of Titanic helped explain why it sank.	The discovery of the father taught that family is important.	The discovery of artifacts helped explain the past.
2. Why do people try to make discoveries?			

Practice Together

Study and Summarize the Ideas Compare the answers for each question. Then summarize. To write your summary, turn the question into a statement. Look for ways in which the ideas are alike, and explain the connection. Here is a summary of the ideas for question 1.

> "Return to Titanic," "The Forgotten Treasure," and "Mysteries of the Ancient Past" all show that discoveries make a difference. Each discovery gave people important information about events, people, and the past.

Try It!

Make a chart to collect answers to question 2. Summarize them. You may want to use this frame to help you express your comparison.

"Return to *Titanic*," "The Forgotten Treasure," and "Mysteries of the Ancient Past" all show why people keep trying to make discoveries. In "Return to *Titanic*," people want _____. In "The Forgotten Treasure," people want _____, and in "Mysteries of the Ancient Past," they want _____.

Academic Vocabulary
- **discover** (dis-**ku**-vur) *verb*
  To **discover** means to find out something you didn't know before.
- **organize** (**or**-gu-nīz) *verb*
  To **organize** is to put things in a certain order.

The Drive to Discover

GUIDING QUESTION How do discoveries change us and the world?

Reflect on Your Reading

Think back on your reading of the unit selections. Discuss what you did to understand what you read.

Focus on Genre **Organization of Ideas**

In this unit, you learned about some ways writers organize their ideas. Choose a selection from the unit, and draw a diagram or other graphic that shows its organization. It could be a time line, a chart, or even a picture. Use your drawing to explain the organization of the selection to a partner.

Reading Strategy **Ask Questions**

As you read the selections, you learned to ask and answer questions. Explain to a partner how you will use this strategy in the future.

Explore the

Throughout this unit, you have been thinking about the drive to discover. Choose one of these ways to explore the Guiding Question:

- **Discuss** With a group, discuss the Guiding Question. Remember, there can be many answers. What's yours? Give details from the selections that support your idea.
- **Role-Play** Imagine if people or characters from two different selections could meet and discuss the Guiding Question. With a partner, role-play their discussion. For example, what would Robert Ballard and Howard Carter say to each other?
- **Draw** Create a visual interpretation of your answer to the Guiding Question.

Book Talk

Which Unit Library book did you choose? Explain to a partner what it taught you about discoveries.

UNIT LIBRARY

Content Library

Leveled Library

Free, 2007, Elizabeth Rosen. Mixed Media, courtesy of Morgan Gaynin Inc., New York.

▲ Critical Viewing What is the artist's message in this image?

Struggle for Freedom

GUIDING QUESTION

How far will people go for the sake of freedom?

Read More!

Content Library

The Anti-Slavery Movement
by Ann M. Rossi

Leveled Library

The Time Machine
by H.G. Wells, adapted by Les Martin

Letters from Rifka
by Karen Hesse

Franklin D. Roosevelt
by Laura Hamilton Waxman

Internet
InsideNG.com

- Go to the Digital Library to explore why some people seek freedom.
- Learn about struggles for freedom in the United States.
- Listen to freedom songs.

Focus on Genre

Organization of Ideas

► **Cause and Effect**

A common text structure for nonfiction is **cause and effect**. A cause is the reason something happens. An effect is what happens as a result of the cause. Effects often become causes of something else that happens. Writers use cause and effect to explain why things happen.

How It Works

Before reading, preview the text to figure out how the writer **arranged** the information and ideas. This will help you follow the text and understand it better.

Clue words can help you determine if a writer used cause and effect as a text structure. Read this example.

Fight for Freedom

Sanjana lived in a country that was ruled by the king of another country. The king was unfair. Because of this, people wanted to fight him.

Sanjana did not believe war was the right way to get freedom, so she encouraged people to fight with their money, not with weapons. She told people not to pay tax money to the king. If people did not pay the king, then he might change how he was treating people.

As a result of this protest, the king got angry. His reaction led to tougher times. But Sanjana encouraged the people not to give up. They did not pay their taxes, and they disobeyed laws for many years.

Finally, since the king was not getting what he wanted, he made a peaceful agreement with the people. Everyone was glad they had followed Sanjana's plan. Consequently, they asked her to be one of the leaders of her country.

Clue words help you find causes and effects:

as a result	if/then
because	led to
because of	since
caused	so
consequently	therefore

A cause may lead to more than one effect. Sanjana's plan first led to tougher times. Then it led to peace.

Academic Vocabulary

● **arrange** (u-rānj) *verb*
To **arrange** means to put things in a certain order.

Practice Together

Read the following passage aloud. As you read, listen for clues that help you identify cause-and-effect relationships. Remember that effects often become new causes.

Gandhi in South Africa

When he was a young man, Mohandas Gandhi worked as a lawyer in South Africa, where many people from India lived and worked. He thought the laws there treated Indians unfairly and often harshly. Gandhi reasoned that if a law was unjust, then it was OK to break that law. He therefore urged people to break unfair laws. Indians followed his advice. As a result, South Africa changed its laws and gave Indians more rights.

When Gandhi returned to India, he saw unfair laws there. So he began to lead peaceful protests in India. Consequently, the laws in India changed, too.

▲ Gandhi helped change unfair laws in South Africa in the early 1900s.

Try It!

Read the following passage aloud. What are the causes and effects? How do you know?

Peaceful Protests

Henry David Thoreau is a famous American writer of the nineteenth century. He wrote that if each person acts peacefully against an unfair law, then the law eventually would be changed.

Mohandas Gandhi read Thoreau's essays and agreed with them. Therefore, he used the ideas in his fight for civil rights.

Later, because of Thoreau and Gandhi, Martin Luther King, Jr., led peaceful protests in the United States. He encouraged African Americans to protest against unfair laws. These protests led to new laws that were more fair.

▲ The ideas of Thoreau inspired Mohandas Gandhi and Martin Luther King, Jr.

Focus on Vocabulary

Use Context Clues for Unfamiliar Words

On-page clues to the meaning of a word are called **context** clues. There are several different kinds of **context** clues.

Type of Clue	What It Does	Signal Words	Example
Definition clue	Explains the word directly in the text	*is, are, was, called, refers to, means*	**Slavery** *refers to* people owning other people and forcing them to work.
Restatement clue	Gives the meaning in a different way, usually after a comma	*or*	American slaves were **emancipated**, *or* freed, in 1865.
Synonym clue	Gives a word or phrase that means almost the same thing	*also, like*	*Like* other farm workers, the **laborers** picked cotton.
Antonym clue	Gives a word or phrase that means almost the opposite of the word	*but, unlike*	**Enslaved** people, *unlike* free people, cannot leave their jobs.
Example clue	Gives an example of what the word means	*for example, including, such as*	When slaves ran away, they faced **punishment**, *such as* beatings.

How the Strategy Works

When you read, you may come to a word that you don't know. Look for **context** clues to help you figure out the meaning.

1. Read the words nearby, and look for signal words.
2. Predict what the word means.
3. Try out your predicted meaning to see if it makes sense.

Use the strategy to figure out the meaning of each underlined word.

Where Arianna lived, soldiers <u>monitored</u>, or watched, everyone all the time. The soldiers did <u>unjust</u> things, such as taking food from Arianna's restaurant without paying for it. Her brother was <u>incarcerated</u> for a small crime, but others were left free for the same crime. Arianna and her family wanted a better life. They became <u>refugees</u>, which means they went to a new country to be free.

Strategy in Action

" I see the word *or* after *monitored*. It could be a signal word for a restatement clue. *Monitored* could mean 'watched.' That makes sense. "

☑ **REMEMBER** You can use **context** clues to figure out the meanings of unfamiliar words.

Academic Vocabulary

• **context** (**kon**-tekst) *noun*
   Context refers to the parts nearby that help explain the meaning.

Practice Together

Read this passage aloud. Look at each underlined word. Use **context** clues
to figure out its meaning.

A Divided Country

When Chang was a child, his country was <u>divided</u> into two parts: the North
and the South. Each part of the country had its own government. Chang
and his family lived in the South. People were free there, unlike the North,
where they were <u>restricted</u>. The two areas fought for many years. Finally, the
North was <u>victorious</u> and took control of the entire country. Chang and his
family <u>fled</u>, or left, the country in search of freedom.

Try It!

Read this passage aloud. What is the meaning of each underlined word?
How can you tell?

Fight for Freedom

Joseph and his family lived on a rich, <u>prosperous</u> island in the Caribbean.
When he was young, he was free. When he grew up, a new government
controlled the island. People who were born in the country and were <u>native</u> to
it, like Joseph and his family, were forced to work for no pay.

Joseph and his family should have been protected from <u>abuse</u>, but they
received unfair treatment. Finally, they <u>rebelled</u>. They fought the government
for many years and finally won. They began a new government. They gave their
free, <u>independent</u> country a new name.

Escaping to Freedom

by Daniel Schulman

Build Background

Learn About Slavery

Until the mid-1800s, many landowners in the Americas used slave labor on their farms. Life was very hard for the enslaved people.

Digital Library

InsideNG.com
▶ View the video.

▲ **Slave houses in 1860**

Connect

Discussion What traits did people need if they wanted to help enslaved people reach safety? Brainstorm and make a list. Then tell which traits you have.

Traits
1. Courage
2. Ability to keep secrets
3. Concern about people
4. Ability to solve problems

Language & Grammar

Summarize

CD

Listen to a formal presentation. Then listen to a summary of the presentation.

FORMAL PRESENTATION and SUMMARY

The Underground Railroad

The Underground Railroad was not a real railroad. It was a system of trails for slaves in America who ran away. The slaves followed the trails to Canada, where slavery was illegal.

Summary of "The Underground Railroad"

The Underground Railroad was a system of trails that helped runaway slaves in America escape to Canada.

Use Nouns in the Subject and Predicate

Remember, a complete sentence has a subject and a predicate.

The runaway slaves wanted freedom.
<u>subject</u>   <u>predicate</u>

- Often, the most important word in the subject is a **noun**.

    EXAMPLE   The runaway **slaves** wanted freedom.

- A **noun** can also be the object of an action verb. To find the object, turn the verb into a question: "Wanted what?"

    EXAMPLE   The runaway slaves **wanted freedom**.
    <u>verb</u>   <u>object</u>

- Many English sentences follow this pattern: subject → verb → object.

    EXAMPLE   Many **people** in the North **opposed slavery**.
    <u>subject</u>   <u>verb</u>   <u>object</u>

Practice Together

Say each sentence. Tell whether the underlined noun is a subject or an object.

1. Slave traders captured <u>people</u> in Africa.
2. <u>Ships</u> carried some captives to America.
3. Colonists bought the <u>slaves</u>.
4. Many enslaved people tended <u>crops</u> in the fields.
5. Other <u>captives</u> did chores inside houses.

Try It!

Read each sentence. Write *subject* or *object* on a card for the underlined noun. Hold up the card as you say the sentence.

6. Many <u>people</u> hated slavery.
7. Some of these people helped <u>runaways</u>.
8. These brave Americans joined a special <u>organization</u>.
9. <u>Members</u> of the organization secretly helped the enslaved people.
10. The <u>runaways</u> received food.
11. The tired <u>people</u> also received shelter.
12. Often, the assistance saved their <u>lives</u>.

▲ **Enslaved people pick cotton.**

Tell About a Topic

SUMMARIZE

You learned facts about the Underground Railroad on pages 354–355.
Review what you learned. Then think about other facts you may already
know about the topic.

List facts you know about the Underground Railroad.

The Underground Railroad
1. People helped slaves escape to the North.
2. It was dangerous.
3. Slaves and their helpers could be punished.

Review your notes. Think about the information. When you feel ready, tell
the information to a partner.

Now listen as your partner summarizes what you said. Switch roles.

HOW TO SUMMARIZE A PRESENTATION

1. Identify the topic.
2. Identify the main idea, or what the presentation mostly says about the topic.
3. Stay focused on what is important. Leave out details that are interesting but not important.

People gave food to the hungry, tired runaways. They gave them safe places to rest or sleep during the day.

People gave the runaways food and shelter.

USE PRECISE NOUNS

When you make a presentation or summarize ideas, state the information
clearly. Use precise **nouns** in the subjects and predicates of your sentences.

Not Precise: A **woman** helped other **people** .

Precise: **Harriet Tubman** helped other enslaved **people** .

Prepare to Read

Learn Key Vocabulary

Rate and Study the Words Rate how well you know each word. Then:

1. Pronounce the word. Say it aloud several times. Spell it.
2. Study the example.
3. Tell more about the word.
4. Practice it. Make the word your own.

Key Words

assist (u-sist) *verb*
▶ page 366

To **assist** means to help. The father **assists** his son with an assignment when he has trouble understanding it.

capture (kap-chur) *noun*
▶ page 364 *verb* ▶ page 367

1 *verb* To **capture** means to take by force. The farmer **captured** a raccoon. **2** *noun* A **capture** is the act of catching something. Soon after the **capture**, he released the raccoon.

escape (is-kāp) *verb* ▶ page 362
noun ▶ page 365

1 *verb* To **escape** means to get away. People **escaped** the burning building. **2** *noun* An **escape** is the act of getting away from something. We heard about their successful **escape**.

freedom (frē-dum) *noun*
▶ page 362

Freedom is the state of being free. The bird was released and given **freedom**.

reward (ri-word) *noun*
▶ page 364

Lost Dog

REWARD OFFERED

A **reward** is money given for helping someone. We offered a **reward** to anyone who could find our lost dog.

right (rīt) *noun*
▶ page 362

A **right** is the power a person has because of a country's rules. In 1920 American women got the **right** to vote.

slave (slāv) *noun*
▶ page 362

A **slave** is someone who belongs to another person and who works without pay. Owners forced **slaves** to work.

travel (tra-vul) *verb*
▶ page 364

To **travel** means to go from one place to another place. People can **travel** over land by car, train, or wagon.

Practice the Words Write a sentence for each Key Word. Include context clues. Copy the sentences, but put a blank in place of the Key Word. Ask a partner to fill in the words.

The owner forced the _____ to work in the fields.

358 Unit 6 Struggle for Freedom

Reading Strategy: Determine Importance

As you read nonfiction, decide what is important so you can remember it. One way to do this is to summarize as you read.

Reading Strategy
Determine Importance

HOW TO SUMMARIZE NONFICTION

1. Read the title, headings, and first paragraph. Look for clues that tell you what the selection is mostly about.
2. As you read, pause after each paragraph to decide what the author wants you to know about the topic. Record your ideas.
3. Then use your notes as guides to tell what the author mostly is saying about the topic.

Strategy in Action

Here's how one student summarized.

Look Into the Text

section heading

Bonds of Slavery

"The heading tells me that the topic is slavery."

In 1830, Josiah Henson was 41 years old. A life of slavery was all he had ever known. Born in Maryland, Henson was taken from his family as a child. He was bought and sold many times.

Henson lived on a plantation, or large farm, in Kentucky. He had a wife and four children. He tried to buy his way out of slavery, but his owner, Amos Riley, tricked him. Riley kept the money that Henson paid for his freedom, but he did not let Henson go.

"These important details about Henson's life relate to the topic."

Summary Planner

Title: Escaping to Freedom
Topic: Slavery

Paragraph 1:
Josiah Henson was bought and sold many times as a slave.

+

Paragraph 2:

+
(to end of selection)
=
Summary of Selection: _____

Practice Together

Read the passage again, and summarize the second paragraph. Follow the steps in the How-To box.

Focus on Genre

Biography

A biography is the story of a person's life, written by another person. In biographies, writers often use a **cause**-and-**effect** text structure to show why events happened in a person's life.

> One day Henson learned some troubling news. He learned that Riley planned to sell him. . . .
>
> Henson could not accept this, so he made a plan for his family to escape.

What clue word signals the cause-and-effect relationship in the passage?

Your Job as a Reader

Reading Strategy: Determine Importance

As you read, stop after each paragraph and record what is most important. After reading, use your Summary Planner to tell what the selection mostly is telling you about the topic.

> Paragraph 3:
> Riley planned to sell Henson, so Henson decided to escape with his family.

Escaping to Freedom

by Daniel Schulman

Until 1865, most African Americans were not free. They were **slaves** with no **rights**. Their owners forced them to work without pay. They could be sold and sent far away from their families. Many African Americans decided their only chance for **freedom** was to **escape**.

Bonds of Slavery

In 1830, Josiah Henson was 41 years old. A life of slavery was all he had ever known. Born in Maryland, Henson was taken from his family as a child. He was bought and sold many times.

Henson lived on a plantation, or large farm, in Kentucky. He had a wife and four children. He tried to buy his way out of slavery, but his owner, Amos Riley, tricked him. Riley kept the money that Henson paid for his freedom, but he did not let Henson go.

Bad News

One day Henson learned some **troubling news**. He learned that Riley planned to sell him. Henson would have to move to Louisiana, and he might never see his wife and children again! Henson could not **accept** this, so he made a plan for his family to escape.

▲ Josiah Henson in later life

Key Vocabulary
slave *n.*, someone who belongs to another and works without pay
right *n.*, the power a person has because of the rules of a country
freedom *n.*, the state of being free
escape *v.*, to get away

In Other Words
troubling news upsetting information
accept agree to

Many men, women, and children worked as slaves on large farms like this one.

Historical Background

Slavery was not common in North America until 1793. That is when Eli Whitney invented a cotton gin. This machine made cotton a popular crop. Many people used slaves to work on their farms. In 1865, the Thirteenth Amendment made slavery against the law in the United States.

Cotton gin

Before You Move On

1. **Paraphrase** What was Henson's life like? Tell about it in your own words.
2. **Cause and Effect** What happened that made Henson decide to **escape** from the Riley farm?

The Path to Freedom

One dark night, Henson and his family left their home. He carried his two youngest children in a backpack. The family **boarded** a small boat and crossed the Ohio River into Indiana.

Once in Indiana, the family had to move slowly. They had to be careful not to be seen. Some slave owners **offered** **rewards** for the **capture** of escaped slaves. If the family was found, they might be returned to Riley. To make sure no one saw them, Henson's family often **traveled** at night and slept during the day.

100 DOLLARS
REWARD!

Ranaway from the subscriber on the 27th of July, my Black Woman, named

EMILY,

Seventeen years of age, well grown, black color, has a whining voice. She took with her one dark calico and one blue and white dress, a red corded gingham bonnet; a white striped shawl and slippers. I will pay the above reward if taken near the Ohio river on the Kentucky side, or **THREE HUNDRED DOLLARS**, if taken in the State of Ohio, and delivered to me near Lewisburg, Mason County, Ky.   **THO'S. H. WILLIAMS.**
August 4, 1853.

▲ Some slave owners posted signs that offered rewards for the capture of runaway slaves.

Key Vocabulary
reward *n.*, the money given for helping someone else
capture *n.*, the act of catching and keeping a person or animal
travel *v.*, to go from one place to another place

In Other Words
boarded got into
offered said they would pay

Free at Last

The family traveled by wagon, by boat, and on foot. They traveled toward Canada, where slavery was not allowed. Along the way, people helped the family. Some people gave them food, and others hid them in barns.

The family **set foot** in Canada more than a month after their **daring** **escape**. The first words that Henson **exclaimed** when he got there were, "I am free!"

▲ People led escaped slaves through forests and other places on the path to freedom.

▲ People hid escaped slaves in wagons and other secret places.

In Other Words
set foot arrived
daring brave and dangerous
exclaimed said

Before You Move On

1. **Cause and Effect** Why did the family have to **travel** slowly?
2. **Inference** Why do you think people helped the family along the way?

Freedom Train

How was Henson's family able to make the trip to freedom? They traveled by the Underground Railroad, which was not really a railroad and did not go underground, either. The Underground Railroad was a set of paths made of people who helped slaves run away.

People along the Underground Railroad **assisted** runaways. They gave them food and a place to stay. They carried runaways closer to freedom in boats or wagons.

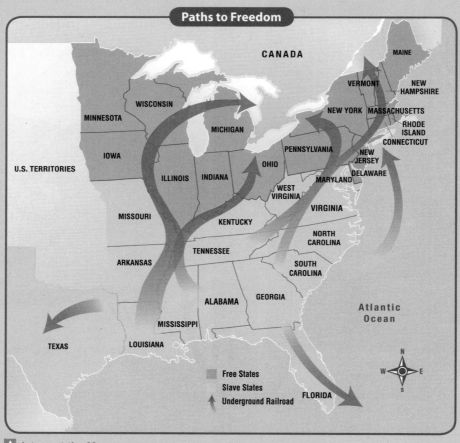

Paths to Freedom

▲ Interpret the Map Choose one path of the Underground Railroad. Name all the states it went through.

Key Vocabulary
assist *v.*, to help

Historical Background
The Underground Railroad helped between 40,000 and 100,000 slaves escape. Some people, like Harriet Tubman, escaped and then returned to the southern states to help others find freedom.

Secret Paths to Freedom

The Underground Railroad was secret. We do not know all of the paths that people traveled, but we do know that the Underground Railroad helped many slaves escape to freedom. Some **journeys** took a month. Others took a year or more. Some runaways were **captured** or died along the way. The Underground Railroad shows how far people will go for freedom. ❖

Some people in the Underground Railroad had hidden rooms where escaped slaves could stay.

Key Vocabulary
capture *v.*, to take by force

In Other Words
journeys trips

Before You Move On

1. **Summarize** What was the Underground Railroad?
2. **Inference** How do you think **slaves** felt as they **traveled** on the Underground Railroad? Why?

Follow the Drinking Gourd

A Traditional Song

Follow the drinking gourd!

Follow the drinking gourd!

For the old man is a-waiting for to carry you to freedom

If you follow the drinking gourd.

5 When the sun comes back and the first quail calls,

Follow the drinking gourd.

For the old man is a-waiting for to carry you to freedom

If you follow the drinking gourd.

In Other Words

a-waiting for to carry waiting
  to take
quail bird

Background Note

A gourd is a hard-shelled fruit. Some
dry gourds can be used like a cup.
The pattern of stars called the Big
Dipper looks like a drinking gourd.
People can use the Big Dipper to
find their way north at night because
it points to the North Star.

Before You Move On

1. **Metaphor** What do you think the
   "old man" represents in this song?
2. **Mood** The mood of a song is the
   feeling the writer gives it. What is
   the mood of this song?

Connect Reading and Writing

Vocabulary
assisted
capture
escape
freedom
rewards
rights
slaves
traveled

CRITICAL THINKING

1. **SUM IT UP** Make a Venn Diagram. Compare people in the past who wanted **freedom** with people who seek equal **rights** today.

Venn Diagram

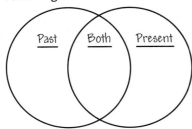

Past   Both   Present

2. **Interpret** Suppose you lived in the 1830s and saw a poster offering a **reward** for a runaway **slave**. How would you react? Explain why.

3. **Describe** How would you describe people who joined the Underground Railroad to **assist** **slaves**? Give three adjectives.

4. **Infer** Look at the map on page 366. Do you think it was easier for Henson to **escape** than for many other **slaves**? Explain.

READING FLUENCY

Intonation Read the passage on page 583 to a partner. Assess your fluency.

1. I read
   a. great   **b.** OK   **c.** not very well

2. What I did best in my reading was _____.

READING STRATEGY

Determine Importance
Show your notes to a partner. Explain how summarizing helped you decide what was important as you read.

VOCABULARY REVIEW

Oral Review Read the paragraph aloud. Add the vocabulary words.

To _____ from slavery, Josiah Henson _____ to Canada, which did not allow slavery. In Canada, African Americans had the same _____, or legal powers, as other citizens. Enslaved people who avoided _____ and reached Canada got their liberty, or _____. Although many owners offered _____, Canada would not return escaped _____. Henson then _____ former slaves.

Written Review Imagine that you live in the past and that you **travel** from town to town to speak out against slavery. Write your speech. Use at least five vocabulary words.

WRITE ABOUT THE GUIDING QUESTION

Explore the Struggle for Freedom
How does "Follow the Drinking Gourd" go with "**Escaping** to **Freedom**"? Reread both texts. Find examples in each one to support your ideas.

Connect Across the Curriculum

Analyze Text Structure: Cause and Effect

> **Academic Vocabulary**
> ● **arrange** (u-rānj) *verb*
>   To **arrange** means to put things in a
>   certain order.

How Is Writing Organized? Some nonfiction writers use cause and effect to structure, or **arrange**, their ideas. They use the structure to explain why something happens and how one event leads to another.

Sometimes a single cause has more than one effect. Sometimes two or more causes lead to one effect.

Practice Together

Read and Notice Read the paragraph from "Escaping to Freedom." Notice how different **causes** lead to the **effect**.

> Until 1865, most African Americans were not free. They were slaves with no rights. Their owners forced them to work without pay. They could be sold and sent far away from their families. Many African Americans decided their only chance for freedom was to escape.

Make a Chart You can use a Cause-Effect Organizer to show how events are related. List each cause and effect from the paragraph above.

Cause-Effect Organizer

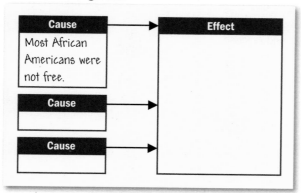

Try It!

Work with a partner. Choose another passage from "Escaping to Freedom." Identify the causes and effects. **Arrange** them in a chart to show how they relate.

Use Context Clues

> **Academic Vocabulary**
> • **context** (**kon**-tekst) *noun*
> Context refers to the parts nearby that help explain the meaning.

A **definition clue** explains an unfamiliar word directly in the text.
A **restatement clue** gives the meaning in a different way.

Look at the **context** clues in this sentence from "Escaping to Freedom."
Notice how the phrase "or large farm" restates the meaning of *plantation*.

> EXAMPLE   Henson lived on a <u>plantation</u>, or large farm, in Kentucky.

Figure Out Word Meanings Use **context** clues to figure out the meaning of each underlined word. Write a definition of the word.

1. The slaves had many <u>hardships</u>, or difficulties, in their lives.
2. The Underground Railroad <u>enabled</u>, or allowed, many slaves to escape.
3. <u>Underground</u> often refers to something that is secret.
4. A <u>conductor</u> on the Underground Railroad was a person who led slaves to safety.

Write Sentences Write a new sentence for each underlined word above.

Research the Underground Railroad

HISTORY

> **Academic Vocabulary**
> • **source** (**sors**) *noun*
> A **source** is the book or other text that you used to gather information.

1 Select a Topic With a group, brainstorm topics related to the Underground Railroad. Choose a specific topic to research.

2 Conduct Research Use the Internet or library books to learn more about the topic. Take notes from different **sources**.

> **Internet InsideNG.com**
> ⊘ Find out more about the Underground Railroad.

▲ Harriet Tubman led many to freedom on the Underground Railroad.

3 Write a Report Organize your notes so they follow a logical order. Then state the main ideas and support each one with facts, details, and examples. Write an introduction that will get readers' attention. End your report with a conclusion that restates the main points. Finally, list the **sources** you used in your research.

Listening/Speaking

Dramatize a Song

DRAMA

> **Academic Vocabulary**
> • **interpret** (in-**tur**-prut) *verb*
>   To **interpret** means to explain or tell what
>   something means.

As a group, analyze song lyrics—the words that make up a song. Then give
a dramatic reading to show your interpretation of the song.

1 **Read and Interpret** Reread the traditional song "Follow the Drinking
Gourd." Notice that the lyrics include some unusual words and phrases.
They are unusual because we do not use them every day. Use a chart
like this to **interpret** the words and phrases. Compare the words
and phrases in the lyrics with how people today might express the
same idea.

Song Lyrics Chart

Lyrics	In Other Words
Follow the drinking gourd	Follow the Big Dipper
the old man is a-waiting	the old man is waiting

2 **Discuss the Song** With a group, discuss how the unusual words and
phrases affect the song. What mood, or feeling, do they give the song?

3 **Prepare a Presentation** Plan to give a dramatic reading of the song.
Think about actions and facial expressions that go with the words. Show
how you **interpret** the
song. Practice a few times.

4 **Present the Song** Give
your dramatic reading.

• Speak clearly and loudly
  enough so your audience
  can hear you.

• Use a tone that
  expresses the feelings
  of the song.

• Do not speak too quickly
  or too slowly.

▲ The drinking gourd refers to the group of
stars known as the Big Dipper.

Summarize

Pair Talk Work with a partner to summarize one section of "Escaping to Freedom." Use subject and object pronouns correctly. Share your summary with the class.

> We read the first section, "Bonds of Slavery."

> Josiah Henson was a slave in Kentucky. He tried to buy his freedom. Josiah's owner took the money but didn't release him.

Write About Freedom

Study the Models When you write about an important topic like freedom, you want your readers to understand all your ideas. Use pronouns correctly so that your readers know whom or what you are talking about.

NOT OK

Jonathan Walker was born in 1799. **Him** opposed slavery strongly. Walker worked hard to try to stop **them**. Once, Walker helped seven slaves escape. The slaves sailed from Florida to freedom in the Bahamas. The authorities caught Walker and punished **us**. The incident did not stop **her**, however. For many years, **they** traveled around America and spoke out against slavery.

> The reader thinks: "I'm confused. I can't tell whom the writer is talking about."

OK

My aunt and my grandmother came to the United States from Saudi Arabia. **They** were amazed at all the freedom here. In Saudi Arabia, **they** could not drive a car or have a job. Everyone expected **them** to stay home most of the time. Now my aunt has a job. **She** works as an Arabic language teacher. Aunt Nadia loves **it**. **She** teaches **us** Arabic, too!

> This writer uses correct **subject pronouns and object pronouns**. It's easy to tell whom the writer is talking about.

Revise It Look back at the NOT OK passage. Work with a partner to revise it. Fix subject and object pronouns.

WRITE ON YOUR OWN Write about something you have done or would like to do to improve the rights or freedoms of others. Use subject and object pronouns correctly.

REMEMBER

	Singular					Plural		
Subject Pronouns	I	you	he	she	it	we	you	they
Object Pronouns	me	you	him	her	it	us	you	them

Brave Butterflies

by Susan Blackaby

Butterfly, 1978, Tamás Galambos. Oil on canvas, private collection.

SELECTION 2 OVERVIEW

▶ **Build Background**

▶ **Language & Grammar**
Make Comparisons
Use Pronouns in the Subject and Predicate

▶ **Prepare to Read**
Learn Key Vocabulary
Learn a Reading Strategy
Determine Importance

▶ **Read and Write**
Focus on Genre
Short Story
Apply the Reading Strategy
Determine Importance
Critical Thinking
Reading Fluency
Read with Expression
Vocabulary Review
Write About the Guiding Question

▶ **Connect Across the Curriculum**
Literary Analysis
Analyze Text Structure: Cause and Effect
Analyze the Topic
Vocabulary Study
Use Context Clues
Research/Speaking
Research Freedom Seekers
Language and Grammar
Make Comparisons
Writing and Grammar
Write About a New Home

Build Background

Tour an Island Country

The Dominican Republic is an island in the Caribbean Sea. The country has an interesting past and present.

Digital Library

InsideNG.com
⊙ View the video.

▲ A port on the island of the Dominican Republic

Connect

T Chart What do you think of the Dominican Republic? What would you like and dislike? Work with a group. List positive and negative impressions of the Dominican Republic.

T Chart

Positive	Negative
climate mountains	poverty politics

Language & Grammar

Make Comparisons

Listen to the chant. Listen again and chime in.

CHANT

What's the Difference?

The United States
And the Dominican Republic
Are as different as can be.
They are both in the
Americas, but one
Shares an island with Haiti.

Americans
Have beaches, mountains,
Deserts, hills, and plains.
Dominicans
Have beaches, mountains,
And fruit called plantains.

1 TRY OUT LANGUAGE
2 LEARN GRAMMAR
3 APPLY ON YOUR OWN

Use Pronouns in the Subject and Predicate

- Use a **subject pronoun** as the subject of a sentence.

  EXAMPLE   The red-roofed **house** is beautiful.
  It is on the beach in Tunisia.
  subject

- Use an **object pronoun** as the object of the verb in the predicate.

  EXAMPLES   Rodrigo owned an **apartment** in Cuba.
  He left **it** ten years ago.
  object

  I know many **people** in Mali.
  I visit **them** often.
  object

Singular Pronouns	
Subject	**Object**
I	me
you	you
he	him
she	her
it	it

Plural Pronouns	
Subject	**Object**
we	us
you	you
they	them

Practice Together

Say each pair of sentences. Choose the correct pronoun. Then tell whether it is a subject or an object pronoun.

1. My uncle's house is in the mountains. (He/She) built it forty years ago.
2. Our cousins live in the Dominican Republic. We call (us/them) every week.
3. Tía Jacinta is staying at our house. Mamá invited (him/her).
4. You and your family have a nice apartment. Do many people visit (me/you)?
5. I don't live far from you. (We/You) should visit me.

Try It!

Read each pair of sentences. Write the correct pronoun on a card. Hold up the card as you say the sentence. Then tell whether the pronoun is a subject or an object pronoun.

6. Margarita has a house in the Caribbean. We visit (him/her).
7. Father and I swim in the water. The sea amazes (us/you)!
8. Sebastian is Margarita's neighbor. We see (him/it) every day.
9. Sometimes Margarita and Sebastian discuss the government in their country. (He/They) like it.
10. Margarita asks us questions about the United States. (She/It) is interested in our country.

▲ The house is colorful. Do you like it?

Compare Homes

MAKE COMPARISONS

People have many different kinds of homes, and you can compare them.
Try one of these ideas:

- Compare your home with another home or an imaginary home.
- Compare your current home with one you used to live in.
- Compare the two most unusual homes you have seen.

Start your comparison with a Venn Diagram. In the outside sections, tell how the homes are different. In the center section, tell how the homes are the same or similar.

▲ This unusual house was built to look like a car.

Venn Diagram

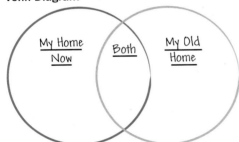

Use your diagram to organize your ideas about the two homes. Then share your comparison with a group.

HOW TO MAKE COMPARISONS

1. Tell how things are alike. Use words like *all*, *both*, *the same*, *similar*, and *too*.

2. Tell how things are different. Use words like *differ*, *different*, *only* and *but*.

> My new home is smaller than my old one, but it has a pretty garden.

USE PRONOUNS CORRECTLY

When you make your comparison, be sure to use the correct **subject pronouns** and **object pronouns**.

EXAMPLES   **My parents** sold our **house** in Venezuela.
They didn't need **it** anymore.

Odette visits **relatives** in Haiti.
She visits **them** in Haiti.

Prepare to Read

Learn Key Vocabulary

Rate and Study the Words Rate how well you know each word. Then:

1. Pronounce the word. Say it aloud several times. Spell it.
2. Study the example.
3. Tell more about the word.
4. Practice it. Make the word your own.

Key Words

arrest (u-rest) *verb*
▶ page 382

To **arrest** means to put someone in jail. A police officer **arrests** a suspect and puts handcuffs on him.

dictator (dik-tā-tur) *noun*
▶ page 382

A **dictator** is a person who leads a country without sharing power. Most **dictators** do not allow others to make decisions for the country.

hopeful (hōp-ful) *adjective*
▶ page 388

Someone who is **hopeful** is full of good thoughts about what will happen. This girl is **hopeful** about winning the contest.

journal (jur-nul) *noun*
▶ page 382

A **journal** is a record of someone's thoughts, feelings, and actions. Some people write in their **journal** almost every day.

organize (or-gu-nīz) *verb*
▶ page 382

To **organize** means to plan and set up something. The man **organizes** the people to support a cause.

politics (pah-lu-tiks) *noun*
▶ page 385

Politics is the business of government. Members of Congress talk about issues of national and international **politics**.

rescue (res-kyū) *noun*
▶ page 388

A **rescue** is the act of saving someone or something from danger. The **rescue** was daring and successful.

violent (vī-u-lunt) *adjective*
▶ page 389

Something that is **violent** uses force. **Violent** storms like tornadoes can damage buildings and kill people.
Synonyms: **cruel, fierce**
Antonyms: **peaceful, gentle**

Practice the Words Make a Word Map for each Key Word. Then compare your maps with a partner's.

Definition	Characteristics
to put in jail	involves police; relates to crime
	Word **arrest**
She was arrested for stealing a bicycle.	She got a bicycle for her birthday.
Example	Non-example

Word Map

Reading Strategy: Determine Importance

When you read, look for the main ideas and the most important details. The author may not state them directly, so look for clues to determine what they are.

HOW TO IDENTIFY MAIN IDEAS AND DETAILS

1. Turn the title into a question.

2. Look for information to answer your question. Record what you find.

3. Think about how the details answer your question. Write one or two sentences to state the main ideas.

Strategy in Action

Here's how one student identified main ideas and details.

Look Into the Text

Kiki, that rascal, had escaped when I opened the door. She scampered across the lawn and slipped into the Garcías' yard.

I followed her and searched the bushes next to the house. When I finally spotted her, I had to bend low to reach her. She pawed at my outstretched fingers. I was about to call to her when I heard two men's voices drifting through the open window above my head. They were talking about my father. I froze.

"Alberto Pérez is involved," said Mr. García.

> These details seem important. I will add them to the chart.

Main-Idea Chart

Title: Brave Butterflies
Question: How can butterflies be brave? What brave thing did they do?

Detail: Two men are talking about the girl's father and she stops to listen.

Detail: Her father is involved in something.

Detail:

Main Idea:

Practice Together

Make a Main-Idea Chart like the one above. Follow the steps in the How-To box as you read the selection. Record important details and state the main ideas.

Short Story

A short story is a kind of narrative fiction. The actions of the **characters** make up the plot. A character who tells the story is the **narrator**.

> The voices became muffled as the men moved through the house, and I heard the front door open. I stayed in my hiding place until I saw Mr. García and the man drive away. Then I scooped up Kiki and sneaked back home.

Short stories often have a cause-and-effect structure. The reason for each action is a cause. What happens because of the action is an effect.

Your Job as a Reader

Reading Strategy: Determine Importance

As you read, look for details that will help you identify main ideas. Record the details in your Main-Idea Chart. Use them to help you state main ideas.

Detail: The girl hides until the men drive away.

Brave Butterflies
by Susan Blackaby

Butterfly, 1978, Tamás Galambos. Oil on canvas, private collection.

▲ **Critical Viewing: Design** Why do you think the artist made the butterfly in this painting larger than the leaves?

Online Coach

"Kitty . . . Here, kitty kitty . . ."

Kiki, that rascal, had escaped when I opened the door. She **scampered** across the lawn and slipped into the Garcías' yard.

I followed her and searched the bushes next to the house. When I finally **spotted** her, I had to bend low to reach her. She pawed at my outstretched fingers. I was about to call to her when I heard two men's voices drifting through the open window above my head. They were talking about my father. I froze.

"Alberto Pérez is involved," said Mr. García. "He has been seen with those who are foolish enough to **organize** in the name of *Las Mariposas*. I've heard he keeps a **journal** about their activities. It's only a matter of time until we **arrest** him. In the meantime, I'm **keeping my eye on** him."

"Why should we wait?" the other voice asked. "We should get our hands on that journal now. Think of the reward!" he said.

García laughed. "There's no harm in conducting a surprise search. It's a good way to find out what information he has."

I was stunned! I never suspected that Mr. García was a member of the secret police!

Key Vocabulary

dictator *n.*, a person who leads a country completely

organize *v.*, to plan and set up

journal *n.*, a record of one's thoughts and feelings

arrest *v.*, to put someone in jail

In Other Words

scampered ran
spotted found
keeping my eye on watching

Historical Background

Las Mariposas (the Butterflies) was the code name for the three Mirabal sisters who opposed the dictator, Rafael Trujillo. They were killed on November 25, 1960. In their memory, November 25 is International Day for the Elimination of Violence Against Women.

The voices became **muffled** as the men moved through the house, and I heard the front door open. I stayed in my hiding place until I saw Mr. García and the other man drive away. Then I scooped up Kiki and sneaked back home.

Home, 2006, Elizabeth Rosen. Acrylic on wood, collection of the artist.

▲ **Critical Viewing: Setting** How does this image relate to the setting of the story? Explain.

In Other Words
muffled hard to understand

At dinner I couldn't eat. My stomach **churned**, and my throat felt raw. Papi chatted with Carlos about baseball as if **he didn't have a care in the world**. Mami, always on the alert, reached over and felt my forehead. Her thin fingers tipped my chin to the light. I looked into her eyes and saw the fear and worry that I had not recognized before.

"Early bedtime for you," she said.

Normally I would **protest**. I had just turned thirteen, and Mami still treated me like a child. But now I simply nodded, not trusting myself to speak.

Madre Protectora II, 2007, Felix Berroa. Acrylic and oil on canvas, collection of the artist.

▲ **Critical Viewing: Character** How do these people feel about each other? Why do you think that?

In Other Words
churned was upset
he didn't have a care in the world nothing was wrong
protest disagree

I awoke in the middle of the night and looked outside. A dim light **flickered** in one of the Garcías' windows, a watchful eye spying on us. In the **study**, I could hear Papi and Mami talking in low whispers. I tiptoed down the hallway and stood in the shadows.

"Alberto, please, you must be more careful," Mami pleaded. "Getting involved in **politics** is risky. Think of our friends who have gone to prison or disappeared. Think of the Mirabal sisters. **We could suffer the same fate**."

"I am thinking of them," said Papi. "I am thinking of the courage that the Mirabals—those brave *Mariposas*—

> "...you must be more careful," Mami pleaded.

showed in standing up to the dictator. And I am thinking of our children's future. Just imagine what it would be like to live in freedom."

"But Alberto, these are **violent** and dangerous times," said Mami. "Everyone in the Dominican Republic is **caught in an iron grip of fear**. I share your dream, but I'm afraid of what could happen."

"And I'm afraid of what could happen if we do nothing," said Papi.

I tiptoed back to my room and curled up with Kiki under my chin. I didn't sleep for a long time, and when I did, I dreamed of butterflies, their wings flickering in the sunshine.

Key Vocabulary
politics *n.*, the business of government
violent *adj.*, using force

In Other Words
flickered shone
study office
We could suffer the same fate. The same thing could happen to us.
caught in an iron grip of fear very scared

Before You Move On

1. **Paraphrase** What does the girl learn at the García house? What does she learn in her own house?
2. **Cause and Effect** Why does the girl go to bed early?
3. **Inference** Why does the girl dream of butterflies?

A week later, Mr. García **carried out his threat**. When Carlos and I got home from school, the car I had seen before was parked out in front of the Garcías' house. Once we were safely inside, I grabbed Carlos's arm and hurried him into the kitchen, where Mami was cooking.

"Mr. García is going to search the house," I said. "Is Papi's journal here?"

Mami looked startled. Then she answered, "Yes, Ana, but it is well hidden. I don't know where it is."

"I do," I said.

I hurried to Papi's study and pulled up the loose **floorboard** underneath the desk.

The thin, worn notebook was wrapped in cloth.

"Carlos, quick," I said. "Hand me your baseball bat."

I was replacing the floorboard when Mr. García pounded on the door. Carlos answered and then stepped aside as Mr. García and several of the men in his **squad** entered the house. Mami came from the kitchen, wiping her hands on her apron.

"Good evening, Mrs. Pérez." Mr. García smiled, but his eyes were as cold as steel.

"Good evening," said Mami. "If you're looking for Alberto, I'm afraid he isn't here."

"Oh, we know that, Mrs. Pérez," said Mr. García. "He was seen leaving the university just a little while ago.

In Other Words
carried out his threat did what he
   said he was going to do
floorboard part of the floor
squad group

▲ **Critical Viewing: Mood** How does this image make you feel? Why?

Unless he stops somewhere on the way home, he should be here in fifteen or twenty minutes."

"I'm sure he will come straight home," said Mami.

"We will soon see," said Mr. García. "In the meantime, my men will have a look around." Mami, Carlos, and I sat in the dining room while Mr. García's men opened drawers and cupboards. They pulled the books off the bookshelf and threw the pillows off the furniture.

"So, Carlos," sneered Mr. García, "I hear that you are the fourth Alou brother. I suppose you are **hopeful** that you will be asked to **play ball** in the United States in a few years."

"Yes sir," said Carlos, twirling his baseball bat between his knees.

Just then Kiki danced across the floor. We watched as she **swatted** a big wad of tape between her paws. One flick sent it tumbling under a **bureau**.

Mr. García frowned.

I held my breath.

Papi came through the door, right on time.

> ## " . . . my men will have a look around."

Key Vocabulary
hopeful *adj.*, full of good thoughts about what will happen

In Other Words
play ball be on a professional baseball team
swatted hit
bureau set of drawers

Historical Background
Brothers Matty, Felipe, and Jesus Alou all moved from the Dominican Republic to the United States to play professional baseball. One season they all played for the San Francisco Giants. Then they played for different teams. Felipe went on to become a baseball manager.

Late that night, when the police were finally gone, Papi came into my room.

"You were very brave, Ana," he said. "Carlos and Mami tell me that you were the one who came to the **rescue**."

"We all did, Papi," I said. "Carlos wrapped your notebook around the handle of his bat and Mami helped me retape it. Even Kiki helped. She hid the old tape under the bureau."

"But you knew what was coming," said Papi. "You **hover around** us, watching and waiting."

"Kind of like a butterfly," I said. ❖

Vegetation, 1978, Tamás Galambos. Oil on canvas, private collection.

🔺 **Critical Viewing: Design** What details do you notice in the painting? How do they affect the overall feeling?

Before You Move On

1. **Confirm Prediction** Was your prediction correct? What happened that you did not expect?
2. **Paraphrase** How does Ana come to the **rescue**?

Farah Ahmedi

by Libby Lewis

Farah Ahmedi was born in Afghanistan. Although her country was at war, she had a happy life with her father, mother, brothers, and sisters.

But when Farah was seven years old, something terrible happened. As she crossed a field, she stepped on a **land mine**, and it exploded. Farah survived, but she lost her left leg. She had to get a **prosthetic** leg to help her walk.

Then, two years later, a bomb hit her house. It killed her father and sisters.

A few months later, her brothers left home and were never heard from again.

Farah and her mother were alone.

At this time, the laws in Afghanistan said women could not go anywhere in public without a male relative. Farah and her mother could not go to work, school, or even the store.

Farah and her mother decided they had to leave their country in order to be free.

They crossed into Pakistan by walking over the mountains. The path was steep, and it was a risk with Farah's prosthetic leg. But she did not let it slow her down.

Farah and her mother made it safely to Pakistan. After many more hardships, they came to the United States.

Today, Farah and her mother live in Illinois. She works with an international group that clears **minefields** around the world. She also runs a foundation to help other **amputees**.

"I lost my leg, I lost my family, I am out from my country, but I never gave up," Farah says. "And I will keep going."

In Other Words
land mine bomb
prosthetic false, artificial
minefields areas with bombs
amputees people who have lost
   body parts

Before You Move On

1. **Recall and Interpret** Why did Farah and her mother walk over the mountains to Pakistan? Was this a good thing for them to do? Why or why not?

2. **Character** What kind of person is Farah Ahmedi? What details make you think this?

Connect Reading and Writing

Vocabulary

arrest

dictator

hopeful

journal

organize

politics

rescue

violent

CRITICAL THINKING

1. **SUM IT UP** Make a Beginning-Middle-End chart for the selection. Use the chart to retell the story.

Beginning-Middle-End Chart

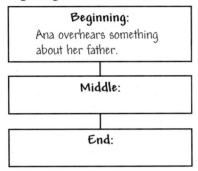

Beginning:
Ana overhears something about her father.

Middle:

End:

2. **Speculate** Do you think Mr. García will ever **arrest** Ana's father? Explain.

3. **Generalize** Think about what you read about the **dictator** in this story and what you know about other **dictators**. Tell two things that are true for all or most dictators.

4. **Compare** Both Ana and Farah experienced **violent** situations. Do you think one situation was worse than the other? Explain.

READING FLUENCY

Expression Read the passage on page 584 to a partner. Assess your fluency.

1. I read
   a. great   **b.** OK   **c.** not very well

2. What I did best in my reading was _____.

READING STRATEGY

Determine Importance
During reading, how did you identify main ideas and details? With a partner, share one example.

VOCABULARY REVIEW

Oral Review Read the paragraph aloud. Add the vocabulary words.

Alberto Pérez keeps a _____ about some people who are active in _____. Those heroes try to come to the _____, to save their country from Trujillo's iron grip. Trujillo was the _____ of the Dominican Republic from 1930 to 1961. If people tried to _____ against him, the police could _____ them. Police actions could be mean and _____. In May 1961, Trujillo himself was murdered, but problems continued. Not until many years later, when fair elections began, could people begin to be _____ about the future.

Written Review Imagine that you are living in the Dominican Republic during the 1950s and are **organizing** against the government. Write a report. Use five vocabulary words.

WRITE ABOUT THE GUIDING QUESTION

Explore the Struggle for Freedom
What do you think the Pérez family is willing to do for the sake of freedom from the **dictator**? Use details from the text to support your response.

Connect Across the Curriculum

Analyze Text Structure: Cause and Effect

> **Academic Vocabulary**
> • **demonstrate** (de-mun-strāt) *verb*
>   To **demonstrate** means to prove or make clear.

How Is Writing Organized? You often read about causes and effects in stories. Sometimes a situation leads to a character taking action. The action is the effect, or the result of the cause. Sometimes an effect influences another event later in the story. Look for causes and effects in this part of the selection.

> Kiki, that rascal, had escaped when I opened the door. She scampered across the lawn and slipped into the Garcías' yard.
>
> I followed her and searched the bushes next to the house. . . . I was about to call to her when I heard two men's voices drifting through the open window . . .

In this example, the cause is opening the door. The effect is that the cat escapes and runs into the neighbor's yard. This action influences what happens later: Ana overhears two men talking about her father.

Practice Together

Use a Cause-and-Effect Chain A Cause-and-Effect Chain helps **demonstrate** how some events influence other events. Begin by writing the first cause in the first box. Write the effect in the next box, and so on. Compare this chain with the text above. What would go in the next box?

Cause-and-Effect Chain

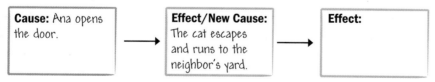

| Cause: Ana opens the door. | → | Effect/New Cause: The cat escapes and runs to the neighbor's yard. | → | Effect: |

Try It!

Create a Cause-and-Effect Chain Work with a partner. Choose another part of the story. Make a Cause-and-Effect Chain. **Demonstrate** how causes influence later events in the story.

Use Context Clues

> **Academic Vocabulary**
> ● **explain** (ik-**splān**) *verb*
> When you **explain** an idea, you make it clear so people can understand it.

When you come to an unfamiliar word in the text, you can look for context clues that **explain** the meaning. A **synonym clue** gives a word or phrase that means almost the same as the unfamiliar word. An **antonym clue** gives a word or phrase that means the opposite of the unfamiliar word.

Figure Out the Meaning Tell the meaning of each underlined word. **Explain** how you used the context clues.

1. I never <u>suspected</u> that Mr. García was a member of the secret police. It was unbelievable!
2. "You must be more careful," Mami pleaded. "Getting involved in politics is <u>risky</u>."
3. Mami looked <u>startled</u> at first, but then tried to calm herself.
4. Mr. García <u>sneered</u> and made fun of Carlos's dreams of playing baseball.

Research Freedom Seekers

HISTORY

> **Academic Vocabulary**
> ● **source** (sors) *noun*
> A **source** is the book or other text that you used to gather information.

❶ Conduct Research Find out about other people or groups that have fought for human rights, as the Mirabal sisters did. Use different **sources** of information, including history books, the Internet, and experts.

> **Internet** InsideNG.com
> ⌁ Experience the stories of other freedom-seeking groups around the world.

❷ Collect Facts Gather narrative accounts about the group you researched. Plan a presentation. Organize your ideas. Collect pictures, maps, and other visuals that you can use in your talk.

❸ Make a Narrative Presentation Begin by providing background information so listeners can imagine the events. Give a narrative account of the group you chose. Include interesting details. Explain why people should know about the group.

▲ Artist Elsa Nuñez honored the Mirabal sisters by painting this monument in Santo Domingo in the Dominican Republic.

Analyze the Topic

> **Academic Vocabulary**
> ● **topic** (tah-pik) *noun*
>   A **topic** is the subject of a piece of writing or of a discussion.

A **topic** of a story is what the story is about. Different writers can write about the same **topic** in a short story, a news article, a personal narrative, or another genre. When you compare the information that different authors present, you can learn a lot more about the **topic**.

Practice Together

Begin a Comparison Chart The **topic** of "Brave Butterflies" is life under a cruel government. The biography of Farah Ahmedi has the same **topic**. You can compare how the two selections discuss this **topic**. Begin by reading this passage from "Brave Butterflies."

> "But Alberto, these are violent and dangerous times," said Mami. "Everyone in the Dominican Republic is caught in an iron grip of fear."

▲ Rafael Trujillo was dictator in the Dominican Republic until 1961.

Use a Comparison Chart to record your ideas. Think about what kind of writing each one represents. Add notes about the information that the writers include.

Comparison Chart

Selection	Kind of Writing	Information
"Brave Butterflies"	fiction short story	Dominicans were afraid of the government.
"Farah Ahmedi"		

Try It!

Complete the Chart Add more information from each selection to complete your chart.

Analyze Topics Use your charts to analyze the two selections. Why do you think the authors chose the genres they did to discuss the **topic**? What did you learn about life under a cruel government?

Make Comparisons

Compare and Share Compare the experience of the Pérez family with the experiences of enslaved Americans seeking freedom. Share your comparison with a partner. Use pronouns correctly.

> Ana's family is afraid of being arrested or killed by the secret police. Runaway slaves were afraid of being caught.

Write About a New Home

Study the Models When you write about personal experiences, you want readers to be interested. Vary your sentences and use pronouns to take the place of nouns. Be sure to use the right pronouns so readers won't get confused.

NOT OK

> Two years ago, my parents and I arrived in New York. Our relatives met my parents and me at the airport. My relatives took my parents and me to their house. My parents and I stayed there for several months before finding an apartment. The apartment was not very big, but we liked the apartment. The apartment was not far from our relatives' house. My parents and I got to see our relatives often.

The writer repeats the same words, and the sentences sound too similar. The reader thinks: "**I can't understand this.**"

OK

> Two years ago, my parents and I arrived in New York. Our relatives met **us** at the airport. Where do you think **they** took **us**? To their house! **We** stayed there for several months before finding an apartment. Our apartment wasn't very big, but we liked **it**. Best of all, **it** was close to our relatives' house, and **we** got to see **them** often.

The writer uses a mix of nouns and **pronouns** as well as different kinds of sentences. The writing is more interesting.

Add Sentences Think of two sentences to add to the OK model above. Use subject pronouns and object pronouns correctly.

✎ **WRITE ON YOUR OWN** Think about a time in your life when you moved to a new place or thought about moving. Write about the experience. Pay attention to subject and object pronouns.

REMEMBER

	Singular					Plural		
Subject Pronouns	I	you	he	she	it	we	you	they
Object Pronouns	me	you	him	her	it	us	you	them

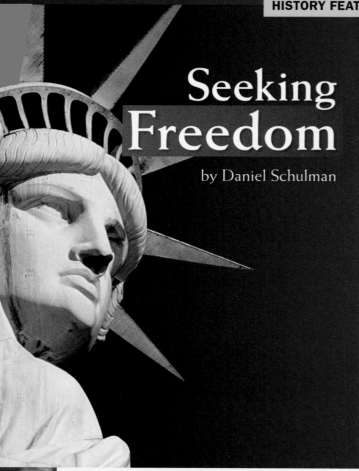

Seeking Freedom

by Daniel Schulman

Build Background

Connect

Anticipation Guide What will people do for freedom? Tell whether you agree or disagree with each statement.

Anticipation Guide

	Agree	Disagree
1. It is OK to break the law if you are fighting for human rights.	____	____
2. People should be willing to give up their rights in exchange for safety and security.	____	____

Talk About Rights

People all over the world have certain needs and wants. Look at the photos, and discuss how people stand up for their rights.

Digital Library

InsideNG.com
↗ View the images.

▲ Journalists fight for rights in Pakistan.

Language & Grammar

Express Opinions

CD

Listen to the information. Then listen to the opinions.
What do you think?

INFORMATION and OPINIONS

Myanmar is a country in Southeast Asia. People there are not allowed to express their opinions in public about the government or to vote for their own government.

In September of 2007, thousands of people marched in the streets of Myanmar. They protested peacefully against the government. The government arrested many people. Some people were beaten or even killed.

In my opinion, all people should have the freedom to say what they think about their government.

Use Possessive Nouns

Use a **possessive noun** to show that someone owns, or possesses, something.

	How to Make the Noun Possessive	Examples
One Owner	Add **'s**.	A country's government is democratic if the people vote for the leaders.
More Than One Owner	Add **'** if the noun ends in **-s**.	The citizens' rights are important.
	Add **'s** if the noun does not end in **-s**.	The people's votes count.

EXAMPLES   **The laws of the nation** are fair. The **nation's** laws are fair.

People obey **the laws of the rulers**. People obey the **rulers'** laws.

Practice Together

Change the words in each box to form a phrase with a possessive noun. Say the phrase. Then say the complete sentence.

1. | the great-grandmother of Lena | _____ escaped from East Germany and came to the United States.

2. | the fight of African Americans | _____ for equal rights was difficult.

3. | the journey of my grandparents | _____ to the United States was long.

4. | the father of Tchin | _____ is an activist in Myanmar.

5. | the rights of women | Susan B. Anthony fought for _____ in the 1800s.

Try It!

Change the words in each box to form a phrase with a possessive noun. Write the phrase on a card. Then say the sentence with the phrase.

6. | the protest of the monks | Did you hear about _____ in Myanmar?

7. | the desire of people | It is important to understand _____ for liberty.

8. | the Constitution of this country | _____ protects our rights and freedoms.

9. | the governments of some countries | _____ don't allow people to express opinions in public.

10. | the citizens of East Germany | _____ gained the right to travel to the West in 1989.

▲ For many years, the Berlin Wall limited East Germans' freedom.

Discuss Ideas About Freedom

EXPRESS OPINIONS

Imagine that you live in a country that does not allow its citizens to be free. How far would you go to fight for your rights? What would you do?

As a class, form two groups. With your group, brainstorm a list of tasks and dangers that someone might face in the fight for human rights. Write the list in your own notebook. Check off the tasks and dangers you would be willing to face.

Tasks and Dangers	Yes or No?
1. Go to prison	
2. Face armed soldiers	
3. Risk death	

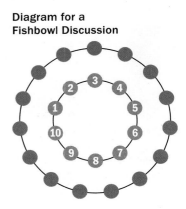

Diagram for a Fishbowl Discussion

Now have a "fishbowl" discussion with the other group. Form a circle with your chairs. Face inward, toward the center of the circle. The other group forms a circle around you. The outside group listens as your group members exchange opinions about fighting for human rights.

Switch positions and listen to the other group's discussion. How is it different from your group's discussion?

HOW TO EXPRESS OPINIONS

1. Tell what you think about something. Use expressions like *I think*, *I believe*, *In my opinion*, and *For me*.

2. If you have the same opinion as someone else, you can say "I agree." If you have a different opinion, you can say "I disagree."

> In my opinion, freedom is more important than anything else.

> I agree.

USE POSSESSIVE NOUNS

In your discussion, you may talk about people's experiences or countries' actions. Be sure to use **possessive nouns** correctly.

EXAMPLE   My **family's** escape from Afghanistan was difficult.

Learn Key Vocabulary

Rate and Study the Words Rate how well you know each word. Then:

1. Pronounce the word. Say it aloud several times. Spell it.
2. Study the example.
3. Tell more about the word.
4. Practice it. Make the word your own.

Key Words

government
(**gu**-vurn-munt) *noun* ▸ page 404

The people who control the country according to certain laws are the **government**. Washington, DC, is the center of the U.S. **government**.

law (law) *noun*
▸ page 404

The **law** is a country's rules. A police officer reminds people to follow the **law**.

leader (**lē**-dur) *noun*
▸ page 406

A **leader** is a person in charge of others. The **leader** of our hiking club decides which trail we will take.

opinion (u-**pin**-yun) *noun*
▸ page 405

An **opinion** is a belief or a view about a topic. My friends share their **opinions** about fashion.

protest (**prō**-test) *verb*
▸ page 409 *noun* ▸ page 410

1 *verb* To **protest** means to make a statement against an idea. The students **protested** against school spending cuts. **2** *noun* A **protest** is a display of strong feelings.

public (**pu**-blik) *noun*
▸ page 412

When you are in **public**, you are in an area that is open to others. Even though we held our family gathering in **public**, the setting felt private.

responsibility
(ri-**spont**-su-**bi**-lu-tē) *noun* ▸
page 404

A **responsibility** is something you should do because it is right. It is my **responsibility** to walk the dog every day.

system (**sis**-tum) *noun*
▸ page 408

A **system** is a way of doing things. An assembly line is a factory **system** that usually saves time and money.

Practice the Words Work with a partner to complete an Expanded Meaning Map for each Key Word.

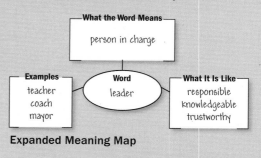

Expanded Meaning Map

Reading Strategy: Determine Importance

As you read, look for details that relate to your own life. This will make the text more meaningful to you.

Reading Strategy
Determine Importance

HOW TO DETERMINE WHAT IS IMPORTANT TO YOU

1. Identify the topic. Note what the author is writing about.

2. Decide on your purpose. Figure out what you want to know about the topic.

3. Focus on your purpose. Look for details that tell you what you want to know about the topic.

Strategy in Action

Here's how one student determined what is important.

Look Into the Text

"The writer is mostly telling about freedom in the United States."

   The people who built the government of the United States more than 200 years ago knew that freedom was important. They wrote . . . the Constitution, and it explains how the government should work. Part of the Constitution is the Bill of Rights. It lists freedoms that all Americans share.   **Detail**

"I want to know more about Americans' freedoms."

   People who have freedom also have responsibilities. One responsibility is knowing that others have rights, too. We should not hurt others or break the law, but we are free to make choices.   **Detail**

"Now I know more about the rights and responsibilities of freedom."

Practice Together

Read the passage again, and make notes on any ideas that relate to your own life.

Focus on Genre

History Feature

History features tell about real people and real events from the recent past or long ago. History features often contain **cause**-and-**effect** relationships about important events and ideas.

> Some countries do not have laws that protect people's freedom. What do people in those countries do to find freedom?
>
> Sometimes people leave their homes.

Your Job as a Reader

Reading Strategy: Determine Importance

As you read, look for details that fit your purpose.

> The text says that sometimes people leave their homes. I want to know why people leave their homes.

Seeking
Freedom

by Daniel Schulman

Throughout history, people have searched for freedom and found it in different ways.

Online Coach

A Plan for Freedom

The people who built the **government** of the United States more than 200 years ago knew that freedom was important. They wrote on paper their ideas for a free country. This paper is the Constitution, and it explains how the government should work. Part of the Constitution is the Bill of Rights. It lists freedoms that all Americans share.

People who have freedom also have **responsibilities**. One responsibility is knowing that others have rights, too. We should not hurt others or break the **law**, but we are free to make choices.

▼ This shows the beginning of the U.S. Constitution. The actual document, including the Bill of Rights, is several pages. Some additional laws, or amendments, have been added more recently.

Historical Background

The Constitution explains the powers of the U.S. government. It became law in 1789. The Bill of Rights contains the first ten amendments, or changes, to the Constitution. The amendments protect the rights of every U.S. citizen. They were added in 1791.

Some Freedoms in the Bill of Rights

Freedom of Speech
People can say what they think, without fear. This means people can disagree with one another or the government about what should be done.

Freedom of the Press
News reporters can tell the news as they see it. This helps people understand events and form their own **opinions**.

Freedom of Religion
People can choose their religion. In free countries, there are often many different religions.

Before You Move On

1. **Explain** What does it mean to have **responsibilities** as well as rights?
2. **Interpret** What are some of the freedoms that U.S. citizens share?

Key Vocabulary
opinion *n.*, a belief or view about a topic

In Other Words
News reporters People who write news stories

Seeking Freedom

Some countries do not have laws that protect people's freedoms. What do people in those countries do to find freedom?

Sometimes people leave their homes. They might move to a country with more freedom, but this can be very hard. People who move to a new country might have to learn a new language and way of life.

Reasons to Leave Home

Millions of people have left their homes in search of freedom. Often they want freedom to practice their religion or the freedom to pick their **leaders**. People move for freedom of speech and freedom of the press. People also move because they want a better education or jobs.

People Who Have Moved for Freedom

English, 1600s

The Pilgrims began to leave for the Americas in 1620. They left England because they were not allowed to practice their religion.

Germans, 1930s

Many Germans, especially Jews, left Germany because of a **cruel** government. They moved to other countries to find freedom.

Key Vocabulary
leader *n.*, a person in charge of others

In Other Words
cruel mean and hurtful

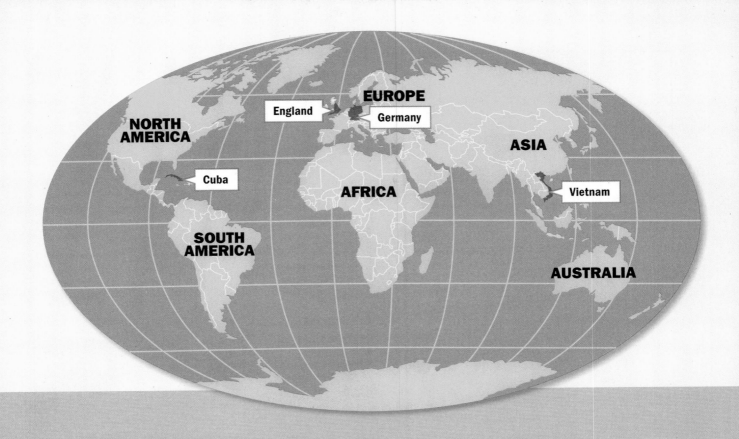

NORTH AMERICA

EUROPE

England

Germany

ASIA

Cuba

AFRICA

Vietnam

SOUTH AMERICA

AUSTRALIA

Cubans, 1960s

Many Cubans left their island country in the 1960s. They left because their government did not allow them to pick their leaders.

Vietnamese, 1970s

Many people from Vietnam left to escape war. People there were also not free to speak out or to choose their work.

Before You Move On

1. **Recall and Interpret** Why is it hard for most people to move to a new country?

2. **Categorize** What are four reasons that people might leave their home countries?

▲ Nelson Mandela spent 28 years in prison for speaking about freedom.

AFRICA

South Africa

Working for Freedom at Home

People do not always leave their country to find freedom. Sometimes they struggle for it at home. That happened in South Africa. About 20 years ago, South Africa had a **system** called apartheid, which means "separation." Apartheid was a set of unfair laws. These laws took away freedoms from some people because of the color of their skin.

Nelson Mandela fought against apartheid. He was even **jailed** for speaking out, but he won! Apartheid laws were changed. Like many others, Mandela thought freedom was **worth fighting** for.

Key Vocabulary
system *n.*, a way of doing things

In Other Words
jailed put in jail
worth fighting important enough to fight

Students Speak Out

In 1989, thousands of Chinese students gathered in Tiananmen Square in Beijing, China, to **peacefully protest** unfair laws. They wanted more freedom from their government.

The students did not **succeed** because China's government sent in the army to stop the students. Hundreds of students were killed. People in China still do not have many freedoms.

ASIA

China

▲ Students in Tiananmen Square carried signs asking for fair laws.

Before You Move On

1. **Vocabulary** What is apartheid? What clues in the text help you know the definition?
2. **Cause and Effect** What happened when students **protested** in Tiananmen Square?

Key Vocabulary

protest *v.*, to make a strong statement against an idea or action

In Other Words

peacefully quietly and calmly
succeed get what they wanted

The Right to Vote

People in the United States have struggled for the freedom we have now. For many years women could not vote, and they did not have the same rights as men.

Women who wanted to vote began to join together. They held meetings and **protests**. Some were even **arrested** and jailed. On August 26, 1920, women in the United States finally **gained** the right to vote.

▲ This Suffrage Badge was produced around 1910 to encourage women to fight for the right to vote.

▲ In the early 1900s, women protested to gain the right to vote. This photo shows Mrs. Herbert Carpenter leading a march on Fifth Avenue in New York City to gain women's rights.

Key Vocabulary
protest *n.*, a display of strong feelings against an idea or action

In Other Words
arrested taken away by the police
gained won, got

Freedom for All

African Americans in the United States did not always have the same freedoms as other Americans. Many were kept from voting. Some were not allowed to go to good schools. Others were not allowed to use or enjoy the same things as white people.

In the 1960s, people protested. They said African Americans should have the same rights as all Americans. These protests helped change the laws.

▲ On August 28, 1963, Dr. Martin Luther King, Jr., spoke to more than 200,000 people during the March on Washington to demand equal rights for all citizens.

Before You Move On

1. **Conclusion** Why did many American women **protest** against the **government** in the early 1900s?
2. **Compare and Contrast** Why did African Americans **protest** in the 1960s? How were their goals similar to and different from the goals of women in the early 1900s?

The Search for Freedom Continues

Today freedom is spreading around the world. **Until recently**, people in Afghanistan had very few freedoms. Women were not allowed to go to school or work, and they could not be seen in **public**. Men were **punished** or killed if they did not follow the government's rules.

Countries around the world helped the people of Afghanistan. Now they have important rights and a new **constitution**.

It says that citizens have the right to vote. They can choose who will stand up and speak for them. The new constitution says that girls can go to school. It also says that women can work and move freely in public.

All around the world, people **seek** freedom to make their own choices. ❖

▼ Girls in Afghanistan now have the right to go to school.

ASIA

Afghanistan

Key Vocabulary
public *n.*, an area open to everyone

In Other Words
Until recently Not many years ago
punished hurt
constitution list of rules that says what can happen in the country
seek look for; try to get

Before You Move On

1. **Evidence and Conclusion** What information shows that freedom is spreading around the world?
2. **Judgment** How is the new constitution of Afghanistan better or worse for the country?

Connect Reading and Writing

Vocabulary
governments

laws

leaders

opinion

protests

public

responsibility

systems

CRITICAL THINKING

1. **SUM IT UP** Make an outline to record the ideas in each section of the text. Use your outline to sum up the selection.

   Outline

   I. A Plan for Freedom
      A.
      B.
   II.
      A.

2. **Explain** What can people do if the **leaders** or **laws** of their country are unjust? Support your ideas with examples from the text.

3. **Infer** The U.S. **government** is based on the Constitution. Why do you think this document has worked so well for more than 200 years?

4. **Analyze** Review your Anticipation Guide on page 396. Do you want to change your **opinions**? Discuss in a group.

READING FLUENCY

Phrasing Read the passage on page 585 to a partner. Assess your fluency.

1. I read
   a. great   **b.** OK   **c.** not very well

2. What I did best in my reading was _____.

READING STRATEGY

Determine Importance
Did you find details in the text that you wanted to know? Did this help you understand the text? Share one example.

VOCABULARY REVIEW

Oral Review Read the paragraph aloud. Add the vocabulary words.

> Mohandas Gandhi and Martin Luther King, Jr., believed that the people who ran their _____ had made rules, or _____, that failed to protect everyone. Their countries' political _____, or ways of doing things, needed to change. Gandhi and King took _____ for forcing change. They spoke in _____, not just in private, about unjust conditions and became great _____ for people. They organized peaceful marches and _____ to help create change. In the _____ of many people, Gandhi and King are heroes of freedom.

Written Review Think of a **responsibility** that someone has in a free country. Write a paragraph about it. Use at least five vocabulary words.

WRITE ABOUT THE GUIDING QUESTION

Explore the Struggle for Freedom
Why is freedom worth fighting for? Reread the selection and write your **opinion** about the worth of freedom. Use evidence from the text.

Analyze Text Structure: Cause and Effect

Academic Vocabulary
- **demonstrate** (de-mun-strāt) *verb*
  To **demonstrate** means to prove or make clear.

How Is Writing Organized? Nonfiction texts often **demonstrate** cause-and-effect relationships. Words and phrases such as *because*, *the reason*, *since*, and *as a result* signal cause and effect.

Practice Together

Read and Notice Read this passage from "Seeking Freedom." It explains why people might leave their home country for a new home. Notice the **signal word**.

> People move for freedom of speech and freedom of the press. People also move **because** they want a better education or jobs.

Use a Chart You can use a Cause-and-Effect Chart to **demonstrate** how events and ideas are related. Paraphrase the cause and effect from the paragraph above.

Cause-and-Effect Chart

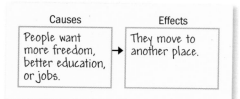

Causes	Effects
People want more freedom, better education, or jobs.	They move to another place.

▲ Many Kurdish people were forced to leave their homes in Iraq.

Identify Cause and Effect As a group, read the first two paragraphs on page 406. Make a Cause-and-Effect Chart to **demonstrate** how the ideas are related.

Try It!

Work with a partner. Find another passage in "Seeking Freedom" that **demonstrates** cause and effect. Record the information in a chart.

Use Context Clues

> **Academic Vocabulary**
> ● **context** (kon-tekst) *noun*
> Context refers to the parts nearby that help explain the meaning.

An **example clue** illustrates the meaning of another word in the text. The words *for example*, *including*, and *such as* signal an example clue.

Figure Out Word Meanings Work with a partner. Use **context** clues to figure out the meaning of each underlined word. Write the definition, and check it in a dictionary.

1. Many people want <u>liberties</u> such as freedom of speech, freedom of religion, and freedom of the press.

2. Some people take <u>drastic</u> actions, such as crossing the ocean in a small boat, to find freedom.

3. People may have many <u>hurdles</u> in a new country, including learning a new language and way of life.

4. People have to make <u>adjustments</u> to a new place. For example, they may be able to see friends and family only occasionally.

Research Constitutional Rights

SOCIAL SCIENCE

> **Academic Vocabulary**
> ● **interview** (in-tur-vyū) *noun*
> In an **interview**, one person finds out about another person by asking questions.

❶ Conduct Research With a partner, find out more about one of the ten amendments in the Bill of Rights. Focus on just one amendment. Use textbooks or the Internet for your research.

> **Internet InsideNG.com**
> ➋ Explore the Bill of Rights.

❷ Plan an Interview With your partner, write three questions to ask in an **interview** . Form questions that relate to the amendment you studied. For example: "What does the right to bear arms mean to you?"

❸ Conduct an Interview Present your questions to a parent or other adult in an **interview** . Record the answers.

❹ Write a Report Put your questions and answers together so they make sense to you.

Distinguish Facts and Opinions

> **Academic Vocabulary**
> • **fact** (fakt) *noun*
>   A **fact** is a piece of information that is true.

Nonfiction texts such as "Seeking Freedom" give **facts** about ideas and events. Sometimes nonfiction writers include opinions. They may express their own views of certain ideas or events. They also may report other people's opinions.

A **fact** is a statement that can be proved as true or false. Numbers and dates often signal statements of **fact**.

An opinion is a statement of what a person thinks or believes. Opinions often include signal words like *think*, *believe*, *want* or *like*. Descriptive words such as *good, wise,* or *foolish* may signal opinions, too.

▲ Protesters in Pakistan state their opinions.

Practice Together

Read and Discuss In a group, read the examples of **fact** and opinion from "Seeking Freedom." Then read and discuss the explanation. It tells how the example is **fact** or opinion.

Fact-and-Opinion Chart

	Fact	Opinion
Example	"Part of the Constitution is the Bill of Rights."	"Sometimes people leave their homes. They might move to a country with more freedom, but this can be very hard."
Why?	You can look at the Constitution to see if this is a true statement.	You cannot prove whether the statement is true. You can interpret the words <u>very hard</u> in different ways.

Try It!

Find Facts and Opinions Reread "Seeking Freedom." Identify more **facts** and opinions. List them in a chart like the one above.

Express Opinions

Group Share With a group, discuss the different stories in "Seeking Freedom." Which part did you find the most interesting or inspiring? Take turns sharing opinions and commenting on the ideas of others. Use possessive words correctly.

> I think the part about Nelson Mandela's life was the most inspiring.

> The part about girls' rights in Afghanistan inspired me the most.

Write About Human Rights

Study the Models When you write about important ideas, you want readers to understand what you write. Be sure to show ownership correctly.

NOT OK

Martin Luther King is one of **Americas** heroes. **His** speeches were powerful and effective. **His** efforts to change conditions for African Americans were very important. He inspired African Americans to fight peacefully for **their** rights. During **Kings** time, the **countrys** laws did not apply equally to everyone. Because of him, many things changed, and many **African Americans** lives improved.

> The reader thinks: "**Some sentences are confusing because apostrophes are missing in the possessive nouns.**"

OK

Martin Luther King is one of **America's** heroes. His speeches were powerful and effective. His efforts to change conditions for African Americans were very important. He inspired African Americans to fight peacefully for their rights. During **King's** time, the **country's** laws did not apply equally to everyone. Because of him, some things changed and many **African Americans'** lives improved.

> The reader thinks: "**Now it's clear that these words are possessive nouns.**"

Revise It Work with a partner to revise this passage. Add an apostrophe to fix each possessive noun.

Glorias family escaped from Cuba and came to the United States on a raft. My arrival was similar to her experience. I came from Haiti on Papas small boat. Our journey was scary! Waves crashed over the boats side. We used buckets to scoop the water out. When we finally arrived, we were so relieved to see our relatives faces.

REMEMBER

Add **'s** or **'** to a noun to show ownership.
- Pablo**'s** book
- the leaders**'** ideas
- the men**'s** rights

✏ **WRITE ON YOUR OWN** Imagine that you and your family are fighting for human rights. Describe what happens. Include possessive words.

Compare Across Texts

Compare Writing on the Same Topic

"Escaping to Freedom," "Brave Butterflies," and "Seeking Freedom" all tell about people's struggles for **freedom** . Compare how writing about the topic of **freedom** is different in these texts.

How It Works

Collect and Organize Ideas   To compare ideas across several texts, organize them in a Comparison Chart. What are the big ideas in the selections? What details does each writer include about the topic?

Comparison Chart

Writing about Freedom	Escaping to Freedom	Brave Butterflies	Seeking Freedom
big ideas	how Matthew Henson gained freedom	how Ana saves her father from being arrested	how different people have gained freedom
details			

Practice Together

Study and Compare the Ideas   Analyze how the selections talk about **freedom** . Then write a paragraph that compares them. Here is a paragraph that compares the big ideas in the selections.

> The three selections are all about the topic of freedom. "Escaping to Freedom" tells about the events in Matthew Henson's life. "Brave Butterflies" tells how Ana saves her father from being arrested. "Seeking Freedom" explains how different groups of people have gained freedom.

Try It!

Complete the Comparison Chart. Then use the ideas to write a paragraph that compares the details. You may want to use this frame.

The three selections are all about freedom. In "Escaping to Freedom," the author tells _____ . An example is _____ . In "Brave Butterflies," the main character tells _____ . An example is _____ . In "Seeking Freedom," the author describes _____ . An example is _____ .

Academic Vocabulary
- **freedom** (frē-dum) *noun*
  If you have **freedom**, you are not limited in what you do.

Struggle for Freedom

GUIDING QUESTION How far will people go for the sake of freedom?

UNIT LIBRARY

Content Library

THE ANTI-SLAVERY MOVEMENT

Leveled Library

Reflect on Your Reading

Think back on your reading of the unit selections. Discuss what you did to understand what you read.

Focus on Genre **Organization of Ideas**

In this unit, you learned how writers use cause and effect to organize their ideas. Choose a selection from the unit, and make a Cause-and-Effect Chain that shows how the text is organized. Use your graphic to explain the organization to a partner.

Reading Strategy **Determine Importance**

As you read the selections, you learned to summarize, identify main ideas and details, and determine what is important. Explain to a partner how you will use this strategy in the future.

Explore the

Throughout this unit, you have been thinking about freedom. Choose one way to explore the Guiding Question:

- **Discuss** With a group, discuss the Guiding Question. Talk about personal qualities, such as vision, courage, or an ability to plan, that can help people in the struggle for human rights.
- **Create a Journal** Imagine that you live in a country with a terrible dictator. Write a journal of your experiences. Explain what you will do for freedom.
- **Draw** Create a visual interpretation of your answer to the Guiding Question. Explain to a partner how your artwork is a picture of your response.

Book Talk

Which Unit Library book did you choose? Explain to a partner what it taught you about the need for freedom.

An astronomer looks at a cloud of gas and dust called the Rho Ophiuchus.

Star Power

GUIDING QUESTION

Why are both storytellers and scientists drawn to the stars?

Read More!

Content Library

Missions in Space
by Stephen Currie

Leveled Library

The War of the Worlds
by H.G. Wells, adapted by Mary Ann Evans

Stargirl
by Jerry Spinelli

**The Man Who Went to
the Far Side of the Moon**
by Bea Uusma Schyffert

Internet
InsideNG.com

⊘ Go to the Digital Library
to learn about the universe.

⊘ View images of space.

⊘ Learn about
space explorations.

Focus on Genre

Author's Purpose

▶ **Persuasive Writing**

Every author has a **purpose**, or reason, for writing. Some purposes are to
- give information or explain
- entertain, describe, or express personal feelings
- persuade readers to think or act in a certain way
- tell readers how to do something.

How It Works

Before you read a text, preview it to determine the author's purpose. Understanding the purpose can help you **evaluate** the information.

Persuasive Writing The author's purpose in the passage below is to persuade readers that the U.S. space program is important. As you read, **evaluate** how well the author accomplishes this purpose. Study the facts, or ideas that can be proved. **Evaluate** the author's opinions, or ideas. Then decide if the author persuaded you.

Bold Frontiers

In 1961, President Kennedy announced an exciting plan: "I believe that this nation should commit itself to achieving the goal . . . of landing a man on the moon and returning him safely to the earth."

The United States met the goal. In 1969, men walked on the moon for the first time.

Now it is time for our country to become fearless again! We need to put citizens like us on the moon. This is an amazing time in history. We should be able to move humans across the solar system.

We landed people on the moon. We must become bold again!

> Loaded words make readers feel emotions such as anger, fear, and pride. Loaded words support the writer's purpose of persuading the reader.

Academic Vocabulary
- **evaluate** (i-**val**-yu-wāt) *verb*
  To **evaluate** means to judge something's value or worth.

Practice Together

Read the following persuasive passage aloud. As you read, consider the facts and opinions. Determine if the author achieves the purpose.

Kids in Space, Now!

If there can be a Teacher-in-Space program, then there should be a Kids-in-Space program. We kids want to enjoy the amazing thrill and excitement of zooming into space. Kids from all over the country would try out. We're already experts at going to school, so we can easily spend a year in a training program to go into space. We study science and math, two important subjects for space travel. The thrill of flying into space in a space shuttle would be too fantastic to miss.

▲ Kids at space camp love the challenge of space training.

Try It!

Read this persuasive passage aloud. Does the author persuade you? Which facts and opinions are most persuasive?

Junk Yard in the Sky

Since 1957, people have put more than 5,000 satellites in space. These machines float above Earth. They help us talk to each other, track weather, and study space. But only about 600 are being used. The rest are junk. And some of it is dangerous, zooming along at thousands of miles per hour! It could be life-threatening to astronauts. The U.S. Space Command tracks this space junk so that it doesn't run into the path of active satellites. What a waste of time and effort! If we can launch rockets and set up space stations, then we should be able to pick up all of that garbage. Let's get someone to clean it up!

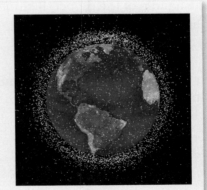

▲ This computer-made image shows all the junk being tracked around Earth.

Focus on Vocabulary

Use Context Clues for Multiple-Meaning Words

Many English words have more than one meaning. They are called **multiple-meaning words**. In the dictionary, the different meanings are numbered.

> EXAMPLE   I made a **table** with facts about the planets.
> I worked at the kitchen **table**.

How the Strategy Works

As you read, you may find a multiple-meaning word and may not know which meaning is being used. The best way to figure out the **appropriate** meaning is to use context clues. Follow these steps:

1. Look at other words in the sentence.
2. Read the sentences that come before and after to find more clues.
3. Use the clues to determine a meaning that makes sense.
4. Replace the word with the meaning, and say the sentence. If it does not make sense, look in a dictionary for more meanings.

Use the strategy to figure out the meaning of each underlined word.

Stars in the night sky look like tiny <u>points</u> of light. The North Star, however, is more than a twinkling dot. Throughout history, people have used the North Star to determine which direction is north. This bright star is located in a group of stars called the Little Dipper. It is at the <u>tip</u> of the handle of the dipper. It shines above the North Pole, the most northern <u>point</u> on Earth.

Strategy in Action

" The words *tiny* and *dot* in the first two sentences are clues. They tell me that *points* probably means 'small spots.' "

☑ **REMEMBER** You can use context clues to figure out the **appropriate** meaning of a multiple-meaning word.

Academic Vocabulary

● **appropriate** (u-prō-prē-ut) *adjective*
If something is **appropriate**, it is correct for the situation.

Practice Together

Read this passage aloud. Look at each underlined word. Use context clues to figure out the correct meaning of the multiple-meaning word.

Light Show

Are you a <u>fan</u> of the night sky? On clear, starry nights, do you like to look up at the sparkling <u>show</u>? Ancient people liked to look at the sky. They noticed that groups of stars formed shapes and <u>figures</u>.

Over time, people learned more and more about the night sky. They invented <u>instruments</u>, like the telescope, to study distant objects in the sky.

Today, people continue to explore the sky to learn about the universe. They also enjoy <u>just</u> looking up at the twinkling, <u>bright</u> lights!

Try It!

Read this passage aloud. What is the meaning of each underlined word? How do you know?

Colorful Planets

The planets come in a rainbow of colors. Earth usually appears <u>light</u> blue with <u>patches</u> of white in photos. What about some of the other planets? Mars is fiery <u>orange</u> and red. Venus and Saturn tend to be pale yellow. Jupiter, the largest planet, has orange and white <u>bands</u>.

▲ The red-orange color of Mars comes from the rusty soil and dust on its surface.

The Earth Under Sky Bear's Feet

Native American Poems of the Land

by Joseph Bruchac

illustrations by Thomas Locker

Build Background

Connect

In the past, people noticed that some stars seemed to form patterns or shapes in the sky. These are called constellations. People gave each constellation a name, such as Orion or Leo, and created stories about the characters.

Group Discussion What do you know about the constellations? Share stories or other information you may know about them. Then vote on your favorite constellation picture. Explain your choice.

Digital Library

InsideNG.com
View the images.

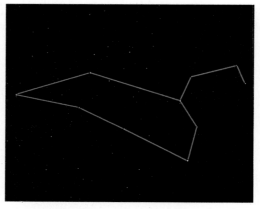

▲ This constellation is known as Leo, the lion.

Language & Grammar

Describe

CD

Look at the picture and listen to the description.
Then describe something in the picture.

PICTURE PROMPT

It is so clear tonight. I wish you could see the stars. They look like diamonds scattered across the sky.

Use Prepositions

Prepositions show how two objects or ideas are related.

- Some show location: We sat **on** the bench.
  The stars were **above** us.

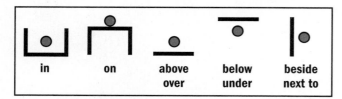

in	on	above over	below under	beside next to

- Some show direction: Mom came **through** the door.
  She walked **down** the stairs.

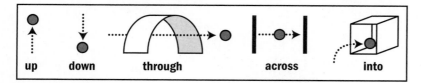

up	down	through	across	into

- Some show time: We saw some constellations **at** nine o'clock.
- Some show origin: That constellation is **from** a Greek myth.

Practice Together

Add a preposition to complete each sentence. Say the sentence.

1. There is a telescope _____ the roof of our school.
2. Last week, my class climbed _____ the stairs to the roof.
3. We learned about the telescope _____ a professor.
4. We each got to look _____ the telescope.
5. It was exciting to see the stars _____ us.

Try It!

Read each incomplete sentence. On a card, write a preposition to complete the sentence. Then hold up the card as you say the sentence with the preposition.

6. Do you like to sleep _____ the stars?
7. You can lie _____ the soft ground.
8. You can look _____ the whole sky.
9. Thousands of lights twinkle _____ your head.
10. You can watch them glow _____ midnight.

▲ The girl studies the sky through a telescope.

Tell About the Sky

DESCRIBE

Pretend that you are sitting under a starry sky. Close your eyes and imagine it. What do you see and hear? What do you feel and smell?

Make a list of words and phrases that tell about the scene.

> 1. black sky
> 2. bright stars
> 3. bugs chirping
> 4. cold air on my skin
> 5. the wind in the trees

Use your list to help you create a description. Then describe the sky to a partner.

HOW TO DESCRIBE

1. Tell what something or someone is like.
2. Give details.
3. Use descriptive words.

The bright stars are above the trees.

USE PREPOSITIONS

Prepositions can help you describe things in a clear way.

EXAMPLES   I climbed **up** a steep hill with my backpack.

A cold wind blew **through** the trees.

The bright stars sparkled **above** me.

▲ The night sky sparkles above the trees.

Prepare to Read

Learn Key Vocabulary

Rate and Study the Words Rate how well you know each word. Then:

1. Pronounce the word. Say it aloud several times. Spell it.
2. Study the example.
3. Tell more about the word.
4. Practice it. Make the word your own.

Key Words

advice (ud-**vīs**) *noun*
► page 440

Advice is a suggestion or an idea that helps someone decide what to do. Family members can give you **advice** when you have a problem.

continue (kun-**tin**-yū) *verb*
► page 436

To **continue** means to keep going. The highway **continues** for miles.
Synonyms: **go on, last**
Antonym: **discontinue**

hunter (**hun**-tur) *noun*
► page 436

A **hunter** is a person who looks for wild animals to capture or kill. A skilled **hunter** may use a bow and arrows to hunt.

remain (ri-**mān**) *verb*
► page 438

To **remain** means to stay in the same place. The dog is learning to **remain** in one spot when told.
Synonym: **stay**
Antonym: **leave**

roam (**rōm**) *verb*
► page 434

To **roam** means to wander or to travel without any particular place to go. Wild animals **roam** freely.
Synonyms: **stray, drift**

scatter (**ska**-tur) *verb*
► page 438

To **scatter** means to throw or drop many things over a wide area. The leaves **scatter** across the street.
Synonyms: **spread, toss, sprinkle**

tale (**tāl**) *noun*
► page 436

A **tale** is a story. The children enjoy listening to the **tale**.
Synonym: **story**

track (**trak**) *noun*
► page 436

A **track** is a footprint or a mark left by something as it moves over a surface. When you look at animal **tracks**, you can tell what kind of animal was in the area.

Practice the Words Work with a partner. Write a question using at least one Key Word. Answer your partner's question using a different Key Word. Keep going until you have used each word twice.

Questions	Answers
What did the hunters find?	They found deer tracks.

Reading Strategy: Make Inferences

When you make an inference, you figure something out based on information and experience. Suppose a friend tells you he will come over at five o'clock. You may infer that he means five o'clock in the evening, not in the morning. You make inferences like this when you read, too.

Reading Strategy
Make Inferences

How to MAKE INFERENCES

1. Look for ideas and information that the author emphasizes.
2. Think about what your own experience tells you.
3. Combine what you know with what you read, and figure out what the author means but hasn't said directly.

Strategy in Action

Here's how one student made inferences.

Look Into the Text

What I read:
The girl wants to go inside. She is afraid of the dark.

"*Akhsotha*," the girl said. "My grandmother, we must go into the lodge before it is dark. I'm afraid of the night."

Grandmother shook her head. "*Iah*, if we go in too soon, we will not see Sky Bear." Grandmother looked up into the sky. The pattern of stars that shaped the Great Bear was bright. "Soon she will roam around the skyland."

"I know many young children who are afraid of the dark. So I think the girl is young."

Practice Together

Read this passage about Sky Bear again, and make an inference of your own. Follow the steps in the How-To box. Use sticky notes to keep track of ideas and information in the text.

Focus on Genre

Myth

A myth is a fictional narrative. The author's purpose is to explain something about the world. A myth usually gives a supernatural, or nonscientific, explanation for something in nature.

> Long ago,
>
> three hunters and their little dog
>
> found the tracks of a giant bear. . . .
>
> That bear was Sky Bear,
>
> running on through the stars.

Your Job as a Reader

Reading Strategy: Make Inferences

As you read, make inferences by combining information in the text with what you already know.

What I read:

Sky Bear is running through the stars.

Sky Bear is really a group of stars.

The Earth
Under Sky Bear's Feet

Native American Poems of the Land

by Joseph Bruchac

illustrations by Thomas Locker

Grandmother sat in front of the lodge. The small girl beside her watched. The old woman's strong hands finished the weaving of the ash splint basket. The glow of the setting sun reflected from the surface of the river. Autumn leaves **swirled** in the **current**.

"*Akhsotha*," the girl said. "My grandmother, we must go into the lodge before it is dark. I'm afraid of the night."

Grandmother shook her head. "*Iah*, if we go in too soon, we will not see Sky Bear." Grandmother looked up into the sky. The pattern of stars that shaped the Great Bear was bright. "Soon she will **roam** around the skyland."

"Does Sky Bear see everything from up there? Does she hear what we say?"

"*Hen*, Granddaughter. As she travels the sky this whole earth is stretched beneath her feet. Listen. I will share with you some of the stories our old people tell about what Sky Bear sees and hears through the night."

Key Vocabulary
roam *v.*, to wander or travel

In Other Words
swirled turned around and around
current flow of the river water
Akhsotha My grandmother
  (in Mohawk)
Iah No (in Mohawk)
Hen Yes (in Mohawk)

Cultural Background

The characters in this tale are Iroquois, a native people from New York state. The grandmother is making a basket with thin strips of ash wood. The strips are called *splints*. The characters speak Mohawk, one of several Iroquois languages.

Before You Move On

1. **Explain** Why does Grandmother want to stay outside longer?
2. **Character's Point of View** Why does Grandmother want to tell her granddaughter stories about Sky Bear?

Most people have seen the Big Dipper. Native Americans call this star pattern Sky Bear. The Mohawk people tell this **tale** of how Sky Bear formed.

Sky Bear

Long ago,

three **hunters** and their little dog

found the **tracks** of a giant bear.

They followed those tracks

5   all through the day

and even though it was almost dark

they did not stop, but **continued** on.

They saw that bear now, climbing up

a hill, which **glittered**

10   with new-fallen snow.

They ran hard to catch it,

but the bear was too fast.

They ran and they ran, climbing

up and up until one of the hunters said,

15   "Brothers, look down."

They did and saw they

were high above Earth.

That bear was Sky Bear,

running on through the stars.

20   Look up now

and you will see her,

circling the sky.

Key Vocabulary

tale *n.*, a story

hunter *n.*, someone who hunts wild animals

track *n.*, a mark left by something; a footprint

continue *v.*, to keep going

In Other Words

glittered was shiny

circling going in a circle around

Before You Move On

1. **Recall and Interpret** Based on this **tale**, how was the Big Dipper formed?

2. **Figurative Language** When the **hunters** see Sky Bear "running through the stars," what picture do you see in your mind? Is this a good way to describe what they see? Explain.

The Earth Under Sky Bear's Feet   **437**

The Cochiti Pueblo of New Mexico tell this brief story.
It explains how all star patterns formed.

The Scattered Stars

Why are the stars
scattered all through the sky?
Sky Bear says it happened long ago,
when the people **came**
5 **from the underworld**.
Our Mother, the Mother
of All the People,
gave one little girl named *Ko-tci-man-yo*
a bag made of white **cotton**
10 for her to carry.
Do not open this bag, Our Mother said.
But as they walked for many days,
Ko-tci-man-yo felt that bag grow heavy.

One night, when they stopped,
15 *Ko-tci-man-yo* climbed up to a hill
where no one could see her,
and then she untied the many **knots**
to take just one small look inside.
But when she **loosened** the last knot,
20 the bag popped open
and bright things began to escape
to the sky.

Ko-tci-man-yo quickly closed that bag,
but only a few of the stars **remained**
25 to be placed in patterns in the sky.
All the others scattered.
They are still that way
because **of her curiosity**.

Key Vocabulary
scatter *v.*, to throw or drop many things over a wide area
remain *v.*, to stay in the same place

In Other Words
came from the underworld first came to the land
cotton cloth, fabric
knots places where the bag was tied
loosened untied
of her curiosity she was curious

Before You Move On

1. **Summarize** According to this Cochiti **tale**, how did star patterns form?
2. **Cause and Effect** Why does the girl open the bag? What happens when she does?

This Lenape story tells about a group of seven stars. The Lenape people are from the Eastern Woodlands of the United States.

The Seven Mateinnu

Long ago, seven **wise men**
lived among the people.
They knew so much that everyone
was always asking them for **advice**.

5 They grew so tired that
they decided to hide from the people,
and **turned themselves
into** seven big stones.
But before too long,
10 the people found them,
and because they were stones,
they had to sit and listen
to everyone ask for help.

They tried a second time to hide,
15 and turned into seven cedar trees.
But once again,
the people found them,
and because they were **rooted**,
they still had to listen.

20 At last they **accepted**
that they could not hide.
They changed themselves
into seven stars dancing in the middle
of the sky.

25 Each night the people look up to them
and see the answers to their questions
in the light of those stars. ❖

Key Vocabulary
advice *n.*, ideas that help
someone decide what to do

In Other Words
wise men men who gave good
advice
turned themselves into became
rooted attached to the ground
accepted knew it was true

Before You Move On

1. **Problem and Solution** Why do the seven wise men want to hide? How do they solve the problem?

2. **Personification** How are the wise men still like people after they turn into rocks, trees, and stars? How are they different?

The Earth Under Sky Bear's Feet   **441**

"There can be as much to see in the living night as in the more familiar light of day."

—Joseph Bruchac

About the Author

Joseph Bruchac

Joseph Bruchac (1942–) is a storyteller and a poet. He loves nature and the stories about nature that he learned from his Native American ancestors. Bruchac believes that everything in nature has its own story to tell.

Bruchac tells readers, "keep listening, listen to the voices of others, listen to the sounds of nature around us, and listen to your heart. Everything is there."

Connect Reading and Writing

Vocabulary
advice
continues
hunter
remains
roams
scatter
tale
tracks

CRITICAL THINKING

1. SUM IT UP Choose one myth. Complete a Beginning-Middle-End Chart. Use your chart to retell the **tale**.

Beginning-Middle-End Chart

Myth Title: Sky Bear

Beginning:
Three hunters and a dog follow bear tracks.

Middle:

End:

2. Infer Why did people use stories long ago to explain mysteries such as why stars are **scattered** across the sky?

3. Analyze What does "The Seven Mateinnu" tell you about people and their need to seek **advice** about the world? Use examples from the text.

4. Generalize Why do people **continue** to tell old myths?

READING FLUENCY

Expression Read the passage on page 586 to a partner. Assess your fluency.

1. I read
   a. great   **b.** OK   **c.** not very well

2. What I did best in my reading was _____.

READING STRATEGY

Make Inferences
With a partner, share two inferences you made in this selection. Tell what information you used to make the inferences.

VOCABULARY REVIEW

Oral Review Read the paragraph aloud. Add the vocabulary words.

> Here is a short _____: A deer family _____ the fields. The father deer, a buck, sees something moving in the grass ahead. He signals his family to _____. They quickly take his _____. The buck stays, or _____, and watches as a _____ comes near. The buck runs, leaving _____ in the dirt. He leaps into the sky. The buck _____ in this way, leaping from star to star. Whenever you see a shooting star, the buck is running.

Written Review Look back at the illustrations of the stars in the selection. Write a caption for each picture. Use at least four vocabulary words.

 **WRITE ABOUT THE** GUIDING QUESTION

Explore the Power of the Stars
Why do people look for patterns in the stars and then create **tales** about those patterns? Support your explanation with examples from the text.

Connect Across the Curriculum

Compare Myths

Academic Vocabulary
- **compare** (kum-**pair**) *verb*
  When you **compare** two things, you think about how they are alike and different.

Myths are old stories that attempt to explain mysteries of the natural world, such as why rainbows appear or why zebras have stripes. All the myths in "The Earth Under Sky Bear's Feet" tell about stars. Each myth explains why a group of stars forms a certain pattern.

People from different cultures created the myths, so each story is different. Look back at the selection to see which group of people told each myth.

Practice Together

Compare Myths Choose two of the myths. Use a Venn Diagram to **compare** them. In the middle section, write how the myths are alike. In the outside section, write how they are different.

Venn Diagram

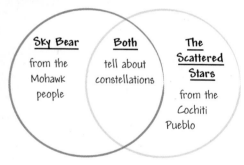

Sky Bear
from the Mohawk people

Both
tell about constellations

The Scattered Stars
from the Cochiti Pueblo

Try It!

Write About Myths Write a comparison-contrast paragraph about the two myths. Write sentences about how the myths are alike and how they are different. Use the Venn Diagram to help you organize information about the similarities and differences. At the end of the paragraph, include a few sentences that tell which myth you like the best, and why.

Compare Ideas Read your paragraph aloud. Listen to your classmates' paragraphs to determine their ideas. **Compare** your ideas with theirs and discuss the differences.

Use Context Clues

Academic Vocabulary
- **appropriate** (u-**prō**-prē-ut) *adjective*
  If something is **appropriate**, it is correct for the situation.

Multiple-meaning words have more than one meaning. In a dictionary, the meanings are numbered. Context clues are hints in a text that help you figure out the **appropriate** meaning.

Dictionary Entries

hide (hīd) *verb* **1** to go where no one can see you   *noun* **2** an animal's skin

knot (not) *noun* **1** the tied ends of rope or string   **2** unit used to measure a ship's speed

lodge (loj) *verb* **1** to become fixed in one place and not move   *noun* **2** a small house or cabin

tracks (traks) *noun* **1** the rails a train rides on   **2** marks left by an animal

Determine Meanings Find each of these words in the selection. Determine which meaning applies in the text. Use context clues.

1. lodge, p. 434   **2.** tracks, p. 436   **3.** knot, p. 438   **4.** hide, p. 440

Research Stories About Stars

SOCIAL SCIENCE

Academic Vocabulary
- **locate** (lō-kāt) *verb*
  To **locate** something is to find it.

❶ Plan Your Research **Locate** information about a constellation. Narrow your topic and **locate** one story that people in the past told about the constellation. Use books, or look online.

> **Internet** InsideNG.com
> ➋ Find out about constellations.

❷ Prepare Your Materials Read the story. Then write it in your own words. Make a poster with a picture of the constellation and your story.

❸ Share the Story Post your work in a "Constellation Corner."

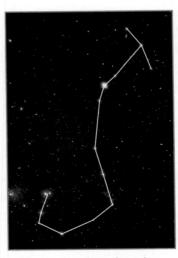
▲ These stars form Scorpius, the scorpion.

Literary Analysis

Analyze Mood and Tone

> **Academic Vocabulary**
> • **discuss** (di-**skus**) *verb*
>   When you **discuss** something, you talk about it.

All writing has a **mood** and **tone**. The mood of a text is the feeling you get when you read it. For example, the mood of a story may make you feel happy, scared, curious, excited, sad, optimistic, or angry. The tone of a text is the author's attitude toward the topic. For example, the author's attitude might be serious, playful, respectful, positive, humorous, or bitter.

Practice Together

Read this excerpt from "The Scattered Stars."

> One night, when they stopped,
> *Ko-tci-man-yo* climbed up to a hill
> where no one could see her,
> and then she untied the many knots
> to take just one small look inside.
> But when she loosened the last knot,
> the bag popped open
> and bright things began to escape
> to the sky.

Notice how the writer chooses words that set a certain mood. The girl didn't just look in the bag. She took "just one small look." And the bag didn't just open. It "popped open." These words give the writing a mood of childlike wonder.

Now think about the tone, or how the author feels about the characters and the topic. This writer has a respectful tone as he explains reasons for *Ko-tci-man-yo*'s actions.

Try It!

Analyze Another Myth With a partner, choose another myth. **Discuss** the mood and the tone of the text. Then **discuss** how the author communicates this mood and tone. Compare your ideas with your classmates' ideas. Do you agree on the mood and tone?

Describe

Describe a Picture Look back at the illustrations for the three myths. Decide which one is your favorite. Then describe it. Use prepositions to add details to your sentences.

> Three men climb up a hill. There is a bear in the sky.

Write About a Character in Space

Study the Models When you write a story, you can use prepositional phrases to add interesting details.

NOT OK

> Rana fell asleep. She started to dream. She zoomed through a galaxy. The view was amazing. Rana's home planet looked like a tiny, blue ball.

These are not enough details. The reader wonders: "**What did she dream about? What was she traveling in?**"

OK

> Rana fell asleep **at ten o'clock**. She started to dream **about an unusual journey across the Milky Way**. She zoomed **through the galaxy in a silver spacecraft with wings** as bright as stars. The view **of Earth from space** was amazing. Rana's home planet looked like a tiny, blue ball.

Here, the writer uses **prepositional phrases** to add details and make the writing more interesting.

Add Sentences Think of two sentences to add to the OK model above. Use prepositional phrases to add details.

✎ **WRITE ON YOUR OWN** Imagine a character who is traveling in space. Write about what happens. Use prepositions like the ones below to add details to your sentences.

REMEMBER

Location	Direction	Time	Origin
in/on above/over below/under beside/next to	up/down through across into	at in on	from

▲ The astronaut floats in space.

A Universe of Stars

by Ellen Fried

Build Background

Meet Some Astronomers

Astronomers are scientists who study the stars, the planets, and other objects in space. Famous astronomers like Galileo Galilei have helped us understand the universe.

Digital Library

InsideNG.com
▶ View the video.

◀ Unlike others of his time, Galileo Galilei believed the Earth moved around the sun.

Connect

KWLS Chart What do you know about the stars and space? What would you like to know? Create a KWLS Chart. Fill in the last two columns after you read the selection.

KWLS Chart

WHAT I KNOW	WHAT I WANT TO KNOW	WHAT I LEARNED	WHAT I STILL WANT TO LEARN
The sun is a star.	How big is the sun?		

Language & Grammar

Define and Explain

CD

Study the images and listen to the explanation.
Then explain something about one of the images.

PICTURE PROMPT

In 2006, NASA launched New Horizons, a spacecraft that will study Pluto and the Kuiper belt. The Kuiper belt is a group of icy objects outside the orbit of Neptune. Astronomers believe that studying these objects will help them better understand how our solar system began.

Charon, one of Pluto's moons

Pluto

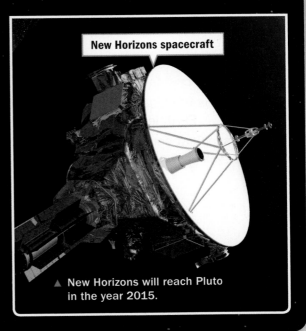

New Horizons spacecraft

▲ New Horizons will reach Pluto in the year 2015.

Use Pronouns in Prepositional Phrases

A **prepositional phrase** is a group of words. It begins with a **preposition** and ends with a **noun** or an **object pronoun**.

EXAMPLES   The planets travel **around** the **sun**.

Stars and planets are interesting **to me**.

I like to read **about them**.

Object Pronouns	
Singular	**Plural**
me	us
you	you
him, her, it	them

Practice Together

Say each pair of sentences. Add an object pronoun to the second sentence.

1. I need a book about an astronomer. Can you find one for _____?

2. Here is a book about Caroline Herschel. Do you know about _____?

3. I have heard of the astronomer William Herschel. Was Caroline related to _____?

4. She was his sister. She lived with _____ in England about 200 years ago.

5. He taught her about astronomy. This book is about both of _____.

Try It!

Read each pair of sentences. Write an object pronoun on a card. Then hold up the card as you say the second sentence with the object pronoun.

6. We studied the planets in class. I'm very interested in _____.

7. My favorite planet is Jupiter. I know a lot about _____.

8. Did you know that Jupiter has more than 60 moons? I can name some of them for _____.

9. Jupiter is the largest planet. Compared to _____, Earth looks tiny.

10. Let's look at some images of Jupiter online. That will be fun for _____!

▲ Jupiter is the fifth planet from the sun. The distant planet is 484 million miles from it.

Explain Something About Space

DEFINE AND EXPLAIN

What do you know about space? Tell a partner something you know about a planet, a spacecraft, an astronomer, or a similar topic.

First, review the information in your science textbook or another source. Make an outline to organize your thoughts.

Outline

I. The Solar System
   A. the sun
   B. planets that orbit the sun
      1. Mercury
      2. Venus
      3. Earth
      4. Mars
      5. Jupiter
      6. Saturn
      7. Uranus
      8. Neptune

Check your outline to see if there are any words or phrases you may need to define for your partner. Write their meanings on your outline. If you need help with the definitions, use a dictionary.

Explain the information to your partner. Define the difficult words.

How To DEFINE AND EXPLAIN

1. **Define:** As you give information, tell the meaning of any difficult words or phrases.
2. **Explain:** Give more details or examples to make the definition clear.

> To orbit means to move around an object. Earth orbits the sun.

USE PRONOUNS IN PREPOSITIONAL PHRASES

When you give an explanation, make sure you use the correct **object pronoun** after a **preposition**.

EXAMPLES   Earth goes **around** the sun once a year.
              Earth goes **around** **it** once a year.

Prepare to Read

Learn Key Vocabulary

Rate and Study the Words Rate how well you know each word. Then:

1. Pronounce the word. Say it aloud several times. Spell it.
2. Study the example.
3. Tell more about the word.
4. Practice it. Make the word your own.

Key Words

distance (dis-tunts) *noun*
▶ page 457

Distance is the area between two points. The **distance** between Earth and the sun is 93 million miles.

orbit (or-but) *verb*
▶ page 461

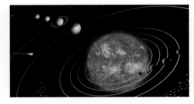

To **orbit** means to move in an almost circular path around another object. It takes Earth about 365 days to **orbit** the sun.

space (spās) *noun*
▶ page 456

Space is the area beyond Earth. Scientists send special ships into **space** to learn about other planets and the moon.

telescope (te-lu-skōp) *noun*
▶ page 459

A **telescope** is a tool you can look through to make faraway things look bigger. You can use a **telescope** to look at the moon.

temperature (tem-pur-chur) *noun* ▶ page 460

The **temperature** is how hot or cold something is. We measure **temperature** using a thermometer.

unit (yū-nit) *noun*
▶ page 458

A **unit** is a certain amount used in measuring. An inch is a common **unit** used to measure small objects.

universe (yū-nu-vurs) *noun*
▶ page 456

The **universe** is everywhere and includes Earth, all other planets, and all stars.

vary (vair-ē) *verb*
▶ page 460

To **vary** means to be different from others. Snowflakes **vary** from one another so that no two are alike.

Practice the Words Make a Word Map for each Key Word. Then compare your maps with a partner's.

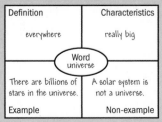

Definition	Characteristics
everywhere	really big
Word universe	
There are billions of stars in the universe.	A solar system is not a universe.
Example	Non-example

Word Map

Reading Strategy: Make Inferences

Writers don't always tell you everything you need to know. Sometimes you need to fill in the missing information, or make inferences, when you read.

Reading Strategy
Make Inferences

HOW TO MAKE INFERENCES

1. As you read, notice the details in the text.
2. Think about what the author suggests but does not state directly. What could you add? Write an inference to fill in the information.
3. Think again. Are you sure your information is correct?
4. Keep reading to find more details.

Strategy in Action

Here's how one student made an inference.

Look Into the Text

If you stand outside on a clear, dark night, far away from any city lights, you may see a pale band of light stretching across the sky. The band of light is the Milky Way. The glow is from a huge number of stars.

Long ago, people could use only their eyes to study the sky. Over time, more powerful tools have allowed us to look farther and farther out into the universe. We've learned so much about space, but there is *much* more left to explore.

What the text says: The Milky Way is a band of light in the sky.

What I think: The Milky Way is far away from Earth.

"I'll keep reading to find more details about the Milky Way."

Practice Together

Read the passage again, and make an inference of your own. Follow the steps in the How-To box.

Science Article

A science article gives information about the world around us. It contains many facts and **scientific terms**. An author writes a science article to inform and explain.

> Each star is a giant, fiery ball of gases. Our sun is a star. It is made mostly of hydrogen and helium gases. The sun is extremely hot. Huge columns of gas sometimes leap from the surface.

Your Job as a Reader

Reading Strategy: Make Inferences

As you read, make inferences. If you are not sure about an inference, make a note so that you can confirm it later.

What the text says: Our sun is a star. It is made mostly of hydrogen and helium gases.

What I think: All stars are made of these gases.

A Universe of Stars

by Ellen Fried

The Night Sky

If you stand outside on a clear, dark night, far away from any city lights, you may see a **pale band** of light stretching across the sky. The band of light is the Milky Way. The **glow** is from a huge number of stars.

Long ago, people could use only their eyes to study the sky. Over time, more powerful tools have allowed us to look farther and farther out into the **universe**. We've learned so much about **space**, but there is *much* more **left** to explore.

On dark and cloudless nights, people can view the stars. ▶

Key Vocabulary

universe *n.*, everywhere, including Earth, the planets, and the stars

space *n.*, the area beyond Earth

In Other Words

pale band light-colored strip
glow soft, steady light
left still

What Is a Star?

In the night sky, stars look like tiny diamonds **fastened** to the ceiling. They seem peaceful, timeless, and unchanging. In reality, stars are huge. They are scattered through **vast distances** in space. They're not timeless but are always changing, and those changes can be **violent**.

Each star is a giant, **fiery** ball of gases. Our sun is a star. It is made mostly of hydrogen and helium gases. The sun is **extremely** hot. Huge columns of gas sometimes **leap** from the surface.

Our sun is so big that a million Earths could fit inside it. More than a hundred Earths could stretch side by side across it. Other stars look much smaller than our sun, but that is because they are much farther away from us than the sun is.

▼ Hot streams of gas leap from the surface of the sun.

Key Vocabulary

> **distance** *n.*, the area between two points

In Other Words

fastened stuck
vast large, great
violent strong, forceful
fiery burning
extremely very
leap jump

Before You Move On

1. **Simile** How are stars "like tiny diamonds fastened to the sky"? How is this comparison not true?
2. **Summarize** What is a star?

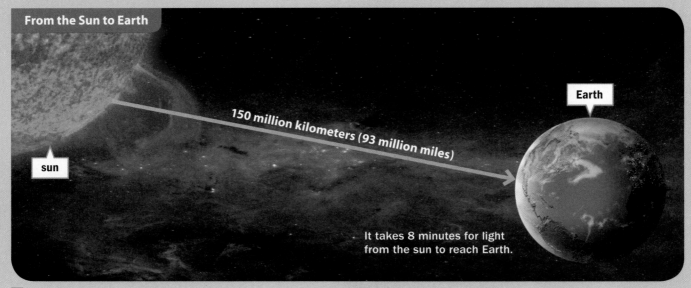

From the Sun to Earth

150 million kilometers (93 million miles)

sun

Earth

It takes 8 minutes for light from the sun to reach Earth.

▲ Interpret the Diagram What does 150 million kilometers or 93 million miles represent?

Measuring the Universe

Distances in space are so great that scientists use a special **unit** to measure them. This unit of measurement is based on how fast light travels.

Light is the fastest moving thing we know. It takes about 8 minutes for light to travel from the sun to Earth. That's a distance of 150 million kilometers (93 million miles). You might say that the sun is 8 light-minutes from Earth.

It takes years for the light from other stars to reach us. We use a unit called a light-year to measure the distance between Earth and those other stars. A light-year is the distance that light travels in a year.

We cannot travel to the stars. We cannot even send **space probes** that far away. To learn about other stars, scientists study the light and other energy that travels through space and reaches us on Earth.

Key Vocabulary
unit *n.*, a certain amount used in measuring

In Other Words
space probes spacecraft without people

Scoping the Sky

Long ago, people studied the stars just by eye. They noticed that stars seem to move across the sky and that groups of stars **formed patterns**. They gave names to the patterns. A group of stars that forms a pattern is a constellation. Knowing the constellations helped people travel at night.

In the 1600s scientists started using **telescopes** to look at the sky. Since then, telescopes have become more powerful. They allow us to see things that are very far away. Other tools let us study the light that telescopes **collect**.

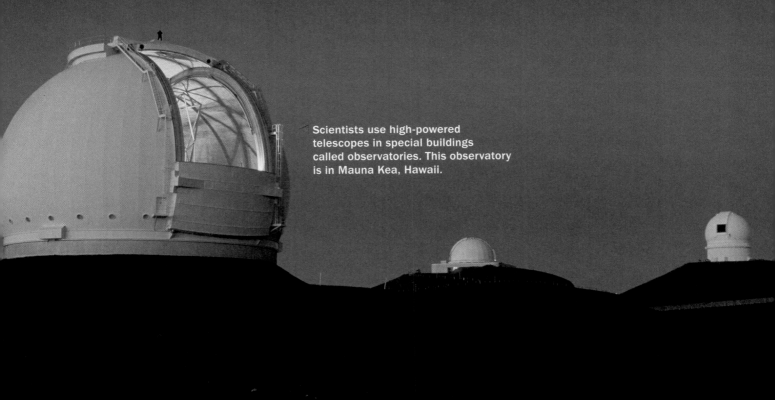

Scientists use high-powered telescopes in special buildings called observatories. This observatory is in Mauna Kea, Hawaii.

Before You Move On

1. **Explain** What **unit** do scientists use to measure **distances** in **space**? Explain what it means.
2. **Compare and Contrast** What is different about how people studied the stars long ago and the way they study them now? What is the same?

Key Vocabulary
telescope *n.*, a tool you can look through to make faraway things look bigger

In Other Words
formed patterns looked like shapes
collect bring together in one place

Star Variety

Stars **vary** greatly in how much light they give off. Our sun looks bright only because it is so close. Some stars give off thousands of times more light than the sun. Other stars give off much less light.

Stars also give off different colors of light. Our sun gives off mostly yellow light. Some stars give off mostly red light. Others give off mostly white or blue light.

The surface **temperature** of stars varies, too. The surface temperature of our sun is about 5,500°C (10,000°F). Some stars are much hotter. Others are only half as hot. Usually, the hotter a star is, the brighter it is. This isn't always true, though.

Also, stars vary in size. **Dwarf** stars are small compared to other stars. Giant stars are very large. The sun is a smaller star.

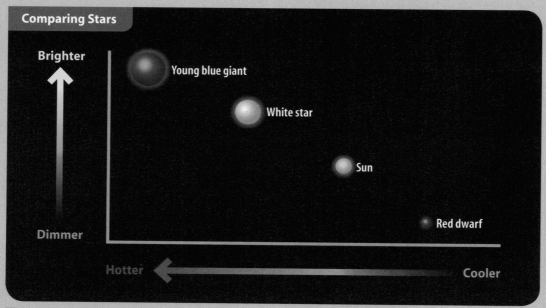

Comparing Stars

Brighter

Young blue giant

White star

Sun

Red dwarf

Dimmer

Hotter   Cooler

△ Interpret the Chart Which is hotter, a young blue giant star or a red dwarf star?

Key Vocabulary
vary *v.*, to be different from others
temperature *n.*, how hot or cold something is

In Other Words
Dwarf Small

Our Place in Space

The universe is huge, and our place in it is small. Earth is just one of the planets that **orbit** the sun. The sun is just one of a great many stars in the Milky Way, and the Milky Way is just one of more than a hundred billion **galaxies** in space.

There is so much more to learn about stars and the universe. The more we study the night sky, the more we will uncover. ❖

▲ A telescope in space took this photo of the universe. It shows galaxies stretching out over billions of light-years.

In Other Words
galaxies groups of stars

Before You Move On
1. **Categorize** Name three ways that stars **vary**.
2. **Evidence and Conclusion** Why does the author say that our place in the **universe** is small? What details support this idea?

THE ASTRONOMER

BY AESOP

There was once a famous **astronomer** who attracted many visitors. Scientists came from far and wide to listen to him speak about the night sky.

One clear night, the astronomer took some visitors for a walk. He described each planet and named each constellation, but he did not watch where he was going.

Suddenly, the astronomer stumbled, fell forward, and landed face down in a muddy **ditch**. He slowly got up. His clothes were wet and his body was **bruised**.

The poor man limped back to the road. There, clear as day, was a rock in the path.

A visitor **remarked**, "You see great things in the sky, but you should see the small things at your feet, too."

MORAL: As you think about the great things in life, don't **ignore** the small things.

In Other Words
astronomer scientist who studied the stars
ditch hole in the ground
bruised hurt
remarked said
ignore forget about

Before You Move On

1. **Cause and Effect** Why did the astronomer fall down? What happened after he fell?
2. **Paraphrase** Restate the moral, or lesson, of this fable.

Connect Reading and Writing

Vocabulary

distances

orbit

space

telescopes

temperatures

unit

universe

vary

CRITICAL THINKING

1. SUM IT UP With a partner, complete your KWLS Chart from page 448. Add facts you learned about **space** and information you still want to learn.

KWLS Chart

WHAT I KNOW	WHAT I WANT TO KNOW	WHAT I LEARNED	WHAT I STILL WANT TO LEARN
The sun is a star.	How big is the sun?	A million Earths could fit in the sun.	How long will our sun last?

2. Speculate Review the information on page 457 about the size of the sun. Then look at page 460. About how many Earths could fit in a young blue giant?

3. Compare "A Universe of Stars" and "The Astronomer" both tell about scientists studying the **universe**. Do the authors feel the same way about this topic? Explain.

4. Infer How have **telescopes** changed our understanding of the **universe**?

READING FLUENCY

Phrasing Read the passage on page 587 to a partner. Assess your fluency.

1. I read

    a. great   **b.** OK   **c.** not very well

2. What I did best in my reading was _____.

READING STRATEGY

Make Inferences
With a group, share inferences you made and how your inferences changed as you read more details.

VOCABULARY REVIEW

Oral Review Read the paragraph aloud. Add the vocabulary words.

Scientists use a variety of tools and methods to study the stars and other objects in _____. They use a _____ of measurement called the light-year to determine the vast _____ to some stars. Scientists look through _____ and launch rockets. Rockets carry probes that gather data about the _____. Rockets also place satellites that _____ Earth. The purpose of satellites can _____. For example, some satellites gather _____ and other weather data.

Written Review Imagine that you have just discovered an object in **space** such as a new planet. Write a description of it using five vocabulary words.

 **WRITE ABOUT THE** GUIDING QUESTION

Explore the Power of the Stars
Do you think it is important to study the **universe**? Why or why not? Support your opinion with evidence from the text.

Connect Across the Curriculum

Analyze Style

> **Academic Vocabulary**
> ● **style** (stī-ul) *noun*
> A **style** is a certain way of expressing an idea.

What Is Style? Different singers may sing the same song in different ways. One sings it slowly and softly. Another sings it as a fast rap. The way they sing is their **style** .

An author's **style** is the way the author expresses an idea. The author of a children's book may write in short sentences that rhyme. A science author may write in long sentences full of technical terms.

Practice Together

Read and Discuss Read this passage from "A Universe of Stars." Notice the author's **style** . She

- uses some everyday words and some technical terms
- writes with short sentences and long sentences
- starts the sentences in different ways
- uses **descriptive words** to keep readers interested
- repeats **important words** to make sure readers understand the main idea.

> In the night sky, stars look like tiny diamonds fastened to the ceiling. They seem peaceful, timeless, and unchanging. In reality, stars are huge. They are scattered through vast distances in space. They're not timeless but are always changing, and those changes can be violent.

Try It!

Choose Another Selection Look back at a selection you read before. Analyze the author's **style** for that selection. Take notes on what you find.

- What type of words does the author use? What effect do they have?
- What important words or phrases does the author repeat?
- What types of sentences are in the selection? What effect do they have?

Share Your Findings Discuss your selection, and tell about the author's **style** .

Use Context Clues

Academic Vocabulary
- **appropriate** (u-**prō**-prē-ut) *adjective*
  If something is **appropriate**, it is correct for the situation.

A multiple-meaning word has more than one meaning. You can use context clues to figure out the **appropriate** meaning. Then you can check the definition using a dictionary.

The full moon looks <u>odd</u> behind the clouds.

Dictionary Entry

odd (od) *adjective* **1** strange or unusual **2** not able to be divided by two

The sentence is about the moon. This context helps you figure out the **appropriate** meaning of *odd*: The moon looks strange behind the clouds.

Define Words Find each of these words on page 456. Write the context clues. Then look up the word in a dictionary, and copy the **appropriate** definition.

1. stand **2.** clear **3.** band **4.** left

Research Energy

HEALTH & SCIENCE

Academic Vocabulary
- **fact** (fakt) *noun*
  A **fact** is a piece of information that is true.

1 **Conduct Research** The sun is the source of most energy on Earth. Energy is stored and changes form when it is used. Work with a group to learn **facts** about the sun's energy. Focus on one way that energy changes form. Record where you get your **facts** so you can go back to the original source for details.

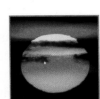

▲ The sun is an important source of energy.

Internet InsideNG.com
 Find out how the sun's energy is transformed.

2 **Organize Your Ideas** Make a drawing to show how energy is stored and how it changes from one form to another. Start with the sun. Label each step. Then organize the key ideas in your talk to go with your drawing.

3 **Share What You Learned** Display your drawing. Present the **facts** and details you learned. Take turns reading the labels in order. Emphasize each point so your listeners will understand the key ideas.

Analyze Author's Purpose

Academic Vocabulary

- **evaluate** (i-**val**-yu-wāt) *verb*
  To **evaluate** means to judge something's value or worth.

Before authors write, they think about what to tell readers and why. Their purpose, or reason, for writing helps them decide on the genre, or form of writing, to use. For example, an author can write

- an article to **inform** readers about the stars
- an essay to **persuade** readers to study astronomy
- a story or play about the constellations to **entertain** readers
- a manual to **explain** how to operate a telescope.

If you know the author's purpose, it can help you **evaluate** the text. For example, if the author's purpose is to inform, you can decide if you learned something from the text.

To determine the author's purpose, look at the information and ideas the author includes. Think about whether the selection is fiction or nonfiction. Ask yourself: "Does the author want to tell me a story? Explain, describe, or express something? Persuade me to do something?"

Practice Together

Analyze the Fable Reread the fable "The Astronomer." A fable is a fictional story with a moral, or lesson. The author tells the story to teach readers a lesson. Decide whether the author was successful.

Try It!

Analyze Another Selection Read the passage below. What is the author's purpose? **Evaluate** if the author achieved the purpose.

Scientists think there may be liquid water on Mars. They have known that water vapor and ice are on the planet, but, until recently, there was no reason to think there was liquid water. Spacecraft took photos of the planet over a period of several years. By comparing these photos, scientists noticed that material was moved from one place to another. They believe liquid water moved the material. They also believe there may be more water under the ground. They hope to learn more in future experiments.

Define and Explain

Partner Share Look in the selection for a difficult word or phrase that you learned. Then share with a partner. Define the difficult term. Explain its meaning. Use prepositional phrases to add details.

> A light-minute is the distance that light travels in one minute. Light travels from the sun to Earth in about eight minutes.

Write About an Adventure

Study the Models When you write about an adventure, include details. This will make your work interesting for readers. One way to add details is to use prepositional phrases.

NOT OK

> I read a science fiction book about explorers in space. The crew traveled far. They landed. They could land because they had special equipment. One crew member fell. The others searched for him.

The reader thinks: **"It's hard to picture this. There are not enough details."**

OK

> I read a science fiction book about explorers in space. The crew traveled through many galaxies to an unknown planet. They landed on its hard, rocky surface. They could land on the planet because they had special equipment. One crew member fell into a deep crater. The others looked for him.

The writer adds interesting details in **prepositional phrases**.

Add Sentences Think of two sentences to add to the OK model above. Include descriptive prepositional phrases.

WRITE ON YOUR OWN Write about an adventure on a real planet or an imaginary planet. Use prepositional phrases to help make your writing interesting.

REMEMBER
There are singular and plural object pronouns.

Singular	Plural
me	us
you	you
him, her, it	them

◄ This image shows an imaginary planet.

Not-So-Starry Nights

Light Pollution Turns Night into Day

by Sharon Guynup

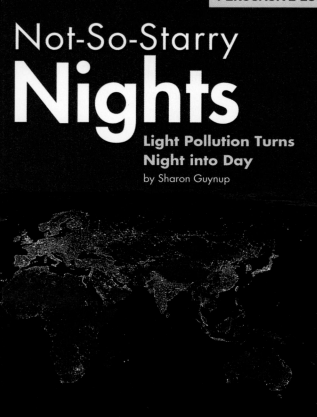

SELECTION 3 OVERVIEW

▶ **Build Background**

▶ **Language & Grammar**
Persuade
Use Participles

▶ **Prepare to Read**
Learn Key Vocabulary
Learn a Reading Strategy
Make Inferences

▶ **Read and Write**
Focus on Genre
Persuasive Essay
Apply the Reading Strategy
Make Inferences
Critical Thinking
Reading Fluency
Read with Intonation
Vocabulary Review
Write About the Guiding Question

▶ **Connect Across the Curriculum**
Literary Analysis
Analyze Persuasive Techniques
Vocabulary Study
Use Context Clues
Research/Media
Analyze Media
Listening/Speaking
Deliver a Persuasive Presentation
Language and Grammar
Persuade
Writing and Grammar
Write About the Night Sky

Build Background

Connect

Anticipation Guide What do you think about the environment? Tell whether you agree or disagree with these statements.

Anticipation Guide

	Agree	Disagree
1. Environmental problems hurt humans more than animals.	_____	_____
2. Outdoor lighting is not a problem for wildlife.	_____	_____
3. Most electricity is produced in a way that doesn't harm the environment.	_____	_____

Learn About Night Lights

About a century ago, people in the United States could see hundreds of twinkling stars at night. Today, artificial lights in cities make it difficult to see most of the stars at night.

Digital Library

InsideNG.com
⊘ View the video.

▲ Artificial lights block our view of the stars.

Language & Grammar

Persuade

CD

Listen to the chant. Listen again and join in.
Then listen to a persuasive argument.

CHANT and PERSUASIVE ARGUMENT

What Is It Worth?

A tossed bottle,
A thrown cup,
Polluted water—
Clean it up!

What is it worth
To us on Earth
To clean our atmosphere?
We must reduce the garbage
That pollutes the land and air!

1 TRY OUT LANGUAGE
2 LEARN GRAMMAR
3 APPLY ON YOUR OWN

Use Participles

You can make your sentences more interesting by adding **participles**.
A **participle** is a verb form that can be used as an adjective.

EXAMPLES   The bird landed in the water. People had **polluted** the water.
                                                       verb

          The bird landed in the **polluted** water.
                                      adjective

          The bird picked up a cup. The cup was **floating**.
                                                verb

          The bird picked up a **floating** cup.
                                adjective

- The **present participles** of regular and irregular verbs end in -**ing**.
- The **past participles** of regular verbs end in -**ed**.
- The **past participles** of irregular verbs usually have a new spelling.

Regular Verb	Irregular Verb	Present Participle	Past Participle
	break	break**ing**	broken
damage		damag**ing**	damag**ed**
discard		discard**ing**	discard**ed**
leak		leak**ing**	leak**ed**
litter		litter**ing**	litter**ed**
	tear	tear**ing**	torn

Practice Together

Combine each pair of sentences. Move the underlined participle to tell
about a noun in the other sentence. Say the new sentence.

1. A group is cleaning the beach. The beach is <u>littered</u> with trash.
2. Some volunteers pick up glass. People had <u>broken</u> the glass.
3. Others collect food. People had <u>discarded</u> it.
4. One person found a sandal. Someone had <u>torn</u> it.

Try It!

Write the underlined participle. Combine the
sentences and hold up the participle as you
say it in the new sentence.

5. We repair items so we can use them
   again. The items were <u>damaged</u>.
6. I fixed an umbrella. Someone had
   <u>broken</u> it.
7. My mom mended a shirt. I had <u>torn</u> it.
8. My sister repaired a hose. The hose
   was <u>leaking</u>.

▲ Someone will fix this
broken cup.

Give a Persuasive Speech

PERSUADE

Think about the chant on page 469. What would you do to improve the environment? What is Earth worth to you? How important is it to you?

Work in small groups. Discuss environmental problems and solutions. Record your ideas on a chart.

Idea Chart

Problem	Action Needed	Why It's Important
People are cutting down forests faster than new trees can grow.	use less paper, recycle paper	Forests provide homes for animals. Forests protect soil from washing away.
The air is polluted.		
People are overfishing.		

Focus on one problem. Then write a speech to persuade others to help solve the problem.

HOW TO PERSUADE

1. State your opinion.

2. Give reasons for your opinion.

3. Use persuasive words like *must*, *have to*, and *should*.

4. Tell why your opinion or plan of action is important.

5. Tell how it will help others.

> We should use shopping bags made of cloth. This will help save trees.

After you finish the speech, decide which group member will present it to the class.

USE PARTICIPLES

When you try to persuade people, you need to use effective and interesting sentences. Using **participles** adds interest and convincing details to your sentences.

Not as Interesting: We must save the waters of our lake.

More Interesting: We must save the **sparkling** waters of our lake.

Learn Key Vocabulary

Rate and Study the Words Rate how well you know each word. Then:

1. Pronounce the word. Say it aloud several times. Spell it.
2. Study the example.
3. Tell more about the word.
4. Practice it. Make the word your own.

Rating Scale

1 = I have never seen this word before.

2 = I am not sure of the word's meaning.

3 = I know this word and can teach the word's meaning to someone else.

Key Words

benefit (be-nu-fit) *noun*
▶ page 476

A **benefit** is something that is helpful. Fresh air and exercise are two **benefits** of hiking.

environment (in-vī-run-munt) *noun* ▶ page 478

An **environment** is the area where plants and animals live and grow. Plants grow well in a healthy **environment**.

migrate (mī-grāt) *verb*
▶ page 480

To **migrate** means to move from one place to another. These birds **migrate** to a warm climate for the winter.

pollution (pu-lü-shun) *noun*
▶ page 476

Pollution is waste that harms nature. Trash is one form of **pollution**.

protect (pru-tekt) *verb*
▶ page 481

To **protect** means to keep safe. The mother bird **protects** her chicks from danger.
Synonym: **save**

reduce (ri-düs) *verb*
▶ page 483

To **reduce** means to have fewer or less of something. The box is too heavy for her to carry, so her friend helps **reduce** the heavy load.
Antonym: **increase**

release (ri-lēs) *verb*
▶ page 478

To **release** means to let out. When you **release** an animal into the wild, you let it go free.

wasted (wāst-ud) *adjective*
▶ page 478

Something that is **wasted** is not needed. Food that you throw away instead of eating is **wasted**.

Practice the Words Make a chart to tell how you feel about each word. Is your response positive, negative, or neither? Explain. Compare your chart with a partner's and discuss.

Word	Positive (+) Negative (-) Neither (=)	Reason
release	+	I think it is good to release animals.

Connotation Chart

Reading Strategy: Make Inferences

When you read, pay attention to details in different parts of the text. Put ideas together to make inferences. Then build on your inferences to get more meaning from the text.

Reading Strategy
Make Inferences

How to MAKE INFERENCES

1. Notice the details in the text. Think about what you know.

2. Put the ideas together to figure out what the author did not say directly.

3. Keep reading. Notice other details. Remember the inference you made.

4. Put the new ideas together and build on your earlier inference.

Strategy in Action

Here's how one student made inferences.

Look Into the Text

What I read: People had a twinkling view of the sky.

One hundred years ago, everyone had a twinkling view of the night sky. At that time, people could see about 1,500 stars. Today, only one in ten Americans has a beautiful, starry view. People in cities see a glowing orange sky and just a few dozen stars instead.

Astronomers were the first to notice the growing problem of light pollution. They began to realize it in the 1970s.

"I know that stars twinkle. I infer that people used to be able to see a lot of stars."

What I read: One in ten people has a beautiful, starry view.

"A starry view must also mean that they can see a lot of stars in the sky."

Practice Together

Reread the passage above, and make an inference. Follow the steps in the How-To box.

Persuasive Essay

A persuasive essay is a short piece of nonfiction writing about one subject. The author's purpose is to convince you of something. The author expresses an opinion and supports it with **facts and examples**.

> About one-third of all lighting in the United States is wasted. Wasted light costs billions of dollars per year. It also harms the environment.
>
> Electricity comes from power plants. . . . Power plants burn coal, which pollutes the air.

Reading Strategy: Make Inferences

As you read, use information from the text to make inferences. Think about what you know, too. Build on your inferences.

INFORMATION IN THE TEXT:

There is wasted light.

Electricity comes from power plants.

Power plants burn coal.

YOU INFER:

Wasted light harms the environment because it causes power plants to burn more coal.

Not-So-Starry Nights

Light Pollution Turns Night into Day

by Sharon Guynup

▲ This photo from space shows how bright the lights from cities are.

The Sky as a Natural Resource

A star-filled sky is a magnificent sight. It is also an important part of our lives. By studying the sky, we learn about our place in the universe.

Animals also need the night sky. Some animals use the stars to **find their way**. Others depend on the dark to feel safe.

This natural **wonder**, like many others, is in danger from human activity. Light **pollution** is changing our view of the night. We must change our ways, or we will lose the **benefits** of the starry sky.

History of the Problem

One hundred years ago, everyone **had a twinkling view of** the night sky. At that time, people could see about 1,500 stars. Today, only one in ten Americans has a beautiful, starry view. People in cities see a glowing orange sky and just a few dozen stars instead.

Astronomers were the first to notice the growing problem of light pollution. They began to realize it in the 1970s. They were shocked when they looked into their telescopes and saw that some of the stars and planets that they had studied were gone. They were still there, of course, but city lights made them impossible to see.

Nights started to get brighter more than a century ago. The first long-lasting lightbulb was invented in 1879. Companies began to **install** electric power lines across the country. More and more people used electricity for lighting.

At the same time, the population grew. Many people moved to the United States. In 1900, there were 76 million Americans. There are more than 300 million today. More people now live in cities and suburbs, and their lights create light pollution.

Key Vocabulary
pollution *n.*, waste that harms nature
benefit *n.*, something that is helpful

In Other Words
find their way know which direction to go
wonder resource
had a twinkling view of could see stars in
install put up

▲ This photo was taken on August 14, 2003. It shows the night sky over Ontario, Canada, **during a blackout**.

▲ This photo was taken the next night. It shows how the night sky looks when there are many lights on.

Before You Move On

1. **Inference** How is the sky in danger from human activity?
2. **Evidence and Conclusion** How did astronomers first learn about light **pollution**?

In Other Words

during a blackout when electricity was not available

Science Background

A lightbulb uses electricity to heat a thin strip of material that glows brightly. The material lasts a long time before it burns out. The glass bulb is filled with a mostly harmless gas.

What Causes Light Pollution?

Light pollution is caused by excess light that is **beamed** into the sky. The extra light shines from houses, office buildings, streetlights, and sports fields. It reflects onto low clouds, causing a sky glow that **blots out** the stars.

Bad **light fixtures** cause much of the problem. Most of the **murky** glow in the night sky is **wasted** light, according to David Crawford. He is the director of the International Dark-Sky Association, an organization that is working to stop light pollution. Crawford says that lights should point at the ground, not at the sky.

About one-third of all lighting in the United States is wasted. Wasted light costs billions of dollars per year. It also harms the **environment**.

Electricity comes from power plants. Half of the country's power plants burn coal, which pollutes the air. The power plants **release** sulfur dioxide and carbon dioxide. Sulfur dioxide creates harmful acid rain. Carbon dioxide traps heat near the Earth's surface, causing global warming.

Key Vocabulary
wasted *adj.*, not needed
environment *n.*, the area where plants and animals live and grow
release *v.*, to let out

In Other Words
beamed sent
blots out makes it hard to see
light fixtures streetlights, spotlights, and other sources of light
murky dull

The more electricity people use, the more power plants have to produce. That means more air pollution.

Science Background

Sunlight heats Earth's surface. Some heat goes out into space, but most stays close to Earth. Gases, including carbon dioxide, soak up the heat. As more gases are released into the air, they keep more and more heat close to Earth. Earth becomes warmer than usual.

Before You Move On

1. **Cause and Effect** How does **wasted** light cause light **pollution**?
2. **Evaluating Sources** Do you agree with David Crawford that lights should point at the ground and not at the sky? Why or why not?

Animals at Risk

Light pollution also harms wildlife. "Animals depend on patterns of light and dark," says Travis Longcore. He is an **ecologist** with the Urban Wildlands Group. According to Longcore, lighting up the night changes the way animals **behave**.

Light pollution has the worst effect on birds. Many birds **migrate** at night and use the stars like street signs to find their way. Bright lights sometimes confuse birds in flight. Lights from buildings and towers attract the birds. The birds **veer off course**, and sometimes whole **flocks** of birds crash.

▲ Millions of migratory birds crash into buildings each year and die. The birds in this photo were all killed in Toronto, Canada, while migrating one year.

Key Vocabulary
  migrate *v.*, to move from one place to another

In Other Words
ecologist environmental scientist
behave act
veer off course fly in the wrong direction
flocks groups

In 1954, a flock of birds followed the spotlights at a U.S. Air Force base in Georgia. They flew straight into the ground. About 50,000 birds died.

Hundreds of **bird species** in North America die from light pollution. Some of these species are **endangered**, as Michael Mesure explains. Mesure is president of Canada's Fatal Light Awareness Program. His group helps **protect** migrating birds.

In Other Words
bird species types of birds
endangered rare, at risk of dying out

Before You Move On

1. **Explain** How can light **pollution** harm birds that **migrate** at night?
2. **Viewing** How does the photo of the birds illustrate the ideas in the text?

Turtles in Danger

Light pollution is also bad for other **nocturnal animals**. Female sea turtles come **ashore** at night and lay their eggs in the sand.

Beach hotels want people to enjoy the outdoors at night. They light up the beaches. But turtles do not feel safe on brightly lighted beaches. They will not come to shore to lay their eggs.

Turtles must be allowed to nest each year. There are only seven species of sea turtles, and all of them are endangered. It is important for them to lay eggs.

Hatchlings need a dark night sky, too, just as the female turtles do. When baby turtles hatch, they need to crawl to the water. Starlight and moonlight shining on the water pull them toward the sea. Light coming from land leads them the wrong way. As a result, the turtles wander into streets and parking lots and get lost. There, they **risk getting run over** by cars.

▼ Sea turtle hatchlings crawl toward the water.

In Other Words
nocturnal animals animals that are active at night
ashore onto the beach
Hatchlings Baby turtles
risk getting run over are in danger of being killed

Taking Back the Night

We need to stop light pollution. It is an easy problem to fix, says Crawford.

Cities need to use lamps that don't waste light. Special streetlights can shine light directly downward. **Individuals** and businesses must use fewer lights. We need to leave many parking lots and office buildings dark at night.

Some states have already passed lighting laws. Hundreds of communities have, too. Miami and other cities have already bought new streetlights. Toronto is trying to **reduce** city lights during bird migration season.

These steps will help, but everyone needs to help stop this problem. "**At the flick of a switch**, this problem could disappear," says Mesure. ❖

About the Author

Sharon Guynup

Sharon Guynup (1958–) is a science writer, editor, and photographer. She especially enjoys writing about nature. Guynup's stories have appeared in many science magazines. She travels all over the world for her assignments.

"Hiking deep in the rainforest or snorkeling along coral reefs gave me a deep love of nature," Guynup says. "Much of my work explores ways we need to protect wildlife—and this beautiful planet we all share."

Key Vocabulary
reduce *v.*, to have fewer of something

In Other Words
Individuals People
At the flick of a switch By turning lights off

Before You Move On

1. **Paraphrase** Use your own words to tell why light **pollution** is bad for turtles.
2. **Interpret** How can lighting laws **reduce** the problem of light **pollution**?

Preserving the Rural Environment

by Anthony Arrigo

Snyderville Basin, Utah – Ten years ago, county officials acted to preserve our view of the beautiful, star-filled night skies.

They set up laws for outdoor lighting. The laws say all outdoor lights must be directed downward. **Flood lights** are not allowed.

Unfortunately, people did not pay much attention to the laws. Now our **basin** is flooded with light.

The county must start **enforcing** the lighting laws.

And since the county created the problem, it should help fix it.

Homeowners who replace their bad lights within a year should pay 50 percent of the cost. The county should pay the rest.

People who wait a year to buy new lights should pay 75 percent. Those who wait for more than two years should pay the whole amount.

We must act now. We must prevent our beautiful area from becoming another **blemish** along the **interstate**.

Snyderville Basin at night

In Other Words

Flood lights Lights that shine up into the sky
basin valley
enforcing making people follow
blemish ugly mark
interstate road, highway

Before You Move On

1. **Main Idea and Details** What problem in Snyderville Basin is this editorial about?
2. **Opinion** Do you agree with the author's solution? Explain your answer.

Connect Reading and Writing

Vocabulary
benefit
environment
migrate
pollution
protect
reduce
released
wasted

CRITICAL THINKING

1. SUM IT UP Make a Proposition-Support Diagram with the writer's ideas about light **pollution**. Use the diagram to summarize the selection with a partner.

Proposition-Support Diagram

Proposition: We must stop light pollution.
Support 1:
Support 2:
Support 3:

2. Analyze Look again at your Anticipation Guide about the **environment** from page 468. Evaluate your answers. Discuss your thinking with a group.

3. Synthesize How is the problem of **wasted** light connected to animals?

4. Compare Compare the author's purpose for the two texts. Which text is more persuasive? Explain.

READING FLUENCY

Intonation Read the passage on page 588 to a partner. Assess your fluency.

1. I read
   a. great   **b.** OK   **c.** not very well

2. What I did best in my reading was _____.

READING STRATEGY

> **Make Inferences**
> Explain how building on your inferences helped you better understand the text.

VOCABULARY REVIEW

Oral Review Read the paragraph aloud. Add the vocabulary words.

> I found a sick bird. When it got better, I _____ it into the air. That night, I saw a program on TV about light _____ . I learned how unused, or _____, light not only harms the _____, but also confuses birds. As birds _____, they use the stars to guide them. Artificial lights can cause them to go the wrong way. I want to help and _____ birds, so I wrote a letter to the mayor. I said that the city should find out if it shines too much light at night. If it does, it should _____ the glow. I explained why this would be a big _____ to the birds in our area.

Written Review Imagine that your city passed laws against **wasted** light. What would the sky look like? Write a description. Use four vocabulary words.

 **WRITE ABOUT THE** **GUIDING QUESTION**

Explore the Power of the Stars
Is lighting up the night sky worth the **benefit** to humans, or is it too harmful to the **environment**? Write a persuasive paragraph to explain what you think. Use examples from the text.

Analyze Persuasive Techniques

> **Academic Vocabulary**
> • **analyze** (a-nu-līz) *verb*
>   To **analyze** means to break down information into parts to understand it better.

Authors use certain techniques to get readers to think or act a certain way. Usually, they state their position or belief about a topic. They often use words like *must* and *should* to state a position.

Then authors give evidence to support their position. They may give facts, examples, statements from experts, or photographs to prove that something is true. When you read a persuasive essay, you have to **analyze** the evidence and decide if you agree with the author's position.

▲ **Should leaders in Los Angeles, California think about reducing light pollution?**

Practice Together

Begin a Chart Reread page 483. Make a chart to **analyze** the persuasive techniques the author uses. List the author's position and evidence that supports it.

Persuasive Techniques Chart

Author's Position	Evidence to Support
Everyone should help reduce wasted light.	Miami bought streetlights that do not waste light.

Discuss Decide if you agree with the author.

Try It!

Complete the Chart Read "Not-So-Starry Nights" again. Work with your partner to complete your chart. List other positions that the author states and any supporting evidence for those positions. Then tell what you think.

Use Context Clues

Academic Vocabulary
- **locate** (lō-kāt) *verb*
  To **locate** something is to find it.

Jargon is specialized language used by members of a particular group, such as scientists, musicians, or chefs. The underlined word below has a special meaning. **Locate** context clues to figure it out.

Most asteroids—small, rocky objects in space—are in the asteroid <u>belt</u> between Mars and Jupiter.

Dictionary Entry

belt (belt) *noun* **1** a strip of material worn around the waist **2** an area full of a particular thing

The context clues *asteroid, Mars,* and *Jupiter* help you determine that the second definition fits the text.

Define Words With a partner, look in the text for each word below that is used to talk about electricity. **Locate** clues to determine the correct meaning. Then find the word in a dictionary. Copy the definition that fits the text.

1. lines, p. 476   **2.** fixtures, p. 478   **3.** power, p. 478   **4.** plants, p. 478

Analyze Media

MEDIA &
TECHNOLOGY

Academic Vocabulary
- **evaluate** (i-**val**-yu-wāt) *verb*
  To **evaluate** means to judge something's value or worth.

People do not always agree about environmental issues. How do you know what to believe when you hear or see messages in the media?

1 **Conduct Research** Find out about an environmental issue, such as water pollution or clear-cutting forests. Look for articles or ads in magazines or other media, including the Internet.

2 **Study the Message** Read, view, or listen to the article or ad. **Evaluate** it for facts that can be proved, such as data. Also look for clues that express opinions. List important details. What audience do you think the writer wants to persuade?

3 **Discuss Your Findings** Share the article or ad and your notes. How effective is the article or ad? How well does it work for the audience?

Listening/Speaking

Deliver a Persuasive Presentation

SOCIAL SCIENCE

Academic Vocabulary
- **fact** (fakt) *noun*
  A **fact** is a piece of information that is true.

How would you like to help reduce light pollution in your community? Make a persuasive presentation for city leaders!

1 **Begin Your Research** Work with a partner. Notice the streetlights and other outdoor lights in your community. Brainstorm ways to reduce light pollution.

2 **Identify Your Audience** Find out who could take action to solve the problem. Your audience might be a person, such as the mayor or a business owner, or a group, such as the city council.

3 **State Your Position** Write a statement that expresses an opinion about the topic. You should use this as an interesting introduction for your presentation.

4 **Collect Data** Find **facts** to support your position, such as how laws in other towns have helped. Organize your **facts** and make notes for your presentation. Make or find charts, drawings, or other visuals. Include photos, if possible, and quotes from experts. Then write a conclusion that restates your position in a powerful way.

Presentation Planner

Introduction:
Statement: Light pollution is costly and harms the environment.

Middle:
Facts:

Conclusion:

▲ Make notes for your presentation.

5 **Give Your Presentation** Make your presentation to the class. Speak clearly and slowly. Make eye contact with listeners.

6 **Analyze Persuasive Techniques** Listen carefully as other students give their presentations. Afterward, identify the most persuasive parts.

Persuade

Role-Play Work in a group of three. The citizen wants more laws to protect the environment. The business owner does not want more laws. They both try to persuade the mayor. Use participial phrases in your role-play.

> Looking at the lake, I saw trash in the water.

Write About the Night Sky

Study the Models When you write about the night sky, make your sentences interesting. Add details to give readers a clearer picture of what you mean, and vary your sentences. Use participial phrases to help.

NOT OK

My family went camping last summer. We drove to the mountains. We arrived at night. We were amazed by the sky. We had never seen so many stars! The twinkling stars seemed to wink at us.

> The reader thinks: "The sentences are too much the same, and the details are not interesting."

OK

Sitting outside our tent one night, we saw an amazing sight. Looking up, we noticed a shooting star! It looked like a ball of fire with a glowing tail. The star, dragging a thin stream of light behind it, zoomed through the sky. Thrilled by the sight, I clapped my hands and shouted, "Wow!"

> This writer uses participial phrases to create interesting sentences. The reader thinks: "The details really help me picture the star."

Revise It Look back at the NOT OK passage. Work with a partner to revise it. Place each participial phrase near the noun or pronoun it tells about.

WRITE ON YOUR OWN Write about something you have seen in the night sky. Use participial phrases to help you write interesting sentences.

REMEMBER

Place each phrase near the noun or pronoun it describes.

Shining brightly, the full moon lighted the path.

The full moon lighted the path **covered with leaves.**

Compare Across Texts

Compare an Author's Works

All of the stories in "The Earth Under Sky Bear's Feet" were written by Joseph Bruchac. Compare different **elements** in this author's works.

How It Works

Collect and Organize Ideas To compare **elements** across texts, organize information in a chart. List the setting, characters, and plot for each story.

Comparison Chart

Element	Sky Bear	The Scattered Stars	The Seven Mateinnu
Setting	**When:** long ago, on a winter day **Where:** on a snowy hill, then high above Earth	**When:** long ago **Where:** on a hill	
Characters	hunters, a dog, and a bear		
Plot	The hunters and their dog chase a bear. The bear changes into a pattern of stars.		

Practice Together

Write a Review When you review two stories, you compare the information in them. You also tell how you feel about them.

> "Sky Bear" and "The Scattered Stars" take place long ago on a hill. In both stories, something unrealistic happens that relates to the stars. I like "The Scattered Stars" because it shows what happens if someone is very curious.

Try It!

Review the information in your completed chart. Write a report that compares the **elements** of all three stories and tells what you think of them. You may want to use this frame as a guide.

All three stories take place _____. In all of the stories, something unrealistic happens. The most unrealistic story is _____ because _____. The story I like best is _____ because _____.

Academic Vocabulary
- **element** (e-lu-munt) *noun*
  An **element** is a basic part of a whole.

Star Power

GUIDING QUESTION Why are both storytellers and scientists drawn to the stars?

UNIT LIBRARY

Content Library

MISSIONS IN SPACE

Leveled Library

The War of the Worlds

JERRY SPINELLI

the man who went to the far side of the moon

Reflect on Your Reading

Think back on your reading of the unit selections. Discuss what you did to understand what you read.

Focus on Genre **Author's Purpose**

In this unit, you learned about author's purpose. Choose a selection. At the top of a card, complete this sentence: *The author's purpose is to _____.* Explain how you identified the author's purpose. Then explain the author's purpose to a partner.

Reading Strategy **Make Inferences**

As you read, you learned to make inferences. Explain to a partner how you will use this strategy.

Explore the

In this unit, you have been thinking about stars. Choose one way to explore the Guiding Question:

- **Discuss** With a group, discuss the Guiding Question. Use what you know from your own life and details from the selections to support your ideas.
- **Panel Discussion** Organize a class panel discussion called "Why I Am Drawn to the Stars." Participate as a scientist, storyteller, or poet on the panel or as a member of the audience. If you are on the panel, explain why the stars attract you.
- **Write and Share** Write your own star myth. Or research something you would like to know about the stars and write a brief report. Share your story or report with a group. Then post your work in the classroom for others to read.

Book Talk

Which Unit Library book did you choose? Explain to a partner what it taught you about star power.

Spirit of Harlem, 2005, Louis Delsarte. Glass Mosaic, North Fork Bank, New York.

▲ **Critical Viewing** What does the style of this mosaic tell you about the artist? Explain.

Art and Soul

What do we learn about people from their artful expressions?

Read More!

Content Library

Johan Reinhard: Discovering Ancient Civilizations
by Rebecca L. Johnson

Leveled Library

WJHC on the Air!
by Jane Smith Fisher and Kirsten Petersen

When Marian Sang
by Pam Muñoz Ryan

Sadako and the Thousand Paper Cranes
by Eleanor Coerr

Internet
InsideNG.com

- Go to the Digital Library to uncover ideas about art.
- View an art exhibit.
- Explore music and dance from around the world.

Focus on Genre

Text Features

▶ **In Fiction**
▶ **In Nonfiction**

Writers use text features in fiction and nonfiction. They **select** the best features to add to their writing and to help readers understand.

How It Works

Before you read, look at the text features to see how the text is organized. As you read, use the features to help guide you through the text.

Text Features in Fiction The **titles** of stories and novels often tell what the story is about. **Paragraphs** separate the ideas in a story into understandable parts. Fiction often has **illustrations**, which help readers visualize the characters and events.

Text Features in Nonfiction Like fiction, nonfiction texts have titles and paragraphs. They often have other kinds of text features, too. Look at the **headings** and the **photo** and **caption** in this nonfiction text:

Origami
> The title tells what the text is about.

Origami is the Japanese art of paper folding. It is more than 400 years old. Artist Robert J. Lang has been doing origami since he was six. He is a master of the art.

Origami As Art

Lang can create many shapes. He can form flowers, birds, frogs, butterflies, and other creatures. He also makes origami shapes of buildings, including the Empire State Building.

▲ Lang makes a figure of two dancers from two rectangular sheets of paper.

> **Photos and captions give extra information or help explain the text.**

Origami As Science
> A heading tells the main idea of a section.

Using math and computers for origami has brought it to a new level. Scientists can use origami to help design medical and safety devices. Lang used it to help design a giant telescope.

Academic Vocabulary
● **select** (su-**lekt**) *verb*
  To **select** something means to choose it.

Practice Together

Read the following passage aloud. As you read, look for text features that the writer used to organize the text and help make it clear.

Louis Armstrong

Early Days

Louis Armstrong was born in New Orleans in 1901. He showed musical talent early. He was a street performer as a kid. He danced and sang for pennies. Then he got his first horn. He soon became known as a great jazz player.

▲ Louis Armstrong was generous, especially toward other musicians.

New Jazz

After becoming famous in New Orleans, Armstrong traveled to Chicago to play jazz and then to New York City. Before long, he was playing music around the world. Armstrong was a technical master and a creative genius. No one could match his spirit, but many musicians copied his style.

Try It!

Read the following passage aloud. What text features did the writer use? How do they help guide you through the text?

Public Expression

Painting on Walls

Graffiti means words or pictures drawn on public buildings. It has been around since paintings were drawn on cave walls. Today, many people see graffiti as a crime. Graffiti artists often work at night to avoid being caught. They write names, messages, or symbols.

▲ Murals decorate buildings in Philadelphia.

Murals

When does painting a building become art and not a crime? For many years, Philadelphia had a big graffiti problem. Then the city tried something new—a mural-making program. The program director invited graffiti artists to help paint murals. The program has been very successful.

Go Beyond the Literal Meaning

Writers choose words carefully to **communicate** their ideas in interesting ways. They often use **figurative language**, or words and phrases that have meanings outside of their exact definitions.

Idioms are one kind of figurative language. An idiom is a group of words that, together, **communicate** a different meaning than what the words mean by themselves. For example, *David is* **out of shape** means "David needs to exercise."

A **metaphor** is another kind of figurative language. A metaphor compares two unlike things. Metaphors often say that one thing *is* the other. For example, *The room was a* **boiling pot ready to explode** means "People in the room showed anger or other strong feelings."

How the Strategy Works

When you read, you may come to a phrase that does not make sense. Use context to figure out the meaning.

> EXAMPLE   Tish can be loud. She often shouts **at the top of her lungs**.

1. Look at sentences nearby. See if they give clues to the meaning.
2. Predict a literal meaning that might fit in the context.
3. Reread the sentence to see if your definition makes sense. If it does not, ask someone to explain the phrase.

Use the strategy to figure out the meaning of each underlined phrase.

> **M**y best friend's father is a talented gardener. People say that he has a green thumb. He certainly can make plants grow!
> Every year he enters the garden show. This year, his entry stole the spotlight. It won first prize. It was so amazing that everyone wanted to see it. You would be blown away if you saw it!

Strategy in Action

" The first sentence says that he is a talented gardener. It sounds like *having a green thumb* means 'he is a good gardener.' That meaning makes sense."

☑ **REMEMBER** Use context to figure out the meaning of figurative language.

Academic Vocabulary
- **communicate** (ku-**myū**-nu-kāt) *verb*
  When you **communicate**, you share information.

Practice Together

Read this passage aloud. Look at each underlined phrase. Use context to figure out the meaning.

Develop Your Talent

Everyone has talent of some kind. Some people are talented artists or musicians. Others are good at sports. Skateboarding, for example, might be a <u>piece of cake</u> for those people!

Some people have no talent for sports. Instead, they might be good at solving problems. Their talent is to <u>think outside the box</u>!

Once you find your talent, you need to develop it. You have to <u>feed and water it</u> by practicing often. You also should listen to people's advice for how to improve. Sometimes that can be <u>hard to swallow</u>. But when you see the results, you will feel good about your success. Then you can <u>pat yourself on the back</u>!

Try It!

Read this passage aloud. What is the meaning of each underlined phrase? How do you know?

The Cure

Arturo felt <u>down in the dumps</u>. He had no energy. He could not <u>put his finger on it</u>, but he just did not feel right. Then he remembered he had not played music for a couple of weeks. Music was <u>the best medicine</u>. It always made him feel better.

▲ Arturo plays a trombone.

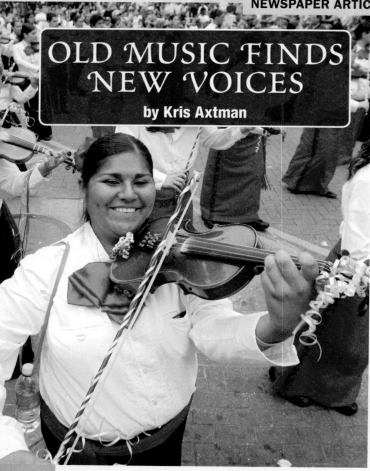

NEWSPAPER ARTICLE

OLD MUSIC FINDS NEW VOICES

by Kris Axtman

SELECTION 1 OVERVIEW

▶ **Build Background**

▶ **Language & Grammar**
Use Appropriate Language
Use Complete Sentences

▶ **Prepare to Read**
Learn Key Vocabulary
Learn a Reading Strategy
Synthesize

▶ **Read and Write**
Focus on Genre
Newspaper Article
Apply the Reading Strategy
Synthesize
Critical Thinking
Reading Fluency
Read with Appropriate Phrasing
Vocabulary Review
Write About the Guiding Question

▶ **Connect Across the Curriculum**
Literary Analysis
Analyze News Media
Vocabulary Study
Interpret Metaphors
Listening/Speaking
Share Information
Recite Songs
Language and Grammar
Use Appropriate Language
Writing and Grammar
Write About Music

Build Background

Explore the Arts

Artists express their ideas and feelings through their art. They also express their culture. Take a look at some artful expressions from around the world.

Connect

Quickwrite How do you express yourself? Do you write, draw, sing, play an instrument, play a sport? Take three minutes to write your answer. You will refer to it later.

Digital Library

InsideNG.com
● View the video.

▲ Mexican dancers and musicians perform at a concert in Hawaii.

Language & Grammar

Use Appropriate Language 🔵 CD

Listen to three different people talk about the painting.
How are their word choices and expressions different?

PICTURE PROMPT

Vahine No Te Tiare (Woman with a Flower), 1891.
Paul Gauguin. Oil on canvas, Ny Carlsberg Glyptotek, Copenhagen, Denmark.

To my left you'll see the portrait *Woman with a Flower* by Paul Gauguin. He painted it in 1891 when he was living in Tahiti.

Look at this painting. It's called *Woman with a Flower* because she's holding a flower in her hand.

Wow! Look at this painting by Paul Gauguin. I love the colors.

Use Complete Sentences

Remember, a complete sentence has two parts: the **subject** and the **predicate**.

> EXAMPLE   **The artist** **paints interesting images.**

- A **statement** is a sentence that tells something. In a statement, the subject usually comes before the predicate.

> EXAMPLE   **The name of the artist** **is Paul Gauguin.**

- A **simple sentence** is a sentence with one subject and one predicate.

> EXAMPLE   **Many of Gauguin's paintings** **hang in museums.**

Practice Together

Say each group of words. Add a subject or a predicate. Say the complete sentence. Then name the subject and the predicate in the sentence.

1. love art.
2. Every weekend we
3. My neighbor Marcus
4. express many feelings.
5. paints pictures of mountains.
6. The paintings
7. is a good artist.
8. My favorite artist

Try It!

Read each group of words. Write a subject or a predicate on a card. Hold up the card as you say the complete sentence. Then name the subject and the predicate in the sentence.

9. makes clay pots.
10. His studio
11. loves to sing.
12. are in a museum.
13. Those beautiful paintings
14. creates murals.
15. Her voice
16. The recital

▲ Sol LeWitt created this colorful sculpture.

Make a Presentation

USE APPROPRIATE LANGUAGE

We all express ourselves in different ways. Think about how you express yourself. Do you like to draw or paint? Do you act, sing, or play an instrument? Interview a partner. Start by listing interview questions like these:

Questions

How do you express yourself?
Why do you enjoy . . . . ?
When did you start . . . ?
Where did you learn . . . ?

Take notes as your partner answers the questions. Then use your notes to prepare a presentation for the class. Before you give your presentation, consider the way you spoke during the interview. Then consider the language you will use when you speak to the class.

HOW TO USE APPROPRIATE LANGUAGE

1. Use words that match the audience and the occasion.
- Use formal language when you give a presentation. Formal language is proper and polite.
- Use informal language when you talk with a friend. Informal language uses familiar expressions and ordinary, everyday words.

2. Use appropriate facial expressions, body language, tone, and volume.
- In a formal situation, look serious. Stand up straight. Make eye contact. Speak loudly and clearly enough for the audience to hear you.
- In an informal situation, you can act more relaxed and less serious. You can speak with more emotion.

> Good afternoon, everyone. Today I would like to tell you about Ahmad.

USE COMPLETE SENTENCES

When you give your presentation, be sure to use complete sentences. Remember, a complete sentence has a **subject** and a **predicate**.

EXAMPLE   **Ahmad** **writes poems in Arabic.**

Prepare to Read

Learn Key Vocabulary

Rate and Study the Words Rate how well you know each word. Then:

1. Pronounce the word. Say it aloud several times. Spell it.
2. Study the example.
3. Tell more about the word.
4. Practice it. Make the word your own.

Key Words

approve (u-**prüv**) *verb*
▶ page 506

To **approve** means to think something is good or right. The teacher **approves** the work I did.

career (ku-**rear**) *noun*
▶ page 507

A **career** is a job someone trains for and does full-time. This man went to veterinary school and now has a **career** working with animals.

competition
(kom-pu-**ti**-shun) *noun* ▶ page 507

A **competition** is a contest. The runners are in **competition** to win the race or to improve their time.
Synonyms: **game, challenge**

concert (**kont**-surt) *noun*
▶ page 507

A **concert** is an event where people play music for an audience. The orchestra is giving a **concert**.
Synonyms: **show, performance**

instrument (**int**-stru-munt)
noun ▶ page 509

An **instrument** is something you play to make music. Guitars and violins are both stringed **instruments**.

preserve (pri-**zurv**) *verb*
▶ page 508

To **preserve** means to save. The grandmother **preserves** a special tradition by sharing it with her granddaughter.
Synonym: **protect**

roots (rüts) *noun*
▶ page 506

Roots are a person's family traditions and culture. My family is from India. I am so proud of my Indian **roots**.

support (su-**port**) *verb*
▶ page 508

To **support** means to help. People **support** friends and family when they encourage or comfort each other.
Synonym: **assist**

Practice the Words Make a Vocabulary Example Chart for each Key Word. Then compare your chart with a partner's.

Word	Definition	Example from My Life
approve	to think something is good or right	My teacher approved the plans for my project.

Vocabulary Example Chart

Reading Strategy: Synthesize

When you draw conclusions about something you read, you think about what the text says, together with what you know. Then you draw conclusions, or decide what you believe, about what the text says.

Reading Strategy
Synthesize

HOW TO DRAW CONCLUSIONS

1. As you read, notice important details in the text.

2. Think about your own experience related to the text.

3. Put the details together with your experience. Decide what you believe about the text. That is your conclusion.

Strategy in Action

Here's how one student drew conclusions.

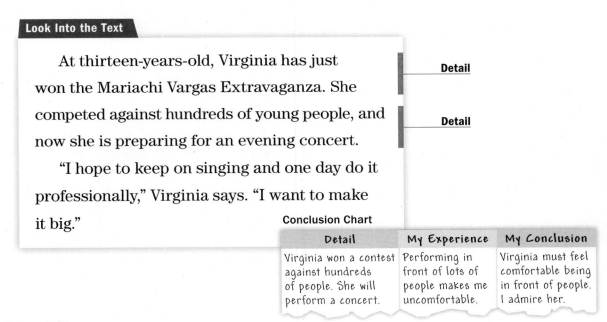

Look Into the Text

At thirteen-years-old, Virginia has just won the Mariachi Vargas Extravaganza. She competed against hundreds of young people, and now she is preparing for an evening concert.

"I hope to keep on singing and one day do it professionally," Virginia says. "I want to make it big."

Detail

Detail

Conclusion Chart

Detail	My Experience	My Conclusion
Virginia won a contest against hundreds of people. She will perform a concert.	Performing in front of lots of people makes me uncomfortable.	Virginia must feel comfortable being in front of people. I admire her.

Practice Together

Reread the passage above. Follow the steps in the How-To box to draw a conclusion of your own. Record your ideas in a Conclusion Chart.

Newspaper Article

Newspaper articles provide facts about recent topics and events. The reporter's purpose is to inform readers.

A newspaper article begins with a **headline**, which tells what the article is about and grabs the reader's interest. A **deck** is a short introduction to the article. A **byline** identifies the writer of the article.

Old Music Finds New Voices

headline

Mexico's traditional mariachi music is a hit again—with Hispanic youngsters in the United States. It connects them to their roots.

deck

by Kris Axtman

byline

Your Job as a Reader

Reading Strategy: Synthesize

As you read, combine details and your experience to draw conclusions. Record your ideas in a Conclusion Chart.

OLD MUSIC FINDS NEW VOICES

by Kris Axtman

Online Coach

High school group Mariachi Nuevo Santander from Roma, Texas, performs in Atlanta, Georgia.

Old Music Finds New Voices

*Mexico's traditional mariachi music is **a hit** again — with Hispanic youngsters in the United States. It connects them to their **roots**.*

by Kris Axtman
Staff writer of *The Christian Science Monitor*

San Antonio - Virginia Stille can't decide on the right shade of lipstick. She doesn't want anything too bright, but the color must be bright enough to show up on stage.

"What about this one, Mom?" she calls.

Mom **approves**, and Virginia puts on the lipstick. Just as she's about to stand up, someone asks her to sing.

Now, that's something Virginia is not **indecisive** about.

She begins slowly: *"Rebozo, Rebozo."* Then she sings more quickly: *"de Santa María."*

Key Vocabulary

roots *n.*, a person's family traditions and culture

approve *v.*, to think something is good or right

In Other Words

a hit popular
indecisive unsure
Rebozo, Rebozo . . . de Santa María Shawl, shawl . . . of Santa María (in Spanish)

At thirteen-years-old, Virginia has just won the Mariachi Vargas Extravaganza. She **competed** against hundreds of young people, and now she is preparing for an evening **concert**.

"I hope to keep on singing and one day do it **professionally**," Virginia says. "I want to **make it big**."

While it may be hard to imagine a mariachi singer making a lot of money, mariachi is growing more popular in the United States. Plus, mariachi is **hip** with the youngsters here.

Many Mexican American teens are thinking about **careers** in mariachi. Schools offer courses in mariachi music, and **competitions** are spreading across the country as more and more Hispanic teens become interested in their culture.

"I like to tell stories," says Victoria Acosta, who won competitions even before she was a teen. "When I'm singing, it's like I'm telling a story. There are sad songs, and happy songs, and love songs. There are all different kinds of stories to tell."

Valerie Vargas and her group Mariachi Las Altenas win a competition in Houston, Texas.

Before You Move On

1. **Personal Experience** Have you ever been in a **competition**? What did you like about it? What did you not like?
2. **Explain** Why is mariachi music popular with some young people?

Key Vocabulary

concert *n.*, an event where people play music for an audience

career *n.*, a job someone trains for and does full-time

competition *n.*, a contest

In Other Words

competed took part in the contest
professionally as my job
make it big become famous
hip popular at this time

When Victoria was just 4 years old, she fell in love with mariachi music. She **begged** her parents for lessons.

A member of the all-female group Mariachi Altenas performs in Little Rock, Arkansas.

Her parents **supported** her. "We need to do our part to **preserve** our culture," says her father, Ruben Acosta. He is a **fifth-generation Mexican American**. "Mariachi music is so beautiful. We want to make sure it doesn't die out."

Spanish is not spoken in many homes like the Acostas'. Both parents only know a little of the language. Their children are learning Spanish for the first time through mariachi music.

Maria Elena Gonzales tells about the song she just sang. "It's about a shepherd who sings to his sheep," she says. "I don't really know Spanish, so I think that's what it's about."

Her family speaks Spanish when they are together. Maria Elena says she never paid attention. "I guess I never really wanted to know what they were saying."

She and her best friend, Lizzette Abreu, began learning mariachi songs just two years ago. "I grew to love it," says Lizzette. She is dressed in white lace-up boots and a white *traje de charro*. This is a female style of the mariachi suit. "When I sing, I feel like I am in Mexico."

Key Vocabulary
support *v.*, to help
preserve *v.*, to save

In Other Words
begged asked
fifth-generation Mexican American
    person whose great-great grandparents
    came to the U.S. from Mexico
traje de charro cowboy costume
    (in Spanish)

A young musician tunes his **guitarrón** with the help of a friend. This special type of guitar plays low notes. It is used mostly in mariachi music.

Her mother was surprised at Lizzette's interest in mariachi. Lucila Ruiz moved to Houston 37 years ago from Mexico City. "When she used to listen to mariachi music in her room, I told her: '[Turn] it off. We're from here now,'" says Ms. Ruiz. "But I could see she really felt it in her heart, and so I'm proud of her."

When Jorge Perez first started to play mariachi, he says, "I had to learn to like the music." He puts on his felt hat and grabs his **instrument**. "My grandpa used to play the guitar and sing. When he found out I was playing in a mariachi band, it surprised him a lot."

"Don't ask me why, but when I'm playing, I feel a lot closer to my Mexican roots." ❖

Key Vocabulary
instrument *n.*, something that you play to make music

In Other Words
guitarrón large guitar (in Spanish)

Before You Move On

1. **Opinion** Do you think families should **support** young people who want to learn mariachi? Why or why not?
2. **Text Features** What additional information does the caption tell you about a *guitarrón*?

When I Sing/ Cuando Canto

by Juanita Ulloa

When I sing, I see the sky
and its color becomes more beautiful.
When I sing, I feel inspired and my soul
fills with love.

5 When I sing, I fly high and my wings
are made of light.
I feel inspired when I sing
with love.
That's why I sing, because
10 it's my passion.

*Cuando canto, veo el cielo
y es mas bello su color.
Cuando canto, me emociono y en mi
alma hay solo amor.*

5 *Cuando canto, vuelo alto y mis alas
son de luz.
Yo me siento inspirada cuando canto
con amor.
Es por eso que canto, porque
10 es mi pasión.*

About the Songwriter

Juanita Ulloa

Juanita Ulloa was 8 years old when her family moved to Mexico City. "My dad would take me to hear mariachi bands. I remember those powerful voices and how their music would just soar."

Later, Ulloa studied music at college. Now, she performs with a mariachi group and writes music. Her song *"Cuando Canto"* won a prize at the Latin American Song Festival in 2001.

In Other Words

inspired like I want to do something important
my passion something I really love to do

Before You Move On

1. **Metaphor** What does the singer mean when she says, "I fly high and my wings are made of light"?
2. **Interpret** What is this song about? What message does the singer want to give people?

Connect Reading and Writing

CRITICAL THINKING

1. **SUM IT UP** Create a Main-Idea Diagram. List the main idea of the selection and details that **support** it. Use your diagram to sum up the selection.

Main-Idea Diagram

Main Idea:
Detail:
Detail:

2. **Describe** Use details in the photos and the text to describe what a mariachi performer typically wears during a **competition**.

3. **Generalize** The performers in the selection like to feel close to their **roots**. Do you think this is true for others who perform ethnic music in the United States? Explain.

4. **Compare** How do the mariachi musicians and Juanita Ulloa feel about their music? How can feelings like these help **preserve** mariachi music?

READING FLUENCY

Phrasing Read the passage on page 589 to a partner. Assess your fluency.

1. I read
   a. great   **b.** OK   **c.** not very well

2. What I did best in my reading was _____.

READING STRATEGY

Synthesize
During reading, how did you draw conclusions? Share one conclusion with a partner and explain how you made it.

VOCABULARY REVIEW

Oral Review Read the paragraph aloud. Add the vocabulary words.

> There are many ways to keep, or _____, the customs of a culture. One way is to study folk dancing and make it a profession, or _____. Some people have selected Irish step dancing. American square dancing is also popular and has its _____ in step dancing. The fiddle, a fun and lively _____, is used with both forms of dance. My friends _____ of my interest in folk dancing. They will _____ me by coming to my next _____. At my last _____, I got a silver medal!

Written Review Imagine that you want a **career** as a mariachi performer. Write a list of goals. Use four vocabulary words.

 **WRITE ABOUT THE** **GUIDING QUESTION**

Explore Art and Soul
Why is music an important way for people to express themselves? **Support** your ideas with examples from the selection and your own life.

Connect Across the Curriculum

Analyze News Media

> **Academic Vocabulary**
> • **report** (ri-**port**) *verb*
>   When you **report** on an event, you describe what happened.

Articles in news publications **report** facts about events. Facts are statements that can be proved as true or false. Dates, places, and data suggest facts. Articles can include opinions, too. Most opinion statements use words like *think, believe,* or *like.*

Because people read news publications for information, a reporter can focus people's attention on a topic or issue by writing about it. The facts and opinions that the reporter presents also help people form opinions about the topic or issue.

Practice Together

Read and Discuss This news feature is from a music magazine. Notice the **facts** . Then notice how the writer **reports** people's **opinions** .

"He's the best guitar player in the world," one fan said. "I think he has natural talent."

I interviewed Miguel's parents after the show. They told me that Miguel practices at least three hours every day. His guitar coach confirmed this. "Miguel does seem to have a gift, but he works hard, too. I give him very difficult exercises and he works on them all week. At his next lesson, I can tell he learned from the exercises."

Miguel has performed in more than ten cities in the past year. Everywhere he goes, fans scream for more. He just might be the country's next great talent.

The reporter of this article focuses on the guitar player Miguel. What opinions might people have about Miguel after they read this article?

Try It!

Work with a partner. Find facts and opinions in the news article "Old Music Finds New Voices." Then think about what topic the reporter wants people to focus on. What opinion do you have about this topic because of the article?

Interpret Metaphors

Academic Vocabulary
- **interpret** (in-**tur**-prut) *verb*
  To **interpret** means to explain or tell what something means.

A metaphor compares two things that are not really alike. Metaphors often suggest that one thing is another thing or that it has the qualities of something else. The speaker of "When I Sing" compares herself to a bird. She compares her wings to beams of light.

> When I sing, I fly high and my wings are made of light.

The speaker does not mean that she really flies. She means that singing makes her feel like she is flying. Her wings are not really made of light. They just feel like they have no substance, or matter.

Interpret Metaphors Find each metaphor in the passage below. What two things does it compare? In a small group, explain how you **interpret** the metaphor and how it helps you understand the text.

> When I play my guitar, my fingers are butterflies.
> They float on the strings. The music becomes a satin
> blanket. I sway my head in the sea of music.

Share Information

ART

Academic Vocabulary
- **communicate** (ku-**myū**-nu-kāt) *verb*
  When you **communicate**, you share information.

What artistic skills do you have? **Communicate** to your group how to do one skill.

1. **Prepare Directions** Think about something you know how to do well, such as tuning a guitar or making an origami figure. How would you **communicate** the process to others? Identify the key steps. Decide what you can bring to illustrate the skill, too.

2. **Share Your Skill** Work in a small group. Give precise directions for others to follow.

▲ Musicians demonstrate how to play a traditional musical instrument in China.

Recite Songs

MUSIC

Academic Vocabulary
- **select** (su-**lekt**) *verb*
  To **select** something means to choose it.

When you recite a poem or song, you memorize it first. Then you say it aloud for others to hear.

1 **Choose a Song** **Select** a song or poem that you know well and that you can share. Try to **select** one that is meaningful to you. It should be short enough to memorize. Songs or poems that have a strong rhythm, or beat, are easier to memorize. Rhyming words—words like *sky* and *fly* or *friend* and *send*—also make a song or poem easier to remember.

2 **Practice** Learn the poem or song lyrics until you do not need to read the words. Then practice reciting it with emotion, or feeling.

3 **Share Your Song** Recite your poem or song lyrics to a group. Be sure to tell the title and the name of the songwriter or poet.

- Say the words clearly so listeners can understand them.
- Use an appropriate tempo, or timing. Do not speak too quickly or too slowly.
- Speak at the right volume: loud enough that people can hear you, but not too loud.
- Use meaningful phrasing. Let people hear the rhythm of the poem or lyrics. Pause at the right times. Stress the right words.
- Express the meaning and emotion of the poem or lyrics. Use the appropriate tone and movements with your hands and face.

4 **Discuss** Which songs did you enjoy most? What did you like about them?

▲ It is easier to memorize a short poem with a strong rhythm and rhyming words.

Use Appropriate Language

Role-Play Work with a partner. Imagine you are one of the singers or musicians in the selection. Your partner discusses your music with you as a friend and then as a reporter from a serious news program. Switch roles. Speak in complete sentences.

> Mr. Perez, what do you like most about mariachi music?

> I feel a connection to Mexico when I play.

Write About Music

Study the Models When you write about music you like, you want to share your ideas. Be sure to use complete sentences so your readers do not become confused.

NOT OK

Bluegrass music began in the southern United States. Some common bluegrass instruments. Banjo, guitar, and fiddle. A blend of English, Irish, Scottish, and African American music. It is sometimes called "mountain music." Because early bluegrass musicians wrote songs about their life in the mountains and the country.

> The writer confuses the reader by using fragments instead of complete sentences.

OK

Bluegrass music began in the southern United States. **Some common bluegrass instruments include the banjo, guitar, and fiddle. Bluegrass is a blend of English, Irish, Scottish, and African American music.** It is sometimes called "mountain music" because early bluegrass musicians wrote songs about their life in the mountains and the country.

> The writer fixes fragments by adding missing **subjects** and missing verbs in **predicates**.

Revise It Work with a partner to revise this passage. Fix the fragments.

Mariachi is music from Mexico. Very popular now among young people. Learning to sing and play the songs. Mexican American kids are especially interested in this traditional music. They learn the words to the old songs in Spanish. Although many of them do not speak Spanish at home.

WRITE ON YOUR OWN What kind of music do you like? Write a paragraph about it. Make sure every sentence expresses a complete thought.

REMEMBER

To fix a fragment, you can
- add a **subject** or a **predicate**
- combine sentences.

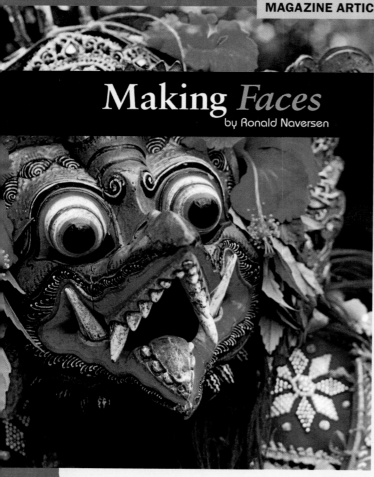

Making *Faces*
by Ronald Naversen

Build Background

Talk About Costumes

Costumes change the way you look and feel. Look at the photos. Make a list of reasons that people wear costumes or masks.

Digital Library

InsideNG.com
▶ View the images.

◀ A costumed performer gets ready for a festival in Japan.

Connect

Class Survey Find out the most common reasons that people wear masks or special clothing. Survey the class. Use a chart to record the results.

Survey Tally

Did you wear a mask or special clothing . . . ?	Responses	Total
to perform a play or dance	ⅢⅡ ///	8
as a uniform		
to a dress-up party		
for a certain holiday		

Language & Grammar

Use Appropriate Language CD

Listen to the actors. Listen to the people in the audience.
Notice the differences in their word choices and expressions.

PICTURE PROMPT

At the Theater

▲ Actors perform the story of
the Monkey King, a popular
story from China.

Use Compound Sentences

An **independent clause** expresses a complete thought. It can stand alone as a sentence. When you join two independent clauses, you make a **compound sentence**.

The words *and*, *but*, and *or* are **conjunctions**. They join the two clauses. A comma (,) comes before the conjunction.

> EXAMPLE   **Leon puts on the green mask**, **and** **I put on the blue one**.

- Use *and* to join similar or related ideas.

> EXAMPLE   Jorge cuts out the mask, **and** Maya paints it.

- Use *but* to join different or opposite ideas.

> EXAMPLE   Tessa thinks the mask is scary, **but** I think it looks funny.

- Use *or* to show a choice.

> EXAMPLE   You can wear the mask, **or** you can hang it on a wall.

Practice Together

Say each pair of sentences. Combine them with *and*, *but*, or *or* to make a compound sentence. Say the sentence.

1. People wear masks during celebrations. They have parades.
2. Some masks are old. Other masks are new.
3. Do you like traditional masks? Do you prefer new ones?
4. A mask might be made of paper. A mask might be made of wood.
5. Some masks are supposed to scare people. People still enjoy them.

▲ This is a Day of the Dead mask, and it is from Mexico City.

Try It!

Read each pair of sentences. Combine the pair using *and*, *but*, or *or* to make a compound sentence. Write the conjunction on a card. Then hold up the card as you say the sentence.

6. I might wear a clown mask for the parade. I might wear a tiger mask.
7. My father bought a dancer's mask in Guatemala. He bought a theater mask in Japan.
8. You can buy a carnival mask in Puerto Rico. You can find one on the Internet.
9. We have three African masks on our living room wall. They are all handmade.
10. I like all the masks. My favorite is the long, thin one with the surprised expression.

Talk About It!

USE APPROPRIATE LANGUAGE

People who like masks sometimes collect them. What interests you? What do you collect, or what would you like to collect?

With a group, talk about your ideas. Find out what your classmates are interested in, too. Do any of them have collections? Record the information on a chart.

Class Chart

Name	Collects . . .	Wants to collect . . .	Why?
Sonja		coins from around the world	She wants to have one coin from every country.
Henry	comic books		He wants to be an artist.

As a group, prepare a formal presentation about what you discussed. Choose one person in the group to give the presentation to the class.

HOW TO USE APPROPRIATE LANGUAGE

1. When you talk to your classmates in a small group, use informal language. Relax and be casual. Speak in a normal tone of voice.
2. When you give a presentation in front of a large group, use formal language. Stand up straight. Look serious. Make eye contact with the audience. Speak loudly and clearly.

> I collect comic books, but I want to collect baseball cards.

> The members of my group have many interests, and those interests are all different.

USE COMPOUND SENTENCES

Use the **conjunctions** *and*, *but*, and *or* to combine some of the sentences in your presentation. Your talk will sound better and will be more interesting.

Just OK: Boris collects postcards. He always buys some when he goes on vacation. He asks other people to send postcards to him.

Better: Boris collects postcards. He always buys some when he goes on vacation, **and** he asks other people to send postcards to him.

Prepare to Read

Learn Key Vocabulary

Rate and Study the Words Rate how well you know each word. Then:

1. Pronounce the word. Say it aloud several times. Spell it.
2. Study the example.
3. Tell more about the word.
4. Practice it. Make the word your own.

Key Words

belief (bu-lēf) *noun*
▶ page 525

A **belief** is a feeling that something is true or right. One **belief** is that your wish comes true if you break a wishbone and get the bigger part.

carve (karv) *verb*
▶ page 525

To **carve** means to cut shapes from a material like stone or wood. The artist uses sharp tools to **carve** this sculpture.
Synonym: **cut**

collect (ku-lekt) *verb*
▶ page 524

To **collect** means to gather things of interest. This boy **collects** stamps.

costume (kos-tüm) *noun*
▶ page 532

A **costume** is a set of clothes that someone wears to look like another person. You can dress up in a **costume** for a special occasion.

decorate (de-ku-rāt) *verb*
▶ page 526

To **decorate** means to add things to make something look better. The baker **decorates** the fancy dessert.

design (di-zīn) *noun*
▶ page 531

A **design** is a drawing or a pattern. The tiles are placed so they form a colorful **design**.

mask (mask) *noun*
▶ page 524

A **mask** is something a person wears to hide his or her face. The girl will wear a **mask** to a dress-up party.

perform (pur-form) *verb*
▶ page 528

To **perform** means to dance, sing, act, or play music for an audience. Students **perform** on stage for special events.

Practice the Words Work with a partner. Write a question using two Key Words. Answer your partner's question using a different Key Word. Keep going until you have used all of the words twice.

Questions	Answers
Where will you wear the mask that you carved from wood?	I will wear it to perform.

Reading Strategy: Synthesize

A generalization is a statement that applies to many situations. When you read, you may form generalizations. Take ideas from the text, along with your own knowledge, and form a new idea that applies to many situations.

HOW TO FORM GENERALIZATIONS

1. As you read, look for details that are about the same idea.

2. Add related examples from your own experience or knowledge.

3. Create a statement that seems true for both the author's examples and your examples.

Strategy in Action

Here's how one student formed a generalization.

Look Into the Text

One of my favorite trips was to Bali. It is an island in Indonesia that is famous for its wooden masks. There I learned how to carve wooden masks .

Carving masks is hard work. After the masks are carved, artists paint them with many colors. They use 15 to 20 coats of paint to get each mask just right. Some artists add hair or jewels.

"The text gives details about making masks."

Generalization Chart

Details in Text:
Carving masks is hard. Artists paint them with many coats of paint. Some artists add decorations.
My Experiences:
I make bracelets. It takes a lot of work to get them just right. The bracelets are so pretty that it is worth the time.
Generalization:
People will spend a lot of time to make something if they like what they make.

Practice Together

Reread the passage above and follow the steps in the How-To box to make another generalization. Record the information in a Generalization Chart.

Magazine Article

Most magazine articles are nonfiction. Many have **headings** to divide the text into readable parts. The text may be set in easy-to-read columns.

Articles also use **photos** and **captions** to make the text more interesting and to help readers understand more about the topic.

My Collection ‹ heading

My young neighbor was shocked. It was her first visit to my house, and everywhere she turned, another strange face stared back at her.

◄ In ancient Greece, actors wore masks like this one. They played different characters by changing their masks. — caption

photo

Reading Strategy: Synthesize

As you read, bring together different ideas to create generalizations. Work out ideas on a Generalization Chart.

Full of *Spirit*

One of my favorite trips was to Bali. It is an island in Indonesia that is famous for its wooden masks. There I learned how to **carve** wooden masks.

Carving masks is hard work. After the masks are carved, artists paint them with many colors. They use 15 to 20 **coats** of paint to get each mask just right. Some artists add hair or jewels.

The masks are used in plays about good and evil. People in Bali believe that the character's **spirit** lives in each mask. Wearing masks helps people act as those characters.

Many cultures have similar **beliefs** about the power of masks.

An actor from Bali wears a mask in a play. The mask helps the actor show the spirit of the character. ▶

Before You Move On

1. **Author's Point of View** Why does the author think that **masks** have power?

2. **Steps in a Process** How does an artist in Bali make a wooden **mask**? List three steps in order.

Festival *Faces*

People in Bhutan, a small **nation** in Asia, use masks to tell stories, too. The people there hold festivals to keep evil spirits away and bring good **fortune**.

At the festivals, dancers wear masks that show spirits, **demons**, and other characters. The masks are carved out of wood, and then they are painted and **decorated**.

The audience knows each character by its mask. That helps people follow the stories. These dances tell favorite tales from their religion, known as Buddhism. These stories tell how to lead a good life.

Festival dancers in Bhutan wear masks that help the audience follow the story.

A masked dancer from Bhutan performs a jumping dance. ▶

Key Vocabulary
decorate *v.*, to add things to make something look better

In Other Words
nation country
fortune luck
demons evil creatures, monsters

Cultural Background
Buddhism is a religion and a set of beliefs. A Buddhist is someone who follows the ideas of Siddhartha Gautama, a prince and teacher who lived in India and Nepal about 2500 years ago. Buddhism spread through Asia and the rest of the world.

Before You Move On

1. **Details** How do people in Bhutan use **masks** at festivals?
2. **Recall and Interpret** Why does each character have its own **mask**? How does this help the audience?

Facing *Change*

The Dogon people live in West Africa. They make many different kinds of masks that **differ** from village to village. Some masks are twice as tall as a man. Others look like cloth bags covered with shells. Some have tall, thin wood pieces on top. Some are simple wooden faces.

Masks are especially important for rituals that honor the dead. Dancers **perform** in masks when someone dies. They dance on the roof of the person's house to show respect for the dead person.

The Dogon also wear masks to dance at festivals. Doing so helps keep Dogon traditions alive. That's important to many Dogon, since the world keeps changing, and they don't want their ways to die out.

The Dogon wear masks at festivals. The masks are an important part of their tradition. ▷

Key Vocabulary
perform *v.*, to dance, sing, act, or play music for an audience

In Other Words
differ are different

Wearing the *Wolf*

Masks are not the only way that people make faces. Some people put paint or ink on their faces to change the way they look.

The Northern Arapaho people in Wyoming do that. They wear paint and **headgear** to look like wolves.

The wolf is special to them because the Northern Arapaho see wolves as teachers.

Watching wolves taught them to hunt and showed them how to share food.

Now the Arapaho honor wolves with dances they perform at **gatherings** called powwows. Face paint helps dancers **look the part**.

▼ A Northern Arapaho man wears a wolf headdress and face paint. He is ready for a powwow, or gathering.

In Other Words
headgear special hats
gatherings meetings
look the part seem like wolves

Before You Move On

1. **Make a Connection** How does a Dogon dancer show respect for someone who dies? How would you show respect?
2. **Viewing** Look at the photo of the Northern Arapaho man. Describe how he has made himself look like a wolf.

▼ Face paint helps the Karo people stand out from neighboring groups.

Standing *Out*

The Karo are a people from the East African country of Ethiopia who also paint themselves.

They live near a larger group of people. Since both groups speak similar languages, the Karo could easily blend into the larger group and lose their culture.

Instead, they want to **stand out**. To do so, they **smear** white and yellow paint on their faces. Sometimes they add dots and lines. Their face paint says, "Look at me. I am proud to be Karo!"

In Other Words
stand out be different
smear spread, wipe

Read My *Face*

The Maori are a people in New Zealand. To them, **designs** on a face tell a story. One side of a man's face tells about his father's family, and the other side tells about his mother's family. Women also wear these designs. But they do not have as many as men.

Maori face decorations **are permanent**. Artists cut the designs into the skin. Then they put color into the cuts to make blue-black marks.

The process takes a long time and is very painful, yet the Maori accept the pain because the designs are signs **of belonging to** the group.

▼ The Maori wear permanent designs on their faces. The designs tell about a person's family.

In Other Words
are permanent do not come off
of belonging to that they are a part of

Before You Move On

1. **Compare and Contrast** How are face painting **designs** similar for the Karo and Maori? How are they different?
2. **Analyze** What clues tell you that face **designs** are important to the Maori people?

Familiar *Faces*

I travel far and wide to see masks, but I can also find masks and decorated faces here at home, too. Kids wear masks with **costumes**, and sports fans paint their faces in the colors of their team.

All over the world, a new face is a chance to act like a new person. That is why making faces has such power! ❖

The author **poses** with some of the masks **from his collection**. ▼

Key Vocabulary
costume *n.*, clothes that someone wears to look like another person

In Other Words
poses has his picture taken
from his collection that he collected

Before You Move On

1. **Personal Experience** Tell about a time when you wore a **mask** or a **costume**, or tell about one you would like to wear.
2. **Author's Purpose** Why do you think the author wrote this article? What do you think was his main purpose?

Connect Reading and Writing

Vocabulary
beliefs
carve
collect
costumes
decorated
design
masks
perform

CRITICAL THINKING

1. **SUM IT UP** Create a T Chart. List the people and places discussed in the selection. Write notes about their **masks**. Use your chart to sum up the selection.

T Chart

People or Place	Their Masks
Bali	carved wooden masks

2. **Analyze** Why do you think many people make **masks** to express their **beliefs** about important matters like good and evil and death?

3. **Draw Conclusions** The author **collects** **masks** from around the world. What does this activity say about him?

4. **Explain** The Karo and the Maori **decorate** their faces with **designs** for a special reason. What is it?

READING FLUENCY

Intonation Read the passage on page 590 to a partner. Assess your fluency.

1. I read
   a. great   **b.** OK   **c.** not very well

2. What I did best in my reading was _____.

READING STRATEGY

Synthesize
With a partner, share one generalization you made while reading. What ideas did you bring together?

VOCABULARY REVIEW

Oral Review Read the paragraph aloud. Add the vocabulary words.

> Some Native American groups in the Northwest make _____ to wear on their faces and _____ to wear as special clothing. One dance they _____ is called the Winter Dance. The masks are _____ with different colors. Artists cut, or _____, masks inside of masks. The _____ on the outside is an animal and on the inside is a human. The masks are based on the powerful _____ of the Native Americans. Because the masks are unusual, many people _____ them.

Written Review Choose a **belief** you have, such as a belief in friendship or hard work. Draw a **mask** that expresses your belief. Then write a description of the mask. Use five vocabulary words.

 **WRITE ABOUT THE** **GUIDING QUESTION**

Explore Artful Expressions
What did you learn about the **beliefs** of some mask makers from reading this selection? Include examples from the selection in your response.

Analyze Author's Purpose and Tone

Academic Vocabulary

- **identify** (ī-**den**-tu-fī) *verb*
  To **identify** means to find out or to show what something is.

An author may want to inform, entertain, or persuade readers. The author's **purpose** often determines the **tone**. Tone is the author's attitude toward the topic.

- If the author mainly wants to entertain readers, the tone may be friendly and cheerful. The author may use everyday language, descriptive words, and short sentences.

- If the author wants to inform readers, the tone may be serious. The author may use words that are specific, accurate, and technical.

- If the author wants to persuade readers, the tone may be strong and forceful. The author may use words like *must* or *should*.

Practice Together

Read and Discuss Read the passage below. Notice the **everyday language and descriptive words and phrases** . Discuss how they express a friendly tone. **Identify** the author's purpose.

> The storage room in our museum is going to burst at the seams pretty soon! Our collection of masks is growing way too fast . When we started, we had about 25 masks from different places in Asia. Then the museum director visited Italy and returned with dozens of elegant, richly decorated masks. Then she went to Kenya, where she bought hundreds of traditional carved wood masks. Some have animal features. Others have scary, painted designs. Every time the director goes on a trip, she brings back more masks. If this keeps up, we'll need a whole new museum just for masks!

Try It!

Read and Discuss Reread "Making Faces." **Identify** the purpose and tone. What words and phrases help you **identify** the tone?

Analyze Idioms

> **Academic Vocabulary**
> • **communicate** (ku-**myū**-nu-kāt) *verb*
> When you **communicate**, you share information.

An **idiom** is a group of words that, together, **communicates** a meaning that is different from what the words mean by themselves.

> EXAMPLE   I laugh when my brother looks at me and <u>makes a face</u>.

The context of this sentence tells you that to "make a face" means to change expression.

Interpret Idioms Use context clues to figure out the meaning of each underlined phrase. Tell the meaning it **communicates** . Then use the idiom to express your own ideas.

1. When the author travels, he <u>keeps an eye out</u> for interesting masks to add to his collection.
2. He looks for unusual masks that <u>stand out</u> from others.
3. It <u>costs him an arm and a leg</u> to buy a rare and valuable mask.
4. Once when the author lost a mask, he <u>turned his place upside down</u> looking for it.

Present a Story

DRAMA

> **Academic Vocabulary**
> • **create** (krē-**āt**) *verb*
> To **create** means to make something new.

❶ **Find a Story** Work with a group. Find or write a story to act out.

❷ **Design Masks** Use art materials to **create** masks for the characters. Decorate the masks with meaningful symbols that match the characters in your story.

❸ **Plan Your Presentation** Decide who will play each character. How will you show the setting and plot? When you have finished planning, then you can practice presenting the story.

❹ **Present and Discuss** Use your masks to act out the story for an audience. Discuss how the symbols express the different characters.

▲ A man in Maranhão, Brazil, acts out a story about an ox.

Research/Speaking

Explore Ancient Greek Drama

HISTORY

Academic Vocabulary
- **element** (e-lu-munt) *noun*
  An **element** is a basic part of a whole.

Ancient Greek plays often told stories of popular characters. Many plays that were written 2,500 years ago are still performed today.

Movies and TV use some **elements** of ancient Greek drama. Find out how ancient Greek drama affects modern cultures.

▲ These masks, which represent tragedy and comedy, come from ancient Greek theater.

❶ **Choose a Topic** Work with a partner. Select one question to guide your research:

- What characters in movies or TV shows are based on characters from ancient Greek drama? How are the stories similar and different?
- Who were the main playwrights, or writers of plays, in ancient Greece? Why are they important today?
- What was the *chorus* in ancient Greek drama? How is this **element** used today?
- What were ancient Greek stages, costumes, and props like? How are these **elements** different today?
- How did the government of ancient Greece affect its theater? How was that government similar to the U.S. government?

❷ **Conduct Research** Look through books and magazines. Use the table of contents, index, and other parts of books to locate information. Skim and scan the text to get answers to your questions.

❸ **Plan a Talk** Gather information for an oral report. Include facts and details that will interest listeners. Find or create visuals, such as pictures, maps, or charts.

❹ **Give Your Report** Display your visuals. Use them as you deliver your report.

Use Appropriate Language

Act It Out With a group, create a short play to present to the class. Use the masks you made on page 535. Present your play, and then discuss it with the audience. Use appropriate language for each occasion. Use some compound sentences.

> We wrote this play "The Sisters," and we hope you enjoy it.

Write About Your Interests

Study the Models When you write about something you enjoy doing, you can make your writing more interesting by using a blend of short and long sentences.

NOT OK

> Masks are beautiful and I love to make them and I enjoy wearing them. I wear my own masks in parades or at parties, I let other kids wear them, too. My friends love my masks and sometimes they try to make their own masks and they ask me what to do. I show them the materials they will need, I explain all the steps to them.

The sentences go on and on. The reader thinks: "I can't understand this."

OK

> Masks are beautiful. I love to make them, and I enjoy wearing them. I wear my own masks in parades or at parties, and I let other kids wear them, too. My friends love my masks. Sometimes they try to make their own masks, but they always ask me what to do. I show them the materials they will need, and I explain all the steps to them.

The sentences are different lengths, and the text flows smoothly. There are no run-on sentences.

Revise It Work with a partner to revise this passage. Fix run-on sentences or overly long sentences.

> I collect stamps and I have relatives in South America and they send me letters and postcards. They always choose the most interesting stamps, some of the stamps have photos of famous people on them, some show famous buildings. I also belong to a stamp club and we meet once a month and we share our stamp collections with one another.

WRITE ON YOUR OWN Write about something you do that expresses your personality and interests. Include short and long sentences. Watch out for run-on sentences.

REMEMBER
- A **conjunction** joins the two clauses in a compound sentence.
- Usually, a comma (,) comes before the conjunction:
  > I have a hat collection, **and** my brother collects rocks.

Wings

Written and illustrated by Christopher Myers

SELECTION 3 OVERVIEW

▶ **Build Background**

▶ **Language & Grammar**
Retell a Story
Use Complex Sentences

▶ **Prepare to Read**
Learn Key Vocabulary
Learn a Reading Strategy
Synthesize

▶ **Read and Write**
Focus on Genre
Short Story
Apply the Reading Strategy
Synthesize
Critical Thinking
Reading Fluency
Read with Expression
Vocabulary Review
Write About the Guiding Question

▶ **Connect Across the Curriculum**
Literary Analysis
Compare Characters
Analyze Plot Events
Vocabulary Study
Analyze Similes
Research/Speaking
Research Greek Myths
Language and Grammar
Retell a Story
Writing and Grammar
Write About Myths

Build Background

Explore Flying Machines

Look at pictures of early flying machines. How do you think they worked?

Digital Library
InsideNG.com
◉ View the images.

◀ A pilot tries to take off in his glider.

Connect

Sort Drawings What kind of flying machine would you invent? Make a sketch of it. Then, as a group, form categories based on how the inventions look or move. Sort the sketches.

Category Web

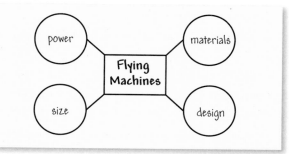

Language & Grammar

1 TRY OUT LANGUAGE
2 LEARN GRAMMAR
3 APPLY ON YOUR OWN

Retell a Story

Listen to the rap. Listen again and chime in.
Then listen to a story and a retelling of the story.

RAP and STORY

Let Me Tell It!

Let me tell the story
Because I know how it goes.
I'll introduce the setting
And the heroes.
I'll tell all the events
For as far as they extend,
Because I like the story,
Especially the end.

◀ In the story, the girl
dreams she is flying.

Use Complex Sentences

- A clause has a **subject** and a **verb**. An **independent clause** can stand alone as a sentence.

  EXAMPLE   **The girl** **runs** fast.
  independent clause

- A **dependent clause** also has a **subject** and a **verb**. It cannot stand alone because it begins with a **conjunction**. *After, although, because, before, since, until,* and *when* are conjunctions.

  EXAMPLE   **because** **she** **wants** to escape
  dependent clause

- You can use a conjunction to link a dependent clause to an independent clause. The new sentence is complete, and it is called a **complex sentence**.

  EXAMPLE   **The girl** **runs** fast **because** **she** **wants** to escape.
  independent clause   dependent clause

Practice Together

Match each independent clause in column 1 to a dependent clause in column 2. Say the complex sentence.

1. I have wanted to fly
2. I can't fly
3. My father can fly
4. He felt like a bird
5. I will learn to hang glide
6. He will go hang gliding this weekend

a. although he doesn't have wings.
b. when I am old enough.
c. after he took hang gliding lessons.
d. because I don't have wings.
e. unless it rains.
f. since I was a small child.

▲ People can enjoy the feeling of flying when they learn how to hang glide.

Try It!

Match each independent clause in column 1 to a dependent clause in column 2. Write the complex sentence on a card. Hold up the card as you say the sentence.

7. I flew in an airplane
8. I would like to be a pilot
9. You have to get a lot of training
10. Sometimes I watch planes
11. I have been interested in aviation
12. I may go to flight school

a. since I was little.
b. when they fly overhead.
c. because it is an exciting job.
d. when I went to visit my uncle.
e. before you can fly a plane.
f. unless I get interested in something else.

Tell What Happened

RETELL A STORY

Did you enjoy the rap and the story you listened to on page 539? How would you retell the story? What would you say?

First, think about what happened. Make a time line to help you remember which event happened first, next, and so on.

Time Line

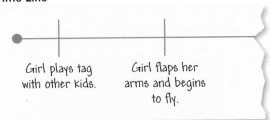

Girl plays tag with other kids.

Girl flaps her arms and begins to fly.

Look at the events on your time line. Think about how you could tell each part in your own words. Practice your version of the story. Be sure to tell the events in the right order.

Now retell the story to a partner. Speak with enthusiasm. Use facial expressions to show emotions and gestures to show action. You may even want to act out parts of the story.

How To RETELL A STORY

1. Recall the sequence of events.

2. Say the events in your own words. Use words that tell time order.

3. Speak clearly and with expression.

4. Use facial expressions and gestures.

> The girl was running very fast because the boy was chasing her. She started to do this (flaps arms).

USE COMPLEX SENTENCES

When you retell your story, use **complex sentences** to express some of the actions and events. This will show how events are related. It will also make your story sound smooth.

Simple Sentences: The girl was very surprised.
She floated up into the air.

Complex Sentence: The girl was very surprised when she floated up into the air.

Prepare to Read

Learn Key Vocabulary

Rate and Study the Words Rate how well you know each word. Then:

1. Pronounce the word. Say it aloud several times. Spell it.
2. Study the example.
3. Tell more about the word.
4. Practice it. Make the word your own.

Key Words

complain (kum-plān) *verb*
▶ page 546

To **complain** means to say that you are unhappy about something. I **complained** that it was not fair I had to take out the trash by myself.

drift (drift) *verb*
▶ page 548

To **drift** means to move along slowly in the air or on water. She **drifts** down the river, carried along by the current.
Synonym: **float**

droop (drüp) *verb*
▶ page 548

To **droop** means to hang down. The branches of the tree **droop** to the ground.
Synonyms: **bend, sink**

impressed (im-prest) *verb*
▶ page 548

If you are **impressed**, you are strongly affected by something. The audience is very **impressed** by the musicians.

proud (prowd) *adjective*
▶ page 546

If you are **proud**, you are feeling happy about yourself. I felt **proud** when I won the prize.
Antonym: **ashamed**

struggle (stru-gul) *verb*
▶ page 548

To **struggle** means to try hard. I **struggle** to beat my uncle at arm wrestling.
Synonyms: **work, fight**

useless (yūs-lus) *adjective*
▶ page 546

If something is **useless**, it is of no use. A broken cell phone is **useless**.
Antonym: **useful**

whisper (whis-pur) *verb*
▶ page 546

To **whisper** means to speak very quietly. I **whisper** the secret to my friend so no one else can hear.
Antonym: **shout**

Practice the Words Make a Key Vocabulary Chart for the Key Words. Compare your chart with a partner's.

Word	Synonyms	Definition	Sentence or Picture
complain	protest	to say something is wrong	I complain about getting up at 5 in the morning.

Key Vocabulary Chart

Reading Strategy: Synthesize

When you read two or more texts about the same topic, you can compare how the authors express ideas. Comparing across texts is one way to synthesize.

Reading Strategy
Synthesize

HOW TO COMPARE ACROSS TEXTS

1. Read the first text. Use a Comparison Chart to record information about the text and to determine the theme.
2. Read the second text. Add to the Comparison Chart.
3. Note the similarities and differences between the texts.

Strategy in Action

Here's how one student began to compare across two texts.

Look Into the Text

Wings

"Look at that strange boy!"

Everyone from the neighborhood is pointing fingers and watching the sky.

"How's he doing that?"

They stretch their necks and shake their heads.

Ikarus Jackson, a new boy on my block, is flying above the rooftops.

"People think the boy's actions are unusual."

Comparison Chart

	Wings	Icarus and Daedalus
Setting		
Characters	Ikarus Jackson, a flying boy	
Problem	People think he is strange.	
Solution		
Theme		
Similarities		
Differences		

Practice Together

First read "Wings." Then read "Icarus and Daedalus." Follow the steps in the How-To box to compare the two texts.

Short Story

A short story is brief narrative fiction. It often focuses on one event. You learn about the main character through the event.

Paragraphs separate story ideas into understandable parts. Writers may include **pull quotes** with interesting text from the story. Pull quotes catch the reader's attention. Short stories also may have illustrations for interest.

> They stretch their necks and shake their heads.
>
> ---
>
> ### Look at that strange boy!
>
> *pull quote*
>
> ---
>
> Ikarus Jackson, a new boy on my block, is flying above the rooftops. He is swooping and diving, looping past people's windows and over the crowd.

paragraph

Your Job as a Reader

Reading Strategy: Synthesize

As you read "Wings," write notes in a Comparison Chart. Then do the same for the myth. When you've finished reading both selections, note their similarities and differences.

Wings

Written and illustrated by
Christopher Myers

Set a Purpose
Ikarus, the new boy at school, has a problem.
Find out what it is.

"Look at that strange boy!"

Everyone from the neighborhood is pointing fingers and watching the sky.

"How's he doing that?"

They stretch their necks and shake their heads.

Ikarus Jackson, a new boy on my block, is flying above the rooftops. He is swooping and diving, looping past people's windows and over the crowd.

I don't think he's strange.

Ikarus Jackson, the fly boy, came to my school last Thursday. His long, strong, **proud** wings followed wherever he went.

The whole school was **staring eyes and wagging tongues**. They **whispered** about his wings and his hair and his shoes. Like they whisper about how quiet I am.

Look at that strange boy!

Our teacher **complained** that the other kids couldn't help but gawk and stare. He said that Ikarus's wings blocked the blackboard and made it hard for the students to pay attention.

The teacher told Ikarus to leave class until he could **figure out** what to do with his wings. He left the room quietly, dragging his feathers behind him. One boy **snickered**.

At recess the snicker grew into a giggle and spread across the playground. Soon all the kids were laughing at Ikarus Jackson's "**useless**" wings. I thought that if he flew just once everyone would stop laughing. Ikarus looked up, flapped his wings a couple of times, then jumped into the air.

Key Vocabulary
proud *adj.*, feeling happy about yourself
whisper *v.*, to speak very quietly
complain *v.*, to say you are unhappy about something
useless *adj.*, of no use

In Other Words
staring eyes and wagging tongues looking at him and talking about him
figure out decide
snickered laughed

Before You Move On

1. **Narrator's Point of View** Who is telling the story? What clues in the story and the picture help you know?

2. **Problem and Solution** What is Ikarus's problem? How do you think he should solve it?

He swept through the schoolyard like a slow-motion instant replay. But the other kids were not **impressed**. One girl grabbed the basketball. A boy stuffed the handball in his pocket. Somebody nagged, "Nobody likes a **show-off**."

Their words sent Ikarus **drifting** into the sky, away from the glaring eyes and the pointing fingers.

I waited for them to point back at me as I watched Ikarus float farther and farther away.

Walking home from school, I knew how he felt, how lonely he must be. Maybe I should have said something to those mean kids.

I knew how he felt . . .

I ran through the streets with my eyes to the sky, searching the clouds for Ikarus.

He **struggled** to stay in the air. His wings **drooped** and his head hung low. He landed heavily on the edge of a building and sat with the pigeons. Pigeons don't **make fun of people**.

A policeman passing by blew his whistle.

"You with the wings, come down from there! **Stay yourself** on the ground. You'll get in trouble. You'll get hurt."

It seemed to me Ikarus was already in trouble and hurt. Could the policeman put him in jail for flying, for being too different?

Key Vocabulary
impressed *v.*, strongly affected by something
drift *v.*, to move along slowly in the air
struggle *v.*, to try hard
droop *v.*, to hang down

In Other Words
show-off person who tries to get attention
make fun of people cause people to feel hurt
Stay yourself Get down

Before You Move On

1. **Perspectives** How would you feel at this point if you were Ikarus?
2. **Confirm Prediction** Was your prediction correct? What happened that you did not expect?

When the neighborhood kids saw the policeman yelling at him, they **exploded** with laughter. Ikarus dropped to the ground.

"Stop!" I cried. "Leave him alone." And they did.

I called to Ikarus and he **sailed** closer to me. I told him what someone should have long ago: "Your flying is beautiful."

For the first time, I saw Ikarus smile. At that moment I forgot about the kids who had laughed at him and me. I was just glad that Ikarus had found his wings again.

"Look at that amazing boy!" I called to all the people on the street as I pointed to my new friend Ikarus **swirling** through the sky. ❖

In Other Words
exploded burst out loudly
sailed flew
swirling flying in circles

About the Author

Christopher Myers

Christopher Myers has been around storytellers his entire life. His grandfather was a great storyteller. His father, Walter Dean Myers, is an award-winning author.

Christopher Myers is a writer and an illustrator. He began by drawing pictures for his father's books. Now he writes and illustrates his own stories. Myers says that he was different growing up. He wants kids to know that it's OK to be different. He says, "The things that make you *you* are the things that you need to be proud of. [They] are the things . . . to be celebrated."

Before You Move On

1. **Confirm Prediction** Did you predict what happened to Ikarus? What happened that you did not expect?
2. **Character's Motive** Why do you think the narrator does what she does at the end of the story?
3. **Predict** What will change for Ikarus and the narrator if the story continues?

ICARUS AND DAEDALUS
a Greek myth

When the famous builder, Daedalus, went to Crete, he built an amazing **labyrinth** for the king. It had twists and turns. It had **corridors that coiled** in dizzy circles like the spirals on a seashell.

King Minos hid the Minotaur, a creature with a bull's head and a man's body, in the **maze**.

Every seven years, the king did something horrible. He fed youths from Athens to the Minotaur. A man named Theseus wanted to stop this terrible practice, so he entered the maze and killed the beast. Daedalus had told him how to escape from the maze.

King Minos was angry, and he locked Daedalus and his son, Icarus, in a tower.

From the tower, Icarus watched the seabirds **whirl** over the water every day. One day a thought came to Daedalus. He and Icarus could fly to freedom!

Father and son began to gather feathers

In Other Words
laybrinth place with twisting passages
corridors that coiled hallways that turned
maze confusing passages
whirl fly quickly in circles

from the birds that landed at their window. When Daedalus had a pile of feathers, he **stitched** them together, and he used candle wax to fasten the ends. Then he attached the wings to **harnesses** that he had cleverly made from his sandals.

Icarus helped his father with his harness. Then he put on his own set of wings. Just before their escape, Daedalus warned his son, "You must not fly too high. The sun will melt the wax."

The two men **soared** out over the sea. Icarus fluttered his wings joyfully. He felt like a leaf playing in the wind. As he flapped higher and higher, he forgot his father's warning.

Suddenly a drop of hot wax trickled down his arm. A feather dropped from one wing. More feathers **wafted** down like snow.

"Fly lower, Icarus!" Daedalus shouted. But it was too late. He watched helplessly

In Other Words
stitched joined, sewed
harnesses straps
soared flew smoothly
wafted floated

as his son drifted away, out of sight.

Daedalus whirled high and low searching for Icarus. He **skimmed above** the sea, calling his son's name. Soon he spotted **dozens** of feathers floating sadly on the waves.

Daedalus flew to the island of Sicily where he built a **temple** in honor of his beautiful son, Icarus. ❖

Greek Myths

Myths are stories about events that happened long ago. Many myths tell how things in nature came to be. Others explain why people do things in a certain way.

Some myths tell the adventures of gods or famous people from long ago. Most heroes in myths were brave warriors, but Daedalus was an architect and inventor. No one knows if he was a real person. If he was, he may have built some of the oldest buildings in Greece.

Greek myths are still popular. The stories continue to be told in plays, movies, books, poems, and art.

In Other Words
skimmed above flew close to
dozens a lot
temple building to honor a god
or hero

Before You Move On

1. **Explain** Tell how Daedalus plans to escape from the tower with his son.
2. **Cause and Effect** Why does Daedalus tell Icarus not to fly too close to the sun? What happens when Icarus forgets this warning?

Connect Reading and Writing

Vocabulary
complains
drifts
droop
impressed
proud
struggles
useless
whispers

CRITICAL THINKING

1. **SUM IT UP** Make a Venn Diagram to compare Ikarus and Icarus. Use it to help you retell the stories.

Venn Diagram

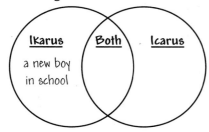

Ikarus / Both / Icarus
a new boy in school

2. **Infer** "Wings" is about a boy who **struggles** because he is different. What is the author's message? Support your answer with examples.

3. **Paraphrase** Why did Icarus **drift** out of his father's sight? Use your own words to tell what happened.

4. **Speculate** Do you think the teacher, the policeman, and the kids in "Wings" will be **impressed** with Ikarus at the end of the story? Explain.

READING FLUENCY

Expression Read the passage on page 591 to a partner. Assess your fluency.

1. I read
   a. great   **b.** OK   **c.** not very well

2. What I did best in my reading was _____.

READING STRATEGY

> **Synthesize**
> Tell a partner one comparison you made between "Icarus and Daedalus" and "Wings."

VOCABULARY REVIEW

Oral Review Read the paragraph aloud. Add the vocabulary words.

> Zephyr is a great trapeze artist. He is a _____ member of a circus troupe that performs around the world. Zephyr practices every day. He never _____ about the hard work. He _____ to improve at every practice session. Sometimes when he has trouble doing a new trick, his spirits _____. He _____ quietly to himself, "I can't do this. It's _____!" But everyone else is _____ with Zephyr's talent. He swings, swirls, and _____ through the air like a beautiful bird.

Written Review Imagine yourself flying over a city or an ocean. Write a paragraph. Tell what thoughts would come to you as you **drift** through the sky. Use five vocabulary words.

WRITE ABOUT THE **GUIDING QUESTION**

Explore Art and Soul

How does Ikarus Jackson **struggle** to express himself? What artful expression does he make? Use details from "Wings" to explain your answer.

Connect Across the Curriculum

Literary Analysis

Compare Characters

Academic Vocabulary
- **interpret** (in-**tur**-prut) *verb*
  To **interpret** means to explain or tell what something means.

Sometimes writers refer to a person, place, or thing that is not specifically described in the text. This is called an **allusion**. Readers have to **interpret** the allusion.

> **EXAMPLE** Dillon, a real Superman, finished his homework, walked the dog, and made dinner all before seven o'clock.

Here, the author alludes to Superman to tell about Dillon's amazing character. The author assumes that readers know Superman is a hero who does things quickly and well.

Practice Together

Compare Characters Read this passage and think about the **allusions**.

> Molly was the Daedalus of her class. Whenever there was a school project, everyone wanted to be in her group. Molly was able to create interesting and original plans in a few hours. But even Molly had a wax wings project. She and her group built a model covered with birdseed. They displayed it outdoors. Before lunch, the birds had eaten the entire model!

Discuss Daedalus was a great builder and inventor. What does the allusion tell you about Molly? The wax wings were Daedalus's invention that ended badly. How does this allusion help you understand Molly's project?

Try It!

Compare Characters The name of the main character in "Wings" is an allusion to the myth about Icarus. **Interpret** the allusion by answering these questions:

- What are the characteristics of the original Icarus?
- How are the two characters, Ikarus and Icarus, alike?
- What does the allusion communicate about the theme?
- How does the allusion help you understand the story?

Analyze Similes

> **Academic Vocabulary**
> • **compare** (kum-**pair**) *verb*
> When you **compare** two things, you think about how they are alike and different.

A **simile** is one kind of figurative language. It **compares** two unlike things, usually with the words *like*, *as*, or *than*. Similes help readers visualize the meaning.

EXAMPLE   He swept through the schoolyard <u>like a slow-motion instant replay</u>.

This simile **compares** the way Ikarus moves to a sports video played at slow speed. The two things are alike because they both have slow, repeated movements. The simile can help you imagine what Ikarus looks like.

Interpret Similes Work with a partner. Find these similes. Copy and complete the chart.

Simile Chart

Simile	What It Compares	How They're Alike
like the spirals on a seashell, p. 552		
like a leaf playing in the wind, p. 553		
like snow, p. 553		

Research Greek Myths

HISTORY

> **Academic Vocabulary**
> • **belief** (bu-**lēf**) *noun*
> A **belief** is a feeling that something is true or right.

Many English words and phrases come from Greek myths—fictional stories of gods and heroes. The word *atlas*, for example, is named for the Titan Atlas, who had to carry the heavens on his shoulders. Many ancient Greeks held the **belief** that the stories were true.

1 **Conduct Research** Use books or the Internet to find more examples of words and phrases from Greek myths. Choose one example and learn about the myth it comes from.

2 **Share Your Findings** Tell about the word or phrase you researched. Retell the myth. Include details about the characters, setting, and plot.

▲ A statue of Atlas

Literary Analysis

Analyze Plot Events

> **Academic Vocabulary**
> • **series** (sear-ēz) *noun*
>   A **series** is a group of related things that are put in a certain order.

The **plot** of a story is the **series** of events that happen. The story often starts with an **exposition**, or introduction. Often the plot involves a problem to be solved. The events build up to the **climax**, or most intense part. The final events finish the story and resolve the problem.

Practice Together

Plot a Story You can use a plot diagram to show the key parts of a story. Compare this Plot Diagram with "Wings." Notice that the story begins with a problem. Then the rising action, which is a **series** of events, leads to the climax. The events after the climax are the falling action.

Plot Diagram

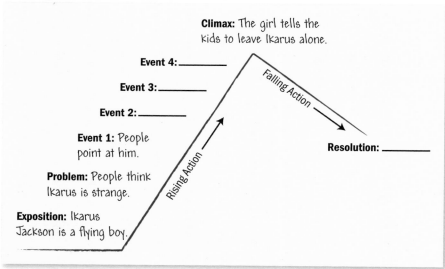

Try It!

Complete the Diagram Copy the Plot Diagram. Work with a partner to complete the missing events and the resolution.

Retell the Story Use your completed diagram to retell the story to another group. Be sure to include all of the main events. Tell how one event leads to another.

Retell a Story

Partner Story Exchange With a partner, take turns retelling the myth. Speak clearly. Use gestures and facial expressions. Tell events in order. Include some complex sentences.

> Daedalus and Icarus were locked in a tower because Daedalus made the king angry.

Write About Myths

Study the Models When you write a myth, keep your readers interested by using a variety of sentences. Mix short, simple sentences with compound and complex sentences.

NOT OK

> Ajit read about Icarus and Daedalus. He wanted to read another myth. He went online. He found a Web site with myths from all over the world. He printed out a story about a flying horse named Pegasus. He loved the story. He wanted to read an illustrated version of it. He hurried to the library. It was still open.

> The writer uses **too many short sentences.**

OK

> **After** Ajit read about Icarus and Daedalus, he wanted to read another myth. He went online **and** found a Web site with myths from all over the world. He printed out a story about a flying horse named Pegasus. He loved the story, **but** he wanted to read an illustrated version of it. He hurried to the library **since** it was still open.

> The writer uses **conjunctions to combine sentences.**

Revise It Work with a partner to revise the following passage. Fix fragments. Use conjunctions to combine sentences.

> Mount Olympus is in the sky. It is beautiful. Because the Greek gods live there. One day, a man named Bellerophon tried to ride Pegasus to Mount Olympus. When the mighty god Zeus saw Bellerophon. He became angry. Zeus made an insect sting Pegasus. Bellerophon fell off Pegasus's back.

▲ Pegasus

REMEMBER
- Use conjunctions to combine sentences.
- A compound sentence uses the conjunctions **and**, **but**, or **or**.

  Daedalus made wings, **and** he escaped.
- A complex sentence uses conjunctions like **because**, **since**, or **when**.

  Daedalus made wings **because** he wanted to escape.

✎ WRITE ON YOUR OWN Think of a myth you have read, or create your own. Write it, using short and long sentences.

Compare Across Texts

Compare Themes

"Old Music Finds New Voices," "Making Faces," and "Wings" tell about how people **communicate** with expressions of art. Compare the themes in these texts.

How It Works

Collect and Organize Ideas Work with a group. Think about the author's messages, or themes, for each selection. Remember that selections often have more than one theme. Collect your ideas in a chart.

Comparison Chart

Old Music Finds New Voices	Making Faces	Wings
People express themselves through playing music.	People express themselves through making and wearing masks.	People express themselves with their unique abilities.

Practice Together

Study and Explain Choose one theme from each selection. Then write a comparison paragraph. First, write a sentence that tells how all the themes are similar or related. Then tell how each is unique, or different from the others. Here is a comparison paragraph for one set of themes.

> "Old Music Finds New Voices," "Making Faces," and "Wings" all tell how people express themselves. In "Old Music Finds New Voices," people tell stories with music. People in "Making Faces" wear masks to act out stories. In "Wings," a boy expresses himself by flying.

Try It!

Write a comparison paragraph about another set of themes you collected. You may want to use this frame to help you express your comparison.

One theme of the three selections is _____ . In "Old Music Finds New Voices," _____ . In "Making Faces," _____ . In "Wings," _____ .

Academic Vocabulary

- **communicate** (ku-**myū**-nu-kāt) *verb*
  When you **communicate**, you share information.

Art and Soul

GUIDING QUESTION What do we learn about people from their artful expressions?

UNIT LIBRARY

Content Library

Leveled Library

Reflect on Your Reading

Think back on your reading of the unit selections. Discuss what you did to understand what you read.

Focus on Genre **Text Features**

In this unit, you studied the text features in a newspaper article, a magazine article, and a short story. List as many features as you can. Then explain to a partner how each feature helped you understand the information in the selections.

Reading Strategy **Synthesize**

As you read, you learned how to synthesize information. Explain to a partner how you will use this strategy in the future.

Explore the **GUIDING QUESTION**

Throughout this unit, you have been learning about artful expressions. Choose one of these ways to explore the Guiding Question:

- **Discuss** With a group, discuss what you have learned about how people use art to express themselves. Give supporting details from the selections.
- **Share Your Art** Think about an art form that expresses who you are, such as playing an instrument or telling jokes. Describe your art to a group, and show an example of it.
- **Display Art** Show an example of art that you like. Tell how it expresses the artist's culture or personal beliefs and feelings.

Book Talk

Which Unit Library book did you choose? Explain to a partner what it taught you about expressions of art.

READING FLUENCY

What Is Reading Fluency?

Reading fluency is the ability to read smoothly and expressively with clear understanding. Fluent readers are able to better understand and enjoy what they read. Use the strategies that follow to build your fluency in these four key areas:

- accuracy and rate
- phrasing
- intonation
- expression

How to Improve Accuracy and Rate

Accuracy is the correctness of your reading. Rate is the speed of your reading.

How to read accurately:

- Use correct pronunciation.
- Emphasize correct syllables.
- Recognize most words.

How to read with proper rate:

- Match your reading speed to what you are reading. For example, if you are reading an exciting story, read slightly faster. If you are reading a sad story, read slightly slower.
- Recognize and use punctuation.

Test your accuracy and rate:

- Choose a text you are familiar with, and practice reading it aloud or silently multiple times.
- Keep a dictionary with you while you read, and look up words you do not recognize.
- Use a watch or clock to time yourself while you read a passage.
- Ask a friend or family member to read a passage for you, so you know what it should sound like.

Use the formula below to measure a reader's accuracy and rate while reading aloud. For passages to practice with, see **Reading Fluency Practice**, pp. 568–591.

Accuracy and Rate Formula

words attempted in one minute	−	number of errors	=	words correct per minute (wcpm)

How to Improve Intonation

Intonation is the rise and fall in the pitch or tone of your voice as you read aloud. Pitch and tone both mean the highness or lowness of the sound.

How to read with proper intonation:

- Change the sound of your voice to match what you are reading.
- Make your voice flow, or sound smooth while you read.
- Make sure you are pronouncing words correctly.
- Raise the sound of your voice for words that should be stressed, or emphasized.
- Use proper rhythm and meter.
- Use visual clues. (see box below)

Visual Clue and Meaning	Example	How to Read It
Italics: draw attention to a word to show special importance	She is *smart*.	Emphasize "smart."
Dash: shows a quick break in a sentence	She is—smart.	Pause before saying "smart."
Exclamation: can represent energy, excitement, or anger	She is smart!	Make your voice louder at the end of the sentence.
All capital letters: can represent strong emphasis, or yelling	SHE IS SMART.	Emphasize the whole sentence.
Bold facing: draws attention to a word to show importance	She is **smart**.	Emphasize "smart."
Question mark: shows curiosity or confusion	She is smart?	Raise the pitch of your voice slightly at the end of the sentence.

Use the rubric below to measure how well a reader uses intonation while reading aloud. For intonation passages, see **Reading Fluency Practice**, pp. 568–591.

Intonation Rubric		
1	**2**	**3**
The reader's tone does not change. The reading all sounds the same.	The reader's tone changes sometimes to match what is being read.	The reader's tone always changes to match what is being read.

How to Improve Phrasing

Phrasing is how you use your voice to group words together.

How to read with proper phrasing:

- Use correct rhythm and meter by not reading too fast or too slow.
- Pause for key words within the text.
- Make sure your sentences have proper flow and meter, so they sound smooth instead of choppy.
- Make sure you sound like you are reading a sentence instead of a list.
- Use punctuation to tell you when to stop, pause, or emphasize. (see box below)

Punctuation	How to Use It
. period	stop at the end of the sentence
, comma	pause within the sentence
! exclamation point	emphasize the sentence and pause at the end
? question mark	emphasize the end of the sentence and pause at the end
; semicolon	pause within the sentence between two related thoughts
: colon	pause within the sentence before giving an example or explanation

One way to practice phrasing is to copy a passage, then place a slash (/), or pause mark, within a sentence where there should be a pause. One slash (/) means a short pause. Two slashes (//) mean a longer pause, such as a pause at the end of a sentence.

Read aloud the passage below, pausing at each pause mark. Then try reading the passage again without any pauses. Compare how you sound each time.

There are many ways / to get involved in your school / and community. // Joining a club / or trying out for a sports team / are a few of the options. // Volunteer work can also be very rewarding. // You can volunteer at community centers, / nursing homes, / or animal shelters. //

Use the rubric below to measure how well a reader uses phrasing while reading aloud. For phrasing passages, see **Reading Fluency Practice**, pp. 568–591.

Phrasing Rubric		
1	2	3
Reading is choppy. There are usually no pauses for punctuation.	Reading is mostly smooth. There are some pauses for punctuation.	Reading is very smooth. Punctuation is being used properly.

How to Improve Expression

Expression in reading is how you use your voice to express feeling.

How to read with proper expression:

- Match the sound of your voice to what you are reading. For example, read louder and faster to show strong feeling. Read slower and quieter to show sadness or seriousness.
- Match the sound of your voice to the genre. For example, read a fun, fictional story using a fun, friendly voice. Read an informative, nonfiction article using an even tone and a more serious voice.
- Avoid speaking in monotone, which is using only one tone in your voice.
- Pause for emphasis and exaggerate letter sounds to match the mood or theme of what you are reading.

Practice incorrect expression by reading this sentence without changing the tone of your voice: *I am so excited!*

Now read the sentence again with proper expression: *I am so excited!* The way you use your voice while reading can help you to better understand what is happening in the text.

For additional practice, read the sentences below aloud with and without changing your expression. Compare how you sound each time.

- I am very sad.
- That was the most *boring* movie I have ever seen.
- We won the game!

Use the rubric below to measure how well a reader uses expression while reading aloud. For expression passages, see **Reading Fluency Practice**, pp. 568–591.

Expression Rubric

1	2	3
The reader sounds monotone. The reader's voice does not match the subject of what is being read.	The reader is making some tone changes. Sometimes, the reader's voice matches what is being read.	The reader is using proper tones and pauses. The reader's voice matches what is being read.

Practice Intonation: "Growing Together"

Intonation is the rise and fall in the pitch or tone of your voice as you read aloud. Use this passage to practice reading with proper intonation. Print a copy of this passage from InsideNG.com to help you monitor your progress.

He stands up as I run to him. I cry angry tears.

A moment like this comes for every immigrant child.

It is hard to leave a home you know. It is even harder to make another place home. Everything is new. Everything is strange. Everything is different.

I tell Papi how I feel.

"I hate it here! I am not like them, and they are not like me!" I say to him.

Papi pulls out a handkerchief and hands it to me.

My father, the gardener, looks at me intently for a few moments. Then he asks, "Carmita, do you remember our mango tree in Cuba?"

"Yes," I sniff. I am curious now.

"Do you know what it means to graft a tree?"

I nod. "You take a branch from one tree and attach it to another tree. The branch and the tree grow together. Right?"

"*Sí*, that is right," Papi says.

My father tells me that I am like a branch from that Cuban mango tree. He says Georgia is like the magnolia tree. I must wait. Eventually, the mango and magnolia will grow together.

From "Growing Together," page 12

Practice Expression: "Kids Like Me"

Expression in reading is how you use your voice to express feeling. Use this passage to practice reading with proper expression. Print a copy of this passage from **InsideNG.com** to help you monitor your progress.

Q: What advice do you have for people who move to the United States?

Eunji: Ask many questions. That way, you learn about the person you are talking to. You can also learn about American culture.

Hewan: Quickly make friends in order to learn the language and culture. With their help, it is easier to settle into a new country. Friends can also make it easier to adjust to the different customs and ideas.

Liban: Be yourself. That is the main thing. Do not put yourself down. Do not let anybody put you down. Work hard. Talk to people. Ask for help if you need it. Say what you want to say (other than bad words).

Adib: Play sports to meet new people. Make an effort to be social and talk with people in your classes. This is hard at first.

Anne Rose: Get involved in everything you can. The more things you get into, the more opportunities you have to learn, understand, and appreciate life.

Manuel: I have one piece of advice. Don't be lazy!

From "Kids Like Me," page 30

Practice Phrasing: "Familiar Places"

Phrasing is how you use your voice to group words together. Use this passage to practice reading with proper phrasing. Print a copy of this passage from **InsideNG.com** to help you monitor your progress.

Familiar sounds can make a new place feel like home.

When a language is new to you, the words can look so different. Sometimes it is nice to see your native language.

Korean people who move to Koreatown agree. In Koreatown, you can find words in English and Korean. Read the *hangul* signs. Buy a book in Korean. Find a Korean newspaper.

Familiar words can make a new place feel like home.

Everyone likes to celebrate! There are always many reasons to have fun. Some celebrations are more familiar, though.

Every September, the people of Little Italy hold a festival. Look at the decorations and watch the parade. Then eat *cannoli* while you dance and sing Italian songs.

Familiar celebrations can make a new place feel like home.

Familiar foods, sounds, and celebrations can make you feel at home in a new neighborhood. As new people move in, the neighborhood will continue to change and become their home, too.

From "Familiar Places," page 48

Practice Expression: "The Secret Water"

Expression in reading is how you use your voice to express feeling. Use this passage to practice reading with proper expression. Print a copy of this passage from **InsideNG.com** to help you monitor your progress.

Then the Voice of the Mountain shouts, "Shu Fa, you told my secret! Now you must live in my river forever."

Shu Fa cries. She begs the Voice to let her say goodbye to her family. The Voice grumbles, "Go, but you must return here tonight."

Shu Fa runs back to the village. "What can I do?" she asks herself. "I do not want to live in the river!" She decides to tell Uncle about the problem.

Uncle thinks for a few minutes. Then he says, "I have a plan."

Uncle works all day to carve a statue out of stone. The statue looks just like Shu Fa. He thinks the statue will trick the Voice of the Mountain.

"I just need one thing," Uncle tells Shu Fa. He cuts Shu Fa's long, white hair and attaches it to the statue. Then he places the statue in the river. Water flows over the statue. It carries the white hair over the mountain like a waterfall.

The Voice of the Mountain sees the statue. It says, "Hello, Shu Fa!"

The trick worked!

From "The Secret Water," page 74

Practice Phrasing: "How Do We Use Water?"

Phrasing is how you use your voice to group words together. Use this passage to practice reading with proper phrasing. Print a copy of this passage from **InsideNG.com** to help you monitor your progress.

An incredible amount of water covers Earth. Look at a globe. The blue area represents the water. There are about 200 billion liters (53 billion gallons) of water for each person on Earth!

There is not always enough water to drink, however.

Most of Earth's water is salty ocean water. Salt water is fine for sea creatures. But it is not fine for humans and most other animals.

Only 3 percent of Earth's water is fresh water. Fresh water is an important resource that we need every day.

We need to drink fresh water to live. All day, we lose water from our bodies. We lose it when we sweat and when we get rid of waste. We drink water to replace the water we lose.

From "How Do We Use Water?," page 92

Practice Intonation: "Water at Work"

Intonation is the rise and fall in the pitch or tone of your voice as you read aloud. Use this passage to practice reading with proper intonation. Print a copy of this passage from **InsideNG.com** to help you monitor your progress.

At 5 a.m. it is still dark outside. But Kevin Aiken has been awake for an hour. Kevin is a farmer. He grows cherries near Wenatchee, Washington. In the orchard, Kevin stops at an irrigation pipe. He turns a big wheel on the pipe. Water spouts from sprinklers under the cherry trees.

This area does not have enough rainfall to grow fruit trees. Instead, Kevin uses water from the Columbia River to water the trees. Pumps move the river water to the cherry trees.

Farther down the Columbia River is the city of Pasco, Washington. Roberto López plays basketball at his school there. Roberto stops for a drink of water. The water in the water fountain comes from the Columbia River.

Before the water reaches Roberto's school, though, it has to be cleaned. People cannot safely drink water directly from rivers. The water is treated at a water treatment plant first.

From "Water at Work," page 110

Practice Phrasing: "Volcano!"

Phrasing is how you use your voice to group words together. Use this passage to practice reading with proper phrasing. Print a copy of this passage from **InsideNG.com** to help you monitor your progress.

About 1,500 of Earth's volcanoes are active. An active volcano is one that can erupt lava.

Some volcanoes make runny lava. The lava flows fast, like pancake batter. It piles up in thin layers. Over time, it forms low, wide mountains.

Other volcanoes erupt thick lava. It flows slowly, like toothpaste. It piles up in thick layers. Over time, it forms tall, steep mountains.

Volcanoes are found all over Earth. Some form on land. Others rise up from the bottom of the ocean.

Most volcanoes are near the Pacific Ocean. They form a circle of volcanoes known as the Ring of Fire.

These volcanoes are found in areas where big pieces of Earth's surface, or plates, meet. Many volcanoes are formed along such plate boundaries.

From "Volcano!," page 136

Practice Expression: "Fleeing Katrina"

Expression in reading is how you use your voice to express feeling. Use this passage to practice reading with proper expression. Print a copy of this passage from InsideNG.com to help you monitor your progress.

I went home. But it wasn't home. Home isn't really there anymore.

Mud was caked everywhere on the ground. Things were brown and gray, not green as they used to be. It was like I stepped into some other reality. This wasn't the St. Bernard I remembered.

We turned into my neighborhood, and it was strange. Usually, I see green grass, green bushes, green shrubs, and trees. Now, the salt water had killed all of those things. It was brown now, an old, dry brown.

Dad stopped the truck in the middle of the street, and we spilled out.

When mom walked onto the porch and looked through the front room door, I knew she wasn't expecting what she saw. And the smell was horrible. Mold and rotten food and mud scents mixing together.

From "Fleeing Katrina," page 156

Practice Intonation: "Earthquake"

Intonation is the rise and fall in the pitch or tone of your voice as you read aloud. Use this passage to practice reading with proper intonation. Print a copy of this passage from **InsideNG.com** to help you monitor your progress.

In the early dawn, confused and frightened, we gathered at Portsmouth Square. All of Chinatown must have been there.

"You must go to Golden Gate Park!" shouted the policeman.

"The city is on fire. Go quickly now!"

Dark smoke hurt our eyes. Gritty dust filled the air, our mouths and noses, too.

The earth shook again. We stopped, and watched in fear as buildings crumbled around us.

Elder Brother, Younger Brother, and I cleared a path for the cart carrying MaMa and PoPo and our belongings.

We were hot and thirsty until we shed the extra clothing and drank some cold tea.

In the early-morning rush to leave, we had not eaten anything.

PoPo gave us crackers and dried fruit.

Up the steep hills, across the city, we pushed and pulled the heavy cart.

From "Earthquake," page 178

Practice Expression: "Frankenstein"

Expression in reading is how you use your voice to express feeling. Use this passage to practice reading with proper expression. Print a copy of this passage from **InsideNG.com** to help you monitor your progress.

My name is Victor Frankenstein. I created an evil monster. The terrible things that the creature has done are all because of me. No one else must ever know how to do what I have done—I will take that secret with me to my grave.

After many years of study, I had discovered how to bring something to life. I was eager to use what I had learned, so I devoted two years to making a new creature out of bones and body parts from graveyards and slaughterhouses.

At last, my experiment was ready. An enormous, lifeless creature lay on the table in my lab. I thought my creation would show the world what a great scientist I was. I did not know how wrong I was!

From "Frankenstein," page 210

Practice Phrasing: "Film Fright"

Phrasing is how you use your voice to group words together. Use this passage to practice reading with proper phrasing. Print a copy of this passage from **InsideNG.com** to help you monitor your progress.

The first motion pictures were made in the 1890s. They were usually very short and simple. Some were only thirty seconds long! People were fascinated with moving images.

In 1910, Thomas Edison made the movie *Frankenstein*. It was only sixteen minutes. It terrified moviegoers, though. In the 1920s, a horror movie revolution began. People made numerous silent horror films.

Movie studios made many popular monster movies from 1920 to 1950. In 1931, Universal Studios released *Dracula* and *Frankenstein*. These films were two of the most successful horror movies of the time. The studios also made movies about other characters. These characters included the Wolf Man, the Invisible Man, and the Creature from the Black Lagoon.

From "Film Fright," page 232

Practice Intonation: "Mister Monster"

Intonation is the rise and fall in the pitch or tone of your voice as you read aloud. Use this passage to practice reading with proper intonation. Print a copy of this passage from **InsideNG.com** to help you monitor your progress.

DR. FRANKENSTEIN. [*speaking angrily to* MS. ROSARIO] My name is Dr. Victor Frankenstein. You stole my creation!

MS. ROSARIO. [*surprised*] Your what?

DR. FRANKENSTEIN. My creation! I put him together from a hundred dead bodies! I created him. I did not give you permission to use him in your commercial.

[YGOR *enters the office, pulling on the rope.* THE MONSTER *is offstage, at the other end of the rope.*]

DR. FRANKENSTEIN. [*pointing at* YGOR] You! You stole my creature to make money!

YGOR. We need the money. Do you know how much it will cost to keep this monster?

[*As* YGOR *argues with the doctor, he drops the rope mistakenly. The rope disappears.*]

YGOR. The cost of food alone will break our backs!

DR. FRANKENSTEIN. That's my problem! I created him. I gave him life!

YGOR. Oh, yes, you gave him life. But did you give him love? Did you give him a name? Did you give him breakfast?

From "Mister Monster," page 254

Practice Intonation: "Return to *Titanic*"

Intonation is the rise and fall in the pitch or tone of your voice as you read aloud. Use this passage to practice reading with proper intonation. Print a copy of this passage from InsideNG.com to help you monitor your progress.

Titanic was the largest ship in the world—as long as four city blocks. Many people called it the "wonder ship." It was like a floating palace, with a swimming pool, carved wood, and fancy gold lights. It also had many rich and famous passengers who wanted to be the first to ride on this great ship.

Titanic set off for New York. At first, the ride was like a party. By April 14, the ship was in the middle of the Atlantic Ocean. That night, the weather was clear, and stars twinkled against the dark sky. On the ship, people danced late into the night. No one knew that danger was near.

Shortly before midnight, a sailor on lookout saw something in the darkness. He knew it could be only one thing. It was an iceberg, a floating mountain of ice. The sailor raised the alarm : "Iceberg ahead!" Next, the crew tried to turn *Titanic* away from the iceberg, but it was too late. Finally, the ship scraped along the ice.

The problem did not seem too bad at first. Then water started pouring into the ship, and nothing could stop it. The ship was going to sink!

From "Return to *Titanic*," page 286

Practice Expression: "The Forgotten Treasure"

Expression in reading is how you use your voice to express feeling. Use this passage to practice reading with proper expression. Print a copy of this passage from InsideNG.com to help you monitor your progress.

Once there was a hunter who lived with his wife and their four sons. Each son had eyes like shiny black stones. The hunter looked at his sons and smiled. "Some men have gold, but my sons are better than gold. They are my treasures."

The hunter's wife was going to have a fifth baby. Sometimes she could feel it kick. "It will be another boy," she would say. "Another fine boy, just like his brothers."

Every morning, the hunter said to his family, "You are all my treasures. If you care about me, remember me always."

Every morning, his sons would say, "Father, we do not need to remember you. Every day you go out, but every day you come back. You are always here, so how could we ever forget you?"

From "The Forgotten Treasure," page 306

Practice Phrasing: "Mysteries of the Ancient Past"

Phrasing is how you use your voice to group words together. Use this passage to practice reading with proper phrasing. Print a copy of this passage from **InsideNG.com** to help you monitor your progress.

Who built the pyramids, and why did they build them? What lies inside these mysterious buildings? These are some of the questions that scientists and historians try to answer.

Archaeologists study objects from the past to learn about the people who made or used those objects and left them behind when they died. Archaeologists gather clues in many places. They look in old buildings. They also look for objects buried under the ground. Archaeologists often have to dig to find what they are looking for.

The objects that archaeologists study are called artifacts. Artifacts are clues that tell archaeologists how people lived in ancient times.

Artifacts can take many shapes. Old toys and games are artifacts. Statues and other art objects, baskets, bowls, and mummies are also artifacts. When artifacts are broken, archaeologists try to put the pieces back together.

From "Mysteries of the Ancient Past," page 328

Practice Intonation: "Escaping to Freedom"

Intonation is the rise and fall in the pitch or tone of your voice as you read aloud. Use this passage to practice reading with proper intonation. Print a copy of this passage from InsideNG.com to help you monitor your progress.

One dark night, Henson and his family left their home. He carried his two youngest children in a backpack. The family boarded a small boat and crossed the Ohio River into Indiana.

Once in Indiana, the family had to move slowly. They had to be careful not to be seen. Some slave owners offered rewards for the capture of escaped slaves. If the family was found, they might be returned to Riley. To make sure no one saw them, Henson's family often traveled at night and slept during the day.

The family traveled by wagon, by boat, and on foot. They traveled toward Canada, where slavery was not allowed. Along the way, people helped the family. Some people gave them food, and others hid them in barns.

The family set foot in Canada more than a month after their daring escape. The first words that Henson exclaimed when he got there were, "I am free!"

From "Escaping to Freedom," page 360

Practice Expression: "Brave Butterflies"

Expression in reading is how you use your voice to express feeling. Use this passage to practice reading with proper expression. Print a copy of this passage from **InsideNG.com** to help you monitor your progress.

I awoke in the middle of the night and looked outside. A dim light flickered in one of the Garcías' windows, a watchful eye spying on us. In the study, I could hear Papi and Mami talking in low whispers. I tiptoed down the hallway and stood in the shadows.

"Alberto, please, you must be more careful," Mami pleaded. "Getting involved in politics is risky. Think of our friends who have gone to prison or disappeared. Think of the Mirabal sisters. We could suffer the same fate."

"I am thinking of them," said Papi. "I am thinking of the courage that the Mirabals—those brave Mariposas—showed in standing up to Trujillo. And I am thinking of our children's future. Just imagine what it would be like to live in freedom."

From "Brave Butterflies," page 380

Practice Phrasing: "Seeking Freedom"

Phrasing is how you use your voice to group words together. Use this passage to practice reading with proper phrasing. Print a copy of this passage from **InsideNG.com** to help you monitor your progress.

Some countries do not have laws that protect people's freedoms. What do people in those countries do to find freedom?

Sometimes people leave their homes. They might move to a country with more freedom, but this can be very hard. People who move to a new country might have to learn a new language and way of life.

Millions of people have left their homes in search of freedom. Often they want freedom to practice their religion or the freedom to pick their leaders. People move for freedom of speech and freedom of the press. People also move because they want a better education or jobs.

From "Seeking Freedom," page 402

Practice Expression: "The Earth Under Sky Bear's Feet"

Expression in reading is how you use your voice to express feeling. Use this passage to practice reading with proper expression. Print a copy of this passage from **InsideNG.com** to help you monitor your progress.

Long ago,

three hunters and their little dog

found the tracks of a giant bear.

They followed those tracks

all through the day

and even though it was almost dark

they did not stop, but continued on.

They saw that bear now, climbing up

a hill, which glittered

with new-fallen snow.

They ran hard to catch it,

but the bear was too fast.

They ran and they ran, climbing

up and up until one of the hunters said,

"Brothers, look down."

They did and saw they

were high above Earth.

That bear was Sky Bear,

running on through the stars.

Look up now

and you will see her,

circling the sky.

From "The Earth Under Sky Bear's Feet," page 432

Practice Phrasing: "A Universe of Stars"

Phrasing is how you use your voice to group words together. Use this passage to practice reading with proper phrasing. Print a copy of this passage from **InsideNG.com** to help you monitor your progress.

If you stand outside on a clear, dark night, far away from any city lights, you may see a pale band of light stretching across the sky. The band of light is the Milky Way. The glow is from a huge number of stars.

Long ago, people could use only their eyes to study the sky. Over time, more powerful tools have allowed us to look farther and farther out into the universe. We've learned so much about space, but there is *much* more left to explore.

In the night sky, stars look like tiny diamonds fastened to the ceiling. They seem peaceful, timeless, and unchanging. In reality, stars are huge. They are scattered through vast distances in space. They're not timeless but are always changing, and those changes can be violent.

From "A Universe of Stars," page 454

Practice Intonation: "Not-So-Starry Nights"

Intonation is the rise and fall in the pitch or tone of your voice as you read aloud. Use this passage to practice reading with proper intonation. Print a copy of this passage from **InsideNG.com** to help you monitor your progress.

Astronomers were the first to notice the growing problem of light pollution. They began to realize it in the 1970s. They were shocked when they looked into their telescopes and saw that some of the stars and planets that they had studied were gone. They were still there, of course, but city lights made them impossible to see.

Nights started to get brighter more than a century ago. The first long-lasting lightbulb was invented in 1879. Companies began to install electric power lines across the country. More and more people used electricity for lighting.

At the same time, the population grew. Many people moved to the United States. In 1900, there were 76 million Americans. There are more than 300 million today. More people now live in cities and suburbs, and their lights create light pollution.

From "Not-So-Starry Nights," page 474

Practice Phrasing: "Old Music Finds New Voices"

Phrasing is how you use your voice to group words together. Use this passage to practice reading with proper phrasing. Print a copy of this passage from **InsideNG.com** to help you monitor your progress.

Many Mexican American teens are thinking about careers in mariachi. Schools offer courses in mariachi music, and competitions are spreading across the country as more and more Hispanic teens become interested in their culture.

"I like to tell stories," says Victoria Acosta, who won competitions even before she was a teen. "When I'm singing, it's like I'm telling a story. There are sad songs, and happy songs, and love songs. There are all different kinds of stories to tell."

When Victoria was just 4 years old, she fell in love with mariachi music. She begged her parents for lessons.

Her parents supported her. "We need to do our part to preserve our culture," says her father, Ruben Acosta. He is a fifth-generation Mexican American. "Mariachi music is so beautiful. We want to make sure it doesn't die out."

From "Old Music Finds New Voices," page 504

Practice Intonation: "Making Faces"

Intonation is the rise and fall in the pitch or tone of your voice as you read aloud. Use this passage to practice reading with proper intonation. Print a copy of this passage from **InsideNG.com** to help you monitor your progress.

My young neighbor was shocked. It was her first visit to my house, and everywhere she turned, another strange face stared back at her. There were big faces and small faces. Some were bright, and others were plain. At last, she said, "You really have an interesting place here!"

I collect masks, so my house is filled with them. I have about 150. Masks amaze me with their power. They change how people look and act!

I take trips to study masks. In Greece, I watched people make masks that were just like masks used in ancient times. Back then, actors wore masks in plays. Different masks helped actors play more than one part.

My trip to Romania was great, too. There I saw masks change people into hairy, wild men. To celebrate the start of spring, people put on these masks and then run through the streets.

From "Making Faces," page 522

Practice Expression: "Wings"

Expression in reading is how you use your voice to express feeling. Use this passage to practice reading with proper expression. Print a copy of this passage from **InsideNG.com** to help you monitor your progress.

I ran through the streets with my eyes to the sky, searching the clouds for Ikarus.

He struggled to stay in the air. His wings drooped and his head hung low.

He landed heavily on the edge of a building and sat with the pigeons. Pigeons don't make fun of people.

A policeman passing by blew his whistle.

"You with the wings, come down from there! Stay yourself on the ground. You'll get in trouble. You'll get hurt."

It seemed to me Ikarus was already in trouble and hurt. Could the policeman put him in jail for flying, for being too different?

When the neighborhood kids saw the policeman yelling at him, they exploded with laughter. Ikarus dropped to the ground.

"Stop!" I cried. "Leave him alone." And they did.

From "Wings," page 544

Glossary

The definitions in this glossary are for words as they are used in the selections in this book. Use the Pronunciation Key below to help you use each word's pronunciation. Then read about the parts of an entry.

Pronunciation Key

Symbols for Consonant Sounds				Symbols for Short Vowel Sounds		Symbols for R-controlled Sounds		Symbols for Variant Vowel Sounds	
b	box	p	pan	a	hat	ar	barn	ah	father
ch	chick	r	ring	e	bell	air	chair	aw	ball
d	dog	s	bus	i	chick	ear	ear	oi	boy
f	fish	sh	fish	o	box	ír	fire	ow	mouse
g	girl	t	hat	u	bus	or	corn	oo	book
h	hat	th	earth			ur	girl	ü	fruit
j	jar	th	father	**Symbols for Long Vowel Sounds**				**Miscellaneous Symbols**	
k	cake	v	vase						
ks	box	w	window	ā	cake			shun	fraction
kw	queen	wh	whale	ē	key			chun	question
l	bell	y	yarn	ī	bike			zhun	division
m	mouse	z	zipper	ō	goat				
n	pan	zh	treasure	yū	mule				
ng	ring								

• Academic Vocabulary

Certain words in this glossary have a red dot indicating that they are academic vocabulary words. These are the words that you will use as you study many different subjects in school.

Parts of an Entry

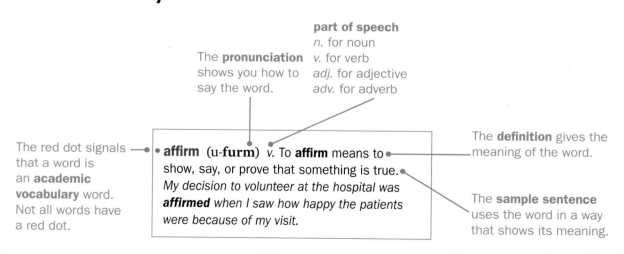

part of speech
n. for noun
The **pronunciation** *v.* for verb
shows you how to *adj.* for adjective
say the word. *adv.* for adverb

The **definition** gives the meaning of the word.

The red dot signals that a word is an **academic vocabulary** word. Not all words have a red dot.

• **affirm** (u-**furm**) *v.* To **affirm** means to show, say, or prove that something is true. *My decision to volunteer at the hospital was **affirmed** when I saw how happy the patients were because of my visit.*

The **sample sentence** uses the word in a way that shows its meaning.

A

active (**ak**-tiv) *adj.* Something that is **active** is likely to move or to show action. *Children are **active** when they run and play games outside.*

actor (**ak**-tur) *n.* An **actor** is a person who acts in a movie or play. *The **actors** are working on a new movie.*

• **adjust** (u-**just**) *v.* To **adjust** means to change in order to become comfortable with something. *I hope I can **adjust** to my new school.*

advice (ad-**vīs**) *n.* **Advice** is a suggestion or an idea that helps someone decide what to do. *Family members can give you **advice** when you have a problem.*

agree (u-**grē**) *v.* When you **agree** with someone, you have the same ideas. *A handshake shows that people **agree** to something.*

alarm (u-**larm**) *n.* An **alarm** warns people of danger. *A smoke detector is one kind of **alarm**.*

alive (u-**līv**) *adj.* Something that is living is **alive**. *The girl looks happy to be **alive**.*

amazed (u-**māzd**) *adj.* To be **amazed** means to be very surprised. *They are **amazed** that the experiment worked so well.*

amount (u-**mount**) *n.* An **amount** is the total number or quantity. *There is a large **amount** of wood in this pile.*

• **analyze** (**a**-nu-līz) *v.* To **analyze** means to break down information into parts to understand it better. *Our science class will **analyze** cell structures using a microscope.*

ancient (**ānt**-shunt) *adj.* If something is **ancient**, it is very old. *People built this **ancient** temple long ago.*

angry (**ang**-grē) *adj.* When you are **angry**, you are mad at someone or something. *An **angry** leopard hisses a warning.*

• **apply** (u-**plī**) *v.* To **apply** means to ask for or to request something. *People often fill out forms when they **apply** for a job.*

• **appreciate** (u-**prē**-shē-āt) *v.* To **appreciate** means to care about something or someone. *A boy gives flowers to his mom to show that he **appreciates** her.*

• **appropriate** (u-**prō**-prē-ut) *adj.* If something is **appropriate**, it is correct for the situation. *Lisa's blue dress is **appropriate** to wear to the wedding.*

approve (u-**prüv**) *v.* To **approve** means to think something is good or right. *The teacher **approves** the work I did.*

archaeologist (ar-kē-ah-lu-jist) *n.* An **archaeologist** studies the way people lived in the past. *Bones, buildings, and tools help **archaeologists** learn about the past.*

• **arrange** (u-**rānj**) *v.* To **arrange** means to put things in a certain order. *The librarian will **arrange** the books on the shelves at the library.*

arrest (u-**rest**) *v.* To **arrest** means to put someone in jail. *When police officers **arrest** a suspect, they may use handcuffs.*

arrive (u-**rīv**) *v.* To **arrive** means to reach a place. *A plane **arrives** at an airport.*

artifact (**ar**-ti-fakt) *n.* An **artifact** is an object, or the remains of one, that represents a culture. *An old statue is an **artifact**.*

• **assist** (u-**sist**) *v.* To **assist** means to help. *The father **assists** his son with an assignment when he has trouble understanding it.*

audience (**aw**-dē-unts) *n.* An **audience** is a group of people who watch or listen to something. *The **audience** claps during the show.*

• **available** (u-**vā**-lu-bul) *adj.* When something is **available**, it is here and ready for use. *Fresh fruit is **available** in the summer.*

B

beautiful (**byū**-ti-ful) *adj.* Something that is **beautiful** is very pretty. *The flowers are **beautiful**.*

• **belief** (bu-**lēf**) *n.* A **belief** is a feeling that something is true or right. *One **belief** is that your wish comes true if you break a wishbone and get the bigger part.*

• **benefit** (**ben**-e-fit) *n.* A benefit is something that is helpful. *Fresh air and exercise are two **benefits** of hiking.*

bury (**bair**-ē) *v.* To **bury** means to place in the ground. *The dog **buries** a bone.*

• **Academic Vocabulary**

Glossary

C

capture (**kap**-chur) **1** *v.* To **capture** means to take by force. *The farmer **captured** a raccoon.* **2** *n.* A **capture** is the act of catching something. *Soon after the **capture**, he released the raccoon.*

career (ku-**rear**) *n.* A **career** is a job someone trains for and does full-time. *This man went to veterinary school and now has a **career** working with animals.*

carefully (**kair**-foo-lē) *adv.* To act **carefully** means to act with care. *You should carry the eggs **carefully** so they do not break.*

carve (**karv**) *v.* To **carve** means to cut shapes from a material like stone or wood. *The artist used sharp tools to **carve** a sculpture.*

• **category** (**ka**-tu-gor-ē) *n.* A **category** is a group of items that are related in some way. *Cheetahs and leopards belong to the same **category** of big cats.*

change (**chānj**) *n.* A **change** is something new and different. *A sudden **change** in weather can surprise people!*

character (**kair**-ik-tur) *n.* A **character** is someone in a story. *He acted out the role of the main **character** in the play.*

civilization (si-vu-lu-**zā**-shun) *n.* A **civilization** is the culture of a specific place, time, or group of people. *Greece has a very old **civilization**.*

• **classic** (**kla**-sik) *adj.* Something that is **classic** is old but good. ***Classic** cars are expensive if they are in good shape.*

clue (**klü**) *n.* A **clue** is a piece of information that leads to a solution. *A police detective looks for **clues** to the crime.*

• **collapse** (ku-**laps**) *v.* To **collapse** means to fall down. *The old building **collapsed**.*

• **collect** (ku-**lekt**) *v.* To **collect** means to gather things of interest. *The boy **collects** postage stamps from around the world.*

commercial (ku-**mur**-shul) *n.* A **commercial** is an ad on TV or the radio. *Most TV **commercials** show products that viewers can buy.*

• **communicate** (ku-**myū**-ni-kāt) *v.* When you **communicate**, you share information. *The pilot used the loud speaker to **communicate** with the passengers.*

• **community** (ku-**myū**-ni-tē) *n.* A **community** is a place where people live, work, and carry out their daily lives. *Some **communities** have outdoor markets.*

• **compare** (kum-**pair**) *v.* When you **compare** two things, you think about how they are alike and different. *I would like to **compare** the apple pie to the blueberry pie to find out which one tastes better.*

competition (kom-pe-**ti**-shun) *n.* A **competition** is a contest. *The runners are in **competition** to win the race or to improve their time.*

complain (kum-**plān**) *v.* To **complain** means to say that you are unhappy about something. *I **complained** that it was not fair I had to take out the trash by myself.*

concert (**kont**-surt) *n.* A **concert** is an event where people play music for an audience. *The orchestra is giving a **concert**.*

confused (kun-**fyūzd**) *adj.* To be **confused** means to be unsure or not clear. *We could not follow the recipe because we were **confused** by the instructions.*

• **context** (**kon**-tekst) *n.* **Context** refers to the parts nearby that help explain the meaning. *Paul knows to use the **context** to help him understand what a new word means.*

continue (kun-**tin**-yū) *v.* To **continue** means to keep going. *The highway **continues** for miles.*

costume (**kos**-tüm) *n.* A **costume** is a set of clothes that someone wears to look like another person. *You can dress up in a **costume** for a special occasion.*

• **create** (krē-**āt**) *v.* To **create** means to make something new. *The artist **creates** a work of art in his studio.*

creature (**krē**-chur) *n.* A **creature** is a real or imaginary living thing. *A dragon is an imaginary **creature**.*

crop (**krop**) *n.* **Crops** are plants that farmers grow. *Corn, beans, and peaches are different **crops**.*

- **culture** (**kul**-chur) *n.* The ideas and way of life for a group of people make up their **culture**. *Baseball and jazz are both part of American **culture**.*

curious (**kyoor**-ē-us) *adj.* If you are **curious**, you want to know more about something. *A **curious** person shows interest in things.*

D

dangerous (**dān**-jur-us) *adj.* Something that is **dangerous** is not safe. *It is **dangerous** to walk barefoot near broken glass. You could cut yourself.*

decorate (**de**-ku-rāt) *v.* To **decorate** means to add things to make something look better. *The baker **decorates** the fancy dessert.*

- **define** (dē-**fīn**) *v.* When you **define** something, you tell what it means. *I have to **define** eight new words for homework.*

- **demonstrate** (**de**-mun-strāt) *v.* To **demonstrate** means to prove or make clear. *As the team coach, Mike **demonstrates** how to kick the soccer ball.*

depend (dē-**pend**) *v.* When you **depend** on something, you need it. *Babies **depend** on their parents for everything.*

- **design** (di-**zīn**) *n.* A **design** is a drawing or a pattern. *The tiles are placed so they form a colorful **design** on the surface.*

destroy (di-**stroi**) *v.* To **destroy** something means to take it apart or to ruin it. *Workers **destroyed** the old building.*

dictator (**dik**-tā-tur) *n.* A **dictator** is a person who leads a country without sharing power. *Most **dictators** do not allow others to make decisions for the country.*

different (**dif**-er-ent) *adj.* Something that is **different** is not the same. *A red flower in a field of orange tulips is **different** from the others.*

disappear (dis-u-**pear**) *v.* To **disappear** means to no longer be seen. *When the bell rang, the students left quickly. They **disappeared**.*

- **discover** (dis-**ku**-vur) *v.* To **discover** means to find something that is lost or hidden. *The boy **discovers** a starfish at the beach.*

- **discuss** (di-**skus**) *v.* When you **discuss** something, you talk about it. *My teacher likes to **discuss** the classroom rules every morning.*

distance (**dis**-tunts) *n.* **Distance** is the area between two points. *The **distance** between Earth and the sun is 93 million miles.*

drift (**drift**) *v.* To **drift** means to move along slowly in the air or on water. *She **drifts** down the river on a raft, carried along by the current.*

droop (**drüp**) *v.* To **droop** means to hang down. *The branches of the tree **droop** to the ground.*

E

earthquake (**urth**-kwāk) *n.* An **earthquake** is a sudden shaking of the earth. *Strong **earthquakes** cause damage to roads and buildings.*

electricity (ē-lek-**tri**-si-tē) *n.* **Electricity** is a form of energy. *Lamps and computers use **electricity** to work.*

- **element** (**e**-le-ment) *n.* An **element** is a basic part of a whole. *Pitching is one **element** of a baseball game.*

- **environment** (en-**vī**-run-ment) *n.* An **environment** is the area where plants and animals live and grow. *Plants grow well in a healthy **environment**.*

- **equipment** (ē-**kwip**-ment) *n.* Tools or machines for a certain use are **equipment**. *Hospitals have **equipment** for treating people who are sick or hurt.*

erupt (ē-**rupt**) *v.* To **erupt** means to break open or shoot out suddenly. *When a volcano **erupts**, lava and ash shoot out.*

escape (es-**kāp**) **1** *v.* To **escape** means to get away. *People **escaped** the burning building.* **2** *n.* An **escape** is the act of getting away from something. *We heard about their successful **escape**.*

evacuate (ē-**va**-kyū-āt) *v.* To **evacuate** means to leave or to get out. *The woman **evacuated** the building when the fire alarm rang.*

• evaluate (ē-**val**-yu-wāt) v. To **evaluate** means to judge something's value or worth. *The coach will* ***evaluate*** *all students who want to play basketball.*

evil (**ē**-vul) adj. Something that is **evil** is very bad or harmful. *Some people believe rattlesnakes are* ***evil*** *because their bite is dangerous.*

experiment (eks-**spair**-i-ment) n. An **experiment** is an activity that someone does to test an idea. *The students are doing an* ***experiment*** *in their science class.*

• explain (eks-**splān**) v. When you **explain** an idea, you make it clear so people can understand it. *Lucy* ***explains*** *the rules of the game to her sister.*

• explanation (ek-splu-**nā**-shun) n. An **explanation** is a statement that makes an idea clear. *Her* ***explanation*** *makes the directions easy to understand.*

explorer (eks-**splor**-ur) n. An **explorer** travels somewhere to study something. ***Explorers*** *find out what is special about a new place.*

F

• fact (**fakt**) n. A **fact** is a piece of information that is true. *It is a proven* ***fact*** *that Earth revolves around the sun.*

familiar (fu-**mil**-yur) adj. Something that is **familiar** is already known. *He was happy to see a* ***familiar*** *face at the party.*

famous (**fā**-mus) adj. Something that is **famous** is very well known. *Many people have seen the* ***famous*** *Statue of Liberty.*

fascinated (fa-su-**nā**-tud) adj. To be **fascinated** means to be very interested in something. *The student is* ***fascinated*** *by the model.*

festival (**fes**-tu-vul) n. A **festival** is a special event or party. *Dancers perform at the* ***festival***.

flow (**flō**) v. To **flow** means to move freely. *A river* ***flows*** *without stopping.*

• force (**fors**) **1** v. To **force** means to push. *Too much weight* ***forces*** *the ice loose.* **2** n. A **force** is a great power in nature. *The* ***force*** *sent ice flying.*

forest (**for**-ust) n. A **forest** is a place that has lots of trees. *Many* ***forests*** *have been cut down to make room for new buildings.*

forget (for-**get**) v. When you **forget** something, you stop thinking about it. *The boy leaves without his shoes. He* ***forgets*** *them.*

fortunate (**for**-chu-nut) adj. Someone who is **fortunate** is lucky. *The family is* ***fortunate*** *that their house did not burn in the fire.*

• freedom (**frē**-dum) n. If you have **freedom** you are not limited in what you do. *The bird was released and given* ***freedom***.

frightened (**frī**-tund) adj. To be **frightened** is to be afraid or scared. *When I'm* ***frightened*** *at the movies, I cover my face with my hands.*

future (**fyū**-chur) n. The **future** is what will happen in the time to come. *I am going to a concert at some time in the near* ***future***.

G

• generate (**je**-nu-rāt) v. To **generate** means to make something. *Windmills* ***generate*** *energy that people can use.*

• globe (**glōb**) n. A **globe** is a model of Earth. *A* ***globe*** *shows the shape of the land. The blue represents oceans.*

goods (**goodz**) n. **Goods** are things that people buy and sell. *Stores sell* ***goods***. *For this meaning,* **goods** *is always plural.*

government (**gu**-vurn-munt) n. The people who control the country according to certain laws are the **government**. *Washington, DC, is the center of the U.S.* ***government***.

H

hideous (**hi**-dē-us) adj. Something that is **hideous** is very ugly. *A mask can make someone look* ***hideous***.

hopeful (**hōp**-ful) adj. Someone who is **hopeful** is full of good thoughts about what will happen. *The girl is* ***hopeful*** *about winning the contest.*

• Academic Vocabulary

hunter (**hun**-tur) *n.* A **hunter** is a person who looks for wild animals to capture or kill. *A skilled hunter may use a bow and arrows to hunt.*

hurricane (**hur**-u-kān) *n.* A **hurricane** is an ocean storm with strong winds. *From space, a hurricane looks like a spiral of white clouds.*

I

• **identify** (ī-**den**-tu-fī) *v.* To **identify** means to find out or to show what something is. *Some scientists try to identify how germs make people sick.*

• **immigrant** (**i**-mu-grunt) *n.* An **immigrant** is a person who comes to live in a new country. *Immigrants say a pledge, or promise, when they become citizens.*

impressed (im-**prest**) *adj.* If you are **impressed**, you are strongly affected by something. *The audience was very impressed by the talented musicians.*

instrument (**int**-stru-munt) *n.* An **instrument** is something you play to make music. *Guitars and violins are both stringed instruments.*

• **interpret** (in-**tur**-prut) *v.* To **interpret** means to explain or tell what something means. *Paul has to interpret the directions for me.*

• **interview** (**in**-tur-vyū) *n.* In an **interview**, one person finds out about another person by asking questions. *The reporter gathered information in the interview and then wrote the news article.*

J

journal (**jur**-nul) *n.* A **journal** is a record of someone's thoughts, feelings, and actions. *Some people write in their journal almost every day.*

L

law (**law**) *n.* The **law** is a country's rules. *A police officer reminds people to follow the law.*

layer (**lā**-ur) *n.* A **layer** is a section that is on top of or under another. *The cake has many layers, with frosting in between.*

leader (**lē**-dur) *n.* A **leader** is a person in charge of others. *The leader of our hiking club decides which trail we will take.*

learn (**lurn**) *v.* To **learn** means to know about a subject by studying or practicing it. *You can learn many things by reading.*

leave (**lēv**) *v.* When you **leave** a place, you go away from it. *A bird leaves its nest to find food.*

levee (**le**-vē) *n.* A **levee** is a structure that keeps a river from flooding. *If rainfall is heavy for a long time, a river could rise and the water could spill over the levee.*

• **locate** (**lō**-kāt) *v.* To **locate** something is to find it. *The woman tried to locate her missing purse.*

lonely (**lōn**-lē) *adj.* To be **lonely** means to be alone, without friends. *Do you feel lonely when your friends are away?*

loss (**laws**) *n.* When you no longer have something important, you feel the **loss**. *A terrible loss is the death of a loved one.*

M

mascot (**mas**-kot) *n.* A **mascot** is a character that represents an organization. *The basketball team's mascot cheers for the team.*

mask (**mask**) *n.* A **mask** is something a person wears to hide his or her face. *The girl will wear a mask to a dress-up party.*

material (mu-**tear**-ē-ul) *n.* **Materials** are things you need to make a product or to do a project. *Paint and brushes are materials you need for painting.*

• **migrate** (**mī**-grāt) *v.* To **migrate** means to move from one place to another. *Some birds migrate to a warm climate for the winter.*

N

• **narrative** (**nair**-u-tiv) **1** *adj.* **Narrative** writing tells a story. **2** *n.* A **narrative** tells a story. *My narrative about life in another country won first place in the narrative writing contest.*

• **Academic Vocabulary**

Glossary

native (**nā**-tiv) *adj.* Something that belongs to you because of where you were born is **native** to you. *People wave flags from their **native** countries.*

necessity (ni-**se**-su-tē) *n.* A **necessity** is an item that someone needs. *Food and water are the most basic **necessities** of life.*

neighborhood (**nā**-bur-hood) *n.* A **neighborhood** is a place where people live and work together. *Most families know each other in our **neighborhood** in Boston.*

O

ocean (**ō**-shun) *n.* An **ocean** is a large area or body of salt water. ***Oceans** cover most of Earth.*

offstage (awf-**stāj**) *adv.* To be **offstage** means to be at the side of the stage. *The dancer waits **offstage** and gets ready to perform.*

opinion (u-**pin**-yun) *n.* An **opinion** is a belief or a view about a topic. *My friends share their **opinions** about fashion.*

opportunity (ah-pur-**tü**-nu-tē) *n.* An **opportunity** is a good chance to do something. *A sign in the window tells about a job **opportunity** at the restaurant.*

orbit (**or**-but) *v.* To **orbit** means to move in an almost circular path around another object. *It takes Earth about 365 days to **orbit** the sun.*

ordinary (**or**-du-nair-ē) *adj.* An **ordinary** thing is plain. *The brown box looks **ordinary**.*

• **organize** (**or**-gu-nīz) *v.* To **organize** means to plan and set up something. *The leader **organizes** the people to support a cause.*

original (u-**rij**-u-nul) *adj.* Something that is **original** is the first of its kind. *Mary Shelley's novel is the **original** story of Frankenstein.*

P

passenger (**pa**-sen-jur) *n.* When you ride in a car, boat, or other vehicle, you are a **passenger**. *The bus driver took ten **passengers** to the school.*

perfect (**pur**-fikt) *adj.* Something that is **perfect** is just right. *The girl made a **perfect** dive into the water.*

perform (pur-**form**) *v.* To **perform** means to dance, sing, act, or play music for an audience. *Students **perform** on stage for special events.*

plan (plan) *n.* A **plan** is an idea about how to do something. *The architect's drawings show the **plans** for building a new house.*

politics (**pah**-lu-tiks) *n.* **Politics** is the business of government. *Members of Congress talk about issues of national and international **politics**.*

pollution (pu-**lū**-shun) *n.* **Pollution** is waste that harms nature. *Trash is one form of **pollution**.*

population (pah-pyu-**lā**-shun) *n.* **Population** means the number of people who live somewhere. *Many people live in New York City. It has a large **population**.*

power (**pow**-ur) *n.* **Power** is energy that makes things work. *A dam collects water to use as a source of **power**.*

prepare (pri-**pair**) *v.* To **prepare** means to get ready. *Dad is **preparing** vegetables for dinner tonight.*

preserve (pri-**zurv**) *v.* To **preserve** means to save. *A grandmother **preserves** a family tradition by sharing it with her granddaughter.*

problem (**prah**-blum) *n.* A **problem** is something that is wrong. A **problem** needs to be solved or fixed. *The driver has a **problem** because his truck is stuck in the mud.*

process (**prah**-ses) *n.* A **process** is a set of actions taken to get a certain result. *Making homemade jam is a difficult **process**.*

protect (pru-**tekt**) *v.* To **protect** means to keep safe. *The mother bird **protects** her chicks from danger.*

protest (**prō**-test) **1** *v.* To **protest** means to make a statement against an idea. *The students **protested** against school spending cuts.* **2** *n.* A **protest** is a display of strong feelings. *The students led a **protest**.*

• **Academic Vocabulary**

proud (**prowd**) *adj.* If you are **proud**, you are feeling happy about yourself. *I felt **proud** when I won the prize.*

public (**pu**-blik) *n.* When you are in **public**, you are in an area that is open to others. *Even though we held our family gathering in **public**, the setting felt private.*

pyramid (**pear**-u-mid) *n.* A **pyramid** is a building with a square base and four sides that are triangles. *Egypt has many ancient **pyramids**.*

R

rainfall (**rān**-fawl) *n.* **Rainfall** is the total rain, snow, or sleet that falls in a period of time. *There has been a lot of **rainfall** this year.*

• **record** (ri-**kord**) *v.* To **record** means to put something in writing. *The weather scientist **records** how much rain falls in one month.*

reduce (ri-**düs**) *v.* To **reduce** means to have fewer or less of something. *The box was too heavy for her to carry so her friend helped in order to **reduce** the heavy load.*

• **relate** (ri-**lāt**) *v.* When you **relate** two things, you think about how they are connected. *Boats and trains both **relate** to the topic of transportation.*

relative (**re**-lu-tiv) *n.* A family member is a **relative**. *The mother and daughter are **relatives**.*

• **release** (ri-**lēs**) *v.* To **release** means to let out. *When you **release** an animal into the wild, you let it go free.*

remain (ri-**mān**) *v.* To **remain** means to stay in the same place. *My dog is learning to **remain** in one spot when I tell him.*

remember (ri-**mem**-bur) *v.* When you **remember** something, you think of it again later. *A soldier went to the monument to **remember** his friend who died.*

• **report** (ri-**port**) *v.* When you **report** on an event, you describe what happened. *I will **report** the lost dog to the police.*

rescue (**res**-kyū) *n.* A **rescue** is the act of saving someone or something from danger. *The **rescue** was daring and successful.*

• **resource** (**rē**-sors) *n.* A **resource** is something that people need and use. *Air, soil, and water are natural **resources**.*

• **response** (ri-**sponts**) *n.* A **response** is what people think or say about something. *She raises her hand to give a **response** to the question.*

responsibility (ri-spont-su-**bi**-lu-tē) *n.* A **responsibility** is something you should do because it is right. *It is my **responsibility** to walk the dog every day.*

reward (ri-**ward**) *n.* A **reward** is money given for helping someone. *We offered a **reward** to anyone who could find our lost dog.*

right (**rīt**) *n.* A **right** is the power a person has because of a country's rules. *In 1920 American women got the **right** to vote.*

roam (**rōm**) *v.* To **roam** means to wander or to travel without any particular place to go. *Wild animals **roam** freely.*

roots (**rüts**) *n.* **Roots** are a person's family traditions and culture. *My family is from India. I am so proud of my Indian **roots**.*

S

safely (**sāf**-lē) *adv.* To do something **safely** is to do it without danger. *The girl worked **safely** by protecting her eyes from the chemicals.*

scatter (**ska**-tur) *v.* To **scatter** means to throw or drop many things over a wide area. *The leaves **scatter** across the street.*

scientist (**sī**-un-tist) *n.* A person who studies science is a **scientist**. *The **scientist** uses a microscope to study small objects up close.*

• **Academic Vocabulary**

search (surch) **1** *v.* When you **search** for something, you look for it. *You might search for something you lost.* **2** *n.* A **search** is also the act of looking for something. *We organized a search for the missing dog.*

secret (sē-krut) **1** *adj.* Something that is **secret** is hidden from others. **2** *n.* A **secret** is something you hide from others. *Can you keep a secret?*

• **select** (su-lekt) *v.* To **select** something means to choose it. *You may select five books to borrow from the library.*

• **series** (sear-ēz) *n.* A **series** is a group of related things that are put in a certain order. *There is a concert series for children in the park this summer.*

• **sequence** (sē-kwens) *n.* The **sequence** of events is the order in which the events happen. *Sarah must remember the right sequence of numbers to open her lock.*

severe (su-vear) *adj.* Something that is **severe** is very serious or dangerous. *Dad could not read because he had a severe headache.*

shelter (shel-tur) *n.* A **shelter** is a place where people can safely stay. *An umbrella provides shelter from the rain.*

• **similar** (si-mu-lur) *adj.* Things that are **similar** are almost the same. *Oranges and tangerines are similar fruits.*

skeleton (ske-lu-tun) *n.* A **skeleton** is the set of bones in an animal or a person. *The model shows a human skeleton.*

slave (slāv) *n.* A **slave** is someone who belongs to another person and who works without pay. *Owners forced slaves to work.*

• **source** (sors) *n.* A **source** is the book or other text that you used to gather information. *My source of information is an encyclopedia.*

• **space** (spās) *n.* **Space** is the area beyond Earth. *Scientists send special ships into space to learn about other planets and the moon.*

• **specific** (spi-si-fik) *adj.* Something that is **specific** is exact. *Dr. Gonzales gave specific directions about which medicine to take.*

statue (sta-chü) *n.* A **statue** is a model of a person or thing. *The monument has a statue of Abraham Lincoln.*

strange (strānj) *adj.* Something that is **strange** is not familiar. *The reflection in this mirror is strange. I look so much taller.*

• **structure** (struk-chur) *n.* **Structure** is the way something is organized or put together. *The structure of the building is strong.*

struggle (stru-gul) *v.* To **struggle** means to try hard. *I struggle to beat my uncle at arm wrestling.*

• **style** (stī-ul) *n.* A **style** is a certain way of expressing an idea. *Salsa is one style of dance.*

successful (suk-ses-ful) *adj.* To be **successful** means to have a good result or to be well liked. *The team was successful at the science fair.*

• **support** (su-port) *v.* To **support** means to help. *People support friends and family when they encourage or comfort each other.*

surface (sur-fus) *n.* The **surface** is the outside part of something. *The surface of the lake is calm.*

system (sis-tum) *n.* A **system** is a way of doing things. *An assembly line is a factory system that usually saves time and money.*

T

tale (tāl) *n.* A **tale** is a story. *The children enjoy listening to the tale.*

telescope (te-lu-skōp) *n.* A **telescope** is a tool you can look through to make faraway things look bigger. *You can use a telescope to look at the moon.*

temperature (tem-pur-chur) *n.* The **temperature** is how hot or cold something is. *We measure temperature using a thermometer.*

• **Academic Vocabulary**

terror (**tair**-ur) *n.* To feel **terror** means to have much fear. *The frightened man runs away from the bear in terror.*

• **theme** (**thēm**) *n.* A **theme** is the main message of a story. *The theme of the school play is to always ask for help when you need it.*

tomb (**tüm**) *n.* A **tomb** is a grave, or a special place for the body of a dead person. *The inside of the tomb looked almost like someone's living room.*

• **topic** (**tah**-pik) *n.* A **topic** is the subject of a piece of writing or of a discussion. *Meg's teacher said the topic for the day was how to write complete sentences.*

track (**trak**) *n.* A **track** is a footprint or a mark left by something as it moves over a surface. *When you look at animal tracks, you can tell what kind of animal was in the area.*

• **tradition** (**tru**-**di**-shun) *n.* A **tradition** is an activity or belief that people share for many years. *It is a tradition for our family to celebrate Kwanzaa every December.*

travel (**tra**-vul) *v.* To **travel** means to go from one place to another place. *People can travel over land by car, train, or wagon.*

treasure (**tre**-zhur) *n.* A **treasure** is something very special and important. *The old gold coins are part of a famous treasure.*

treat (**trēt**) *v.* When you **treat** something, you change it. *You can use a special cleaner to treat a stain on clothing.*

U

understand (un-dur-**stand**) *v.* To **understand** something is to know it well. *A teacher understands a math problem can explain it to the students.*

unit (**yū**-nit) *n.* A **unit** is a certain amount used in measuring. *An inch is a common unit used to measure small objects.*

universe (**yū**-nu-vurs) *n.* The **universe** is everywhere and includes Earth, all other planets, and all stars.

untouched (un-**tucht**) *adj.* Something that is **untouched** is not changed or hurt in any way. *Few areas of the world have been untouched by humans.*

useless (**yūs**-lus) *adj.* If something is **useless**, it is of no use. *A broken cell phone is useless.*

V

value (**val**-yū) *n.* A **value** is something that people care about. *Respect is an important value in Japan.*

• **vary** (**vair**-ē) *v.* To **vary** means to be different from others. *Snowflakes vary from one another so that no two are alike.*

village (**vi**-lij) *n.* A **village** is a very small town. *Not many people live in farming villages, where homes are separated by large areas of land.*

violent (**vī**-u-lunt) *adj.* Something that is **violent** uses force. *Violent storms like tornadoes can damage buildings and kill people.*

volcano (vol-**kā**-nō) *n.* A **volcano** is an opening in Earth from which lava, ash, and steam escape. *The state of Hawaii has several volcanoes.*

W

warning (**wor**-ning) *n.* A **warning** is a sign that something bad may happen. *The road sign gives us a warning that a railroad crossing is ahead.*

wasted (**wāst**-ud) *adj.* Something that is **wasted** is not needed. *Food that you throw away instead of eating is wasted.*

whisper (**whis**-pur) *v.* To **whisper** means to speak very quietly. *I whisper the secret to my friend so no one else can hear.*

worry (**wur**-ē) *v.* To **worry** about something means to feel unhappy and afraid about what may happen. *People often worry when they are late.*

wreck (**rek**) *n.* A **wreck** is what is left after a crash. *A shipwreck is a broken ship that crashed.*

• Academic Vocabulary

• Academic Vocabulary Master Word List

adaptation	contrast	goal	purpose
adjust	convince	generate	react
adjustment	couple	globe	record
affect	create	identify	refer
aid	credit	illustrate	reflect
amend	culture	image	region
analyze	data	immigrant	relate
appeal	debate	impact	release
application	decision	individual	report
apply	define	inevitable	research
appreciate	definition	integrate	resource
approach	demonstrate	interpret	response
appropriate	describe	interview	result
area	design	involve	role
arrange	despite	issue	route
assignment	device	job	section
assist	discover	judgment	select
associate	discuss	literal	sequence
assume	distinguish	locate	series
attach	effect	location	similar
available	effectively	logical	situation
awareness	element	media	solve
belief	emerge	migrate	source
benefit	encounter	model	space
bond	energy	modify	specific
capable	ensure	narrative	structure
category	environment	negative	style
challenge	equipment	obvious	summarize
chapter	establish	organize	support
characteristic	evaluate	origin	survive
classic	evidence	original	symbol
collapse	exact	outcome	team
collect	experiment	perspective	technical
communicate	expert	plan	technique
community	explain	position	technology
compare	explanation	positive	temporary
compound	express	predict	theme
concentrate	fact	presentation	topic
conflict	feature	process	tradition
connect	focus	professional	trait
connotation	force	promote	unique
context	freedom	propaganda	vary

• Words in red appear in Level C.

A

Alliteration The repetition of the same sounds (usually consonants) at the beginning of words that are close together. **Example:** Molly makes magnificent mousse, though Pablo prefers pecan pie.

See also **Repetition**

Allusion A key form of literary language, in which one text makes the reader think about another text that was written before it. Allusion can also mean a reference to a person, place, thing, or event that is not specifically named. **Example:** When Hannah wrote in her short story that vanity was the talented main character's "Achilles heel," her teacher understood that Hannah was referring to a character in a Greek myth. So, she suspected that the vanity of the main character in Hannah's short story would prove to be the character's greatest weakness.

See also **Connotation; Literature; Poetry**

Article A short piece of nonfiction writing on a specific topic. Articles appear in newspapers and magazines.

See also **Expository nonfiction; Nonfiction**

Autobiography The story of a person's life, written by that person. **Example:** Mahatma Gandhi wrote an autobiography titled *Gandhi: An Autobiography: The Story of My Experiments With Truth*.

See also **Diary; Journal; Personal narrative**

B

Biographical fiction A fictional story that is based on real events in the life of a real person. **Example:** Although the book *Farmer Boy* by Laura Ingalls Wilder is about her husband's childhood, the conversations between characters are from the author's imagination. They are based on what she thought the characters might have said at the time.

See also **Biography; Fiction**

Biography The story of a person's life, written by another person.

See also **Autobiography; Biographical fiction**

C

Character A person, an animal, or an imaginary creature in a work of fiction.

See also **Characterization; Character traits**

Characterization The way a writer creates and develops a character. Writers use a variety of ways to bring a character to life: through descriptions of the character's appearance, thoughts, feelings, and actions; through the character's words; and through the words or thoughts of other characters.

See also **Character; Character traits; Motive**

Character traits The special qualities of personality that writers give their characters.

See also **Character; Characterization**

Climax The turning point or most important event in a plot.

See also **Falling action; Plot; Rising action**

Complication See **Rising action**

Conflict The main problem faced by a character in a story or play. The character may be involved in a struggle against nature, another character, or society. The struggle may also be between two elements in the character's mind.

See also **Plot**

Connotation The feelings suggested by a word or phrase, apart from its dictionary meaning. **Example:** The terms "used car" and "previously owned vehicle" have different connotations. To most people, the phrase "previously owned vehicle" sounds better than "used car."

See also **Denotation; Poetry**

D

Denotation The dictionary meaning of a word or phrase. Denotation is especially important in functional texts and other types of nonfiction used to communicate information precisely.

See also **Connotation; Functional text; Nonfiction**

Descriptive language Language that creates a "picture" of a person, place, or thing—often using words that appeal to the five senses: sight, hearing, touch, smell, and taste. **Example:** The bright, hot sun beat down on Earth's surface. Where once a vibrant lake cooled the skin of hippos and zebras, only thin, dry cracks remained, reaching across the land like an old man's fingers, as far as the eye could see. The smell of herds was gone, and only silence filled the space.

See also **Imagery**

Dialogue What characters say to each other. Writers use dialogue to develop characters, move the plot forward, and add interest. In most writing, dialogue is set off by quotation marks; in play scripts, however, dialogue appears without quotation marks.

Diary A book written by a person about his or her own life as it is happening. Unlike an autobiography, a diary is not usually meant to be published. It is made up of entries that are written shortly after events occur. The person writing a diary often expresses feelings and opinions about what has happened.

See also **Autobiography; Journal**

Literary Terms

Drama A kind of writing in which a plot unfolds in the words and actions of characters performed by actors.
See also **Genre; Play; Plot**

E

Essay A short piece of nonfiction, normally in prose, that discusses a single topic without claiming to do so thoroughly. Its purpose may be to inform, entertain, or persuade.
See also **Nonfiction; Photo-essay; Topic**

Exposition The rising action of a story in which characters and the problems they face are introduced.
See also **Rising action**

Expository nonfiction Writing that gives information and facts. It is usually divided into sections that give information about subtopics of a larger topic.
See also **Article; News feature; Nonfiction; Report; Textbook; Topic**

Exaggeration Figurative language that makes things seem bigger than they really are in order to create a funny image in the reader's mind. **Example:** My eyes are so big they pop out of my face when I get surprised or angry.
See also **Figurative language; Hyperbole**

F

Fable A brief fictional narrative that teaches a lesson about life. Many fables have animals instead of humans as characters. Fables often end with a short, witty statement of their lesson. **Example:** "The Tortoise and the Hare" is a famous fable in which a boastful, quick-moving hare challenges a slow-moving tortoise to a race. Because the overconfident hare takes a nap during the race, the tortoise wins. The moral of the fable is that slow and steady wins the race.
See also **Fiction; Folk tale**

Fairy tale See **Fantasy; Folk tale**

Falling action The actions and events in a plot that happen after the climax. Usually, the major problem is solved in some way, so the remaining events serve to bring the story to an end.
See also **Climax; Conflict; Plot, Rising action**

Fantasy Fiction in which imaginary worlds differ from the "real" world outside the text. Fairy tales, science fiction, and fables are examples of fantasy.
See also **Fable; Fiction**

Fiction Narrative writing about imaginary people, places, things, or events.
See also **Biographical fiction; Fable; Fantasy; Folk tale; Historical fiction; Myth; Novel; Realistic fiction; Short story**

Figurative language The use of a word or phrase to say one thing and mean another. Figurative language is especially important in literature and poetry because it gives writers a more effective way of expressing what they mean than using direct, literal language. **Example:** Upon receiving her monthly bills, Victoria complained that she was "drowning in debt."
See also **Exaggeration; Hyperbole; Idiom; Imagery; Literature; Metaphor; Personification; Poetry; Simile; Symbol**

Folk tale A short, fictional narrative shared orally rather than in writing, and thus partly changed through its retellings before being written down. Folk tales include myths, legends, fables, ghost stories, and fairy tales.
See also **Fable; Legend; Myth**

Folklore The collection of a people's beliefs, customs, rituals, spells, songs, sayings, and stories as shared mainly orally rather than in writing.
See also **Folk tale; Legend; Myth**

Functional text Writing in which the main purpose is to communicate the information people need to accomplish tasks in everyday life. **Examples:** résumés, business letters, technical manuals, and the help systems of word-processing programs.

G

Genre A type or class of literary works grouped according to form, style, and/or topic. Major genres include fictional narrative prose (such as short stories and most novels), nonfiction narrative prose (such as autobiographies, diaries, and journals), drama, poetry, and the essay.
See also **Essay; Fiction; Literature; Nonfiction; Poetry; Prose; Style; Topic**

H

Hero or **Heroine** In myths and legends, a man or woman of great courage and strength who is celebrated for his or her daring feats.
See also **Legend; Myth**

Historical fiction Fiction based on events that actually happened or on people who actually lived. It may be written from the point of view of a "real" or an imaginary character, and it usually includes invented dialogue.
See also **Fiction**

Hyperbole Figurative language that exaggerates, often to the point of being funny, to emphasize something. **Example:** When his mother asked how long he had waited for the school bus that morning, Jeremy grinned and said, "Oh, not long. Only about a million years."
See also **Exaggeration; Figurative language**

I

Idiom A phrase or expression that means something different from the word or words' dictionary meanings. Idioms cannot be translated word for word into another language because an idiom's meaning is not the same as that of the individual words that make it up. **Example:** "Mind your p's and q's" in English means to be careful, thoughtful, and behave properly.

Imagery Figurative language that communicates sensory experience. Imagery can help the reader imagine how people, places, and things look, sound, taste, smell, and feel. It can also make the reader think about emotions and ideas that commonly go with certain sensations. Because imagery appeals to the senses, it is sometimes called *sensory language*.

> *See also* **Descriptive language; Figurative language; Symbol**

Interview A discussion between two or more people in which questions are asked and answered so that the interviewer can get information. The record of such a discussion is also called an interview.

J

Jargon Specialized language used by people to describe things that are specific to their group or subject. **Example:** *Mouse* in a computer class means "part of a computer system," not "a rodent."

Journal A personal record, similar to a diary. It may include accounts of actual events, stories, poems, sketches, thoughts, essays, a collection of interesting information, or just about anything the writer wishes to include.

> *See also* **Diary**

L

Legend A very old story, usually written about a hero or heroine or to explain something in nature. Legends are mostly fiction, but some details may be true.

> *See also* **Folk tale; Hero or Heroine; Myth**

Literature Works written as prose or poetry.

> *See also* **Poetry; Prose**

M

Metaphor A type of figurative language that compares two unlike things by saying that one thing is the other thing. **Example:** Dhara says her grandfather can be a real mule when he doesn't get enough sleep.

> *See also* **Figurative language; Simile; Symbol**

Meter The patterning of language into regularly repeating units of rhythm. Language patterned in this way is called *verse*. By varying the rhythm within a meter, the writer can heighten the reader's attention to what is going on in the verse and reinforce meaning.

> *See also* **Poetry; Rhythm**

Mood The overall feeling or atmosphere a writer creates in a piece of writing.

> *See also* **Tone**

Motive The reason a character has for his or her thoughts, feelings, actions, or words. **Example:** Maria's motive for bringing cookies to her new neighbors was to learn what they were like.

> *See also* **Characterization**

Myth A fictional narrative, often a folk tale, that tells of supernatural events as a way of explaining natural events and their relation to human life. Myths commonly involve gods, goddesses, monsters, and superhuman heroes or heroines.

> *See also* **Folk tale; Hero** or **Heroine; Legend**

N

Narrative writing Writing that gives an account of a set of real or imaginary events (the story), which the writer selects and arranges in a particular order (the plot). Narrative writing includes nonfiction works such as news articles, autobiographies, and journals, as well as fictional works such as short stories, novels, and plays.

> *See also* **Autobiography; Fiction; Journal; Narrator; Nonfiction; Plot; Story**

Narrator Someone who gives an account of events. In fiction, the narrator is the teller of a story (as opposed to the real author, who invented the narrator as well as the story). Narrators differ in how much they participate in a story's events. In a first-person narrative, the narrator is the "I" telling the story. In a third-person narrative, the narrator is not directly involved in the events and refers to characters by name or as *he*, *she*, *it*, or *they*. Narrators also differ in how much they know and how much they can be trusted by the reader.

> *See also* **Character; Point of view**

News feature A nonfiction article that gives facts about real people and events.

> *See also* **Article; Expository nonfiction; Nonfiction**

Nonfiction Written works about events or things that are not imaginary; writing other than fiction.

> *See also* **Autobiography; Biography; Diary; Essay; Fiction; Journal; Personal narrative; Photo-essay; Report; Textbook**

Novel A long, fictional narrative, usually in prose. Its length enables it to have more characters, a more complicated plot, and a more fully developed setting than shorter works of fiction.

> *See also* **Character; Fiction; Plot; Prose; Setting; Short story**

O

Onomatopoeia The use of words that imitate the sounds they refer to. **Examples:** *buzz, slam, hiss*

Literary Terms

P

Personal narrative An account of a certain event or set of events in a person's life, written by that person.
    See also **Autobiography; Diary; Journal**

Personification Figurative language that describes animals, things, or ideas as having human traits. **Examples:** In the movie *Babe* and in the book *Charlotte's Web*, the animals are all personified.
    See also **Figurative language**

Persuasive writing Writing that attempts to get someone to do or agree to something by appealing to logic or emotion. Persuasive writing is used in advertisements, editorials, and political speeches.

Photo-essay A short nonfiction piece made up of photographs and captions. The photographs are as important as the words in presenting information.
    See also **Essay; Nonfiction**

Play A work of drama, especially one written to be performed on a stage. **Example:** Lorraine Hansberry's *A Raisin in the Sun* was first performed in 1959.
    See also **Drama**

Plot The pattern of events and situations in a story or play. Plot is usually divided into four main parts: *conflict* (or *problem*), *rising action* (or *exposition* or *complication*), *climax*, and *falling action* (or *resolution*).
    See also **Climax; Conflict; Drama; Falling action; Fiction; Rising action; Story**

Poetry A form of literary expression that uses line breaks for emphasis. Poems often use connotation, imagery, metaphor, symbol, allusion, repetition, and rhythm. Word patterns in poetry include rhythm or meter, and often rhyme and alliteration.
    See also **Alliteration; Connotation; Figurative language; Meter; Repetition; Rhyme; Rhythm**

Point of view The position from which the events of a story seem to be observed and told. A first-person point of view tells the story through what the narrator knows, experiences, concludes, or can find out by talking to other characters. A third-person point of view may be *omniscient*, giving the narrator unlimited knowledge of things, events, and characters, including characters' hidden thoughts and feelings. Or it may be *limited* to what one or a few characters know and experience. **Example** of First-Person Point of View: I'm really hungry right now, and I can't wait to eat my lunch. **Example** of Third-Person Limited Point of View: Olivia is really hungry right now and she wants to eat her lunch. **Example** of Third-Person Omniscient Point of View: Olivia is really hungry right now and she wants to eat her lunch. The other students are thinking about their weekend plans. The teacher is wondering how she will finish the lesson before the bell rings.
    See also **Character; Fiction; Narrator**

Propaganda A type of persuasion that twists or doesn't tell the whole truth. Types of propaganda include *glittering generalities* (using impressive words to skip past the truth), *transfers* (using appealing ideas or symbols that aren't directly related to the topic), *testimonials* (using the words of famous people), *plain folks* (showing that a product or idea has the same values as the audience), *bandwagon* (claiming that everyone else is doing it), and *name calling*.
    See also **Persuasive writing**

Prose A form of writing in which the rhythm is less regular than that of verse and more like that of ordinary speech.
    See also **Poetry; Rhythm**

Proverb A short saying that expresses a general truth. Proverbs are found in many different languages and cultures. **Example:** An apple a day keeps the doctor away.

Purpose An author's reason for writing. Most authors write to entertain, inform, or persuade. **Example:** An author's purpose in an editorial is to persuade the reader to think or do something.
    See also **Expository nonfiction; Narrative writing; Persuasive writing**

R

Realistic fiction Fiction in which detailed handling of imaginary settings, characters, and events produces a lifelike illusion of a "real" world. **Example:** Although Upton Sinclair's *The Jungle* is a work of fiction, the author's graphic, detailed descriptions of the slaughterhouse workers' daily lives led to real changes in the meatpacking industry.
    See also **Fiction**

Repetition The repeating of individual vowels and consonants, syllables, words, phrases, lines, or groups of lines. Repetition can be used because it sounds pleasant, to emphasize the words in which it occurs, or to help tie the parts of a text into one structure. It is especially important in creating the musical quality of poetry, where it can take such forms as alliteration and rhyme.
    See also **Alliteration; Poetry; Rhyme**

Report A usually short piece of nonfiction writing on a particular topic. It differs from an essay in that it normally states only facts and does not directly express the writer's opinions.
    See also **Essay; Nonfiction; Topic**

Resolution *See* **Falling action**

Rhyme The repetition of ending sounds in different words. Rhymes usually come at the end of lines of verse, but they may also occur within a line. **Examples:** *look, brook, shook*
    See also **Poetry; Repetition; Rhyme scheme**

Rhyme scheme The pattern of rhymed line endings in a work of poetry or a stanza. It can be represented by giving a certain letter of the alphabet to each line ending on the same rhyme. **Example:** Because the end word of every other line rhymes in the following poem, the rhyme scheme is *abab*:

Winter night falls quick (a)
The pink sky gone, blackness overhead (b)
Looks like the snow will stick (a)
Down the street and up the hill I tread (b)
     See also **Poetry; Rhyme; Stanza**

Rhythm The natural rise and fall, or "beat," of language. Rhythm is present in all language, including speech and prose, but it is most obvious in poetry.
     See also **Meter; Poetry; Prose**

Rising action The part of a plot that presents actions or events that lead to the climax.
     See also **Climax; Conflict; Exposition; Falling action; Plot**

<h2 style="text-align:center"><u>S</u></h2>

Setting The time and place in which the events of a story occur.

Short story A brief, fictional narrative. Like the novel, it organizes the action, thought, and dialogue of its characters into a plot. But it tends to focus on fewer characters and to center on a single event.
     See also **Character; Fiction; Novel; Plot; Story**

Simile A type of figurative language that compares two unlike things by using a word or phrase such as *like*, *as*, *than*, *similar to*, *resembles*, or *seems*. **Examples:** The tall, slim man had arms as willowy as a tree's branches. The woman's temper is like an unpredictable volcano.
     See also **Figurative language; Metaphor**

Song lyrics Words meant to be sung. Lyrics have been created for many types of songs, including love songs, religious songs, work songs, sea chanties, and children's game songs. Lyrics for many songs were shared orally for generations before being written down. Not all song lyrics are lyrical like poems; some are the words to songs that tell a story. Not all poems called songs were written to be sung.
     See also **Folk literature; Poetry**

Speech A message on a specific topic, spoken before an audience; also, spoken (not written) language.

Stanza A group of lines that forms a section of a poem and has the same pattern (including line lengths, meter, and usually rhyme scheme) as other sections of the same poem. In printed poems, stanzas are separated from each other by a space.
     See also **Meter; Poetry; Rhyme scheme**

Story A series of events (actual or imaginary) that can be selected and arranged in a certain order to form a narrative or dramatic plot. It is the raw material from which the finished plot is built. Although there are technical differences, the word *story* is sometimes used in place of *narrative*.
     See also **Drama; Plot**

Style The way a writer uses language to express the feelings or thoughts he or she wants to convey. Just as no two people are alike, no two styles are exactly alike. A writer's style results from his or her choices of vocabulary, sentence structure and variety, imagery, figurative language, rhythm, repetition, and other resources.
     See also **Figurative language; Genre; Imagery; Repetition; Rhythm**

Symbol A word or phrase that serves as an image of some person, place, thing, or action but that also calls to mind some other, usually broader, idea or range of ideas. **Example:** An author might describe doves flying high in the sky to symbolize peace.
     See also **Figurative language; Imagery**

<h2 style="text-align:center"><u>T</u></h2>

Textbook A book prepared for use in schools for the study of a subject.

Theme The underlying message or main idea of a piece of writing. It expresses a broader meaning than the topic of the piece.
     See also **Topic**

Tone A writer's or speaker's attitude toward his or her topic or audience or toward him- or herself. A writer's tone may be positive, negative, or neutral. The words the writer chooses, the sentence structure, and the overall pattern of words convey the intended tone.
     See also **Connotation; Figurative language; Literature; Mood; Rhythm; Topic**

Topic What or who is being discussed in a piece of writing; the subject of the piece.
     See also **Theme**

Index of Skills

LITERARY ANALYSIS

READING

Critical Thinking

Independent Reading

Reading Fluency

Reading Strategies

VOCABULARY

Academic Vocabulary

Key Vocabulary

Word Consciousness

Word-Learning Strategies

LANGUAGE & GRAMMAR

Language Functions

Grammar

see also Writing & Grammar

adjectives 206, 207, 225, 228, 229, 247, 417
  comparative 228, 229, 247
  demonstrative 225
  possessive 417
  predicate 225
adverbs 250, 251, 271
capitalization 8, 44
clauses 540
  dependent 515, 540, 559
  independent 518, 540, 559
conjunctions 518, 537, 540, 559
modifiers *see* adjectives, adverbs
nouns 70, 71, 85, 152, 153, 171, 356, 357, 450, 489
  plural 70, 71, 85
  possessive 398, 399, 417
  precise 85
  singular 70, 71
phrases 450, 451, 467, 515
  participial 489
  prepositional 450, 451, 467
predicates 88, 89, 103, 356, 376, 500, 501, 515
prepositions 428, 429, 447, 450, 451
pronouns 132, 133, 149, 152, 153, 171, 376, 377, 395, 490
  object 373, 376, 377, 395, 450, 451, 467
  plural 373, 376, 377, 395, 467
  singular 373, 376, 377, 395, 467
  subject 132, 133, 149, 152, 153, 171, 373, 376, 377, 395
punctuation
  commas 518
  exclamation points 59
  periods 8, 44, 59
  question marks 59
  quotation marks 102
sentence
  combining 515, 537
  command 44, 45, 59
  complete 88, 89, 103, 500, 501, 515
  complex 540, 541, 559
  compound 518, 519
  exclamation 59
  fragment 515, 559
  question 26, 27, 41, 59
  run-on 537
  simple 500, 541

  statement 8, 9, 23, 26, 27, 41, 44, 45, 59, 500
spelling
  final consonant 70, 85
  plurals 70, 71, 85
subjects 88, 89, 103, 106, 107, 356, 376, 377, 500, 501, 515, 540
subject-verb agreement 106, 107, 121
verbs 88, 106, 107, 470, 471, 540
  action 88, 121, 356
  be 8, 9, 106, 107, 302, 303, 321
  do 106, 107
  have 106, 107, 302, 303, 321
  helping 174, 175, 193
  irregular 324, 325, 345, 470
  is 8, 9, 106
  main 174
  past participle 470, 471
  past tense 282, 283, 299, 302, 303, 321, 324, 325, 345
  present participle 470, 471
  present tense 282, 283, 299, 302, 303, 321, 324, 325, 345
  regular 321, 345, 470

Listening & Speaking

Activities

conversation 131, 133, 149
discussion 22, 37, 39, 61, 67, 81, 84, 86, 91, 101, 120, 123, 133, 168, 170, 189, 191, 192, 195, 223, 224, 244, 245, 269, 273, 297, 301, 303, 317, 321, 341, 354, 372, 396, 399, 415, 417, 419, 426, 446, 464, 469, 471, 485, 486, 487, 491, 512, 513, 534, 535, 537, 556, 561
dramatize 195, 245, 372, 535
give precise directions 57, 513
informational presentation 58, 148, 246, 296, 319, 343, 465, 536
interview 171, 247, 298, 317, 415, 501
narrative presentation 393
persuasive presentation 488
read aloud 3, 5, 19, 55, 65, 67, 99, 117, 127, 129, 145, 167, 189, 191, 200, 201, 203, 221, 243, 244, 267, 268, 269, 277, 295, 317, 341, 351, 353, 369, 391, 413, 423, 425, 443, 444, 463, 485, 495, 497, 533, 555

  recite 514
retell a story 169, 539, 541, 557, 558
role-play 45, 193, 208, 247, 270, 273, 281, 298, 317, 347, 357, 399, 489, 515
tell about a story 271

Strategies

listen for a purpose 3, 7, 25, 27, 43, 65, 69, 87, 101, 102, 103, 105, 120, 131, 151, 173, 200, 205, 227, 249, 277, 281, 298, 301, 323, 351, 355, 357, 375, 397, 399, 444, 449, 469, 487, 488, 499, 513, 515, 539, 541
organize ideas effectively 58, 148, 246, 319, 344, 465
respond to audience questions 147, 246
speak clearly 39, 40, 147, 148, 245, 270, 298, 319, 372, 488, 519
  appropriate language 501
  body language 23, 245, 514
  eye contact 40, 298, 488, 519
  facial expressions 372, 541, 559
  gestures 319, 541, 559
  intonation 298, 514, 519, 541
  nonverbal cues 23, 40, 245, 298, 319, 372, 488, 514, 541, 559
  pace 58, 298, 488, 514
  standard grammatical forms 89
  volume 58, 147, 270, 372, 514, 519

Viewing & Representing

Viewing

analyze visuals
  charts 35, 460
  diagram 458
  graphs 98
  maps 32, 140, 158, 366
critical viewing 0, 62, 196, 307, 308, 309, 311, 312, 314, 348, 381, 383, 384, 387, 389, 492
  character 308, 309, 384
  design 307, 312, 381, 389
  mood 387
  setting 311, 383

Representing

create visuals 61, 123, 195, 347, 373, 419, 491
  brochure 123

charts 58, 120, 536
drawing 195, 273, 465
graph 40
interpretation 347
maps 61, 536
model 148
pictures 148, 319, 393, 536
poster 229, 445
slide show 147

MEDIA & TECHNOLOGY

Media

analyze media 487
film 246
news media 512
TV commercials 269
compare media 170, 272
create media products
movie poster 229
slide show 147
use media for research 58, 169, 170
use media to learn 297

Technology

digital library 1, 6, 24, 42, 63, 68, 86, 104, 125, 130, 150, 172, 197, 204, 226, 248, 275, 280, 300, 322, 349, 354, 374, 396, 421, 426, 448, 468, 493, 498, 516, 538
use the Internet for research 40, 58, 102, 119, 120, 147, 169, 170, 191, 223, 246, 269, 296, 297, 319, 344, 371, 393, 415, 445, 465

RESEARCH & STUDY SKILLS

Projects

analyze media 487
discover tools of the past 319
explore TV commercials 269
explore ancient Greek drama 536
research constitutional rights 415
research earthquakes 192
research energy 465
research floods 119
research freedom seekers 393

research Greek myths 557
research Hurricane Katrina 169
research hydroelectric power 120
research plate tectonics 148
research population change 40
research pyramids 343
research stories about stars 445
research a time period 223
research the Underground Railroad 371
research water use 102
report on a volcano 147
retell a personal narrative 169
tell about traditions 58
write a how-to article 191
write about China 83

Skills

almanac 119
alphabetical order 57, 101, 192
choose a topic 58, 536
collect data 40
collect facts 147, 246, 393
credit sources 371
dictionary 21, 39, 57, 109, 202, 223, 269, 415, 424, 451, 465, 487
evaluate information 147
frame questions 148
generate questions 269
glossary 192
graphic organizers 40, 58, 120
Internet 40, 58, 102, 119, 120, 169, 191, 246, 269, 319, 343, 371, 393, 415, 445, 465
index 192
library/reference resources 83, 119, 120, 192, 371
note cards 83
note taking 102, 120, 148, 319, 371
organize information 58, 120, 147, 148, 191, 465
present information 40, 58, 102, 119, 147, 148, 191, 192, 223, 246, 269, 297, 319, 343, 393, 445, 465, 487, 536, 557
research 40, 58, 83, 102, 119, 120, 147, 148, 169, 170, 191, 192, 223, 246, 269, 297, 319, 343, 344, 371, 393, 415, 445, 465, 487, 488, 491, 536, 557
table of contents 148, 536
thesaurus 101
use multiple sources 120

CAREER AND LIFE SKILLS

give directions to a location 57
learn about careers 275, 298, 323
share safety tips 175, 191
understand constitutional rights 415

INTERDISCIPLINARY STUDIES

Art

artistic expression 498, 513
Egyptian art 344
chart 58, 120

Connect Across the Curriculum

20–23, 38–41, 56–59, 82–85, 100–103, 118–121, 146–149, 168–171, 190–193, 222–225, 244–247, 268–271, 296–299, 318–321, 342–345, 370–373, 392–395, 414–417, 444–447, 464–467, 486–489, 512–515, 534–537, 556–559

Content Library

1, 61, 63, 123, 125, 195, 197, 273, 275, 347, 349, 419, 421, 491, 493, 561

Drama

ancient Greek drama 536
costumes 516
dramatize a song 372
perform a play 270
present a story 535

Health and Science

artificial light pollution 468, 488
constellations 426
early flying machines 538
earthquakes 172, 192
famous astronomers 448
hurricanes 150, 169, 170
hydroelectric power 120
plate tectonics 148
science articles 136, 454
solar energy 465
volcanoes 120, 147
water use 102, 104

WRITING

Acknowledgments, continued from page ii

Blue Cloud Quarterly: "There Is No Word for Goodbye" from THERE IS NO WORD FOR GOODBYE by Mary Tall Mountain. Copyright © 1981 by Mary Tall Mountain. Published by Blue Cloud Quarterly, Marvin, South Dakota. Used by permission. A special thank you to The American Indian Resource Center at the County of Los Angeles Public Library in Huntington Park.

California State University Bakersfield: From "California Odyssey: The 1930's Migration to the Southern San Joaquin Valley" an oral history interview of Ethel Oleta Wever Belezzuoli by Stacey Jagels. Copyright © 1981 by California State University Bakersfield. Used by permission.

The Christian Science Monitor: Adapted from "Old Music Finds New Voices" by Kris Axtman. Reproduced with permission from January 9, 2002 issue of The Christian Science Monitor (www.csmonitor.com). © 2002 The Christian Science Monitor. All rights reserved.

Farrar, Straus and Giroux, LLC: Text and illustrations from EARTHQUAKE by Milly Lee, illustrated by Yangsook Choi. Text copyright © 2001 by Milly Lee. Illustrations copyright © 2001 by Yangsook Choi. Reprinted by permissions of Farrar, Straus and Giroux, LLC.

Houghton Mifflin Harcourt Publishing Company: FRANKENSTEIN MAKES A SANDWICH, copyright © 2006 by Adam Rex, reproduced by permission of Houghton Mifflin Harcourt Publishing Company.

Intercultural Press, a division of Nicholas Brealey Publishing: Adapted from KIDS LIKE ME: VOICES OF THE IMMIGRANT EXPERIENCE by Judith M. Blohm and Terri Lapinsky. Copyright © 2006 by Judith M. Blohm and Terri Lapinsky. Reprinted by permission of Intercultural Press, A Nicholas Brealey Publishing Company, Boston, MA.

Penguin Group (USA), Inc.: TEXT: "The Earth Under Sky Bear's Feet", "Sky Bear", "The Scattered Stars", "The Seven Mateinuu", from THE EARTH UNDER SKY BEAR'S FEET: NATIVE AMERICAN POEMS OF THE LAND by Joseph Bruchac, copyright © 1995 by Joseph Bruchac. Used by permission of Philomel Books, A Division of Penguin Young Readers Group, A Member of Penguin Group (USA) Inc., 345 Hudson Street, New York, NY 10014. All rights reserved. ILLUSTRATIONS: From THE EARTH UNDER BIG SKY BEAR'S FEET: NATIVE AMERICAN POEMS OF THE LAND by Joseph Bruchac, illustrated by Thomas Locker, copyright © 1995 by Thomas Locker, illustrations. Used by permission of Philomel Books, A Division of Penguin Young Reader's Group, A Member of Penguin Group (USA) Inc., 345 Hudson Street, NY 10014. All rights reserved.

Rosen Publishing Group, Inc.: FRANKENSTEIN MEETS THE WOLF MAN by Greg Roza, copyright © 2007 by The Rosen Publishing Group, 29 East 21st Street, New York, NY, 10010, and reprinted with permission.

Scholastic, Inc.: From WINGS by Christopher Myers. Scholastic Inc./Scholastic Press. Copyright © 2000 by Christopher Myers. Reprinted by permission.

Simon & Schuster: "When I Grow Up" by Janet S. Wong. Reprinted with the permission of Margaret K. McElderry Books, an imprint of Simon & Schuster Children's Publishing Division, from A SUITCASE OF SEAWEED AND OTHER POEMS by Janet S. Wong. Copyright © 1996 by Janet S. Wong. All rights reserved.

The Tattoo: "Caught in the Rain" from "Hurricane Journal" by Samantha Perez (www.ReadTheTattoo.com). Copyright © 2005 by The Tattoo. Reprinted with the permission of The Tattoo international teen newspaper.

Ulloa Productions/Vocal Power Productions: "Cuando Canto/When I Sing" by Jaunita Ulloa from JUANITA: MUJERES Y MARIACHI. Copyright © Ulloa Productions. All rights Reserved. Used by permission.

Photographs

2 (b) Mistral images/Index Stock. **3** (b) Stephanie Maze/National Geographic Image Collection. (t) Palemale.com. **5** (t) Bettmann/Corbis. (b) Bob Jacobson/Corbis. **6** (b) Ames L. Stanfield/National Geographic Image Collection. **7** (l) Neil Emmerson/Robert Harding World/Corbis. **8** (b) Wolfgang Kaehler, www.wkaehlerphoto.com. **10** (bc) INSADCO Photography/Alamy Images. (bl) Brian Drouin/National Geographic Image Collection. (mc) Liz Garza Williams. (ml) David Mcnew/Getty Images. (mr) Norbert Rosing/National Geographic Image Collection. (tc) Michael Heinsen/Getty Images. (tl) Michael Durham/Getty Images. (tr) Peter Mason/Getty Images. **17** (c) Carmen Agra Deedy. **18** (bg) sozaijiten/Datacraft/age fotostock. **24** (b) Tom McCarthy/Photo Network/Alamy Images. **25** (t) Danita Delimont/Alamy Images. (m) Gabe Palmer/Corbis. (b) Virgo Productions/zefa/Corbis. **26** (b) Michael Newman/PhotoEdit. **27** (b) Tim Hall/Getty Images. **28** (bc) Jon Feingersh/Image Bank/Getty Images. (bl) James Sugar/National Geographic Image Collection. (mc) Lars Klove/Getty Images. (ml) Ted Spiegel/National Geographic Image Collection. (mr) Liz Garza Williams. (tc) Randy Faris/Corbis. (tl) Ace Stock Limited/Alamy Images. (tr) Drew Hallowell/Getty Images. **35** (b) Aaron Graubart/The Image Bank. **38** (c) Borderlands/Alamy Images. **42** (b) Robert Holmes/Corbis. (bg) Jose Fuste/Raga/Corbis. **43** (b) Richard T. Nowitz/Corbis. **44** (c) Jeff Greenberg/PhotoEdit. **45** (b) Phil Schermeister/Corbis. **46** (bc) Mark Adams/Getty Images. (bl) Mitchell Funk/Getty Images. (mc) Adam Pretty/Getty Images. (ml) Larry Dale Gordon/Image Bank/Getty Images. (mr) Jeff Pullen/The Bridgeman Art Library/Getty Images. (tc) Rob Reichenfeld/Getty Images. (tl) Sam Kittner/National Geographic Image Collection. (tr) Photodisc/Getty Images. **47** (b) Lauren Victoria Burke/AP Images. **48–49** (LesOp) Jose Fuste Raga/Corbis. **50** (b) John Dominis/Time Life Pictures/Getty Images. (c) Lauren Victoria Burke/AP Images. **51** (c) Sandy Felsenthal/Corbis. **52** (c) Jeff Greenberg/The Image Works. **53** (l) Nik Wheeler/Corbis. **54** (c) Bob Krist/Corbis. **56** (r) Sandy Felsenthal/Corbis. **58** (b) Matthew Wakem/Aurora. **65** (r) Taylor S. Kennedy/National Geographic Image Collection. **67** (t) Richard Cummins/Corbis. (b) Novastock/Jupiter Images. **68** (b) Paul Conklin/PhotoEdit. **72** (bc) Image Source Black/Getty Images. (bl) Robert Frerck/Getty Images. (mc) Lwa–Dann Tardif/Corbis. (ml)

Joel Sartore/National Geographic Image Collection. (mr) Todd Gipstein/National Geographic Image Collection. (tc) David Madison/Getty Images. (tl) Richard Norwitz/National Geographic Image Collection. (tr) Zigy Kaluzny/Getty Images. **76** (b) FoodShapes/PunchStock. **83** (b) Angelo Cavalli/Getty Images. **84** (b) Tom Vezo/Peter Arnold, Inc. **86** (b) Digital Stock/Corbis. (bg) Stephen Frink/Photographer's Choice/Getty Images. **87** (bg) imagewerks/Getty Images. **88** (b) Michael Fay/National Geographic Image Collection. **90** (bc) Nicole Duplaix/National Geographic Image Collection. (bl) Ira Block/National Geographic Image Collection. (mc) Brian Drouin/National Geographic Image Collection. (ml) Roy Toft/National Geographic Image Collection. (mr) Image Source Black/Getty Images. (tc) Pritt Vesilind/National Geographic Image Collection. (tl) Steve Wisbauer/Getty Images. (tr) Paul Damien/National Geographic Image Collection. **92** (l) Robert Harding World/Getty Images. **92–93** (LesOp) Brian Hagiwara/Brand X/Corbis. **94** (bg) Brian Hagiwara/Brand X/Corbis. (bl) Rick Doyle/Corbis. (br) Robert Harding World Imagery/Getty Images. **94–95** (c) Corbis. **95** (bg) Brian Hagiwara/Brand X/Corbis. (br) Stockbyte. **96** (bg) Brian Hagiwara/Brand X/Corbis. (bl) Bill Barksdale. (tr) Reed Kaestner/Corbis. **97** (bg) Brian Hagiwara/Brand X/Corbis. (bl) Lester Lefkowitz/Stone. **98** (bg) Brian Hagiwara/Brand X/Corbis. (bl) Kaml Kishore/Reuters/Corbis. (tr) Steven S. Miric/SuperStock. **100** (b) Lester Lefkowitz/Stone/Getty Images. **102** (c) BlueMoon Stock/Alamy Images. **104** (b) C Productions/The Image Bank/Getty Images. (bg) Antonio Mo/Taxi/Getty Images. **105** (c) Robert Harding Picture Library/Alamy Images. **106** (b) Photo by Brent Stirton/Exclusive by Getty Images. **107** (b) Getty Images/MedioImages. **108** (bc) Christina Kennedy/PhotoEdit. (bl) Nicholas Prior/Getty Images. (mc) Michael S. Yamashita/National GeographicImage Collection. (ml) Sarah Leen/National Geographic Image Collection. (mr) Bill Hatcher/National Geographic/Getty Images. (tc) Sheer Photo, Inc/Getty Images. (tl) Derek Croucher/Getty Images. (tr) Skip Brown/National Geographic Image Collection. **110–111** (LesOp) Ryan Fox/Lonely Planet Images. **112** (bg) Panoramic Stock Images. **113** (b) David Mendelson/Masterfile. **114** (b) Richard Gross/Corbis. **115** (b) Matthew Mcvay/Corbis. 116 (b) Bruce Forster/Stone. **119** (b) Joerg Boethling/Peter Arnold, Inc. **120** (c) Harald Sund. **124** (UnitOp) Martin Bernetti/AFP/NewsCom. **127** (r) Bettmann/Corbis. **129** (t) HMS Group Inc./Index Stock. (b) Mario Tama/Getty Images. **130** (b) Steve Raymer/National Geographic Image Collection. (bg) Martin Rietze/Agency Westend 61/Alamy Images. **131** (c) Schafer & Hill/Stone/Getty Images. **132** (b) Martin Gray/NGS Image Collection. **133** (b) Karen Kasmauski/National Geographic Image Collection. **134** (bc) Pixtal/PunchStock. (bl) Martin Rietze/Westend61/Jupiterimages. (mc) Catherine Karnow/National Geographic Image Collection. (ml) Chris Johns/National Geographic Image Collection. (mr) Frank Lukasseck/Corbis. (tl) Brian Gordon Green/National Geographic Image Collection. (tr) Jose Luis Pelaez Inc./Blend Images/Getty Images. (tr) Carsten Peter/National Geographic Image Collection. **136–137** (LesOp) LOOK Die Bildagentur der Fotografen GmbH/Alamy.

407 (l) Colin Braley/Reuters Photo Archive/ NewsCom. (r) Bettmann/Corbis. **408** (t) David Turnley/Corbis. **409** (b) Jacques Langevin/ Corbis Sygma. **410** (l) Mary Evans/The Womens Library/The Image Works. (r) Bettmann/Corbis. **411** (b) Francis Miller/ Stringer/Time Life Pictures. **412** (b) Robert Patrick/Corbis Sygma. **414** (b) Karim Saheb/ AFP/Getty Images. **416** (c) Arif Ali/AFP/Getty Images. **420** (UnitOp) Larry Landolfi/Photo Researchers, Inc. **423** (t) Compliments of Cape Kennedy Space Center Visitor Complex. (b) Compliments of NASA Orbital Debris Program Office. **425** (t) NASA, ESA and A. Nota (STScI/ ESA). (b) Stocktrek/Corbis. **426** (b) Larry Landolfi/Photo Researchers, Inc. (bg) JTB Photo Communications, Inc./Alamy Images. **427** (bl) Motofish Images/Corbis. (bg) Robert Llewellyn/Corbis. **428** (b) Photodisc/Alamy Images. **429** (b) Chris Strong/Photonica/Getty Images. **430** (bc) Tyrone Turner/National Geographic Image Collection. (bl) David Young– Wolff/Photographer's Choice/Getty Images. (mc) Raymond Gehman/National Geographic Image Collection. (ml) TNT Magazine/Alamy Images. (mr) Image Source Pink/Getty Images. (tc) Bill Hatcher/National Geographic Image Collection. (tl) Camille Tokerud/Getty Images. (tr) Robert Ross/Gallo Images ROOTS RF Collection/Getty Images. **432–433** (LesOp) StockTrek/PhotoDisc. **442** (b) Michael Greenlar/The Image Works. **445** (b) Elvele Images/Alamy Images. **447** (b) Digital Vision/ Getty Images. **448** (b) Hulton Archive/Getty Images. (bg) NASA/JPL-Caltech/Corbis. **449** (b) NASA Jet Propulsion Laboratory/ (NASA-JPL). (bg) Jason Reed/PhotoDisc/Getty Images. **450** (b) Trip/Alamy Images. **452** (bc) Jozsef Szentpeteri/National Geographic Image Collection. (bl) AFP/Getty Images. (mc) Comstock Premium/Jupiterimages/Alamy Images. (ml) Peter Cade/Getty Images. (mr) W.E. Garrett/National Geographic Image Collection. (tc) Solar system. (tl) Barry Tessman/National Geographic Image Collection. (tr) NASA. **454–455** (LesOp) Roger Ressmeyer/Corbis. **456** (bg) Steve Cole/ Photographer's Choice. **457** (b) NASA/JPL– Caltech/Corbis. **458** (t) Panoramic Images. **459** (bg) Roger Ressmeyer/Corbis. **461** (bg) Credit: NASA and A. Riess (STScI). **465** (b) Malcolm Schuyl/Peter Arnold, Inc. **468** (b) Owaki/Kulla/Corbis. (bg) Robert Llewellyn/ Corbis. **469** (b) Dennis Scott/Corbis. (bg) Tyrone Turner/National Geographic/Getty Images. **470** (b) Roaring Lion Image Research LLC. **472** (bc) Saeed Khan/AFP/Getty Images. (bl) Karen Kasmauski/National Geographic Image Collection. (mc) Norbert Rosing/National Geographic Image Collection. (ml) Skip Brown/ National Geographic Image Collection. (mr) Digital Vision/Alamy Images. (tc) Raymond Gehman/National Geographic Image Collection. (tl) Pixland/Corbis. (tr) Raymond Gehman/ National Geographic Image Collection. **474–475** (LesOp) NASA Goddard Space Flight Center (NASA–GSFC). **477** (l, r) Todd Carlson. **479** (bg) Creatas Images. **480–481** (b) Mark Thiessen, NGS Staff Photographer. **482** (b) iconsight/Alamy. **483** (c) Sharon Guynup. **484** (c) Brad Mischler Photography. **486** (c) Getty Images/David Lees. **488** (b) MedioImages/Corbis. **494** (c) Robert J. Lang. **495** (t) Time Life Pictures/Getty Images. (b) 2003 City of Philadelphia Mural Arts Program/ Donald Gensler. Photo by Jack Ramsdale. The Mural Arts Program (MAP) is the nation's largest mural program. Since 1984, MAP has created over 2,700 murals and works of public art, which are now part of Philadelphia's civic landscape and a source of inspiration to the thousands of residents and visitors who encounter them, earning Philadelphia international recognition as the "City of Murals." MAP engages over 100 communities each year in the transformation of neighborhoods through the mural-making process. MAP's award-winning, free art education programs annually serve over 3,000 youth at sites throughout the city and at-risk teens through education outreach programs. MAP also serves adult offenders in local prisons and rehabilitation centers, using the restorative power of art to break the cycle of crime and violence in our communities. **497** (t) Drew Kelley Photography/zefa/Corbis. (b) Muntz/ Taxi/Getty Images. **498** (b) Paul Spinelli/ Getty Images. (bg) Glowimages/Getty Images. **499** (tl) The Bridgeman Art Library International. **500** (b) Barry Winiker/Index Stock Imagery. **502** (bc) Image Source Black/ Getty Images. (bl) Brooke Slezak/Getty Images. (mc) Getty Images. (ml) Getty Images. (mr) Walter Hodges/Getty Images. (tc) Amy White & Al Petteway/National Geographic Image Collection. (tl) Bill Frymire/Alamy Images. (tr) Tui De Roy/Getty Images. **504–505** (LesOp) AP Photo/Eric Gay. **506** (t) www .mariachimusic.com. **506–507** (bg) Don Klumpp/Iconica. **507** (r) AP Photo/The Houston Chronicle, Melissa Phillip. **508** (l) AP Photo/David Quinn. **508–509** (bg) Don Klumpp/Iconica. **509** (t) AP Photo/Jeff Geissler. **510** (b) Vocal Power Productions. (bg) Stuart Westmorland/Corbis. **513** (b) Getty Images/National Geographic Creative. **514** (b) image100/Alamy Images. **516** (b) Ernst Haas/ Ernst Haas/Getty Images. (bg) PictureNet/ Corbis. **517** (t) Dean Conger/Corbis. **518** (c) age fotostock/SuperStock. **520** (bc) Michael Newman/PhotoEdit. (bl) Bilderlounge/Tips RF/ Jupiterimages. (mc) Tim Pannell/Corbis. (ml) Raul Touzon/National Geographic Image Collection. (mr) Cro Magnon/Alamy. (tc) Bruce Dale/National Geographic Image Collection. (tl) Jupiterimages/Creatas/Alamy Images. (tr) Cathy Melloan/PhotoEdit. **522** (l) Dmitri Kessel/Time Life Pictures/Getty Images. **522– 523** (LesOp) J.D. Heaton/AGE Fotostock. **524** (l) David Samuel Robbins/Photographer's Choice. (t) Dmitri Kessel/Stringer/Time Life Pictures. **525** (bg) Hilarie Kavanagh/Stone. **526–527** (r) David Samuel Robbins/ Photographer's Choice. **528** (b) Eric Meola/ Image Bank. **529** (b) Kevin R. Morris/Corbis. **530** (t) Gavin Hellier/Robert Harding World Imagery. **531** (b) Mike Powell/Stone. (cr) Press Association Incorporated. **532** (bg) Jeff Garner/Southern Illinois University at Carbondale. **535** (b) Felipe Goifman/Peter Arnold, Inc. **536** (t) Lanny Ziering/Brand X/ Corbis. **538** (b) Imagno/Getty Images. **538– 539** (bg) Hiroshi Higuchi/Photographer's Choice/Getty Images. **539** (c) flashfilm/Stone/ Getty Images. **540** (c) Skip Brown/National Geographic Image Collection. **542** (bc) Tomasz Tomaszewski/National Geographic Image Collection. (bl) Phil Cawley/Alamy. (mc) Liz Garza Williams. (ml) Ed Bock/Corbis. (mr) Tim Pannell/Corbis. (tc) Rich Reid/National Geographic Image Collection. (tl) Randy Faris/ Corbis. (tr) Jason Edwards/National Geographic Image Collection. **548** (c) Johnny Thompson. **551** (t) Scholastic Inc. **552–554** ("Icarus and Daedalus") Johnny Thompson. **557** (b) Todd Gipstein/National Geographic Image Collection. **559** (b) Ron Brown/SuperStock.

Fine Art

xxiv *Tia's Kitchen*, 2003, Patssi Valdez. Acrylic on canvas, courtesy of Patricia Correia Gallery, Santa Monica, California. **62** *The Last Salmon Run* (detail), 1990, Alfredo Arreguin, private collection. **196** *Untitled*, 1982, Jerry Uelsmann, photograph. **307** *Extended Family*, 2006, Jimoh Buraimoh. Beads on board, Via Mundi Gallery, Atlanta, Georgia. **308** *African Hunter*, 2002, Emmanuel Yeboa. Oils and batik on calico, courtesy of Novica, Los Angeles. **309** *Through the Window*, 1992, Tilly Willis, Oil on canvas, private collection/ The Bridgeman Art Library. **311** *African Sunset*, 2005, Angel Ferreira. Oil on canvas, collection of the artist. **312** Nigerian Egungun costume, Yoruba Culture, courtesy of Hamill Gallery, Boston. **313** Nigerian divination tray, Yoruba culture, courtesy of Hamill Gallery, Boston. **314** *Father and Son*, 1989, Paul Nzalamba. Batik, collection of the artist, courtesy of Nzalamba Art Works, Los Angeles. **348** *Free*, 2007, Elizabeth Rosen. Mixed media, courtesy of Morgan Gaynin Inc., New York. **364–365** *The Underground Railroad Aids the Runaway Slave*, John Davies (20th Century)/Superstock. **380–381** *Butterfly*, 1978, Tamas Galambos. Oil on canvas, © private collection/Bridgeman Art Library/Superstock. **383** *Home*, 2006, Elizabeth Rosen. Acrylic on wood, collection of the artist, courtesy of Morgan Gaynin Inc., New York. **384** *Madre Protectora II*, 2007, Felix Berroa. Acrylic and oil on canvas, collection of the artist, courtesy of Hummingbird Lane Art Gallery, Dahlonega, Georgia. **387** *Journey*, 2000, Rafael Lopez. Acrylic on canvas, collection of the artist. **389** *Vegetation*, 1978, Tamas Galambos, © private collection/Bridgeman Art Library. **492** *Spirit of Harlem*, 2005, Louis Delsarte. Glass mosaic, North Fork Bank, New York, New York. **499** *Vahine No Te Tiara (Woman with a Flower)*, 1891, Paul Gaugin (1848–1903) Oil on canvas, Ny Carlsberg Glypotek, Denmark/ Bridgeman Art Library.

Illustrations

12–17 ("Growing Together") David Diaz. **30–36** ("Kids Like Me" collage illustrations) Jane Sterrett. **32** (world map) Mapping Specialists. **74–80** ("The Secret Water") Jean and Mou–sien Tseng. **87** ("Watery Facts") Walt Curlee. **136** (how volcanoes are formed) Precision Graphics. **139** (how volcanoes are formed) Precision Graphics. **205** (spooky house) Daniele Montella. **210–219** ("Frankenstein") Craig Phillips. **213b** (Arctic Circle locator map) Mapping Specialists. **227** ("Monster Ball" poster) Tim Gabor. **254–266** ("Mr. Monster") Keith Graves. **316** (girl in woods) Amanda Hall. **360–361** (slaves escaping at sunset) Janice Northcutt Huse. **362** (Josiah Henson portrait) Janice Northcutt Huse. **367** (people hiding in basement/Underground Railroad) Janice Northcutt Huse. **411** (U.S. locator globe) Mapping Specialists. **462** (astronomer) Igor Oleynikov. **499** (people in museum) Steve Bjorkman. **546–548** (feathers only) Gail Armstrong. **551** (feathers) Gail Armstrong. **552–554** ("Icarus and Daedalus") Gail Armstrong.

California English–Language Arts Content Standards

Unit 1   Finding Your Own Place

Unit Launch

2–3	**Focus on Genre: Organization of Ideas (Comparison and Contrast)**	• **Reading 2.1** Identify structural patterns found in informational text (e.g., compare and contrast, cause and effect, sequential or chronological order, proposition and support) to strengthen comprehension.
4–5	**Focus on Vocabulary: Use Context Clues for Multiple-Meaning Words**	• **Reading 1.4** Use knowledge of antonyms, synonyms, homophones, and homographs to determine the meanings of words. • **Reading 1.6** Use sentence and word context to find the meaning of unknown words. • **Reading 1.7** Use a dictionary to learn the meaning and other features of unknown words. • **Reading 1.6** Distinguish and interpret words with multiple meanings.

Selection 1   Growing Together

6	**Connect**	• **Listening and Speaking 1.2** Connect and relate prior experiences, insights, and ideas to those of a speaker. • **Reading 2.2** Use appropriate strategies when reading for different purposes (e.g., full comprehension, location of information, personal enjoyment).
7–9	**Language & Grammar: Express Ideas and Feelings**	• **Listening and Speaking 1.0** Students listen critically and respond appropriately to oral communication. They speak in a manner that guides the listener to understand important ideas by using proper phrasing, pitch, and modulation. • **Listening and Speaking 1.9** Read prose and poetry aloud with fluency, rhythm, and pace, using appropriate intonation and vocal patterns to emphasize important passages of the text being read. • **Listening and Speaking 2.4** Recite brief poems (i.e., two or three stanzas), soliloquies, or dramatic dialogues, using clear diction, tempo, volume, and phrasing.
	Use Statements with *Am, Is, Are*	• **Written and Oral English Language Conventions 1.1** Understand and be able to use complete and correct declarative, interrogative, imperative, and exclamatory sentences in writing and speaking. • **Written and Oral English Language Conventions 1.3** Identify and use regular and irregular verbs, adverbs, prepositions, and coordinating conjunctions in writing and speaking.
10	**Key Vocabulary**	• Learn meaning and pronunciation for vocabulary words central to the understanding and discussion of the selection. • **Reading 1.7** Use a dictionary to learn the meaning and other features of unknown words.
11	**Reading Strategy: Plan Your Reading**	• **Reading 2.4** Recall major points in the text and make and modify predictions about forthcoming information. • **Reading 2.2** Use appropriate strategies when reading for different purposes (e.g., full comprehension, location of information, personal enjoyment). • **Reading 2.3** Make and confirm predictions about text by using prior knowledge and ideas presented in the text itself, including illustrations, titles, topic sentences, important words, and foreshadowing clues.
12	**Focus on Genre: Personal Narrative**	• **Reading 3.1** Distinguish common forms of literature (e.g., poetry, drama, fiction, nonfiction).
	Your Job as a Reader	• **Reading 2.2** Use appropriate strategies when reading for different purposes (e.g., full comprehension, location of information, personal enjoyment). • **Reading 2.3** Make and confirm predictions about text by using prior knowledge and ideas presented in the text itself, including illustrations, titles, topic sentences, important words, and foreshadowing clues.

California English–Language Arts Content Standards, continued

13–18	**Reading Selection**	• **Reading 2.2** Ask questions and support answers by connecting prior knowledge with literal information found in, and inferred from, the text.
		• **Reading 2.3** Demonstrate comprehension by identifying answers in the text.
		• **Reading 2.4** Recall major points in the text and make and modify predictions about forthcoming information.
		• **Reading 2.6** Extract appropriate and significant information from the text, including problems and solutions.
		• **Reading 2.2** Use appropriate strategies when reading for different purposes (e.g., full comprehension, location of information, personal enjoyment).
		• **Reading 2.3** Make and confirm predictions about text by using prior knowledge and ideas presented in the text itself, including illustrations, titles, topic sentences, important words, and foreshadowing clues.
19	**Connect Reading and Writing:**	
	Critical Thinking	• **Reading 2.2** Ask questions and support answers by connecting prior knowledge with literal information found in, and inferred from, the text.
		• **Reading 2.3** Demonstrate comprehension by identifying answers in the text.
		• **Reading 2.6** Extract appropriate and significant information from the text, including problems and solutions.
		• **Listening and Speaking 2.3** Deliver oral summaries of articles and books that contain the main ideas of the event or article and the most significant details.
	Reading Fluency	• **Reading 1.3** Read aloud narrative and expository text fluently and accurately and with appropriate pacing, intonation, and expression.
		• **Reading 1.1** Read narrative and expository text aloud with grade-appropriate fluency and accuracy and with appropriate pacing, intonation, and expression.
	Reading Strategy	• **Reading 2.4** Recall major points in the text and make and modify predictions about forthcoming information.
		• **Reading 2.2** Use appropriate strategies when reading for different purposes (e.g., full comprehension, location of information, personal enjoyment).
	Vocabulary Review	• Use vocabulary central to the understanding and discussion of the selection.
		• **Reading 1.6** Use sentence and word context to find the meaning of unknown words.
	Write About the GQ	• **Writing 2.2a** Write responses to literature: Demonstrate an understanding of the literary work.
		• **Writing 2.2b** Write responses to literature: Support judgments through references to both the text and prior knowledge.
20	**Literary Analysis: Analyze Narrator's Point of View**	• **Reading 3.6** Identify the speaker or narrator in a selection.
21	**Vocabulary Study: Use Context Clues**	• **Reading 1.4** Use knowledge of antonyms, synonyms, homophones, and homographs to determine the meanings of words.
		• **Reading 1.6** Use sentence and word context to find the meaning of unknown words.
		• **Reading 1.6** Distinguish and interpret words with multiple meanings.
21	**Literary Analysis: Analyze Text Structure (Compare and Contrast)**	• **Reading 2.1** Identify structural patterns found in informational text (e.g., compare and contrast, cause and effect, sequential or chronological order, proposition and support) to strengthen comprehension.
22	**Literary Analysis: Analyze Poetry**	• **Reading 3.1** Distinguish common forms of literature (e.g., poetry, drama, fiction, nonfiction).

23	**Language & Grammar: Express Ideas and Feelings**	• **Listening and Speaking 1.0** Students listen critically and respond appropriately to oral communication. They speak in a manner that guides the listener to understand important ideas by using proper phrasing, pitch, and modulation. • **Written and Oral English Language Conventions 1.1** Understand and be able to use complete and correct declarative, interrogative, imperative, and exclamatory sentences in writing and speaking. • **Written and Oral English Language Conventions 1.3** Identify and use regular and irregular verbs, adverbs, prepositions, and coordinating conjunctions in writing and speaking. • **Listening and Speaking 1.1** Ask thoughtful questions and respond to relevant questions with appropriate elaboration in oral settings.
23	**Writing and Grammar: Write About Someone You Know**	• **Writing 2.1a** Write narratives: Relate ideas, observations, or recollections of an event or experience. • **Writing 2.1c** Write narratives: Use concrete sensory details. • **Written and Oral English Language Conventions 1.3** Identify and use regular and irregular verbs, adverbs, prepositions, and coordinating conjunctions in writing and speaking.
Selection 2		**Kids Like Me**
24	**Connect**	• **Listening and Speaking 1.2** Connect and relate prior experiences, insights, and ideas to those of a speaker. • **Reading 2.2** Use appropriate strategies when reading for different purposes (e.g., full comprehension, location of information, personal enjoyment).
25–27	**Language & Grammar: Ask and Answer Questions** **Use Questions and Statements**	• **Listening and Speaking 1.0** Students listen critically and respond appropriately to oral communication. They speak in a manner that guides the listener to understand important ideas by using proper phrasing, pitch, and modulation. • **Written and Oral English Language Conventions 1.1** Understand and be able to use complete and correct declarative, interrogative, imperative, and exclamatory sentences in writing and speaking. • **Written and Oral English Language Conventions 1.1** Use simple and compound sentences in writing and speaking. • **Listening and Speaking 1.1** Ask thoughtful questions and respond to relevant questions with appropriate elaboration in oral settings.
28	**Key Vocabulary**	• Learn meaning and pronunciation for vocabulary words central to the understanding and discussion of the selection. • **Reading 1.7** Use a dictionary to learn the meaning and other features of unknown words.
29	**Reading Strategy: Plan Your Reading**	• **Reading 2.2** Use appropriate strategies when reading for different purposes (e.g., full comprehension, location of information, personal enjoyment).
30	**Focus on Genre: Interview** **Your Job as a Reader**	• **Reading 3.1** Distinguish common forms of literature (e.g., poetry, drama, fiction, nonfiction). • **Reading 2.1** Identify structural patterns found in informational text (e.g., compare and contrast, cause and effect, sequential or chronological order, proposition and support) to strengthen comprehension. • **Reading 2.2** Use appropriate strategies when reading for different purposes (e.g., full comprehension, location of information, personal enjoyment).

31–36	**Reading Selection**	• **Reading 2.2** Ask questions and support answers by connecting prior knowledge with literal information found in, and inferred from, the text.

- **Reading 2.3** Demonstrate comprehension by identifying answers in the text.
- **Reading 2.6** Extract appropriate and significant information from the text, including problems and solutions.
- **Reading 2.2** Use appropriate strategies when reading for different purposes (e.g., full comprehension, location of information, personal enjoyment).
- **Reading 2.3** Make and confirm predictions about text by using prior knowledge and ideas presented in the text itself, including illustrations, titles, topic sentences, important words, and foreshadowing clues.
- **Reading 2.5** Compare and contrast information on the same topic after reading several passages or articles.

37   Connect Reading and Writing:

Critical Thinking

- **Listening and Speaking 2.3** Deliver oral summaries of articles and books that contain the main ideas of the event or article and the most significant details.
- **Reading 2.2** Ask questions and support answers by connecting prior knowledge with literal information found in, and inferred from, the text.
- **Reading 2.3** Demonstrate comprehension by identifying answers in the text.
- **Reading 2.6** Extract appropriate and significant information from the text, including problems and solutions.

Reading Fluency

- **Reading 1.3** Read aloud narrative and expository text fluently and accurately and with appropriate pacing, intonation, and expression.
- **Reading 1.1** Read narrative and expository text aloud with grade-appropriate fluency and accuracy and with appropriate pacing, intonation, and expression.

Reading Strategy

- **Reading 2.4** Recall major points in the text and make and modify predictions about forthcoming information.
- **Reading 2.2** Use appropriate strategies when reading for different purposes (e.g., full comprehension, location of information, personal enjoyment).

Vocabulary Review

- Use vocabulary central to the understanding and discussion of the selection.
- **Reading 1.6** Use sentence and word context to find the meaning of unknown words.

Write About the GQ

- **Writing 2.2a** Write responses to literature: Demonstrate an understanding of the literary work.
- **Writing 2.2b** Write responses to literature: Support judgments through references to both the text and prior knowledge.

38   Literary Analysis: Analyze Text Structure (Compare and Contrast)

- **Reading 2.5** Compare and contrast information on the same topic after reading several passages or articles.

39   Vocabulary Study: Use Context Clues

- **Reading 1.4** Use knowledge of antonyms, synonyms, homophones, and homographs to determine the meanings of words.
- **Reading 1.6** Use sentence and word context to find the meaning of unknown words.
- **Reading 1.7** Use a dictionary to learn the meaning and other features of unknown words.
- **Reading 1.6** Distinguish and interpret words with multiple meanings.

39   Listening/Speaking: Use Cultural Expressions

- **Listening and Speaking 1.3** Identify how language usages (e.g., sayings, expressions) reflect regions and cultures.
- **Listening and Speaking 1.7** Emphasize points in ways that help the listener or viewer to follow important ideas and concepts.
- **Listening and Speaking 1.9** Use volume, pitch, phrasing, pace, modulation, and gestures appropriately to enhance meaning.

40	**Research/Speaking:** **Research Population Change**	• **Listening and Speaking 1.8** Clarify and enhance oral presentations through the use of appropriate props (e.g., objects, pictures, charts). • **Writing 1.7** Use various reference materials as an aid to writing (e.g., dictionary, thesaurus, card catalog, encyclopedia, online information). • **Listening and Speaking 1.7** Emphasize points in ways that help the listener or viewer to follow important ideas and concepts. • **Listening and Speaking 2.2b** Make informational presentations: Include facts and details that help listeners to focus.
41	**Language & Grammar:** **Ask and Answer Questions**	• **Written and Oral English Language Conventions 1.1** Understand and be able to use complete and correct declarative, interrogative, imperative, and exclamatory sentences in writing and speaking. • **Listening and Speaking 1.0** Students listen critically and respond appropriately to oral communication. They speak in a manner that guides the listener to understand important ideas by using proper phrasing, pitch, and modulation. • **Listening and Speaking 1.1** Ask thoughtful questions and respond to relevant questions with appropriate elaboration in oral settings.
41	**Writing and Grammar:** **Write a Message**	• **Writing 2.3a** Write personal and formal letters, thank-you notes, and invitations: Show awareness of the knowledge and interests of the audience and establish a purpose and context. • **Writing 2.3b** Write personal and formal letters, thank-you notes, and invitations: Include the date, proper salutation, body, closing, and signature. • **Written and Oral English Language Conventions 1.1** Understand and be able to use complete and correct declarative, interrogative, imperative, and exclamatory sentences in writing and speaking. • **Written and Oral English Language Conventions 1.1** Use simple and compound sentences in writing and speaking.
Selection 3		**Familiar Places**
42	**Connect**	• **Listening and Speaking 1.2** Connect and relate prior experiences, insights, and ideas to those of a speaker. • **Listening and Speaking 1.8** Use details, examples, anecdotes, or experiences to explain or clarify information.
43–45	**Language & Grammar:** **Give Commands** **Use Statements and Commands**	• **Listening and Speaking 1.0** Students listen critically and respond appropriately to oral communication. They speak in a manner that guides the listener to understand important ideas by using proper phrasing, pitch, and modulation. • **Listening and Speaking 2.4** Recite brief poems (i.e., two or three stanzas), soliloquies, or dramatic dialogues, using clear diction, tempo, volume, and phrasing. • **Written and Oral English Language Conventions 1.1** Understand and be able to use complete and correct declarative, interrogative, imperative, and exclamatory sentences in writing and speaking. • **Written and Oral English Language Conventions 1.1** Use simple and compound sentences in writing and speaking.
46	**Key Vocabulary**	• Learn meaning and pronunciation for vocabulary words central to the understanding and discussion of the selection. • **Reading 1.7** Use a dictionary to learn the meaning and other features of unknown words.
47	**Reading Strategy:** **Plan Your Reading**	• **Reading 2.2** Use appropriate strategies when reading for different purposes (e.g., full comprehension, location of information, personal enjoyment). • **Reading 2.3** Make and confirm predictions about text by using prior knowledge and ideas presented in the text itself, including illustrations, titles, topic sentences, important words, and foreshadowing clues.
48	**Focus on Genre:** **Expository Nonfiction** **Your Job as a Reader**	• **Reading 3.1** Distinguish common forms of literature (e.g., poetry, drama, fiction, nonfiction). • **Reading 2.2** Use appropriate strategies when reading for different purposes (e.g., full comprehension, location of information, personal enjoyment). • **Reading 2.3** Make and confirm predictions about text by using prior knowledge and ideas presented in the text itself, including illustrations, titles, topic sentences, important words, and foreshadowing clues.

Unit 1   Finding Your Own Place, continued

49–54	**Reading Selection**	• **Reading 2.2** Ask questions and support answers by connecting prior knowledge with literal information found in, and inferred from, the text. • **Reading 2.3** Demonstrate comprehension by identifying answers in the text. • **Reading 2.5** Distinguish the main idea and supporting details in expository text. • **Reading 2.6** Extract appropriate and significant information from the text, including problems and solutions. • **Reading 2.2** Use appropriate strategies when reading for different purposes (e.g., full comprehension, location of information, personal enjoyment).
55	**Connect Reading and Writing:**	
	Critical Thinking	• **Listening and Speaking 2.3** Deliver oral summaries of articles and books that contain the main ideas of the event or article and the most significant details. • **Reading 2.3** Demonstrate comprehension by identifying answers in the text. • **Reading 2.6** Extract appropriate and significant information from the text, including problems and solutions.
	Reading Fluency	• **Reading 1.3** Read aloud narrative and expository text fluently and accurately and with appropriate pacing, intonation, and expression. • **Reading 1.1** Read narrative and expository text aloud with grade-appropriate fluency and accuracy and with appropriate pacing, intonation, and expression.
	Reading Strategy	• **Reading 2.2** Use appropriate strategies when reading for different purposes (e.g., full comprehension, location of information, personal enjoyment).
	Vocabulary Review	• Use vocabulary central to the understanding and discussion of the selection. • **Reading 1.6** Use sentence and word context to find the meaning of unknown words.
	Write About the GQ	• **Writing 2.2a** Write responses to literature: Demonstrate an understanding of the literary work. • **Writing 2.2b** Write responses to literature: Support judgments through references to both the text and prior knowledge.
56	**Literary Analysis:** **Analyze Text Structure** **(Main Idea)**	• **Reading 2.5** Distinguish the main idea and supporting details in expository text. • **Reading 2.1** Identify structural patterns found in informational text (e.g., compare and contrast, cause and effect, sequential or chronological order, proposition and support) to strengthen comprehension.
57	**Vocabulary Study:** **Use Context Clues**	• **Reading 1.4** Use knowledge of antonyms, synonyms, homophones, and homographs to determine the meanings of words. • **Reading 1.6** Use sentence and word context to find the meaning of unknown words. • **Reading 1.7** Use a dictionary to learn the meaning and other features of unknown words. • **Reading 1.6** Distinguish and interpret words with multiple meanings.
57	**Writing/Speaking:** **Give Directions**	• **Listening and Speaking 1.4** Give precise directions and instructions.
58	**Research/Speaking:** **Tell About Traditions**	• **Listening and Speaking 1.6** Use traditional structures for conveying information. (e.g., cause and effect, similarity and difference, posing and answering a question). • **Listening and Speaking 1.8** Use details, examples, anecdotes, or experiences to explain or clarify information. • **Listening and Speaking 1.9** Use volume, pitch, phrasing, pace, modulation, and gestures appropriately to enhance meaning. • **Listening and Speaking 2.2c** Incorporate more than one source of information (e.g., speakers, books, newspapers, television, or radio reports). • **Writing 1.7** Use various reference materials (e.g., dictionary, thesaurus, card catalog, encyclopedia, online information) as an aid to writing.

59	**Language & Grammar:** **Give Commands**	• **Listening and Speaking 1.0** Students listen critically and respond appropriately to oral communication. They speak in a manner that guides the listener to understand important ideas by using proper phrasing, pitch, and modulation.
		• **Written and Oral English Language Conventions 1.1** Understand and be able to use complete and correct declarative, interrogative, imperative, and exclamatory sentences in writing and speaking.
		• **Listening and Speaking 1.1** Ask thoughtful questions and respond to relevant questions with appropriate elaboration in oral settings.
59	**Writing and Grammar:** **Write About a Special Event**	• **Written and Oral English Language Conventions 1.1** Understand and be able to use complete and correct declarative, interrogative, imperative, and exclamatory sentences in writing and speaking.
		• **Written and Oral English Language Conventions 1.1** Use simple and compound sentences in writing and speaking.
		• **Writing 2.1a** Write narratives: Relate ideas, observations, or recollections of an event or experience.

Compare Across Texts

| 60 | **Compare People** | • **Reading 2.5** Compare and contrast information on the same topic after reading several passages or articles. |

Unit Wrap-Up

61	**Reflect on Your Reading**	• **Reading 2.2** Ask questions and support answers by connecting prior knowledge with literal information found in, and inferred from, the text.
		• **Reading 2.2** Use appropriate strategies when reading for different puropses (e.g., full comprehension, location of information, personal enjoyment).
	Explore the GQ/Book Talk	• **Reading 2.3** Demonstrate comprehension by identifying answers in the text.
		• **Reading 2.6** Extract appropriate and significant information from the text, including problems and solutions.
		• **Reading 2.1** Identify structural patterns found in informational text (e.g., compare and contrast, cause and effect, sequential or chronological order, proposition and support) to strengthen comprehension.
		• **Listening and Speaking 2.3** Deliver oral summaries of articles and books that contain the main ideas of the event or article and the most significant details.

For additional coverage of the Written and Oral English Language Conventions and the Writing Applications standards, see the California standards maps in the Writing book.

Unit 2   Water for Life

Unit Launch

64–65	**Focus on Genre: Fiction and Nonfiction**	• **Reading 3.1** Distinguish common forms of literature (e.g., poetry, drama, fiction, nonfiction).
		• **Reading 3.3** Determine what characters are like by what they say or do and by how the author or illustrator portrays them.
		• **Reading 2.1** Identify structural patterns found in informational text (e.g., compare and contrast, cause and effect, sequential or chronological order, proposition and support) to strengthen comprehension.
66–67	**Focus on Vocabulary: Relate Words**	• **Reading 1.4** Use knowledge of antonyms, synonyms, homophones, and homographs to determine the meanings of words.
		• **Reading 1.5** Demonstrate knowledge of levels of specificity among grade-appropriate words and explain the importance of these relations (e.g., *dog/mammal/animal/living things*).
		• **Reading 1.6** Use sentence and word context to find the meaning of unknown words.
		• **Writing 1.3** Understand the structure and organization of various reference materials (e.g., dictionary, thesaurus, atlas, encyclopedia).
		• **Reading 1.2** Apply knowledge of word origins, derivations, synonyms, antonyms, and idioms to determine the meaning of words and phrases.

Selection 1   **The Secret Water**

68	**Connect**	• **Listening and Speaking 1.2** Connect and relate prior experiences, insights, and ideas to those of a speaker.
		• **Writing 2.2** Write descriptions that use concrete sensory details to present and support unified impressions of people, places, things, or experiences.
		• **Reading 2.2** Use appropriate strategies when reading for different purposes (e.g., full comprehension, location of information, personal enjoyment).
69–71	**Language & Grammar: Express Needs and Wants**	• **Listening and Speaking 1.0** Students listen critically and respond appropriately to oral communication. They speak in a manner that guides the listener to understand important ideas by using proper phrasing, pitch, and modulation.
		• **Listening and Speaking 1.9** Read prose and poetry aloud with fluency, rhythm, and pace, using appropriate intonation and vocal patterns to emphasize important passages of the text being read.
		• **Listening and Speaking 2.4** Recite brief poems (i.e., two or three stanzas), soliloquies, or dramatic dialogues, using clear diction, tempo, volume, and phrasing.
	Use Nouns	• **Written and Oral English Language Conventions 1.1** Use simple and compound sentences in writing and speaking.
		• **Written and Oral English Language Conventions 1.8** Spell correctly one-syllable words that have blends, contractions, compounds, orthographic patterns (e.g., *qu*, consonant doubling, changing the ending of a word from *-y* to *-ies* when forming the plural), and common homophones (e.g., *hair-hare*).
		• **Written and Oral English Language Conventions 1.7** Spell correctly roots, inflections, suffixes and prefixes, and syllable constructions.
72	**Key Vocabulary**	• Learn meaning and pronunciation for vocabulary words central to the understanding and discussion of the selection.
		• **Reading 1.7** Use a dictionary to learn the meaning and other features of unknown words.
73	**Reading Strategy: Monitor Your Reading**	• **Reading 2.2** Use appropriate strategies when reading for different purposes (e.g., full comprehension, location of information, personal enjoyment).
		• **Reading 2.4** Evaluate new information and hypotheses by testing them against known information and ideas.

74	Focus on Genre: Legend	• **Reading 3.1** Distinguish common forms of literature (e.g., poetry, drama, fiction, nonfiction).
	Your Job as a Reader	• **Reading 3.2** Comprehend basic plots of classic fairy tales, myths, folktales, legends, and fables from around the world. • **Reading 2.2** Use appropriate strategies when reading for different purposes (e.g., full comprehension, location of information, personal enjoyment). • **Reading 3.1** Describe the structural differences of various imaginative forms of literature, including fantasies, fables, myths, legends, and fairy tales.
75–80	Reading Selection	• **Reading 2.2** Ask questions and support answers by connecting prior knowledge with literal information found in, and inferred from, the text. • **Reading 2.3** Demonstrate comprehension by identifying answers in the text. • **Reading 2.4** Recall major points in the text and make and modify predictions about forthcoming information. • **Reading 2.6** Extract appropriate and significant information from the text, including problems and solutions. • **Reading 2.2** Use appropriate strategies when reading for different purposes (e.g., full comprehension, location of information, personal enjoyment). • **Reading 2.3** Make and confirm predictions about text by using prior knowledge and ideas presented in the text itself, including illustrations, titles, topic sentences, important words, and foreshadowing clues. • **Reading 3.3** Use knowledge of the situation and setting and of a character's traits and motivations to determine the causes for that character's actions.
81	Connect Reading and Writing:	
	Critical Thinking	• **Listening and Speaking 2.3** Deliver oral summaries of articles and books that contain the main ideas of the event or article and the most significant details. • **Reading 2.2** Ask questions and support answers by connecting prior knowledge with literal information found in, and inferred from, the text. • **Reading 2.3** Demonstrate comprehension by identifying answers in the text. • **Reading 2.6** Extract appropriate and significant information from the text, including problems and solutions.
	Reading Fluency	• **Reading 1.3** Read aloud narrative and expository text fluently and accurately and with appropriate pacing, intonation, and expression. • **Reading 1.1** Read narrative and expository text aloud with grade-appropriate fluency and accuracy and with appropriate pacing, intonation, and expression.
	Reading Strategy	• **Reading 2.2** Use appropriate strategies when reading for different purposes (e.g., full comprehension, location of information, personal enjoyment). • **Reading 2.4** Evaluate new information and hypotheses by testing them against known information and ideas.
	Vocabulary Review	• Use vocabulary central to the understanding and discussion of the selection. • **Reading 1.6** Use sentence and word context to find the meaning of unknown words.
	Write About the GQ	• **Writing 2.2a** Write responses to literature: Demonstrate an understanding of the literary work. • **Writing 2.2b** Write responses to literature: Support judgments through references to both the text and prior knowledge.

82	**Literary Analysis: Analyze Plot**	• **Reading 3.2** Comprehend basic plots of classic fairy tales, myths, folktales, legends, and fables from around the world. • **Reading 3.2** Identify the main events of the plot, their causes, and the influence of each on future actions.
83	**Vocabulary Study: Create Word Categories**	• **Reading 1.5** Demonstrate knowledge of levels of specificity among grade-appropriate words and explain the importance of these relations (e.g., *dog/mammal/animal/living things*).
83	**Research/Writing: Write About China**	• **Writing 2.1a** Provide a context within which an action takes place. • **Writing 2.2** Write descriptions that use concrete sensory details to present and support unified impressions of people, places, things, or experiences. • **Writing 1.7** Use various reference materials as an aid to writing (e.g., dictionary, thesaurus, card catalog, encyclopedia, online information).
84	**Listening/Speaking: Compare Tales Across Cultures**	• **Reading 3.4** Compare and contrast tales from different cultures by tracing the exploits of one character type and develop theories to account for similar tales in diverse cultures (e.g., trickster tales). • **Listening and Speaking 1.6** Use traditional structures for conveying information (e.g., cause and effect, similarity and difference, posing and answering a question).
85	**Language & Grammar: Express Needs and Wants**	• **Listening and Speaking 1.0** Students listen critically and respond appropriately to oral communication. They speak in a manner that guides the listener to understand important ideas by using proper phrasing, pitch, and modulation. • **Listening and Speaking 2.2** Plan and present dramatic interpretations of experiences, stories, poems, or plays with clear diction, pitch, tempo, and tone. • **Written and Oral English Language Conventions 1.1** Use simple and compound sentences in writing and speaking.
85	**Writing and Grammar: Write About a Situation**	• **Written and Oral English Language Conventions 1.8** Spell correctly one-syllable words that have blends, contractions, compounds, orthographic patterns (e.g., *qu*, consonant doubling, changing the ending of a word from *-y* to *-ies* when forming the plural), and common homophones (e.g., *hair-hare*). • **Written and Oral English Language Conventions 1.1** Use simple and compound sentences in writing and speaking. • **Written and Oral English Language Conventions 1.7** Spell correctly roots, inflections, suffixes and prefixes, and syllable constructions. • **Writing 2.1a** Write narratives: Relate ideas, observations, or recollections of an event or experience. • **Writing 2.1b** Write narratives: Provide a context to enable the reader to imagine the world of the event or experience.
Selection 2		**How Do We Use Water?**
86	**Connect**	• **Listening and Speaking 1.2** Connect and relate prior experiences, insights, and ideas to those of a speaker. • **Listening and Speaking 1.1** Ask thoughtful questions and respond to relevant questions with appropriate elaboration in oral settings. • **Reading 2.2** Use appropriate strategies when reading for different purposes (e.g., full comprehension, location of information, personal enjoyment).

87–89	Language & Grammar: Give Information	• **Listening and Speaking 1.0** Students listen critically and respond appropriately to oral communication. They speak in a manner that guides the listener to understand important ideas by using proper phrasing, pitch, and modulation.
		• **Listening and Speaking 1.9** Read prose and poetry aloud with fluency, rhythm, and pace, using appropriate intonation and vocal patterns to emphasize important passages of the text being read.
		• **Listening and Speaking 2.4** Recite brief poems (i.e., two or three stanzas), soliloquies, or dramatic dialogues, using clear diction, tempo, volume, and phrasing.
	Use Complete Sentences	• **Written and Oral English Language Conventions 1.1** Understand and be able to use complete and correct declarative, interrogative, imperative, and exclamatory sentences in writing and speaking.
		• **Written and Oral English Language Conventions 1.4** Identify and use subjects and verbs correctly in speaking and writing simple sentences.
		• **Listening and Speaking 1.4** Identify the musical elements of literary language (e.g., rhymes, repeated sounds, instances of onomatopoeia).
		• **Written and Oral English Language Conventions 1.1** Use simple and compound sentences in writing and speaking.
		• **Listening and Speaking 2.2b** Make informational presentations: Include facts and details that help listeners to focus.
90	Key Vocabulary	• Learn meaning and pronunciation for vocabulary words central to the understanding and discussion of the selection.
		• **Reading 1.7** Use a dictionary to learn the meaning and other features of unknown words.
91	Reading Strategy: Monitor Your Reading	• **Reading 1.6** Use sentence and word context to find the meaning of unknown words.
		• **Reading 2.2** Use appropriate strategies when reading for different purposes (e.g., full comprehension, location of information, personal enjoyment).
92	Focus on Genre: Social Science Article	• **Reading 3.1** Distinguish common forms of literature (e.g., poetry, drama, fiction, nonfiction).
		• **Reading 2.1** Identify structural patterns found in informational text (e.g., compare and contrast, cause and effect, sequential or chronological order, proposition and support) to strengthen comprehension.
	Your Job as a Reader	• **Reading 2.2** Use appropriate strategies when reading for different purposes (e.g., full comprehension, location of information, personal enjoyment).
93–98	Reading Selection	• **Reading 2.2** Ask questions and support answers by connecting prior knowledge with literal information found in, and inferred from, the text.
		• **Reading 2.3** Demonstrate comprehension by identifying answers in the text.
		• **Reading 2.5** Distinguish the main idea and supporting details in expository text.
		• **Reading 2.6** Extract appropriate and significant information from the text, including problems and solutions.
		• **Reading 2.2** Use appropriate strategies when reading for different purposes (e.g., full comprehension, location of information, personal enjoyment).
		• **Reading 2.6** Distinguish between cause and effect and between fact and opinion in expository text.

California English–Language Arts Content Standards, continued

99 **Connect Reading and Writing:**

Critical Thinking
- **Listening and Speaking 2.3** Deliver oral summaries of articles and books that contain the main ideas of the event or article and the most significant details.
- **Reading 2.2** Ask questions and support answers by connecting prior knowledge with literal information found in, and inferred from, the text.
- **Reading 2.3** Demonstrate comprehension by identifying answers in the text.
- **Reading 2.6** Extract appropriate and significant information from the text, including problems and solutions.
- **Reading 2.2** Use appropriate strategies when reading for different purposes (e.g., full comprehension, location of information, personal enjoyment).

Reading Fluency
- **Reading 1.3** Read aloud narrative and expository text fluently and accurately and with appropriate pacing, intonation, and expression.
- **Reading 1.1** Read narrative and expository text aloud with grade-appropriate fluency and accuracy and with appropriate pacing, intonation, and expression.

Reading Strategy
- **Reading 1.6** Use sentence and word context to find the meaning of unknown words.
- **Reading 2.2** Use appropriate strategies when reading for different purposes (e.g., full comprehension, location of information, personal enjoyment).

Vocabulary Review
- Use vocabulary central to the understanding and discussion of the selection.
- **Reading 1.6** Use sentence and word context to find the meaning of unknown words.

Write About the GQ
- **Writing 2.2a** Write responses to literature: Demonstrate an understanding of the literary work.
- **Writing 2.2b** Write responses to literature: Support judgments through references to both the text and prior knowledge.

100 **Literary Analysis:**
Analyze Text Structure
(Main Idea and Details)
- **Reading 2.5** Distinguish the main idea and supporting details in expository text.
- **Reading 2.1** Identify structural patterns found in informational text (e.g., compare and contrast, cause and effect, sequential or chronological order, proposition and support) to strengthen comprehension.
- **Writing 2.4** Write summaries that contain the main ideas of the reading selection and the most significant details.

101 **Vocabulary Study:**
Use Synonyms
- **Reading 1.4** Use knowledge of antonyms, synonyms, homophones, and homographs to determine the meanings of words.
- **Reading 1.2** Apply knowledge of word origins, derivations, synonyms, antonyms, and idioms to determine the meaning of words and phrases.
- **Reading 1.5** Use a thesaurus to determine related words and concepts.

101 **Listening/Speaking:**
Conduct a Survey
- **Listening and Speaking 1.3** Respond to questions with appropriate elaboration.
- **Listening and Speaking 1.1** Ask thoughtful questions and respond to relevant questions with appropriate elaboration in oral settings.

102 **Research/Writing:**
Research Water Use
- **Writing 1.1a** Create a single paragraph: Develop a topic sentence.
- **Writing 1.1b** Create a single paragraph: Include simple supporting facts and details.
- **Writing 1.5** Quote or paraphrase information sources, citing them appropriately.
- **Writing 2.3a** Write information reports: Frame a central question about an issue or situation.
- **Writing 2.3b** Write information reports: Include facts and details for focus.
- **Written and Oral English Language Conventions 1.4** Use parentheses, commas in direct quotations, and apostrophes in the possessive case of nouns and in contractions.

| 103 | Language & Grammar: Give Information | • **Listening and Speaking 1.0** Students listen critically and respond appropriately to oral communication. They speak in a manner that guides the listener to understand important ideas by using proper phrasing, pitch, and modulation.
• **Written and Oral English Language Conventions 1.1** Understand and be able to use complete and correct declarative, interrogative, imperative, and exclamatory sentences in writing and speaking.
• **Written and Oral English Language Conventions 1.4** Identify and use subjects and verbs correctly in speaking and writing simple sentences.
• **Written and Oral English Language Conventions 1.1** Use simple and compound sentences in writing and speaking.
• **Listening and Speaking 2.2b** Make informational presentations: Include facts and details that help listeners to focus. |
| 103 | Writing and Grammar: Write About Water | • **Written and Oral English Language Conventions 1.1** Understand and be able to use complete and correct declarative, interrogative, imperative, and exclamatory sentences in writing and speaking.
• **Written and Oral English Language Conventions 1.4** Identify and use subjects and verbs correctly in speaking and writing simple sentences.
• **Writing 1.1a** Create a single paragraph: Develop a topic sentence.
• **Writing 1.1b** Create a single paragraph: Include simple supporting facts and details.
• **Written and Oral English Language Conventions 1.1** Use simple and compound sentences in writing and speaking. |

Selection 3		**Water at Work**
104	Connect	• **Listening and Speaking 1.2** Connect and relate prior experiences, insights, and ideas to those of a speaker. • **Reading 2.2** Use appropriate strategies when reading for different purposes (e.g., full comprehension, location of information, personal enjoyment).
105–107	Language & Grammar: Elaborate	• **Listening and Speaking 1.0** Students listen critically and respond appropriately to oral communication. They speak in a manner that guides the listener to understand important ideas by using proper phrasing, pitch, and modulation. • **Listening and Speaking 1.8** Use details, examples, anecdotes, or experiences to explain or clarify information.
	Make Subjects and Verbs Agree	• **Written and Oral English Language Conventions 1.2** Identify subjects and verbs that are in agreement and identify and use pronouns, adjectives, compound words, and articles correctly in writing and speaking. • **Written and Oral English Language Conventions 1.4** Identify and use subjects and verbs correctly in speaking and writing simple sentences. • **Listening and Speaking 2.3** Make descriptive presentations that use concrete sensory details to set forth and support unified impressions of people, places, things, or experiences • **Written and Oral English Language Conventions 1.3** Identify and use regular and irregular verbs, adverbs, prepositions, and coordinating conjunctions in writing and speaking.
108	Key Vocabulary	• Learn meaning and pronunciation for vocabulary words central to the understanding and discussion of the selection. • **Reading 1.7** Use a dictionary to learn the meaning and other features of unknown words.
109	Reading Strategy: Monitor Your Reading	• **Reading 1.6** Use sentence and word context to find the meaning of unknown words. • **Reading 2.2** Use appropriate strategies when reading for different purposes (e.g., full comprehension, location of information, personal enjoyment).
110	Focus on Genre: Social Science Article	• **Reading 2.5** Distinguish the main idea and supporting details in expository text. • **Reading 3.1** Distinguish common forms of literature (e.g., poetry, drama, fiction, nonfiction). • **Reading 2.1** Identify structural patterns found in informational text (e.g., compare and contrast, cause and effect, sequential or chronological order, proposition and support) to strengthen comprehension.
	Your Job as a Reader	• **Reading 1.6** Use sentence and word context to find the meaning of unknown words. • **Reading 2.2** Use appropriate strategies when reading for different purposes (e.g., full comprehension, location of information, personal enjoyment).

California English–Language Arts Content Standards, continued

111–116	Reading Selection	• **Reading 2.2** Ask questions and support answers by connecting prior knowledge with literal information found in, and inferred from, the text. • **Reading 2.3** Demonstrate comprehension by identifying answers in the text. • **Reading 2.5** Distinguish the main idea and supporting details in expository text. • **Reading 2.6** Extract appropriate and significant information from the text, including problems and solutions. • **Reading 2.7** Follow simple multiple-step written instructions (e.g., how to assemble a product or play a board game). • **Reading 2.2** Use appropriate strategies when reading for different purposes (e.g., full comprehension, location of information, personal enjoyment).
117	**Connect Reading and Writing:**	
	Critical Thinking	• **Listening and Speaking 2.3** Deliver oral summaries of articles and books that contain the main ideas of the event or article and the most significant details. • **Reading 2.3** Demonstrate comprehension by identifying answers in the text. • **Reading 2.4** Recall major points in the text and make and modify predictions about forthcoming information. • **Reading 2.6** Extract appropriate and significant information from the text, including problems and solutions.
	Reading Fluency	• **Reading 1.3** Read aloud narrative and expository text fluently and accurately and with appropriate pacing, intonation, and expression. • **Reading 1.1** Read narrative and expository text aloud with grade-appropriate fluency and accuracy and with appropriate pacing, intonation, and expression.
	Reading Strategy	• **Reading 1.6** Use sentence and word context to find the meaning of unknown words. • **Reading 2.2** Use appropriate strategies when reading for different purposes (e.g., full comprehension, location of information, personal enjoyment).
	Vocabulary Review	• Use vocabulary central to the understanding and discussion of the selection. • **Reading 1.6** Use sentence and word context to find the meaning of unknown words.
	Write About the GQ	• **Writing 1.1b** Create a single paragraph: Include simple supporting facts and details. • **Writing 2.2a** Write responses to literature: Demonstrate an understanding of the literary work. • **Writing 2.2b** Write responses to literature: Support judgments through references to both the text and prior knowledge.
118	**Literary Analysis:** **Analyze Text Structure** **(Main Idea and Details)**	• **Reading 2.5** Distinguish the main idea and supporting details in expository text. • **Reading 2.1** Identify structural patterns found in informational text (e.g., compare and contrast, cause and effect, sequential or chronological order, proposition and support) to strengthen comprehension.
119	**Vocabulary Study:** **Use Synonyms and Antonyms**	• **Reading 1.4** Use knowledge of antonyms, synonyms, homophones, and homographs to determine the meanings of words. • **Reading 1.2** Apply knowledge of word origins, derivations, synonyms, antonyms, and idioms to determine the meaning of words and phrases.
119	**Research/Speaking:** **Research Floods**	• **Writing 1.3** Understand the structure and organization of various reference materials (e.g., dictionary, thesaurus, atlas, encyclopedia). • **Writing 1.8** Understand the organization of almanacs, newspapers, and periodicals and how to use those print materials. • **Listening and Speaking 2.3** Deliver oral summaries of articles and books that contain the main ideas of the event or article and the most significant details.

120	**Research/Speaking:** **Discuss Hydroelectric Power**	• **Writing 1.3** Understand the structure and organization of various reference materials (e.g., dictionary, thesaurus, atlas, encyclopedia). • **Listening and Speaking 1.11** Distinguish between the speaker's opinions and verifiable facts. • **Listening and Speaking 1.6** Use traditional structures for conveying information (e.g., cause and effect, similarity and difference, posing and answering a question). • **Listening and Speaking 2.2c** Incorporate more than one source of information (e.g., speakers, books, newspapers, television, or radio reports).
121	**Language & Grammar:** **Elaborate**	• **Listening and Speaking 1.0** Students listen critically and respond appropriately to oral communication. They speak in a manner that guides the listener to understand important ideas by using proper phrasing, pitch, and modulation. • **Written and Oral English Language Conventions 1.4** Identify and use subjects and verbs correctly in speaking and writing simple sentences. • **Listening and Speaking 1.8** Use details, examples, anecdotes, or experiences to explain or clarify information. • **Written and Oral English Language Conventions 1.3** Identify and use regular and irregular verbs, adverbs, prepositions, and coordinating conjunctions in writing and speaking.
121	**Writing and Grammar:** **Write About a Day at a River**	• **Written and Oral English Language Conventions 1.2** Identify subjects and verbs that are in agreement and identify and use pronouns, adjectives, compound words, and articles correctly in writing and speaking. • **Written and Oral English Language Conventions 1.4** Identify and use subjects and verbs correctly in speaking and writing simple sentences. • **Written and Oral English Language Conventions 1.3** Identify and use regular and irregular verbs, adverbs, prepositions, and coordinating conjunctions in writing and speaking. • **Writing 2.1a** Relate ideas, observations, or recollections of an event or experience.

Compare Across Texts

122	**Compare Ideas**	• **Reading 2.5** Compare and contrast information on the same topic after reading several passages or articles.

Unit Wrap-Up

123	**Reflect on Your Reading**	• **Reading 2.2** Ask questions and support answers by connecting prior knowledge with literal information found in, and inferred from, the text. • **Reading 3.1** Distinguish common forms of literature (e.g., poetry, drama, fiction, nonfiction). • **Reading 2.1** Identify structural patterns found in informational text (e.g., compare and contrast, cause and effect, sequential or chronological order, proposition and support) to strengthen comprehension. • **Reading 2.5** Compare and contrast information on the same topic after reading several passages or articles. • **Reading 3.1** Describe the structural differences of various imaginative forms of literature, including fantasies, fables, myths, legends, and fairy tales. • **Reading 2.2** Use appropriate strategies when reading for different purposes (e.g., full comprehension, location of information, personal enjoyment).
	Explore the GQ/Book Talk	• **Reading 2.3** Demonstrate comprehension by identifying answers in the text. • **Reading 2.6** Extract appropriate and significant information from the text, including problems and solutions. • **Listening and Speaking 2.3** Deliver oral summaries of articles and books that contain the main ideas of the event or article and the most significant details.

For additional coverage of the Written and Oral English Language Conventions and the Writing Applications standards, see the California standards maps in the Writing book.

Unit 3   Natural Forces
Unit Launch

126–127	Focus on Genre: Narrative Writing (Fiction and Nonfiction)	• **Reading 3.1** Distinguish common forms of literature (e.g., poetry, drama, fiction, nonfiction). • **Reading 3.3** Determine what characters are like by what they say or do and by how the author or illustrator portrays them.
128–129	Focus on Vocabulary: Use Word Parts	• **Reading 1.6** Use sentence and word context to find the meaning of unknown words. • **Reading 1.8** Use knowledge of prefixes (e.g., *un-, re-, pre-, bi-, mis-, dis-*) and suffixes (e.g., *-er, -est, -ful*) to determine the meaning of words. • **Reading 1.3** Use knowledge of root words to determine the meaning of unknown words within a passage.

Selection 1   Volcano!

130	Connect	• **Listening and Speaking 1.2** Connect and relate prior experiences, insights, and ideas to those of a speaker. • **Writing 2.2** Write descriptions that use concrete sensory details to present and support unified impressions of people, places, things, or experiences. • **Reading 2.2** Use appropriate strategies when reading for different purposes (e.g., full comprehension, location of information, personal enjoyment).
131–133	Language & Grammar: Engage in Conversation	• **Listening and Speaking 1.0** Students listen critically and respond appropriately to oral communication. They speak in a manner that guides the listener to understand important ideas by using proper phrasing, pitch, and modulation. • **Listening and Speaking 1.3** Respond to questions with appropriate elaboration. • **Listening and Speaking 1.9** Read prose and poetry aloud with fluency, rhythm, and pace, using appropriate intonation and vocal patterns to emphasize important passages of the text being read. • **Listening and Speaking 1.1** Ask thoughtful questions and respond to relevant questions with appropriate elaboration in oral settings. • **Listening and Speaking 2.4** Recite brief poems (i.e., two or three stanzas), soliloquies, or dramatic dialogues, using clear diction, tempo, volume, and phrasing.
	Use Subject Pronouns	• **Written and Oral English Language Conventions 1.2** Identify subjects and verbs that are in agreement and identify and use pronouns, adjectives, compound words, and articles correctly in writing and speaking.
134	Key Vocabulary	• Learn meaning and pronunciation for vocabulary words central to the understanding and discussion of the selection. • **Reading 1.7** Use a dictionary to learn the meaning and other features of unknown words.
135	Reading Strategy: Make Connections	• **Reading 2.2** Use appropriate strategies when reading for different purposes (e.g., full comprehension, location of information, personal enjoyment).
136	Focus on Genre: Science Article	• **Reading 2.1** Use titles, tables of contents, chapter headings, glossaries, and indexes to locate information in text.
	Your Job as a Reader	• **Reading 3.1** Distinguish common forms of literature (e.g., poetry, drama, fiction, nonfiction). • **Reading 2.2** Use appropriate strategies when reading for different purposes (e.g., full comprehension, location of information, personal enjoyment).
137–144	Reading Selection	• **Reading 2.2** Ask questions and support answers by connecting prior knowledge with literal information found in, and inferred from, the text. • **Reading 2.3** Demonstrate comprehension by identifying answers in the text. • **Reading 2.6** Extract appropriate and significant information from the text, including problems and solutions. • **Reading 2.2** Use appropriate strategies when reading for different purposes (e.g., full comprehension, location of information, personal enjoyment). • **Reading 2.6** Distinguish between cause and effect and between fact and opinion in expository text.

145   Connect Reading and Writing:

Critical Thinking
- **Listening and Speaking 2.3** Deliver oral summaries of articles and books that contain the main ideas of the event or article and the most significant details.
- **Reading 2.2** Ask questions and support answers by connecting prior knowledge with literal information found in, and inferred from, the text.
- **Reading 2.3** Demonstrate comprehension by identifying answers in the text.
- **Reading 2.6** Extract appropriate and significant information from the text, including problems and solutions.

Reading Fluency
- **Reading 1.3** Read aloud narrative and expository text fluently and accurately and with appropriate pacing, intonation, and expression.
- **Reading 1.1** Read narrative and expository text aloud with grade-appropriate fluency and accuracy and with appropriate pacing, intonation, and expression.

Reading Strategy
- **Reading 2.2** Use appropriate strategies when reading for different purposes (e.g., full comprehension, location of information, personal enjoyment).

Vocabulary Review
- Use vocabulary central to the understanding and discussion of the selection.
- **Reading 1.6** Use sentence and word context to find the meaning of unknown words.

Write About the GQ
- **Writing 2.2a** Write responses to literature: Demonstrate an understanding of the literary work.
- **Writing 2.2b** Write responses to literature: Support judgments through references to both the text and prior knowledge.

146   Literary Analysis: Analyze Text Structure (Cause and Effect)
- **Reading 2.1** Identify structural patterns found in informational text (e.g., compare and contrast, cause and effect, sequential or chronological order, proposition and support) to strengthen comprehension.
- **Reading 2.6** Distinguish between cause and effect and between fact and opinion in expository text.

147   Vocabulary Study: Use Word Parts
- **Reading 1.6** Use sentence and word context to find the meaning of unknown words.
- **Reading 1.3** Use knowledge of root words to determine the meaning of unknown words within a passage.

147   Research/Media: Report on a Volcano
- **Listening and Speaking 1.8** Clarify and enhance oral presentations through the use of appropriate props (e.g., objects, pictures, charts).
- **Writing 1.7** Use various reference materials as an aid to writing (e.g., dictionary, thesaurus, card catalog, encyclopedia, online information).
- **Listening and Speaking 2.2b** Make informational presentations: Include facts and details that help listeners to focus.
- **Listening and Speaking 2.2c** Make informational presentations: Incorporate more than one source of information (e.g., speakers, books, newspapers, television, or radio reports).

148   Research/Speaking: Research Plate Tectonics
- **Reading 2.1** Use titles, tables of contents, chapter headings, glossaries, and indexes to locate information in text.
- **Listening and Speaking 1.6** Provide a beginning, a middle, and an end, including concrete details that develop a central idea.
- **Listening and Speaking 1.7** Use clear and specific vocabulary to communicate ideas and establish the tone.
- **Writing 1.6** Locate information in reference texts by using organizational features (e.g., prefaces, appendixes).
- **Writing 2.3a** Write information reports: Frame a central question about an issue or situation.
- **Writing 2.3b** Write information reports: Include facts and details for focus.
- **Listening and Speaking 2.2b** Make informational presentations: Include facts and details that help listeners to focus.

Unit 3   Natural Forces, continued

149	Language & Grammar: Engage in Conversation	• **Listening and Speaking 1.0** Students listen critically and respond appropriately to oral communication. They speak in a manner that guides the listener to understand important ideas by using proper phrasing, pitch, and modulation. • **Listening and Speaking 1.3** Respond to questions with appropriate elaboration. • **Written and Oral English Language Conventions 1.2** Identify subjects and verbs that are in agreement and identify and use pronouns, adjectives, compound words, and articles correctly in writing and speaking. • **Listening and Speaking 1.1** Ask thoughtful questions and respond to relevant questions with appropriate elaboration in oral settings.
149	Writing and Grammar: Write About an Interesting Place	• **Written and Oral English Language Conventions 1.2** Identify subjects and verbs that are in agreement and identify and use pronouns, adjectives, compound words, and articles correctly in writing and speaking. • **Written and Oral English Language Conventions 1.1** Use simple and compound sentences in writing and speaking. • **Writing 2.1a** Write narratives: Relate ideas, observations, or recollections of an event or experience.

Selection 2		**Fleeing Katrina**
150	Connect	• **Listening and Speaking 1.2** Connect and relate prior experiences, insights, and ideas to those of a speaker. • **Reading 2.2** Use appropriate strategies when reading for different purposes (e.g., full comprehension, location of information, personal enjoyment).
151–153	Language & Grammar: Ask and Answer Questions	• **Listening and Speaking 1.0** Students listen critically and respond appropriately to oral communication. They speak in a manner that guides the listener to understand important ideas by using proper phrasing, pitch, and modulation. • **Listening and Speaking 1.3** Respond to questions with appropriate elaboration. • **Listening and Speaking 1.9** Read prose and poetry aloud with fluency, rhythm, and pace, using appropriate intonation and vocal patterns to emphasize important passages of the text being read. • **Listening and Speaking 1.1** Ask thoughtful questions and respond to relevant questions with appropriate elaboration in oral settings. • **Listening and Speaking 2.4** Recite brief poems (i.e., two or three stanzas), soliloquies, or dramatic dialogues, using clear diction, tempo, volume, and phrasing.
	Use Correct Pronouns	• **Written and Oral English Language Conventions 1.2** Identify subjects and verbs that are in agreement and identify and use pronouns, adjectives, compound words, and articles correctly in writing and speaking. • **Written and Oral English Language Conventions 1.4** Identify and use subjects and verbs correctly in speaking and writing simple sentences.
154	Key Vocabulary	• Learn meaning and pronunciation for vocabulary words central to the understanding and discussion of the selection. • **Reading 1.7** Use a dictionary to learn the meaning and other features of unknown words.
155	Reading Strategy: Make Connections	• **Reading 2.2** Use appropriate strategies when reading for different purposes (e.g., full comprehension, location of information, personal enjoyment).
156	Focus on Genre: Journal	• **Reading 3.1** Distinguish common forms of literature (e.g., poetry, drama, fiction, nonfiction). • **Reading 2.1** Identify structural patterns found in informational text (e.g., compare and contrast, cause and effect, sequential or chronological order, proposition and support) to strengthen comprehension.
	Your Job as a Reader	• **Reading 2.2** Use appropriate strategies when reading for different purposes (e.g., full comprehension, location of information, personal enjoyment).

157–166	**Reading Selection**	• **Reading 2.2** Ask questions and support answers by connecting prior knowledge with literal information found in, and inferred from, the text.
		• **Reading 2.3** Demonstrate comprehension by identifying answers in the text.
		• **Reading 2.4** Recall major points in the text and make and modify predictions about forthcoming information.
		• **Reading 2.6** Extract appropriate and significant information from the text, including problems and solutions.
		• **Reading 2.2** Use appropriate strategies when reading for different purposes (e.g., full comprehension, location of information, personal enjoyment).
		• **Reading 2.3** Make and confirm predictions by using prior knowledge and ideas presented in the text itself, including illustrations, titles, topic sentences, important words, and foreshadowing clues.
167	**Connect Reading and Writing:**	
	Critical Thinking	• **Listening and Speaking 2.3** Deliver oral summaries of articles and books that contain the main ideas of the event or article and the most significant details.
		• **Reading 2.2** Ask questions and support answers by connecting prior knowledge with literal information found in, and inferred from, the text.
		• **Reading 2.3** Demonstrate comprehension by identifying answers in the text.
		• **Reading 2.6** Extract appropriate and significant information from the text, including problems and solutions.
		• **Reading 2.2** Use appropriate strategies when reading for different purposes (e.g., full comprehension, location of information, personal enjoyment).
	Reading Fluency	• **Reading 1.3** Read aloud narrative and expository text fluently and accurately and with appropriate pacing, intonation, and expression.
		• **Reading 1.1** Read narrative and expository text aloud with grade-appropriate fluency and accuracy and with appropriate pacing, intonation, and expression.
	Reading Strategy	• **Reading 2.2** Use appropriate strategies when reading for different purposes (e.g., full comprehension, location of information, personal enjoyment).
	Vocabulary Review	• Use vocabulary central to the understanding and discussion of the selection.
		• **Reading 1.6** Use sentence and word context to find the meaning of unknown words.
	Write About the GQ	• **Writing 2.2a** Write responses to literature: Demonstrate an understanding of the literary work.
		• **Writing 2.2b** Write responses to literature: Support judgments through references to both the text and prior knowledge.
168	**Literary Analysis: Analyze Facts and Opinions**	• **Listening and Speaking 1.11** Distinguish between the speaker's opinions and verifiable facts.
		• **Reading 2.6** Distinguish between cause and effect and between fact and opinion in expository text.
169	**Vocabulary Study: Use Word Parts**	• **Reading 1.8** Use knowledge of prefixes (e.g., *un-*, *re-*, *pre-*, *bi-*, *mis-*, *dis-*) and suffixes (e.g., *-er*, *-est*, *-ful*) to determine the meaning of words.
		• **Reading 1.3** Use knowledge of root words to determine the meaning of unknown words within a passage.
169	**Research/Speaking: Retell a Personal Narrative**	• **Listening and Speaking 2.1a** Provide a context for an incident that is the subject of the presentation.
		• **Listening and Speaking 2.1b** Provide insight into why the selected incident is memorable.
		• **Listening and Speaking 1.8** Use details, examples, anecdotes, or experiences to explain or clarify information.
		• **Listening and Speaking 2.1a** Make narrative presentations: Relate ideas, observations, or recollections about an event or experience.
		• **Listening and Speaking 2.1b** Make narrative presentations: Provide a context that enables the listener to imagine the circumstances of the event or experience.
		• **Listening and Speaking 2.1c** Make narrative presentations: Provide insight into why the selected event or experience is memorable.

Unit 3 Natural Forces, continued

170	Media/Speaking: Compare Media Accounts	• **Listening and Speaking 1.10** Compare ideas and points of view expressed in broadcast and print media. • **Listening and Speaking 1.10** Evaluate the role of the media in focusing attention on events and in forming opinions on issues.
171	Language & Grammar: Ask and Answer Questions	• **Listening and Speaking 1.0** Students listen critically and respond appropriately to oral communication. They speak in a manner that guides the listener to understand important ideas by using proper phrasing, pitch, and modulation. • **Listening and Speaking 1.3** Respond to questions with appropriate elaboration. • **Written and Oral English Language Conventions 1.2** Identify subjects and verbs that are in agreement and identify and use pronouns, adjectives, compound words, and articles correctly in writing and speaking. • **Written and Oral English Language Conventions 1.4** Identify and use subjects and verbs correctly in speaking and writing simple sentences. • **Listening and Speaking 1.1** Ask thoughtful questions and respond to relevant questions with appropriate elaboration in oral settings.
171	Writing and Grammar: Write About a Natural Disaster	• **Written and Oral English Language Conventions 1.2** Identify subjects and verbs that are in agreement and identify and use pronouns, adjectives, compound words, and articles correctly in writing and speaking. • **Written and Oral English Language Conventions 1.4** Identify and use subjects and verbs correctly in speaking and writing simple sentences. • **Writing 2.1a** Write narratives: Relate ideas, observations, or recollections of an event or experience.

Selection 3 — Earthquake

172	Connect	• **Listening and Speaking 1.2** Connect and relate prior experiences, insights, and ideas to those of a speaker. • **Reading 2.2** Use appropriate strategies when reading for different purposes (e.g., full comprehension, location of information, personal enjoyment).
173–175	Language & Grammar: Give Advice	• **Listening and Speaking 1.0** Students listen critically and respond appropriately to oral communication. They speak in a manner that guides the listener to understand important ideas by using proper phrasing, pitch, and modulation. • **Listening and Speaking 1.9** Read prose and poetry aloud with fluency, rhythm, and pace, using appropriate intonation and vocal patterns to emphasize important passages of the text being read. • **Written and Oral English Language Conventions 1.1** Understand and be able to use complete and correct declarative, interrogative, imperative, and exclamatory sentences in writing and speaking. • **Listening and Speaking 1.4** Give precise directions and instructions. • **Listening and Speaking 2.4** Recite brief poems (i.e., two or three stanzas), soliloquies, or dramatic dialogues, using clear diction, tempo, volume, and phrasing.
	Use Helping Verbs	• **Written and Oral English Language Conventions 1.4** Identify and use subjects and verbs correctly in speaking and writing simple sentences. • **Written and Oral English Language Conventions 1.3** Identify and use regular and irregular verbs, adverbs, prepositions, and coordinating conjunctions in writing and speaking.
176	Key Vocabulary	• Learn meaning and pronunciation for vocabulary words central to the understanding and discussion of the selection. • **Reading 1.7** Use a dictionary to learn the meaning and other features of unknown words.
177	Reading Strategy: Make Connections	• **Reading 1.6** Use sentence and word context to find the meaning of unknown words. • **Reading 2.2** Use appropriate strategies when reading for different purposes (e.g., full comprehension, location of information, personal enjoyment).
178	Focus on Genre: Historical Fiction Your Job as a Reader	• **Reading 3.1** Distinguish common forms of literature (e.g., poetry, drama, fiction, nonfiction). • **Reading 2.2** Use appropriate strategies when reading for different purposes (e.g., full comprehension, location of information, personal enjoyment).

179–188	**Reading Selection**	• **Reading 2.2** Ask questions and support answers by connecting prior knowledge with literal information found in, and inferred from, the text.
• **Reading 2.3** Demonstrate comprehension by identifying answers in the text.
• **Reading 2.4** Recall major points in the text and make and modify predictions about forthcoming information.
• **Reading 2.6** Extract appropriate and significant information from the text, including problems and solutions.
• **Reading 2.2** Use appropriate strategies when reading for different purposes (e.g., full comprehension, location of information, personal enjoyment).
• **Reading 2.3** Make and confirm predictions by using prior knowledge and ideas presented in the text itself, including illustrations, titles, topic sentences, important words, and foreshadowing clues.
189	**Connect Reading and Writing:**	
	Critical Thinking	• **Listening and Speaking 2.3** Deliver oral summaries of articles and books that contain the main ideas of the event or article and the most significant details.
• **Reading 2.2** Ask questions and support answers by connecting prior knowledge with literal information found in, and inferred from, the text.
• **Reading 2.3** Demonstrate comprehension by identifying answers in the text.
• **Reading 2.6** Extract appropriate and significant information from the text, including problems and solutions.
	Reading Fluency	• **Reading 1.3** Read aloud narrative and expository text fluently and accurately and with appropriate pacing, intonation, and expression.
• **Reading 1.1** Read narrative and expository text aloud with grade-appropriate fluency and accuracy and with appropriate pacing, intonation, and expression.
	Reading Strategy	• **Reading 2.2** Use appropriate strategies when reading for different purposes (e.g., full comprehension, location of information, personal enjoyment).
	Vocabulary Review	• Use vocabulary central to the understanding and discussion of the selection.
• **Reading 1.6** Use sentence and word context to find the meaning of unknown words.
	Write About the GQ	• **Writing 2.2a** Write responses to literature: Demonstrate an understanding of the literary work.
• **Writing 2.2b** Write responses to literature: Support judgments through references to both the text and prior knowledge.
190	**Literary Analysis: Analyze Setting and Character**	• **Reading 3.3** Determine what characters are like by what they say or do and by how the author or illustrator portrays them.
• **Reading 3.2** Identify the main events of the plot, their causes, and the influence of each on future actions.
• **Reading 3.3** Use knowledge of the situation and setting and of a character's traits and motivations to determine the causes for that character's actions.
191	**Vocabulary Study: Use Word Parts**	• **Reading 1.8** Use knowledge of prefixes (e.g., *un-, re-, pre-, bi-, mis-, dis-*) and suffixes (e.g., *-er, -est, -ful*) to determine the meaning of words.
• **Reading 1.3** Use knowledge of root words to determine the meaning of unknown words within a passage.
191	**Research/Writing: Write a How-To Article**	• **Writing 1.3** Understand the structure and organization of various reference materials (e.g., dictionary, thesaurus, atlas, encyclopedia).
• **Writing 1.3** Use traditional structures for conveying information (e.g., chronological order, cause and effect, similarity and difference, posing and answering a question).
• **Writing 1.7** Use various reference materials (e.g., dictionary, thesaurus, card catalog, encyclopedia, online information) as an aid to writing.
• **Reading 2.7** Follow multiple-step instructions in a basic technical manual (e.g., how to use computer commands or video games).

California English–Language Arts Content Standards, continued

192	**Research/Speaking: Research Earthquakes**	• **Writing 1.3** Understand the structure and organization of various reference materials (e.g., dictionary, thesaurus, atlas, encyclopedia). • **Reading 2.1** Use titles, tables of contents, chapter headings, glossaries, and indexes to locate information in text. • **Writing 1.6** Locate information in reference texts by using organizational features (e.g., prefaces, appendixes). • **Listening and Speaking 1.8** Use details, examples, anecdotes, or experiences to explain or clarify information. • **Listening and Speaking 2.2a** Make informational presentations: Frame a key question.
193	**Language & Grammar: Give Advice**	• **Listening and Speaking 1.0** Students listen critically and respond appropriately to oral communication. They speak in a manner that guides the listener to understand important ideas by using proper phrasing, pitch, and modulation. • **Written and Oral English Language Conventions 1.4** Identify and use subjects and verbs correctly in speaking and writing simple sentences. • **Listening and Speaking 1.1** Ask thoughtful questions and respond to relevant questions with appropriate elaboration in oral settings. • **Listening and Speaking 1.4** Give precise directions and instructions. • **Written and Oral English Language Conventions 1.3** Identify and use regular and irregular verbs, adverbs, prepositions, and coordinating conjunctions in writing and speaking.
193	**Writing and Grammar: Write Advice**	• **Written and Oral English Language Conventions 1.4** Identify and use subjects and verbs correctly in speaking and writing simple sentences. • **Writing 2.3a** Write personal and formal letters, thank-you notes, and invitations: Show awareness of the knowledge and interests of the audience and establish a purpose and context. • **Writing 2.3b** Write personal and formal letters, thank-you notes, and invitations: Include the date, proper salutation, body, closing, and signature. • **Written and Oral English Language Conventions 1.3** Identify and use regular and irregular verbs, adverbs, prepositions, and coordinating conjunctions in writing and speaking.

Compare Across Texts

194	**Compare How Information Is Presented**	• **Reading 3.1** Distinguish common forms of literature (e.g., poetry, drama, fiction, nonfiction). • **Writing 1.1b** Create a single paragraph: Include simple supporting facts and details. • **Reading 2.5** Compare and contrast information on the same topic after reading several passages or articles.

Unit Wrap-Up

195	**Reflect on Your Reading**	• **Reading 2.2** Ask questions and support answers by connecting prior knowledge with literal information found in, and inferred from, the text. • **Reading 2.3** Demonstrate comprehension by identifying answers in the text. • **Reading 2.6** Extract appropriate and significant information from the text, including problems and solutions. • **Reading 3.1** Distinguish common forms of literature (e.g., poetry, drama, fiction, nonfiction). • **Reading 2.2** Use appropriate strategies when reading for different purposes (e.g., full comprehension, location of information, personal enjoyment). • **Reading 2.5** Compare and contrast information on the same topic after reading several passages or articles.
	Explore the GQ/Book Talk	• **Listening and Speaking 2.3** Deliver oral summaries of articles and books that contain the main ideas of the event or article and the most significant details.

For additional coverage of the Written and Oral English Language Conventions and the Writing Applications standards, see the California standards maps in the Writing book.

198–201	Focus on Genre: Elements of Fiction (Plot, Characters, and Setting)	• **Reading 3.1** Distinguish common forms of literature (e.g., poetry, drama, fiction, nonfiction). • **Reading 3.2** Comprehend basic plots of classic fairy tales, myths, folktales, legends, and fables from around the world. • **Reading 3.3** Determine what characters are like by what they say or do and by how the author or illustrator portrays them. • **Reading 3.1** Describe the structural differences of various imaginative forms of literature, including fantasies, fables, myths, legends, and fairy tales. • **Reading 3.2** Identify the main events of the plot, their causes, and the influence of each on future actions. • **Reading 3.3** Use knowledge of the situation and setting and of a character's traits and motivations to determine the causes for that character's actions.
202–203	Focus on Vocabulary: Use Word Parts	• **Reading 1.6** Use sentence and word context to find the meaning of unknown words. • **Reading 1.7** Use a dictionary to learn the meaning and other features of unknown words. • **Reading 1.8** Use knowledge of prefixes (e.g., *un-, re-, pre-, bi-, mis-, dis-*) and suffixes (e.g., *-er, -est, -ful*) to determine the meaning of words. • **Reading 1.3** Use knowledge of root words to determine the meaning of unknown words within a passage.

Selection 1 Frankenstein

204	Connect	• **Listening and Speaking 1.2** Connect and relate prior experiences, insights, and ideas to those of a speaker. • **Reading 2.2** Use appropriate strategies when reading for different purposes (e.g., full comprehension, location of information, personal enjoyment).
205–207	Language & Grammar: Describe People and Places	• **Listening and Speaking 1.0** Students listen critically and respond appropriately to oral communication. They speak in a manner that guides the listener to understand important ideas by using proper phrasing, pitch, and modulation. • **Listening and Speaking 1.9** Read prose and poetry aloud with fluency, rhythm, and pace, using appropriate intonation and vocal patterns to emphasize important passages of the text being read. • **Listening and Speaking 2.3** Make descriptive presentations that use concrete sensory details to set forth and support unified impressions of people, places, things, or experiences
	Use Adjectives	• **Written and Oral English Language Conventions 1.2** Identify subjects and verbs that are in agreement and identify and use pronouns, adjectives, compound words, and articles correctly in writing and speaking. • **Written and Oral English Language Conventions 1.3** Identify and use regular and irregular verbs, adverbs, prepositions, and coordinating conjunctions in writing and speaking.
208	Key Vocabulary	• Learn meaning and pronunciation for vocabulary words central to the understanding and discussion of the selection. • **Reading 1.7** Use a dictionary to learn the meaning and other features of unknown words.
209	Reading Strategy: Visualize	• **Reading 2.4** Recall major points in the text and make and modify predictions about forthcoming information. • **Reading 2.2** Use appropriate strategies when reading for different purposes (e.g., full comprehension, location of information, personal enjoyment).

Unit 4 Creepy Classics, continued

210	**Focus on Genre: Fantasy**	• **Reading 3.1** Distinguish common forms of literature (e.g., poetry, drama, fiction, nonfiction). • **Reading 3.1** Describe the structural differences of various imaginative forms of literature, including fantasies, fables, myths, legends, and fairy tales.
	Your Job as a Reader	• **Reading 2.2** Use appropriate strategies when reading for different purposes (e.g., full comprehension, location of information, personal enjoyment).
211–220	**Reading Selection**	• **Reading 2.2** Ask questions and support answers by connecting prior knowledge with literal information found in, and inferred from, the text. • **Reading 2.3** Demonstrate comprehension by identifying answers in the text. • **Reading 2.4** Recall major points in the text and make and modify predictions about forthcoming information. • **Reading 2.6** Extract appropriate and significant information from the text, including problems and solutions. • **Reading 3.3** Determine what characters are like by what they say or do and by how the author or illustrator portrays them. • **Reading 3.6** Identify the speaker or narrator in a selection. • **Reading 2.2** Use appropriate strategies when reading for different purposes (e.g., full comprehension, location of information, personal enjoyment). • **Reading 2.3** Make and confirm predictions by using prior knowledge and ideas presented in the text itself, including illustrations, titles, topic sentences, important words, and foreshadowing clues.
221	**Connect Reading and Writing:** **Critical Thinking**	• **Listening and Speaking 2.3** Deliver oral summaries of articles and books that contain the main ideas of the event or article and the most significant details. • **Reading 2.2** Ask questions and support answers by connecting prior knowledge with literal information found in, and inferred from, the text. • **Reading 2.3** Demonstrate comprehension by identifying answers in the text. • **Reading 2.4** Recall major points in the text and make and modify predictions about forthcoming information. • **Reading 2.6** Extract appropriate and significant information from the text, including problems and solutions. • **Reading 3.1** Describe the structural differences of various imaginative forms of literature, including fantasies, fables, myths, legends, and fairy tales.
	Reading Fluency	• **Reading 1.3** Read aloud narrative and expository text fluently and accurately and with appropriate pacing, intonation, and expression. • **Reading 1.1** Read narrative and expository text aloud with grade-appropriate fluency and accuracy and with appropriate pacing, intonation, and expression.
	Reading Strategy	• **Reading 2.2** Use appropriate strategies when reading for different purposes (e.g., full comprehension, location of information, personal enjoyment).
	Vocabulary Review	• Use vocabulary central to the understanding and discussion of the selection. • **Reading 1.6** Use sentence and word context to find the meaning of unknown words.
	Write About the GQ	• **Writing 2.2a** Write responses to literature: Demonstrate an understanding of the literary work. • **Writing 2.2b** Write responses to literature: Support judgments through references to both the text and prior knowledge.
222	**Literary Analysis: Analyze Character Development**	• **Reading 3.3** Determine what characters are like by what they say or do and by how the author or illustrator portrays them. • **Reading 3.3** Use knowledge of the situation and setting and of a character's traits and motivations to determine the causes for that character's actions. • **Listening and Speaking 2.2a** Make informational presentations: Frame a key question.

223	**Vocabulary Study:** **Use Word Parts**	• **Reading 1.7** Use a dictionary to learn the meaning and other features of unknown words. • **Reading 1.8** Use knowledge of prefixes (e.g., *un-*, *re-*, *pre-*, *bi-*, *mis-*, *dis-*) and suffixes (e.g., *-er*, *-est*, *-ful*) to determine the meaning of words. • **Reading 1.3** Use knowledge of root words to determine the meaning of unknown words within a passage.
223	**Research/Writing:** **Research a Time Period**	• **Writing 1.1** Select a focus, an organizational structure, and a point of view based upon purpose, audience, length, and format requirements. • **Writing 1.7** Use various reference materials as an aid to writing (e.g., dictionary, thesaurus, card catalog, encyclopedia, online information). • **Writing 2.3b** Write information reports: Include facts and details for focus.
224	**Literary Analysis:** **Analyze Theme**	• **Reading 3.3** Determine what characters are like by what they say or do and by how the author or illustrator portrays them. • **Reading 3.4** Determine the underlying theme or author's message in fiction and nonfiction text.
225	**Language & Grammar:** **Describe People and Places**	• **Listening and Speaking 1.0** Students listen critically and respond appropriately to oral communication. They speak in a manner that guides the listener to understand important ideas by using proper phrasing, pitch, and modulation. • **Listening and Speaking 2.3** Make descriptive presentations that use concrete sensory details to set forth and support unified impressions of people, places, things, or experiences • **Written and Oral English Language Conventions 1.2** Identify subjects and verbs that are in agreement and identify and use pronouns, adjectives, compound words, and articles correctly in writing and speaking. • **Written and Oral English Language Conventions 1.3** Identify and use regular and irregular verbs, adverbs, prepositions, and coordinating conjunctions in writing and speaking.
225	**Writing and Grammar:** **Write About a** **Creepy Situation**	• **Written and Oral English Language Conventions 1.2** Identify subjects and verbs that are in agreement and identify and use pronouns, adjectives, compound words, and articles correctly in writing and speaking. • **Writing 2.2** Write descriptions that use concrete sensory details to present and support unified impressions of people, places, things, or experiences. • **Written and Oral English Language Conventions 1.1** Use simple and compound sentences in writing and speaking. • **Written and Oral English Language Conventions 1.3** Identify and use regular and irregular verbs, adverbs, prepositions, and coordinating conjunctions in writing and speaking. • **Writing 2.1a** Write narratives: Relate ideas, observations, or recollections of an event or experience.
Selection 2		**Film Fright**
226	**Connect**	• **Listening and Speaking 1.2** Connect and relate prior experiences, insights, and ideas to those of a speaker. • **Reading 2.2** Use appropriate strategies when reading for different purposes (e.g., full comprehension, location of information, personal enjoyment).

California English–Language Arts Content Standards, continued

227–229	Language & Grammar: Make Comparisons	• **Listening and Speaking 1.0** Students listen critically and respond appropriately to oral communication. They speak in a manner that guides the listener to understand important ideas by using proper phrasing, pitch, and modulation. • **Listening and Speaking 1.9** Read prose and poetry aloud with fluency, rhythm, and pace, using appropriate intonation and vocal patterns to emphasize important passages of the text being read. • **Listening and Speaking 1.1** Ask thoughtful questions and respond to relevant questions with appropriate elaboration in oral settings. • **Listening and Speaking 2.4** Recite brief poems (i.e., two or three stanzas), soliloquies, or dramatic dialogues, using clear diction, tempo, volume, and phrasing.
	Use Adjectives to Make Comparisons	• **Written and Oral English Language Conventions 1.2** Identify subjects and verbs that are in agreement and identify and use pronouns, adjectives, compound words, and articles correctly in writing and speaking. • **Written and Oral English Language Conventions 1.3** Identify and use regular and irregular verbs, adverbs, prepositions, and coordinating conjunctions in writing and speaking. • **Written and Oral English Language Conventions 1.7** Spell correctly roots, inflections, suffixes and prefixes, and syllable constructions.
230	Key Vocabulary	• Learn meaning and pronunciation for vocabulary words central to the understanding and discussion of the selection. • **Reading 1.7** Use a dictionary to learn the meaning and other features of unknown words.
231	Reading Strategy: Visualize	• **Reading 2.2** Use appropriate strategies when reading for different purposes (e.g., full comprehension, location of information, personal enjoyment).
232	Focus on Genre: Feature Article	• **Reading 3.1** Distinguish common forms of literature (e.g., poetry, drama, fiction, nonfiction).
	Your Job as a Reader	• **Reading 2.2** Use appropriate strategies when reading for different purposes (e.g., full comprehension, location of information, personal enjoyment).
233–242	Reading Selection	• **Reading 2.2** Ask questions and support answers by connecting prior knowledge with literal information found in, and inferred from, the text. • **Reading 2.3** Demonstrate comprehension by identifying answers in the text. • **Reading 2.5** Distinguish the main idea and supporting details in expository text. • **Reading 2.6** Extract appropriate and significant information from the text, including problems and solutions. • **Reading 2.7** Follow simple multiple-step written instructions (e.g., how to assemble a product or play a board game). • **Listening and Speaking 1.4** Identify the musical elements of literary language (e.g., rhymes, repeated sounds, instances of onomatopoeia). • **Reading 2.2** Use appropriate strategies when reading for different purposes (e.g., full comprehension, location of information, personal enjoyment).

243   Connect Reading and Writing:

Critical Thinking

- **Listening and Speaking 2.3** Deliver oral summaries of articles and books that contain the main ideas of the event or article and the most significant details.
- **Reading 2.2** Ask questions and support answers by connecting prior knowledge with literal information found in, and inferred from, the text.
- **Reading 2.3** Demonstrate comprehension by identifying answers in the text.
- **Reading 2.6** Extract appropriate and significant information from the text, including problems and solutions.
- **Reading 2.2** Use appropriate strategies when reading for different purposes (e.g., full comprehension, location of information, personal enjoyment).
- **Reading 2.4** Evaluate new information and hypotheses by testing them against known information and ideas.

Reading Fluency

- **Reading 1.3** Read aloud narrative and expository text fluently and accurately and with appropriate pacing, intonation, and expression.
- **Reading 1.1** Read narrative and expository text aloud with grade-appropriate fluency and accuracy and with appropriate pacing, intonation, and expression.

Reading Strategy

- **Reading 2.2** Use appropriate strategies when reading for different purposes (e.g., full comprehension, location of information, personal enjoyment).

Vocabulary Review

- Use vocabulary central to the understanding and discussion of the selection.
- **Reading 1.6** Use sentence and word context to find the meaning of unknown words.

Write About the GQ

- **Writing 2.2a** Write responses to literature: Demonstrate an understanding of the literary work.
- **Writing 2.2b** Write responses to literature: Support judgments through references to both the text and prior knowledge.

244   Literary Analysis: Analyze Rhythm in Poetry

- **Reading 3.1** Distinguish common forms of literature (e.g., poetry, drama, fiction, nonfiction).
- **Reading 3.5** Recognize the similarities of sounds in words and rhythmic patterns (e.g., alliteration, onomatopoeia) in a selection.
- **Listening and Speaking 1.4** Identify the musical elements of literary language (e.g., rhymes, repeated sounds, instances of onomatopoeia).
- **Listening and Speaking 1.9** Read prose and poetry aloud with fluency, rhythm, and pace, using appropriate intonation and vocal patterns to emphasize important passages of the text being read.
- **Listening and Speaking 1.9** Use volume, pitch, phrasing, pace, modulation, and gestures appropriately to enhance meaning.
- **Listening and Speaking 2.4** Recite brief poems (i.e., two or three stanzas), soliloquies, or dramatic dialogues, using clear diction, tempo, volume, and phrasing.

245   Vocabulary Study: Use Latin and Greek Roots

- **Reading 1.7** Use a dictionary to learn the meaning and other features of unknown words.
- **Reading 1.8** Use knowledge of prefixes (e.g., un-, re-, pre-, bi-, mis-, dis-) and suffixes (e.g., -er, -est, -ful) to determine the meaning of words.
- **Reading 1.3** Use knowledge of root words to determine the meaning of unknown words within a passage.
- **Reading 1.4** Know common roots and affixes derived from Greek and Latin and use this knowledge to analyze the meaning of complex words (e.g., international).

245   Literary Analysis: Analyze Structure of Poetry

- **Listening and Speaking 2.2** Plan and present dramatic interpretations of experiences, stories, poems, or plays with clear diction, pitch, tempo, and tone.
- **Listening and Speaking 1.9** Use volume, pitch, phrasing, pace, modulation, and gestures appropriately to enhance meaning.
- **Listening and Speaking 2.4** Recite brief poems (i.e., two or three stanzas), soliloquies, or dramatic dialogues, using clear diction, tempo, volume, and phrasing.

Unit 4 Creepy Classics, continued

246	**Research/Speaking:** **Research a Special Effects Technique**	• **Listening and Speaking 1.7** Use clear and specific vocabulary to communicate ideas and establish the tone. • **Listening and Speaking 1.8** Clarify and enhance oral presentations through the use of appropriate props (e.g., objects, pictures, charts). • **Writing 1.1** Select a focus, an organizational structure, and a point of view based upon purpose, audience, length, and format requirements. • **Writing 1.7** Use various reference materials (e.g., dictionary, thesaurus, card catalog, encyclopedia, online information) as an aid to writing. • **Writing 2.3b** Write information reports: Include facts and details for focus. • **Listening and Speaking 1.9** Use volume, pitch, phrasing, pace, modulation, and gestures appropriately to enhance meaning. • **Listening and Speaking 2.2b** Make informational presentations: Include facts and details that help listeners to focus.
247	**Language & Grammar:** **Make Comparisons**	• **Listening and Speaking 1.0** Students listen critically and respond appropriately to oral communication. They speak in a manner that guides the listener to understand important ideas by using proper phrasing, pitch, and modulation. • **Written and Oral English Language Conventions 1.2** Identify subjects and verbs that are in agreement and identify and use pronouns, adjectives, compound words, and articles correctly in writing and speaking. • **Written and Oral English Language Conventions 1.3** Identify and use regular and irregular verbs, adverbs, prepositions, and coordinating conjunctions in writing and speaking.
247	**Writing and Grammar:** **Write to Compare Monsters**	• **Written and Oral English Language Conventions 1.2** Identify subjects and verbs that are in agreement and identify and use pronouns, adjectives, compound words, and articles correctly in writing and speaking. • **Writing 2.2** Write descriptions that use concrete sensory details to present and support unified impressions of people, places, things, or experiences. • **Written and Oral English Language Conventions 1.3** Identify and use regular and irregular verbs, adverbs, prepositions, and coordinating conjunctions in writing and speaking. • **Written and Oral English Language Conventions 1.7** Spell correctly roots, inflections, suffixes and prefixes, and syllable constructions.

Selection 3 — Mister Monster

248	**Connect**	• **Listening and Speaking 1.2** Connect and relate prior experiences, insights, and ideas to those of a speaker. • **Reading 2.2** Use appropriate strategies when reading for different purposes (e.g., full comprehension, location of information, personal enjoyment).
249–251	**Language & Grammar:** **Describe an Event or Experience**	• **Listening and Speaking 1.0** Students listen critically and respond appropriately to oral communication. They speak in a manner that guides the listener to understand important ideas by using proper phrasing, pitch, and modulation. • **Listening and Speaking 2.3** Make descriptive presentations that use concrete sensory details to set forth and support unified impressions of people, places, things, or experiences • **Listening and Speaking 2.1a** Make narrative presentations: Relate ideas, observations, or recollections about an event or experience.
	Use Adverbs	• **Written and Oral English Language Conventions 1.3** Identify and use regular and irregular verbs, adverbs, prepositions, and coordinating conjunctions in writing and speaking.
252	**Key Vocabulary**	• Learn meaning and pronunciation for vocabulary words central to the understanding and discussion of the selection. • **Reading 1.7** Use a dictionary to learn the meaning and other features of unknown words.
253	**Reading Strategy:** **Visualize**	• **Reading 1.6** Use sentence and word context to find the meaning of unknown words. • **Reading 2.2** Use appropriate strategies when reading for different purposes (e.g., full comprehension, location of information, personal enjoyment).

254	**Focus on Genre: Play**	• **Reading 3.1** Distinguish common forms of literature (e.g., poetry, drama, fiction, nonfiction). • **Reading 3.1** Describe the structural differences of various imaginative forms of literature, including fantasies, fables, myths, legends, and fairy tales.
	Your Job as a Reader	• **Reading 2.2** Use appropriate strategies when reading for different purposes (e.g., full comprehension, location of information, personal enjoyment).
255–266	**Reading Selection**	• **Reading 2.2** Ask questions and support answers by connecting prior knowledge with literal information found in, and inferred from, the text. • **Reading 2.3** Demonstrate comprehension by identifying answers in the text. • **Reading 2.4** Recall major points in the text and make and modify predictions about forthcoming information. • **Reading 2.6** Extract appropriate and significant information from the text, including problems and solutions. • **Reading 2.2** Use appropriate strategies when reading for different purposes (e.g., full comprehension, location of information, personal enjoyment). • **Reading 2.3** Make and confirm predictions by using prior knowledge and ideas presented in the text itself, including illustrations, titles, topic sentences, important words, and foreshadowing clues. • **Reading 3.3** Use knowledge of the situation and setting and of a character's traits and motivations to determine the causes for that character's actions.
267	**Connect Reading and Writing:**	
	Critical Thinking	• **Reading 2.2** Ask questions and support answers by connecting prior knowledge with literal information found in, and inferred from, the text. • **Reading 2.3** Demonstrate comprehension by identifying answers in the text. • **Reading 2.6** Extract appropriate and significant information from the text, including problems and solutions. • **Listening and Speaking 2.3** Deliver oral summaries of articles and books that contain the main ideas of the event or article and the most significant details.
	Reading Fluency	• **Reading 1.3** Read aloud narrative and expository text fluently and accurately and with appropriate pacing, intonation, and expression. • **Reading 1.1** Read narrative and expository text aloud with grade-appropriate fluency and accuracy and with appropriate pacing, intonation, and expression.
	Reading Strategy	• **Reading 2.2** Use appropriate strategies when reading for different purposes (e.g., full comprehension, location of information, personal enjoyment).
	Vocabulary Review	• Use vocabulary central to the understanding and discussion of the selection. • **Reading 1.6** Use sentence and word context to find the meaning of unknown words.
	Write About the GQ	• **Writing 2.2a** Write responses to literature: Demonstrate an understanding of the literary work. • **Writing 2.2b** Write responses to literature: Support judgments through references to both the text and prior knowledge.
268	**Literary Analysis: Compare Literature**	• **Reading 2.5** Compare and contrast information on the same topic after reading several passages or articles.
269	**Vocabulary Study: Use Word Parts**	• **Reading 1.7** Use a dictionary to learn the meaning and other features of unknown words. • **Reading 1.8** Use knowledge of prefixes (e.g., *un-, re-, pre-, bi-, mis-, dis-*) and suffixes (e.g., *-er, -est, -ful*) to determine the meaning of words. • **Reading 1.3** Use knowledge of root words to determine the meaning of unknown words within a passage.
269	**Research/Speaking: Explore TV Commercials**	• **Listening and Speaking 1.8** Clarify and enhance oral presentations through the use of appropriate props (e.g., objects, pictures, charts). • **Listening and Speaking 2.2a** Make informational presentations: Frame a key question. • **Writing 1.1** Select a focus, an organizational structure, and a point of view based upon purpose, audience, length, and format requirements.

Unit 4 Creepy Classics, continued

270	Listening/Speaking: Perform a Play	• **Listening and Speaking 1.8** Clarify and enhance oral presentations through the use of appropriate props (e.g., objects, pictures, charts). • **Listening and Speaking 2.2** Plan and present dramatic interpretations of experiences, stories, poems, or plays with clear diction, pitch, tempo, and tone. • **Listening and Speaking 1.9** Use volume, pitch, phrasing, pace, modulation, and gestures appropriately to enhance meaning.
271	Language & Grammar: Describe an Event or Experience	• **Listening and Speaking 1.0** Students listen critically and respond appropriately to oral communication. They speak in a manner that guides the listener to understand important ideas by using proper phrasing, pitch, and modulation. • **Listening and Speaking 2.3** Make descriptive presentations that use concrete sensory details to set forth and support unified impressions of people, places, things, or experiences. • **Listening and Speaking 2.1a** Make narrative presentations: Relate ideas, observations, or recollections about an event or experience. • **Written and Oral English Language Conventions 1.3** Identify and use regular and irregular verbs, adverbs, prepositions, and coordinating conjunctions in writing and speaking.
271	Writing and Grammar: Write About a Performance	• **Writing 2.2** Write descriptions that use concrete sensory details to present and support unified impressions of people, places, things, or experiences. • **Writing 2.1a** Write narratives: Relate ideas, observations, or recollections of an event or experience. • **Written and Oral English Language Conventions 1.3** Identify and use regular and irregular verbs, adverbs, prepositions, and coordinating conjunctions in writing and speaking.

Compare Across Texts

272	Compare Themes in Different Media	• **Reading 3.4** Determine the underlying theme or author's message in fiction and nonfiction text. • **Reading 2.5** Compare and contrast information on the same topic after reading several passages or articles.

Unit Wrap-Up

273	Reflect on Your Reading	• **Reading 2.2** Ask questions and support answers by connecting prior knowledge with literal information found in, and inferred from, the text. • **Reading 2.6** Extract appropriate and significant information from the text, including problems and solutions. • **Reading 2.2** Use appropriate strategies when reading for different purposes (e.g., full comprehension, location of information, personal enjoyment). • **Reading 2.5** Compare and contrast information on the same topic after reading several passages or articles. • **Reading 3.2** Identify the main events of the plot, their causes, and the influence of each on future actions.
	Explore the GQ/Book Talk	• **Listening and Speaking 2.3** Deliver oral summaries of articles and books that contain the main ideas of the event or article and the most significant details.

For additional coverage of the Written and Oral English Language Conventions and the Writing Applications standards, see the California standards maps in the Writing book.

Unit 5   The Drive to Discover

Unit Launch

276–277 **Focus on Genre: Organization of Ideas (In Sequence, By Main Ideas and Details)**	• **Reading 3.1** Distinguish common forms of literature (e.g., poetry, drama, fiction, nonfiction). • **Reading 2.1** Identify structural patterns found in informational text (e.g., compare and contrast, cause and effect, sequential or chronological order, proposition and support) to strengthen comprehension.
278–279 **Focus on Vocabulary: Use Word Parts**	• **Reading 1.6** Use sentence and word context to find the meaning of unknown words. • **Reading 1.8** Use knowledge of prefixes (e.g., *un-, re-, pre-, bi-, mis-, dis-*) and suffixes (e.g., *-er, -est, -ful*) to determine the meaning of words. • **Reading 1.3** Use knowledge of root words to determine the meaning of unknown words within a passage.

Selection 1   Return to *Titanic*

280 **Connect**	• **Listening and Speaking 1.2** Connect and relate prior experiences, insights, and ideas to those of a speaker. • **Reading 2.2** Use appropriate strategies when reading for different purposes (e.g., full comprehension, location of information, personal enjoyment).
281–283 **Language & Grammar: Ask for and Give Information**	• **Listening and Speaking 1.0** Students listen critically and respond appropriately to oral communication. They speak in a manner that guides the listener to understand important ideas by using proper phrasing, pitch, and modulation. • **Listening and Speaking 1.3** Respond to questions with appropriate elaboration. • **Listening and Speaking 1.9** Read prose and poetry aloud with fluency, rhythm, and pace, using appropriate intonation and vocal patterns to emphasize important passages of the text being read. • **Listening and Speaking 1.1** Ask thoughtful questions and respond to relevant questions with appropriate elaboration in oral settings. • **Listening and Speaking 2.4** Recite brief poems (i.e., two or three stanzas), soliloquies, or dramatic dialogues, using clear diction, tempo, volume, and phrasing.
Use Present and Past Tense Verbs	• **Written and Oral English Language Conventions 1.3** Identify and use past, present, and future verb tenses properly in writing and speaking. • **Written and Oral English Language Conventions 1.3** Identify and use regular and irregular verbs, adverbs, prepositions, and coordinating conjunctions in writing and speaking. • **Written and Oral English Language Conventions 1.7** Spell correctly roots, inflections, suffixes and prefixes, and syllable constructions.
284 **Key Vocabulary**	• Learn meaning and pronunciation for vocabulary words central to the understanding and discussion of the selection. • **Reading 1.7** Use a dictionary to learn the meaning and other features of unknown words.
285 **Reading Strategy: Ask Questions**	• **Reading 2.2** Ask questions and support answers by connecting prior knowledge with literal information found in, and inferred from, the text. • **Reading 2.3** Demonstrate comprehension by identifying answers in the text. • **Reading 2.2** Use appropriate strategies when reading for different purposes (e.g., full comprehension, location of information, personal enjoyment).
286 **Focus on Genre: History Article**	• **Reading 2.2** Ask questions and support answers by connecting prior knowledge with literal information found in, and inferred from, the text. • **Reading 3.1** Distinguish common forms of literature (e.g., poetry, drama, fiction, nonfiction). • **Reading 2.1** Identify structural patterns found in informational text (e.g., compare and contrast, cause and effect, sequential or chronological order, proposition and support) to strengthen comprehension.
Your Job as a Reader	• **Reading 2.3** Demonstrate comprehension by identifying answers in the text. • **Reading 2.2** Use appropriate strategies when reading for different purposes (e.g., full comprehension, location of information, personal enjoyment).

Unit 5 The Drive to Discover, continued

287–294	Reading Selection	• **Reading 2.2** Ask questions and support answers by connecting prior knowledge with literal information found in, and inferred from, the text. • **Reading 2.3** Demonstrate comprehension by identifying answers in the text. • **Reading 2.5** Distinguish the main idea and supporting details in expository text. • **Reading 2.6** Extract appropriate and significant information from the text, including problems and solutions. • **Reading 2.1** Identify structural patterns found in informational text (e.g., compare and contrast, cause and effect, sequential or chronological order, proposition and support) to strengthen comprehension. • **Reading 2.2** Use appropriate strategies when reading for different purposes (e.g., full comprehension, location of information, personal enjoyment).
295	Connect Reading and Writing:	
	Critical Thinking	• **Listening and Speaking 2.3** Deliver oral summaries of articles and books that contain the main ideas of the event or article and the most significant details. • **Reading 2.2** Ask questions and support answers by connecting prior knowledge with literal information found in, and inferred from, the text. • **Reading 2.3** Demonstrate comprehension by identifying answers in the text. • **Reading 2.6** Extract appropriate and significant information from the text, including problems and solutions. • **Reading 2.1** Identify structural patterns found in informational text (e.g., compare and contrast, cause and effect, sequential or chronological order, proposition and support) to strengthen comprehension.
	Reading Fluency	• **Reading 1.3** Read aloud narrative and expository text fluently and accurately and with appropriate pacing, intonation, and expression. • **Reading 1.1** Read narrative and expository text aloud with grade-appropriate fluency and accuracy and with appropriate pacing, intonation, and expression.
	Reading Strategy	• **Reading 2.2** Ask questions and support answers by connecting prior knowledge with literal information found in, and inferred from, the text. • **Reading 2.3** Demonstrate comprehension by identifying answers in the text. • **Reading 2.2** Use appropriate strategies when reading for different purposes (e.g., full comprehension, location of information, personal enjoyment).
	Vocabulary Review	• Use vocabulary central to the understanding and discussion of the selection. • **Reading 1.6** Use sentence and word context to find the meaning of unknown words.
	Write About the GQ	• **Writing 2.2a** Write responses to literature: Demonstrate an understanding of the literary work. • **Writing 2.2b** Write responses to literature: Support judgments through references to both the text and prior knowledge.
296	Literary Analysis: Analyze Text Structure (Sequence)	• **Reading 2.1** Identify structural patterns found in informational text (e.g., compare and contrast, cause and effect, sequential or chronological order, proposition and support) to strengthen comprehension.
297	Vocabulary Study: Use Word Parts	• **Reading 1.6** Use sentence and word context to find the meaning of unknown words. • **Reading 1.8** Use knowledge of prefixes (e.g., *un-*, *re-*, *pre-*, *bi-*, *mis-*, *dis-*) and suffixes (e.g., *-er*, *-est*, *-ful*) to determine the meaning of words. • **Reading 1.3** Use knowledge of root words to determine the meaning of unknown words within a passage.

297	Media/Speaking: View the Wreck of Titanic	• **Listening and Speaking 1.3** Respond to questions with appropriate elaboration. • **Writing 1.7** Use various reference materials as an aid to writing (e.g., dictionary, thesaurus, card catalog, encyclopedia, online information). • **Listening and Speaking 1.1** Ask thoughtful questions and respond to relevant questions with appropriate elaboration in oral settings.
298	Listening/Speaking: Conduct a Career Interview	• **Listening and Speaking 1.1** Retell, paraphrase, and explain what has been said by a speaker. • **Listening and Speaking 1.7** Use clear and specific vocabulary to communicate ideas and establish the tone. • **Listening and Speaking 1.1** Ask thoughtful questions and respond to relevant questions with appropriate elaboration in oral settings. • **Listening and Speaking 1.2** Summarize major ideas and supporting evidence presented in spoken messages and formal presentations.
299	Language & Grammar: Ask for and Give Information	• **Listening and Speaking 1.0** Students listen critically and respond appropriately to oral communication. They speak in a manner that guides the listener to understand important ideas by using proper phrasing, pitch, and modulation. • **Listening and Speaking 1.3** Respond to questions with appropriate elaboration. • **Written and Oral English Language Conventions 1.3** Identify and use past, present, and future verb tenses properly in writing and speaking. • **Listening and Speaking 1.1** Ask thoughtful questions and respond to relevant questions with appropriate elaboration in oral settings. • **Written and Oral English Language Conventions 1.3** Identify and use regular and irregular verbs, adverbs, prepositions, and coordinating conjunctions in writing and speaking.
299	Writing and Grammar: Write About the Past	• **Writing 2.2** Write descriptions that use concrete sensory details to present and support unified impressions of people, places, things, or experiences. • **Written and Oral English Language Conventions 1.3** Identify and use past, present, and future verb tenses properly in writing and speaking. • **Writing 2.1a** Relate ideas, observations, or recollections of an event or experience. • **Written and Oral English Language Conventions 1.3** Identify and use regular and irregular verbs, adverbs, prepositions, and coordinating conjunctions in writing and speaking. • **Written and Oral English Language Conventions 1.7** Spell correctly roots, inflections, suffixes and prefixes, and syllable constructions.

Selection 2	**The Forgotton Treasure**

300	Connect	• **Listening and Speaking 1.2** Connect and relate prior experiences, insights, and ideas to those of a speaker. • **Reading 2.2** Use appropriate strategies when reading for different purposes (e.g., full comprehension, location of information, personal enjoyment).
301–303	Language & Grammar: Engage in Discussion	• **Listening and Speaking 1.0** Students listen critically and respond appropriately to oral communication. They speak in a manner that guides the listener to understand important ideas by using proper phrasing, pitch, and modulation. • **Listening and Speaking 1.3** Respond to questions with appropriate elaboration. • **Listening and Speaking 1.9** Read prose and poetry aloud with fluency, rhythm, and pace, using appropriate intonation and vocal patterns to emphasize important passages of the text being read. • **Listening and Speaking 1.1** Ask thoughtful questions and respond to relevant questions with appropriate elaboration in oral settings. • **Listening and Speaking 2.4** Recite brief poems (i.e., two or three stanzas), soliloquies, or dramatic dialogues, using clear diction, tempo, volume, and phrasing.
	Use Verb Tense: *Be* and *Have*	• **Written and Oral English Language Conventions 1.3** Identify and use past, present, and future verb tenses properly in writing and speaking. • **Written and Oral English Language Conventions 1.3** Identify and use regular and irregular verbs, adverbs, prepositions, and coordinating conjunctions in writing and speaking.

Unit 5	The Drive to Discover, continued	
304	Key Vocabulary	• Learn meaning and pronunciation for vocabulary words central to the understanding and discussion of the selection. • **Reading 1.7** Use a dictionary to learn the meaning and other features of unknown words.
305	Reading Strategy: Ask Questions	• **Reading 2.2** Ask questions and support answers by connecting prior knowledge with literal information found in, and inferred from, the text. • **Reading 2.3** Demonstrate comprehension by identifying answers in the text. • **Reading 2.2** Use appropriate strategies when reading for different purposes (e.g., full comprehension, location of information, personal enjoyment).
306	Focus on Genre: Folk Tale	• **Reading 2.2** Ask questions and support answers by connecting prior knowledge with literal information found in, and inferred from, the text. • **Reading 3.1** Distinguish common forms of literature (e.g., poetry, drama, fiction, nonfiction). • **Reading 3.1** Describe the structural differences of various imaginative forms of literature, including fantasies, fables, myths, legends, and fairy tales.
	Your Job as a Reader	• **Reading 2.3** Demonstrate comprehension by identifying answers in the text. • **Reading 2.2** Use appropriate strategies when reading for different purposes (e.g., full comprehension, location of information, personal enjoyment).
307–316	Reading Selection	• **Reading 2.2** Ask questions and support answers by connecting prior knowledge with literal information found in, and inferred from, the text. • **Reading 2.3** Demonstrate comprehension by identifying answers in the text. • **Reading 2.4** Recall major points in the text and make and modify predictions about forthcoming information. • **Reading 2.6** Extract appropriate and significant information from the text, including problems and solutions. • **Reading 2.2** Use appropriate strategies when reading for different purposes (e.g., full comprehension, location of information, personal enjoyment). • **Reading 2.3** Make and confirm predictions by using prior knowledge and ideas presented in the text itself, including illustrations, titles, topic sentences, important words, and foreshadowing clues.

317	**Connect Reading and Writing:**	
	Critical Thinking	• **Listening and Speaking 2.3** Deliver oral summaries of articles and books that contain the main ideas of the event or article and the most significant details.
		• **Reading 2.2** Ask questions and support answers by connecting prior knowledge with literal information found in, and inferred from, the text.
		• **Reading 2.3** Demonstrate comprehension by identifying answers in the text.
		• **Reading 2.6** Extract appropriate and significant information from the text, including problems and solutions.
		• **Reading 2.2** Use appropriate strategies when reading for different purposes (e.g., full comprehension, location of information, personal enjoyment).
		• **Reading 2.5** Compare and contrast information on the same topic after reading several passages or articles.
	Reading Fluency	• **Reading 1.3** Read aloud narrative and expository text fluently and accurately and with appropriate pacing, intonation, and expression.
		• **Reading 1.1** Read narrative and expository text aloud with grade-appropriate fluency and accuracy and with appropriate pacing, intonation, and expression.
	Reading Strategy	• **Reading 2.2** Ask questions and support answers by connecting prior knowledge with literal information found in, and inferred from, the text.
		• **Reading 2.3** Demonstrate comprehension by identifying answers in the text.
		• **Reading 2.2** Use appropriate strategies when reading for different purposes (e.g., full comprehension, location of information, personal enjoyment).
	Vocabulary Review	• Use vocabulary central to the understanding and discussion of the selection.
		• **Reading 1.6** Use sentence and word context to find the meaning of unknown words.
	Write About the GQ	• **Writing 2.2a** Write responses to literature: Demonstrate an understanding of the literary work.
		• **Writing 2.2b** Write responses to literature: Support judgments through references to both the text and prior knowledge.
318	**Literary Analysis: Analyze Text Structure (Sequence)**	• **Reading 3.2** Comprehend basic plots of classic fairy tales, myths, folktales, legends, and fables from around the world.
		• **Reading 2.1** Identify structural patterns found in informational text (e.g., compare and contrast, cause and effect, sequential or chronological order, proposition and support) to strengthen comprehension.
		• **Reading 3.2** Identify the main events of the plot, their causes, and the influence of each on future actions.
319	**Vocabulary Study: Use Word Parts**	• **Reading 1.8** Use knowledge of prefixes (e.g., *un-*, *re-*, *pre-*, *bi-*, *mis-*, *dis-*) and suffixes (e.g., *-er*, *-est*, *-ful*) to determine the meaning of words.
		• **Written and Oral English Language Conventions 1.7** Spell correctly roots, inflections, suffixes and prefixes, and syllable constructions.
319	**Research/Speaking: Discover Tools of the Past**	• **Listening and Speaking 1.8** Clarify and enhance oral presentations through the use of appropriate props (e.g., objects, pictures, charts).
		• **Listening and Speaking 1.9** Use volume, pitch, phrasing, pace, modulation, and gestures appropriately to enhance meaning.
		• **Listening and Speaking 2.3** Deliver oral summaries of articles and books that contain the main ideas of the event or article and the most significant details.
320	**Literary Analysis: Analyze Theme**	• **Reading 3.3** Determine what characters are like by what they say or do and by how the author or illustrator portrays them.
		• **Reading 3.4** Determine the underlying theme or author's message in fiction and nonfiction text.
		• **Reading 3.2** Identify the main events of the plot, their causes, and the influence of each on future actions.

California English–Language Arts Content Standards, continued

| 321 | Language & Grammar: Engage in Discussion | • **Listening and Speaking 1.0** Students listen critically and respond appropriately to oral communication. They speak in a manner that guides the listener to understand important ideas by using proper phrasing, pitch, and modulation.
• **Listening and Speaking 1.3** Respond to questions with appropriate elaboration.
• **Written and Oral English Language Conventions 1.3** Identify and use past, present, and future verb tenses properly in writing and speaking.
• **Listening and Speaking 1.1** Ask thoughtful questions and respond to relevant questions with appropriate elaboration in oral settings.
• **Written and Oral English Language Conventions 1.3** Identify and use regular and irregular verbs, adverbs, prepositions, and coordinating conjunctions in writing and speaking. |
| 321 | Writing and Grammar: Write About the Past | • **Writing 2.1a** Write narratives: Provide a context within which an action takes place.
• **Written and Oral English Language Conventions 1.3** Identify and use past, present, and future verb tenses properly in writing and speaking.
• **Written and Oral English Language Conventions 1.3** Identify and use regular and irregular verbs, adverbs, prepositions, and coordinating conjunctions in writing and speaking. |

Selection 3 — Mysteries of the Ancient Past

322	Connect	• **Listening and Speaking 1.2** Connect and relate prior experiences, insights, and ideas to those of a speaker. • **Reading 2.2** Use appropriate strategies when reading for different purposes (e.g., full comprehension, location of information, personal enjoyment).
323–325	Language & Grammar: Define and Explain	• **Listening and Speaking 1.0** Students listen critically and respond appropriately to oral communication. They speak in a manner that guides the listener to understand important ideas by using proper phrasing, pitch, and modulation. • **Listening and Speaking 1.9** Read prose and poetry aloud with fluency, rhythm, and pace, using appropriate intonation and vocal patterns to emphasize important passages of the text being read. • **Listening and Speaking 1.8** Use details, examples, anecdotes, or experiences to explain or clarify information.
	Use Past Tense Verbs	• **Written and Oral English Language Conventions 1.3** Identify and use past, present, and future verb tenses properly in writing and speaking. • **Written and Oral English Language Conventions 1.3** Identify and use regular and irregular verbs, adverbs, prepositions, and coordinating conjunctions in writing and speaking.
326	Key Vocabulary	• Learn meaning and pronunciation for vocabulary words central to the understanding and discussion of the selection. • **Reading 1.7** Use a dictionary to learn the meaning and other features of unknown words.
327	Reading Strategy: Ask Questions	• **Reading 2.2** Ask questions and support answers by connecting prior knowledge with literal information found in, and inferred from, the text. • **Reading 2.3** Demonstrate comprehension by identifying answers in the text. • **Reading 2.2** Use appropriate strategies when reading for different purposes (e.g., full comprehension, location of information, personal enjoyment).
328	Focus on Genre: History Article	• **Reading 2.5** Distinguish the main idea and supporting details in expository text. • **Reading 3.1** Distinguish common forms of literature (e.g., poetry, drama, fiction, nonfiction). • **Reading 2.1** Identify structural patterns found in informational text (e.g., compare and contrast, cause and effect, sequential or chronological order, proposition and support) to strengthen comprehension.
	Your Job as a Reader	• **Reading 2.2** Ask questions and support answers by connecting prior knowledge with literal information found in, and inferred from, the text. • **Reading 2.3** Demonstrate comprehension by identifying answers in the text. • **Reading 2.2** Use appropriate strategies when reading for different purposes (e.g., full comprehension, location of information, personal enjoyment).

329–340	**Reading Selection**	• **Reading 2.2** Ask questions and support answers by connecting prior knowledge with literal information found in, and inferred from, the text. • **Reading 2.3** Demonstrate comprehension by identifying answers in the text. • **Reading 2.5** Distinguish the main idea and supporting details in expository text. • **Reading 2.6** Extract appropriate and significant information from the text, including problems and solutions. • **Reading 2.2** Use appropriate strategies when reading for different purposes (e.g., full comprehension, location of information, personal enjoyment).
341	**Connect Reading and Writing:**	
	Critical Thinking	• **Reading 2.2** Ask questions and support answers by connecting prior knowledge with literal information found in, and inferred from, the text. • **Reading 2.3** Demonstrate comprehension by identifying answers in the text. • **Reading 2.6** Extract appropriate and significant information from the text, including problems and solutions. • **Listening and Speaking 2.3** Deliver oral summaries of articles and books that contain the main ideas of the event or article and the most significant details.
	Reading Fluency	• **Reading 1.3** Read aloud narrative and expository text fluently and accurately and with appropriate pacing, intonation, and expression. • **Reading 1.1** Read narrative and expository text aloud with grade-appropriate fluency and accuracy and with appropriate pacing, intonation, and expression.
	Reading Strategy	• **Reading 2.2** Ask questions and support answers by connecting prior knowledge with literal information found in, and inferred from, the text. • **Reading 2.3** Demonstrate comprehension by identifying answers in the text. • **Reading 2.2** Use appropriate strategies when reading for different purposes (e.g., full comprehension, location of information, personal enjoyment).
	Vocabulary Review	• Use vocabulary central to the understanding and discussion of the selection. • **Reading 1.6** Use sentence and word context to find the meaning of unknown words.
	Write About the GQ	• **Writing 2.2a** Write responses to literature: Demonstrate an understanding of the literary work. • **Writing 2.2b** Write responses to literature: Support judgments through references to both the text and prior knowledge.
342	**Literary Analysis:** **Analyze Text Structure** **(Main Idea and Details)**	• **Reading 2.5** Distinguish the main idea and supporting details in expository text. • **Reading 2.1** Identify structural patterns found in informational text (e.g., compare and contrast, cause and effect, sequential or chronological order, proposition and support) to strengthen comprehension.
343	**Vocabulary Study:** **Use Word Parts**	• **Reading 1.8** Use knowledge of prefixes (e.g., *un-*, *re-*, *pre-*, *bi-*, *mis-*, *dis-*) and suffixes (e.g., *-er*, *-est*, *-ful*) to determine the meaning of words. • **Reading 1.3** Use knowledge of root words to determine the meaning of unknown words within a passage.
343	**Research/Speaking:** **Research Pyramids**	• **Listening and Speaking 1.6** Provide a beginning, a middle, and an end, including concrete details that develop a central idea). • **Listening and Speaking 1.5** Present effective introductions and conclusions that guide and inform the listener's understanding of important ideas and evidence. • **Listening and Speaking 2.2b** Include facts and details that help listeners to focus. • **Listening and Speaking 2.3** Deliver oral summaries of articles and books that contain the main ideas of the event or article and the most significant details.
344	**Listening/Speaking:** **Explore Egyptian Art**	• **Listening and Speaking 1.8** Clarify and enhance oral presentations through the use of appropriate props (e.g., objects, pictures, charts). • **Listening and Speaking 1.9** Use volume, pitch, phrasing, pace, modulation, and gestures appropriately to enhance meaning. • **Listening and Speaking 2.2a** Make informational presentations: Frame a key question.

Unit 5 The Drive to Discover, continued

345	Language & Grammar: Define and Explain	• **Listening and Speaking 1.0** Students listen critically and respond appropriately to oral communication. They speak in a manner that guides the listener to understand important ideas by using proper phrasing, pitch, and modulation. • **Listening and Speaking 1.8** Use details, examples, anecdotes, or experiences to explain or clarify information. • **Written and Oral English Language Conventions 1.3** Identify and use past, present, and future verb tenses properly in writing and speaking. • **Written and Oral English Language Conventions 1.3** Identify and use regular and irregular verbs, adverbs, prepositions, and coordinating conjunctions in writing and speaking.
345	Writing and Grammar: Write About the Past and Present	• **Writing 2.2** Write descriptions that use concrete sensory details to present and support unified impressions of people, places, things, or experiences. • **Written and Oral English Language Conventions 1.3** Identify and use past, present, and future verb tenses properly in writing and speaking. • **Writing 2.1a** Relate ideas, observations, or recollections of an event or experience. • **Written and Oral English Language Conventions 1.3** Identify and use regular and irregular verbs, adverbs, prepositions, and coordinating conjunctions in writing and speaking.

Compare Across Texts

346	Compare Important Ideas	• **Reading 3.1** Distinguish common forms of literature (e.g., poetry, drama, fiction, nonfiction). • **Reading 2.5** Compare and contrast information on the same topic after reading several passages or articles.

Unit Wrap-Up

347	Reflect on Your Reading	• **Reading 2.2** Ask questions and support answers by connecting prior knowledge with literal information found in, and inferred from, the text. • **Reading 2.6** Extract appropriate and significant information from the text, including problems and solutions. • **Reading 2.1** Identify structural patterns found in informational text (e.g., compare and contrast, cause and effect, sequential or chronological order, proposition and support) to strengthen comprehension. • **Reading 2.2** Use appropriate strategies when reading for different purposes (e.g., full comprehension, location of information, personal enjoyment). • **Reading 2.5** Compare and contrast information on the same topic after reading several passages or articles.
	Explore the GQ/Book Talk	• **Listening and Speaking 2.3** Deliver oral summaries of articles and books that contain the main ideas of the event or article and the most significant details.

For additional coverage of the Written and Oral English Language Conventions and the Writing Applications standards, see the California standards maps in the Writing book.

350–351	Focus on Genre: Organization of Ideas (Cause and Effect)	• **Reading 3.1** Distinguish common forms of literature (e.g., poetry, drama, fiction, nonfiction). • **Reading 2.1** Identify structural patterns found in informational text (e.g., compare and contrast, cause and effect, sequential or chronological order, proposition and support) to strengthen comprehension. • **Reading 2.6** Distinguish between cause and effect and between fact and opinion in expository text.
352–353	Focus on Vocabulary: Use Context Clues for Unfamiliar Words	• **Reading 1.6** Use sentence and word context to find the meaning of unknown words.

Selection 1 — Escaping to Freedom

354	Connect	• **Listening and Speaking 1.2** Connect and relate prior experiences, insights, and ideas to those of a speaker. • **Reading 2.2** Use appropriate strategies when reading for different purposes (e.g., full comprehension, location of information, personal enjoyment).
355–357	Language & Grammar: Summarize	• **Listening and Speaking 1.0** Students listen critically and respond appropriately to oral communication. They speak in a manner that guides the listener to understand important ideas by using proper phrasing, pitch, and modulation. • **Listening and Speaking 1.9** Read prose and poetry aloud with fluency, rhythm, and pace, using appropriate intonation and vocal patterns to emphasize important passages of the text being read. • **Listening and Speaking 1.2** Summarize major ideas and supporting evidence presented in spoken messages and formal presentations.
	Use Nouns in the Subject and Predicate	• **Written and Oral English Language Conventions 1.2** Identify subjects and verbs that are in agreement and identify and use pronouns, adjectives, compound words, and articles correctly in writing and speaking.
358	Key Vocabulary	• Learn meaning and pronunciation for vocabulary words central to the understanding and discussion of the selection. • **Reading 1.7** Use a dictionary to learn the meaning and other features of unknown words.
359	Reading Strategy: Determine Importance	• **Reading 2.1** Use titles, tables of contents, chapter headings, glossaries, and indexes to locate information in text. • **Reading 2.2** Use appropriate strategies when reading for different purposes (e.g., full comprehension, location of information, personal enjoyment). • **Listening and Speaking 2.3** Deliver oral summaries of articles and books that contain the main ideas of the event or article and the most significant details.
360	Focus on Genre: Biography	• **Reading 2.1** Use titles, tables of contents, chapter headings, glossaries, and indexes to locate information in text. • **Reading 3.1** Distinguish common forms of literature (e.g., poetry, drama, fiction, nonfiction). • **Reading 2.1** Identify structural patterns found in informational text (e.g., compare and contrast, cause and effect, sequential or chronological order, proposition and support) to strengthen comprehension.
	Your Job as a Reader	• **Reading 2.2** Use appropriate strategies when reading for different purposes (e.g., full comprehension, location of information, personal enjoyment). • **Listening and Speaking 2.3** Deliver oral summaries of articles and books that contain the main ideas of the event or article and the most significant details.

Unit 6	Struggle for Freedom, continued	
361–368	Reading Selection	• **Reading 2.2** Ask questions and support answers by connecting prior knowledge with literal information found in, and inferred from, the text. • **Reading 2.3** Demonstrate comprehension by identifying answers in the text. • **Reading 2.6** Extract appropriate and significant information from the text, including problems and solutions. • **Reading 2.2** Use appropriate strategies when reading for different purposes (e.g., full comprehension, location of information, personal enjoyment). • **Reading 2.6** Distinguish between cause and effect and between fact and opinion in expository text.
369	Connect Reading and Writing:	
	Critical Thinking	• **Listening and Speaking 2.3** Deliver oral summaries of articles and books that contain the main ideas of the event or article and the most significant details. • **Reading 2.2** Ask questions and support answers by connecting prior knowledge with literal information found in, and inferred from, the text. • **Reading 2.3** Demonstrate comprehension by identifying answers in the text. • **Reading 2.6** Extract appropriate and significant information from the text, including problems and solutions.
	Reading Fluency	• **Reading 1.3** Read aloud narrative and expository text fluently and accurately and with appropriate pacing, intonation, and expression. • **Reading 1.1** Read narrative and expository text aloud with grade-appropriate fluency and accuracy and with appropriate pacing, intonation, and expression.
	Reading Strategy	• **Reading 2.1** Use titles, tables of contents, chapter headings, glossaries, and indexes to locate information in text. • **Listening and Speaking 2.3** Deliver oral summaries of articles and books that contain the main ideas of the event or article and the most significant details. • **Reading 2.2** Use appropriate strategies when reading for different purposes (e.g., full comprehension, location of information, personal enjoyment).
	Vocabulary Review	• Use vocabulary central to the understanding and discussion of the selection. • **Reading 1.6** Use sentence and word context to find the meaning of unknown words.
	Write About the GQ	• **Writing 2.2a** Write responses to literature: Demonstrate an understanding of the literary work. • **Writing 2.2b** Write responses to literature: Support judgments through references to both the text and prior knowledge.
370	Literary Analysis: Analyze Text Structure (Cause and Effect)	• **Reading 2.1** Identify structural patterns found in informational text (e.g., compare and contrast, cause and effect, sequential or chronological order, proposition and support) to strengthen comprehension. • **Reading 2.6** Distinguish between cause and effect and between fact and opinion in expository text.
371	Vocabulary Study: Use Context Clues	• **Reading 1.6** Use sentence and word context to find the meaning of unknown words.
371	Research/Writing: Research the Underground Railroad	• **Writing 1.1** Select a focus, an organizational structure, and a point of view based upon purpose, audience, length, and format requirements. • **Writing 1.5** Quote or paraphrase information sources, citing them appropriately. • **Writing 1.7** Use various reference materials as an aid to writing (e.g., dictionary, thesaurus, card catalog, encyclopedia, online information). • **Writing 2.3b** Write information reports: Include facts and details for focus.
372	Listening/Speaking: Dramatize a Song	• **Listening and Speaking 1.9** Read prose and poetry aloud with fluency, rhythm, and pace, using appropriate intonation and vocal patterns to emphasize important passages of the text being read. • **Listening and Speaking 1.3** Identify how language usages (e.g., sayings, expressions) reflect regions and cultures. • **Listening and Speaking 2.4** Recite brief poems (i.e., two or three stanzas), soliloquies, or dramatic dialogues, using clear diction, tempo, volume, and phrasing.

373	**Language & Grammar:** **Summarize**	• **Listening and Speaking 1.0** Students listen critically and respond appropriately to oral communication. They speak in a manner that guides the listener to understand important ideas by using proper phrasing, pitch, and modulation. • **Written and Oral English Language Conventions 1.2** Identify subjects and verbs that are in agreement and identify and use pronouns, adjectives, compound words, and articles correctly in writing and speaking. • **Listening and Speaking 1.2** Summarize major ideas and supporting evidence presented in spoken messages and formal presentations.
373	**Writing and Grammar:** **Write About Freedom**	• **Writing 2.2** Write descriptions that use concrete sensory details to present and support unified impressions of people, places, things, or experiences. • **Written and Oral English Language Conventions 1.2** Identify subjects and verbs that are in agreement and identify and use pronouns, adjectives, compound words, and articles correctly in writing and speaking. • **Writing 2.1a** Write narratives: Relate ideas, observations, or recollections of an event or experience.
Selection 2		**Brave Butterflies**
374	**Connect**	• **Listening and Speaking 1.2** Connect and relate prior experiences, insights, and ideas to those of a speaker. • **Reading 2.2** Use appropriate strategies when reading for different purposes (e.g., full comprehension, location of information, personal enjoyment).
375–377	**Language & Grammar:** **Make Comparisons**	• **Listening and Speaking 1.0** Students listen critically and respond appropriately to oral communication. They speak in a manner that guides the listener to understand important ideas by using proper phrasing, pitch, and modulation. • **Listening and Speaking 1.9** Read prose and poetry aloud with fluency, rhythm, and pace, using appropriate intonation and vocal patterns to emphasize important passages of the text being read. • **Listening and Speaking 2.4** Recite brief poems (i.e., two or three stanzas), soliloquies, or dramatic dialogues, using clear diction, tempo, volume, and phrasing.
	Use Pronouns in the **Subject and Predicate**	• **Written and Oral English Language Conventions 1.2** Identify subjects and verbs that are in agreement and identify and use pronouns, adjectives, compound words, and articles correctly in writing and speaking.
378	**Key Vocabulary**	• Learn meaning and pronunciation for vocabulary words central to the understanding and discussion of the selection. • **Reading 1.7** Use a dictionary to learn the meaning and other features of unknown words.
379	**Reading Strategy:** **Determine Importance**	• **Reading 2.2** Use appropriate strategies when reading for different purposes (e.g., full comprehension, location of information, personal enjoyment). • **Writing 2.4** Write summaries that contain the main ideas of the reading selection and the most significant details.
380	**Focus on Genre:** **Short Story**	• **Reading 3.1** Distinguish common forms of literature (e.g., poetry, drama, fiction, nonfiction). • **Reading 2.1** Identify structural patterns found in informational text (e.g., compare and contrast, cause and effect, sequential or chronological order, proposition and support) to strengthen comprehension. • **Reading 3.1** Describe the structural differences of various imaginative forms of literature, including fantasies, fables, myths, legends, and fairy tales.
	Your Job as a Reader	• **Reading 2.2** Use appropriate strategies when reading for different purposes (e.g., full comprehension, location of information, personal enjoyment). • **Writing 2.4** Write summaries that contain the main ideas of the reading selection and the most significant details.

Unit 6 Struggle for Freedom, continued

381–390	**Reading Selection**	• **Reading 2.2** Ask questions and support answers by connecting prior knowledge with literal information found in, and inferred from, the text. • **Reading 2.3** Demonstrate comprehension by identifying answers in the text. • **Reading 2.4** Recall major points in the text and make and modify predictions about forthcoming information. • **Reading 2.6** Extract appropriate and significant information from the text, including problems and solutions. • **Reading 2.2** Use appropriate strategies when reading for different purposes (e.g., full comprehension, location of information, personal enjoyment). • **Reading 2.3** Make and confirm predictions by using prior knowledge and ideas presented in the text itself, including illustrations, titles, topic sentences, important words, and foreshadowing clues.
391	**Connect Reading and Writing:**	
	Critical Thinking	• **Reading 2.2** Ask questions and support answers by connecting prior knowledge with literal information found in, and inferred from, the text. • **Reading 2.3** Demonstrate comprehension by identifying answers in the text. • **Reading 2.6** Extract appropriate and significant information from the text, including problems and solutions. • **Reading 2.4** Evaluate new information and hypotheses by testing them against known information and ideas. • **Reading 2.5** Compare and contrast information on the same topic after reading several passages or articles. • **Listening and Speaking 2.3** Deliver oral summaries of articles and books that contain the main ideas of the event or article and the most significant details.
	Reading Fluency	• **Reading 1.3** Read aloud narrative and expository text fluently and accurately and with appropriate pacing, intonation, and expression. • **Reading 1.1** Read narrative and expository text aloud with grade-appropriate fluency and accuracy and with appropriate pacing, intonation, and expression.
	Reading Strategy	• **Reading 2.2** Use appropriate strategies when reading for different purposes (e.g., full comprehension, location of information, personal enjoyment). • **Writing 2.4** Write summaries that contain the main ideas of the reading selection and the most significant details.
	Vocabulary Review	• Use vocabulary central to the understanding and discussion of the selection. • **Reading 1.6** Use sentence and word context to find the meaning of unknown words.
	Write About the GQ	• **Writing 2.2a** Write responses to literature: Demonstrate an understanding of the literary work. • **Writing 2.2b** Write responses to literature: Support judgments through references to both the text and prior knowledge.
392	**Literary Analysis: Analyze Text Structure (Cause and Effect)**	• **Reading 3.2** Identify the main events of the plot, their causes, and the influence of each on future actions.
393	**Vocabulary Study: Use Context Clues**	• **Reading 1.6** Use sentence and word context to find the meaning of unknown words.

393	**Research/Speaking:** **Research Freedom Seekers**	• **Listening and Speaking 1.8** Clarify and enhance oral presentations through the use of appropriate props (e.g., objects, pictures, charts). • **Listening and Speaking 2.1a** Make brief narrative presentations: Provide a context for an incident that is the subject of the presentation. • **Listening and Speaking 2.1b** Make brief narrative presentations: Provide insight into why the selected incident is memorable. • **Listening and Speaking 2.1b** Make narrative presentations: Provide a context that enables the listener to imagine the circumstances of the event or experience. • **Listening and Speaking 2.1c** Make narrative presentations: Provide insight into why the selected event or experience is memorable. • **Listening and Speaking 2.2c** Incorporate more than one source of information (e.g., speakers, books, newspapers, television, or radio reports).
394	**Literary Analysis:** **Analyze the Topic**	• **Reading 2.5** Compare and contrast information on the same topic after reading several passages or articles.
395	**Language & Grammar:** **Make Comparisons**	• **Listening and Speaking 1.0** Students listen critically and respond appropriately to oral communication. They speak in a manner that guides the listener to understand important ideas by using proper phrasing, pitch, and modulation. • **Written and Oral English Language Conventions 1.2** Identify subjects and verbs that are in agreement and identify and use pronouns, adjectives, compound words, and articles correctly in writing and speaking.
395	**Writing and Grammar:** **Write About a New Home**	• **Writing 2.1a** Write narratives: Provide a context within which an action takes place. • **Written and Oral English Language Conventions 1.2** Identify subjects and verbs that are in agreement and identify and use pronouns, adjectives, compound words, and articles correctly in writing and speaking. • **Writing 2.1a** Write narratives: Relate ideas, observations, or recollections of an event or experience.

Selection 3   Seeking Freedom

396	**Connect**	• **Listening and Speaking 1.2** Connect and relate prior experiences, insights, and ideas to those of a speaker. • **Reading 2.2** Use appropriate strategies when reading for different purposes (e.g., full comprehension, location of information, personal enjoyment).
397–399	**Language & Grammar:** **Express Opinions**	• **Listening and Speaking 1.0** Students listen critically and respond appropriately to oral communication. They speak in a manner that guides the listener to understand important ideas by using proper phrasing, pitch, and modulation. • **Listening and Speaking 1.3** Respond to questions with appropriate elaboration. • **Listening and Speaking 1.9** Read prose and poetry aloud with fluency, rhythm, and pace, using appropriate intonation and vocal patterns to emphasize important passages of the text being read. • **Listening and Speaking 1.1** Ask thoughtful questions and respond to relevant questions with appropriate elaboration in oral settings.
	Use Possessive Nouns	• **Written and Oral English Language Conventions 1.2** Identify subjects and verbs that are in agreement and identify and use pronouns, adjectives, compound words, and articles correctly in writing and speaking. • **Written and Oral English Language Conventions 1.4** Use parentheses, commas in direct quotations, and apostrophes in the possessive case of nouns and in contractions.
400	**Key Vocabulary**	• Learn meaning and pronunciation for vocabulary words central to the understanding and discussion of the selection. • **Reading 1.7** Use a dictionary to learn the meaning and other features of unknown words.
401	**Reading Strategy:** **Determine Importance**	• **Reading 2.2** Use appropriate strategies when reading for different purposes (e.g., full comprehension, location of information, personal enjoyment).

California English–Language Arts Content Standards, continued

402	**Focus on Genre:** **History Feature**	• **Reading 2.1** Identify structural patterns found in informational text (e.g., compare and contrast, cause and effect, sequential or chronological order, proposition and support) to strengthen comprehension.
		• **Reading 3.1** Distinguish common forms of literature (e.g., poetry, drama, fiction, nonfiction).
	Your Job as a Reader	• **Reading 2.2** Use appropriate strategies when reading for different purposes (e.g., full comprehension, location of information, personal enjoyment).
		• **Reading 2.6** Distinguish between cause and effect and between fact and opinion in expository text.
403–412	**Reading Selection**	• **Reading 2.2** Ask questions and support answers by connecting prior knowledge with literal information found in, and inferred from, the text.
		• **Reading 2.3** Demonstrate comprehension by identifying answers in the text.
		• **Reading 2.6** Extract appropriate and significant information from the text, including problems and solutions.
		• **Reading 2.2** Use appropriate strategies when reading for different purposes (e.g., full comprehension, location of information, personal enjoyment).
		• **Reading 2.6** Distinguish between cause and effect and between fact and opinion in expository text.
413	**Connect Reading and Writing:**	
	Critical Thinking	• **Reading 2.2** Ask questions and support answers by connecting prior knowledge with literal information found in, and inferred from, the text.
		• **Reading 2.3** Demonstrate comprehension by identifying answers in the text.
		• **Reading 2.6** Extract appropriate and significant information from the text, including problems and solutions.
		• **Listening and Speaking 2.3** Deliver oral summaries of articles and books that contain the main ideas of the event or article and the most significant details.
	Reading Fluency	• **Reading 1.3** Read aloud narrative and expository text fluently and accurately and with appropriate pacing, intonation, and expression.
		• **Reading 1.1** Read narrative and expository text aloud with grade-appropriate fluency and accuracy and with appropriate pacing, intonation, and expression.
	Reading Strategy	• **Reading 2.2** Use appropriate strategies when reading for different purposes (e.g., full comprehension, location of information, personal enjoyment).
	Vocabulary Review	• Use vocabulary central to the understanding and discussion of the selection.
		• **Reading 1.6** Use sentence and word context to find the meaning of unknown words.
	Write About the GQ	• **Writing 2.2a** Write responses to literature: Demonstrate an understanding of the literary work.
		• **Writing 2.2b** Write responses to literature: Support judgments through references to both the text and prior knowledge.
414	**Literary Analysis:** **Analyze Text Structure** **(Cause and Effect)**	• **Reading 2.1** Identify structural patterns found in informational text (e.g., compare and contrast, cause and effect, sequential or chronological order, proposition and support) to strengthen comprehension.
		• **Reading 2.6** Distinguish between cause and effect and between fact and opinion in expository text.
415	**Vocabulary Study:** **Use Context Clues**	• **Reading 1.6** Use sentence and word context to find the meaning of unknown words.
415	**Research/Writing:** **Research Constitutional Rights**	• **Writing 1.1** Select a focus, an organizational structure, and a point of view based upon purpose, audience, length, and format requirements.
		• **Writing 2.3a** Write information reports: Frame a central question about an issue or situation.
416	**Literary Analysis:** **Distinguish Facts and Opinions**	• **Reading 3.1** Distinguish common forms of literature (e.g., poetry, drama, fiction, nonfiction).
		• **Reading 2.6** Distinguish between cause and effect and between fact and opinion in expository text.

417	**Language & Grammar:** **Express Opinions**	• **Listening and Speaking 1.0** Students listen critically and respond appropriately to oral communication. They speak in a manner that guides the listener to understand important ideas by using proper phrasing, pitch, and modulation.
		• **Listening and Speaking 1.3** Respond to questions with appropriate elaboration.
		• **Listening and Speaking 1.1** Ask thoughtful questions and respond to relevant questions with appropriate elaboration in oral settings.
		• **Written and Oral English Language Conventions 1.2** Identify subjects and verbs that are in agreement and identify and use pronouns, adjectives, compound words, and articles correctly in writing and speaking.
417	**Writing and Grammar:** **Write About Human Rights**	• **Writing 2.1a** Write narratives: Provide a context within which an action takes place.
		• **Written and Oral English Language Conventions 1.2** Identify subjects and verbs that are in agreement and identify and use pronouns, adjectives, compound words, and articles correctly in writing and speaking.
		• **Writing 2.1a** Write narratives: Relate ideas, observations, or recollections of an event or experience.
		• **Writing 2.1b** Write narratives: Provide a context to enable the reader to imagine the world of the event or experience.
		• **Written and Oral English Language Conventions 1.4** Use parentheses, commas in direct quotations, and apostrophes in the possessive case of nouns and in contractions.

Compare Across Texts

418	**Compare Writing on the Same Topic**	• **Writing 1.1b** Create a single paragraph: Include simple supporting facts and details.
		• **Reading 2.5** Compare and contrast information on the same topic after reading several passages or articles.

Unit Wrap-Up

419	**Reflect on Your Reading**	• **Reading 2.2** Ask questions and support answers by connecting prior knowledge with literal information found in, and inferred from, the text.
		• **Reading 2.6** Extract appropriate and significant information from the text, including problems and solutions.
		• **Reading 2.1** Identify structural patterns found in informational text (e.g., compare and contrast, cause and effect, sequential or chronological order, proposition and support) to strengthen comprehension.
		• **Reading 2.2** Use appropriate strategies when reading for different purposes (e.g., full comprehension, location of information, personal enjoyment).
		• **Reading 2.5** Compare and contrast information on the same topic after reading several passages or articles.
	Explore the GQ/Book Talk	• **Listening and Speaking 2.3** Deliver oral summaries of articles and books that contain the main ideas of the event or article and the most significant details.

For additional coverage of the Written and Oral English Language Conventions and the Writing Applications standards, see the California standards maps in the Writing book.

Unit 7 Star Power

Unit Launch

424–425	**Focus on Vocabulary: Use Context Clues for Multiple-Meaning Words**	• **Reading 1.6** Distinguish and interpret words with multiple meanings.

Selection 1 | The Earth Under Sky Bear's Feet

426	**Connect**	• **Listening and Speaking 1.2** Connect and relate prior experiences, insights, and ideas to those of a speaker. • **Reading 2.2** Use appropriate strategies when reading for different purposes (e.g., full comprehension, location of information, personal enjoyment). • **Listening and Speaking 1.1** Ask thoughtful questions and respond to relevant questions with appropriate elaboration in oral settings.
427–429	**Language & Grammar: Describe**	• **Listening and Speaking 1.0** Students listen critically and respond appropriately to oral communication. They speak in a manner that guides the listener to understand important ideas by using proper phrasing, pitch, and modulation. • **Listening and Speaking 1.1** Retell, paraphrase, and explain what has been said by a speaker. • **Listening and Speaking 2.3** Make descriptive presentations that use concrete sensory details to set forth and support unified impressions of people, places, things, or experiences
	Use Prepositions	• **Written and Oral English Language Conventions 1.3** Identify and use past, present, and future verb tenses properly in writing and speaking.
430	**Key Vocabulary**	• Learn meaning and pronunciation for vocabulary words central to the understanding and discussion of the selection. • **Reading 1.7** Use a dictionary to learn the meaning and other features of unknown words.
431	**Reading Strategy: Make Inferences**	• **Reading 2.2** Use appropriate strategies when reading for different purposes (e.g., full comprehension, location of information, personal enjoyment).
432	**Focus on Genre: Myth**	• **Reading 3.1** Distinguish common forms of literature (e.g., poetry, drama, fiction, nonfiction).
	Your Job as a Reader	• **Reading 2.2** Use appropriate strategies when reading for different purposes (e.g., full comprehension, location of information, personal enjoyment).
433–442	**Reading Selection**	• **Reading 2.2** Ask questions and support answers by connecting prior knowledge with literal information found in, and inferred from, the text. • **Reading 2.3** Demonstrate comprehension by identifying answers in the text. • **Reading 2.2** Use appropriate strategies when reading for different purposes (e.g., full comprehension, location of information, personal enjoyment).

443 Connect Reading and Writing:

Critical Thinking	• **Reading 2.2** Ask questions and support answers by connecting prior knowledge with literal information found in, and inferred from, the text.
	• **Reading 2.3** Demonstrate comprehension by identifying answers in the text.
Reading Fluency	• **Reading 2.6** Extract appropriate and significant information from the text, including problems and solutions.
	• **Reading 1.1** Read narrative and expository text aloud with grade-appropriate fluency and accuracy and with appropriate pacing, intonation, and expression.
Reading Strategy	• **Reading 2.2** Use appropriate strategies when reading for different purposes (e.g., full comprehension, location of information, personal enjoyment).
Vocabulary Review	• Use vocabulary central to the understanding and discussion of the selection.
	• **Reading 1.6** Use sentence and word context to find the meaning of unknown words.
Write About the GQ	• **Writing 2.2b** Write responses to literature: Support judgments through references to both the text and prior knowledge.

444	**Literary Analysis: Compare Myths**	• **Reading 3.1** Describe the structural differences of various imaginative forms of literature, including fantasies, fables, myths, legends, and fairy tales.
		• **Reading 3.4** Compare and contrast tales from different cultures by tracing the exploits of one character type and develop theories to account for similar tales in diverse cultures (e.g., trickster tales).
445	**Vocabulary Study: Use Context Clues**	• **Reading 1.6** Distinguish and interpret words with multiple meanings.
445	**Research/Speaking: Research Stories About Stars**	• **Writing 1.1** Select a focus, an organizational structure, and a point of view based upon purpose, audience, length, and format requirements.
446	**Literary Analysis: Analyze Mood and Tone**	• **Reading 3.5** Define figurative language (e.g., simile, metaphor, hyperbole, personification) and identify its use in literary works.
447	**Language & Grammar: Describe**	• **Listening and Speaking 1.1** Retell, paraphrase, and explain what has been said by a speaker.
		• **Listening and Speaking 1.3** Respond to questions with appropriate elaboration.

Selection 2		**A Universe of Stars**
448	**Connect**	• **Listening and Speaking 1.2** Connect and relate prior experiences, insights, and ideas to those of a speaker.
		• **Reading 2.2** Use appropriate strategies when reading for different purposes (e.g., full comprehension, location of information, personal enjoyment).
449-451	**Language & Grammar: Define and Explain**	• **Listening and Speaking 1.0** Students listen critically and respond appropriately to oral communication. They speak in a manner that guides the listener to understand important ideas by using proper phrasing, pitch, and modulation.
		• **Listening and Speaking 1.8** Use details, examples, anecdotes, or experiences to explain or clarify information.
	Use Pronouns in Prepositional Phrases	• **Written and Oral English Language Conventions 1.2** Identify subjects and verbs that are in agreement and identify and use pronouns, adjectives, compound words, and articles correctly in writing and speaking.
		• **Written and Oral English Language Conventions 1.3** Identify and use regular and irregular verbs, adverbs, prepositions, and coordinating conjunctions in writing and speaking.
452	**Key Vocabulary**	• Learn meaning and pronunciation for vocabulary words central to the understanding and discussion of the selection.
		• **Reading 1.7** Use a dictionary to learn the meaning and other features of unknown words.
453	**Reading Strategy: Make Inferences**	• **Reading 2.2** Use appropriate strategies when reading for different purposes (e.g., full comprehension, location of information, personal enjoyment).

Unit 7   Star Power, continued

454	**Focus on Genre:** **Science Article**	• **Reading 3.1** Distinguish common forms of literature (e.g., poetry, drama, fiction, nonfiction).
	Your Job as a Reader	• **Reading 2.2** Use appropriate strategies when reading for different purposes (e.g., full comprehension, location of information, personal enjoyment).
455–462	**Reading Selection**	• **Reading 2.2** Ask questions and support answers by connecting prior knowledge with literal information found in, and inferred from, the text. • **Reading 2.3** Demonstrate comprehension by identifying answers in the text. • **Reading 2.6** Extract appropriate and significant information from the text, including problems and solutions. • **Reading 2.2** Use appropriate strategies when reading for different purposes (e.g., full comprehension, location of information, personal enjoyment).
463	**Connect Reading and Writing:**	
	Critical Thinking	• **Reading 2.2** Ask questions and support answers by connecting prior knowledge with literal information found in, and inferred from, the text. • **Reading 2.3** Demonstrate comprehension by identifying answers in the text. • **Reading 2.6** Extract appropriate and significant information from the text, including problems and solutions. • **Listening and Speaking 2.3** Deliver oral summaries of articles and books that contain the main ideas of the event or article and the most significant details.
	Reading Fluency	• **Reading 1.1** Read narrative and expository text aloud with grade-appropriate fluency and accuracy and with appropriate pacing, intonation, and expression.
	Reading Strategy	• **Reading 2.2** Use appropriate strategies when reading for different purposes (e.g., full comprehension, location of information, personal enjoyment).
	Vocabulary Review	• Use vocabulary central to the understanding and discussion of the selection. • **Reading 1.6** Use sentence and word context to find the meaning of unknown words.
	Write About the GQ	• **Writing 2.2a** Write responses to literature: Demonstrate an understanding of the literary work. • **Writing 2.2b** Write responses to literature: Support judgments through references to both the text and prior knowledge.
464	**Literary Analysis: Analyze Style**	• **Reading 2.5** Compare and contrast information on the same topic after reading several passages or articles.
465	**Vocabulary Study:** **Use Context Clues**	• **Reading 1.4** Use knowledge of antonyms, synonyms, homophones, and homographs to determine the meanings of words. • **Reading 1.6** Use sentence and word context to find the meaning of unknown words. • **Reading 1.6** Distinguish and interpret words with multiple meanings.
465	**Research/Speaking:** **Research Energy**	• **Listening and Speaking 1.6** Use traditional structures for conveying information (e.g., cause and effect, similarity and difference, posing and answering a question). • **Listening and Speaking 1.7** Emphasize points in ways that help the listener or viewer to follow important ideas and concepts. • **Listening and Speaking 2.2b** Make informational presentations: Include facts and details that help listeners to focus. • **Listening and Speaking 2.2c** Make informational presentations: Incorporate more than one source of information (e.g., speakers, books, newspapers, television or radio reports).
466	**Literary Analysis:** **Analyze Author's Purpose**	• **Reading 3.1** Distinguish common forms of literature (e.g., poetry, drama, fiction, nonfiction). • **Reading 3.1** Describe the structural differences of various imaginative forms of literature, including fantasies, fables, myths, legends, and fairy tales.
467	**Language & Grammar:** **Define and Explain**	• **Listening and Speaking 1.8** Use details, examples, anecdotes, or experiences to explain or clarify information.

467	**Writing and Grammar: Write About an Adventure**	• **Written and Oral English Language Conventions 1.2** Identify subjects and verbs that are in agreement and identify and use pronouns, adjectives, compound words, and articles correctly in writing and speaking. • **Written and Oral English Language Conventions 1.3** Identify and use regular and irregular verbs, adverbs, prepositions, and coordinating conjunctions in writing and speaking.
Selection 3		**Not-So-Starry Nights**
468	**Connect**	• **Listening and Speaking 1.2** Connect and relate prior experiences, insights, and ideas to those of a speaker. • **Reading 2.2** Use appropriate strategies when reading for different purposes (e.g., full comprehension, location of information, personal enjoyment).
469–471	**Language & Grammar: Persuade**	• **Listening and Speaking 1.0** Students listen critically and respond appropriately to oral communication. They speak in a manner that guides the listener to understand important ideas by using proper phrasing, pitch, and modulation.
472	**Key Vocabulary**	• Learn meaning and pronunciation for vocabulary words central to the understanding and discussion of the selection. • **Reading 1.7** Use a dictionary to learn the meaning and other features of unknown words.
473	**Reading Strategy: Make Inferences**	• **Reading 2.2** Use appropriate strategies when reading for different purposes (e.g., full comprehension, location of information, personal enjoyment).
474	**Focus on Genre: Persuasive Essay**	• **Reading 3.1** Distinguish common forms of literature (e.g., poetry, drama, fiction, nonfiction). • **Reading 2.1** Identify structural patterns found in informational text (e.g., compare and contrast, cause and effect, sequential or chronological order, proposition and support) to strengthen comprehension.
	Your Job as a Reader	• **Reading 2.2** Use appropriate strategies when reading for different purposes (e.g., full comprehension, location of information, personal enjoyment).
475–484	**Reading Selection**	• **Reading 2.2** Ask questions and support answers by connecting prior knowledge with literal information found in, and inferred from, the text. • **Reading 2.3** Demonstrate comprehension by identifying answers in the text. • **Reading 2.2** Use appropriate strategies when reading for different purposes (e.g., full comprehension, location of information, personal enjoyment).
485	**Connect Reading and Writing:**	
	Critical Thinking	• **Reading 2.3** Demonstrate comprehension by identifying answers in the text. • **Reading 2.6** Extract appropriate and significant information from the text, including problems and solutions. • **Listening and Speaking 2.3** Deliver oral summaries of articles and books that contain the main ideas of the event or article and the most significant details.
	Reading Fluency	• **Reading 1.1** Read narrative and expository text aloud with grade-appropriate fluency and accuracy and with appropriate pacing, intonation, and expression.
	Reading Strategy	• **Reading 2.2** Use appropriate strategies when reading for different purposes (e.g., full comprehension, location of information, personal enjoyment).
	Vocabulary Review	• Use vocabulary central to the understanding and discussion of the selection. • **Reading 1.6** Use sentence and word context to find the meaning of unknown words.
	Write About the GQ	• **Writing 2.2a** Write responses to literature: Demonstrate an understanding of the literary work. • **Writing 2.2b** Write responses to literature: Support judgments through references to both the text and prior knowledge.
486	**Literary Analysis: Analyze Persuasive Techniques**	• **Reading 2.1** Identify structural patterns found in informational text (e.g., compare and contrast, cause and effect, sequential or chronological order, proposition and support) to strengthen comprehension.

California English–Language Arts Content Standards, continued

For additional coverage of the Written and Oral English Language Conventions and the Writing Applications standards, see the California standards maps in the Writing book.

Unit Launch

494–495	**Focus on Genre: Text Features (Fiction and Nonfiction)**	• **Reading 2.1** Use titles, tables of contents, chapter headings, glossaries, and indexes to locate information in text.
496–497	**Focus on Vocabulary: Go Beyond the Literal Meaning**	• **Reading 3.5** Define figurative language (e.g., simile, metaphor, hyperbole, personification) and identify its use in literary works.

Selection 1 — Old Music Finds New Voices

498	**Connect**	• **Listening and Speaking 1.2** Connect and relate prior experiences, insights, and ideas to those of a speaker. • **Reading 2.2** Use appropriate strategies when reading for different purposes (e.g., full comprehension, location of information, personal enjoyment).
499–501	**Language & Grammar: Use Appropriate Language**	• **Listening and Speaking 1.0** Students listen critically and respond appropriately to oral communication. They speak in a manner that guides the listener to understand important ideas by using proper phrasing, pitch, and modulation. • **Listening and Speaking 1.7** Use clear and specific vocabulary to communicate ideas and establish the tone. • **Listening and Speaking 1.9** Read prose and poetry aloud with fluency, rhythm, and pace, using appropriate intonation and vocal patterns to emphasize important passages of the text being read. • **Listening and Speaking 2.1** Make brief narrative presentations.
	Use Complete Sentences	• **Written and Oral English Language Conventions 1.1** Understand and be able to use complete and correct declarative, interrogative, imperative, and exclamatory sentences in writing and speaking.
502	**Key Vocabulary**	• Learn meaning and pronunciation for vocabulary words central to the understanding and discussion of the selection. • **Reading 1.7** Use a dictionary to learn the meaning and other features of unknown words.
503	**Reading Strategy: Synthesize**	• **Reading 2.4** Recall major points in the text and make and modify predictions about forthcoming information. • **Reading 2.2** Use appropriate strategies when reading for different purposes (e.g., full comprehension, location of information, personal enjoyment). • **Reading 2.4** Evaluate new information and hypotheses by testing them against known information and ideas.
504	**Focus on Genre: Newspaper Article**	• **Reading 2.1** Use titles, tables of contents, chapter headings, glossaries, and indexes to locate information in text. • **Reading 3.5** Define figurative language (e.g., simile, metaphor, hyperbole, personification) and identify its use in literary works.
	Your Job as a Reader	• **Reading 2.2** Use appropriate strategies when reading for different purposes (e.g., full comprehension, location of information, personal enjoyment). • **Reading 2.4** Evaluate new information and hypotheses by testing them against known information and ideas.
505–510	**Reading Selection**	• **Reading 2.2** Ask questions and support answers by connecting prior knowledge with literal information found in, and inferred from, the text. • **Reading 2.3** Demonstrate comprehension by identifying answers in the text. • **Reading 2.2** Use appropriate strategies when reading for different purposes (e.g., full comprehension, location of information, personal enjoyment).

California English–Language Arts Content Standards, continued

511 Connect Reading and Writing:

Critical Thinking	• **Reading 2.2** Ask questions and support answers by connecting prior knowledge with literal information found in, and inferred from, the text. • **Reading 2.3** Demonstrate comprehension by identifying answers in the text. • **Reading 2.6** Extract appropriate and significant information from the text, including problems and solutions.
Reading Fluency	• **Reading 1.1** Read narrative and expository text aloud with grade-appropriate fluency and accuracy and with appropriate pacing, intonation, and expression.
Reading Strategy	• **Reading 2.4** Recall major points in the text and make and modify predictions about forthcoming information. • **Reading 2.2** Use appropriate strategies when reading for different purposes (e.g., full comprehension, location of information, personal enjoyment). • **Reading 2.4** Evaluate new information and hypotheses by testing them against known information and ideas.
Vocabulary Review	• Use vocabulary central to the understanding and discussion of the selection. • **Reading 1.6** Use sentence and word context to find the meaning of unknown words.
Write About the GQ	• **Writing 2.2a** Write responses to literature: Demonstrate an understanding of the literary work. • **Writing 2.2b** Write responses to literature: Support judgments through references to both the text and prior knowledge.

512	**Literary Analysis:** **Analyze News Media**	• **Reading 2.4** Evaluate new information and hypotheses by testing them against known information and ideas.
513	**Vocabulary Study:** **Interpret Metaphors**	• **Reading 3.5** Define figurative language (e.g., simile, metaphor, hyperbole, personification) and identify its use in literary works.
513	**Listening/Speaking:** **Share Information**	• **Listening and Speaking 1.4** Give precise directions and instructions.
514	**Listening/Speaking:** **Recite Songs**	• **Listening and Speaking 2.2** Plan and present dramatic interpretations of experiences, stories, poems, or plays with clear diction, pitch, tempo, and tone. • **Reading 3.1** Describe the structural differences of various imaginative forms of literature, including fantasies, fables, myths, legends, and fairy tales. • **Listening and Speaking 2.4** Recite brief poems (i.e., two or three stanzas), soliloquies, or dramatic dialogues, using clear diction, tempo, volume, and phrasing.
515	**Language & Grammar:** **Use Appropriate Language**	• **Listening and Speaking 1.7** Emphasize points in ways that help the listener or viewer to follow important ideas and concepts. • **Listening and Speaking 1.9** Use volume, pitch, phrasing, pace, modulation, and gestures appropriately to enhance meaning.

Selection 2		Making Faces
516	Connect	• **Reading 2.2** Use appropriate strategies when reading for different purposes (e.g., full comprehension, location of information, personal enjoyment). • **Listening and Speaking 1.2** Connect and relate prior experiences, insights, and ideas to those of a speaker.
517–519	Language & Grammar: Use Appropriate Language	• **Listening and Speaking 1.0** Students listen critically and respond appropriately to oral communication. They speak in a manner that guides the listener to understand important ideas by using proper phrasing, pitch, and modulation. • **Listening and Speaking 1.7** Emphasize points in ways that help the listener or viewer to follow important ideas and concepts. • **Listening and Speaking 1.9** Use volume, pitch, phrasing, pace, modulation, and gestures appropriately to enhance meaning.
	Use Compound Sentences	• **Written and Oral English Language Conventions 1.1** Use simple and compound sentences in writing and speaking. • **Written and Oral English Language Conventions 1.3** Identify and use regular and irregular verbs, adverbs, prepositions, and coordinating conjunctions in writing and speaking.
520	Key Vocabulary	• Learn meaning and pronunciation for vocabulary words central to the understanding and discussion of the selection. • **Reading 1.7** Use a dictionary to learn the meaning and other features of unknown words.
521	Reading Strategy: Synthesize	• **Reading 2.2** Use appropriate strategies when reading for different purposes (e.g., full comprehension, location of information, personal enjoyment). • **Reading 2.5** Compare and contrast information on the same topic after reading several passages or articles.
522	Focus on Genre: Magazine Article	• **Reading 2.1** Use titles, tables of contents, chapter headings, glossaries, and indexes to locate information in text. • **Reading 2.5** Compare and contrast information on the same topic after reading several passages or articles.
	Your Job as a Reader	• **Reading 2.2** Use appropriate strategies when reading for different purposes (e.g., full comprehension, location of information, personal enjoyment).
523–532	Reading Selection	• **Reading 2.2** Ask questions and support answers by connecting prior knowledge with literal information found in, and inferred from, the text. • **Reading 2.3** Demonstrate comprehension by identifying answers in the text. • **Reading 2.2** Use appropriate strategies when reading for different purposes (e.g., full comprehension, location of information, personal enjoyment).

Unit 8 Art and Soul, continued

533	**Connect Reading and Writing:**	
	Critical Thinking	• **Reading 2.2** Ask questions and support answers by connecting prior knowledge with literal information found in, and inferred from, the text. • **Reading 2.3** Demonstrate comprehension by identifying answers in the text. • **Reading 2.6** Extract appropriate and significant information from the text, including problems and solutions. • **Reading 2.2** Use appropriate strategies when reading for different purposes (e.g., full comprehension, location of information, personal enjoyment). • **Reading 2.4** Evaluate new information and hypotheses by testing them against known information and ideas. • **Listening and Speaking 2.3** Deliver oral summaries of articles and books that contain the main ideas of the event or article and the most significant details.
	Reading Fluency	• **Reading 1.1** Read narrative and expository text aloud with grade-appropriate fluency and accuracy and with appropriate pacing, intonation, and expression.
	Reading Strategy	• **Reading 2.2** Use appropriate strategies when reading for different purposes (e.g., full comprehension, location of information, personal enjoyment). • **Reading 2.4** Evaluate new information and hypotheses by testing them against known information and ideas.
	Vocabulary Review	• Use vocabulary central to the understanding and discussion of the selection. • **Reading 1.6** Use sentence and word context to find the meaning of unknown words.
	Write About the GQ	• **Writing 2.2a** Write responses to literature: Demonstrate an understanding of the literary work. • **Writing 2.2b** Write responses to literature: Support judgments through references to both the text and prior knowledge.
534	**Literary Analysis:** **Analyze Author's Purpose and Tone**	• **Reading 3.1** Distinguish common forms of literature (e.g., poetry, drama, fiction, nonfiction)
535	**Vocabulary Study:** **Analyze Idioms**	• **Reading 3.5** Define figurative language (e.g., simile, metaphor, hyperbole, personification) and identify its use in literary works.
535	**Listening/Speaking:** **Present a Story**	• **Listening and Speaking 2.1c** Make narrative presentations: Provide insight into why the selected event or experience is memorable.
536	**Research/Speaking:** **Explore Ancient Greek Drama**	• **Writing 1.6** Locate information in reference texts by using organizational features (e.g., prefaces, appendixes). • **Listening and Speaking 2.2b** Make informational presentations: Include facts and details that help listeners to focus.
537	**Language & Grammar:** **Use Appropriate Language**	• **Listening and Speaking 1.7** Emphasize points in ways that help the listener or viewer to follow important ideas and concepts. • **Listening and Speaking 1.9** Use volume, pitch, phrasing, pace, modulation, and gestures appropriately to enhance meaning.
537	**Writing and Grammar:** **Write About Your Interests**	• **Written and Oral English Language Conventions 1.1** Use simple and compound sentences in writing and speaking. • **Written and Oral English Language Conventions 1.3** Identify and use regular and irregular verbs, adverbs, prepositions, and coordinating conjunctions in writing and speaking.

Selection 3 Wings

538	**Connect**	• **Listening and Speaking 1.2** Connect and relate prior experiences, insights, and ideas to those of a speaker. • **Reading 2.2** Use appropriate strategies when reading for different purposes (e.g., full comprehension, location of information, personal enjoyment).

539–541	Language & Grammar: Retell a Story	• **Listening and Speaking 1.0** Students listen critically and respond appropriately to oral communication. They speak in a manner that guides the listener to understand important ideas by using proper phrasing, pitch, and modulation. • **Listening and Speaking 1.6** Provide a beginning, a middle, and an end, including concrete details that develop a central idea.
	Use Complex Sentences	• **Written and Oral English Language Conventions 1.3** Identify and use regular and irregular verbs, adverbs, prepositions, and coordinating conjunctions in writing and speaking.
542	Key Vocabulary	• Learn meaning and pronunciation for vocabulary words central to the understanding and discussion of the selection. • **Reading 1.7** Use a dictionary to learn the meaning and other features of unknown words.
543	Reading Strategy: Synthesize	• **Reading 2.2** Use appropriate strategies when reading for different purposes (e.g., full comprehension, location of information, personal enjoyment). • **Reading 2.5** Compare and contrast information on the same topic after reading several passages or articles.
544	Focus on Genre: Short Story	• **Reading 2.5** Compare and contrast information on the same topic after reading several passages or articles.
	Your Job as a Reader	• **Reading 2.2** Use appropriate strategies when reading for different purposes (e.g., full comprehension, location of information, personal enjoyment).
545–554	Reading Selection	• **Reading 2.2** Ask questions and support answers by connecting prior knowledge with literal information found in, and inferred from, the text. • **Reading 2.3** Demonstrate comprehension by identifying answers in the text. • **Reading 2.6** Extract appropriate and significant information from the text, including problems and solutions. • **Reading 2.2** Use appropriate strategies when reading for different purposes (e.g., full comprehension, location of information, personal enjoyment). • **Reading 2.3** Make and confirm predictions about text by using prior knowledge and ideas presented in the text itself, including illustrations, titles, topic sentences, important words, and foreshadowing clues.
555	**Connect Reading and Writing:**	
	Critical Thinking	• **Reading 2.3** Demonstrate comprehension by identifying answers in the text. • **Reading 2.6** Extract appropriate and significant information from the text, including problems and solutions. • **Listening and Speaking 2.3** Deliver oral summaries of articles and books that contain the main ideas of the event or article and the most significant details.
	Reading Fluency	• **Reading 1.1** Read narrative and expository text aloud with grade-appropriate fluency and accuracy and with appropriate pacing, intonation, and expression.
	Reading Strategy	• **Reading 2.2** Use appropriate strategies when reading for different purposes (e.g., full comprehension, location of information, personal enjoyment).
	Vocabulary Review	• Use vocabulary central to the understanding and discussion of the selection. • **Reading 1.6** Use sentence and word context to find the meaning of unknown words.
	Write About the GQ	• **Writing 2.2a** Write responses to literature: Demonstrate an understanding of the literary work. • **Writing 2.2b** Write responses to literature: Support judgments through references to both the text and prior knowledge.
556	Literary Analysis: Compare Characters	• **Reading 3.3** Determine what characters are like by what they say or do and by how the author or illustrator portrays them. • **Reading 3.3** Use knowledge of the situation and setting and of a character's traits and motivations to determine the causes for that character's actions.
557	Vocabulary Study: Analyze Similes	• **Reading 3.5** Recognize the similarities of sounds in words and rhythmic patterns (e.g., alliteration, onomatopoeia) in a selection.

California English–Language Arts Content Standards, continued

Unit 8   Art and Soul, continued

557	**Research/Speaking:** **Research Greek Myths**	• **Listening and Speaking 2.1c** Make brief narrative presentations: Include well-chosen details to develop character, setting, and plot. • **Reading 1.2** Apply knowledge of word origins, derivations, synonyms, antonyms, and idioms to determine the meaning of words and phrases.
558	**Literary Analysis:** **Analyze Plot Events**	• **Reading 3.2** Comprehend basic plots of classic fairy tales, myths, folktales, legends, and fables from around the world. • **Listening and Speaking 2.1c** Make brief narrative presentations: Include well-chosen details to develop character, setting, and plot. • **Reading 3.2** Identify the main events of the plot, their causes, and the influence of each event on future actions.
559	**Language & Grammar:** **Retell a Story**	• **Listening and Speaking 1.6** Provide a beginning, a middle, and an end, including concrete details that develop a central idea.
559	**Writing & Grammar:** **Write About Myths**	• **Written and Oral English Language Conventions 1.1** Use simple and compound sentences in writing and speaking.

Compare Across Texts

560	**Compare Themes**	• **Reading 3.4** Determine the underlying theme or author's message in fiction and nonfiction text. • **Reading 2.5** Compare and contrast information on the same topic after reading several passages or articles.

Unit Wrap-Up

561	**Reflect on Your Reading**	• **Reading 2.2** Use appropriate strategies when reading for different purposes (e.g., full comprehension, location of information, personal enjoyment).
	Explore the GQ/Book Talk	• **Reading 2.4** Recall major points in the text and make and modify predictions about forthcoming information. • **Reading 2.6** Extract appropriate and significant information from the text, including problems and solutions. • **Reading 2.4** Evaluate new information and hypotheses by testing them against known information and ideas. • **Reading 3.1** Describe the structural differences of various imaginative forms of literature, including fantasies, fables, myths, legends, and fairy tales.

For additional coverage of the Written and Oral English Language Conventions and the Writing Applications standards, see the California standards maps in the Writing book.